Enduring Controversies in Military History

ENDURING CONTROVERSIES IN MILITARY HISTORY

Critical Analyses and Context

Volume 1

Spencer C. Tucker, Editor

An Imprint of ABC-CLIO, LLC
Santa Barbara, California • Denver, Colorado

Library of Congress Cataloging-in-Publication Data

Names: Tucker, Spencer, 1937– author.
Title: Enduring controversies in military history : critical analyses and context /
    Spencer C. Tucker, editor.
Description: Santa Barbara, California : ABC-CLIO [2017] | Includes
    bibliographical references and index.
Identifiers: LCCN 2016047936 (print) | LCCN 2016052968 (ebook) |
    ISBN 9781440841194 (set : alk. paper) | ISBN 9781440848131
    (volume 1 : alk. paper) | ISBN 9781440848148 (volume 2 : alk. paper) |
    ISBN 9781440841200 (ebook)
Subjects: LCSH: Military history. | Military policy.
Classification: LCC D25 .T828 2017 (print) | LCC D25 (ebook) | DDC 355.009—dc23
LC record available at https://lccn.loc.gov/2016047936

ISBN: 978-1-4408-4119-4 (set)
      978-1-4408-4813-1 (vol. 1)
      978-1-4408-4814-8 (vol. 2)
      978-1-4408-4120-0 (ebook)

21   20   19   18   17   1   2   3   4   5

This book is also available as an eBook.

ABC-CLIO
An Imprint of ABC-CLIO, LLC

ABC-CLIO, LLC
130 Cremona Drive, P.O. Box 1911
Santa Barbara, California 93116-1911
www.abc-clio.com

This book is printed on acid-free paper ∞

Manufactured in the United States of America

For Jinwung Kim, professor of history and distinguished scholar of Korean history at Kyungpook National University, Republic of Korea

CONTENTS

INTRODUCTION

Historians interpret events differently. All of us approach subjects from different points of view based on our own life experiences, training, knowledge, and biases, whether these are recognized or not. Obviously the passage of time provides a clearer perspective as to the importance and impact of a particular event, while new evidence in the form of memoirs and documents—often appearing decades or even generations after the event itself—allows for fresh assessment of it.

After consulting with other scholars and historians, I have assembled a collection of essays treating 64 topics in the long history of world conflict that have been the subject of different interpretations. The essays selected range in time from ancient history to the contemporary world: from the Peloponnesian War to whether women in the U.S. military should be allowed to serve in combat units.

The topics are arranged in loose chronological fashion, grouped in seven major eras: ancient Greece and Rome (500 BCE–500 CE), 5 topics; the Middle Ages (500–1500), 6 topics; the emergence of modern Europe and the Americas (1500–1825), 10 topics; the rise of imperialism and nationalism (1825–1914), 11 topics; the world at war (1914–1945), 12 topics; the Cold War (1945–1991), 12 topics; and the new millennium (1991–present), 8 topics. Each topic has a brief introduction and a background essay.

Some of the background essays are relatively short; others, such as that on the Vietnam War, are necessarily longer because the essays themselves make reference to events without necessarily explaining what they were. Following the background essay, each topic has between two and five position essays. An expansive list of books for further reading on the subject closes out each topic.

Some topics lent themselves to different approaches. Among these are the topics that address the key factors behind the fall of the Roman Empire and the primary causes of World War I. Here the authors address the one central issue that they believe was paramount.

Other topics lent themselves to pro and con approaches. Examples of this include whether it would have been better from a military standpoint for Britain and

France to have gone to war with Germany in October 1938 at the time of the Munich Conference rather than in September 1939, when war was thrust upon them with the German invasion of Poland; whether U.S. president Harry S. Truman was justified in relieving General Douglas MacArthur from his commands of U.S. forces in the Pacific and the United Nations Command during the Korean War; and whether the United States was justified in dropping atomic bombs on Japan.

The reader will find much of interest here. Thus, in the discussion of the use of the atomic bombs against Japan, one author notes that aircraft flying from U.S. Navy and Royal Navy carriers had largely severed interisland traffic and that Japan's land transportation net had also been badly disrupted. Massive firebomb raids by B-29 Superfortress bombers had largely burned out the major Japanese major cities, and the Japanese people were on a starvation diet.

But would these circumstances have been sufficient to bring surrender? Japan had assembled large numbers of suicide craft and kamikaze aircraft with which to contest any American landing attempt, and a number of its military leaders were determined that Japanese honor could be met only by a fight to the last. There is also controversy within a controversy regarding estimates of probable American casualties in an invasion of the Japanese home islands. Certainly, given Japanese resistance at places such as Iwo Jima and Okinawa, casualties would have been heavy.

In these circumstance Emperor Hirohito, himself a controversial figure for his role in the war, found his voice, for the atomic bombs gave him the excuse to take into his own hands the difficult decision to surrender. But fanatics among the generals were determined that his remarks not be heard by the Japanese people. A military putsch that included an attempt to assassinate the emperor was averted only by the narrowest of margins.

Were there not also other factors at play in the employment of the atomic bombs? It is certainly worth pointing out the savage nature of the fighting in the Pacific theater with no holds barred and war to the knife hilt. Was the atomic bomb simply an additional degree in the already existing horror? The bomb's high cost and lengthy development and its availability probably furthered the inevitability of its use. Certainly, President Truman remarked afterward that he had no qualms about the decision, but others in authority who knew of the bomb opposed its use. Were geopolitical factors at play? The American capacity for strategic bombing had been strikingly demonstrated in the Pacific theater, and now the atomic bomb was added to the equation. Thus, to what extent was employing the bomb an opening salvo of the Cold War, designed as a signature warning to the leadership of the Soviet Union? All of these factors were at play to some degree. They and other matters are all discussed in the essays on this topic. Here, as with the other topics, it will be up to the reader to decide.

In my editing of entries I have made stylistic and formatting changes. I have, however, taken special care not to interfere with the authors' points of view.

Assisting me in the topic selection were military historians Dr. Timothy C. Dowling; Dr. Jerry Morelock, Colonel, U.S. Army Rtd; and Dr. David T. Zabecki, Major General, U.S. Army Rtd. I am especially grateful to my associate of long standing with ABC-CLIO projects, Dr. Paul G. Pierpaoli Jr. He wrote a large number of the topic introductions as well as some of the essays.

Hopefully students and academics and others with a general interest in military history will find this work informative in its factual content but also useful in understanding how historians approach topics and inform others about the rich fabric that is our shared history.

Spencer C. Tucker

PART I

ANCIENT GREECE AND ROME
(500 BCE–500 CE)

1. What Was the Primary Cause of the Peloponnesian War?

The Peloponnesian War began in 431 BCE and ended in 404 BCE. The conflict pitted democratic Athens and its allies against warlike Sparta and its allies. It was an especially bloody war that would forever change ancient Greece and the dynamics between the Athenians and Spartans. The Peloponnesian War was as much a clash of cultures as it was a struggle for mastery of the ancient Greek world. For many years, Sparta had been known for its unparalleled military prowess; indeed, its entire social and political structure was geared toward defense and war. Athens, on the other hand, had been aggregating power not so much by its army but instead through increased trade, mastery of the seas, skillful diplomacy, and the force of new ideas. In the end the conflict fundamentally reordered the Greek world, reducing Athens's strength and prestige while making Sparta the leading Greek power. The war also had profound economic consequences particularly for Athens, which never regained its prewar prosperity. The reasons behind the war are numerous, and since the Athenian general and historian Thucydides wrote about the conflict in the fifth century BCE, scholars ever since have been fascinated by this struggle.

Each perspective essay in this part attempts to isolate the primary catalysts for the war. In the first essay, Dr. Lee L. Brice views the war primarily through the prism established by Thucydides, arguing that the conflict was caused chiefly by Sparta's fears of growing Athenian power and Athenian imperialism. He further asserts that Sparta was also propelled toward war by its allies and that the most immediate catalyst for conflict was Athens's war against its former ally, Potidaea. Dr. Lee W. Eysturlid, in the second essay, ultimately asserts that the primary causes of the conflict were intractable cultural and economic differences between Athens and Sparta. These differences had been building for years and made war nearly inevitable. Dr. James B. McNabb echoes some of the same sentiments but specifically asserts that neither the leaders of Sparta nor Athens could avoid war because of widening cultural and social differences between them and because of Athens's growing maritime power and trade. More immediately, the growing competition between Corinth, an ally of Sparta, and Athens served as one of the principal causes of the conflict. Notably, McNabb also focuses on

The charismatic Athenian Pericles was one of the great leaders of ancient Greece. An able general and statesman, his death produced a void that his successors were unable to fill and was certainly a factor in the Athenian defeat in the Peloponnesian War. (Library of Congress)

the differences between Athens and Sparta in the cultural and educational spheres. The former was becoming more reliant on science and philosophy, while the latter clung to the status quo of myth and superstition.

Background Essay

Between 431 and 404 BCE, the Peloponnesian War raged throughout Greece and the Aegean Sea and even as far west as Sicily as Sparta and its allies in the Peloponnesian League fought against what had become the Athenian Empire. It was to be a rather unconventional war in which Sparta, with the best Greek army, faced Athens, with the best Greek navy, but Athens had the additional advantages of offensive mobility by sea and plenty of funds. Many Greek cities and even Persia became involved in the war, which thus had an impact on nearly every part of the Greek world. The war ended in defeat for Athens and dissolution of its empire.

Throughout the period after 478 Athens had become increasingly powerful, mainly by drawing on the Delian League, a network of alliances that had evolved into an empire. After a series of what appeared as provocations by Spartan allies, Sparta, led by King Archidamus, declared Athens in violation of the existing peace treaty from the First Peloponnesian War, and fighting began in 431.

According to the primary source chronicler for this period, the Greek historian Thucydides, Archidamus planned to draw the Athenians out to battle and win a swift victory on land that would result in the collapse of the Delian League. Pericles, the leader of Athens, advised his fellow citizens to remain behind their walls, secure with their large wealth reserves, to maintain the fleet and import food but also to raid the coastline of Peloponnesian League members.

The first phase of the war, sometimes called the Archidamian War, lasted 10 years and began with a Spartan invasion of Athenian territory. Pericles pursued his semidefensive strategy with great effect. The invasion raided Attica but left Athens itself untouched, and after some desultory destruction the Spartans withdrew. The next year while the Athenians remained behind their walls, a plague struck Athens and reduced its population. This not only affected the numbers of men it could field but also cost the city-state its most capable leader, Pericles, in 429.

During the early years of the war both sides enjoyed victories, but the Athenian occupation of Pylos and the capture of some Spartan citizens compelled the nearby Spartans to sue for peace in 425. The Athenians, seeing their advantage, refused. Sparta responded by campaigning in the northern Aegean and eventually capturing Amphipolis in 422. This success led directly to the Peace of Nicias, which was intended to restore the status quo, with both sides returning captured territory.

The treaty may not have been fully implemented, but it initiated a period of uneasy peace during which Athens sought to expand its empire by alliance with Argos, the conquest of Melos, and then a great expedition to Sicily in 415. That campaign in the west proved costly to Athens, as its huge expeditionary force was defeated at Syracuse in 413. That led to the end of the peace and the beginning of the second phase of the war, called the Decelean War.

During the siege of Syracuse Sparta was not idle, having invaded Attica again and occupying a fort at Decelea. Sparta also focused on building up its own fleet to take advantage of the battered state of the Athenian Navy. A significant portion of the Athenian fleet was destroyed in the attack on Sicily. Also, in the aftermath of the defeat at Syracuse several members of the Delian League revolted, and this further occupied Athenian attention. Between 411 and 408, Athens experienced a coup d'état in favor of an oligarchy and then a restoration of democracy, the continued rebellion of several allies, and food shortages caused by Spartan naval successes. However, a major Athenian naval victory in the Battle of Cyzicus in 410 decimated the Spartan fleet and revived Athenian hopes of winning the war.

Despite the fact that Athens had secured its supply lines and even reclaimed a few of its subject states, political squabbling among the Athenians hampered their military progress, and the Spartans, with financial resources provided by the Persians, continued to apply pressure. Athens achieved its last significant victory in the war in the Battle of Arginusae in 406, but even that triumph was marred by the execution of several Athenian generals for reportedly failing to recover and bury their dead. The following year, the Spartan commander Lysander crushed the Athenian fleet in the Battle of Aegospotami. Sparta than cut off Athens's food imports and besieged the city by land, forcing it to surrender in 404.

Sparta spared Athens from utter destruction, although Corinth and other Spartan allies had urged such action. Under the conditions of surrender Athens lost its overseas possessions, its Long Walls, and most of its fleet. The Delian League was also dissolved. The golden age of Athens and its empire was over. Despite this conclusion, Sparta had difficulty exploiting its victory in the decades that followed. In this way, the Peloponnesian War only led to a longer period of wearing conflict among the Greek city-states.

James B. Tschen-Emmons and Lee L. Brice

Perspective Essay 1. Greek Fears over Growing Athenian Power

The Greek historian Thucydides, primary chronicler of the Peloponnesian War, is correct in attributing the conflict chiefly to Spartan fear of growing Athenian power. The Peloponnesian War, fought throughout the Greek world from 431 to 404 BCE between Sparta and its allies on the one side and the Athenian Empire on the other, was a significant event in the history of ancient Greece. By the time it ended, the war had directly affected nearly every part of the Greek world from the Black Sea to Sicily and had also drawn the Persian Empire back into Greek affairs. Although the fighting was triggered by the Theban attack on Plataea in 431, the underlying causes of this war have remained a matter of debate among scholars.

Thucydides was an Athenian who wrote *The Peloponnesian War* during the war or in the years soon after it ended. He made an effort to record and analyze events and present facts in unbiased fashion. In his account he states that he interviewed participants when possible, considered varying accounts for veracity, and tried in his record of speeches to adhere to the original intended spirit. This detailed method led later historians to credit Thucydides with having been the father of a scientific, historical method.

In the beginning of *The Peloponnesian War,* Thucydides reports that there were four "openly acknowledged events" (in Aegina, Epidamnus, Megara, and Potidaea) contributing to the declaration of war but that the genuine underlying cause of the war was Spartan fear of growing Athenian power. He reasserts this twice more in the course of his history. Although it may be hard to imagine Spartans afraid of any other city, it is easier to understand when one realizes that these fears grew out of experiences following the creation of the Delian League in 478 under Athenian leadership. While the growing power of Athens did cause concern, it was only the four events to which Thucydides refers that brought Spartan fears to the fore and resulted in war.

During the nearly 50-year period after the Battle of Plataea in 479, Athens had become increasingly powerful mainly by drawing on the Delian League, its alliance network. The league had evolved by 446 into an Athenian Empire. At the same time, while Sparta had undergone some internal difficulties, it nonetheless remained leader of the loose alliance known as the Peloponnesian League. A period of low-level conflict between members of the Delian and Peloponnesian Leagues that began in 461 over Athenian expansion on the mainland ended without serious result in 446 with the Thirty Years' Peace.

In the years that followed the peace, Athens, led by its great leader Pericles, grew ever stronger and wealthier. Athens also imposed its laws, garrisons, and form of government on members of the empire. It even forced rebellious member cities back into the Delian League. Athens also tried to increase its influence with Greek cities in the western Mediterranean by initiating new colonies such as Thurii and making alliances with other cities such as in Akarnania. This imperial activity heightened the concerns of other Greek city-states, including Sparta and several of its allies. Athenian power created apprehension but did not lead to conflict until a series of incidents and grievances triggered Spartan action.

The first of the four events that Thucydides reports as having led to the war originated in the island of Aegina. It appears that leaders of the island community near Athens complained to other Greeks that they were not free from Athenian influence as promised in the peace treaty of 446. There was not much Aegina could do about this, however. When its leaders originally appealed to Sparta for assistance remains a mystery, but the complaints did increase other Greeks' concerns about Athenian influence.

The second event reported by Thucydides began in Epidamnus, a small Greek city on the Adriatic coast and a colony of Corcyra. A civil war between pro-oligarchy and prodemocracy supporters broke out in 435. The prodemocracy side sought support and ended up turning to Corinth, the city that had originally founded Corcyra. Corinth was an oligarchy, but it was also a long-term enemy of Corcyra and so supported the prodemocracy faction. The Corcyreans resented what they perceived as meddling, and armed conflict broke out between the two cities. Corcyra fared poorly in the fighting, however, and eventually made an alliance with Athens, despite the risk of breaking the Thirty Years' Peace should Athens engage in battle against Corinth. In 433 Corcyra, with Athenian assistance, defeated Corinth at sea. Already anxious of Athenian influence, Corinth saw Athenian intervention as a threat and complained to Sparta, leader of the Peloponnesian League. The Spartans may have been concerned, but they did not declare war.

The next event, the date of which is uncertain, occurred in the city of Megara, located between Athens and Corinth. Megara had been an early member of the Peloponnesian League but in 460 joined the Delian League. It remained in that alliance until 446, when it rejoined the Peloponnesian League. Under Pericles's direction, Athens charged Megara with religious crimes for cultivating sacred land and issued the Megarian Decree that included several restrictions, the most important banning Megarian merchants from Athenian marketplaces and all Delian League ports. The advantage of such a measure for Athens was that it allowed Athens to inflict harm on a member of the Peloponnesian League without violating the peace treaty. Megara was a maritime trading city, and many important Greek ports were in the Delian League, so this decree was potentially damaging. Despite repeated requests, Athens would not rescind the decrees, which rose out of events sometime between 435 and 432. The Megarians appealed first to Corinth and then to Sparta for assistance.

The fourth event occurred in the northern Aegean at Potidaea. This city in the Chalcidice Peninsula was a former colony of Corinth but also a member of the Delian League. Despite its alliance with Athens, Potidaea and Corinth maintained close political and economic ties. In 433–432 as a result in part of suspicions about the activity of Macedon, Athens demanded in decrees that Potidaea dismiss its Corinthian magistrates and submit to Athenian authority. When this demand was rebuffed, Athens attacked and then laid siege to its ally. With active support from Corinth and Perdiccas II, the king of Macedon, the Potidaeans held out for two years. In support of its former colony, Corinth appealed to Sparta repeatedly for the Peloponnesian League to wage war against Athens. These calls were without success until the Megarian envoys added their own appeal. This coupled with the general climate of anxiety finally led Sparta to declare war in late 432.

It is important to understand why Sparta was apprehensive about Athens, despite having the best army in Greece and with great influence in mainland Greek affairs. When Sparta had made peace with Athens to end interleague conflict (the First Peloponnesian War) in 446, it did so on terms that suggested that it did not fear any city-state. What probably caused the Spartan leadership increasing apprehension was Athenian activity outside of mainland Greece in the years that followed the peace. Athens had actively forced its will on the member states of its empire. The best example was the Samian War of 440–439, when Samos and Byzantium revolted unsuccessfully. Soon afterward, Athens strengthened its position in the north by founding Amphipolis in Thrace and sponsoring a mission by Pericles into the Black Sea. Athens had also become more active in the west, seeking connections and allies on the Adriatic coast and in southern Italy. All of this activity must have increased Spartan anxiety.

Additionally, Spartan leaders may well have become worried about their city-state's own position vis-à-vis Athens, for Spartan leaders could well worry that Athens was becoming far more powerful than Sparta. In the competitive culture of ancient Greece, especially when Sparta had dominated Athens militarily for so long, such unequal status was alarming to Spartans who had seldom shied away from such competition. Thucydides's reference to fear of Athens's growing power included concern of the increase in Athenian stature and status among Greeks. Given the threats to its military dominance and status, it is not difficult to see why Sparta and its allies might have worried about the growing strength of the Athenian empire. Thucydides's analysis has stood the test of time.

Lee L. Brice

Perspective Essay 2. The Significance of Cultural and Economic Differences

The primary causes of the Peloponnesian War were the cultural and economic differences that had existed between Athens and Sparta for more than a century. The conflict was all but inevitable, and because the war resulted from intrinsic differences, it was destined to be particularly violent and prolonged.

In the Greek classical era, Athens appears as both appealing and repulsive. It is regarded as the birthplace of democracy and Western cultural tradition. Athens was the home to philosophy, drama, and comedy and early notions of science. It was a dynamic place, full of energy and creativity. It was also, however, both a slave-owning society and one that treated women with little dignity. One must also remember that Athens was a deeply religious place, with great festivals for the numerous gods and goddesses. But what is also true is that Athens had created a military-commercial empire that dominated the Aegean-Greek world. Proud of their city, their culture, and their wealth, Athenians increasingly saw themselves as distinct from and superior to their fellow Greeks.

The Athenian notion of democracy was at the core of their difference. Although Athens possessed an aristocracy, the preference for the assigning of offices by a lottery system excluded those aristocrats from winning offices by even democratic means. Court cases concerning property, especially between the aristocrats, had moved to jury trials in which paid volunteer juries of average citizens sat in judgment. For this reason, Athens's nobles competed with each other in the courts rather than in politics. Only in the election of the *strategos,* or military leaders, could the aristocracy find an outlet for its energies and talents. Athens therefore embraced a distinct, if incomplete, notion of equality for all people.

The Athenians built a very successful and unique system by which they might be first among equals in at least half of the Greek world. Their manipulation of the Delian League from a defensive confederacy against Persia to a trade federation with Athens at the forefront brought them great power through wealth in trade. Athenian power made it possible for the imposition of democracy on the Greek states that joined the league as well as those that rebelled. By the start of the Peloponnesian War, it would have been clear to any observer that growing Athenian power, especially in material wealth and naval strength, was a threat. It would thus be natural for Sparta and Corinth, oligarchies and arguably fearful of change, to see Athens as an inherent agent of change and threat to their very existence.

About 100 miles from Athens, the region of the Lacedaemonians, or Spartans, stood in stark contrast. First, there was not a Spartan "city" to speak of but rather numerous modest villages. This lack of a focusing city, as with Athens, was more than compensated for by the Spartan culture. The privileges and responsibilities of a full-fledged Spartiate, or citizen, were extended only to a few. For these men, that status brought great rigors from youth onward. Its unique constitution essentially made Sparta an army with an attached state. The great helot (slave) population that supported the near full-time soldiering of the Spartiates also required a full-time police force to keep it from rebelling.

This invincible warrior spirit inherent in the Spartiates also bred out of them interest in trade and the arts. A good example was the emphasis on the Laconian way of speaking. Great emphasis was placed on and pride taken in conveying what needed to be known with the fewest words possible, hence the word "laconic." When the Spartan commander Lysander reported the Athenian capitulation at the end of the Peloponnesian War, the entire message sent home was "Athens taken." The story told after the event is that when the leaders in Sparta received his message, they were disappointed at his overuse of words, a simple "taken" being sufficient.

The Spartans also lacked the notion of democracy possessed by Athens. Sparta had two kings who acted as rotating executives. Real authority, as laid down by Lycurgus, the creator of Sparta, lay with five elected officials known as *ephors,* who essentially guided internal affairs. They were long tenured and acted as judges, who in the eyes of the other Greeks wielded great and unassailable power. The actual assembly of full Spartiates voted on issues of importance, such as whether to declare war. This was done not by anonymous voting but by shouting, the loudest carrying the day.

The Spartan male lived in a barracks, even when married; ate at the common mess; and remained removed from economic activities. Helots were assigned to each Spartiate to farm and provide the food necessary for daily life.

Thus, the Athenians and Spartans were different in many important ways. Athens the democracy, open to the absolute participation of all of its citizens through the use of the lottery of office, was in stark contrast to the essentially oligarchic Sparta. While the Athenians remained very specific in their notions of who and who was not a citizen, the nobility of any single citizen was of little importance. For the Spartiate the opposite was true, with a clear line between full-blooded Spartans and the rest of the people. Secondary citizens called *perioeci,* while free men, where not citizens. The Athenians also engaged readily in the dynamic enterprise of commerce and international trade. The city was born of this trade, especially in higher-value items such as olive oil. Success in commerce saw the Athenians take to the sea, opening the city to an influx of ideas and change that accompanied such trade. Sparta rejected trade as beneath Spartiate dignity, unworthy of serious engagement.

Unfortunately for the Greek world, both Athenians and Spartans were similar in their devotion to their own uniqueness and the need to maintain it. Added to this was the reality that the two city-states were hypercompetitive, both among themselves and with their neighbors. Eventually each came to see the other Greek states as either vassals or allies. In the end, the maintenance of their own unique nature required the domination of the rest of Greece.

Sparta's nature made it oligarchic and warlike. It could not tolerate any state that did not accept its status as the primary power in the Peloponnese and later in greater Greece. For good or bad this made sense, for the system had created a rigid social structure and bred its people to dedication to the state, even to celebrate death in its service and disgrace if failing to be successful. How could such a people accept others as equals or, worse still, superiors? Sparta dominated its alliance system, known as the Peloponnesian League, even though the sum of its members greatly outnumbered the Spartans. Sparta, especially after the wars with the Persians that preceded the Peloponnesian War, insisted on a dominant position in Greece. The Spartans then were the rulers of old Greece, even as the new Greece of Athens and the Aegean rose.

The Athenians were hypercompetitive as well. Athens's desire to dominate the trade of the Aegean and the fleet resources necessary to maintain power led it to seek to dominate its partners. Like the Spartans, the Athenians developed a clear devotion to the importance of their city. Athenians also had the good fortune of discovering rich silver mines. This wealth made possible the city-state's initial rise as a naval power, which in turn enabled its commercial dominance. Originally formed as a defensive confederation against the Persians, the Athenian-led Delian League provided the basis for realization of Athenian aspirations.

How could the Athenians, believing in their own importance if not superiority, not be expected to seek to lead the numerous smaller Greek states in an alliance system in which only Athens possessed real military power? Once inside the league, the member states, with few exceptions, gave up their ships and rowers and paid tribute to Athens, which controlled the increasing naval power. Resigning from the league became impossible, because for the Athenians to have allowed optional membership would have been akin to the Spartans allowing optional membership in their alliance system.

The events that unfolded in the years before the Peloponnesian War were therefore simply catalysts in igniting a conflict that already existed. When the Spartans dismissed an Athenian force sent to help them subdue a helot uprising, it was taken as an insult. When Themistocles rejected the Spartan demand that Athens not build walls to Piraeus, which would protect the city from a potential siege, how could it not be seen by the Spartans as a threat? The existence of dynamic, democratic, and invasive Athens was a threat to the very nature of Sparta, and their unwillingness to change made the Athenians an ever-growing threat. In the end the Spartans and the Athenians had become so different in what made them "Greek" that they no longer had enough in common to avoid a clash.

Lee W. Eysturlid

Perspective Essay 3. The Impact of Cultural and Political Change on Athenian-Spartan Rivalry

The primary cause of the Peloponnesian War (431–404 BCE) was the rising power of an increasingly imperialistic Athens and the inability of Athenian and Spartan leaders to find a peaceful way forward. A historic shift was slowly taking shape as early philosophy and science, largely being cultivated within the spheres of Athenian influence, challenged the traditional domain of myth and supernatural explanation. Moreover, the historic shift was met with a regional systemic shift in terms of the political and military power structure of the Archaic Era of early Greece (800–480 BCE) as the trading and sea-power legacy of Corinth, in loose conjunction with Spartan land power, was being eclipsed by a rising Athenian trading and naval enterprise.

In Western civilization, ancient Greece represents the transition from a world based largely on supernatural explanation, as in "everything is attributable to the will of the gods" to the follow-on eras with an increased focus on philosophical and scientific explanation. A philosophical explanation, according to this tradition, is one that seeks to uncover the reasons for an event or an occurrence. Why did the horse break its leg? A supernatural explanation would claim that it was the will of the gods, while a philosophical explanation would attempt to uncover the logical aspects of the mishap, as in the following observation: "The horse's leg broke because of the misstep by the animal into a hole on the road." From this viewpoint there are reasons why things happen, and man, imbued with the faculty of reasoning, can examine and understand those reasons, which provide a greater clarity and understanding of the world in which he or she inhabits. One can imagine the unease that this type of change represented to those holding on to the exclusive use of supernatural explanation in human affairs in ancient Greece. At that point in human history, philosophical explanation was widely regarded as blasphemy.

Athens served as a symbol of the philosophical tradition that was challenging the long-held values of the old order throughout ancient Greece. Sparta, with an army that had been respected for centuries, along with Corinth and its supporters, represented the vanguard of the old order. The status quo was rigidly entrenched in a hierarchical sociopolitical order that required constant vigilance in two regards. First, agriculture served as the center of life in ancient Greece, and any problems in the harvest presented potentially dire consequences for the survival of the surrounding community. So important was a Greek community's agricultural sector that Spartan military strategy was based primarily on the ability of the army to advance swiftly to a foe's territory and destroy the opponent's crops. Moreover, a recurring problem for the communities of ancient Greece was the rapidly growing population in relation to the available food supply. This concern for the scarcity of food kept the interaction of the various ancient Greek communities at a tense and unpredictable level. When Athens began provisioning its community with wheat from the Black Sea region and possessed the most powerful navy to protect those imports, the Spartan military strategy of attacking crops was less potent.

Athens also represented a challenge to the status quo with its promotion of the concept of *demos kratos* (people power). The concept of democracy was not well received in Sparta, where the workers and the helots, or slaves, vastly outnumbered the Spartan citizen-warriors on an order of 10 to 1. From the perspective of Sparta, empowering a vast array of individuals within a community brought with it significant potential for instability and, in the extreme case, open revolt. In sum, Athens represented major challenges to the status quo with its promotion of philosophy over religion and its support for democracy over a closely monitored societal hierarchy of privilege and power. As it increasingly controlled the seas and was less susceptible to Spartan military pressure, particularly in regard to its food supply, Athens was less compelled to moderate its expansive behavior.

To better understand the outbreak of the Peloponnesian War, it is also necessary to examine the influence of the Persian invasions on the expansion of the power of Athens and of Athenian control over the Delian League and its subsequent assertive relations with its neighbors in the half century before the war. In the Persian Wars (499–449 BCE), Persia launched a series of military campaigns and operations against Greece. The Persian invasions united many of the Greek city-states. Once that threat had been neutralized, the Greek regional system settled into the newly won peace and revolved around two alliances: the Delian League, which was led by Athens, and the Peloponnesian League, led by Sparta.

Athens took an assertive approach in its dealings with Delian League affairs, for it quickly transferred the league's treasury from Delos to Athens and required tribute be paid to it by league members. Furthermore, all league finances were to be conducted in Athenian currency, as the league was transformed from an instrument aimed at blocking Persian encroachment into one that would expand Athenian power and influence. While concern arose across Greece and throughout the Mediterranean world about this new Athenian assertiveness, many others believed it far better to have a powerful Greek navy operating in the eastern Mediterranean than one from Persia. Sparta continued to maintain the region's premier land army in the region and retained the capability of destroying Athens in a direct land campaign. At the same time, Athenian sea power, while always a concern, was not viewed at the time as a significant and direct threat to Spartan security.

By the mid-fifth century BCE, Sparta had been a powerful military force in Greece for several centuries and, with an extended lineage of military effectiveness, knew well the pluses and minuses that accompanied the use of military force. During these years, Sparta had developed a military capability that was tied to a mature and keen understanding of how to defend the community. Spartans were not quick to resort to war and were able to understand when a potential enemy was attempting to coerce them with bluster and bluff, as opposed to when a potential enemy actually threatened their survival. The Spartan leadership was acutely aware of and well versed in the vulnerabilities of the community and knew that certain aspects of their security would have to be defended by use of force if and when they came under threat.

One such vital interest was the land bridge leading onto the Peloponnesus landmass from the rest of Greece. Strategically located along this narrow land bridge was the city-state and Spartan ally, Corinth. Corinth enjoyed a long history of economic development and sea trade and was at one point considered the richest of all Greek communities. Sparta kept a watchful eye on this important land bridge, as it represented the only land route for an enemy invasion of Sparta itself. Similarly, the Spartan leadership kept tabs on the political, economic, and security developments within Corinth and the key community adjoining the Isthmus of Corinth at Megara.

As Persian forces withdrew at the close of the Persian Wars, the new political alliance structure came into being. This created a regional system of two separate groups and was referred to as dual hegemony. Leading one of the centers of power were Sparta and Corinth and other members of the Peloponnesian League. This group was dominant on the land of the Peloponnesus and in Attica as well as in the Mediterranean Sea in waters, colonies, and trade west of Greece. The second grouping was composed of Athens and the Delian League. It was focused in the Aegean Sea and associated colonies involved with trade east of Greece and extending north to the Black Sea.

Although the dual hegemony idea seemed to have resolved the issues between the old order and the new, because Corinth had extensive trading interests and because Athens was intent on expanding its areas of influence, Athens and Corinth were soon again in competition across the ancient Mediterranean world. Two locations provided a flashpoint of this friction as Athens sought to expand north as well as west into the Ionian Sea and into Sicily and Italy. In the northern Aegean, Athens attempted to expel Corinthian influence from Potidaea and successfully fought a combined force from Corinth and Macedon. In the west, the presence of the Athenian fleet in the Battle of Sybota in 433 BCE allowed Corcyra to effectively block Corinth's advance on the city-state.

After having significantly weakened Corinth, Athens again attempted to expand its influence in the Megara basin with the issuance in 432 BCE of what became known as the Megarian Decree. This essentially cut off Megara from trade with any member of the Delian League, which included virtually all trade outlets in the Aegean Sea and the Black Sea, including the trade in wheat. Moreover, Corinth, which guarded the strategic land approach to Sparta, was simply too valuable an ally for Sparta to allow Athens to undermine.

Following these events, Corinthian leaders requested a meeting of the Peloponnesian League in Sparta to address what they argued were unacceptable provocations. After hearing arguments from the Corinthians as well as an uninvited delegation from Athens, the Spartan Assembly voted to declare war against Athens. This began the Peloponnesian War, which would eventually destroy Athenian power.

James Brian McNabb

Further Reading

Bagnall, Nigel. *The Peloponnesian War: Athens, Sparta, and the Struggle for Greece.* New York: Thomas Dunne Books, 2006.

Brice, Lee L., and Jennifer Roberts, eds. *Recent Directions in the Military History of the Ancient World.* Claremont, CA: Regina Books, 2011.

Buckler, John. *Aegean Greece in the Fourth Century BC.* Leiden, Netherlands: Brill, 2003.

Cartwright, David. *A Historical Commentary on Thucydides.* Ann Arbor: University of Michigan Press, 1997.

de Ste. Croix, G. E. M. *The Origins of the Peloponnesian War.* London: Duckworth, 1972.

Fornara, Charles W., and Loren J. Samons II. *Athens from Cleisthenes to Pericles.* Berkeley: University of California Press, 1991.

Hanson, Victor Davis. *A War Like No Other: How the Athenians and Spartans Fought the Peloponnesian War.* New York: Random House, 2006.

Hornblower, Simon. *A Commentary on Thucydides.* 3 vols. Oxford: Oxford University Press, 1991, 1996, 2009.

Hornblower, Simon. *The Greek World, 479–323 BC.* 4th ed. New York: Routledge, 2011.

Jones, W. T., and Robert J. Fogelin. *A History of Western Philosophy: The Classical Mind.* 2nd ed. Belmont, CA: Wadsworth, 1969.

Kagan, Donald. *The Fall of the Athenian Empire.* Ithaca, NY: Cornell University Press, 1987.

Kagan, Donald. *On the Origins of War and the Preservation of Peace.* New York: Anchor Books, 1996.

Kagan, Donald. *The Outbreak of the Peloponnesian War.* Ithaca, NY: Cornell University Press, 1969.

Kagan, Donald. *Pericles of Athens and the Birth of Democracy.* New York: Free Press, 1998.

Kagan, Donald. *The Peloponnesian War.* New York: Viking, 2003.

Kennel, Nigel M. *Spartans: A New History.* Malden, MA: Wiley-Blackwell, 2010.

Lazenby, J. F. *The Peloponnesian War: A Military Study.* New York: Routledge, 2004.

Lendon, J. E. "Athens and Sparta and the Coming of the Peloponnesian War." In *The Cambridge Companion to the Age of Pericles,* edited by Loren J. Samos II, 258–281. Cambridge: Cambridge University Press, 2007.

Lendon, J. E. *Song of Wrath: The Peloponnesian War Begins.* New York: Basic Books, 2010.

Martin, Thomas R. *Ancient Greece*. New Haven, CT: Yale University Press, 1996.

Morpeth, Neil. *Thucydides' War: Accounting for the Faces of Conflict*. New York: OLMS, 2006.

Rhodes, P. J. *A History of the Classical Greek World, 478–323 BC*. 2nd ed. Malden, MA: Wiley-Blackwell, 2010.

Sealey, Raphael. "The Causes of the Peloponnesian War." *Classical Philology* 70(2) (April 1975): 89–109.

Taylor, Martha. *Thucydides, Pericles, and the Idea of Athens in the Peloponnesian War*. Cambridge: Cambridge University Press, 2009.

Thucydides. *History of the Peloponnesian War*. Translated by Rex Warner. London: Penguin, 1972.

Thucydides. *The Landmark Thucydides*. Edited by Robert Strassler. New York: Free Press, 1998.

Tritle, Lawrence A. *A New History of the Peloponnesian War*. Malden, MA: Wiley-Blackwell, 2010.

Vasiliev, Aleksander Aleksandrovich. *History of the Byzantine Empire, 324–1453*. Madison: University of Wisconsin Press, 1952.

Walbank, F. W. *The Hellenistic World*. Cambridge, MA: Harvard University Press, 1993.

Welwei, Karl-Wilhelm. "The Peloponnesian War and Its Aftermath." In *A Companion to the Classical Greek World*, edited by Konrad Kinzl, 526–543. Malden, MA: Wiley-Blackwell, 2006.

2. WHY DID ALEXANDER THE GREAT'S EMPIRE FALL APART SO SOON AFTER HIS DEATH?

As incredible as the meteoric rise of Alexander the Great's empire was, its swift demise was equally dramatic. Indeed, Alexander spent less time governing his newly won domain than he did creating it. His imprint on the Greek world was nevertheless enormous and long-lasting. His conquests led to the diffusion of Greco-Buddhism and the eastern expansion of Greek culture, which in turn created a new Hellenistic civilization. Alexander founded at least 20 different cities that bore his name, including Egypt's Alexandria. Taught by the great Greek philosopher Aristotle, Alexander above all was an extraordinary military leader and would serve as a model military commander for many centuries after his death. In the wake of the conqueror's death in 323 BCE, his empire was split among several of his generals, thus permanently dividing it; the empire went on to endure as independent states. Given the mysteries surrounding the young ruler's death, it is perhaps not surprising that scholars have debated not only how Alexander died but also how his empire might have fared had he lived.

Dr. Peter Green, in the first perspective essay, argues that Alexander was too preoccupied with the process of conquest itself and too disinterested in governing newly won territory, meaning that his impressive land gains were rather ephemeral. He saw himself more as a Homeric warrior-king than a ruler of a vast empire. Furthermore, Green points out that many of Alexander's conquests were tenuous or incomplete and that he included too few fellow Greeks in his inner circle of advisers. For Dr. Jeanne Reames, the question of the empire's fall begs another question: would it have survived even had Alexander lived? Reames not only examines the competition among Alexander's general staff, his lack of an heir, and the sheer size of his domain but also asserts that his empire might have been in trouble even before he died. Notions of kingship in Macedonia and in the East were far different, and Alexander never successfully melded these divergent understandings of rulership. In the third essay, Dr. Ian Worthington cites several factors in the demise of Alexander's empire. First, there were the immense difficulties of administering territory that stretched from Greece in the west to Pakistan in the east. Added to this, Alexander's empire was extremely diverse, and many of his subjects had a long history of resisting invaders. Worthington further argues that the ambitions of Alexander's generals and their animosity toward one another also led to the collapse of the empire. But perhaps the greatest factor in the empire's demise was the fact that Alexander left no undisputed successor.

Background Essay

Alexander III (356–323 BCE) was the king of Macedonia (336–332), the pharaoh of Egypt (332–323), the king of Persia (330–323), and the king of Asia (331–323). His conquests and his military abilities rank him as one of history's truly great captains. His vision of a unified people and his role in spreading Greek culture changed the Mediterranean world and ushered in the Hellenistic period, warranting him the appellation of "the Great."

Alexander was born in Pella, Macedonia, in 356 BCE to Philip II, king of Macedonia, and Olympias of Epirus. Bright and charismatic, Alexander had the philosopher Aristotle as his teacher after 342. Although as a boy Alexander had a tumultuous relationship with his father, much of his later success is attributable to Philip's training and generals. Philip created the superb Macedonian Army that his son used to conquer the known world. Philip also secured control of Greece, an essential prelude to an invasion of the Persian Empire.

Alexander proved himself as a military commander, having charge of the Macedonian left-wing cavalry in Philip's victory over the allied Greeks in the Battle of Chaeronea (August 338). In 337 Alexander fled with Olympias to Epirus following a violent quarrel between her and Philip. Both returned to Pella some months later.

Philip was preparing to invade Persia when he was assassinated in July 336. Suspicions swirled around Alexander and Olympias, but the succession was not contested, and Alexander became king. Before he could carry out his father's plan of invading Persia, Alexander first shored up his power base in northern Greece. In 335 he won a series of victories in Thessaly, Boeotia, and Illyria, and he brutally suppressed a revolt in Thebes, after which he razed the city.

In 334 Alexander set out to invade the Persian Empire, the world's largest. Departing Macedonia with an army of Macedonian and Greek soldiers drawn from the League of Corinth, the confederation Philip had created after his victory at Chaeronea in 338, Alexander crossed the Hellespont (Dardanelles) into Asia Minor with the aim of first liberating the small Greek city-states of Asia Minor. His army was small for the task ahead of it: only some 30,000 infantry and 5,000 cavalry. What moved his men was Alexander's leadership. He shared their hardships and was always in the thick of the fray.

The Persian satraps (governors) of Asia Minor assembled a much larger force to fight Alexander and waited for him on the east bank of the Granicus River. In May 334 Alexander personally led his cavalry across the river into the Persian line, and the Macedonians achieved a stunning victory. This dramatic triumph established Alexander as a bold commander and inspired fanatical devotion to him among his men.

After freeing the Ionian cities from Persian control, Alexander won successive battles and sieges in central Turkey, and in September the swift-moving Alexander surprised the Persian defenders of the Cilician Gates (near Bolkar Daglari) and seized that vital pass without a fight. Alexander then moved against the main Persian army under Emperor Darius III. The decisive Battle of Issus (November 333) again proved Alexander's reputation. Darius escaped, but Alexander captured Darius's family and all of his baggage, later marrying one of Darius's daughters. Alexander refused an offer from Darius of 10,000 talents (300 tons) in gold.

Alexander then pushed south. In one of the great siege operations in all history, he took Tyre and Gaza at the end of 332. All Phoenicia passed under his control, an essential prelude to a new invasion of Persia as far as his lines of communication back to Greece were concerned. He then occupied Egypt, traveling into the desert to consult the oracle of Ammon at Siwa (331), where he was greeted by the priest as the son of Ammon (Zeus to the Greeks). It is not clear whether Alexander believed in his own divinity.

Detail of a mosaic depicting Alexander the Great on horseback at the Battle of Issus (333 BCE). A brilliant military commander, Alexander conquered Persia and spread Greek culture throughout much of the known world. (Jupiterimages)

Learning that Darius had put together a huge new army, Alexander departed Egypt and marched north into southern Mesopotamia in the spring of 331. Alexander and his army crossed the Tigris River that September, and in the Battle of Gaugamela (Arbela) in October 331 with about 50,000 men, he again defeated King Darius III's force, variously estimated at between 250,000 and 1 million men. Alexander's victory ended the Persian Empire.

Later in 331 Alexander captured Babylon and then Susa. Cities rallied to him, knowing of his leniency and toleration of their gods if they surrendered and of terrible punishments if they resisted. In December in a lightning strike, Alexander secured the Persian Gates and then occupied and sacked the Persian capital of Persepolis, one of the blemishes on his career (the reasons remain in dispute). When Darius was killed in 330 by members of his own entourage, Alexander became king.

Alexander shocked his Macedonians by adopting Persian dress and ceremonies and by advancing Persians to high posts. He insisted that his generals take Persian wives. Aristotle had told him to treat the Persians as slaves, but Alexander had a wider vision in which all men would be bound by a common culture (that of Greece) and have equal opportunity based on their deeds.

Alexander now ruled the greatest empire of antiquity, but he wanted more. He campaigned along the southern shores of the Caspian Sea. Suppressing a plot from among his senior officers, he ordered the execution of both Philotas and his father Parmenion in December 330. In 329 Alexander invaded southern Afghanistan and Badakshan. Wherever he went he founded new cities, many of them named for him (the most famous was Alexandria in Egypt). He then campaigned along the Oxus River before besieging and capturing the reputedly impregnable fortresses of the Sogdian Rock and the Chiorenes Rock in 327. He then married Roxanne, daughter of the lord of the Sogdian Rock, reportedly to secure an heir, for Alexander had a male lover in his general Hephaestion. That same year Alexander crushed a plot against him from among the corps of pages, executing its leader.

Alexander invaded India by the Khyber Pass, crossed the Indus River (April 326 BCE), and defeated King Porus in the Battle of the Hydaspes (May). That July Alexander's army mutinied, refusing to proceed farther. Alexander then led his army in a difficult and nearly disastrous march across the Gedrosian desert in Buluchistan during September–November 325, returning to Persepolis in January 324. He then crushed another mutiny against his assimilationist policies in the army. He arrived in Babylon (spring 323), evidently intent on making it his capital. In June 323 after a night of heavy banqueting, Alexander took ill for several days. He died on June 13, 323. At his death, he was 32 years old.

Alexander was a general of unmatched leadership who excelled in every type of combat, including sieges and irregular warfare. A master of logistics, he also possessed a keen administrative sense. He was never defeated in battle. It was not just that Alexander conquered much of the known world, for his reign also ushered in a new era in which Greek culture spread to new areas. The rulers who followed him adopted similar court practices and continued his Hellenizing policy.

Following Alexander's death, first Perdiccas and then Antigonus the One-Eyed endeavored to maintain the unity of the empire. Soon, however, a dozen of Alexander's leading generals (the Diadochi, or successors) were fighting for control of the state. Although skillful generals, none had Alexander's vision or genius. By 309 Alexander's direct family had been eliminated, and the contenders believed themselves strong enough to claim the title of king in their own areas of the Hellenistic world. Alexander's vision of a universal commonwealth was thus lost. By 176 the three major power centers of the Hellenistic empire were Macedon, Egypt, and the Seleucid Empire.

Despite the breakup of Alexander's empire, the cultural impact of his conquests was immense. The fusion of the Greek culture with that of the Persians has been called "Hellenistic" and impacted virtually all areas, including the arts but also education, government, and even city planning. The impact of Hellenistic culture was still evident in the Byzantine Empire of the mid-15th century.

Spencer C. Tucker

Perspective Essay 1. Alexander's Obsession with Conquest

Augustus, the first Roman emperor (and no mean empire builder) is noted as having been surprised "that Alexander did not regard it as a greater task to set in order the empire which he had won than to win it" (Plutarch, *Moralia,* 207d 8). This accurately addresses Alexander's central weakness, which so far as his legend went was also his strength. For him, the overriding obsession was conquest in itself. He saw himself as a Homeric hero, an avatar of Achilles, a king and warrior whose glorious renown (*kleos*) came solely from dazzling military achievements. Conquering the Persian Empire was not sufficient. In Babylon during the last two years of his life, he was feverishly planning the conquest of North Africa and then Spain, Italy, and Sicily. On his deathbed he was discussing the logistics of an assault on the Arabian Peninsula. The administration of these, as of his earlier conquered territories, came very low on his list of priorities.

Worse, when we consider the durability of his arrangements, was the fact that in many ways even Alexander's conquests were inadequate, incomplete, or sometimes nonexistent. He carved his narrow route of victories from the Granicus River to western India, but many areas remained at best semipacified, and revolts flared up in his wake as he moved on. The only area that actively welcomed him was Egypt, where Persian rule had, unusually, been oppressive. India, Bactria (modern-day Afghanistan), and much of Iran were never properly subdued. Alexander's notion of administration was to leave the local system and local officials in place but to put reliable Macedonian governors in on top of them to make sure that taxes and tribute were channeled in the right direction—that is, primarily to the invaders.

We have to remember that for a century or so Greek rhetoricians such as Isocrates had been preaching a debased form of Panhellenism, a crusade to unite the eternally quarreling Greek states. Revenge must be secured for Xerxes I's attempt to invade Greece a century and a half earlier, for his destruction of Athens, and for the burning of Greek temples. How better to achieve this end than, collectively, to invade and conquer the Achaemenid Empire? The Greeks believed the Persian regime to be fabulously wealthy, its rulers despotic and cowardly, and its soldiers no match for Greek troops. What the Greek world was being offered was a free pass for morally justified conquest followed by systematic colonial exploitation with no end in sight. The temptation was great; the irony was that the ones who carried it out were not the southern Greeks—though many of them considered the idea—but rather their northern neighbors, the Macedonians.

This kingdom of highland toughs, lowland farmers, and wine-swilling local barons had been taken in hand by Alexander's father Philip, heir to the Argead royal house, who had refashioned Macedonia into a powerful military state with a near-professional army maintained by wealth extracted from the Thracian gold and silver mines. In less than half a century Macedonia became the dominant power in Greece. This was sealed in a devastating victory over the combined southern states at Chaeronea in 338 BCE.

After this victory, the invasion of Persia was only a matter of time. Philip intended to lead it, but he fell to an assassin's dagger at the wedding of his daughter, and his son Alexander (who had always believed the conquest of Persia to be his own sacred destiny) took the throne and proceeded to make his destiny reality.

However, Alexander's (and his father's) previous dealings with the southern Greek states left him with a problem. The Macedonians had not only defeated them in battle and deprived them of their cherished independence; when one of them, famous Thebes, showed signs of revolt—and, worse, publicly insulted Alexander— he retaliated by destroying the city, with huge loss of life. The Greeks never forgave him. They detested him, and he never trusted them. As a result, there were few southern Greek volunteers for the great Persian expedition (Sparta refused to participate altogether), and those who came were kept out of the front line. Rather than use the Greek fleet to assault the ports of the eastern Aegean, Alexander sent it home and captured the ports out from landward. His Greek personal secretary, Eumenes, was the one non-Macedonian player after his death in the fight for the succession.

Thus, all responsibility throughout the dozen years of the Persian expedition rested with Alexander's corps of Macedonian officers. The only Greeks in his inner circle were private friends, scientists, literary guests, and the expedition's chroniclers. When toward the end Alexander inevitably ran short of trustworthy Macedonians to leave in place as governors and other staff in conquered territories, rather than turn to Greeks he started a policy of using the equivalent Persians he had conquered; he even began training young Persians to take the place of Macedonian officers and adopted Persian court protocol for himself.

The battle-hardened Macedonians who had fought their way to the Hindu Kush and beyond with Alexander hated this new turn of events. They had joined the expedition to make their fortunes; their commander's dreams of unending world conquest—especially now that he began to show signs of megalomania and delusions of godhead—had no attraction for them whatsoever. If Alexander had not looted the Persian treasuries of their immense stores of gold and silver and used this to bribe his troops wholesale to go on, the expedition might well have ground to a halt two or three years earlier than it did. As it was, three monsoons and a final battle, that of the Hydaspes (Jhelum) River (326), fought in a welter of mud, blood, and driving rain against enemies supported by wound-maddened elephants, finally caused his proud veterans to mutiny and refuse to proceed farther.

Alexander, furious but defeated, marched his men back as far as Babylon, where, as we have seen, he found himself incapable of giving up his dreams of conquest.

All of this was cut short in 323 by his premature death: there were rumors, not surprisingly, that he had been poisoned, though a combination of wounds, tropical diseases, and alcoholism may well have been responsible.

On Alexander's death all his grandiose schemes were cancelled, literally, overnight. Revolts broke out in Greece and the East. His senior officers, whom he had kept in control like a lion tamer, now spent four decades fighting for the spoils of conquest, and the survivors ended as kings themselves, in Macedonia, Egypt, and Asia. These Hellenistic kingdoms lasted for three centuries. But Alexander himself had never truly had a real empire, only insecure and unsettled conquests, to be battled for by his greedy and ambitious successors.

Peter Green

Perspective Essay 2. Deep-Seated Cultural Differences in Alexander's Empire

Alexander's conquest of Asia is sometimes presented as a triumphal march from battlefield victory to battlefield victory. Yet while he was an outstanding strategist with a real gift for second-guessing (and therefore psyching out) his military opponents, when it came to politics, Alexander was not yet the equal of his father, Philip II of Macedon. Of course, all things considered, Alexander was still young— invading Asia at only 22 years of age—and his views grew more complex (and more cynical) over time as he faced the increasingly thorny problem of ruling the multinational empire he had just acquired.

Conquest had been the easy part. We need only point to recent struggles in the Middle East to realize that winning battles in this region is easier than keeping the peace afterward. Yet it is peacekeeping that allows an empire to survive.

For all Alexander's ability to solve logistical puzzles and pull tactical rabbits out of his helmet, the one problem he never truly solved was combining traditional Oriental (Eastern) and Occidental (Western) views on rule. Western views tended to regard the ruler as first among equals. For instance, all a Macedonian subject had to do before addressing his king was to remove his hat. After that, he could speak to him face-to-face, joke with him, and touch and even scold him. In fact, Macedonian kings were not addressed as "king," because a man who needed the title wasn't fit to be a king. Macedonians expected their king to be approachable. He acted not only as priest, war leader, and policy maker but also even as hunting companion and drinking buddy. Kings led battles from the front, visited the hospital tent afterward, and, when the going got tough, offered encouragement even to the lowest foot soldier. Kings also had a sacred duty to sit as judge and hear cases—and, according to Plutarch in his *Moralia,* might be told "to stop kinging it" by their subjects if they decided to pack up early. In two generations, Macedon went from this rough-and-ready highland kingdom to a world-spanning empire. It is little wonder if Alexander struggled with that transformation.

By contrast, the Achaemenid Persian Empire had existed for two centuries, itself inheriting a millennia-old Mesopotamian tradition of rule. Reliefs at the Persian capital of Persepolis depict themes of eternity and universality, and all figures appearing in the same frame as a king are smaller than he is. An extensive court bureaucracy was necessary to administrate such a large multinational empire, and only six people had unrestricted access to the king, whose proper title was *shahan-shah* (king of kings, or great king), because other kings acted as governors under his authority. While the great king was not himself considered to be a god (unlike the Egyptian pharaoh), the *proskynesis* (a specific bow of respect) offered to him by his subjects was certainly seen by Westerners as offered only to gods—and according to the Roman biographer Nepos, the Greeks refused to perform it for a man. In terms of power over their lives, the average Persian subject might see little difference between the great king and a god. The great king embodied the will of the Zoroastrian god Ahura Mazda, much as the Persian Abbasid caliphs of the medieval world would later be called "shadows of God (Allah) on Earth."

Thus, a short 20-something young man with a sunburn who dressed no differently than his own officers did not—to the Persians—seem like a real king. They had a difficult time taking him seriously. Understanding this and fearing a succession of revolts in his rear, Alexander attempted to introduce some Persian procedures into his own court, but they were received with grumbling at best and outright rejection at worst.

Alexander's problem was not conquering Persia—it was successfully ruling an empire made up of both Easterners and Westerners. Easterners regarded Westerners as uncultured brute animals, while Westerners regarded Easterners as groveling weaklings and "natural slaves" (in Aristotle's terminology). These were hardly grounds for mutual respect and cooperation.

Given this, the fracture of Alexander's empire after his death was hardly a surprise. Yes, his failure to marry young and produce a viable heir—not to mention his preference for conquest, glory, and adventure over the daily grind of actual rule— certainly contributed. Yet the real difficulty was more pervasive and involved deep-seated cultural differences.

The Occident and the Orient have always been uncomfortable bed partners, and in fact Alexander's empire broke apart along predictable geographical lines that mirrored age-old cultural divisions. Bactria (modern-day Afghanistan) became its own kingdom influenced by the Greco-Macedonians but with a unique flavor,

India tore away under the rule of Candra Gupta Maurya (Chandragupta), and Alexander's own marshals divided up the rest. Seleucus I Nicator held the Near and Middle East (the heart of the old Persian Empire), Ptolemy I Soter took Egypt, and the Antigonids seized Macedonia. There were other smaller kingdoms too, such as Pergamum and even Greece itself (the Achaean League). If the Romans would later have more luck at holding things together, even their empire never extended as far to the east as Alexander reached.

The primary difficulty faced by Alexander—and the reason his empire was neither long-lived nor ultimately successful—involved deep-seated cultural differences. These differences still dog modern political intercourse between the West and the Middle East. Is a more equal democratic approach to rule correct, or is a more absolute and theocratic approach correct? The answer to that question is as much historical and anthropological as philosophical.

Jeanne Reames

Perspective Essay 3. The Problem of Succession

Alexander III (the Great) of Macedonia died in Babylon in June 323 BCE. The most widely accepted explanation for his death is acute alcoholic pancreatitis, and probably contributing to his demise was a constitution weakened by wounds (some nearly fatal) suffered in battles and sieges. By the time of his death Alexander had extended the Macedonian Empire from Greece in the west to what the Greeks called "India" (Pakistan) in the east, and he had done so in a reign of only 13 years (336–323) after invading Asia in 334.

There was no undisputed successor to Alexander; his wife Roxana was still pregnant when he died. Hence, immediately on his death it was left to his senior staff at Babylon to decide the future of the Macedonian Empire. They held a meeting at which they divided Alexander's empire into a number of different areas, each of them ruling over one of these areas. For example, Ptolemy I Soter received Egypt (and founded the Ptolemaic dynasty), and Antipater (whom Alexander had left behind as a regent of Greece) was given Macedonia and Greece. Thus ended the single Macedonian Empire.

The ambitions and rival personalities of the generals soon surfaced, and the settlement at Babylon broke down within three years. During the next 30 years or so these men (in some cases along with their sons) would wage a series of bloody wars (the so-called Wars of the Successors) to gain control of their previous comrades' areas until eventually the great kingdoms of the Hellenistic period (such as Ptolemaic

Egypt and Seleucid Syria) came into being. Thus, what happened to Alexander's empire is easy enough to comprehend, but the big question is why it did not remain intact and disintegrated so quickly.

One answer is that Alexander acquired his empire, especially in Asia, by conquest. Although he had tried to reconcile the various peoples of Asia to his rule, he could not boast a record of success, and he had faced a number of revolts, especially in Bactria, Sogdiana, and "India." Hence, the conquered peoples would have taken advantage of Alexander's death and the rivalries of his senior staff to bring an end to Macedonian rule.

Added to this explanation was the sheer size of the empire. The principal reason for the collapse of the Roman Empire was its vast size, even though it later split between east and west and was administered by more than one ruler, whereas the existence of Alexander's empire depended solely on him. The Persian kings soon discovered that their empire was too large for one man to govern effectively, and Darius I had split it into 20 satrapies (or provinces), each ruled by a satrap (or governor). This middle-management position meant that the satrap was subservient to the great king of Persia but had virtually a free hand to govern his satrapy as he saw fit, thus easing the burden on the great king. Alexander maintained the satrap system, but the difference was that many of his satraps showed him little loyalty. Hence, he was constantly faced with challenges in administering an empire that, unlike the Persian kings, he had to deal with himself. His empire thus grew too big for one person to control effectively.

The above factors played some role in the collapse of Alexander's empire, but Alexander left no clear successor, and the personal rivalries among his generals are probably more important. Alexander had been advised to marry and produce an heir when he became king before he left for Asia in 334, but he had ignored that advice. It was not until 327 that he married a Bactrian princess named Roxana, a marriage that did not sit well with his men given her ethnicity. Alexander already had a half brother, Arrhidaeus, who was living in Pella (the Macedonian capital) and was Macedonian. Since Roxana was pregnant as Alexander lay dying in 323, his generals asked him to whom he would leave his empire. He replied "to the best."

When Roxana gave birth to a son, Alexander IV, shortly after her husband died, the problem of the succession intensified. Alexander the Great's son was of course a baby (a regent would be needed until he became of age), whereas Arrhidaeus was already old enough to become king.

There was also the problem of Alexander's enigmatic answer "to the best." The king had given his signet ring to Perdiccas, his second-in-command, shortly before dying. Perdiccas interpreted this gesture, together with these last words, to mean that he was to succeed Alexander. The other generals did not agree. In truth, during the past several years personality clashes and rivalries had been increasing among Alexander's generals.

While there were individual generals who might want to rule the sort of empire that Alexander had established, despite the problems inherent in this as outlined above, no one general was acceptable to Alexander's senior staff. Hence, one group of generals supported the rights of Philip III Arrhidaeus (as he came to be known) to the Macedonian throne, while a rival group supported those of Alexander IV. Both Philip III and Alexander IV were soon put to death, leaving the generals to continue battling for more territory and power.

Without a proper heir to the throne and given the lack of unity among Alexander's generals, the rapid disintegration of his empire was inevitable.

Ian Worthington

Further Reading

Austin, M. M. *The Hellenistic World from Alexander to the Roman Conquest: A Selection of Ancient Sources in Translation.* Cambridge: Cambridge University Press, 2006.

Bosworth, Albert B. *Alexander and the East: The Tragedy of Triumph.* Oxford: Oxford University Press, 2001.

Bosworth, Albert B. *Conquest and Empire: The Reign of Alexander the Great.* Cambridge: Cambridge University Press, 1988.

Bugh, Glenn Richard. *The Cambridge Companion to the Hellenistic World.* New York: Cambridge University Press, 2006.

Burn, A. *Alexander the Great and the Hellenistic Empire.* 2nd ed. London: English Universities Press, 1951.

Daskalakis, A. *Alexander the Great and Hellenism.* Thessaloniki: Institute for Balkan Studies, 1966.

Engels, Donald W. *Alexander the Great and the Logistics of the Macedonian Army.* Berkeley: University of California Press, 1978.

Fuller, J. F. C. *The Generalship of Alexander the Great.* New York: Da Capo, 1990.

Green, Peter. *Alexander the Great and the Hellenistic Age: A Short History.* London: Phoenix, 2008.

Green, Peter. *Alexander of Macedon, 356–323 B.C.: A Historical Biography.* Berkeley: University of California Press, 1991.

Green, Peter. *Alexander to Actium: The Historical Evolution of the Hellenistic Age.* Berkeley: University of California Press, 1990.

Gruen, Erich S. *The Hellenistic World and the Coming of Rome.* Berkeley: University of California Press, 1986.

Hammond, N. G. L. *Alexander the Great: King, Commander, and Statesman.* 3rd ed. London: Bristol Classical, 1996.

Hammond, N. G. L. *The Genius of Alexander the Great.* Chapel Hill: University of North Carolina Press, 1997.

Hammond, N. G. L. *The Macedonian State: Origins, Institutions, and History.* Oxford: Oxford University Press, 1989.

Kern, Paul Bentley. *Ancient Siege Warfare*. Bloomington: Indiana University Press, 1999.

Lane Fox, Robin. *Alexander the Great*. London: Penguin, 2005.

McCrindle, J. W. *The Invasion of India by Alexander the Great as Described by Arrian, Q Curtius, Diodorus, Plutarch, and Justin*. Westminster, UK: Archibald Constable, 1993.

Plutarch. *The Life of Alexander*. New York: Modern Library, 2004.

Quintus, Curtius Rufus. *The History of Alexander*. New York: Penguin Classics, 1984.

Renault, Mary. *The Nature of Alexander*. New York: Pantheon Books, 1976.

Sekunda, Nick, and John Warry. *Alexander the Great: His Armies and Campaigns, 332–323 B.C.* London: Osprey, 1988.

Worthington, Ian. *Alexander the Great: Man and God*. Harlow, UK: Longman, 2004.

3. Why Was the Carthaginian General Hannibal So Successful against Roman Armies but Ultimately Defeated in His War against Rome?

Even today, ancient sources on Hannibal, the Carthaginian general who inflicted such costly setbacks on Rome during the Second Punic War (218–201 BCE), are required reading for students of military history. His brilliant victories at the Trebbia River, Lake Trasimene, and Cannae—to name three classic examples—have become legendary, so much so that modern military leaders such as German general Alfred Graf von Schlieffen, who devised the Schlieffen Plan prior to World War I, based some of his plans on those used by Hannibal. Roman forces, however, countered Hannibal's strategic and tactical brilliance by fighting a grinding war of attrition against Carthage, successfully laying siege to and eventually recapturing many cities that had defected to the Carthaginian side during the war. The enormity of Rome's losses during much of the conflict cannot be denied, however, nor can Hannibal's role in those losses be minimized. Despite Hannibal's smashing victories and Rome's heavy losses, Rome not only survived but also eventually won its war with Carthage. How could a general so brilliant, with so many important victories, lose?

Dr. Dexter Hoyos, in the first perspective essay, maintains that Hannibal's aim was not wholesale domination of Rome but rather its reduction to a Carthaginian satellite.

Hannibal set out to do this by destroying Rome's armies, luring its allies to switch allegiances, and ultimately forcing Rome to sue for peace. He failed because Roman resistance defied even the worst defeat in the field but also because he made tactical mistakes. He sent more forces to other theaters than to Italy, underestimated the loyalty of Rome's Italian allies, and eschewed besieging Rome itself. Dr. Garrett G. Fagan focuses on Hannibal's strategy to incite the Italian allies against Rome. Hannibal was largely unsuccessful in accomplishing this, and the strategy became more of a nuisance than a threat once the war moved into Spain. Because his strategy in Italy relied so heavily on reducing Rome's ability to draw men from its allies, Hannibal's inability to effect widespread defections doomed him to failure. Rome had cultivated its relationship with its allies so well and for so long that by and large they remained loyal. For Dr. Jessica H. Clark, military success was not the key to overall victory. She cites several factors that led to Hannibal's defeat, among them differing opinions of how to force a surrender. When Rome refused to capitulate, Hannibal believed that victory in the field would decide the final outcome, but Rome persevered, even after sustaining tremendous losses. In addition, Rome successfully moved the focus of the war out of Italy and into Spain, thereby dividing Carthaginian forces and resources.

Background Essay

The Second Punic War, which lasted from 218 to 201 BCE, was the middle of three wars between the Roman Republic and Carthage for control of the Mediterranean world. During the second war the legendary Carthaginian general Hannibal led his troops to several impressive victories, but Carthage ultimately succumbed to the growing power of Rome.

After losing Sicily to the Roman Republic at the end of the First Punic War (264–241 BCE), Carthage had to deal with a mercenary revolt. Rome took advantage of the situation, securing the island of Sardinia from Carthage in 238. To compensate for their losses, the Carthaginians began to extend their territorial holdings in Spain. Initially under the command of General Hamilcar Barca and afterward under his son-in-law Hasdrubal, the Carthaginians conquered a large part of the Iberian Peninsula. Anxious to establish their own contacts in Spain, Rome entered the Iberian Peninsula from Gaul as the Carthaginians were consolidating the south. In 226 Carthage and Rome reached an agreement in which Carthage agreed to stay south of the Ebro River in northern Spain, while Rome was to stay north of it.

In 221, Hamilcar's son Hannibal was chosen to command the Carthaginian Army. Hannibal quickly focused his attention on the Spanish town of Saguntum

A first-century BCE bust of Hannibal Barca (247–182 BCE). Leader of Carthaginian forces against Rome in the Second Punic War, Hannibal was one of history's great captains and certainly the most dangerous foe Rome ever faced. (The LIFE Picture Collection/Getty Images)

south of the Ebro, which had allied itself with Rome in an attempt to fend off Carthage. Hannibal viewed that alliance as a violation of the 226 treaty and responded by laying siege to the city in 219; he captured it eight months later. As the siege continued, a militant faction came to power in Rome and declared war against Carthage in 218.

Carthage had lost control of the waters of the northwestern Mediterranean, so Hannibal decided to preempt a Roman invasion of Spain by moving his forces overland in an invasion of Italy. Surprising almost everyone by this bold move, he defeated all resistance and, by November 218, moved his army, complete with elephants, through the Alps into northern Italy. Fighting local tribes in the mountains, coupled with the onset of winter weather, resulted in the deaths of many of his men, but he entered Italy with about 20,000 infantry and 6,000 cavalry. Hannibal's strategy was to provoke the subject tribes of Italy into revolt against Rome, which would simultaneously weaken their power and enlarge his. His apparent goal was not to destroy Rome as a major power but instead to limit the Romans to the Italian Peninsula and regain territory lost since the first war.

During the next few years Hannibal rampaged through Italy, defeating Roman forces in the Battle of the Trebbia in December 218 and the Battle of Lake Trasimene in June 217. At Cannae in August 216, he won one of history's most brilliant victories by executing a double envelopment of the Roman forces in which he inflicted an estimated 50,000 casualties while losing only about 6,000 of his own men. After that debacle, the new Roman commander Quintus Fabius Maximus Cunctator decided that the best way to fight Hannibal was to avoid pitched battles. Indeed, the Latin agnomen *cunctator* means "delayer" and references his strategy of securing the cities and attacking the Carthaginian supply lines. Indeed, he is regarded by many as the father of guerrilla warfare. As a result, Hannibal did not secure as many allies from among the Italian cities as he had hoped, nor did he have a sufficient siege train to assault the well-defended Roman-allied cities. He had to content himself with living off the countryside and attacking the occasional city, usually with mixed results.

Meanwhile in Sicily, Syracuse had broken its alliance with Rome and joined the Carthaginians in 214. Under the command of Marcus Claudius Marcellus, the Romans attacked in 213. The defenders were assisted by mechanical artillery developed by the famed scientist Archimedes. A lengthy siege ensued, combined with campaigning against Carthaginian troops and numerous hostile towns. In 211 the Romans took Syracuse, and by 210 all of Sicily was under Roman control. Besides the overseas expeditions to Sicily, the Romans also campaigned in Sardinia and Illyria (present-day Albania).

In Spain, Rome committed its reconstituted military, attempting to deny Hannibal his base of operations. Hannibal's brother Hasdrubal fought a long and inconclusive campaign against Roman forces under the brothers Publius Scipio and Gnaeus Scipio. Both Spain and Italy saw much fighting, but no force became dominant until 209, after the son of Publius Scipio came to command in Spain. Scipio Africanus the Elder captured Cartagena, the capital of Carthaginian Spain, and forced Hasdrubal and his brother Mago onto the defensive in southwestern Iberia. In 207 Hasdrubal crossed over the Alps to reinforce his brother, but he was defeated and killed in the Battle of the Metaurus River.

The fighting continued without much success on either side until 206, when Scipio achieved an impressive victory in the Battle of Ilipa and consolidated Roman power in Spain. In 204 he sailed for Africa, where he raised a Numidian ally to aid him. Scipio failed to impose his will on Carthage but caused its leadership to recall Hannibal home to defend the city; Hannibal could not comply, as Rome still controlled the sea. Scipio's capture of Tunis, very near Carthage, caused the Carthaginians to agree to a truce. Hannibal returned to Carthage under the terms of the cease-fire to negotiate with Scipio. When they failed to reach agreement, the two sides fought the Battle of Zama in 202. Scipio, aided by Numidian cavalry, won and became the first Roman to defeat Hannibal in open battle.

Hannibal's defeat at Zama brought the war to an end in 201. Under the peace terms, Carthage lost its possessions in Spain and most of its African empire but maintained its merchant navy (although it was limited to 10 ships) and trading connections. Carthage also was to pay Rome reparations amounting to 10,000 talents (more than 500,000 pounds of silver) over a 50-year period. Still, Carthage was able to recover economically. Fearful of the consequences of this, Rome again went to war with Carthage in the Third Punic War (149–146), resulting in the complete destruction of Rome's rival.

Paul K. Davis

Perspective Essay 1. The Flaws in Hannibal's Great Enterprise

Although Carthaginian military leader Hannibal and his top commanders were away from Carthage for most of the Second Punic War (218–201 BCE), Greek historian Polybius concluded that Hannibal directed all military policy, no doubt through his network of supporters at home and his military lieutenants. This had a direct bearing on why Hannibal was successful for so long and yet ultimately failed. His intent was to force Rome to make peace on Carthaginian terms by inflicting costly defeats and winning over the Italian cities allied with Rome. His strategy came close to success, yet partly because of its inherent limitations and partly through Rome's qualities of resistance, in the end Hannibal failed.

Third-century Carthaginians practiced up-to-date Greek military methods. Hannibal himself judged Alexander the Great and Pyrrhus of Epirus as his greatest predecessors, and his tactical and strategic successes exploited all the features of Hellenistic warfare. Alexander's crucial contribution had been to employ cavalry with greater flexibility than before, especially in attack. Moreover, his infantry arms—light troops and massed phalanx—could also act resourcefully, and he was a master of fast movement both tactically and strategically. These skills required experienced long-service soldiers, not armies intermittently recruited from civilians. Pyrrhus, half a century later, made skillful use of war elephants—at least until the Romans worked out how to cope with them.

Carthage's armies took to war elephants all the more readily, as they were obtainable in Africa. The Carthaginian armies included professional infantry contingents from the western Mediterranean, notably Iberians (the Greek name for Spaniards) from Spain and Ligurians and Gauls from northern Italy. Other infantry came from the Libyan communities under Carthaginian rule. All served for long periods. Carthaginian citizens served as officers. The cavalry consisted primarily of the highly skilled light horsemen from Numidia, located in Africa to the west of Carthage.

Hannibal showed great military adaptability. Surprise moves, both strategic and tactical, were characteristic. He made bold use of ambushes, prompting the Romans to denounce such "Punic treachery." Brilliant battlefield tactics were Hannibal's trademark. No two of his great victories were gained in the same way. In the Battle of the Tagus River in Spain in 220, he let part of the pursuing Carpetanian forces cross over to his bank, then struck these with his elephants and simultaneously loosed cavalry on the Spaniards still in the stream before crossing back to rout the remainder. Against the Romans, both at the Trebbia River in 218 and at Cannae (August 216), he chose to let the Roman infantry launch the attack on his own center and then held them with his infantry center and assaulted their flanks and rear with cavalry and elephants. In 218 the Roman attack proved too forceful to be stalled: the infantry broke through, though the Carthaginians inflicted heavy losses. At Cannae, not only did Hannibal's more flexibly arrayed center hold, but he was also able to launch the flank and rear assault. Such battlefield maneuvers succeeded because all components of the Hannibalic army were well coordinated and officered to a level of sophistication rarely seen again in the ancient world.

Hannibal began the war with a remarkable group of subordinates. These included his nephew Hanno, his brother Mago (during 218–216), his quartermaster general Hasdrubal, and Maharbal. All could be trusted to perform complex missions and act on personal initiative. After Cannae, Mago and then Hanno were entrusted with a secondary army that operated across the south of Italy until 214, winning new allies and harassing Roman interests.

The high point of Hannibal's and Carthage's success followed Cannae. Between then and 212 much of central and southern Italy defected to him, including the ambitious city-states of Capua and Tarentum. Northern Italy's Gauls were largely pro-Carthage. In Spain the Roman invasion ground to a halt and was shattered in 211, while in Sicily a still independent Syracuse allied with Carthage, as did the far more powerful Kingdom of Macedon across the Adriatic. Thus, on every side Carthage and its allies threatened Rome and its remaining allies, largely constricted to central Italy, a scattered number of loyal cities in the south, and western Sicily.

Despite this, Hannibal's great enterprise suffered from a number of flaws. One glaring shortcoming was the small size in 218 of Carthage's once formidable navy. In the First Punic War, the Carthaginians had been able to put hundreds of warships to sea. However, when the Second Punic War began, Carthage had just over 100 warships in Spain and Africa—not all of them fit for action—while the Romans could launch 220. Although their numbers did grow in the next few years, at sea the Carthaginians accomplished little beyond ferrying troops or showing the flag to Sicily, Spain, and some other locations. They could not repel repeated Roman raids on the North African coast, nor did they oppose Scipio's crucial (and very public) crossing to Africa in 204. This had great impact. Most obviously, Hannibal could not invade Italy by sea and had to take the long land route, as did his brother Hasdrubal in 208. Nor could Carthage harass Italy's coasts or impede Roman trade, activities that could have materially aided Hannibal's operations on land.

Although Hannibal had able lieutenants to carry out his plans, Carthaginian military talent in the war was damagingly limited. Even an enterprising subordinate such as Hanno encountered problems in his independent command, and a shattering defeat in Samnium in 214 ended his prospects. Hannibal's other famous lieutenants were killed during the war, or, like Hanno, disappeared from the historical record, replaced by largely anonymous ones. In Italian field operations after 214, only Hannibal himself earns significant mention in the records except for when his brothers operated in northern Italy.

Generals elsewhere were frankly mediocre. Carthage's admiral Bomilcar (Hannibal's brother-in-law) headed the navy's unspectacular efforts. In Spain, Hannibal's brothers Hasdrubal and Mago (who joined Hasdrubal in 215) and their colleague Hasdrubal, son of Gisco, did destroy the overextended Roman forces in 211. But before that his brother Hasdrubal had suffered more than one defeat, and from 209—once the youthful Scipio took command in Spain—each suffered repeated defeats. By 206 all Carthaginian resistance in Spain had collapsed, leaving Scipio free to organize the invasion of Africa. Hannibal's brother Hasdrubal failed to exploit the triumph of 211 to take reinforcements to Italy as he had been ordered to do since 215. When he did at last reach northern Italy, he proved no match for the resourceful consuls of 207, Claudius Nero and Livius Salinator, who finished him at the Metaurus River. When Mago during 205–203 invaded Liguria in northern Italy with substantial forces and funds, he was stymied, crushed, and expelled by moderately competent Roman generals. Hasdrubal, son of Gisco, commanding in North Africa from 205, was catastrophically beaten by Scipio twice in 203, so badly that he committed suicide.

Hannibal himself was limited in his assets. Leaving Spain with 59,000 troops in the summer of 218, he reached the Rhône with 46,000 and descended from the Alps into Italy in the autumn with 20,000 infantry soldiers and 6,000 cavalry. Neither the summer and autumn weather nor Gallic attacks can be held accountable for such losses. Most of his 33,000 losses must have been due to desertion, with many of the African and Spanish rank and file losing heart at the prospect of winter and then Italian warfare. Whatever the reason, these losses radically affected his military potential. The thousands of Gauls who then joined him were warlike but much less disciplined and trustworthy. Had he brought 40,000–50,000 troops from Spain and added the Gauls to them and then Italians defecting after Cannae, his prospects of final victory would have been far greater.

Hannibal also refused to move against Rome itself until it was too late. After his victory in the Battle of Lake Trasimene, he was just five days' march away, the countryside lay open, and the city had virtually no garrison. Even his own officers expected him to march. He did not do so. After Cannae, with no significant Roman forces in his way and few fresh troops in the city, he again rejected such a course of action. On either occasion he only needed to cut Rome off from the hinterland to impress its Italian allies and possibly starve the city into submission. When he did march on Rome in 211, it was a mere feint to try to raise the Roman siege of his principal ally, Capua. The Romans were not fooled, Hannibal withdrew, and Capua surrendered. From then on, despite one or two more victories such as Herdonea (212), Hannibal was strategically on the defensive, confined to the south of Italy.

The overall direction of Carthage's war effort, which Polybius insists lay with Hannibal, also raises questions. Fresh armies were often dispatched to other theaters, notably Spain in 215, Sicily in 213, and Liguria in 205, but only a small body of

4,000 men and some elephants went to Hannibal after Cannae (presumably he chose to rely on recruiting Italians). Yet the 28,000 troops sent to Sicily or even the 21,000 sent to Liguria could have benefited his own operations far more, while in Sicily and Liguria they only met defeat. Hasdrubal's invasion during 208–207 with 30,000 or so men was a communications, strategic, and tactical disaster. Carthaginian naval weakness required him to follow his brother's overland route to northern Italy, with practically no prospect of joining Hannibal (then in Apulia), for everything in between swarmed with war-hardened legions. Likewise, Mago's dispatch to Liguria was a total waste of men and resources.

Hannibal's grand strategy was to inflict such thorough defeats on Rome that allied cities would defect quickly and the Romans would be forced to terms. It is fairly clear that Carthaginian strategy was not to physically destroy Rome but rather to reduce its territories, take over its external possessions, and make it an unthreatening satellite. When the Romans obdurately refused to negotiate, Hannibal had to fall back on a much more grinding strategy to attract Italian support, seek overseas allies so as to multiply and drain Rome's energies, and try for yet another smashing field victory that would force Rome to terms. But even a victory such as Herdonea in 210, as costly to the Romans as Trasimene, led nowhere. Hannibal began to lose his allies, and during 205–203 the Romans were able to keep him confined to Italy so that Scipio could campaign in North Africa.

The other chief factor in Hanibal's ultimate failure was Roman resistance. Even with the loss of perhaps 100,000 Roman and allied Italian troops between 218 and 216, the Romans called up fresh levies, maintained naval dominance and the invasion of Spain, and rid themselves of the new overseas enemies that Hannibal raised against them. In 211 no fewer than 25 legions with Italian-allied contingents were in service, 16 of them in Italy; in 207 there were 23, with 15 in Italy. More and more of Hannibal's allies submitted to Rome. The Romans also found better generals than those of Carthage except Hannibal, notably Claudius Marcellus and Claudius Nero. For Hannibal himself Rome finally found a match in Scipio, a commander no less versatile, risk-taking, and imaginative. At Zama in 202, Hannibal's own tactics of Cannae were turned against him.

Dexter Hoyos

Perspective Essay 2. Why Hannibal Failed to Win the Second Punic War

In November 218 BCE, Carthaginian general Hannibal Barca led his bedraggled, half-starved, and much-depleted army down from the Alps into the northern plain of Italy, then known as Cisalpine Gaul. During the next three years in a series of decisive engagements, Hannibal decimated three Roman armies sent against him: at the Trebbia River in December 218, at Lake Trasimene in June 217, and on August 2, 216, at Cannae in southern Italy. In these three engagements the Romans lost a total of some 100,000 men, including an incumbent consul at Cannae.

Yet these three major battles, although crushingly decisive tactical victories in their own right, decided nothing at the strategic level. The Romans did not sue for peace. Hannibal did not besiege Rome. Indeed, the focus of the war shifted to Spain, where the Romans concentrated on destroying the Punic base of operations in a series of campaigns that lasted until 206 BCE. Hannibal, with his army in Italy, became little more than a nuisance as he wandered the peninsula aimlessly for a period of 13 years, ravaging the countryside and causing little more than embarrassment to the Romans. Recalled in 203 to counter a Roman invasion of Africa that threatened Carthage itself, Hannibal was finally defeated in the Battle of Zama the following year by the Romans under Publius Cornelius Scipio, later dubbed Scipio Africanus (Scipio of Africa) the Elder.

How, from a position of seeming unassailable military strength in 216, could Hannibal have faced ultimate defeat 14 years later? To understand why he failed, we need first to appreciate what Hannibal's war aims were, and to understand those, we need to examine briefly the nature of the Roman-dominated Italy he invaded in 218 BCE.

The Romans had spent just short of 500 years conquering Italy. What is critical is how the Romans treated these conquered people. During their conquest of Latium, the Romans had begun founding new cities of Roman citizens (called "colonies") to guard newly acquired territories. They also entered into bilateral relationships with existing subjugated communities. In typical Roman fashion, these relationships came to be arrayed in a hierarchy of status with regard to each place's standing with Rome.

At the top were the colonies of full Roman citizens who, despite living away from Rome itself, retained all the privileges of Roman citizenship. Initially only newly founded cities were colonies, but the Romans eventually could decree any community in their realm a colony. In the mid-fourth century BCE the Romans added communities "without the vote," also known as the Latin Right. Communities with this status enjoyed most of the privileges of Roman citizenship but could not participate in politics. Also in the same century the Romans began employing the status of *municipium,* which generally denoted a self-governing community in which the elected magistrates, but not the rest of populace, became Roman citizens. Finally, there were treaty states whose privileges and duties were stipulated in a treaty with Rome.

The point of all of this was threefold. First, the conquered people were bound to Rome bilaterally and individually and thus were divided among themselves. Treaties or agreements between themselves that excluded Rome were instant grounds for suspicion if not outright suppression by Rome. Second, the hierarchical nature of the arrangements offered the promise of promotion up the ladder—contingent, of course, on good behavior. Conversely, bad behavior might mean demotion. In this way, the Romans did not have to employ brutal methods of suppression to ensure the loyalty of the conquered Italians. Instead, they could merely hold out the promise of promotion or threaten demotion to get the communities to toe the Roman line. The key here is the remarkable willingness on Rome's part to share the benefits of conquest with the conquered.

The third aspect was perhaps the most important. Whatever the status of the community, it was obligated to provide troops for the Roman Army. Citizens were mustered into legions and noncitizens were mustered into allied contingents under the command of Roman officers called prefects. Until the granting of full Roman citizenship to all freeborn Italians in 90 BCE, Roman armies were equal part citizen legions and allied contingents. By these means, the Romans marshaled the military manpower of the entire Italian Peninsula and could regularly raise armies on a scale unprecedented in the ancient Mediterranean basin up to that point.

This is the Italy that Hannibal invaded in 218 BCE. An assault on Rome directly, in the form of a siege, was not a viable option. Rome had formidable walls that ran in a circuit of some seven miles. Despite Punic experience in siege warfare, to invest Rome posed a considerable risk to Hannibal's army. A relieving army of Roman allies would threaten his rear, possibly hemming in Hannibal's entire army with fortifications of their own. Hannibal's strategy, as it can be inferred from his actions, was to bypass Rome itself, dismantle the Roman Confederation of Italy, and thus cripple or even remove the Roman threat to Carthage's dominance of the western Mediterranean.

Hannibal's strategy was twofold. First, he set out to humiliate the Romans in battle on their own soil and thus make them lose face before their allies and subjects. Second, Hannibal would pose as a liberator of the Italian allies, the man who would release them from under the yoke of Rome. If the allies could be detached from the Romans, the Roman ability to raise armies to replace the ones destroyed by Hannibal would be reduced or removed entirely. A liberated Italy would pose a lesser threat to Hannibal's rear if and when he decided to attack Rome itself.

The first part of Hannibal's strategy is revealed in his eagerness to engage the Romans in large-scale battles as rapidly as he could after he reached Italy. The second part of Hannibal's plan is revealed in a detail documented by Polybius and Livy in their accounts of the Second Punic War. Polybius reports that after the Battle of the Trebbia, Hannibal kept the Roman prisoners in custody on starvation rations but treated the allied prisoners with great kindness and "afterwards called a meeting and addressed them, saying that he had not come to make war on them but on the Romans for their sakes; therefore if they were wise they should embrace his friendship, for he had come first of all to reestablish the liberty of the peoples of Italy and also to help them to recover the cities and territories of which the Romans had deprived them." He then let them return to their homes without ransom, hoping thereby to gain their support against Rome.

Likewise, Polybius relates how, after the Battle of Lake Trasimene, Hannibal gathered all 15,000 prisoners together and poured vitriol over the Romans, whom he retained under guard. Then he again let the Italians return to their homes ransom-free, saying he was here to fight on behalf of the Italians against the Romans. Livy says that he found this detail in the earlier (now lost) history of Fabius Maximus, who had lived through the war. It therefore comes on good authority.

Livy also reports that in the aftermath of Hannibal's great victory of Cannae, he again sent home, without ransom and with a few kind words, the allied Italian troops who had been taken prisoner. The Romans, in contrast, were to remain prisoners until ransomed at fixed sums for cavalry, infantry, and slaves. A delegation was sent to Rome to ratify these terms, accompanied by a Carthaginian noble who was to test the waters for any sign that Rome was willing to negotiate peace. Before even reaching Rome, this noble was met by an official and ordered from Roman territory. The Roman Senate denied the ransom request, and the prisoner delegation was returned to Hannibal's camp.

There were some signs that Hannibal's plan to destroy the Roman Confederation of Italy might work. After the Battle of the Trebbia, Hannibal's depleted army had been massively reinforced by local Gallic volunteers. This is not entirely surprising, since the region had been annexed by Rome only four years earlier, and resistance was still fresh in the population. But now, after Cannae, much of southern Italy joined Hannibal, including the city of Capua in Campania; many tribal peoples in Apulia, Lucania, and Bruttium; and much of Samnium in south-central Italy. Matters looked perilous for Rome.

But the fact is that these defecting regions were all reasonably recent conquests for Rome, brought into the confederation within the previous three generations. In contrast, the heartland of the confederation in Latium and Etruria stood firm. With aid from these regions, the Romans raised new armies to shadow Hannibal in Italy, attack and punish the defecting allies, and campaign in Spain to deny Carthage its base of operations in the war. With these events, Hannibal's war strategy had failed. Hannibal was reduced to a sideshow in Italy, while the Roman war effort concentrated on Punic holdings in Spain and eventually on Africa itself.

Hannibal failed because the Romans had succeeded in carefully building the network of relationships in their confederation during the centuries before he set foot on Italian soil. While some of the newly conquered territories went over to Hannibal in 216, the heartland of the Roman Confederation stood by its obligations to Rome and shut its gates to the Punic invader.

Had Hannibal studied history, he might have rethought his strategy. In 415 BCE, an Athenian armada failed in its attempt to liberate Greek cities oppressed by Syracuse, the strongest city-state on Sicily. Most of the Greek cities of Sicily, terrified by the size of the Athenian force and suspicious of its motives, shut their gates, and the Athenians, operating alone and far from home, were eventually annihilated in 413. Closer to home, in 280 King Pyrrhus of Epirus invaded southern Italy at the invitation of the Greek city of Tarentum. At the head of a large professional Hellenistic army modeled on that of Alexander the Great, Pyrrhus defeated the Romans in Italy at Heraclea in 280 and (possibly) at Asculum the following year. Some southern regions defected to his side. The rest stood by Rome. The Romans thus saw no need to negotiate. After a third battle in 275, Pyrrhus was forced to withdraw.

In other words, the solidarity of the Roman Confederation had already been displayed. Perhaps Hannibal thought that truly crushing defeats inflicted on the Romans would succeed. If so, he miscalculated. As a rule, when foreign commanders at the head of large invading armies claim they are there to help, they will be met with suspicion and hostility. This has happened time and time again. Hannibal, in the end, was a victim of his own ambition.

Garrett G. Fagan

Perspective Essay 3. Beyond Battlefield Success and Failure

Hannibal's battlefield victories were ultimately not the most relevant factors in determining the winning side in the Second Punic War. At least four other issues were more important than battlefield success in shaping the outcome of the war.

First and most important, Hannibal and his Roman counterparts operated under differing notions of what might lead one party to surrender. As a result, although the evidence suggests that Hannibal expected Rome to negotiate after it had suffered a series of crushing losses, the Roman Senate chose the improbable course of continued warfare. Following from this, Hannibal needed to force the conclusion of the war in the field rather than at the negotiating table; this required the maintenance of an extensive network of allies, a task for which Hannibal was ill-prepared. At the same time, the Roman focus on fighting in Spain diverted Carthaginian resources and undercut the significance of Hannibal's Italian successes. Finally, leaders in Carthage proved less resistant to the idea of a negotiated surrender than the Romans had, perhaps recognizing that the acceptance of another defeat against Rome did not mean the end of their society.

The evidence that Hannibal expected Rome to surrender after his initial series of seemingly definitive victories is scant but suggestive. After the fall of Saguntum in 219 BCE, Hannibal had marched with deservedly famous speed against Italy itself. He eluded a Roman force sent to intercept him in southern France and crossed the Alps in 218 to win a minor engagement at the Ticinus River that same year. This was followed by another victory near the Trebbia River. In 217 Hannibal, who was now aided by a growing contingent of Gallic allies, won a significant battle at Lake Trasimene and was able to move without opposition south through the Italian Peninsula. After Trasimene, the Romans briefly embraced a strategy of avoidance under the dictator Quintus Fabius Maximus Cunctator, but since Hannibal spent the same time devastating swaths of rural Italy, Fabius's policies were unpopular at Rome. In 216, the Romans changed their approach and sent two consular armies (a combined eight legions) to meet Hannibal in the southeastern region of Apulia. The result was the devastating defeat in the Battle of Cannae.

In the aftermath of Cannae, Hannibal sent a delegation to negotiate the ransom of his Roman prisoners. The Greek historian Polybius made much of the Senate's refusal to comply, using the episode to illustrate what he presented as the superiority of Rome's governmental system. Of surviving sources, however, only Livy included the relevant detail that Hannibal's embassy included a certain Carthalo, who was from an elite family and was empowered to set the terms of Rome's surrender. This Carthalo may be the same man who enjoyed ties of hospitality with Fabius's father, and some scholars see the choice of Carthalo as indicative of Hannibal's expectation that the Romans might capitulate after their unprecedented losses at Cannae. Another piece of evidence is provided by the treaty concluded between Hannibal and Philip V of Macedon in 215. The terms of the agreement suggest anticipation of a swift resolution of the war. Philip had designs on Illyria and sought to capitalize on Rome's preoccupation with the Carthaginian threat, and both he and Hannibal had good reason to characterize their shared endeavors in vaguely optimistic terms.

Nevertheless, there is good reason to believe that Hannibal would have expected the Romans to yield after Cannae. A set of unwritten rules governed conflicts between polities in the Hellenistic world. Significant among these was the principle that such conflicts aimed to negotiate hierarchies among states rather than to achieve the annihilation of one party by another. Since Hannibal had unquestionably demonstrated the superiority of his armies and of his generalship, this principle ought to have led Rome to seek terms with Carthage. Both ancient and modern commentators have questioned Hannibal's decision not to move against the city of Rome in the immediate aftermath of Cannae; this decision only makes sense if Hannibal sought the surrender rather than the destruction of his opponent. The terms of such surrender, in keeping with Hellenistic precedents (and Rome's own treaty with defeated Carthage in 241), would likely have involved the payment of an indemnity, the return of territories such as Sicily and Sardinia to Punic control, and guarantees for the autonomy of Hannibal's newfound Gallic and Italian allies. Rome would have been reduced to a small regional power, and Carthage could resume its hegemony in the western Mediterranean.

The Roman Senate was unreceptive to warfare on these terms, however. For reasons about which we may only speculate, at some point in its history Rome developed an ethos that precluded the possibility of subordination to another polity. Essentially,

Roman commanders were not empowered to negotiate from a disadvantage, so their only option was to position themselves to advantage prior to opening negotiations (or to buy time with an agreement that the Senate would later repudiate).

Hannibal's victories in the field could not produce the objective he sought. Although he likely could have taken the city in 216 or 215, and perhaps still when he marched almost to its gates in 211, he could not make the Romans admit that they were defeated. Thus, while his Carthaginians were successful against Roman armies on the terms under which Hannibal was fighting, success in the field did not provide the foundation for an ultimate victory in the war by the definition that Rome employed.

As a result, Hannibal found himself fighting a very different war than that which he had begun with such initiative in 218. His armies were largely cut off from the possibility of reinforcement or resupply from Carthage and therefore relied on the allies and the provisions they could win in Italy. After his victory at Cannae, a number of central and southern Italian peoples joined the Cisalpine tribes that had already cast their lot with the Carthaginians, but few of these allies came without a fight. Moreover, as scholars have recently stressed, their numbers should not be overestimated. In the north, the Gallic Boii were effectively able to drive the Romans from Cisalpine Gaul following their victory over a consul-elect in 216. Because this area had only been loosely, and recently, held by Rome, however, the loss was probably not of great strategic significance. The defection of many Campanian cities caused more problems for Rome but required that Hannibal either divide his forces through the emplacement of garrisons or—as proved to be the case in several instances—fail to protect his new allies from Roman reprisals.

Moreover, Rome's decision to return to the Fabian tactics of avoidance and harassment in place of pitched battles undercut Hannibal's ability to live off the land and to maintain his fragile alliances. Although the Carthaginians continued to win victories in the field, the Romans had essentially forced Hannibal to assume a holding pattern. Meanwhile, they could work to increase their own military strength and could focus their military energies on Sicily and, in particular, Spain.

The scale of Rome's commitment to the fighting in Spain is striking, to the point that some researchers have posited that the Second Punic War might best be understood as a struggle for control of the Iberian Peninsula. The more southern and coastal areas of that region had long been involved with Carthaginian trading interests, and in the decade after the First Punic War these interests were supported and greatly extended through the extensive military interventions of Hannibal's father, Hamilcar Barca. Hamilcar's sons and son-in-law continued his strategy and expanded Carthaginian hegemony along the central coast and more inland areas, with a particular focus on Iberian mineral resources. This activity provoked concern in Rome, and in 226 the Romans and Carthaginians allegedly negotiated a nominal boundary between their territorial interests in Spain at the Ebro River. When Hannibal attacked Saguntum in 219, this provided the Roman Senate with a justification for war even though the city was in fact located south of the Ebro. After the city's fall, Hannibal marched for Italy. In the almost 15 years that he would spend on Italian soil, Roman armies would succeed in driving the Carthaginians from Spain.

There is good reason to believe that the Carthaginian leadership viewed Spain as the primary theater of the war. In 218 when Publius Cornelius Scipio (Scipio Africanus the Elder) regained the territory that Hannibal had won north of the Ebro, the Carthaginians responded with a redoubled effort. When Scipio's brother joined him in 217, Roman successes continued, culminating in a significant victory in 215. At this point, the Carthaginians diverted reinforcements originally intended for Hannibal, sending them first to Spain and then to Numidia to fight unsuccessfully against a former Punic ally. Carthage ultimately did muster a sizable army and defeat the two Scipios in 211, at the same time that Hannibal was failing to hold his gains in Campania and the Romans were retaking Sicily.

The Punic victory in Spain was short-lived, however, for after Rome's victories at Syracuse and Capua it was free to send another army westward. It arrived in 210 and in four years of campaigning forced the Carthaginians to abandon the peninsula. It was only in 207 that a Punic army under the command of Hannibal's brother Hasdrubal marched to Italy to reinforce, and hopefully reinvigorate, the war effort there. Hasdrubal's army was crushed in the Battle of the Metaurus River, however, and at the close of 207 the Romans controlled more territory than they had held prior to the commencement of the war.

Hannibal had been in Italy for more than a decade and had likely not been defeated in a single engagement against Roman forces. Paradoxically, his own battlefield victories may have done more harm than good to his efforts to reduce Rome to a minor regional power. Despite his requests, no major reinforcements were forthcoming from Carthage, and resources that might well have allowed him to consolidate his victories in the period 213–209 were diverted to, among other destinations, Spain. Whatever Hannibal's motives in invading Italy—revenge, ambition, empire— once it became clear that they could not be satisfied swiftly, the continued pursuit of such motives was antithetical to the model of maritime and mercantile dominance that Carthage had enacted so successfully in the western Mediterranean since the sixth century. At the risk of reducing a staggeringly complex set of factors to a simplistic bon mot, Hannibal failed in his war against Rome precisely because it was his war, while Carthage, and indeed Rome, were fighting on rather different terms.

In the end, although Carthage accepted defeat in 202, it was hardly the end of that city. The Second Punic War had left Carthage in a position to rebuild its fortunes and reposition itself as an economic power in the Mediterranean world. Without denying the obvious fact that Punic leaders would have preferred to win the war, they were not willing to risk the siege of their city, or even a second major defeat on African soil, in order to do so.

Jessica H. Clark

Further Reading

Bagnall, N. *The Punic Wars: Rome, Carthage, and the Struggle for the Mediterranean.* New York: Thomas Dunne Books, 1990.

Bickerman, E. "Hannibal's Covenant." *American Journal of Philology* 73(1) (1952): 1–23.

Briscoe, J. "The Second Punic War." In *Rome and the Mediterranean to 133 B.C.,* edited by A. E. Astin, F. W. Walbank, M. W. Frederiksen, and R. M. Ogilvie, 44–80. Cambridge Ancient History Vol. 8. Cambridge: Cambridge University Press, 1989.

Cornell, T., ed. *The Second Punic War: A Reappraisal.* London: Institute of Classical Studies, 1996.

Daly, G. *Cannae: The Experience of Battle in the Second Punic War.* London: Routledge, 2003.

Dillon, S., and K. E. Welch, eds. *Representations of War in Ancient Rome.* Cambridge: Cambridge University Press, 2006.

Eckstein, A. M. *Moral Vision in the Histories of Polybius.* Berkeley: University of California Press, 1995.

Erdkamp, P. "Polybius, the Ebro Treaty, and the Gallic Invasion of 225 B.C.E." *Classical Philology* 104(4) (2009): 495–510.

Errington, R. M. "Rome and Greece to 205 B.C." In *Rome and the Mediterranean to 133 B.C.,* edited by A. E. Astin, F. W. Walbank, M. W. Frederiksen, and R. M. Ogilvie, 81–106. Cambridge Ancient History Vol. 8. Cambridge: Cambridge University Press, 1989.

Flower, H. I. *Roman Republics.* Princeton, NJ: Princeton University Press, 2010.

Fronda, M. P. *Between Rome and Carthage: Southern Italy during the Second Punic War.* Cambridge: Cambridge University Press, 2010.

Gargola, D. J. "Mediterranean Empire (264–134)." In *A Companion to the Roman Republic,* edited by N. Rosenstein and R. Morstein-Marx, 147–166. Oxford, UK: Blackwell, 2006.

Goldsworthy, A. *The Fall of Carthage: The Punic Wars, 265–146 BC.* London: Cassell, 2003.

Goldsworthy, A. K. *The Punic Wars.* London: Cassell, 2001.

Hölkeskamp, K.-J. "Conquest, Competition and Consensus: Roman Expansion in Italy and the Rise of the Nobilitas." *Historia* 42(1) (1993): 12–39.

Hoyos, D. *Hannibal's Dynasty: Politics and Power in the Western Mediterranean, 247–183 BC.* London: Routledge, 2005.

Hoyos, D. "Maharbal's Bon Mot: Authenticity and Survival." *Classical Quarterly* 50(2) (2000): 610–614.

Hoyos, D., ed. *The Blackwell Companion to the Punic Wars.* Oxford, UK: Wiley-Blackwell, 2011.

Lancel, S. *Hannibal.* Oxford, UK: Wiley-Blackwell, 1999.

Lazenby, J. F. *Hannibal's War: A Military History of the Second Punic War.* Norman: University of Oklahoma Press, 1978.

Lazenby, J. F. "Rome and Carthage." In *The Cambridge Companion to the Roman Republic,* edited by H. I. Flower, 225–241. Cambridge: Cambridge University Press, 2004.

Lazenby, J. F. "Was Maharbal Right?" In *The Second Punic War: A Reappraisal,* edited by T. Cornell, B. Rankov, and P. Sabin, 39–48. London: Institute of Classical Studies, School of Advanced Study, University of London, 1996.

Livy. *Hannibal's War: Books 21 to 30*. Translated by J. C. Yardley with an introduction and notes by D. Hoyos. Oxford World's Classics. Oxford: Oxford University Press, 2006.

Ma, J. "Fighting Poleis of the Hellenistic World." In *War and Violence in Ancient Greece*, edited by H. van Wees, 337–376. London: Duckworth, 2000.

Miles, R. *Carthage Must Be Destroyed: The Rise and Fall of an Ancient Civilisation*. London: Viking, 2010.

Nicolet, C. *The World of the Citizen in Republican Rome*. Translated by P. S. Falla. Berkeley: University of California Press, 1980.

Palmer, R. E. A. *Rome and Carthage at Peace*. Stuttgart: Franz Steiner, 1997.

Polybius. *The Histories of Polybius*, Vol. 1, Book 3. Translated by Evelyn S. Shuckburgh. London: Macmillan, 1889.

Serrati, J. "Neptune's Altars: The Treaties between Rome and Carthage (509–226 B.C.)." *Classical Quarterly* 56(1) (2006): 113–134.

Wise, Terence, and Mark Healy. *Hannibal's War with Rome: The Armies and Campaigns 216 BC*. Oxford, UK: Osprey, 1999.

4. Why Did Julius Caesar Prevail in the Caesarian-Pompeian Civil War yet Ultimately Lose Support to the Extent that He Was Assassinated by His Own People?

The Caesarian-Pompeian Civil War of 49–45 BCE was one of the last major conflicts to occur prior to the establishment of the Roman Empire. As a civil war, it encompassed political, military, and social dimensions that were tightly intertwined. The war pitted Gaius Julius Caesar and his supporters against Gnaeus Pompeius Magnus (Pompey the Great), who was generally supported by the Roman Senate and many wealthy, conservative Roman citizens. The Senate feared Caesar's popularity and grand ambitions and saw him as a usurper threatening to undue Rome's established sociopolitical system. When these tensions boiled over into war, Caesar's military genius and his well-seasoned troops proved to be more than a match for Pompey's forces; at the same time, Caesar executed a series of brilliant political moves that virtually assured him dominance in Rome once the war was won. The Senate appointed Caesar dictator in 46, empowering him to institute widespread populist reforms, including broadening Roman citizenship and reining in the Senate. Aghast by these moves, Caesar's detractors began plotting his demise. Caesar was assassinated as he made his way to the Senate on March 15, 44. In the end, Caesar's attempt to bring more liberty to Rome failed when he ran afoul of Rome's well-established conservative power brokers.

In the first perspective essay, Robert P. Broadwater asserts that Caesar's assassination was largely a political act. Many senators viewed Caesar's populist sentiments and his attempts to undermine senatorial power as a direct threat to their power and prestige. Indeed, his attempts to centralize power, champion the common people, and circumvent the Senate left his political detractors no choice but to silence him for good. The second essay, written by Raymond Limbach, asserts that Caesar's assassination was chiefly a reflection of Roman society and politics. Caesar, a populist, threatened Rome's long-standing social traditions that had given immense power to a small number of wealthy political elites. Most of these elites were conservative and did not take kindly to Caesar's populist reform measures. In the end, Caesar threatened the Senate and Rome's traditional ruling hierarchy. His greatest mistake was perhaps the fact that he did not purge Rome's old ruling families, which eventually supported attempts to assassinate him. In the third essay, Dr. Allene Phy-Olsen argues that Caesar's outsized personality clashed with traditional Roman values and societal norms, opening him up to animosity among Rome's ruling elite. Caesar's military brilliance and political instincts served him well enough before and during the civil war, but once it ended, his ambition led to his assassination. He fought too many bloody wars of conquest, seemingly to prove his invincibility. Caesar's womanizing and promiscuity also caused problems for him, as they outraged Rome's conservative elites. In the end, more people may have loved Caesar than hated him, but those who hated him held the power to extinguish his ambitions.

Background Essay

During 49–45 BCE, Roman military leaders Gaius Julius Caesar and Gnaeus Pompeius Magnus (Pompey the Great) fought to determine who would control Roman affairs. The Caesarian-Pompeian Civil War, also known as Caesar's Civil War and the Great Roman Civil War, was the last major politico-military conflict in Rome before the establishment of the Roman Empire, to which it directly contributed, but it was also the culmination of a long series of subversions of governmental institutions of the Roman Republic, beginning in the second century BCE.

In the year 59 Caesar, Pompey, and wealthy nobleman Marcus Licinius Crassus had formed the First Triumvirate, in effect dividing power in the Roman Republic between them. Caesar became one of two consuls, followed by a military command in Illyricum, constituting most of the former Yugoslavia and modern-day Albania and Gaul on both sides of the Alps (France and northern Italy). Caesar's subsequent victory over the Gauls added a rich and populous territory, indeed one of the largest territorial additions in Roman history. During the conquest of Gaul his army had grown in strength from 4 to 13 legions.

Pompey had received the governorship of Spain in 55 but exercised it in absentia. In 53 Crassus was killed campaigning in Mesopotamia, and the First Triumvirate came to an end. In 52 amid increasing civil unrest, the Roman Senate appointed Pompey sole consul. A conservative group of senators pressed Pompey to break with Caesar, whose popularity and ambitions the senators greatly feared. The ensuing civil war was thus a test between Caesar and his legions on the one side and supporters and Pompey, his legions, and the politically conservative and socially traditionalist leaders of the Roman Senate on the other side.

The Pompey-dominated Senate demanded that Caesar give up his military command. Caesar was then at Ravenna in Cisalpine Gaul with one legion only. Although willing to yield his command, he wanted another consulship, for without this he would be subject to prosecution by his enemies in the Pompey-controlled Senate for alleged irregularities during his consulship and supposed war crimes during his Gallic campaigns.

Efforts to achieve some sort of compromise failed, and the Senate then invested Pompey with command of all the Roman armed forces. In December 50 the Senate ordered Caesar to give up his military command, disband his legions, and return to Rome. The stage was set for civil war.

Roman law specifically prohibited generals from bringing their legions into Italy proper without approval of the Senate. On the Adriatic, this border was the Rubicon River. In 49 Caesar, announcing that "the die is cast," defied the Senate and crossed that stream. Although he had

Certainly one of history's greatest generals, Julius Caesar established the dictatorship that effectively ended the Roman Republic and produced the Roman Empire. (Corel)

only one legion with him, he retained eight others in Gaul. Ranged against him, Pompey and his allies in the Senate could call on two legions in Italy (eight more were being raised), seven in Spain, and substantial military resources in Greece, the East, and North Africa.

Caesar offset this formidable imbalance by decisive action. Moving swiftly south, he collected additional forces and recruits. Pompey and most of the senators abandoned Rome and fled south to gather additional resources in southern Italy. Pompey expected to raise substantial forces in the eastern Greek provinces and, with control of most of the Roman Navy, institute a blockade of the Italian coasts. In March 49 he sailed from Brundisium for Epirus.

Before Caesar could contemplate proceeding against Pompey in Greece, he had to first eliminate the threat to his rear posed by Pompey's sizable army in Spain. Leaving some forces in Italy, Caesar marched for Spain and was victorious there. Returning to Rome, in January 48 he risked all, for Pompey's ships controlled the Adriatic, and managed to evade Pompey's fleet in a crossing of the Adriatic and land on the coast of Epirus (present-day Albania).

Surprisingly, Pompey, whose forces outnumbered Caesar's forces four to one, failed to press his advantage. That March additional forces arrived for Caesar by sea, but he was still outnumbered two to one. That July Pompey was victorious over Caesar in battle at Dyrrhachium, although Caesar was able to withdraw in good order. The decisive battle occurred at Pharsalus on August 9, 48. Although outnumbered two to one, Caesar attacked and triumphed. Pompey escaped with only a handful of followers, reaching the coast and sailing for Egypt.

Caesar pursued Pompey to Egypt with a small force and there learned that Pompey had been assassinated on the orders of King Ptolemy XII, coruler of Egypt with his sister Cleopatra, who now besieged Caesar at Alexandria. Caesar ably defended a small part of the city, then triumphed in the February 47 Battle of the Nile, with Ptolemy among those slain. Caesar then established firm control over Egypt. At the same time, he became involved romantically with Cleopatra and with her fathered his only known biological son, Ptolemy XV Caesar, known as Caesarion. Caesar and Cleopatra never married, however, owing to Roman law prohibiting marriage with a non-Roman citizen.

Meanwhile, King Pharnaces of Bosporus Cimmerius took advantage of the Roman Civil War to re-create his father's Kingdom of Pontus. Securing reinforcements in Syria, Caesar moved overland and defeated Pharnaces in the Battle of Zela in May 47. This victory was the subject of Caesar's famous message to Rome "Veni, vidi, vici" (I came, I saw, I conquered).

After reorganizing the eastern part of the empire, Caesar returned to Rome, quashed a mutiny among his troops demanding back pay, and then sailed for Africa to do battle with Pompey's forces that had gathered there from throughout the empire. Again outnumbered two to one, Caesar took the offensive and soundly defeated his foes in the Battle of Thapsus in February 46. Returning to Rome, after six months Caesar sailed for Spain and defeated a somewhat larger force under Gaeus Pompeius (Pompey the Younger) near Osuna in southern Spain in March 45.

In July 45 Caesar returned to Rome, where he was recognized as the undisputed ruler and in effect the uncrowned monarch. In 46 he had secured appointment by the Senate as dictator for 10 years. Although the formality of elections continued, Caesar held power. What Caesar intended is unclear. In 44 he caused his dictatorship to be extended for life and secured deification. He seems to have wanted the kingship, but the Roman public apparently opposed this step, and he was not to have the time to convince them otherwise.

Always rational and logical, Caesar carried out extensive reforms. He began projects to restore Corinth and Carthage, the destruction of which had marked the end of Mediterranean trade, as he believed that this would bring employment for the Roman urban poor. He reformed local government by moving toward decentralization, and he also reformed the calendar. (A month in the calendar was renamed July after him.) Caesar made many provincials citizens, including the entire province of Cisalpine Gaul.

Not all Romans approved of Caesar's reforms. Many traditionalists, powerful vested interests, and republicans were upset by his changes and cosmopolitan attitude. Shortly after he extended his dictatorship to life, a group of senators, some of whom had been his supporters and some of whom had been Popmeians whom he had spared, plotted against him. Caesar was assassinated on March 15, 44 BCE, stabbed to death in Rome. Believing that they had killed a tyrant and were restoring liberty, the senators brought anarchy instead. Ultimately the new contest to control the Roman state was won by Caesar's young nephew, adopted son in his will, and legal heir, Gaius Octavius (Octavian). Victorious in the Battle of Actium in 31, he became the first Roman emperor as Augustus.

Spencer C. Tucker

Perspective Essay 1. Caesar's Desire to Usurp Senatorial Powers Brought His Assassination

Julius Caesar prevailed in the Caesarian-Pompeian Civil War, also known as the Great Roman Civil War, for several reasons, but the primary factors were his popularity within Rome and its surrounding areas and the fact that his legions consisted of seasoned veterans. Caesar's military victories in Gaul had made him a hero to the people. His political views, which included plans to eliminate corruption and restore centralized power to the government, struck a chord with many Romans, causing Caesar to be seen as a champion of the people. For this reason, Pompey and the politically conservative members of the Senate found it difficult to raise legions to oppose Caesar from within Rome or its surrounding areas and were forced to flee to provinces in Albania, Greece, Egypt, Africa, and Hispania. This left Caesar in complete control of Rome and its surrounding area, giving his forces a centralized base of operations and meaning that Pompey would be in a position of having to wage war from Roman outposts in order to seize Rome and retake control of the government.

Caesar refused to allow Pompey and his followers the ability to organize and prepare for such a campaign, however. Rather, Caesar took the offensive and marched his legions against the forces loyal to Pompey. In so doing Caesar was able to keep Pompey's followers, known as the Optimates, from being able to concentrate their forces against him.

Caesar's greatest advantage was that the soldiers in his legions were battle-hardened veterans who had served under his direction during his conquest of Gaul. The forces fighting for the Optimates were numerically superior to Caesar's but were largely green and untested. Caesar believed that on the battlefield his veterans would be more than a match for the Optimate forces so long as the odds were not supremely disproportionate. In this he proved prescient, as he was able to deal a decisive defeat to forces twice his own number in size led by Pompey in the Battle of Pharsalus in August 48 BCE. Through the use of interior lines of supply and communication, keeping his opponents from being able to concentrate their forces against him, and by means of the superiority of his battle-hardened legions, Caesar was able to defeat the Optimate forces and seize control of Rome and the Roman government.

Caesar's failure to maintain that control, which ultimately led to his assassination, stemmed from fears in the Senate that he intended to do away with that body and usurp all power himself. Formal governmental power still resided with the Senate. Caesar's titles as consul, tribune, and dictator were honors bestowed by the Senate and were honorary in nature. According to Roman law, his power to rule rested in the consent and will of the Senate.

Caesar sought to circumvent the Senate and gather all power to himself through a series of maneuvers. First, he used his powers as tribune to veto actions of the Senate. Next, he used his censorial powers to make numerous appointments of partisans to the Senate, making that body increasingly subservient to him and his agenda of political reform. He confronted the possibility that another general might try to challenge his power by establishing term limits for governors. He forced the Senate to bestow various titles and honors upon him, such as "Father of the Fatherland" and "Imperator," further consolidating power in his own person. Finally, he forced the passage of laws granting him sole authority to appoint magistrates, consuls, and tribunes. This meant that these posts would no longer be representatives of the people but would instead be puppet representatives of the dictator.

The power of the Senate diminished proportionate to the increased power Caesar took for himself, leading many senators to believe that he intended to do away with the Senate altogether and impose a dictatorship. Led by Cassius Longinus, a group of conspirators calling themselves the Liberatores (liberators), came together under the auspices of restoring republican principles and the republican form of government to Rome. Among those gathered to the liberators' banner in opposition to Caesar was Marcus Brutus, Caesar's own protégé, who had been made governor of Gaul after rejoining Caesar's inner circle following the Battle of Pharsalus.

The timetable of the assassination plot was dictated by Caesar's announced plans to commence a military campaign against the Parthian Empire on March 18, 44. Caesar had appointed loyal leaders of his legions to rule Rome in his absence. The republican senators had been loath to serve under Caesar's decrees, and they were unified in their resistance to place themselves in a subservient position to his underlings. On March 13, Cassius met with the other conspirators to formulate a plan of action. It was decided that Caesar must be assassinated, and the date was set for March 15, known as the Ides of March in the Roman calendar, as Caesar was scheduled to make an appearance before the Senate on that day.

Caesar was well aware that he was hated by many in the Senate, but he inexplicably dismissed his personal security guard shortly before his arrival at the Theatre of Pompey, where the session was to be held. Upon entering the chamber, reportedly Caesar was handed a written warning, which he failed to read. Once in the hall, Caesar was surrounded by between 40 and 60 senators, all holding daggers. Servilius Casca reportedly struck the first blow, wounding Caesar in the shoulder. The other conspirators joined in, slashing and stabbing in such numbers that they inflicted wounds on one another while striking Caesar 23 times and killing him.

Caesar had seized control of the Roman body politic, but his desire to make that power absolute caused him to be viewed by many as a threat to the republic and led to his downfall and assassination. Ironically, Caesar's death did not bring about a restoration of the republic. Instead, it led to yet another civil war, one that would be won by Caesar's grandnephew and adopted son, Gaius Octavius, who would be known to history as Caesar Octavian, the first emperor of Rome as Augustus.

Robert P. Broadwater

Perspective Essay 2. Caesar's Assassination Was Rooted in Roman Society and Politics

Gaius Julius Caesar was born in July 100 BCE and died at the age of 55 on March 15, 44. Although of patrician lineage the family had lost its wealth, and Caesar grew up in an impoverished neighborhood of Rome. This helped form his political attitude and ideas as one of the Populares, understanding the common people and the rough ways of the street, in contrast to his upper-class peers known as Optimates, who were the elite and supported the Old Republic.

Caesar was ambitious, determined to regain his family's status. This he achieved through the Senate and the fixed course of advancement known as the Paths of Honors. The first was service as a tribune. Proving himself in battle, Caesar led from the front and was awarded the *corona civica* (civic crown), an oak wreath similar to the U.S. Medal of Honor today.

The next step in the Path of Honors was the position of quaestor, handling the everyday management of government. Caesar then acquired a coveted foreign assignment in Spain. Before departing, he delivered the funeral oration for his Aunt Julia. Her husband, Marius, had been a champion of the common people, whom the aristocratic Optimates had hated. In his remarks Caesar established himself as a staunch advocate of the Populares. In Spain he also earned a reputation as a fair and just administrator.

In 65 Caesar become an aedile, overseeing street repairs, policing, temple maintenance, and management of public festivals. As a consequence of his lineage, he could not, as he wished, become a "tribune of the Plebs." Caesar arranged festivals like none before, increasing his popularity with the masses.

Elected praetor, Caesar had oversight of judicial functions, including imposition of the death penalty. He immediately gave notice to the Optimates that he would exercise his rights of office on behalf of the people. He then returned to Spain, where he won victories and governed fairly. His troops hailed him as imperator with the prized title "conqueror," eligible for a public triumph through Rome.

In 59 Caesar, Gnaeus Pompeius Magnus (Pompey the Great), and wealthy nobleman Marcus Licinius Crassus formed the First Triumvirate, dividing power in the Roman Republic between them. Caesar became one of two consuls. Cato and Cicero tried but failed to prevent this. As consul, Caesar introduced land reforms to benefit the people, especially military veterans, angering the Optimates. He also improved tax collection.

With the Optimates intriguing against him and his reforms, Caesar secured military command in Illyricum (constituting most of the former Yugoslavia and modern-day Albania) and Gaul on both sides of the Alps (France and northern Italy) and left Rome.

Eight years later Caesar had conquered Gaul, invaded Britain, and subdued the German tribes across the Rhine. Well aware that his enemies in Rome, jealous of his popularity with the people and status of war hero, were intriguing against him and intended to prosecute him for alleged irregularities in Gaul and supposed war crimes, Caesar sought a new office that would give him immunity from prosecution. The Optimates turned to Pompey to support their cause. The Senate rejected an effort to bring about a compromise, and the senators entrusted Pompey with the command of all Roman armies.

Rejecting Senate demands that he disband his own forces, on January 10, 49, Caesar crossed the Rubicon River into Italy, a violation of law, and began the Caesarian-Pompeian Civil War, also known as the Great Roman Civil War. Moving swiftly and gambling boldly, by early 46 Caesar had defeated the forces loyal to Pompey and the Optimates. Pompey and Cato were both dead, and most of their remaining forces fled to Spain. Caesar returned to Rome, pardoning many of his former enemies in a gesture of peace and hoped conciliation. In the summer of 46, Caesar entered Rome in triumph.

The loss of lives in the civil war was immense, and the senators sought stability. Out of fear of retribution by Caesar, the Senate granted him unprecedented powers, including making him dictator for 10 years. Caesar in turn enacted groundbreaking social and civic reforms, altering Roman traditional practice for the benefit of all Roman citizens. His first act was a census of the city, enabling him to cut the grain allocation in half, saving money and implementing efficiency. He planned the increase of the membership of the Senate, undercutting the old traditional ruling families.

Caesar increased the number of middle-class professionals, granting citizenship to teachers and physicians. He also planned a large public library and the codification of Roman law. Thousands of Romans were sent abroad in newly established citizen colonies to increase the influence of Rome beyond the Italian Peninsula. Citizens from the lower classes were resettled to start new lives. Even with all of these changes, the remaining Optimates hoped that Caesar would lay down his dictatorship and that they might bring about the return of the Old Republic ways.

In 45 Caesar departed Rome for Spain and there defeated the remaining Pompeian forces. On his return to Rome, the Senate then bestowed on Caesar more honors, with the titles "liberator" and "imperator." A golden chair was built for him in the Senate. Caesar's birthday became a public holiday, and he was proclaimed father of his country, consul for 10 years, and dictator for life. He was also deified, in defiance of Roman tradition. Many Romans were troubled that Caesar had gone from conquering hero to divine figure.

Caesar was planning a war in the east against the Parthians, who threatened Roman holdings in Asia Minor. The people, especially the Optimates, who wished his death backed the war. Caesar meanwhile began acting more like a king. Ribbons were tied around Caesar's statues signifying kingship, and crowds began to hail him as such. Although offered the crown by Mark Antony, Caesar thrice rejected this. The optimists, however, now believed that there was sufficient popular support for Caesar to become king, and they now decided to assassinate him.

Three groups of individuals participated in the plot: former enemies who had been pardoned; former allies who nonetheless resented Caesar for not purging the old ruling families, as had been past practice; and those who truly believed in the Old Republic and ancient Roman traditions and considered him a threat to these.

Four main figures emerged in the plot: Caius Trebonius, Decimus Brutus, Cassius, and Brutus, a favorite of Caesar who had been given many honors. They knew that they had to act swiftly, prior to Caesar's campaign in the east. They also planned to carry it out in the open to give it a sense of legitimacy. The date selected was March 15, Caesar's last meeting before his planned departure.

On his way to the Senate, a Greek philosophy teacher, Artemidorus, overheard Brutus and his plans, wrote them down, and gave the parchment to Caesar imploring him to read it. Caesar then saw Spurinna, who had warned him of the Ides of March, and called to him that he was not dead, whereupon Spurinna reportedly replied "Yes, the Ides have come, but not yet passed."

Arriving in the Senate, Caius Trebonius pulled Caesar's aide Mark Antony aside. All of the senators stood as Caesar took his seat. Tullius Climber, whose brother Caesar had exiled, pleaded for his pardon, which Caesar dismissed. Climber then grabbed Caesar's toga, the signal for the senators to attack. Caesar initially fought back until weakened by two dozen stab wounds. Brutus approached Caesar to inflict his blow, to Caesar's disbelief. Caesar's last words before Brutus struck were in Greek: "Kai su, teknon?" (Even you, my child?). Brutus then struck his blow. Caesar died at the foot of Pompey's statue, still clutching Artemidorus's warning parchment.

Caesar's death did not bring back the Old Republic envisioned by the plotters. Indeed, it brought about their demise. The conspirators could not control the situation. Mark Antony and Caesar's young nephew and adopted son and legal heir, Gaius Octavius (Octavian), joined forces to crush the optimists. Prolonged warfare followed, with Antony and Octavian dueling for control of the state. Octavian won and became the first of a long line of Roman emperors.

Raymond D. Limbach

Perspective Essay 3. Personality and Policies Doomed Caesar

Throughout the Middle Ages and almost into our own time, the assassination of Gaius Julius Caesar has ranked as the crucial event of Western antiquity, excepting only the crucifixion of Jesus. Why did Caesar, who brought glory and wealth to Rome, prevail in the Caesarian-Pompeian Civil War yet ultimately lose such support that he was assassinated by his own people? Against the backdrop of his age, the answer must lie in the personality of Caesar, both honored and reviled then as he remains today.

Plutarch, the Greek biographer of the first century CE, commended the skill with which Caesar pleaded legal cases. Mercy frequently tempered justice when he pardoned enemies, sparing lives of men later to betray him. He wept when Egyptians, seeking his favor, presented the severed head of his former son-in-law and antagonist, Pompey. After his decisive victory in the Battle of Pharsalus in 48 BCE, Caesar ordered that Brutus, the child of a woman he had loved, be unharmed, despite Brutus's alignment with Pompey.

As military strategist and commander, Caesar ranks with Alexander the Great, whom he emulated. Caesar's soldiers fought bravely for him, even when greatly outnumbered. With associates he was generous, keeping a good table though abstemious himself. After becoming the virtual ruler of Rome, he pleased the plebeians, abundantly providing "bread and circuses." Caesar was a member of a noble but impoverished family and was reared in a depressed Roman neighborhood among Jewish families and foreign residents, and his sympathies often extended beyond patricians. In later years he championed the extension of Roman citizenship to provincials.

Though an unquestioned military genius, Caesar was also an intellect. His writings, as every second-year Latin student discovers, are models of classical style. Caesar was praised for oratory, an art valued in ancient Rome. An astute politician and propagandist, he understood the value of image and reputation.

Perceiving that the days were numbered for the Roman Republic, which then benefited patricians only and was riddled with corruption, Caesar also knew that Rome's institutions were unequipped to govern an expanding empire. As head of state, acclaimed by the plebeians, he was autocratic but pragmatic. Had he survived, his administrative skill would have improved the city and benefited the empire. He projected a library in Rome to rival the splendid one his armies had burned in Alexandria. Other plans were to refine laws, ease debts, and make communications throughout the empire safe and efficient. Caesar also reformed the chaotic Roman calendar. With a few later modifications by Pope Gregory the Great, the Julian calendar is used even today, its seventh month being named after Caesar. Possibly the truest evidence of his discernment was the choice of his great-nephew Octavius as his heir. After upheavals Octavius would become Augustus Caesar, remembered as one of history's great rulers.

From the beginning Caesar's critics enumerated his faults, real or perceived. His justification for conquests rested on flimsy excuses, while he plundered the regions he conquered, enriching himself and his soldiers. Even in a brutal century, the bloodletting of his campaigns sometimes shocked Rome. The Celts suffered genocide, and 1 million people perished in the Gallic Wars, while a like number were enslaved.

Cicero, Rome's famous orator and never an admirer of Caesar, labeled him "that viper we have cherished in our bosom." Suetonius, like Plutarch, living in the first century CE and using records that no longer survive, eagerly reported salacious rumors that circulated in the hotbed of scandal that had become imperial Rome. "Lock up your wives" it was said when Caesar returned from the wars, "for here comes the bald whoremonger." Roman gossips delighted in repeating a calumny from Caesar's youth that he was "every woman's man and every man's woman," though he denied under oath ever being the lover of the king of Bithynia. Suetonius, that "keyhole biographer" of Rome's emperors, pronounced Caesar's assassination justified.

More harmful than rumors was Caesar's sojourn with Cleopatra in Egypt during the civil war. Egypt was viewed as a place of indolent luxury, though Rome had long coveted its riches. Initially Caesar may have ventured there to secure grain and other necessities, but he remained there too long, floating down the Nile with Cleopatra, who bore a child, Caesarion, whom she claimed he had sired.

Caesar's reputation with the Roman elite suffered further when Cleopatra later arrived in the city as his guest. Rather than distance himself from her, he set up her golden statue in the temple of Venus. Patricians whispered that he planned to divorce his proper Roman wife, Calpernia, to marry Cleopatra and move the capital from Rome to Alexandria.

Enemies might have overlooked amorous intrigues but not the honors that the bribed and sycophantic Senate heaped upon Caesar. He was proclaimed dictator for life, an innovation for Rome. In 45 BCE the Senate outdid itself, designating Caesar "Divus Juius," a divinity. Though the divinizing of the living was common in the East, it was not so in Rome. Caesar appeared publicly in the purple robes of a king, a laurel wreath hiding his baldness. Dignitaries complained of his imperious manners, as he remained seated in their presence. It was remembered that not merely barbarians had perished in his campaigns but also Romans themselves had been slain in the civil wars.

A troubling event occurred early in 44 at the Roman ceremony of Lupercalia. Mark Antony, a consul, publicly offered Caesar a kingly crown. He refused it thrice, ordering it sent instead to Jupiter's temple. Enemies were nevertheless convinced that the affair had been staged and that had the assembled crowd approved, Caesar would have eagerly accepted the crown.

Leading conspirators intensified their plans to rid Rome of Caesar. Motives are never simple. Brutus, a student of philosophy, defended assassination as a patriotic act. Cassius loathed Caesar personally, having been passed over for promotion and blaming Caesar for his father's death. Envy stirred others. Idealizing the republic, the conspirators all feared a return to the days of hated Tarquin, Rome's last king. Believing that the death of Caesar would be welcomed, they failed to predict the resulting chaos.

Was it a dramatic necessity that Caesar die so violently? He was no longer a young man but was now a victim of "the falling sickness." His glory days were past; to perish in this way placed a heroic stamp on his legend.

Caesar's reported last words, face-to-face, with the child of his beloved Servilia, widely rumored to be his own son, were not "Et tu Brute." That poignant line is

Shakespearean. Plutarch wrote that Caesar silently collapsed in death against the statue of his old enemy, Pompey. Suetonius reported, as rumor rather than fact, that the last words to Brutus were "Even you, my son?," giving an Oedipal cast to the final sword thrust.

In the centuries since his death, Caesar has been both lauded and abhorred. During the Middle Ages, with a nostalgia for the stability of a vanished Rome, he was held in supreme regard. In his epic work *The Inferno,* Dante placed Brutus and Cassius in the pit of Hell congealed in Satan's mouth beside Judas Iscariot, suffering eternally among those who betray their masters.

With the Renaissance, as exemplified by Shakespeare's play *Julius Caesar,* a more balanced approach to Caesar's memory was evident, recognizing the ambiguities of his career. But in the 18th and 19th centuries, he was again extolled. Even an ardent Republican, Alexander Hamilton, acknowledged Caesar as the greatest man who ever lived. The 19th-century German historian Theodor Mommsen spoke of Caesar as a political genius who had planned a future to benefit all humankind. Mark Twain, with his usual cynicism, observed that Caesar had waged wars against harmless folk, thus conferring the blessings of Roman civilization on their widows and orphans.

The 20th century, with more than its share of tyrants, did not find Caesar especially appealing. Roman scholar Philip Matyzak concluded that history has been kinder to Caesar than he deserved and that his legacy was autocratic government and internecine struggle. Classicist Edith Hamilton described Caesar as one widely regarded as Rome's greatest man, though nobody seemed to know why.

Building on the plans and policies of his great-uncle, Augustus Caesar must also be regarded a part of the legacy in any assessment of Caesar. Under Augustus's rule, channels of culture and communication emerged throughout the Greco-Roman world, which enabled Christianity, a faith appealing to people of many traditions, to spread "in the fullness of time," to use the phrase of St. Paul, a Jew who valued his Roman citizenship. Augustus would inaugurate the relative peace to be enviously remembered ever after as the Pax Romana. Rome would consolidate imperial rule, achieving a multiracial culture and looking ahead to the Europe of modern times.

Allene Phy-Olsen

Further Reading

Adkins, Lesley, and Roy A. Adkins. *Handbook to Life in Ancient Rome.* New York: Oxford University Press, 1994.

Appian. *The Civil Wars.* Translated with an introduction by John Carter. New York: Penguin Classics, 1996.

Blois, Lukas de. *The Roman Army and Politics in the First Century before Christ.* Amsterdam: J. C. Gieben, 1987.

Boardman, John, et al. *The Oxford History of the Roman World.* Oxford: Oxford University Press, 2001.

Brice, Lee L., ed. *Warfare in the Roman Republic: From the Etruscan Wars to the Battle of Actium.* Santa Barbara, CA: ABC-CLIO, 2014.

Caesar, Julius. *The Civil War.* Edited and translated by Jane F. Mitchell. London: Penguin, 1967.

Canfora, Luciano. *Julius Caesar: The Life and Times of the People's Dictator.* Translated by Marian Hill and Kevin Windle. Berkeley: University of California Press, 2007.

Chrissanthos, Stefan G. "Caesar and the Mutiny of 47 B.C." *Journal of Roman Studies* 91 (2001): 63–75.

Everitt, Antony. *Cicero: The Life and Times of Rome's Greatest Politician.* New York: Random House, 2001.

Fields, Nic. *Julius Caesar.* New York: Osprey, 2010.

Fields, Nic. *Pompey.* New York: Osprey, 2012.

Freeman, Philip, *Julius Caesar.* New York: Simon and Schuster, 2009.

Gelzer, Matthias. *Caesar: Politician and Statesman.* Cambridge, MA: Harvard University Press, 1985.

Goldsworthy, Adrian. *Caesar: Life of a Colossus.* New Haven, CT: Yale University Press, 2006.

Goldsworthy, Adrian. *Caesar's Civil War, 49–44 BC.* New York: Osprey, 2002.

Goodman, Rob, and Soni Jimmy. *Rome's Last Citizen: The Life and Legacy of Cato, Mortal Enemy of Caesar.* New York: Thomas Dunne Books, St. Martin's, 2012.

Grant, Michael. *The Army of the Caesars.* New York: Scribner, 1974.

Grant, Michael. *History of Rome.* New York: Scribner, 1978.

Grant, Michael. *Julius Caesar.* New York: M. Evans, 1992.

Gruen, Erich S. *The Last Generation of the Roman Republic.* Berkeley: University of California Press, 1995.

Hamilton, Edith. *The Roman Way to Western Civilization.* New York: New American Library of World Literature, 1957.

Jimenez, Raymond. *Caesar against Rome: The Great Roman Civil War.* Westport, CT: Praeger, 2000.

Keppie, Lawrence. *The Making of the Roman Army: From Republic to Empire.* Norman: University of Oklahoma Press, 1998.

Maatyszak, Philip. *Chronicle of the Roman Republic.* London: Thames and Hudson, 2003.

Meier, Christian. *Caesar: A Biography.* Translated by David McLintock. New York: Basic Books, 1997.

Parenti, Michael. *The Assassination of Julius Caesar: A People's History of Ancient Rome.* New York: New Press, 2003.

Plutarch. *Fall of the Roman Republic.* London: Penguin Classics, 1954.

Plutarch. *Lives of Noble Grecians and Romans.* Edited by John Dryden and Arthur Hugh Clough. New York: Modern Library, 2000.

Scullard, H. H. *From the Gracchi to Nero: A History of Rome from 133 B.C. to A.D. 68.* New York: Routledge, 1991.

Sheppard, Si, and Adam Hook. *Pharsalus 48 BC: Caesar and Pompey—Clash of the Titans.* New York: Osprey, 2006.

Shotter, David. *The Fall of the Roman Republic.* London: Routledge, 1994.

Strauss, Barry. *The Death of Caesar: The Story of History's Most Famous Assassination.* New York: Simon and Schuster, 2015.

Suetonius. *Lives of the Caesars.* Edited by Catharine Edwards. New York: Oxford University Press, 2008.

Weinstock, Stefan. *Divus Julius.* Oxford: Oxford University Press, 1971.

5. What Caused the Fall of the Roman Empire?

The Roman Empire dates to 27 BCE, when Julius Caesar became dictator, and endured for five centuries thereafter. During much of that time Rome was the world's largest city, and at its pinnacle of strength the empire included nearly one-quarter of the world's population. For many years the Roman Empire fielded potent, well-led armies; maintained highly efficient governments; and presided over a robust and expanding economy. It produced enduring works of arts and literature and incubated religious tolerance by assimilating Christianity in the fourth century CE. Indeed, the empire's culture, legal codes, philosophy, and architecture ensured the longevity of Roman values and civilization long after it fell. The fall of the Roman Empire has been attributed to a variety of factors. These include invasions by Germanic peoples, economic decline, overreliance on slave labor, the division of the empire into western and eastern halves in the late 300s, imperial overreach and crippling military spending, government inefficiency and corruption, the dilution of traditional societal values, the weakening of the Roman military, and overreliance on mercenary soldiers.

In the first perspective essay, Dr. Lee W. Eysturlid argues that the decline of the Roman Empire was a century-long process. The empire did not end because of one factor or a single cataclysmic event. He argues that military decline in general and the supplanting of Roman troops by Germanic forces were major reasons for the fall of the empire. He also points out that Rome's decline was precipitated by a decline in civic participation after the introduction of Christianity, a faltering economy, a dwindling population, and disease. The largest contributor, however, was a series of barbarian invasions beginning in the mid-400s. Dr. Kathryn Jasper suggests that

Rome's division into four and then two administrative components diminished the senatorial class, thereby weakening Rome's traditional political values. Rome fell because of a wide array of internal and external threats occurring over an extended period of time. Nevertheless, despite the end of the Western Roman Empire in 476, Roman institutions such as the Catholic Church, legal codes, and local institutions were preserved as part of the successive Germanic kingdoms. Dr. Alexander Mikaberidze asserts that Rome did not decline as much as it transitioned into the Byzantine Empire, which lasted another 1,000 years. The Germanic kingdoms of the West were merely part of the long history of the region and another chapter in the trajectory of Rome's history. At the same time, Rome's transition can also be viewed as a reflection of changing values, cultures, and beliefs that marked the shift from classical antiquity to the Middle Ages.

Background Essay

At its greatest extent, the Roman Empire completely encircled the Mediterranean. One of the largest empires in all of history, it included much of Europe, North Africa, and the Middle East. Most of that territory was acquired under the Roman Republic in the first century CE, but the empire reached its greatest territorial extent under Emperor Trajan (98–117), when it included some 1.93 million square miles (including some 40 countries today), with a population of some 55–100 million people. Even the lower figure would have given it a quarter of the world's total. Certainly it was the largest state in the West until the mid-19th century.

The Roman Empire lasted some 500 years. Its establishment is usually dated from 27 BCE, when Julius Caesar was appointed dictator. With Caesar's assassination in 44 BCE, civil war gripped Rome as rival factions vied for power. The victor in that struggle was Caesar's grandnephew and adopted son Octavian, who ruled Rome from 31 BCE to 14 CE. Known as Augustus, he was careful to portray himself and his government as the reconstitution of the republic—a clever facade that sought to conceal what in reality was an autocracy. Those emperors who had long reigns were careful to secure and retain the support of the Roman legions.

For the next three centuries, a period called the Principate, Roman emperors took the unofficial title *princeps*. Augustus's immediate heirs, the Julio-Claudian dynasty, ruled in much the same guise by playing up the Senate and maintaining power with the personal loyalty of the legions. Among those rulers were some of the more notorious emperors, including Caligula and Nero. For the most part, the Julio-Claudians maintained the size of the empire they had inherited and kept up the facade of the Principate, but they also ruled as autocrats.

View of the Forum in Rome. The Forum was the site of both sacred and secular activities. (Roberto Zilli/Dreamstime.com)

With the death of Nero in 68 and with no clear heir, Rome was plunged into a period of war. The Year of the Four Emperors, as 68–69 came to be known, saw four men rise to the throne and revealed the true power of the Roman Army. The army could even make emperors outside Rome: for example, Emperor Galba was from Spain.

Emperor Vespasian, the last of those four, ruled for 10 years and restored order within the empire. Vespasian and his heirs, the Flavian dynasty, were succeeded by the Antonine dynasty. Nerva, who took over from Domitian in 96, established what came to be called the reign of the Five Good Emperors. To some historians, those emperors represented ideal monarchs in that they ruled with relative justice, looked after the populace, and allowed the Senate to choose their imperial successors.

Marcus Aurelius, the only one of the Five Good Emperors to have a son, not surprisingly made him his heir. Commodus was a poor ruler, and with his death in 192 civil war erupted again. Peace came within a year after the short reign of two emperors. The third emperor in 193, Septimius Severus, inaugurated the Severan dynasty, which ruled until 235.

With Severus, the Roman emperor became an outright ruler supported by the legions. The Senate lost many of its privileges, the Praetorian Guard (the imperial bodyguard) was disbanded and remade with appointments from the legions, and *equites* filled more official positions. The death of the last Severan, Severus Alexander, ushered in 50 years of civil war and rule by so-called barracks emperors.

For 50 years emperors rose and fell, all while devastating the empire and eroding traditional concepts of rule. In 284, one of those soldier-emperors managed to eliminate his rivals and restore order once again. Diocletian, the first emperor of the period known as the Dominate, made important changes in legitimizing his rule. Most significant, Diocletian and his successors made conscious links with religion (Jupiter was Diocletian's patron god) by using their relationship with the gods or God as the foundation for rule.

Diocletian divided the empire into more manageable administrative areas, each headed by either an "augustus" (senior emperor) or by a "caesar" (junior emperor). That system, dubbed the tetrarchy, greatly enhanced both the internal and external security of the empire but did not last. When Diocletian retired, civil war led first to two emperors, one in the east and one in the west, and finally to one, Constantine I, in 324.

The reign of Constantine (308–337) was remarkable on several levels. First, he managed to keep the empire intact despite Germanic encroachment and pressure from Rome's only real rival, the Sassanid Empire of present-day Iraq and Iran. Constantine also legalized Christianity and further enfranchised it by becoming a Christian himself. Like Diocletian, Constantine emphasized his role as God's agent on Earth, which strengthened his authority. With the exception of Emperor Julian, who tried to revive paganism, the succeeding Roman emperors were Christian. Theodosius I made Christianity the official religion of the empire and was the last emperor to rule the entire empire; he divided Rome into eastern and western halves and put his two sons in charge of them. After the collapse of the western portion of the empire in the fifth century CE, the idea of the Roman Empire lived on among the Germanic peoples of Western Europe and in the Byzantine Empire of the east.

Any examination of the late Roman Empire brings up the question of the fall of Rome, that is, when the empire finally collapsed. It has been customary to view the fall of Rome as an event, and scholars have advanced specific dates and reasons. Some advance 476 as the date when Rome fell, when Romulus Augustulus, the last western emperor, was overthrown by the Germanic warrior Odoacer. Historians today increasingly look at the fall of Rome not as an event but instead as a process, one in which the Roman Empire gradually transformed into new polities. In Western Europe various Germanic kingdoms looked to Rome for inspiration, and many considered themselves heirs to Rome. The eastern Byzantine Empire, which lasted until 1453, constituted a second heir and in many ways represented continuity with old Rome. The Byzantines even called themselves "Romans" in Greek. The last heirs to Rome were the Muslims, who beginning in the seventh century swept from Arabia into the west. Each of those peoples preserved aspects of Rome for posterity.

James B. Tschen-Emmons and Spencer C. Tucker

Perspective Essay 1. The Long-Term Decline of the Roman Military

Although the collapse of the Roman Empire was one of the great events in human history, a great deal of disagreement exists as to the exact or singular cause of Rome's demise. Of the major arguments offered for this, likely the strongest are that the empire was undermined over a period of time by a decline in civic participation caused by the rise of Christianity, the decay of the Roman economy and the dwindling of its population, disease, and finally military defeat. Of these, the best argument is that Rome was broken and then drowned in a series of progressively powerful barbarian invasions starting in the mid-fourth century. Repeated military defeats must be viewed in two complementary parts, however. The first is that successful invasions of warlike peoples across the northern frontiers ate away at Roman military strength. The second emerges from the first in that the Roman Army stopped being Roman and became barbarized.

The military collapse and defeat was a 100-year-long process. Rome's descent can be set in the two great and epochal military defeats that imperial armies suffered in the middle of the fourth century. The first was the destruction of the Roman army in the east in the Battle of Maranga in 363, when Emperor Julian lost his life and the bulk of his forces. A shock for the magnitude of the loss, it would have been more likely a mere setback had it not been followed relatively closely by the defeat of another Roman army under the emperor Valens at Adrianople in 378. Again the bulk of the Roman army was annihilated in battle against what the Romans regarded as an inferior enemy. It was a crushing blow in the numbers of men lost and the further undermining of the notion of the superiority of Roman arms. Of more importance than the Battle of Adrianople was the subsequent influx of great numbers of barbarians into Roman territory. The Visigoths' crossing of the Danube and the initial Roman willingness to allow them to settle in the region set the stage for a long series of invasions that would end with the fall of the Western Roman Empire.

The forced entry and mismanaged settlement of the Visigoths should not be seen as simply part of the decline of the Romans from Valens forward. Before the Battle at Adrianople and despite the defeat at Maranga, the Roman Army and the military system that supported it remained intact. The army would show a great deal of resilience and strength in the 30 years between Valen's defeat and the sack of Rome by the Visigoth Alaric. It had been a Roman strength that even despite serious military setbacks, the empire could recover from tactical defeats. This was clear in the raising of new and effective forces even after defeats such as at Cannae in 216 BCE at the hands of Hannibal Barca and at the Teutoburg Forest by the Germans in 9 CE.

By the middle of the third century there is no evidence that the Romans had lost the will to maintain the empire. Rather, after 410 some of that early resilience remained, but especially in the western portion an important difference emerged. This critical exception was the barbarization of the army.

The strength of the army had always been twofold. First was its tactical discipline. Roman battlefield dynamism came from the fact that citizens drawn into service were trained rigorously in the traditional close-order formations of the reformed legion and the maniple (tactical unit). This training was conducted under experienced officers who expected and evoked the strictest discipline. This discipline allowed for the effective deployment of troops on the field and maximized their operational ability. The decline of the legionary army and its clear tactical and operational decay meant that a western Roman emperor could no longer project coherent force along the traditional frontiers. The smaller professional legionary forces, when competently led, had more often than not been the terror of their opponents. This was especially true of the cruder barbarians, whom the legions made short work of on many occasions.

This effectiveness melted away. Even by the fourth century CE, Roman generals still looked to deploy troops in the ancient fashion, which proved less effective than the more dispersed tactics of the enemy. This decline after 410 meant that Rome could not hold on to Britain, which was essentially abandoned, and a few decades later acceded to the loss of the vital African provinces. Most telling is that Britain and Africa were lost not from a series of battlefield defeats but instead simply due to the fact that the Western Roman Empire no longer had effective field armies to deploy to stop it.

During the period after the disaster at Adrianople and the sacking of Rome in 410, the army underwent a clear deterioration. It must be remembered that it was the army of the Eastern Roman Empire that lost at Maranga and Adrianople. However, it was also this army that moved against the rebellious army of the Western Roman Empire in the Balkans and fought at Frigid River in 394. The eastern army, under Emperor Theodosius, was only partly Roman, having a contingent of nearly 20,000 Visigoths who were commanded by and fought as barbarians. They assaulted the western army in column and still routed it, although with severe losses to both sides. The defeat was a humiliation for the once effective and proud western army, and worse was to come for its numbers and reputation in the climatic years between 407 and 410.

The reduction of the imperial frontiers in the north and west resulted from several waves of barbarian invasion between 410 and 440. As a result of population pressures and other barbarian invasions from Asia, numerous German tribes sought to cross into Roman territory. The devastation at the hands of marauding barbarian forces worked to depopulate areas, ruining the networks of cities and agricultural infrastructure that had existed. The theory that the loss of territory and diminution of the frontiers and Roman strength resulted from the empire's depopulation gets things backward. The collapse of population numbers and economic vitality in the regions of Britain, Gaul, northern Italy, the Balkans, and Africa was the direct result of the extensive warfare and plundering that came in the wake of the invasions. This slaughter and displacement of people and destruction of resources added to the decline of the military. The loss of Africa also meant that Rome no longer had naval dominance of the Mediterranean, undermining operational flexibility and trade. Thus, the serious collapse between 440 and 460 was the result of military failure rather than political and economic problems.

It was at that critical juncture that Western Roman military leadership, both in its emperors and generals, failed. Emperor Honorius (r. 395–423) engaged in an active strategy, attempting to meet the barbarians. His strategic efforts might have paid off, at least in the preservation of the heart of the old empire, had he not been betrayed and had the gates of Rome opened to Alaric's Visigoth forces in 410. The failures of General Stilicho are all too apparent, as he allowed himself to be too often interested in the political affairs of the Eastern Roman Empire. Worse, he failed on several occasions, having defeated the forces of Alaric, to pursue and finish him off. It was Alaric who continued to rally the Visigoths and assault Italy. Had Stilicho focused on the defense of Rome and destroyed Alaric, the sack of the city might have been avoided.

After 410 the Roman Army lost any of the tactical advantages that it had possessed over the barbarian armies, because the Roman Army had itself become barbarized. The potentially apocryphal but telling statement of Attila in the Battle of Châlons in 451 makes this evident. In planning the battle, Attila decided to attack the enemy center, where the Alans were stationed, with the intention of defeating them, then pivoting left and hitting the Visigoths in the flank. When asked about the Roman and German forces that faced him on his right, Attila dismissed them as being of little consequence. The great Roman Army no longer existed.

In conclusion, it was the slow devolution of the Roman Army that created the conditions for the fall of the empire. The army was undermined and then irrevocably diluted by the endless influx of barbarians, both as settlers and then as "federates," or allied forces. Whereas the barbarian forces made up roughly a third of the Roman army at Adrianople, it was more than three-quarters of the army at Châlons. The rapid increase of the rough-and-ready barbarian tribesmen fatally undermined the strengths of Roman discipline and logistical depth. Without the army that had made Rome an empire, there was no force left to defend the empire against the ever-increasing pressures of barbarian peoples surging in. Whether the army could have stopped this from happening by choosing different strategies, the barbarization of the army ensured that it would not.

Lee W. Eysturlid

Perspective Essay 2. A Series of Crises

The fall of the Roman Empire was the result of a series of crises in the fifth century from which it would not recover, although Roman culture and institutions continued to influence barbarian rulers and their kingdoms well into the Middle Ages.

The question of how Rome fell demands another question: What do we mean by "Rome"? When we speak about the fall of an empire, the sudden and dramatic collapse of institutions and infrastructures comes to mind; few scholars would disagree that the Roman Empire in the West ended in the fifth century. But, did Rome not also include Romans? Even as emperors invested more heavily in the eastern half of the empire and the imperial government became ever more distant in the West, on the ground thousands of Romans—craftspeople, bureaucrats, merchants, and farmers—clung to their Romanitas (Romanness). They observed traditions of the state religion, they spoke Latin, and they recognized the authority of the emperor and imperial jurisdiction.

The decentralization of the empire with its division into four and then two administrative units meant that the Roman aristocracy, the senatorial class, became increasingly irrelevant in the wider political scene. On the local level it remained influential in perpetuating Roman culture. In addition, under the Christian emperors many members of this aristocracy entered the church hierarchy and as bishops became leaders in the city and the countryside.

By the fifth century the senatorial class, together with other provincials in the West holding Roman citizenship, still maintained Roman institutions and ways of life, which invading barbarian forces themselves had little desire to subvert. Contemporary documents offer conflicting accounts on relations between barbarian tribes and Roman provincials in the West; nonetheless, there survives much evidence indicating that the two groups worked together to preserve Roman customs. The resettlement of the barbarians in the western provinces proved inconvenient (and even disastrous) to the existing population, but many barbarian soldiers strove to demonstrate their Romanitas and to reconcile themselves with the existing Roman aristocracy, many of whom held important ecclesiastical offices. Roman culture and institutions at the local level continued to influence barbarian rulers and their kingdoms for the next several hundred years.

At the macrolevel, however, the Roman Empire disintegrated in the fifth century. The Roman Empire in the East endured for 1,000 years after the western half collapsed but never reclaimed the territory or power of the former empire. The Roman Empire as a superpower ended not because of any single factor but instead due to a maelstrom of internal and external threats. The Romans had faced formidable enemies for centuries, and yet the empire had persevered. Rome did not fall overnight but eventually succumbed to invaders due to years and years of civil war that wore away at the army and the functionality of imperial bureaucracy. From 217 CE to 476 CE, civil war occurred frequently in the Western Roman Empire.

From the reign of Septimius Severus and on into the fifth century, every adult emperor faced at least one challenger. These wars struck at the backbone of the empire, its military. Invaders took advantage of internal weaknesses. Usurpers relied on soldiers' loyalty, and attempts to secure that loyalty disrupted the formal order and maintenance of the Roman military. Moreover, social unrest removed soldiers from the frontiers precisely when their presence was most needed. As Italy and Gaul received numerous hostile invaders, the army could not protect the provincials not only because it was otherwise occupied but also because invasions and violence destroyed the empire's tax base, and this sharply undermined the military. There was also a connection between the empire's failure to repel invaders and civil strife. Challengers to the imperial throne were emboldened by an emperor's inability to fend off invaders, and after each disaster these men attracted new supporters similarly disappointed with the current regime.

The Roman historian Ammianus Marcellinus recorded the movement of the Goths across the Danube in 376 as a mass migration of men, women, and children. According to Ammianus, these peoples sought to escape the Huns and asked Emperor Valens for refuge within the empire. The empire had allowed in such barbarian groups many times in the past, although some historians argue that fourth-century migrations were of a much larger scale. Estimates range between 15,000 and 20,000 fighting men and their families. Valens arranged for the Goths to be transported across the Danube and eventually be settled in the empire, a strategy that would generate tax revenue, increase land cultivation, and, not least of all, provide new fighting forces for the army. Unfortunately for Valens, the plan went awry. Roman forces along the Danube mismanaged the settling of the refugees, who were forced to pay unreasonable prices for food. While the emperor was occupied with the Persians, the Goths rebelled. The conflict escalated, ending in the death of Valens in the Battle of Adrianople in 378.

Migrations after 376 came with greater frequency and involved significant numbers of peoples, and their movements became destructive. In the early fifth century, rather than a single breach of the frontier, migrations occurred frequently and crossed into Italy. Over time the barbarians managed to claim ownership of all the land they occupied, and they quickly converted that property to power. Arguably, the empire expected to retain control of lands granted by treaty, but with the influx of substantial numbers of fighting men on Roman lands, the barbarians soon seized effective power for themselves. By 476, Roman inhabitants of the western provinces were living under new rule.

Around 410, Britain was outside the empire. In northern Gaul the Franks struck at Roman territory, and the central imperial administration failed to stop them. Childeric, who moved from Roman military commander to king, led one group of

Franks and eventually established the Merovingian dynasty that ruled most of Gaul. Childeric had no intention of destroying what survived of Roman infrastructures in Gaul. After Childeric's death his son and heir, Clovis, worked closely with the Gallic aristocracy (many of whom were bishops), seeking thereby to reinforce his own authority and gain the support of locals. Clovis greatly enhanced Frankish power in Gaul while embracing Roman values at the elite level.

The barbarians were hardly strangers to Roman culture. For centuries they had interacted with Romans along the frontiers. Recent archaeological evidence shows indigenous and Roman objects together in burials in frontier zones of Roman Europe, indicating that the barbarian peoples embraced Roman tools and technologies while maintaining their own traditions. To enhance the smooth functioning of the successor kingdoms, barbarian rulers often employed Roman administrative structures and employed Romans in important positions. The Ostrogoths, who ruled in Italy during the late fifth century, relied on aristocratic Romans to run their kingdom as traditional legal and administrative officers of the Roman state. King Theodoric of the Ostrogoths even minted gold coins with the image and name of the eastern emperor.

Barbarian rulers in Spain, Gaul, Italy, and North Africa adopted many Roman approaches to administration and emulated imperial culture. They used Latin, the language of the conquered, for their official documents and law codes. This continued to be true even during the reign of Charlemagne in the late eighth century. However, at some point in the early Middle Ages the distinction between barbarian and Roman disappeared.

The deposition of Emperor Romulus Augustulus in 476 might have gone unnoticed by provincials if it were not for the symbolic importance of the event, because the transformation of the Western Roman Empire had begun long before. The fall of the Roman Empire occurred over many years, not at once. The decline reached its high point in the fifth century, though Romanitas remained a strong influence on barbarian rulers for centuries. Roman institutions and the Latin language persisted in the barbarian kingdoms of the early Middle Ages in spite of Rome's fall.

Kathryn Jasper

Perspective Essay 3. Transition into Byzantium

The fall of the Roman Empire was not actually an end of the once mighty state but instead was a sociopolitical transition that allowed it to endure for another

1,000 years in the east as the Byzantine Empire. The Roman Empire was the largest state Western Eurasia has ever known. Its advanced culture, outstanding road network, and superbly trained professional army allowed Rome to exercise its imperium (power, authority) for more than 400 years. By the second century, it stretched from Hadrian's Wall in northern Britain to the Euphrates River in present-day Iraq.

Two hundred years later the Romans were still expanding, actively pushing the boundaries of their state in every direction. Yet within a generation, the Roman imperium was shaken to its core. In 376 thousands of Goths, one of the Germanic tribes, reached the empire's borders on the Danube River, asking for asylum. Contrary to established Roman policy, they were allowed in without first being subdued militarily and with no provision for Rome to provide them sustenance. Within two years the Goths revolted, defeated and killed the Roman emperor, and effectively initiated decades-long strife with profound consequences. On September 4, 476, 100 years after the Goths crossed the Danube, Romulus Augustus, the last Roman emperor in the West, was deposed.

In 1776 historian Edward Gibbon published *The Decline and Fall of the Roman Empire,* tracing Rome's end. Gibbon lamented the gradual loss of civic virtue among Roman citizens and mainly blamed Christianity and the barbarians for the collapse of the empire. Christianity, the historian claimed, offered an alternative of a better afterlife that fostered apathy to the present in the Roman society, thereby weakening the Roman resolve to fight and defend their realm. The barbarian invasions of the fourth and fifth centuries then drove the last nail in the coffin of the Roman Empire. Indeed, there was a quick succession of emperors who had been brought to power and then overthrown by Germanic forces, the last being Romulus Augustus. The rebel leader, Odoacer, did not appoint another emperor and instead retained power in Italy, marking the fall of the Roman Empire and the start of a long period of political and social turmoil in Europe.

Yet, the reality was much more complex. Odoacer in fact did not simply claim power and instead sought to legitimize it the only way he knew. He had the Roman Senate petition Emperor Zeno of the eastern half of the Roman Empire to recognize his leadership in return for his acknowledging Zeno as sole emperor over the western and eastern empires. The German chieftain needed recognition from Zeno because the eastern emperor, residing in Constantinople, was still acknowledged as the *basileus kai autokrator Rhomaion* (emperor and autocrat of the Romans) and therefore was the source of legitimacy.

Odoacer's petition offers an important insight. Traditional interpretation of the decline of the Roman Empire focused on the western half and had been dominated by the story of imperial Rome—its struggle against Germanic invasions, repeated sacks at the hands of barbarians, and ultimately collapse. This narrative, which can be traced back to Gibbon, played an important role in shaping popular perceptions of the event. Yet, much of this narrative has been revised by modern historians. It is more accurate to argue that the Roman Empire experienced a complex transformation and endured for centuries more.

In the West, the Roman imperium was replaced by a mosaic of new Germanic kingdoms—Franks, Visigoths, Vandals, Ostrogoths, etc.—but these states did not end Roman civilization; instead, they sought to preserve many elements of the Roman past. The political changes set in motion profound social and cultural transformations as the Germanic newcomers and their Roman subjects combined their traditions to develop novel ways of life. The "barbarians" had not intended to destroy all the benefits of the Roman civilization. It was Rome's wealth and comforts that had attracted them in the first place. The German chieftains tried to continue the Roman system with the surviving Roman elites, but sadly their efforts produced mixed results, and the astonishingly sophisticated levels of the Roman civilization had been lost. Nevertheless, there is still plenty of evidence to underscore social and cultural continuity between Rome and its medieval successor states.

In the East there was a different reality. The eastern half of the Roman Empire endured for another 1,000 years before falling to the Ottomans in 1453. During this long history, the Eastern Roman Empire, also called the Byzantine Empire, stood its ground against numerous threats and occasionally shone brilliantly. In the fifth century when the western half was sacked and divided into barbarian kingdoms, the empire endured in the East. In fact, in the sixth century it counterattacked. After a generation of rule by military men who lacked vision and administrative capacity but succeeded in safeguarding the empire, the Byzantine crown passed to Emperor Justinian, who emerged as the greatest ruler of Late Antiquity. Justinian waged decades-long war to reunite the empire as it had been in the days of Augustus. Led by General Flavius Belisarius, the Byzantine armies reclaimed North Africa from the Vandals, Italy from the Ostrogoths, and parts of Spain from the Visigoths. A generation later Emperor Heraclius triumphantly campaigned against Sassanid Persia, restoring the True Cross (which had been earlier captured by the Sassanids) to Jerusalem in a grand ceremony.

This revival of the Roman imperium proved rather short-lived. The success came at a huge cost in effort, time, and expense. By the early seventh century, the resources of the Byzantine Empire were so depleted that successor rulers could not maintain the momentum of reunification. Much of Italy and Spain had succumbed to new barbarian invasions. In addition, the onslaught of the Bulgars and Slavs in the northeast and Muslim Arabs in the south presented new grave threats to the empire. Yet despite the loss of Italy, Spain, Africa, Egypt, and Syria in the seventh century, the empire lived on, recovering its strength. By the eighth century the empire assumed the basic geographic shape it would hold for centuries, and in contrast to the vast lands once ruled by Rome, it was now confined to the eastern Balkans and western Anatolia.

Byzantine success is striking when compared to the fate of the western half of the empire. Both halves of the empire suffered from similar internal weakness, including corrupt and extortionate bureaucracy, population decline, and agricultural regression; some problems, such as theological disputes, were more acute in the East than in the West. Nevertheless, the Byzantine Empire overcame these weaknesses and managed in the 6th and early 7th centuries to not only hold its own against the barbarians in the West and the Sassanids in the East but also to conquer vast new lands. Even in the dark 7th century, when Muslim armies scored a seemingly unending series of victories, the Byzantines succeeded despite territorial losses. Over the next three centuries it successfully repelled continued Muslim attacks and frequently launched counterattacks that held the line between Christendom and Islam in Anatolia until the 11th century.

Along the way, the Byzantines continued to build on their Roman legacy. Emperor Justinian, for example, launched a major administrative overhaul to reduce official corruption, tighten control of provinces, and ensure a steady flow of tax revenue. In 529–533 Justinian also introduced his famous law code, the Corpus Iuris Civilis, that codified Roman legal practices dating back to the 2nd and 3rd centuries. Justinian's law code remains one of history's most influential legal accomplishments, summarizing centuries' worth of Roman law and remaining valid until 1453; it has subsequently influenced almost every legal system in the modern world. Between the 8th and 10th centuries, Byzantium staved off Muslim attacks in Asia Minor and continued to rebuild. After 850 its power shone brightly once more, with military victories bringing new wealth and power to the imperial court.

Aside from prestige and wealth, military victories also gave the emperors the opportunity to consolidate their power. The empire's wealth derived from a prosperous agricultural economy geared toward trade and commerce that depended on a careful balance of state regulation and individual enterprise. Byzantium was at the heart of a vibrant international trade that connected the empire to much of Europe, North Africa, and the Near East. Just like their Roman predecessors, the Byzantine emperors presided over elaborate court ceremonies that sought to convey the sacred and concentrated power of imperial majesty.

Thus, the term "fall of Rome" is misleading. The western half of the Roman Empire was indeed defeated militarily in the fifth century. One must bear in mind, however, that the "fall" did not change every aspect of the life of Roman subjects but instead marked the start of a transformation of Roman society into a different variant of social organization that emerged in the Middle Ages. Above all, we must remember that the empire did endure for another 1,000 years in the East, experiencing new historic highs and lows and developing a vibrant culture and society.

Alexander Mikaberidze

Further Reading

Amory, Patrick. *People and Identity in Ostrogothic Italy, 489–554*. Cambridge: Cambridge University Press, 2003.

Burns, Thomas S. *Rome and the Barbarians, 100BC–400AD.* New York: Johns Hopkins University Press, 2009.

Bury, J. B. *The Invasion of Europe by the Barbarians.* New York: Norton, 2000.

Erdkamp, Paul A. *Companion to the Roman Army.* Malden, MA: Blackwell, 2007.

Ferrill, Arther. *The Fall of the Roman Empire.* London: Thames and Hudson, 1986.

Gibbon, Edward. *The Decline and Fall of the Roman Empire.* New York: Harcourt Brace, 1960.

Goffart, Walter. *Barbarian Tides: The Migration Age and the Later Roman Empire.* Philadelphia: University of Pennsylvania Press, 2006.

Goldsworthy, Adrian. *How Rome Fell: Death of a Superpower.* New Haven, CT: Yale University Press, 2009.

Grant, Micheal. *The Fall of the Roman Empire.* New York: Touchstone Books, 1997.

Halsall, Guy. *Barbarian Migrations and the Roman West, 376–568.* Cambridge: Cambridge University Press, 2007.

Heather, Peter. *Empires and Barbarians: The Fall of Rome and the Birth of Europe.* Oxford: Oxford University Press, 2009.

Heather, Peter. *The Fall of the Roman Empire: A New History of Rome and the Barbarians.* New York: Oxford University Press, 2007.

Jones, A. H. M. *The Later Roman Empire.* Oxford, UK: Basil Blackwell, 1964.

Kulikowski, Michael. *Rome's Gothic Wars: From the Third Century to Alaric.* Cambridge: Cambridge University Press, 2007.

Martin, Thomas R. *Ancient Rome: From Romulus to Justinian.* New Haven, CT: Yale University Press, 2012.

Mathisen, Ralph W. "Peregrini, Barbari, and Cives Romani: Concepts of Citizenship and the Legal Identity of Barbarians in the Later Roman Empire." *American Historical Review* (October 2006): 1011–1040.

Sherwood, Merriam. "Magic and Mechanics in Medieval Fiction." *Studies in Philology* 44 (1947): 567–592.

Southern, Pat. *The Roman Army: A Social and Institutional History.* Santa Barbara, CA: ABC-CLIO, 2006.

Vasiliev, A. *History of the Byzantine Empire, 324–1453.* Madison: University of Wisconsin Press, 1952.

Ward-Perkins, Brian. *The Fall of Rome and the End of Civilization.* Oxford: Oxford University Press, 2005.

Wells, Peter S. *The Barbarians Speak: How the Conquered Peoples Shaped Roman Europe.* Princeton, NJ: Princeton University Press, 1999.

Wirth, Gerhard. "Rome and Its Germanic Partners in the Fourth Century." In *Kingdoms of the Empire: The Integration of Barbarians in Late Antiquity,* edited by Walter Pohl, 13–55. New York: Brill, 1997.

Wood, Ian. *The Merovingian Kingdoms, 450–751.* London: Longman, 1994.

PART II

THE MIDDLE AGES (500–1500)

6. What Is the Explanation for the Rapid Success of the Arab Conquests in the Hundred Years after the Death of Prophet Muhammad?

During the eighth and seventh centuries CE, Arab armies led by the prophet Muham-mad and his successors achieved a series of dramatic military victories across the Middle East and North Africa. The Arab armies also advanced into Europe, Central Asia, and South Asia. Propelled by faith in the new religion of Islam and the desire to spread it to other peoples, these armies' conquests helped form the foundation of Mus-lim civilization, which would further develop and expand under the rule of such dy-nasties as the Abbasids, the Almohads, and the Umayyads. Muhammad began his military campaign in Mecca (in modern-day Saudi Arabia), finally conquering that city in 630. At the time of his death in 632, he had secured virtually all of Arabia and had converted it into a theocratic state. Muhammad's successors carried forth his grand vision, systematically subduing large portions of the known world and moving as far west and north as Spain and France. How the Arab armies made such large military and political gains in so little time is the chief focus of the perspective essays that follow.

In the first essay, Dr. Nancy Stockdale emphasizes the importance of new Muslims' religious fervor as a motivating force and cohesive influence that allowed the Arab armies to expand their territory and power so quickly. She also discusses other factors leading to Arab success. These include innovative cavalry tactics, chiefly charge, and withdraw; the use of camel caravans, making logistics far more efficient; a profession-alized army officer corps; the use of existing government bureaucracies in conquered regions; and relatively evenhanded policies toward conquered subjects. In the second essay, Dr. Richard A. Gabriel asserts that the fusion of religious (Islamic) zeal with traditional Arab practices such as tribal warfare and raiding virtually ensured the success of Arab armies. Muhammad, he points out, believed that Muslims had a sacred right to conduct warfare against unbelievers and to rule over them. Because Islam prohibits forced proselytism, Arab conquerors hoped that once conquered populations saw the advantages of Islam, they would convert on their own accord. Certainly Muhammad's vision of jihad, or holy war, was a driving factor in the success of the Arab conquests.

Background Essay

The wars of Muslim territorial expansion began with Prophet Muhammad and his desire, continued by his followers, to spread their new faith. Inspired by what he believed to have been a series of divine revelations beginning in 610, Muhammad espoused a new monotheist and egalitarian religion known as Islam. In 622 he organized the tribes of Yathrib (now Medina) into a community under the will of God (Allah) as revealed in his teachings. Both prophet and military commander, Muhammad sought to expand the faith by force of arms.

Muhammad's initial military campaign was against the city of Mecca. Beginning in 623, he raided Meccan caravans. In 624 at Badr, he won a decisive victory over a far larger Meccan force. Many people in Arabia chose to see the victory of Muhammad's badly outnumbered and poorly armed and equipped force as a sign from God, adding immensely to his reputation. Withstanding a siege of Medina in 627, Muhammad's forces took the offensive and took Mecca by assault in 630, converting it to Islam.

By the time of Muhammad's death in June 632, he had established control over most of Arabia, which had become a theocratic state. Abu Bakr became the first caliph, or successor, to Muhammad. In the so-called Ridda Wars (632–634), Bakr crushed revolts and reunited the Arab tribes.

The new Arabian state now confronted the two great empires of Persia and Byzantium, both of which had been seriously weakened in fighting each other during 602–628. The Arabs took the offensive in 632 with invasions of both Persian Mesopotamia and Byzantine territory in Palestine and Syria. The Arabs won battles against the Byzantines in 634 and 635, capturing Emesa (Homs) and Damascus.

In mid-August 636, Arab forces decisively defeated a far larger polyglot Byzantine force in a six-day battle in Palestine next to the Yarmouk (Yarmuk, Yarmūk) River. This victory gave the Muslims control of Syria and Palestine.

Turning their attention back to Persia, the Arabs captured the Persian capital of Ctesiphon in 636. During 637–645 the Arabs completed the conquest of Syria and

Palestine. At the same time, during 639–641 they took all of the remainder of Byzantine Mesopotamia.

Egypt was the next Muslim target, beginning in 639. In July 640 the Arabs were victorious over the Byzantines and, following long sieges, captured the cities of Babylon in 641 and Alexandria in 642.

During 640–650 the Arab armies conquered what remained of Persian territory, then solidified their control over what had been the Sassanid Persian Empire, with the Oxus River being the boundary between Arab and Turkish territory.

During 642–643 the Muslims expanded into North Africa from Egypt, capturing Cyrene and Tripoli and then raiding farther west. In 645 the Muslims turned back a Byzantine effort to recapture Alexandria. At the same time, the Arabs took to the sea. They captured Cyprus in 649, raided Sicily in 652, and secured Rhodes in 654. In 655 the Byzantines, personally led by Emperor Constans II, were defeated by the Arabs under Abdullah ibn Sa'd in a battle off the Lycian coast in what was the first great Arab victory at sea. Civil war within the Rashidun Caliphate during 657–661, however, shelved Arab plans to attack Constantinople and brought the division of Islam into Sunni and Shia factions.

A nineteenth-century engraving of the Battle of Lycia or Battle of the Masts (655), in which a Muslim fleet led by Abdallah ibn Sa'd ibn Abi'l Sarh defeated a Byzantine fleet under the personal command of Emperor Constans II. The battle is considered the first decisive Arab victory at sea. (Ridpath, John Clark. *Ridpath's History of the World,* 1901)

During 661–663, Ziyad ibn Abihi carried out the first Muslim raids against India. These penetrated Sind and the lower Indus River Valley. In 664, repeated Muslim invasions of Afghanistan brought the temporary capture of Kabul.

In 668, warfare resumed between the Arabs and the Byzantine Empire. Muslim forces invaded Anatolia, then crossed the Bosporus but were repulsed at Constantinople in 669. In 672 the Byzantines virtually destroyed an Arab fleet in the Sea of Marmora. The Byzantine use of a combustible mixture known as Greek fire, perhaps the first time it was employed in warfare at sea, was a major factor in the victory. The Arabs dispatched other forces and maintained an intermittent land and sea blockade of Constantinople during 673–677, but the war was effectively ended in another Byzantine naval victory in the Sea of Marmora. With the Byzantines also victorious on land, the Arabs agreed to evacuate Cyprus, pay an annual tribute to Constantinople, and maintain the peace for 30 years.

In 674, meanwhile, Arab forces invaded and conquered Transoxiana in Central Asia, while in 681 Arab forces reached Morocco. Byzantine emperor Justinian II renewed the war with the Arabs during 690–692 but was defeated. The Arabs then took all of Armenia. During 690–691 there was civil war within the Umayyad Caliphate.

During 693–698 Arab forces conquered Tunisia. The Arabs ended Byzantine influence in North Africa with the capture of Carthage in 698. By 705, an alliance between the Berbers brought Arab control of all of North Africa.

During 705–715 Caliph al-Walid secured the greatest territorial extent of any Muslim empire under one ruler. His additions included Bokhara, Samarkand, Khwarizm (Kiva), Ferghana, and Tashkent. Muslim forces also raided into Sinkiang as far as Tashkent in 713. Kabul was taken in 708, and the Sind was secured during 708–712. Multan was taken after a long siege, and the Arabs raided into the Punjab.

In 710 having reached the Strait of Gibraltar, Arab forces commenced raids across it into Spain. During 711–712 a sizable Arab force invaded, defeated the Visigoths, and secured all of Spain. That same year, Muslim forces raided north of the Pyrenees for the first time.

Also in 710, Muslim forces invaded Anatolia, conquering Cilicia in 711 and securing partial control of Galatia in 714. The chief Muslim goal remained the acquisition of Constantinople. This great Byzantine capital city controlled the Bosporus and thus access between the Mediterranean and Black Seas and also guarded the entrance to South-Central Europe. Caliph Suleiman mounted the greatest threat to Constantinople in a yearlong siege of 717–718. Suleiman the General commanded the Arab forces but was defeated by the skillful leadership of Emperor Leo III. Leo's victory was decisive, and in 739 his victory on land compelled the Muslims to withdraw from western Asia Minor. In the process he may have saved not only his empire but also West European civilization.

At the same time, the Muslims were crossing into France from Spain. In 719 they took Narbonne, and in 725 they occupied Carcassonne and Nîmes. The next year they advanced up the Rhône River Valley and ravaged Burgundy. In 732 Muslim governor of Spain Abd-ar-Rahman launched a full-scale invasion of Aquitaine. Led by Charles Martel, who was king in all but name, the Franks defeated the Arabs in the Battle of Tours in 732 in what was the deepest Muslim penetration into Europe, east and west. The Muslim threat to Europe had been contained for the time being.

Spencer C. Tucker

Perspective Essay 1. On the Success of the Early Arab Conquests

One of the most dramatic expansions of political and military authority in history, the Arab conquests of the seventh and eighth centuries established the Islamic empires of the early Middle Ages. Expanding their power from their desert base in Arabia to the Iberian Peninsula in Europe, across North Africa and the Middle East, and into the hinterlands of South and Central Asia, the Arabs astounded the world with their destruction of the Sassanid Empire and dramatic conquest of most of the Byzantine Empire. Moreover, their victories drew attention to their new religion of Islam, and their belief system began its ascent as one of the most popular faiths.

Historians have wrestled with the question of how the Arabs were able to conquer such a vast area of the world so quickly. A variety of factors must be considered. Central to discussions about the Arabs' expansion is the role played by Islam in motivating their actions. Indeed, the emergence of Islam in 610 sparked the events that eventually led to the Arab conquests.

The world first heard of Islam through its prophet, Muhammad. He challenged the social and religious order of the pagan Arabian Peninsula with a monotheist message, and as a consequence, the first Muslims were forced to defend themselves from angry elements who wished to destroy the new community of believers. Thus, from the outset the Muslims organized not only as a group following a belief system but also as an assembly forced to defend its right to exist.

After fleeing their home base of Mecca in 622 when threats were made against Muhammad (an event known in Islamic history as the *hijra,* or migration), the Muslims faced organized military attacks by their enemies, the Quraysh tribe and their allies. From the outset, then, the Muslims organized themselves not only as a community of faith but also as a military unit aimed at self-defense. After a series of battles in the 620s the Muslims took Mecca in 630, dedicated its pagan shrines to their monotheistic deity, and made peace with the inhabitants—much to their enemies' surprise.

By the time of his death in 632, Muhammad had entered into alliances with the major tribes of Arabia and militarily defeated those who rejected his authority. However, it was not until after his death that his successors expanded beyond the Arabian Peninsula and challenged the authority of the dominant empires of the era, the Byzantines to the west and the Sassanids (Sassanians) to the east. The Byzantine-Sassanid Wars (a series of conflicts lasting from 502 to 628) exhausted both the Byzantines and the Persians, opening them up to assaults by Arab forces. A variety of other factors, however, accelerated the Arab conquest of the Middle East and beyond.

First of all, the Arabs implemented strategic innovations that were difficult for their enemies to combat. A swift light cavalry famous for its wedge formations fought alongside an infantry that engaged in a technique known as charge and withdrawal, which came so unexpectedly that it confused the enemy. Also, the Muslims used camel caravans to haul their supplies and maintained separate lines of supply for each of their units. This allowed the army to move far faster than the Roman and Persian forces and prevented units from becoming disconnected from their supplies, since fixed supply bases were nonexistent. Such innovative tactics coupled with a professionalized army whose officers commanded on merit (rather than rank) helped the Muslims defeat the more experienced yet cumbersome and jaded Byzantine and Sassanid militaries.

Furthermore, long-standing conflict between the Romans and Persians not only exhausted their militaries but also frustrated significant elements among their vast imperial populations. Nonorthodox Christians and Jews believed themselves overtaxed and otherwise persecuted by the Byzantines, while the Sassanids also alienated their minorities with steep taxes and social penalties. There is strong evidence to suggest that Jews and other minorities sometimes assisted the Muslims, particularly if it meant dealing a blow to their imperial overlords, the Romans and the Persians.

While it may have been relatively easy for the Arab armies to conquer the states immediately surrounding them, their real genius lay in their ability to maintain authority and build the foundational empire of Islamic civilization. The Muslims established their occupying armies in outlying garrisons rather than in the heart of large population centers, making their presence less obtrusive in the daily lives of their new subjects. Moreover, they worked with standing bureaucracies to integrate locals into their administration, giving people a vested interest in maintaining their rule rather than challenging it. Also, the Muslims were slow to proselytize their religion and were tolerant of Jews, Christians, and Zoroastrians living in their lands. This served them well in their ability to expand and maintain their burgeoning empire.

By 750, the Arabs and their allies had expanded their political and military authority over a vast territory that stretched from Spain in Western Europe across North Africa and throughout the Middle East and toward the hinterlands of Central and South Asia. The world was shocked; the Arabs had been nomads in a region that many considered a backwater, and yet they had successfully challenged two of the world's most potent imperial forces and asserted themselves as the creators of what promised to be a powerful empire of their own. Through their innovative tactics, judicious policies toward their subjects, and the luck of facing the Romans and the Persians at a moment of historical exhaustion, the Arabs successfully conquered vast tracts of the world in a relatively short period of time.

Nancy L. Stockdale

Perspective Essay 2. Arab Conquests and the Beginning of Empire

The dream of Arab empire had been conceived in the mind of a single man, Muhammad the prophet, who set in motion the means and motive for the extensive Arab conquest. Religious and economic conflict with his own tribe in Mecca forced Muhammad to flee to Medina, where after a short time he gained converts and was made leader of the tribes there. Muhammad and his followers attacked the caravans of Mecca. This led to war in which Muhammad gained victory in a number of battles, and these victories brought his old relatives, the Quraysh tribe, and other tribal leaders under his rule. This coalition became converts and served as the nucleus of the armies that spread the new religion of Islam.

Muhammad's fusion of religious fervor with the traditional Arab practice of raiding and tribal warfare provided the critical stimulus that motivated the early Arab armies to conquest. A central tenet of Muhammad's new religion was the belief that those who embrace Islam have a sacred right to war against those who are unbelievers and to conquer and rule them in the name of the true God. The purpose of holy war is not to convert the conquered to Islam, for the faith prohibits forced conversions. It is instead the idea of a jihad, a holy war in which God is always on the side of the army of believers. Muhammad himself is said to have proclaimed the doctrine of holy war on his last visit to Mecca. Tradition has it that his last statement to the faithful was that "Muslims should fight all men until they say, 'There is no God but Allah.'"

The Arab armies established the empire of Islam through military conquest before being subsumed into the larger Muslim convert population. The original Arab armies can be said to have existed from 630 to approximately 842 CE, when the Abbasid caliph al-Mutasim introduced the Mamluk institution of enslaved Turkish soldiers who replaced the original Arab contingents in the armies of Islam. Until that time, the armies of Muhammad and his immediate successors almost exclusively consisted of Arabs from Arabia, and between 633 and 656 these armies invaded and conquered large segments of the Byzantine Empire and the Sassanid Empire. Over the next 100 years the Arabs fought three civil wars. The first war replaced the original successors of Muhammad with the Umayyad family, who ruled from Syria from 661 to 750. The Umayyads survived the second civil war (684–692) but were driven from power during the third civil war (744–750) and replaced by the Abbasid family, who ruled from Iraq and retained the caliphate, although in much altered form, until 1250. The Arab invasions set in motion enormous changes and produced a new sociopolitical order that eventually included the whole of the Arabian Peninsula, all the Sassanid lands, and the Syrian and Egyptian provinces of the Byzantine Empire.

The emergence of Islam in Arabia between 570 and 632, the dates of Muhammad's life, brought into being a new social, religious, and military force that swept out of Arabia on the wings of the religious fervor begun by Muhammad himself and collided immediately with the two great powers of the day, the Byzantine and Sassanid Empires. The Byzantine Empire ran from Eastern Europe through the Anatolian Peninsula and then along the Palestinian land bridge and through Egypt on to Libya, to include Syria. The Sassanids controlled all of Iraq and Iran and large areas stretching eastward into Central Asia. One of the more remarkable achievements in military history was the conquest of large areas of these empires in less than 30 years by Arab armies that probably never exceeded 5,000 men at any time.

Both empires were fragile, weakened by long wars between them. From 540 to 629, the Byzantines and Sassanids fought continuous wars in Syria and Iraq. At one time the Sassanid armies washed their weapons in the Mediterranean, occupying Antioch, Alexandria, and Jerusalem only to be driven back by Byzantine emperor Heraclius in 623. The sapping effect of these wars on the empires' strength was exacerbated by religious persecution within the imperial borders. The conflict between Manichaeism and Zoroastrianism, along with the struggles between heretical Christian sects, weakened Sassanid authority, as did the long and bloody persecution of the Monophysites in Egypt by the Christian emperors of Byzantium. Terrible outbreaks of plague and disease struck both empires on and off for half a century, further weakening imperial will. By the time of the Arab invasions, both empires were mere reflections of their former power and relatively easy prey to the wide-ranging *razzias* (raids) of the Arabs.

The Arab invasions were begun by Prophet Muhammad himself who, having come to think of himself as God's true messenger, sent demands to the emperors of the Sassanids and Byzantines demanding that they accept him and his message. In the absence of an imperial reply, Muhammad began the holy wars near the end of his life by sending an army of 3,000 men to attack the Byzantine frontier near the Dead Sea. This force was defeated at Muta. Undeterred, Muhammad sent another force against the border the next year and succeeded in occupying some small settlements of Christians and Jews near the northwest Arabian border. Legend suggests that he was preparing for yet another attack against Byzantium when he died on June 7, 632.

In 634 the Arabs attacked the Byzantine border provinces again, this time with three columns moving through Palestine, destroying a Byzantine garrison en route.

At the same time another Arab army attacked Damascus. The Byzantine relief force was engaged and forced to withdraw. In the meantime, all of Palestine was left defenseless to Arab raids. A year later Damascus fell to the Arabs. The next year the last remaining Byzantine force in Syria was defeated at the Yamuk River, forcing the Byzantine frontier back to the Amanus Mountains. Two years after Yamuk, Jerusalem and Caesaria surrendered to the Arabs. Between 639 and 646, Arab armies proceeded to eradicate the last vestiges of Byzantine rule in what had been Roman Mesopotamia, destroying the old unity of the Roman Mediterranean world forever.

To the east, a series of other Arab victories spelled the end of the Sassanid Empire. The Sassanids were brought under attack in force in 634, and within three years Arab armies had pushed to the edge of Iraq. The Sassanids withdrew beyond the Zagros, leaving the door to Persia open. By 641 a new Arab advance across the Tigris was under way, and within eight years all of Persia was under Arab rule. Arab armies now prepared to push farther eastward across the Oxus, reaching ultimately to India. Far to the west Egypt and Alexandria became major Arab naval bases, extending the influence of Islam to the Mediterranean Sea. In 661 with the coming of Umayyads, the Arab assault turned west once again, occupying Tunisia and the coast of Morocco, and at the end of the century Arab armies crossed into Spain. In less than 40 years, Arab armies had grown from little more than tribal coalitions to masters of an empire.

Richard A. Gabriel

Further Reading

Blankinship, K. *The End of the Jihad State.* Albany: State University of New York Press, 1994

Butler, A. J. *The Arab Conquests of Egypt.* 2nd ed. Brooklyn, NY: A&B Publishing, 1998.

Collins, Roger. *The Arab Conquest of Spain, 710–797.* Oxford, UK: Blackwell, 1989.

Dixon, A. A. *The Umayyad Caliphate, 65–86/684–705.* London: Luzac, 1971.

Donner, Fred. *The Early Islamic Conquests.* Princeton, NJ: Princeton University Press, 1981.

Esposito, John L. *The Oxford History of Islam.* Oxford: Oxford University Press, 2001.

Fregosi, Paul. *Jihad in the West: Muslim Conquests from the 7th to the 21st Centuries.* Amherst, NY: Prometheus Books, 1998.

Gibbon, Edward. *The History of the Decline and Fall of the Roman Empire,* Vol. 6. Edited by J. B. Bury. London: Metthuen, 1912.

Glubb, John Bagot. *The Empire of the Arabs.* Englewood Cliffs, NJ: Prentice Hall, 1963.

Glubb, John Bagot. *The Great Arab Conquests.* London: Hodder and Stoughton, 1963.

Graham, Mark, and Akbar Ahmed. *How Islam Created the Modern World.* Beltsville, MD: Amana Pulications, 2006.

Haldon, J. J. *Byzantium in the Seventh Century.* Cambridge: Cambridge University Press, 1990.

Hodgson, Marshall G. S. *The Venture of Islam,* Vol. 1, *The Classical Age of Islam.* Chicago: University of Chicago Press, 1977.

Hourani, Albert. *A History of the Arab Peoples.* New York: Warner Books, 1991.

Jandora, John. *The March from Medina*. Clifton, NJ: Kingston, 1990.

Kaegi, Walter. *Byzantium and the Early Islamic Conquests*. Cambridge: Cambridge University Press, 1992.

Karsh, Efraim. *Islamic Imperialism: A History*. New Haven, CT: Yale University Press, 2007.

Kennedy, Hugh. *The Armies of the Caliphs: Military and Society in the Byzantine World*. London: Routledge, 2001.

Kennedy, Hugh. *The Great Arab Conquests: How the Spread of Islam Changed the World We Live In*. Cambridge, MA: Da Capo, 2007.

Lewis, Bernard. *The Arabs in History*. Oxford: Oxford University Press, 2002.

Lewis, Bernard. *Islam from the Prophet Mohammed to the Capture of Constantinople: Politics and War*. New York: Oxford University Press, 1987.

McGraw, Donner F. *The Early Islamic Conquests*. Princeton, NJ: Princeton University Press, 1981.

Nicole, David, and Angus McBride. *The Armies of Islam*. London: Osprey, 1982.

Nicolle, David. *Armies of the Muslim Conquest*. London: Osprey, 1993.

Pirenne, Henri. *Mohammed and Charlemagne*. Mineola, NY: Courier Dover Publications, 2001.

Runciman, Steven. *Byzantine Civilization*. New York: Barnes and Noble, 1994.

Shoufani, E. *Al-Riaddah and the Muslim Conquest of Arabia*. Toronto: University of Toronto Press, 1973.

Vasiliev, Alexander Alexandrovich. *History of the Byzantine Empire, 324–1453*. Madison: University of Wisconsin Press, 1990.

Ye'or, Bat. *The Decline of Eastern Christianity: From Jihad to Dhimmitude*. Madison, NJ: Fairleigh Dickinson University Press, 1996.

7. DID CHARLES MARTEL'S VICTORY IN THE BATTLE OF TOURS PREVENT THE ISLAMIC CONQUEST OF CHRISTIAN EUROPE?

The Battle of Tours (also known as the Battle of Poitiers) took place in October 732 near the border between Aquitaine and the Frankish kingdom in modern-day north-central France. The engagement pitted Frankish forces led by Charles Martel against

Abu-ar-Rahman's Muslim troops fighting for the Umayyad Caliphate. The size of Charles's force is thought to have been anywhere from 20,000 to 60,000 or more men. Muslim forces probably numbered close to 50,000 men. Although the Franks were victorious and succeeded in pushing back the Islamic force, historians continue to debate the broader significance of the battle. After the epic clash, the Umayyad army withdrew south and across the Pyrenees Mountains into Spain. There seems to be general consensus that the Battle of Tours helped establish the foundation of the Carolingian Empire and helped ensure Frankish domination of Western Europe for nearly a century. However, whether or not the confrontation at Tours was integral to halting the Islamic conquest of Christian Europe (as contemporaries claimed it to have been) remains a question not easily answered.

In the essays that follow, two historians present their views on this complex subject. Dr. Alexander Mikaberidze asserts that the Battle of Tours was important in the context of a much larger historical process. Most contemporary observers hailed it as a major turning point in Christian Europe's conflict with Islam and viewed Charles as the "savior" of the continent. Mikaberidze argues, however, that Tours did not definitively end the conflict between the Franks and Muslims, pointing out that fighting between the two groups endured for decades after the battle. He concludes that in the long term, the battle changed both the dynamic of the struggle between Christians and Muslims in the West and political conditions within the Frankish state. In his essay, Dr. Spencer C. Tucker points out that the Battle of Tours did not in itself prevent the Muslim conquest of Western Europe. Instead, that engagement was more the product of a Muslim raiding expedition than an actual attempt at conquest. Tucker suggests that the biggest threat to Christian Europe came from the East, where the Ottomans made several attempts to capture the Byzantine capital of Constantinople. He also concludes that Tours made Charles the unparalleled leader of Gaul and helped him establish the Carolingian dynasty, which would reach its pinnacle under his grandson, Charlemagne.

Background Essay

Around the year 710 CE the tide of Arab conquest reached Morocco and the Atlantic Ocean. Utilizing the Berbers (Moors), Muslim governor of Northern Africa Musa ibn Nusair sent them across the straits to Spain. Musa's goal was apparently plunder rather than conquest. The caliph approved a raid only, cautioning Musa not to risk his men in an overseas expedition. Thus in 710, 400 men crossed the Strait of Gibraltar to Spain, pillaged around Algeciras, and then returned to Morocco.

Encouraged by this success and having learned that the Visigothic king of Spain was in the north fighting the Franks, Musa approved an extensive expedition, committing some 7,000 men. This force took the Visigoth capital of Toledo and by the end of 712 conquered all of Spain. Musa then commenced an invasion of Aquitaine across the Pyrenees Mountains, probably still in 712, to eliminate the remnants of the Visigoths. In 717–718, Musa's successor ordered a full-scale raid; this failed, apparently because it became an operation of conquest. In 719 the Muslims took Narbonne, but two years later they met defeat at Toulouse. In 725 the Muslims occupied Carcassonne and Nîmes, and the next year they advanced up the Rhône River Valley and ravaged Burgundy.

The Franks were hardly in a position to oppose the Muslim advance. The ruling Merovingian dynasty was then in decline, and power had effectively passed into the hands of the mayor of the palace. In 714 Charles had assumed this title and was then king in all but name.

In 732 Muslim governor of Spain Abd-ar-Rahman launched a full-scale invasion of Aquitaine, then ruled by Duke Eudo. The Muslim invaders defeated Eudo at Bordeaux and sacked and burned that city. From Bordeaux Abd-ar-Rahman moved north, pillaging and destroying as he advanced. He took Poitiers and moved toward Tours because of reports of that city's wealth. Eudo meanwhile appealed for assistance to Charles, who had been fighting the Germanic tribes along the Danube. Charles agreed to assist in return for Eudo submitting Aquitaine to Frankish control.

An illuminated manuscript depicting Charles Martel, commander of the Franks, in the Battle of Tours in 732. The battle, which was won by the Franks, ended Muslim expansion into Gaul. (The British Library)

Putting together an army, Charles crossed the Loire, probably at Orléans. Abd-ar-Rahman's army, now burdened down by plunder, fell back on Poitiers. The sudden appearance of Charles's force caused consternation among the Muslims, so heavily weighed down with loot that they were no longer mobile. The two armies faced one another for seven days, with Charles waiting for the arrival of reinforcements.

Few details exist concerning the actual battle. It most likely occurred at a site later called Moussais-la-Bataille on October 25, 732. Probably the armies first came into contact near Tours, and Abd-ar-Rahman then withdrew toward Poitiers; when he found that the army's booty had not gotten farther south, he decided to accept battle. As the Muslims were solely an offensive force, this meant an attack. Realizing this, Charles drew up his own forces in a solid phalanx formation, centered on his veterans.

The battle opened with a furious Muslim cavalry charge. Repeated Muslim efforts failed to break the Frankish phalanx, however. Toward dusk, Eudo and a force of Aquitanians turned one of the Muslim flanks and attacked Abd-ar-Rahman's camp, where the bulk of the loot was located. Abd-ar-Rahman died in the battle, which was over by nightfall. The next morning Charles learned that the Muslims had fled south, abandoning the bulk of their plunder. Frankish chroniclers claimed 360,000 Muslims killed against only 1,500 for Charles, but these were probably closer to 2,000 for the Muslims and 500 for the Franks.

There was no pursuit, for Charles's men on foot could not chase down a retiring mounted force, and the capture of the loot prohibited such an operation. Probably Charles also deemed it wise not to remove all Muslim pressure from Eudo in order to ensure his loyalty. Therefore, Charles collected the loot and recrossed the Loire. For his role in the victory, he became known to posterity as Charles Martel (the Hammer).

The Battle of Tours saw the deepest Muslim penetration into Europe, east and west. It might not have saved Western Europe from Arab rule but it did make Charles supreme in Gaul and enabled him to establish the Carolinigian dynasty, which reached its zenith under his grandson, Charlemagne. In 735 Eudo died; Charles overran Aquitaine and compelled Eudo's two sons to pay homage to him. After this Charles undertook several campaigns against the Muslims in the Rhône Valley of such sufficiency that a few years later they withdrew south of the Pyrenees for good.

Spencer C. Tucker

Perspective Essay 1. Part of a Larger Historical Process

Rising amid the deserts of Arabia in the early decades of the seventh century, Islam quickly established itself as a powerful force in the Middle East and beyond.

Following Prophet Muhammad's death in 632, the Muslim Arabs expanded into Syria-Palestine, Iraq, and North Africa, scoring a quick succession of victories. Within 70 years of the prophet's death, Muslim armies had completely destroyed and absorbed the Sassanian Empire; deprived the Byzantine Empire of key provinces in Anatolia, Syria, Palestine, and Egypt; and extended their reach to much of North Africa.

In 711, Muslims crossed the Strait of Gibraltar. The conquest of the Iberian Peninsula proved to be rapid but haphazard. Although the Muslims scored early victories over the Visigoth king Roderic, their advance was complicated by the victory achieved by an Asturian, Pelayo, at Cavadonga (ca. 718) and subsequent revolts throughout Spain. Furthermore, the Muslims themselves were divided by deep-seated internal rivalries.

Nevertheless, the Muslims were eager to push the boundaries of their growing state. In 717, a Muslim expedition under Emir al-Hurr al-Thaqafi crossed the Pyrenees into the Merovingian kingdom of Franks (France), mainly driven by the desire for quick pillaging. Yet, initial successes also enticed the Muslims to move deeper into the Frankish lands, and during 719–720 Muslim forces under Emir al-Samh captured Narbonne, which they turned into a base for future operations.

In June 721 Duke Eudo (Odo) of Aquitaine defeated Muslim forces led by Anbasa ibn Suhaym al-Kalbi in the Battle of Toulouse, the first major Muslim defeat in Western Europe. This defeat delayed but did not stop further Muslim advances into the Frankish land. Muslims continued to conduct a number of raids into the Rhône Valley. Eudo meanwhile sought to exploit his military success to secure his duchy. Threatened by the Umayyad Caliphate in the south and the Merovingian Franks in the north, Eudo chose to negotiate an alliance with the Muslim Berber emir Uthman ibn Naissa (also called Munuza by the Franks), who had rebelled against the Umayyad authority and carved out his own splinter realm in the strategic eastern Spanish highland bordering France. The Umayyad governor of Andalusia (Spain), Emir Abd-ar-Rahman, responded forcefully to this threat: his Umayyad army crushed the revolt and turned its attention against Eudo. In 731 Abd-ar-Rahman led a large Muslim army across the Pyrenees, effectively making the first major effort to expand the Muslim presence north of the mountains. After suffering defeat near Bordeaux, Eudo chose to reconcile with his Frankish foes in order to constrain the Muslim expansion. Pursued by the Muslims as far as Tours, one of the chief religious centers in France, Eudo summoned to his aid Charles Martel, the mayor of the palace of the Merovingian king, who marched against the Muslims in time to save Tours and the treasures of its famous St. Martin Abbey from pillage.

The decisive battle between the armies of Abd-ar-Rahman and Charles took place between the towns of Tours and Poitiers. While the Muslims were largely unacquainted with their Frankish foes, Charles had been preparing for this clash with Muslims for almost a decade, ever since the first Muslim invasion suffered a setback at Toulouse. He seems to have been well aware of the importance of this battle and probably understood that a Christian defeat here would expose all of the Frankish lands—and potentially the rest of Western Europe—to Muslim attacks. Therefore, Charles acted cautiously. He secured high ground where his veteran and heavily armed infantry could resist the renowned Muslim cavalry. The emir took the offensive, sending his cavalry against the Franks. The Muslim cavalry could do nothing against the heavily armed Franks, who, shoulder to shoulder, formed a square at the crucial moment of the battle. In the thick of action Muslim commander Abd-ar-Rahman was killed, further disheartening his warriors. When darkness fell the two armies disengaged, and great was the surprise of the Franks when they discovered at dawn on the following day that the Muslims had abandoned their camp.

The Christian victory at Tours-Poitiers made a great impact on contemporaries. The news of the triumph spread far and wide, reaching as far as northern England, where the Venerable Bede recorded it in his famed *Ecclesiastical History of the English People* (731). Subsequent medieval Christian chronicles described it as the turning point in Christianity's struggle against Islam and praised Charles as the savior of Christian Europe. Similarly, later generations of European writers and historians believed that this battle was a landmark event that marked the high tide of the Muslim advance into Europe. In his famous work *The History of the Decline and Fall of the Roman Empire* (1776–1789), English historian Edward Gibbon argued that the Christian victory at Tours-Poitiers effectively prevented the Muslims from conquering a divided Europe.

The battle did not definitely decide the outcome of the struggle—fighting between Muslims and Franks continued for decades before the Muslims finally ceased raiding north of the Pyrenees. Therefore, it must be looked upon not in isolation, as many Christian apologists have done over the past 1,300 years, but instead as part of a larger historical process. At the same time, despite claims of some modern European and Arab historians, it is difficult to discount this battle as just a minor skirmish where nothing was decided. While it is true that Abd-ar-Rahman's army was a raiding force, not an occupying army, and while the Muslim failure to capture Constantinople in 718 was of greater strategic consequences, Tours-Poitiers still marked an important point in the Christian-Muslim struggles in Western Europe.

In its immediate effect, Charles's victory stopped Abd-ar-Rahman's advance and thereby protected central Frankish lands and their bountiful monasteries. While it was not a crushing defeat of a major Muslim army, the Christian victory at Tours-Poitiers was sufficiently strong to deter Muslims for the next few years. Had the Muslims won the battle, it is difficult to imagine them simply returning home without ever coming back. A similar raiding party across Gibraltar in 711 had whetted Muslim appetite for further conquests in the Iberian Peninsula.

A Muslim victory at Tours-Poitiers would have meant an immense plunder seized on the battlefield and in local monasteries, especially in St. Martin's Abbey.

This would have only excited Abd-ar-Rahman's men to reconnoiter roads farther to the north, hoping to find new targets for future expeditions. And with the Frankish army defeated and the Merovingian court in disarray, the Muslims would have had excellent opportunities to continue expanding into Frankish lands.

The battle at Tours-Poitiers, together with victories over Abd-ar-Rahman's son in 736–737, allowed Charles and his successor, Pippin, to clear southern France from Muslim attackers. This was an important accomplishment. With the start of the Great Berber Revolt in 740 and the Abbasid Revolution in 750, which effectively destroyed the Umayyad Caliphate, the Muslims in Andalusia were no longer in position to seriously threaten Frankish power. Had the Muslims prevailed in 732, their continued presence in southern France would have caused considerable volatility in the Frankish state and prevented Charlemagne from expanding his authority into the Rhineland and Italy and proclaiming empire. Instead, Charles's victory allowed the Franks to increase pressure on their southern foes, recapturing Avignon in 737 and Narbonne in 759 and effectively driving the Muslims across the Pyrenees.

In the long term, the battle changed both the dynamic of the struggle between Christians and Muslims in the West and political conditions within the Frankish state. It was certainly significant in the eventual establishment of the Carolingian dynasty, which by the early ninth century had turned the Frankish kingdom into the most powerful Christian state. During 731–732 the Muslim threat compelled Eudo of Aquitaine to recognize the authority of the Merovingian state, and Charles's victory at Tours-Poitiers only further strengthened the Merovingian control over southwestern France. Continued fighting against the Muslims allowed Charles to consolidate his authority in the state and, most important, pass it on to his descendants. Thus, his son Pippin the Short succeeded him as the powerful mayor of the palace and eventually overthrew the Merovingian dynasty, while Charles's grandson, Charlemagne, established the famed Carolingian Empire that dominated contemporary Western Europe.

Some studies suggest that the consequences of the Battle of Tours were even greater than that. Charles's success against Muslims was crucial in preserving Western Christendom. His victories, starting at Tours-Poitiers, safeguarded Western monasteries and preserved religious and cultural legacies that had shaped Western Europe. Furthermore, there is ample evidence that after 732 Charles sought to strengthen his armed forces. Despite his victory at Tours-Poitiers, he realized the need for an adequate force to deal with the Muslim cavalry. His solution was to form his own heavily armed cavalry. But such a force needed elaborate coats of armor and specially bred horses, while its maintenance costs were prohibitively expensive. Therefore, Charles had to find additional sources of revenue. He soon turned his attention to numerous bishoprics and monasteries that held vast tracts of lands. Charles began the process of seizing church property and distributing it to followers on condition that they would provide military service on horseback. This marked a gradual shift in the Frankish Army. This change from infantry-based army toward cavalry-dominant military was of profound consequence for Europe. The military grants of lands (benefices) created new warriors—knights—and contributed to the development of feudalism that shaped the course of European history over the next several hundred years.

Alexander Mikaberidze

Perspective Essay 2. A Raid Rather Than a Conquest

Charles Martel's victory in the Battle of Tours in October 732 did not in itself prevent the Muslims from conquering Christian Europe. Despite Sir Edward S. Creasy's inclusion of the Battle of Tours in his book as being among the 15 decisive battles in world history and echoes of this sentiment by others, including historians Edward Gibbon and John B. Bury, the Muslim invasion of Gaul from Spain in 732 was more a raid than an attempt to secure and hold territory. The major threat to Christian Europe came in the east, against Constantinople.

For some time Muslim corsairs based in North Africa had raided the coasts of Southern Europe across the Mediterranean, securing both booty and slaves. While extensive and costly to Europe, these were not efforts at conquest. Indeed, North Africa was far removed from the center of Muslim power.

Around the year 710, the tide of Arab conquest had reached Morocco and the Atlantic Ocean. The Berbers, or Moors, supplied the necessary manpower. These peoples were essentially nomadic raiders. To keep them occupied, Musa ibn Nusair, then the Muslim governor of North Africa, turned them against Spain.

Musa apparently sought to plunder rather than conquer Spain. The caliph gave his permission for a raid only, cautioning Musa not to expose his army in an overseas expedition. Thus, in 710 a Muslim force of 400 men crossed the Strait of Gibraltar to Spain, then pillaged around Algeciras before returning to Morocco.

Encouraged by this success and having learned that the Visigothic king of Spain was fighting in the north against the Franks, Musa decided on a larger expedition. He sent to Spain groups of 400 men totaling some 7,000. This force took the Visigoth capital of Toledo, and by the end of 712 the Moors had conquered all of Spain.

No sooner had Spain been overrun than Musa initiated an invasion of Aquitaine across the Pyrenees to eliminate the remnants of the Visigoths. During 717–718, Musa's successor ordered a full-scale raid; this failed, apparently because it became an operation of conquest. In 719 the Muslims took Narbonne in Gaul, then a Mediterranean port, but two years later they were defeated to the north at Toulouse. In

725 the Muslims occupied Carcassonne and Nîmes in southern Gaul, and the next year they advanced up the Rhône River Valley and ravaged Burgundy.

The Franks were hardly in a position to oppose the Muslim advance. The ruling Merovingian dynasty was in decline and effective power had passed to the mayor of the palace. In 714, Charles had assumed this title and was king in all but name.

In 732, Muslim governor of Spain Abd-ar-Rahman launched an invasion of Aquitaine, then ruled by Duke Eudo. The Muslims defeated Eudo at Bordeaux and sacked and burned that city. From Bordeaux, Abd-ar-Rahman moved north, pillaging and destroying as he advanced. After taking Poitiers he moved toward Tours, prompted by reports of that city's wealth.

Eudo meanwhile fled north and appealed for assistance to Charles, who had been fighting the Germanic tribes along the Danube. Charles agreed to assist Eudo on the condition that Aquitaine submit to Frankish control. Eudo agreed, and Charles assembled an army and crossed the Loire, probably at Orléans.

Little is known about the composition of Abd-ar-Rahman's army or its size, which has been variously estimated at 20,000 to 80,000 men, the bulk of whom were probably mounted Moors. They were armed principally with the lance and sword, and most of the men were without body armor. A mule train followed the troops, probably carrying plunder rather than supplies, for the army lived off the land. Its tactics centered on wild, headlong charges.

The Frankish army was basically an infantry force and smaller than that of the invaders. Only the nobles had horses, and these were used only during the march. The Frankish soldiers were armed with swords, daggers, javelins, and two kinds of axes—one for wielding and one for throwing. The men carried shields for protection. The infantry consisted of the general's private army, which had to be constantly employed because it was paid by plunder alone, and a conscript force of poorly armed militia. There was little discipline on either side.

Charles understood the vulnerability of his foe. According to the historian Edward Gibbon, Charles had written to Eudo stating that

> If you follow my advice, you will not interrupt their march, nor precipitate your attack. They are like a torrent, which it is dangerous to stem in its career. The thirst of riches and the consciousness of success, redouble their valour, and valour is of more avail than arms or numbers. Be patient till they have loaded themselves with the encumbrance of wealth. The possession of wealth will divide their counsels and assure your victory.

Such an approach had the advantage for Charles, of course, of wasting large tracts of land belonging to the rebel Duke of Aquitaine.

The sudden appearance of Charles and his men caused consternation among the Muslims, who were so heavily weighed down with loot that they were no longer mobile. Abd-ar-Rahman considered abandoning the plunder but did not, possibly because his men would have refused to obey such an order. The two armies faced one another for seven days, with Charles waiting for the arrival of reinforcements.

Few details exist concerning the actual battle. It most likely occurred at a site later called Moussais-la-Bataille on October 25, 732. Probably the armies first came into contact near Tours, and Abd-ar-Rahman withdrew toward Poitiers; when he found that the army's booty had not gotten farther south, he decided to accept battle. As the Muslims were solely an offensive force, this meant an attack. Realizing this, Charles drew up his own forces in a solid phalanx formation, centered on his veterans.

The battle opened with a furious Muslim cavalry charge. Although they repeated this again and again, the Muslims were unable to break the Frankish phalanx. Toward dusk, Eudo and a force of Aquitanians turned one of the Muslim flanks and launched an attack on Abd-ar-Rahman's camp, where the bulk of the loot was located. Abd-ar-Rahman died in the battle, which was over by nightfall. The next morning, scouts reported to Charles that the foe had fled south, abandoning the bulk of their plunder. Losses were probably some 2,000 for the Muslims and 500 for the Franks.

There was no pursuit, for Charles on foot could not pursue a retiring mounted force, and the capture of the loot prohibited such an operation. Probably Charles also deemed it wise not to remove all Muslim pressure from Eudo in order to ensure his loyalty. So, he collected the loot and recrossed the Loire. For his role in the victory, Charles became known to posterity as Charles Martel (the Hammer).

Historians are sharply divided on the importance of the battle. As recently as 2003 in *Islam at War: A History*, historians George F. Nafziger and Mark W. Walton called it "one of the most significant battles in history." This characterization notwithstanding, modern scholarship tends to view the Muslim invasion as more a foray than an attempt to conquer and hold territory. This can be seen in the size of the Muslim force, the distance from their base, and the plundering and destruction of property. Tours should thus be viewed in context as one of a series of battles that defended Christian Europe from Muslim inroads. Nonetheless, Tours saw the deepest Muslim penetration into Europe, east and west.

While it might not have saved Western Europe from Arab rule, the Battle of Tours did make Charles supreme in Gaul and enabled him to establish the Carolingian dynasty, which reached its zenith under his grandson Charlemagne. In 735 Eudo died, and Charles overran Aquitaine and compelled Eudo's two sons to pay homage to him. After this, Charles undertook several campaigns against the Muslims in the Rhône Valley, who within a few years had withdrawn south of the Pyrenees for good.

The far more serious threat to Christian Europe came in the east against the great Christian outpost of Constantinople, the capital of the crumbling Byzantium Empire. Constantinople, in close proximity to the center of Arab power in the

Middle East, controlled the Bosporus and thus access between the Mediterranean and Black Seas and also guarded the entrance to South-Central Europe. The Muslims first attempted to take the city in 655. They tried again in 669, and thereafter Constantinople came under intermittent Muslim attack. Several attempts to take it in the 670s were turned back when the Byzantines defeated the attackers at sea.

The greatest test for Constantinople to that point came under Caliph Suleiman during August 717–August 718. The Muslim force involved in the Battle of Tours paled next to the 160,000 men and 2,600 ships sent by Suleiman in 717 against Constantinople. After a yearlong siege, the vastly outnumbered Byzantines, led by Emperor Leo III, forced a Muslim withdrawal. Not until 1453 did the Muslims capture Constantinople. Europe was then in a better position to resist, and although the Muslims did overrun the Balkans and for a time threatened Central Europe, they were turned back at Vienna first in 1529 and definitively in 1683. From that point on, the Muslim tide in Europe receded.

Spencer C. Tucker

Further Reading

Bachrach, Bernard. *Early Carolingian Warfare.* Philadelphia: University of Pennsylvania Press, 2001.

Bury, J. B. *The Cambridge Medieval History.* 8 vols. Edited by Henry M. Gwatkin and James P. Whitney. Cambridge: Cambridge University Press, 1957–1967.

Collins, Roger. *The Arab Conquest of Spain.* London: Wiley-Blackwell, 1989.

Copée, Henry. *History of the Conquest of Spain by the Arab-Moors.* 2 vols. Boston: Georgias, 1881.

Creasy, Sir Edward. *The Fifteen Decisive Battles of the World.* New York: Heritage, 1969.

Donner, Fred M. *The Early Islamic Conquests.* Princeton, NJ: Princeton University Press, 1981.

Fouracre, Paul. *The Age of Charles Martel.* London: Longman, 2000.

Gibbon, Edward. *The History of the Decline and Fall of the Roman Empire.* Abridged version. New York: Harper and Brothers, 1857.

Hanson, Victor Davis. *Carnage and Culture: Landmark Battles in the Rise of Western Power.* New York: Doubleday, 2001.

Hitti, Philip K. *History of Syria, Including Lebanon and Palestine.* New York: Macmillan 1951.

Hodgson, Marshall G. S. *The Venture of Islam: Conscience and History in a World Civilization.* Chicago: University of Chicago Press, 1974.

Hourani, Albert. *A History of the Arab Peoples.* New York: Warner, 1992.

Kennedy, Hugh. *Muslim Spain and Portugal: A Political History of al-Andalus.* New York: Longman, 1997.

Lewis, Bernard. *The Arabs in History.* Oxford: Oxford University Press, 1993.

Lowney, Chris. *A Vanished World: Muslims, Christians, and Jews in Medieval Spain.* New York: Oxford University Press, 2006.

Mercier, Maurice, and André Seguin. *Charles Martel et la Bataille de Poitiers.* Paris: P. Guethner, 1944.

Nafziger, George F., and Mark W. Walton. *Islam at War: A History.* Westport, CT: Praeger, 2003.

Santusuosso, Antonio. *Barbarians, Marauders, and Infidels. The Ways of Medieval Warfare.* Boulder, CO: Westview, 2004.

Wallace-Hadrill, J. M. *The Fourth Book of the Chronicle of Fredegar with Its Continuations.* London: Nelson, 1960.

Watson, William E. "The Battle of Tours-Poitiers Revisited." *Providence: Studies in Western Civilization* 2(2) (Fall 1993): 51–68.

White, Lynn, Jr. *Medieval Technology and Social Change.* Oxford: Oxford University Press, 1962.

Wolf, Kenneth Baxter. *Conquerors and Chroniclers of Early Medieval Spain.* Liverpool: Liverpool University Press, 2000.

8. Why Did the Crusades Ultimately Fail to Retain Christian Control of the Holy Land?

The Crusades involved a sequence of religious wars sanctioned by the Roman Catholic Church beginning in 1096 CE. They were waged in an attempt to wrest control of the Holy Land from Muslim control. The Holy Land is defined here as an area generally between the Jordan River and the Mediterranean Sea. At its heart is Palestine, an area that is considered sacred by the world's three largest Abrahamic religions: Judaism, Christianity, and Islam. Individuals involved in fighting Muslim forces were no doubt motivated to do so by strong religious and ideological convictions. But European settlers in the Holy Land also sought to establish control over the region and develop functioning states there. However, these relatively minor states, many of them little more than heavily fortified strips of land along the eastern Mediterranean, did not remain under Christian control for a long period of time. Crusader states were essentially war-ravaged kingdoms characterized by constant conflict with their Muslim neighbors. Despite their ability to control their respective territories, these small states were subjected to repeated attacks and invasions, making them mere garrisons that had to be provisioned from afar. Muslim military power eventually swept away the last of the remaining crusader states in 1291, at which time the whole enterprise of the Crusades was essentially over.

In the first perspective essay, Dr. John France argues that the fragmentation of the Muslim world in the Middle East accounted for the early success of the Crusades. However, when Muslim power was finally consolidated within larger states, their military power was able to overwhelm the Christian forces that remained and drive them from the region. In essence, Muslim unity was key to the end of European control of the Holy Land. In the second perspective essay, Dr. Alan V. Murray points out that the Frankish states, which made up the crusader nations in the Holy Land, were never able to capture the region's major Muslim cities. This ultimately doomed the Crusades to failure. Furthermore, because the crusader states were inherently unstable and had to be constantly reinforced with troops and monetary aid from Europe, they had little chance at long-term success. In the third essay, Dr. Conor Kostick asserts that the inability of the crusaders to take Egypt and the overwhelming amount of regional hostility doomed the crusader states. Their lack of coordination in contrast to growing Muslim military power and unity also played a role in their undoing. Finally, Dr. Nicholas Morton discusses how the rise of the Mongols played a bigger role than that of Islam in destroying the crusader states. Mongol attacks weakened both Christian and Muslim states. However, Mamluk-controlled Egypt, a principal enemy of the Mongols, was able to counter Mongol military power and was also able to easily conquer territories in the Levant.

Background Essay

In the Age of Faith there were many military efforts said to be primarily motivated by Christian fervor and dubbed "crusades." These included the Reconquista in Spain (722–1492), the Albegensian Crusade in France (1209–1229), the Aragonese Crusade (1284–1285), and the Northern Crusade by the Teutonic Knights in the Baltic region during the 12th and 13th centuries. But certainly the best known, most ambitious, least successful, and yet most lastingly influential of the military efforts cloaked in religion were those advanced by the Latin Roman Catholic Church and supported by the Latin West to wrest control from the Muslims of Jerusalem and the Holy Land of Palestine. The term "crusade" comes from the Spanish term *cruzada*, meaning "marked by the cross."

Apart from the stated religious goals of spreading the faith and reclaiming the Holy Land from the "infidels," there were many secular motivations. One was the advance of the Seljuk Turks. In 1070 they had captured Jerusalem, and Christian pilgrims began to tell of repression there. Reportedly one Peter the Hermit brought a letter from Simeon, the patriarch of Jerusalem, to Pope Urban II bearing witness to this.

The Byzantine Empire was weak. This important Christian state guarded access to South-Central Europe and for seven centuries had held back would-be invaders from crossing the narrow straits that separated Asia from Europe. If Constantinople (Istanbul) fell, this would open the floodgates to Muslim expansion into Europe. The threat was such that Byzantine emperor Alexius I Comnenus sent emissaries to Pope Urban II urging that theological and political differences be set aside and that Latin Europe join him in driving back the Turks. Alexius pointed out that it would be better to fight the Turks in Asia than in Europe.

There was also the ambition of the Italian city-states of Venice, Genoa, and Pisa. They sought to extend their commercial reach into the eastern Mediterranean, expanding trade and opening new markets. Finally, there was also the quest for military glory and political advantage by kings and nobles.

The decision rested with Urban II. During March–October 1095 he toured northern Italy and southern France enlisting support. He then called a church council at Clermont in France and there proclaimed a crusade to reclaim the Holy Land. Urban hoped thereby to unite the Christian West under his leadership.

Extraordinary inducements were offered to participants. These included a plenary indulgence remitting all punishment for sin to those who might fall in the war, remission of criminal punishments, and exemption from feudal dues and taxes. Religious frenzy now swept Christian Europe.

There were nine major identified crusades. The First Crusade occurred during 1096–1099. In what became known as the People's Crusade (considered part of the First Crusade), some 40,000 people, mostly unarmed peasants and including women and children, assembled. Alexius urged them to wait for the arrival of the knights, but they crossed the straits into Asia Minor. Their numbers soon dwindled to perhaps 20,000, and almost all of these were either killed or taken prisoner by the Seljuk Turks in battle near Nicaea. Perhaps only 3,000 returned to Constantinople.

Meanwhile, the various state military contingents, ultimately numbering some 50,000 men, arrived at Constantinople during late 1096 and early 1097. Setting out, they besieged and captured Nicaea (1097), Antioch (1098), and the prize of Jerusalem (1098), where they slaughtered perhaps 70,000 Muslims, including women and children as well as Jews.

Following the capture of Jerusalem, most of the crusaders still alive returned home. Those who remained set up small states in the Holy Land. A protracted multifaceted struggle then ensued for control of Mesopotamia from among the crusaders, various Seljuk Turk sultanates, and other Muslim principalities.

The centerpiece of the Second Crusade (1147–1149) was against Damascus, which the Christians invested but failed to capture. In 1153 Baldwin III, the king of

Jerusalem, captured Ascalon, bringing the entire coast of Palestine under his control. In 1169 King Amalric of Jerusalem led a joint crusader-Byzantine expedition against Egypt, which was repulsed.

The Muslims had long fought among themselves, but in 1171 Seljurk Turk general Salah al-din Yusuf ibn Ayyūb, better known as Saladin, established the Ayyubid dynasty in Egypt. Thanks in large part to dissension among the crusaders, Saladin was able to expand his influence from Egypt into Syria and northern Mesopotamia.

In 1187 following Christian attacks on Muslim caravans and towns along the Red Sea, Saladin proclaimed jihad (holy war). Mounting an invasion of Palestine, he laid siege to the crusader stronghold of Tiberius, then destroyed a Christian relief column in the Battle of Hattin (July 3–4). This battle led directly to the Muslim conquest of most of Palestine, the Christian garrisons of which had been badly depleted in putting together the relief force. Saladin took Jerusalem in October.

The Muslim capture of Jerusalem shocked all of Europe and led to the Third Crusade (1189–1192), which involved three of Europe's most powerful rulers: Emperor Frederick I Barbarossa of Germany, King Philippe II Augustus of France, and King Richard I the Lionheart of England. Frederick, however, drowned en route, and his army soon largely disintegrated. The central event of this crusade was the great siege of Acre (August 28, 1189–July 12, 1191). Christian success here helped ensure the survival of a truncated crusader kingdom in the Holy Land for another century.

Philip returned to France, although most of his forces remained behind. Richard thus had sole command of the crusader army. Although he took back much of the coastal area of Palestine and defeated Saladin in pitched battle, Richard failed to recover Jerusalem. In 1192, the two leaders concluded a treaty that granted special rights and privileges to Christian pilgrims to Jerusalem. Saladin died the next year, ensuring the crusader states a short period of relief.

In 1197 Holy Roman emperor Henry VI sent a preliminary German force to the Holy Land that captured Beirut and other coastal cities in 1198. Henry died in 1197, however, temporarily shelving plans for a larger effort.

In 1199 Pope Innocent III appealed for a new crusade to regain Jerusalem. This Fourth Crusade (1202–1204) ended up not in the Holy Land but instead with the sacking by the crusaders of Christian Constantinople. Although it would continue in existence for another two centuries, the Byzantine Empire never really recovered from this blow inflicted by fellow Christians. The empire's territory was now divided between Venice and the Crusader leaders, with the establishment of the Latin empire of Constantinople.

The Fifth Crusade of 1218–1221 resulted in the capture of Acre in November 1219 after a siege that lasted a year and a half, but an effort to conquer Egypt ended in disaster. Holy Roman emperor Frederick II led the Sixth Crusade (1228–1229). Through skillful diplomacy, he opened talks with Sultan al-Kamil and secured the cession of Jerusalem, Nazareth, and Bethlehem and a corridor connecting Jerusalem to the coast.

The Seventh Crusade (1248–1254) was sparked by the destruction of Jerusalem by the Khwarizmians in 1244. Endeavoring to escape the Mongols, who had taken their territory, the Khwarizmians took Jerusalem from the crusaders, sacked the city, and left it in ruins. The Khwarizmians then allied with Egypt against the crusaders, who themselves allied with the emir of Damascus. The two sides met in battle at Gaza later that same year, with the Khwarizmians and Egyptians victorious.

King Louis IX of France (later canonized as Saint Louis) led the Seventh Crusade (1248–1254). His effort to conquer Egypt ended in defeat, with Louis captured. He was forced to pay a considerable ransom and abandon Damietta.

The success of Mamluk leader Baybars in recovering most of the crusader territory in Palestine and Syria prompted Louis IX to again take up the cross in 1270 in the Eighth Crusade. During a siege of Tunis, Louis and much of his force succumbed to the plague. Prince Edward of England (later king as Edward I) then arrived and, in the Ninth Crusade (1271–1272), mounted raids in Palestine, but they had little impact.

In 1289 Mamluk sultan Kala'un captured Tripoli from the crusaders, and two years later the final disaster occurred. After some Christian adventurers attacked a Muslim caravan in Syria, Mamluk sultan Khalil demanded satisfaction. Receiving

Scenes from an illuminated manuscript of the Eighth Crusade showing French king Louis IX of France and his men arriving in Tunis in 1270 and then being attacked by Muslim forces. (The British Library)

none, he marched against the Christian stronghold of Acre, laid siege to it, and took it after 43 days, then allowed his men to massacre or to enslave 60,000 prisoners. Tyre, Haifa, and Beirut soon fell, bringing finis to the crusader kingdoms of the Latin East.

Spencer C. Tucker

Perspective Essay 1. A Degree of Unity on the Muslim Side

The Crusades failed to retain Christian control of the Holy Land largely because the fragmentation of Islam, which made the success of the First Crusade possible, was replaced by a degree of unity. The failure was not inevitable, because random factors and misjudgments, especially military misjudgments, played a major role, while conditions in Europe changed fundamentally.

In 969 the dissident Shiites established a rival Fatimid caliphate challenging Sunni Baghdad, the power of which was disintegrating. Then in 1055 an alien people, the Seljuk Turks, established a sultanate nominally under the caliph of Baghdad but ruled by the Seljuk family. They created a great empire in Persia (present-day Iran) and Iraq that drove the Fatimids from Syria and Palestine and conquered Byzantine Anatolia. In 1092 a successionist struggle developed among the Seljuks, and Byzantine emperor Alexios Komnenos asked the Roman Catholic leader Pope Urban II for Western mercenaries to regain his lost provinces. This triggered the First Crusade (1096–1099). The key factor that brought this huge movement together was the offer of salvation through slaughter, the forgiveness of all sins in return for waging holy war.

The First Crusade was a huge and incoherent collection of armies. Its fighting style depended on a nucleus of heavily armed cavalry, the knights, backed up by a great mass of poorly trained and armed infantry. The Turks were steppe horse archers who surrounded and harassed their enemies, weakening their formations, before charging in to fight at close quarters. The leaders of the First Crusade adapted their fighting methods, using infantry to protect the cavalry from Turkish arrows: this would be the basic fighting formation of the Westerners in the East. Byzantines and Armenians were allies, and Western fleets gave support. Because the Turkish leaders were divided and because the Fatimids were willing to ally with them, the crusaders seized Edessa and Antioch before capturing Jerusalem from the Fatimids in 1099.

Feuding in the sultanate continued until about 1130, by which time the Seljuks had become preoccupied with Persia. This enabled the Western settlers to enlarge the small weak bridgeheads established by the First Crusade into four states:

Antioch, Edessa, Tripoli, and Jerusalem (the biggest). But they lacked manpower and were never able to seize Damascus or Aleppo, especially as they had quarreled with the Byzantines over the establishment of Western rule in Antioch. However, Turkish leaders in the Jazira (the link between Iraq and Syria), freed from Seljuk rule, increasingly sought dominion over the rich cities of Aleppo and Damascus. In 1128 Zangi, the *atabeg* of Mosul, seized Aleppo, legitimizing his rule by posing as the champion of Islam and calling for jihad against the Westerners, though Damascus remained aloof. Even so, he had a huge empire, drawing riches through a well-developed administration.

By comparison, the principalities of Outremer appeared puny. Jerusalem had only about 120,000 European settlers, with as many in the other states combined, but they enjoyed occasional reinforcements from the West. Their states were anchored by fortified cities, and any attempt by Muslims to besiege them would be frustrated by the disciplined field army of the settlers. The first of their states to collapse was Edessa in 1144, whose capital was seized by Zangi only because its army had been lured away. This set a general pattern: Europe was immersed in its own affairs and took Jerusalem for granted until some crisis occurred. In this case the Second Crusade (1145–1149) led by the kings of Germany and France occurred. But its leaders were poor soldiers with no conception of the new unity of Islam. Their armies were driven back from Damascus. This added impetus to the new mood in Islam. Zangi's son Nur al-Din posed as the champion of Islam, adopting an austere lifestyle and patronizing Sunni scholars who had great influence on the affluent urban Arab traders and administrators. The cry of holy war (jihad) thus dissolved many of the tensions in the Islamic world, at the same time embittering relations with the crusaders.

In the 1160s Fatimid Egypt fell into decay, so Jerusalem and Nur al-Din fought for control there. By the time of his death in 1174 the struggle was resolved in favor of the Muslims by their great leader Saladin, who became Nur al-Din's heir. Saladin's cultivation of jihad strengthened his position in a vast empire that stretched from the Nile to the Tigris. But the problem of attacking Jerusalem, with its cities and formidable field army, remained.

In 1187 Saladin gathered an army of 30,000–40,000 men and besieged Tiberias, aiming to lure the Jerusalemite army into trying to relieve the city by marching through a waterless area. He had tried this before, but events in the kingdom now favored him. Its nobility was few in number and divided by feuds. Many of the nobility hated their new king, Guy of Lusignan, who wanted the prestige of a victory over Saladin. As a result his army, desperately thirsty, was massively defeated in the Battle of Hattin on July 3–4. Jerusalem and all the other cities except Tyre, stripped of their garrisons, fell to Saladin. But Hattin was not decisive, because the fall of the kingdom triggered a wave of crusades. The Third Crusade (1189–1192), under Richard the Lionheart, established a new kingdom, a strip along the coast from Tyre to Jaffa, with its capital at Acre.

Richard advocated an attack on Egypt, which was attractive because Saladin's family, the Ayyubids, was divided, with Egypt and Syria at loggerheads. The Fourth Crusade (1204) intended to attack Egypt but diverted to Constantinople. The Fifth Crusade (1213–1221) seized Damietta in Egypt, but its leaders were divided, and the Egyptians used their knowledge of the Nile Delta to force its surrender. The crusade of Louis IX of France (1248–1254) captured Damietta and pushed into the Nile Delta, where it was cut off from its base, with even the king having to pay a ransom. This crusade was unusual in that it had a single commander, but Louis was not an effective military leader. However, behind his defeat lay a very significant development. The Mamluks, the slave-soldiers of the Ayyubids, were chiefly responsible for Louis's defeat. After their victory they deposed the Ayyubids and set up a military republic, choosing a sultan from their own ranks. They quickly developed a formidable standing professional army. In 1229 Emperor Frederick II went on crusade and exploited diplomatic tensions in the Ayyubid family to achieve the liberation of Jerusalem, and in 1241 this was repeated by Richard of Cornwall on his expedition. But factional struggles within the Latin kingdom threw away any opportunity to capitalize on these successes, and in 1244 Jerusalem fell to Islam.

This tide of defeat had a depressing effect on crusading fervor. Moreover, by the 13th century knights who wanted the prestige of crusading could gain the same spiritual benefit by fighting the pagans of Northern Europe, the Moors of Spain, and even heretics within Europe itself. If they were ambitious, they could enter the service of the great kingdoms emerging in Europe. If they were pious, more personal forms of devotion, often associated with the new orders of Saint Francis and Saint Dominic, offered new and less expensive paths to salvation. Thus, when the Mamluks captured Acre, there was no response as there had been in 1144 and 1187. This was in no way inevitable. Hattin could easily have had a different outcome, while Louis failed only narrowly. But Jerusalem was very distant from Europe, and while crusading remained an ideal, in the Middle East the reality was the dominion of the Mamluks, with their professional army and unremitting code of jihad.

John France

Perspective Essay 2. The Nature of the Crusader States

Outremer is a name used in medieval sources and in modern scholarship as a collective term for the four Frankish states established in Syria and Palestine by the First Crusade (1096–1099): the county of Edessa (1097–1150), the principality of Antioch (1098–1287), the Kingdom of Jerusalem (1099–1291), and the county of

Tripoli (1102–1289). The Kingdom of Jerusalem extended over the southern parts of Outremer, in the area historically known as Palestine; the other three states were situated in the north, in areas known historically as Syria and Upper Mesopotamia. During its relatively short existence, the county of Edessa extended much farther to the east than the other Frankish states, well beyond the Euphrates River. An alternative name for the four Frankish principalities in modern historical writing is "crusader states." Although common, this term is less accurate, since after around 1130 extremely few of their Frankish inhabitants were actually crusaders, in the sense of people who had taken a vow to go on crusade. In the Middle Ages the Frankish states were also often collectively known as Syria.

The Franks were never able to capture the major Muslim cities of Aleppo, Hama, Homs, or Damascus. The conquests of Muslim leader Saladin in the late 12th century and of the Mamluk sultanate in the 13th century successively pushed Frankish-held territory farther back toward the west until it was reduced to a series of unconnected coastal strips by the 1280s. Frankish-held territory consisted of several important cities, particularly on the coast. Acre and to a lesser extent Tyre, Tripoli, and Beirut connected with major trade routes from the east and served as commercial centers for luxury products such as spices and textiles as well as local and regional products. These cities also had important industries, as did Antioch and other major towns. The coastal cities attracted settlers from the Italian republics of Genoa, Venice, and Pisa, who received legal and financial privileges and in some places were able to establish their own autonomous quarters. The inland city of Jerusalem, by contrast, had no large-scale industry or trade; its main economic role was to service the royal and ecclesiastical administrations and cater to the important pilgrim traffic from the west.

The Franks constituted a privileged minority in all four states of Outremer. They were the only ethnic group in possession of all legal rights. The majority of the Frankish population lived in urban centers or as garrisons and support personnel in castles. During the initial phase of conquest, the Muslim and Jewish urban populations were largely either massacred or expelled, although the native Christians were allowed to remain, and Jews were later allowed to return. The city of Jerusalem remained (at least in theory) barred to non-Christians. Most rural settlement was in villages, known in Latin as *casalia,* while there were many deserted or seasonally occupied settlements.

The native rural population consisted largely of Muslims (known to the Franks as Saracens) and native Christians of various denominations. There were also smaller rural minorities of Jews and Samaritans in Galilee and Druzes in the mountains of Lebanon. In some cases Franks settled in newly founded villages, such as Magna Mahomeria near Jericho. Sometimes these new settlements were exclusively meant for Franks, but other settlements had mixed communities of Franks and native Christians. Most of the native population, whether Christian, Muslim, or Jewish, employed

Arabic as their everyday language, although a significant number used Syriac, Armenian (notably in the county of Edessa), and Greek (notably in the cities of Antioch and Laodikeia in Syria). The Frankish settlers and their descendants spoke French and wrote Latin, while Italian dialects were also found in the coastal cities where Venetians, Genoese, and Pisans resided, and many other languages were heard from the numerous pilgrims who visited the Holy Land under Frankish rule. However, few Franks seem to have learned Arabic, and such knowledge was often remarked on (and by implication regarded as unusual) in both Western and Arabic sources.

The long-term occupation of these crusader states depended on establishing stability in the region. However, because of the near-constant warfare between Franks and resurgent Muslim states, it became necessary to constantly supply these states with provisions and fresh troops from Europe. Moreover, while Frankish settlers did attempt to populate these regions, their numbers were never significant to establish any long-term roots in the region. Endemic warfare and the lack of stability contributed to this situation. In the end as the Europeans were gradually expelled and their respective countries lost interest in maintaining these small outposts on the periphery of the Mediterranean, the last of the crusader states, the County of Tripoli, fell to Malmuk Egypt in 1289.

Alan V. Murray

Perspective Essay 3. Outnumbered and Surrounded

Was it possible for the Christians to retain control of the Holy Land throughout the Middle Ages? At first glance, the entire crusading project looks far-fetched. Surrounded by powerful Muslim princes and vastly outnumbered, surely it was only a matter of time before the Kingdom of Jerusalem was overrun. Yet to offset the difficulties of being a small settler population in a largely hostile environment, the Franks did have certain advantages over their enemies. According to Archbishop William of Tyre, who wrote a history of the crusader states that he completed near the end of his life (around 1184),

> All the resources of Egypt and its immense wealth served our needs; the frontiers of our realm were safe on that side; there was no enemy to be feared in the south. The sea afforded a safe and peaceful passage to those wishing to come to us. . . . But now, on the contrary, all things have been changed for the worse. The sea refuses to give us peaceful passage, all the regions round about are subject to the enemy, and the neighbouring kingdoms are making preparations to destroy us.

William was correct. In 1187, the great Muslim commander Saladin captured Jerusalem and drove out the Christian rulers of the towns all around the Holy City.

The Franks managed to hold the northern principalities of Tripoli and Antioch and the coastal town of Tyre and regain control of Acre in 1191 with the assistance of the manpower of the Third Crusade. From these bases the Franks launched renewed assaults on the Muslim world but made only gains of limited duration. In 1291, an Egyptian-led army conquered Acre and ended any prospect of a restored crusader kingdom in the Levant.

By the time of the First Crusade, fleets from Italian cities such as Genoa, Pisa, and Venice were the dominant naval force in the Mediterranean. Italian merchants had taken over from Muslim traders as the middlemen of bulk commerce. The support given by the Italian cities to the crusader realm gave it a vital economic underpinning in addition to ensuring the regular arrival of fresh troops and military supplies from Europe. The Christian knights could generally more than hold their own against the equivalent Muslim troops. With their well-trained heavy cavalry and metal armor, so long as the crusaders could fight at close quarters in formation they could generally overcome even quite a large disparity of numbers on the battlefield.

Above all, the Christian states of Outremer benefited from the political divisions of their neighbors. Not only were the Seljuks of Aleppo, Mosul, and Damascus bitter rivals and jealous of their independence, but also a huge fault line lay between the Shiite realm of the Fatimids based in Egypt and the Sunnī principalities to their east.

The equilibrium between Franks and Muslims was unstable, however, because of a growing crisis in Egypt. In the 10th century, the Fatimid realm had been the richest and most successful of Muslim states. The reliability of the Nile flood allowed farmers to grow crops every year without harm to the fertility of the land. Wheat yields were about 10 to 1 (compared to 3 or 4 to 1 for dry farming elsewhere in the Mediterranean). Linen and wool production also provided the rulers of Egypt with important revenues.

Yet from the 1050s, this wealthy and stable state began to fall apart. Environmental change may have been a factor behind this decline, with terrible famines taking place over a number of years following the failure of the Nile to rise. The central tax system never recovered from the increased provincial autonomy that sprang up during the famine years. The Fatimids' distinctive use of a multiethnic army also led to political instability. The idea was that the civil government could play one enslaved ethnic military group against the other and maintain control of them all. But once dominant over their rivals, the strongest of these ethnic armies had the ability to threaten the state.

During the reign of al-Mustansir (1036–1094) it was the Turks who dominated Cairo. They demanded more and more wages and looted treasures from the palace to sell in the capital. Defeat of the Turks by an alliance of other ethnic groups simply brought more looting: the provinces escaped central control, and much land was left uncultivated. Fatimid silver coins were debased at this time to about 30 percent silver, adding to the economic difficulties of the realm.

William of Tyre, looking to explain the decline of the Fatimids, thought it relevant to note that while the farmers of Syria, both Muslim and Christian, were free, those of Egypt were servile. This might be an important point. Land worked by men and women who have a share of the crop shows significant development compared to land worked by those who do not benefit from increased yields.

Whatever the reason or reasons, by 1168 it was clear to the crusaders as well as the Byzantine emperor that, as William of Tyre reports the Byzantines as saying, "it seems impossible that the kingdom [Egypt] can continue long in its present state and the government and dominion over it must of necessity pass to other nations."

The race for Egypt was on. If the Christians gained control of the riches of the Nile and the entire Mediterranean, Outremer would be secure for decades. But the Franks blundered catastrophically by allowing Egypt to fall to a very dangerous opponent, Nur al-Din. Having managed to create a politically united realm of all the northern Syrian cities, Nur al-Din had already subsumed Damascus into his realm, in part because of the failure of the Second Crusade to capture that city in 1148. Now in similar fashion, he was handed an even greater prize.

The key turning point was the year 1168, when King Amalric of Jerusalem attempted a surprise assault on Cairo. Despite a promising beginning, Amalric's dramatic effort resulted in Egypt falling to Nur al-Din, whose general, Shirkuh, was allowed free passage to Cairo to defend the city. Once he had forced Amalric to retreat, Shirkuh decapitated the man he came to assist and installed himself as governor of Egypt on January 19, 1169. Nur al-Din was now master of the entire region of surrounding states of Outremer.

When Saladin seized power following the death of Nur al-Din in 1174, it was only a matter of time before he exploited the advantage of his position. While Saladin consolidated his great realm, bitter factional rivalries saw the Frankish position worsen. But with control over both Egypt and Syria, Saladin's victory of 1187 was almost inevitable.

The contemporary Christian world saw control of Egypt as a crucial strategic goal for the restoration of the Holy Land. Major efforts in 1218–1221 (the Fifth Crusade) and 1248–1254 (the first crusade of Louis IX of France) were undertaken to capture Cairo. With their failure Muslim control of the region was secure, as only the wealth of Egypt could have allowed a Frankish state to support the army size and network of castles needed to survive as a small minority in the region.

Conor Kostick

Perspective Essay 4. The Ascendancy of Mongol Power

On May 28, 1291, forces led by the Mamluk sultan Qalawun breached the city of Acre's final defenses. This crippling blow effectively destroyed the Kingdom of Jerusalem. Acre had been its main city, and its loss shattered any lingering hope that a Christian presence could be maintained in the Holy Land. The remaining settlements were swiftly evacuated. This event marked the end of the Latin East, but it was the product of a much longer period of decline. Many factors had contributed to this process: the Franks were often divided among themselves, fewer crusaders were coming to the East, and many crusades in this period had achieved disappointing results. Even so, one factor more than any other sent the Christian position spiraling to its destruction: the advent of the Mongols.

In 1244, the Latin East was as strong as it ever had been. Following the catastrophic defeats of 1187, when Saladin had almost driven the Franks into the sea, Western Christendom had striven ceaselessly to rebuild its position in the Holy Land. Despite many reverses, by the 1240s the Franks could field a major army, while their lands were defended by some of the most sophisticated fortresses of the medieval era. In addition, the military orders of the Templars, Hospitallers, and Teutonic Knights possessed huge networks of estates in Western Europe that stood ready to pump resources into the Near East should the need arise. Equally as important, the Franks' Muslim neighbors, the rulers of Aleppo, Damascus, and Egypt, were preoccupied with their own rivalries and posed little threat. In this position, there was no reason to believe that the states of Outremer would not remain a permanent feature of the Near Eastern landscape.

Nevertheless, times were changing. In the early 13th century the Mongols swept out of their Asian homelands, carving a brutal path that would extend into the Middle East. In 1258 they conquered Baghdad, and by 1259 they stood ready to invade Syria. With over 100,000 men, the Mongols were stronger militarily than any other power in the region, while the fear they evoked spread far and wide. The Mongols brought about the fall of the Latin East, but they did not do so directly. There was one Mongol attack on the Frankish city of Sidon in August 1260, but this was the extent of their direct assaults on Christian territory. The Mongols were important instead for the events they set in motion.

These began sometime before in the mid-13th century when bands of refugees began to appear in ever-increasing numbers, fleeing from the Mongol onslaught. Among these groups was a force of 20,000 warriors who had escaped the Mongol overthrow of Khwarizm, an empire far to the east. Their arrival tipped the military balance in the

Holy Land. On their journey into the Levant they sacked Frankish-held Jerusalem and then formed an alliance with the sultan of Egypt, giving him sufficient manpower to contemplate a direct assault on his enemies, the Kingdom of Jerusalem and al-Salih Ismail, the ruler of Damascus. The resulting encounter at La Forbie in 1244 was a major defeat for the Frankish-Damascene force. Both armies suffered heavy casualties, territory was lost, and Christian lands were severely weakened by Khwarizmian depredations.

This was not the only significant defeat the Franks suffered at the hands of migrating tribal warriors moving west to evade the Mongols. In 1250 reports were received that Turkmen tribes had twice devastated the lands around Antioch, while in 1261 a major Christian army numbering 900 knights, 1,500 *turcopoles* (locally recruited mounted archers), and 3,000 infantry was defeated by Turkmen forces east of Lake Tiberias. The direct threat posed by the Turkmen was serious enough, but their horsemen also swelled the ranks of neighboring Muslim rulers.

These waves of displaced peoples were merely one of the problems created by the Mongol advances. The form taken by their subsequent invasion into the Near East was to have catastrophic consequences for the Christian position. In 1260 the Mongols invaded Syria, conquering the independent states of Aleppo and Damascus. Crucially, however, the bulk of their forces did not remain to occupy and defend the land but rapidly withdrew when their ruler, Hulegu, was recalled to the east. The Mamluks, who had seized power in Egypt in 1250, feared an invasion and marched out to confront the Mongols but encountered only the greatly reduced Mongol garrison, which they defeated in the Battle of Ayn Jalut (September 3, 1260). The Mamluks followed up this victory by taking large swaths of land in northern Syria, including Damascus and Aleppo. Fearing a renewal of Mongol rule, these cities proved to be more than happy to seek Mamluk protection, effectively giving them a vast territorial power block.

These events changed the balance of power in the Near East. Ultimately through their invasion, the Mongols had swept away a system of weak and divided Muslim city-states and inadvertently established the conditions necessary for the unification of all of the region's Muslim territories under a single Mamluk ruler. Thus, in only one year and with comparatively little fighting, the Mamluks found themselves in possession of lands that almost surrounded the remaining Frankish territory, a process that had taken Saladin almost a decade.

In subsequent years Mamluk policy was driven by fear of a Mongol backlash, and the Mamluks rapidly strengthened their military capacity. The Mongol khans sent some armies against them, but it was to be over 20 years before they dispatched their full strength. In the intervening period the Mamluks, led by Sultan Baybars, used their newly acquired power to dismember the Frankish states. In the 1260s, Frankish castles and cities fell like dominos; even the strongest fortresses did not hold out for long. The unification of so much territorial power under Baybars rendered him a virtually irresistible force, and the Franks did not even consider attempting to meet him in battle. By the 1280s the Frankish states were ready to fall, while the Mamluks were strong enough to confront the full weight of a Mongol horde.

Consequently, while the Mamluks struck many of the actual body blows that destroyed the Latin East, their ability to outcompete the Christian lands owed much to the Mongols. The Mongols had never intended to strengthen the Mamluks, who were their bitter foes, but through their invasion of Syria and then their sudden withdrawal, they had created an opportunity for the Mamluks to grow rapidly in power. Moreover, just as the Mongol invasions established the necessary conditions for the Mamluks' rise, they also ensured that the Franks remained enfeebled. Waves of migrating tribesmen had reduced Frankish manpower and devastated Frankish agriculture. Perhaps just as important, the Mongol invasions had disrupted the Asiatic trade routes that were absolutely vital for Outremer's economic and commercial life. Ultimately, the Mongols had broken upon the Near East like a tidal wave, but like a tidal wave its impact had been uneven. Some were better placed to take advantage of its aftermath than others. It is striking that the notion of Christian-Islamic warfare, which so dominates our modern ideas of the Crusades, hardly had any role to play at all.

Nicholas Morton

Further Reading

Amitai-Preiss, Reuven. *Mongols and Mamluks: The Mamluk-Ilkhanid War, 1260–1281.* Cambridge: Cambridge University Press, 2004.

Armstrong, Karen. *Holy War: The Crusades and Their Impact on Today's World.* New York: Anchor Books, 2001.

Beaune, Colette. *The Birth of an Ideology: Myths and Symbols of Nation in Late Medieval France.* Berkeley: University of California Press, 1991.

Bosworth, Clifford Edmund. *The New Islamic Dynasties.* Edinburgh, UK: Edinburgh University Press, 1996.

Bronstein, Judith. *The Hospitallers and the Holy Land: Financing the Latin East, 1187–1274.* Woodbridge, UK: Boydell, 2005.

Bull, Marcus. *Knightly Piety and the Lay Response to the First Crusade; The Limousin and Gascony, c. 970–c. 1130.* Oxford: Oxford University Press, 1993.

Christiansen, Eric. *The Northern Crusades: The Baltic and the Catholic Frontier, 1100–1525.* London: Penguin, 1997.

Erdmann, Carl. *The Origin of the Idea of the Crusade.* Princeton, NJ: Princeton University Press, 1977.

France, John. *Western Warfare in the Age of the Crusades, 1000–1300.* London: UCL, 1999.

Hamilton, Bernard. *The Leper King and His Heirs.* Cambridge: Cambridge University Press, 2000.

Hardwicke, Mary N. "The Crusader States, 1192–1243." In *A History of the Crusades,* Vol. 2, edited by Kenneth M. Setton, 522–529. Madison: University of Wisconsin Press, 1969.

Harris, Jonathan. *Byzantium and the Crusades.* London: Hambledon, 2003.

Hillenbrand, Carole. *The Crusades: Islamic Perspectives.* New York: Routledge, 1999.

Holt, P. M. *The Eastern Mediterranean Lands in the Period of the Crusades.* Warminster, UK: Aris and Phillips, 1977.

Housley, Norman. *Contesting the Crusades.* Oxford, UK: Wiley-Blackwell, 2006.

Humphreys, R. Stephen. *From Saladin to the Mongols: The Ayyubids of Damascus, 1193–1260.* Albany: State University of New York Press, 1977.

Irwin, Robert. "Iqta and the End of the Crusader States." In *The Eastern Mediterranean Lands in the Period of the Crusades,* edited by Peter M. Holt, 62–73. Warminster, UK: Aris and Phillips, 1977.

Jackson, Peter. *The Mongols and the West, 1221–1410.* Harlow, UK: Pearson Longman, 2005.

Lev, Yaacov. *Saladin in Egypt.* Leiden: Brill, 1999.

Levanoni, Amalia. *A Turning Point in Mamluk History: The Third Reign of al-Nasir Muhammad ibn Qalawun.* Leiden: Brill, 1995.

Lilie, Johannes R. *Byzantium and the Crusader States, 1096–1204.* Oxford, UK: Clarendon, 1993.

Lloyd, Simon. *English Society and the Crusade, 1216–1307.* Oxford: Oxford University Press, 1988.

Morgan, David O. *Medieval Persia, 1040–1797.* London: Longman, 1988.

Morton, Nicholas. *The Medieval Military Orders, 1120–1314.* Harlow, UK: Pearson Longman, 2013.

Pahlitzsch, Johannes, and Daniel Baraz. "Christian Communities in the Latin Kingdom of Jerusalem (1099–1187 CE)." In *Christians and Christianity in the Holy Land: From the Origins to the Latin Kingdoms,* edited by Ora Limor and Guy G. Stroumsa, 205–235. Turnhout, Belgium: Brepols, 2006.

Phillips, Jonathan. *The Crusades, 1095–1197.* New York: Longman, 2002.

Powell, James M. *Anatomy of a Crusade, 1213–1221.* Philadelphia: University of Pennsylvania Press, 1986.

Richard, Jean. *The Crusades, c. 1071–c. 1291.* Translated by Jean Birrell. Cambridge: Cambridge University Press, 1999.

Riley-Smith, Jonathan. *The Crusades: A History.* London: Bloomsbury, 2014.

Riley-Smith, Jonathan. *The Crusades: A Short History.* New Haven, CT: Yale University Press, 2005.

Riley-Smith, Jonathan. *The First Crusaders, 1095–1131.* Cambridge: Cambridge University Press, 1997.

Runciman, Steven. *A History of the Crusades.* 3 vols. Cambridge: Cambridge University Press, 1951–1954.

Selwood, Dominic. *Knights of the Cloister: Templars and Hospitallers in Central-Southern Occitania, c. 1100–c. 1300.* Woodbridge, UK: Boydell, 1999.

Thorau, Peter. *The Lion of Egypt: Sultan Baybars I and the Near East in the Thirteenth Century.* London: Longman, 1992.

Tyerman, Christopher. *England and the Crusades, 1095–1588.* Chicago: University of Chicago Press, 1988.

9. How Did the Mongol Invaders Manage to Conquer and Rule over Much of Asia in the 13th and 14th Centuries?

In the early 13th century, Genghis Khan's forces swept out of Mongolia, conquering China, Persia, Mesopotamia, and swaths of Central Asia and the territories that would later make up Russia. For a relatively short period of time, the resulting Mongol Empire established a stable contiguous nation that allowed for the exchange of goods, technology, commodities, peoples, and ideas across Eurasia. While the Mongols' powerful military force is often emphasized, their willingness to adopt, assimilate, or tolerate the cultural practices of the conquered was also an important feature of their tactics. For example, while most Mongols were shamanists, they generally allowed Buddhists, Christians, and Muslims to observe their own faiths throughout the empire. That tolerance was in evidence at the Mongols' imperial capital of Karakorum, where one could find Buddhist pagodas, a Christian church, and Muslim mosques.

Dr. Nancy Stockdale, in the first perspective essay, asserts that the Mongols' remarkable martial abilities enabled them to establish a far-flung empire. Indeed, their equestrian skills, intelligence gathering, and logistics operations were second to none. Furthermore, their complete and merciless subjugation of enemies who resisted was legendary. So too was their uncanny ability to adopt the cultural practices of the people they had conquered. Dr. Timothy May argues that the Mongols' ingenious military prowess helped them to conquer and rule other peoples with relative ease, as did their willingness and ability to employ administrative personnel from conquered areas and incorporate them into their own imperial administration. Furthermore, when faced with new military technologies, Genghis Khan and his successors studied them carefully and adapted them to meet their own needs. In the third essay, Dr. George Kallander demonstrates that although Mongol armies were often outnumbered by opponents, the Mongols' military prowess and their extensive use of massed equestrian formations enabled them to overcome numeric disadvantages. He also credits peerless military leadership for the Mongols' success at building a vast empire. Meanwhile, earning the support of conquered elites, practicing religious toleration, and implementing efficient imperial administration enabled the Mongols to rule over their

*subjects with relative ease. Finally, Dr. Spencer C. Tucker points out that the Mongols'
overwhelming military power and ingenuity combined with their highly effective intelligence apparatus gave them a key advantage over their adversaries. At the same
time, their employment of mass terror led to high casualty rates and unprecedented
population displacement. Above all, it was the bold leadership abilities of Genghis
Khan that laid the foundations of Mongol military and imperial success.*

Background Essay

Mongol territorial expansion was unlike almost any other. Extremely violent, it
exacted a frightful toll on the conquered peoples, bringing widespread terror and
population displacement on a heretofore unknown scale. During a two-century
span, the Mongols conquered or pillaged much of the known world. As the largest
contiguous land empire in history, the Mongol Empire was second in total area
only to that of the British Empire at the end of the 19th century. At its greatest extent, the Mongol Empire embraced more than 12 million square miles and more
than 100 million people from East Asia to Central Europe.

One man, Temujin, more commonly known as Genghis Khan (Chingghis or
Jenghis Khan), laid the foundation for and initiated this vast enterprise. Before he
came to power, the Mongols were a disparate group of tribes warring largely with
one another. They lived a nomadic existence in Outer Mongolia, the Gobi Desert,
and Inner Mongolia.

Born the son of a chieftain of a Mongol subclan in the Gobi Desert in 1162, as a
teenager Temujin led raids against his enemies. He soon became known for his
boldness, strong leadership, cunning, and astute diplomacy. By 1188 he probably
commanded 20,000 men. His goal was to unify the tribes of Mongolia and then
conquer the neighboring non-Mongolian peoples.

In 1194 Temujin began a series of successful campaigns against the Tatars. During the next two decades he established an empire centered on the Gobi Desert,
with his capital at Karakorum. By 1204 he had taken the name Genghis Khan
(meaning "supreme ruler") and had unified Mongolia.

Genghis Khan began the Mongol conquest of China in late 1205 by invading the
Xi Xia (Western Xia or Tangut) Empire. In 1209 the Chinese acknowledged his
suzerainty. In 1211 Genghis invaded the Jin Empire of northern China, forcing it to
recognize Mongol suzerainty in 1215, although all of China would not be conquered until 1234, after Genghis's death.

Genghis then turned his attention to the Muslim Khwarizm Empire in the area
between the Aral Sea and Afghanistan, invading it in 1219 and securing it as a result

of the 1221 Battle of the Indus. Also in 1221, Genghis sent forces into the southern Caucasus. Passing through Azerbaijan, they spent the winter of 1221–1222 in eastern Armenia and then moved into present-day Georgia. After defeating a Christian force, the Mongols proceeded into southern Russia, subduing the tribes of the Russian steppes. Crossing the Don, the Mongols entered the Crimean Peninsula, then turned north into present-day Ukraine and passed the winter of 1222–1223 by the Black Sea before attacking and nearly annihilating Russian forces in the Battle of the Kalka River. They then returned home, having covered some 4,000 miles.

The Xi Xia Empire had refused to aid the Mongols during Genghis's campaign against the Khwarizm Empire. Indeed, the Tanguts had entered into an alliance with

Battle in which Genghis Wins Power. From the Mongol history *Jami al-Tawarikh*. (Corel)

their former bitter enemy, the Jin Empire, against the Mongols. Genghis struck in late 1226 and annihilated a far larger Tangut army on the western banks of the frozen Huang He. Reportedly, the Mongols counted some 300,000 Tangut dead.

In August 1227 Genghis died, the cause unknown. His son Ögödei succeeded him, and the Mongols then largely destroyed the Xia state. In 1231, the Mongols invaded Koryo (Korea). That same year after forming an alliance with the Songs, Ögödei implemented his father's plans to destroy the Jin Empire. When Ögödei refused to share his conquest of the Jin Empire with the Songs, this brought a protracted struggle (1234–1279) between the Mongols and the Songs.

Ögödei died in 1241, and the war against the Songs was won by his nephews Möngke Khan (r. 1241–1259) and Kublai Khan (r. 1260–1294) and their successors. Kublai conquered Yunnan during 1252–1253, and a subordinate took Tonkin, capturing Thang Long (present-day Hanoi) in 1257. During 1257–1259 Möngke directed a series of effective campaigns against the Songs, but his death from dysentery brought a dynastic struggle in the Mongol Empire and a temporary lull in fighting the Songs. Not until 1268 was Kublai, having defeated his brother in a struggle for power, again able to direct full attention to the Songs. By 1279, the Mongols controlled the entire Song Empire. Kublai had built a large navy, and it played a key role in the Mongol victory.

The Mongols mounted invasions of eastern and northern Rus in 1237–1238 and southern and western Rus in 1239–1240. In 1238–1239 they were in the northern Caucasus, and in 1238–1240 they invaded Cumania and Alania in the western part of the Eurasian steppe. In 1240–1241 Mongol forces under Godan, son of Ögedei, conquered Tibet, and in 1241 the Mongols raided into the Punjab, capturing Lahore.

After consolidating Mongol control over the loose federation of East Slavic tribes of Rus, Sübetei invaded Central Europe in November 1240. The Mongols captured Kiev, defeated a Polish army at Kraków (Cracow) in March 1241, and then defeated a force in Silesia at Liegnitz (Legnica) that April. To the south, the Mongols conquered Transylvania and then reached Buda. Withdrawing before a larger Hungarian force, the Mongols turned and defeated it in the Battle of the Sajó River on April 11. They now held all of Eastern Europe from the Dnieper to the Oder and from the Baltic to the Danube. In four months they had destroyed Christian forces numbering many times their own. The campaign was halted on word of the death 6,000 miles to the east in Karakorum of Ögödei. In March 1242 the Mongol armies withdrew. Having already ravaged most of Hungary and Transylvania, they did the same in present-day Serbia and Bulgaria as they returned east.

The Mongols went on to secure control of all of Russia and would rule it for the next 250 years. They also defeated the Seljuk Turks in 1243, bringing control of Anatolia. In 1257 the Mongols attempted to capture the Kingdom of Champa in present-day central Vietnam but found themselves fighting a protracted guerrilla war.

In 1258 Mongol forces conquered southern Mesopotamia, taking Baghdad and ending the Abbasid Caliphate. But in the Battle of Ain Jalut near Nazareth on September 3, 1260, the Mongols were defeated by the Mamluks. This battle marked both the zenith of Mongol power and the first defeat from which they did not return and prevail. It also shattered the myth of Mongol invincibility and probably prevented a Mongol invasion of Western Europe. Had they taken Egypt, there was little to prevent the Mongols from sweeping across North Africa and then invading southern Spain.

In 1260 Kublai was elected great khan. In 1264 he built a new Chinese-style capital known as Dadu at present-day Beijing, and in 1271 he declared himself emperor, establishing a new Chinese dynasty, the Yuan. Conquering the Southern Songs in 1279, Kublai brought unity to northern and southern China and also proved to be one of China's most capable rulers. His ambitions included not only the Eurasias but also the Japanese archipelago. When diplomacy failed, he sent two large fleets.

The first Mongol invasion, in 1274, was most probably a reconnaissance in force. It encountered strong Japanese resistance and a major storm. Kublai Khan then assembled a vast expeditionary force of perhaps 170,000 men transported in 4,500 ships. On the night of August 14–15, however, a violent storm (the Kamikaze, or Divine Wind) blew in from the north, wrecked most of the Mongol ships, and killed most of the expeditionary force. Those Mongols ashore were easily defeated and enslaved. Japan retained its independence, and later a modernized Japan would seek to reverse the situation and itself control China. The Mongols also suffered rebuff in Syria in 1281.

The Mongols continued their efforts to penetrate Southeast Asia. In 1287 they conquered present-day Myanmar and established a puppet regime there. They also continued their efforts in present-day Vietnam, with mixed results.

In 1294 the Mongol Empire split into separate provinces, or khanates. Mongol territorial gains persisted into the 14th century in China, Persia, and Russia and into the 19th century in India in the Mughal Empire ("Mughal" being the Arabic word for "Mongol"). The longest lived of the successor states to the Mongol Empire was the Crimean Khanate; it was annexed by Russia only in 1783.

Spencer C. Tucker

Perspective Essay 1. Mongol Military Prowess and the Nature of Mongol Rule

Known for their swift and decisive conquest of large swaths of Asia and Europe, the Mongols were feared by their contemporaries because of the brutality they exhibited while conquering some of their most important imperial possessions. Ironically, the Mongols were also known for borrowing and adapting many of the cultural values, traditions, and institutions of these places. In that way, the study of their imperial project gives historians a fine opportunity to assess the significance of cultural borrowing and adaptation among societies.

The Mongols launched their imperial mission in 1206 and within 70 years had created history's largest empire with contiguous borders. Indeed, at the height of their power, the Mongols controlled some 22 percent of Earth's land area. A variety of reasons lay behind this, the most obvious being their remarkable military prowess. They used their peerless equestrian skills, astonishing martial abilities (including masterful mounted archery), and efficient intelligence and supply networks to swiftly take territory. When met by resistance, the Mongols were merciless; collective punishment of any area mounting resistance was commonplace, leading to the massacre of entire communities.

Perhaps the most famous example of brutal destruction wrought by the Mongols was the conquest of Baghdad, then the capital of the Abbasid Empire. A city of more than 1.5 million inhabitants, Baghdad was a cultural, economic, and educational center of Islamic civilization. However, on February 10, 1258, a Mongol army led by Hulegu Khan (grandson of Mongol leader Genghis Khan) invaded the city. Overwhelmed by the Mongol horde, the people of Baghdad stood by as their city was sacked and burned. The Mongols then turned their wrath on the population. Although there are no clear statistics, historians believe that between 200,000 and 1 million people were killed or injured in the massacre, including Caliph al-Mustasim. Baghdad did not recover for centuries thereafter.

In the course of such brutal invasions, the Mongols were responsible for the destruction of many key cultural institutions, including the House of Wisdom, then one of the world's greatest intellectual centers. The Mongols used such force against resisters as a warning to others not to oppose their expansion. However, even in the wake of their destruction, they found tremendous attraction in many of the cultural elements of the societies they conquered. Indeed, the creation of their empire gained an ironic quality; while they destroyed, they also adopted, adapting many elements of the very cultures they displaced.

One of the most dramatic elements of Mongol cultural borrowing and adaptation is in the religious realm. The Mongols began their territorial expansion as animists who relied on shamanism to communicate with the spirit world. However, as they conquered Asia, Eurasia, the Middle East, and parts of Europe, they interacted with many different cultures claiming a variety of faiths. The Mongols took it upon themselves to promote religious tolerance throughout their empire. This tolerance even occurred in places where their destruction had previously victimized religious institutions and leaders.

However, several Mongol leaders went beyond mere toleration of conquered peoples' religions; they embraced these as their own. A good example of this occurred in Tibet, which the Mongols conquered in 1240. During a series of battles, Mongol leader Khoten ordered the destruction of key Buddhist monasteries and temples. However, once he accepted the submission of the Tibetans, he invited monks to explain their faith to him, and eventually he embraced Tibetan Buddhism as his own religion. The same can be said of Islam, a faith system whose adherents suffered greatly with the Mongol invasions, yet Muslims became favored in the Mongol Empire's bureaucratic system, and many leaders, including Uzbek, Tudi Mengu, and Mahmud Ghazan, converted to Islam and became devout Muslims. Moreover, the Arabic script became the standard throughout the empire, adapted by the Mongols for Uyghur and other Turkic languages they carried with them as they conquered the world.

Another area in which the Mongols borrowed—and perhaps improved upon— the cultural institutions of their conquered populations was trade. With their contiguous imperial holdings straddling two continents, the Mongols consolidated existing trade routes along the Silk Road and ensured security with their well-oiled military presence. They borrowed previously instituted trade practices from the Muslim empires, such as paper currency and the check, as a way to make long-distance financial transactions efficient. At the same time, they allowed conquered peoples to mint their own silver coins; this was crucial, for it did not disrupt local economic practices. The Silk Road allowed for easier long-distance international travel. Perhaps the most famous European to travel this storied road was Marco Polo, although Asian and European cultural and economic exchange was far larger than his journey may suggest.

The Mongol invasions were devastating for millions of people throughout Asia and Europe. Most historians estimate that upwards of 40 million people died as a consequence. Ironically, many of the institutions of the conquered—including religion, bureaucracy, and trade patterns—were embraced by the Mongols and became integral to the success of their empire. By examining elements of cultural borrowing and adaptation by the Mongols, historians may touch on some of the more complicated aspects of imperialism and its institutions—the concurrent destruction and maintenance of conquered cultures by their conquerors.

Nancy L. Stockdale

Perspective Essay 2. The Mongol Military Machine

One of the most fascinating aspects of the rise of the Mongol Empire is how a people numbering only about 1 million were able to defeat and rule kingdoms that usually outnumbered them and were more technologically advanced. Scholars such as David Morgan and George Lane have pointed out the Mongols' use of personnel from conquered states and blending of this with an overarching Mongol administration. The key to victory in battle is an effective army. The army created by Genghis Khan during the wars that unified the Mongolian steppes between 1183 and 1204 was unlike any other military force that the world had yet seen.

The organizational genius of Genghis Khan transformed the Mongols from being simply a fierce force of horse archers into a rational army capable of operations every bit as complex as modern mechanized warfare. Beginning in 1202 Temujin, as he was known before becoming Genghis Khan, began to instill discipline on the unruly tribesmen. He forbade them from stopping to plunder enemy camps until the enemy had been completely defeated. This was achieved by promising to divide the loot from the battle equally. Typically, what had happened was that the leaders received the greater portion of the plunder, and the common warrior received what he personally took. Thus, warriors often became distracted in battle upon discovering valuable items. Throughout the medieval world, many battles had been won but then lost because warriors stopped to loot rather than finish off the enemy.

By 1204, the Mongols had become a formidable force but were still underestimated by their opponents. The final opponent the Mongols faced in Mongolia was the Naimans of western Mongolia. After learning that the Naimans planned to attack them, the Mongols marched hundreds of miles across the steppe at the end of winter. The Naimans still had the advantage in that they were on their own territory, and the Mongol horses were weakened from the long march. The Mongols, however, countered this by unveiling new battle formations and disciplined tactics—ones that the Naimans had never seen before. They could not disrupt the Mongols through charges or by feigning retreat and attempting to lure the Mongols into a trap. With the defeat of the Naimans, the Mongols ruled Mongolia.

In 1206 Temujin was crowned as Genghis Khan, meaning "fierce or firm ruler." On assuming power, he divided his armies into decimal units (tens, hundreds, and thousands) and assigned their leaders. Many had been his comrades from the beginning. What separated Genghis Khan from other steppe leaders, and indeed many rulers in the medieval era, was that he did not care about one's lineage. Indeed, Jelme and Subedai (probably the greatest of Mongol generals) were the sons of a blacksmith and began their careers as Genghis Khan's servants. Genghis Khan had a keen eye for talent, and he always rewarded it.

The 1206 *qurilitai* (congress) saw the creation of the *keshik* (bodyguard). Consisting of 10,000 men, it was a formidable force dedicated to protecting the khan. Yet it was more than this. A member of the *keshik* outranked his non-*keshik* equivalent, and it was from this vast pool of talent that the khans chose their generals and governors. Even the earliest generals such as Subedai had served in the *keshik*. Here, members of the bodyguard not only protected the khan but also tended to the khan's flocks and herds of animals, prepared his meals, and performed other mundane duties. The khan thus observe them performing different tasks. He interacted with them and came to know their character and talents. The *keshik* also served as a military school where its members learned how to command and lead men. Thus, the Mongols trained their generals in a consistent manner—something that did not occur in the rest of the medieval world, where command was often haphazard and training was not in a regular manner.

Mongol military supremacy based on fast-moving horse archers and brilliant generals allowed them to utilize their forces to their utmost. On the march their armies could be dozens of miles apart yet still support each other. Furthermore, Genghis Khan and his successors knew their generals well and could trust them to carry out their own initiatives successfully and on schedule. This allowed the Mongols to strike their opponents from multiple directions and also fight on many fronts against several different enemies. Furthermore, the Mongols would occupy only a small amount of territory but destroy a wide swath of land to serve as a buffer zone.

When the Mongols encountered new technologies, they tried to understand and learn how to employ them. The Mongols actively recruited people from the among their opponents, such as oppressed minorities. The Mongols did not seek to make these people fight in the Mongol style and instead allowed them to fight in the manner to which they were already accustomed. Thus, only other nomads filled the horse archer ranks, while sedentary troops filled the roles of engineers, infantry, and heavy cavalry. This allowed the Mongols to maximize the talents and abilities of their armies, employing the right force for the circumstances. In terms of deployment, organization, strategy, and leadership, the Mongols had no equals until the modern era.

Timothy May

Perspective Essay 3. Mongol Conquests and Empire

In 1206 Temujin unified the nomadic tribes in what is today Mongolia, assumed the name and title Genghis Khan, and began launching raids into northern China and Central Asia. His sons and grandsons continued the legacy of conquest, eventually forging the largest land empire in world history. At its height, the Mongol Empire stretched from the Korean Peninsula in the east through China and Central Asia into Russia and Iraq in the west. Mongol armies even reached Eastern Europe, threatening Vienna in 1241.

The Mongols originally preferred oral history to written traditions, so the story of these conquests has largely come down to us through the people the Mongols dominated. Subjugated peoples often emphasized the brutal nature of the invaders. When the Mongol leader Hulegu captured Baghdad in 1258, the Persian historian Abdullah Wassaf wrote that "They swept through the city like hungry falcons attacking a flight of doves, or like raging wolves attacking sheep, with loose reins and shameless faces, murdering and spreading fear. . . . The massacre was so great that the blood of the slain flowed in a river like the Nile." Such poetic narratives, while providing important clues to the physical and psychological toll of the invasions, stereotype the Mongols as bloodthirsty barbarians and do little to advance the Mongol story.

In forging an empire, Genghis Khan and his successors relied first on military strength. Initially, the Mongol Army was small. Historian David Morgan estimates the number of warriors to have been roughly 105,000, whereas Chinese armies could easily reach 1 million or more. Only later did the size of the Mongol Army increase as the Mongols conscripted men of conquered lands to fight. Chinese and Korean forces were co-opted in the failed attempts to invade the Japanese islands in 1274 and 1281, and Uighur and Chinese troops assisted in the 1293 invasion of Java.

Any limitations imposed by manpower quantity were compensated for by military skills. Mongol armies on horseback were premodern weapons of mass destruction, since life on the harsh steppe turned men into skilled warriors. Extreme temperatures did not permit agriculture, and their survival depended on animals for mobility but also for meat, milk, and hides. Horses were particularly important, and Mongols were born, lived, and often died on horseback. These pastoral nomads, who seasonally moved their herds, learned horsemanship and weapon skills, such as firing arrows from galloping horses, at a young age. When confronting sedentary civilizations such as China and Persia, where most of the population spent their time tending the fields and were not professional warriors, the Mongols had a comparative advantage.

Strong, charismatic leadership was necessary to maximize military power and overcome the tendency for tribal groups to splinter. Through warfare, threats, and strategic alliances, Genghis Khan unified the Tatars, the Merkits, the Naimans, and the Keraits, among others, bringing these tribes under the Mongol banner. This unity on the steppe occurred at a moment when much of Eurasia was disunited. Korea was led by a military family that disrupted the traditional defenses of the kingdom. What is today Russia was then composed of a number of principalities ruled by independent families. The various empires of Central Asia and the Middle East, including Qara-Khitai, the Ismaili empire, the Abbasid Caliphate (in Iraq), and even the powerful Kwararazm-shah (Uzbekistan), fell one by one to Mongol armies.

Europe, then largely a collection of small kingdoms, was only saved because Ogadai, the Mongol khan, died in 1241, temporarily ending all military campaigns as the Mongols took up the task of selecting their next leader. Most important, China was divided into competing dynasties, and the northern frontier was open. Traditional Chinese frontier policy fostered division among the nomadic tribes by buying off certain groups and forming alliances against others. This vulnerability at the frontier was a major factor in the rise of the Mongols.

Ruling a massive empire demanded more than military skill and charismatic leadership, and the Mongols were also adept administrators. The Mongols encouraged local elites of conquered lands to help them govern. Kublai Khan recognized the importance of Chinese-style governance, which depended on Confucian-educated literati. To win over this group, he supported Confucian learning and the examination system. In the Ilkhanate, Persian officials continued to run the daily affairs of the government while prospering from Mongol rule.

Gaining support from the conquered elites resulted partly from Mongol tolerance of local religious practices. Although privately disdainful of most religions and generally themselves shamanist, Mongol leaders supported a variety of religions throughout the empire—from Buddhism to Nestorian Christianity—to win over subject populations. In Persia, Mongol rulers converted to Islam in 1295, which probably contributed to the more rapid demise of Mongol power in the Islamic world as opposed to China, where laws were passed to curtail assimilation. Strategic marriages across the empire also contributed to stabilizing Mongol rule. Korean kings married Mongol princesses, bringing the ruling families into a close alliance so that by the end of Mongol rule, Korean royalty spoke Mongolian and followed Mongol customs.

The Mongol Empire was short-lived. Soon the Mongols reverted to their nomadic patterns of distrust and disunity. In many ways, the empire was never a whole but was divided into four khanates. In time as the Mongols weakened through internal feuds or through assimilation, the peoples and civilizations they had conquered and controlled saw this weakness as an opportunity. In less than 100 years, the khanates in China and Persia fell to rising local powers. Some Mongols far from the homeland were wiped out or absorbed into the local populations. Others, such as in China, retreated home to the Mongol steppes. The khanates in Central Asia and Russia survived the longest. Perry Anderson believes this happened because the Mongols were able to maintain their nomadic lifestyle from the steppe lands of Russia without assimilating into the sedentary civilizations they ruled, allowing them to maintain their military superiority much longer.

Why did the Mongols risk so much in this period of extraordinary expansion? The quest for wealth drove them to push into China and beyond. Raids into China and other lands were important sources of riches, and once the Mongols decided to stay rather than retreat, everything was done to foster trade. However, the power balance between sedentary and nomadic pastoral societies tilted in favor of large empires with massive resources such as Russia and China, with the increasing popularity of firearms. Horsemanship lost out to the rifle.

George Kallander

Perspective Essay 4. The Keys to Mongol Military Success

The vast Mongol territorial expansion rested on a remarkably well organized and highly effective army and an efficient intelligence service. Mongol tactics were extremely violent and exacted a frightful toll on the peoples who were conquered, bringing widespread terror and population displacement on a heretofore unknown scale.

One man, Temujin, usually known as Genghis Khan (Chingghis or Jenghis Khan, meaning "supreme leader"), laid the foundation for Mongol military success. While still in his teens, he gained a reputation for boldness, strong leadership, cunning, and astute diplomacy. These became the hallmarks of Mongol success. By 1204 he had unified the diverse tribes of Mongolia through a common-law system and the threat of military action. His administrative system was both efficient and fair, and he promoted toleration of all religions. Taking advantage of the skill in horsemanship instilled in every Mongolian male from youth, Genghis assembled a formidable and highly mobile military force; he then prepared to use it to conquer much of Asia. One of the keys to his success and that of his successors was the ability to learn from other societies and cultures. Thus, Genghis acquired from the Chinese valuable military technologies in tunnel engineering, siege engines, defensive armor, and, most important, the use of gunpowder. The Mongols also employed turncoat Chinese to assist in building a formidable naval force. The Mongol intelligence service was quite extraordinary, enabling the Mongol leadership to develop a far better picture of enemy strengths and weaknesses than the latter had of the Mongols.

The word "horde," the usual descriptor for a Mongol field army, suggests that Mongol field forces were very large and unorganized and that they triumphed as a consequence of superior numbers. This is not true. The largest Mongol force assembled by Genghis Khan for a campaign was for the invasion of Persia and numbered fewer than 240,000 men. Indeed, most Mongol armies numbered fewer than 150,000 men. Mongol military success rested instead on superior homogenous organization, superb training, extraordinary discipline, excellent leadership, and speed of execution.

The Mongol Army was essentially a cavalry force. All males ages 15 to 60 and capable of undergoing rigorous training were eligible for conscription into the military. Raising the requisite forces was never a problem, however, because this was a source of honor in the tribal warrior tradition. Virtually all Mongols learned to ride from childhood. Reared in the harsh conditions of the Gobi Desert, they were accustomed to hardships and were generally in excellent physical condition. Commanders were selected on the basis of demonstrated leadership and courage in battle, and discipline was extraordinary, with complete obedience to orders.

The individual Mongol soldier was probably the best trained of his day in the world. Extensive drill allowed coordinated and complicated battlefield maneuvers, which were controlled by means of signal flags, whistling arrows, and fire arrows. All of this permitted great flexibility on the battlefield.

Winter was no barrier to Mongol movement, and the Mongols often utilized frozen rivers as ready-made highways. Unlike the Huns and the Vikings, the Mongols were adept at military engineering and at siege warfare, including the construction of such artillery as the trebuchet. Mongol cavalry was generally more lightly armed and armored than its counterparts, allowing much swifter movement and maneuver.

Each man was equipped with one or more spare horses, which were herded along behind the supply train. Mongol cavalrymen also carried sufficient basic equipment to maintain themselves in the field. Pillaging as they proceeded, Mongol forces were able to live off the land to a great degree, largely dispensing with supply trains.

Mongol field armies usually operated independently, which made it easier to live off the land. The Mongols employed a highly efficient courier system, enabling the field armies to keep in contact with each other and the Mongol leadership and to coordinate their movements in order to concentrate resources at key locations. Most important, before they undertook a campaign, the Mongols devoted considerable attention to planning, including extensive intelligence collection on the enemy: his strengths and weaknesses and the disposition and size of forces.

The Mongols were particularly adept at siege warfare, which they learned during their early fighting in China. A large yet highly mobile siege train consisting of wagons and pack animals accompanied the field armies and was manned by highly efficient Chinese engineers. Mongol military engineers were among the best in the world. If a city could not be taken by storm, the siege train was brought forward and began operations, while the remainder of the army sought out the enemy field forces. The destruction of the latter generally brought the surrender of the town or city, in which case the besieged were treated with only moderate severity. However, if the besieged location resisted, once it was taken it would be given over to pillage and destruction. Oftentimes, the speed of the Mongol advance obviated the need for siege operations and saw towns and cities taken by surprise. On occasion in an assault, the Mongol forces would herd captives in front of their own assaulting troops, forcing the defenders to first kill their own countrymen in order to get at the attackers. The Mongols also employed fire arrows from horse archers as well as from siege engines. Mongol psychological warfare—in the form of the circulation of stories of what happened to a location when there was opposition and the Mongol willingness to treat leniently those who cooperated with them—often ended resistance before it had begun.

Deception was a key element of Mongol success. Thus, in their invasion of Hungary in 1241, when King Béla IV assembled a far larger force against them, the Mongols withdrew before his cautious advance. Late on April 10 about 100 miles northeast of Pest, the Hungarians encountered and defeated a weak Mongol force defending a bridge at Muhi on the Sajó River, a tributary of the Tisza. Béla then established a strong bridgehead on the east bank of the Sajó and camped for the night, with the bulk of his force on the west bank in a strong defensive position of wagons chained together.

The Mongols struck before dawn on April 11, attacking the Hungarian bridgehead with stones hurled by catapults and with an onslaught of arrows, followed closely by an infantry assault. The defenders fought fiercely, and the Hungarians sortied from the main camp to their aid, only to discover too late that the attack was only a feint. Mongol commander Sübetei had led 30,000 men to ford the river some distance south of the bridge and then came in from the south and rear of the Hungarians. Nearly surrounded, the Hungarians found themselves packed into a small area and were there destroyed by Mongol arrows, stones, and hurled burning naphtha.

Béla managed to escape with some of his men to the north toward Bratislava (Pressburg, Pozsony). Although Mongol losses in the Battle of the Sajó River were heavy, the Hungarian force was virtually destroyed, with between 40,000 and 70,000 dead, including much of the Magyar nobility. Only the Danube River prevented a further Mongol advance. Following this victory, the Mongols now ravaged all of eastern Hungary and Transylvania. With a majority of its settlements having been destroyed and a large portion of the population slain during the Mongol occupation, the Hungarian state would have to be completely reconstituted.

The Mongol conquests had lasting impact. Their vast empire unified large areas of Asia and Eastern Europe. Some of this territory, including significant portions of Russia and China, remains unified today although not under the Mongols, who were ultimately assimilated into the local populations.

Mongol subjugation and rule also had pronounced demographic effects, although scholars disagree on the extent. Some hold that the Mongols caused depopulation on a massive scale and instituted major demographic shifts, such as the movement of the Iranian tribes from Central Asia into modern-day Iran. While the Mongols generally spared the lives of the populations of cities submitting to their rule, it was also common practice for them to slaughter all the inhabitants of those resisting. This, of course, encouraged enemies to surrender, but the effects of such policies could also be devastating. Hungary was said to have lost half of its population of 2 million, while the population of China also fell by half during its half century of Mongol rule. Russia also registered significant losses. Estimates of the number of people killed by the Mongols range from 30 million to 80 million.

Some researchers also claim that the Black Death that devastated much of Europe in the late 1340s may have been the result of Mongol biological warfare. In 1347 the Mongols laid siege to Caffa, a Genoese trading outpost in Crimea. When plague infected the besiegers, they reportedly catapulted some of the corpses of those who had died of the plague over the walls of Caffa, infecting the inhabitants as well. When the Genoese departed by ship they took the plague with them to Italy, where it rapidly spread. The Black Death claimed some 20 million people in Europe and perhaps 75 million worldwide.

Spencer C. Tucker

Further Reading

Allsen, Thomas T. *Culture and Conquest in Mongol Eurasia*. Cambridge: Cambridge University Press, 2004.

Allsen, Thomas T. "The Rise of the Mongolian Empire and Mongolian Rule in North China." In *The Cambridge History of China*, Vol. 6, *Alien Regimes and Border States, 907–1368*, edited by Herbert Franke and Denis Twitchett, 321–413. Cambridge: Cambridge University Press, 1994.

Amitai-Preiss, Reuven. *Mongols and Mamluks: The Mamluk Ilkhanid War, 1260–1281*. Cambridge: Cambridge University Press, 1995.

Amitai-Preiss, Reuven, and David Morgan, eds. *The Mongol Empire and Its Legacy*. Boston: Brill, 1999.

Anderson, Perry. *Passages from Antiquity to Feudalism*. London: NLB, 1974.

Brent, Peter. *Genghis Khan: The Rise, Authority, and Decline of Mongol Power*. New York: McGraw-Hill, 1976.

Chambers, James. *The Devil's Horsemen: The Mongol Invasion of Europe*. New York: Atheneum, 1979.

Curtin, Jeremiah. *The Mongols: A History*. Westport, CT: Greenwood, 1972.

Hartog, Leo de. *Genghis Khan: Conqueror of the World*. London: I. B. Tauris, 2004.

Hildinger, Erik. *Warriors of the Steppe: A Military History of Central Asia, 500 B.C. to A.D. 1700*. New York: Da Capo, 2001.

Jackson, Peter. *The Mongols and the West, 1221–1410*. Harlow, UK: Pearson Longman, 2005.

Juvayni, 'Ala' al-Din, 'Ala Malik. *Genghis Khan: The History of the World Conqueror*. Seattle: University of Washington Press, 1997.

Lane, George. *Daily Life in the Mongol Empire*. Westport, CT: Greenwood, 2006.

Lane, George. *Genghis Khan and Mongol Rule*. Westport, CT: Greenwood, 2004.

May, Timothy. *The Mongol Art of War: Chinggis Khan and the Mongol Military System*. Yardley, PA: Westholme, 2007.

May, Timothy. *The Mongol Conquests in World History*. London: Reaktion Books, 2011.

Morgan, David. *The Mongols*. 2nd ed. Hoboken, NJ: Wiley-Blackwell, 2007.

Prawdin, Michael. *The Mongol Empire: Its Rise and Legacy*. New Brunswick, NJ: Aldine Transaction, 2006.

Ratchnevsky, Paul. *Genghis Khan: His Life and Legacy*. Malden, MA: Blackwell, 2006.

Rossabi, Morris. *Khubilai Khan: His Life and Times*. Berkeley: University of California Press, 1988.

Rossabi, Morris. *The Mongols: A Very Short Introduction*. New York: Oxford University Press, 2012.

Roux, Jean-Paul. *Genghis Khan and the Mongol Empire*. Translated by Toula Ballas. New York: Harry N. Abrams, 2003.

Saunders, John Joseph. *The History of the Mongol Conquests*. Philadelphia: University of Pennsylvania Press, 2001.

Spuler, Bertold. *History of the Mongols: Based on Eastern and Western Accounts of the Thirteenth and Fourteenth Centuries*. Berkeley: University of California Press, 1972.

Turnbull, Stephen. *Genghis Khan and the Mongol Conquests, 1190–1400*. New York: Routledge, 2003.

10. WHY DID CONSTANTINOPLE FALL TO THE OTTOMANS IN 1453?

A seminal event in Western if not world history, the fall of Constantinople, the last bastion of the Byzantine Empire and a city that had withstood enemies for 1,000 years, marked a sea change in the political, cultural, and religious organization of the Mediterranean world. Despite heroism on both sides, the fall of the great city owed much to its earlier struggles against not only Turkish and Arab armies but also revolts in the Balkans, the sack of the city in 1204 by Western crusaders, and internal dynastic squabbles. With its fall the balance of trade shifted, which contributed to European interest in finding alternate routes to Asia. The collapse of Constantinople also precipitated future conflicts between the Ottomans and states farther to the west. The capture of the city by Ottoman armies marked the end of the 1,500-year-old Roman Empire, dealt a major blow to Christendom, and permitted the Ottomans to move more freely into Europe.

In explaining the fall of Constantinople, Dr. Nancy Stockdale examines the endemic fragility within the Byzantine state as well as the rise of Mehmet II, the sultan whose precocious start as ruler quickly dispelled rumors that so young a leader would prove no threat to Constantinople. Outnumbered and with their supplies cut off, the Byzantines did their best to hold out; however, in the end they could not overcome Mehmet's cannon, his ingenuity in moving ships overland, or his crack troops, the Janissaries. Reaching much the same conclusion, Dr. Jim Tschen-Emmons likewise focuses on the weakness of the Byzantines. Charting the city's increasing isolation and weakness caused by the challenges it had faced during the Middle Ages—particularly the sack of 1204 and the reign of Michael VIII Palaeologus, who managed to hold off the west at the expense of his eastern border—he argues that the Byzantines, despite the good luck they had experienced in the past, were no match for the superior forces of the Ottoman Turks.

Background Essay

By 1453 one of few remnants of the once mighty Byzantine Empire, the traditional heir of the eastern Roman realms, was one of the final urban bastions of nominally

Christian Anatolia, Constantinople. The reasons for the fall of this previously wealthy and esteemed medieval city are manifold, including foundations based in religious society, economics, rural agrarian bases as food suppliers, alliance structures, and military shortcomings. To understand the Ottoman conquest of Constantinople requires an understanding of the nature of Byzantium's long territorial decline over multiple centuries.

During the seventh and eighth centuries, the Byzantine Empire suffered considerable territorial losses at the hands of the Arabs in the Levant, North Africa, and eastern Anatolia; meanwhile, the Byzantine military busied itself with campaigns against the Bulgars in the Balkans. In response to these new enemies along its periphery and because of these territorial losses and subsequent shortfalls in tax revenue, Byzantium formulated a system of militarily administrated regions known as *thematas* to replace traditional Roman civil governments as a means to control regional taxation and defense. However effective these new governing structures may have been, given that each region had its own general and concerns, Byzantium was engulfed in internecine and civil wars for much of its remaining history. In spite of tremendous odds, Byzantium survived in a much smaller territorial form, largely dominated by military concerns, whereby nobility aspired to martial careers over purely civil service. The fact that cities likewise shifted from large organized Roman civic centers with grand facilities and public amenities to smaller walled, defensible hilltop fortifications as a means to withstand raids is further evidence of troubled times.

Succession disputes among the Franks, the establishment of the Fatimid Caliphate in Egypt as a check against the Abbasid Caliphate in Baghdad, and the conversion of the Bulgars, Magyars, and Rus to Eastern Orthodox Christianity granted the Byzantine Empire a short reprieve, allowing the Greeks to consolidate their smaller empire in the Mediterranean, the Balkans, Anatolia, and Crimea in the Black Sea. Eastern Orthodoxy emerged renewed following the iconoclasm controversies of the eight and ninth centuries, and although the Orthodox Church was relegated to Constantinople, Eastern Orthodoxy expanded among traditionally pagan peoples outside of former Byzantine territorial possessions.

From the 8th to the 11th centuries, Byzantium faced threats from the Normans, Franks, and Italian states in the Mediterranean; Turkic tribes, Serbs, and Hungarians in the Balkans; and the Armenians and Seljuk Turks in Anatolia. Byzantine dynasties played a dangerous game of directing each enemy against the other through a balance-of-power rendition of diplomacy and shifting alliances. The advent of the *pronoia* land grants to militarily viable local elites, based on tax collection and protection during the 11th and 12th centuries, undermined the free peasant apparatus that was previously the underpinnings of central Byzantine agricultural efficacy and subsequently the Constantinopolitan emperor.

With the papal calls to four crusades, the Comnenid and Angelid dynasties vying for the imperial seat in Constantinople attempted to use Western crusaders as

Sixteenth-century Byzantine fresco from the Church of the Annunciation depicting the 1453 Ottoman siege of Constantinople, in which the Ottomans finally captured the Byzantine capital city. (Ilona Budzbon/iStockphoto.com)

a military tool; these crusaders instead captured former Byzantine possessions in the eastern Mediterranean and eventually sacked the Byzantine capital city for plunder and military funds. By 1204 Constantinople's population had reached approximately 300,000, and the outlying wealthy coastal regions along the Black Sea and Aegean, upon which this veritable city-state relied, largely operated under the auspices of Italian maritime powers. This last great allied Christian military force, sent to combat the Ottoman armies, instead conquered and partitioned Constantinople, crippling the Byzantine capital's administrative capabilities and Orthodox underpinnings. Constantinople's Theodosian Walls, a series of three concentric, terraced, fortified walls, did not stand up to the catapults and rams of the Latin army in 1204. This Latin conquest (e.g., Frankish, Venetian, Lombard, and German) not only usurped Constantinopolitan rule but likewise pushed other Greek dynasties to the Byzantine periphery, where they survived as nominal successor states. Nicaea, Trebizond, and Epirus committed to civil war, succession disputes, and resistance to attempts at imperial unity following Michael VIII Palaeologus's reconquest of the city in 1261.

Moreover, religious differences between Rome and Constantinople, which developed over centuries of disagreements and political struggles, further isolated Byzantium. Iconoclasm controversies, mutual excommunications leading to church schism in 1054, Byzantine losses of patriarchal sees outside Constantinople, and mutual exclusions from church councils eroded the once united Christian apparatus.

During the Councils of Ferrara-Florence from 1438 to 1439, Roman Catholic and Byzantine Orthodox clergy alongside Byzantine emperor John VIII Palaeologus attempted to reconcile the rift between their churches as a precursor to military aid against the encroaching Turkish armies.

Ferrara-Florence was more a political ploy formulated by Cardinal Julian Cesarini and Pope Eugene IV to garner popular support and prestige against the growing threat of the conciliar movement at Basel whereby church councils retained greater authority over the papacy, a movement that was also courting a Byzantine alliance for prestige and not so much a real attempt to materialize a military force to protect the threatened Byzantine capital. Ultimately the councils failed in their purpose; no military aid was sent to Constantinople as a defense against Ottoman invasion. The underlying reason for failure was the councilors' inability to reconcile different interpretations of the *filioque* addition to the Nicene Creed.

Appropriately, the city founded by Emperor Constantine I fell under another emperor by the same name. Constantine XI Palaeologus, brother of John VIII, was the final ruling emperor over Constantinople during the Turkish siege of 1453. As a defensive fortification, Constantinople could not remain resilient against the Ottoman attack, which included cannon as siege instruments, and allowed the Ottomans to quickly penetrate the city's tall, flat medieval walls. New designs for defensive fortifications and castle walls following the siege warfare of the Crusades, when defenders preferred long sloping barriers more readily defensible against infantry charges, were likewise resistant to cannon fire. Constantinople, however, was never retrofitted to accommodate those advances in siege warfare. Already controlling much of Anatolia, Sultan Mehmet II and his army took Constantinople following a short siege from April 6 to May 29, 1453, to be the crowning jewel for the Ottoman Empire.

Bryan Garrett

Perspective Essay 1. The Last Days of the Byzantine Empire

The Ottoman conquest of Constantinople in 1453 radically changed the political and cultural environment of the eastern Mediterranean. Using more sophisticated weapons and deliberate strategies of conquest, the Turkish invaders of the Byzantine Empire took advantage of the disintegration of Greek military and political organization as well as the city's overall decline to destroy decisively the remains of the once-mighty Roman Empire of the East. A marriage of technology, potent leadership, and determined siege tactics allowed the Ottomans to take a city that had remained almost entirely undefeated for a millennium.

That being said, the 1453 Ottoman siege of Constantinople was successful in part due to the fact that the Byzantines had never fully recovered from the only other time the city was conquered—by West European crusaders in 1204. Despite the passage of nearly 250 years, the Christian city on the Bosporus never regained the unity or authority that it possessed before the Fourth Crusade brought chaos and destruction to the central city of Orthodox Christianity. The destruction wrought by the crusaders coupled with 300 years of Turkish (first Seljuk and later Ottoman) invasion of its hinterland and heartland ruined the Byzantines' ability to remain politically unified and economically strong. Moreover, Serbian, Bulgarian, and Latin rivals also jockeyed for positions of power against the Byzantines, further weakening chances for political stability.

As a result, infighting among the powerful had reduced the government to a variety of factions with radically different agendas and strategies for maintaining personal power (rather than imperial unity). This fragmentation was well known to the enemies of the Byzantines, particularly the Ottomans, who had begun their piecemeal conquests of Byzantine territory in the late 13th century. By the year of the Ottoman conquest of Constantinople, the Byzantines had lost almost all of their former territories and were more or less surrounded by their Turkish rivals. However, the Byzantines deluded themselves about their situation in 1451 with the ascension of a new sultan, Mehmet II, who was only 21 years old.

Mehmet II, however, turned out to be a masterful ruler and surrounded himself with outstanding advisers. By 1452 he launched the building of an Ottoman fortress on the European side of the Bosporus, only a few miles from the walls of Constantinople. His great-grandfather, Sultan Beyezid I, had already built Ottoman installations on the Asian side of the straits; with the new European fortress, the Byzantines were militarily surrounded by the Ottomans. This was a brilliant strategy, for it choked the straits and prevented European reinforcements from coming to the military aid of the Byzantines.

Military strangulation was only part of the Ottoman strategy for conquering Constantinople. The Turkish Sultanate was able to amass a much more significant military than the Byzantines. While the Greeks could rely on over 12 miles of highly fortified walls, along with 7,000 troops, 26 ships, and about 50,000 people residing in the city, the Ottomans commanded at least 80,000 troops and over 6,000 Janissaries—their crack military leaders. The Ottomans also had over 100 ships at their disposal. This dramatic military advantage made the Turkish invaders a highly potent force.

The Ottomans were also equipped with significant advantages in military matériel. Central to their success was their possession of a giant cannon cast for the invasion. It was so heavy that it took 60 oxen and 400 men to pull it from Adrianople, where it was cast, to Constantinople for the battle. Alongside this massive piece were many medium-size cannon as well as thousands of mounted cavalry. As the battle approached, the Byzantines came to realize that they were facing a far better prepared army than they expected.

Outmanned, the Byzantines sent men to protect the city's outer walls as the Ottomans approached in early April 1453. The middle walls and the seawalls were less secure; the Byzantines sent troops to protect some of their most prominent palaces and churches rather than these positions. For the first three weeks Ottoman cannon fire assaulted the wall of the city, but they remained stable. Moreover, the Byzantines were able to keep Ottoman ships out of the Golden Horn using a boom. At the beginning of the siege, the Byzantines therefore had hope that they would hold off the invaders.

However, Sultan Mehmet II had an ingenious idea that was launched by the end of April. By creating a road on the north side of the Golden Horn—controlled by the Ottomans—lined with greased logs, the Turks were able to maneuver their ships across land and into the Golden Horn. This allowed the Ottomans the naval ability to block supplies for the Byzantines and was also a dramatic psychological blow that reinforced the Greeks' realization of extreme crisis.

Fierce fighting continued for a month until finally, at the end of May, the Ottomans prepared for a radical no-holds-barred military assault on the city. In the darkness of the early morning hours of May 29, the Ottomans launched a series of assault waves on the city. Waves of infantry and Janissary fighters brutally attacked the city and were met by fierce defensive fighting by the Greeks. However, by the end of that day Ottoman troops had breached enough of the city to raise their standard. Upon seeing this, the Greek defense of the city collapsed. Byzantine control of Constantinople was no more.

After the Ottomans secured the city, Sultan Mehmet II issued a proclamation that allowed its residents to return to their homes and property and to practice their religions and professions unmolested. This was a standard practice of Islamic governance and one that had been successful for the Ottomans and previous Muslim empires in the Middle East. However, the loss of the city—renamed Istanbul by its conquerors—was a devastating blow to Christendom. The Greeks could no longer lay claim to an unbroken chain of authority stretching back to the Roman era. Moreover, the Ottomans took advantage of the symbolism of their victory and declared Istanbul their imperial capital. The Ottoman Empire lasted until 1923.

Nancy L. Stockdale

Perspective Essay 2. The Fall of Constantinople: Event and Process

The fall of Constantinople in May 1453 has rightly been viewed as a pivotal date in European history. Byzantium, renamed Constantinople for Emperor Constantine I, became the capital of the Eastern Roman Empire in May 330. Constantinople enshrined much of classical heritage, tradition, and culture. Even to West Europeans, who often viewed the "Greeks" as effete and weak, the Byzantines retained a certain prestige, enough so that some Western monarchs could decry the loss of the city as a second fall of Rome. Romantic notions aside, the fall of the city to the Ottoman Turks was both an event and a process. Ottoman cannon brought down its walls, but this owed much to the fact that Constantinople was the seat of an empire long in decline. The year 1453 represents not only the loss of a city but also the last vestiges of a 1,000-year-old empire.

Byzantine territory, which once stretched from the Bosporus to Italy, had by the 15th century dwindled largely to Constantinople itself and a few islands in the Aegean Sea. The Byzantines had often fought Islamic invaders, from the Muslim conquest of the 7th century down to the Ottoman siege in 1422, and had withstood these. There was thus some hope that the city could hold out again. Situated precariously within the Ottoman Empire and a site of great strategic and economic importance, it was, however, only a matter of time until it fell.

The siege of Constantinople began in 1452, when Sultan Mehmet II sent across the Bosporus a large force to build siege works. Not long afterward in April 1453, the sultan arrived with his army of nearly 80,000 men. Byzantine pleas for Western aid went largely unheeded except for a company of well-trained Italian mercenaries. Though in poor repair, Constantinople boasted triple walls that had proved strong in the past. The addition of harbor defenses further strengthened the Byzantine position.

Ottoman cannon, obtained from Hungary, pounded away at the walls for nearly two weeks. After gaining control of the harbor—no easy feat—Mehmet's besiegers were well placed for the final assault. Continued artillery fire damaged several sections of the city, and the attackers made their first inroads into Constantinople. The siege dragged on for weeks thanks to an excellent defensive effort by the Byzantines and their Italian mercenaries, but on May 29 the sultan's armies captured a tower and raised the sultan's flag. The ensuing panic hurt the defense, and with the death of Emperor Constantine XI Palaeologus in the fighting and the wounding of the Italian mercenary captain, the city was soon in the sultan's hands.

The taking of Constantinople meant more than the loss of another city to the Ottomans. It also marked the end of an era. With the addition of Constantinople, renamed Istanbul, the Ottoman Turks controlled the Bosporus and, through it, Black Sea trade. This meant that the riches of Asia would now have to be reached by other means; not surprisingly, there was new impetus for Europeans in seeking sea routes to Asia. Constantinople had also been the center of Greek Orthodox Christianity, led by the patriarch of Constantinople. This authority now shifted northward to Russia. Moreover, the rich cultural and intellectual heritage of the Byzantines was now transferred westward.

Much of this had already occurred, however. As the Byzantine Empire had shrunk in size, so too had its resources. Greek intellectuals had looked west for years, helping in the process to invigorate the Renaissance; the Grand Duchy of Muscovy, which embraced Greek Orthodox religious traditions, had been on the rise for some time, and West European sailors had already begun the initial voyages of discovery to find new routes to Asia. The fall of Constantinople accelerated these developments, to be sure, but was not alone in causing them.

At the time of the fall of Constantinople, the Byzantine Empire was little more than that one city. Constantinople found itself in the 11th century sandwiched between Norman and Muslim forces. Emperor Alexius I Comnenus, for example, struggled against the Normans in Sicily as early as 1045. A century later in 1143 a Byzantine effort to regain the island nearly bankrupted the state. The effort of Christian Crusades to regain the Holy Land proved to be a disaster for the Byzantine Empire. Indeed, the Fourth Crusade of 1202–1204 became a West European effort directed against Constantinople itself and greatly weakened the empire.

In the next century the Byzantines were desperate enough to seek alliance with France, the Mongols, and the papacy. Michael VIII Palaeologus, then emperor, had hoped that the pope would aid him; the emperor had also hoped to reconcile the two halves of the Christian world, split during the Great Schism of 1054, but to no avail. External enemies were one problem, but internal enemies were another. From 1321 until 1354 the Byzantines struggled in civil war, a conflict that drew in Turks, Bulgars, and Serbs. Only Ottoman help secured the empire again, but this made the emperor a nominal subject of the sultan. In 1399, Emperor Manuel II Palaeologus left for Europe to enlist Western aid, and though Western kings were impressed with him and lamented his situation, they did not bring help. Constantinople was on its own, and thus in 1452 when the Turks returned, there was little the Byzantines could do but await the inevitable.

James B. Tschen-Emmons

Further Reading

Angold, Michael. *Byzantium: The Bridge from Antiquity to the Middle Ages.* New York: St. Martin's, 2001.

Browning, Robert. *The Byzantine Empire.* London: Weidenfeld and Nicolson, 1980.

Carroll, Margaret G. *A Contemporary Greek Source for the Siege of Constantinople, 1453: The Sphrantzes Chronicle.* Amsterdam: A. M. Hakkert, 1985.

Crowley, Roger. *1453: The Holy War for Constantinople and the Clash of Islam and the West.* New York: Hyperion, 2005.

Gibbon, Edward. *The Decline and Fall of the Roman Empire, 1185–1453.* New York: Modern Library, 1983.

Goodwin, Jason. *Lords of the Horizons: A History of the Ottoman Empire.* New York: Picador, 2003.

Gregory, Timothy E. *A History of Byzantium, 306–1453.* Malden, MA: Blackwell, 2005.

Inalcik, Halil. *The Ottoman Empire: The Classical Age, 1300–1600.* London: Phoenix, 2000.

Kinross, Lord [John Patrick]. *The Ottoman Centuries: The Rise and Fall of the Turkish Empire*. New York: William Morrow, 1977.

Leonard of Chios. *The Siege of Constantinople 1453: Seven Contemporary Accounts*. Translated by J. R. Melville Jones. Amsterdam: Hakkert, 1972.

Nicol, Donald M. *The Last Centuries of Byzantium, 1261–1453*. Cambridge: Cambridge University Press, 1993.

Nicolle, David. *Constantinople, 1453*. Westport, CT: Praeger, 2005.

Nicolle, David, John Haldon, and Stephen Turnbull. *The Fall of Constantinople: The Ottoman Conquest of Byzantium*. New York: Osprey, 2007.

Norwich, John Julius. *A Short History of Byzantium*. New York: Vintage, 1998.

Norwich, John Julius. *Byzantium: The Decline and Fall*. New York: Knopf, 1995.

O'Shea, Stephen. *Sea of Faith: Islam and Christianity in the Medieval Mediterranean World*. Vancouver, BC: Douglas and McIntyre, 2006.

Ostrogorsky, George. *History of the Byzantine State*. New Brunswick, NJ: Rutgers University Press, 1969.

Runciman, Steven. *The Fall of Constantinople, 1453*. Cambridge: Cambridge University Press, 1965.

The Siege of Constantinople 1453: Seven Contemporary Accounts. Translated by J. R. Melville Jones. Amsterdam: Hakkert, 1972.

Southern, Richard W. *Western Society and the Church in the Middle Ages*. Harmondsworth, UK: Penguin, 1970.

Treadgold, Warren T. *A History of the Byzantine State and Society*. Stanford, CA: Stanford University Press, 1997.

11. Why Did England Win the Major Battles but France Win the Hundred Years' War?

The Hundred Years' War was a major conflict between France and England that waxed and waned between 1337 and 1453. The main causes of the war were chiefly feudal and dynastic. When the conflict began, England was far better prepared for war than the French; England's government and military were better organized, and it enjoyed both technological and tactical superiority. France, however, had a much larger population and greater resources, which would permit it to finally fend off the English for good by the early 1450s. In the end, even though the English won all of the war's major battles, they ultimately did not prevail in the war. Although it ended in a stalemate of sorts, the Hundred Years' War precipitated a long-running rivalry between the French and English that endured until the early years of the 20th century. The war was nonetheless transformative—it witnessed the ebb of feudal armies and the rise of professionalized forces and saw the waning of aristocratic hegemony and the ascendance of democratization within ranks of the military. Why the conflict ended as it did has attracted scholarly attention for centuries.

In the first perspective essay, Dr. Skip Knox asserts that France did not win the war; rather, the English simply gave up. England's chief war goal, winning the French Crown, entailed ruling all of France, which it was simply unable to do. The English, he argues, were never able to destroy France's ability to wage war, which resulted in a strategic stalemate. Dr. Spencer C. Tucker suggests that the war stirred significant nationalism in France, a development that the English were unable to effectively counteract. Beginning with the reign of Charles V, France introduced significant military and government reforms that would give the French an edge during the last decades of the conflict. Dr. John A. Wagner echoes Dr. Tucker's findings concerning improvements in France's military technology and governmental controls over the long haul and asserts that under Charles V, France wisely eschewed pitched battles, which left the English on the defensive. Better-fortified towns and redoubts, improved artillery, and the employment of handguns also helped the French stave off English attacks, argues Wagner.

Background Essay

The Hundred Years' War was the most important Anglo-French conflict of the Middle Ages. Lasting from 1337 to 1453 (thus actually 116 years), the war had complex roots. It was the last and perhaps most violent stage of an enduring conflict that stemmed from the fact that the English king at the time was a vassal of the French king for Guyenne (part of the region of Aquitaine in southwestern France).

By the early 14th century, however, many new areas of contention had developed: control of Flanders (vital for the English wool market), a succession war in Brittany, the revival of the Auld Alliance between the Scots and the French that caught the English in a vise, control of the English Channel and the North Sea, and from 1328 the French dynastic conflict.

The last son of French king Philip IV had died without an heir. The closest male in a collateral line was Edward III of England, Philip's grandson through Philip's daughter (Isabelle of France, who had married King Edward II of England). Edward III had a valid claim on the French Crown, but French lords were unwilling to accept the idea that he might become their king. In order to reject his claim, French lawyers drew on old Salic Law, which stated that property could not descend through a female.

Philip VI of Valois, Philip IV's nephew, was consequently chosen as French king. Despite the disparity in power between England and France (France was the wealthiest and most populous country in Western Europe), England was ready to support the claim of its popular king Edward III. In 1337, Philip VI seized Edward's fiefs in France. This marked the official beginning of the war. The ensuing conflict can be divided into four phases.

During the first phase, from 1337 to 1360, France suffered repeated military disasters in the Battle of Sluys in 1340, the Battle of Crécy in 1346, and the Battle of Poitiers in 1356 at the hands of Edward the Black Prince. The Treaty of Brétigny (1360) concluded this phase of the war and gave England a third of French territory.

During the second phase, from 1360 to 1415, French armies gradually recovered lost territory. As a consequence, at the end of French king Charles V's reign in 1380, England had lost most of its holdings in the French interior, which meant that it controlled only a few ports. Neither France nor England was able to prosecute the war to its end because of internal difficulties. In France, the intermittent stability of Charles VI prompted a power struggle between the dukedoms of Orléans and Burgundy. Those struggles grew into a full-scale civil war, weakening France considerably. England also faced internal turmoil, including the Peasants' Revolt of 1381, but central authority was reestablished under the kings Henry IV and Henry V.

Miniature of the Battle of Poitiers, September 19, 1356, from Jean de Froissart's *Chronicles*, ca. 1415. A pivotal engagement of the Hundred Years' War, the battle was a devastating defeat for King John II of France at the hands of the English under Edward the Black Prince. (The British Library)

During the third phase of the war, from 1415 to 1429, Henry V seized the opportunity presented by French anarchy. Henry crushed the French Royal Army in the Battle of Agincourt in 1415. He conquered Normandy and used diplomacy (namely an alliance with the Burgundians) to force Charles VI in 1420 to sign the Treaty of Troyes, which disinherited Charles's son. Henry then married Charles's daughter. In 1422 his infant son, Henry VI, was declared king of England as well as of France. Yet most of southern France remained loyal to Charles VII, the Dauphin, who was nicknamed the "king of Bourges" (his tiny capital). England now controlled northern France and had nearly rid itself of Charles VII when French heroine Joan of Arc boosted France's fortunes once again.

In the final stage of the Hundred Years' War, from 1429 to 1453, French troops defeated the English in the siege of Orléans and the Battle of Patay in 1429, the Battle of Formigny in 1450, and the Battle of Castillon in 1453. In 1435 Charles VII signed the Peace of Arras with Burgundy, which destroyed the Burgundian-English alliance. France had rallied around the nationalist concept of the kingdom as a united nation, with the *goddons* (the English) as foreigners to be swept away. Between 1449 and 1453, England lost all its territories in France except for the tiny foothold of Calais. The Hundred Years' War had definitively come to an end by 1475, when Louis XI of France prevented an English invasion by bribing English king Edward IV into returning to England.

Fewer than 20 major battles occurred during the Hundred Years' War, which nevertheless saw innumerable skirmishes. Towns were more often taken by surprise or treason than by siege. English raids (there were five between 1339 and 1360) often had a greater psychological than physical impact, and the employment of a scorched earth policy by French kings proved to be a useful deterrent.

The Hundred Years' War led to further political unrest in the Wars of the Roses (1455–1487) in England and the War of the Public Weal (1465) in France. The Hundred Years' War also had a disastrous impact on France's wealthy citizens; the defeats of the 14th century and the widespread destruction across France, combined with the Black Death, paralyzed the economy. Not until the middle of the 15th century did French trade return to the levels of 1300.

The war also proved to be costly for England's 3 million inhabitants. As long as the booty flowed from France, English kings enjoyed the support of the English Parliament, but any setback could provoke a change of dynasty, as with the House of Lancaster in 1400 and the House of York in 1455.

Although the Hundred Years' War was a chaotic conflict between kings, with no definitive peace at its end, its principal legacies were the development of modern centralized monarchies and the two kingdoms' transformation into bona fide nation-states.

Paul K. Davis and Stanley Sandler

Perspective Essay 1. England's Failure to Win the War

France did not so much win the Hundred Years' War as England failed to win it. There were several reasons for this. First, victory meant winning the French Crown; second, securing victory meant having to rule France, and this proved to be too much for English resources; and third, the English, despite their victories, never destroyed the French capacity to wage war. French war aims, on the other hand, were more modest and local; they wanted the Crown to remain French and also wanted to receive homage for the Duchy of Gascony.

Two critical points in the war explain its outcome. Both occurred when it seemed to all that the English had won or were on the verge of winning the war. The first occurred in the wake of the victory at Poitiers in 1356, and the second came after the victory at Agincourt in 1415.

The Battle of Poitiers occurred a decade after the equally significant Battle of Crécy (1346), and the two should be considered jointly. In each, thousands of French soldiers were killed, and many more were captured. Poitiers was all the more devastating because of the losses a decade earlier; moreover, at Poitiers the English captured French king John II and his son, taking them to captivity in London. By 1358, France was in utter disarray. Not only had much of the French nobility been killed or captured, along with vast wealth plundered or taken in ransom, but there was widespread rebellion in France. It is therefore easy to see why King Edward III (r. 1327–1377) of England decided to launch what he hoped would be a final blow in 1359.

Edward raised an army, landed in France, and marched on Rheims, where the kings of France were traditionally crowned. Yet a year later, the Treaty of Bretigny suspended the conflict on the basis of the status quo, despite the fact that Edward lost no battle and returned to England with his army.

The cause of this development can be found in the three factors previously enumerated. First, despite Crécy and Poitiers and the destruction wrought by these battles, Edward could win the war only if he was crowned king of France. He was thus forced to invade and not merely win on the battlefield but also capture the city of Rheims to make good his claim to be the king of France. This he was unable to accomplish because of the other two factors. England had in fact not destroyed the ability of the French king (a young Charles V) to raise another army. France was much larger than England in size, population, and wealth. Thus, the French were able to send a force to Rheims sufficient to prevent a quick English victory. Edward could not lay siege to Rheims because of precarious supply lines, and in any case it was December before he had reached Rheims. He had to abandon his objective and raid into Burgundy just to keep his large army supplied. The next spring he tried to besiege Paris, but the Dauphin (the future Charles VI) simply took position behind the city walls, forcing Edward to give up that attempt within a week. Not long after, the English effort was crippled by a terrible storm. Edward returned to England and opened negotiations for a truce.

Here all three factors were in play. Edward failed to destroy the ability of the French to raise sufficient forces to hold key points, he was unable to control enough of northern France to use it as a base for further operations, and by making the attainment of the Crown, which was a political objective, the definition of victory, he essentially made the military objective nothing less than total victory.

Agincourt illustrates these factors as well. Although the battle itself was important, it was the aftermath that is of most interest here. As at Crécy and Poitiers, the French nobility suffered heavy casualties, leaving France—and particularly northern France—bereft of leaders. There is no doubt that the battle had an immediate and serious effect on the ability of the French to wage war. It did not, however, mean that the French could not raise more forces. They could, and they did.

After Agincourt, Henry V (r. 1413–1433) managed to extricate his little army from France and return to England, having secured for England the port of Harfleur. He needed to do much more, which is why he returned in 1417. The weakened French forces could not resist, and Henry was able to carry out his strategic plan to occupy all of northern France, culminating in the capitulation of Rouen at the end of 1418. England effectively made Normandy a province, appointing a lieutenant governor there in 1419.

Later that year the Duke of Burgundy was assassinated by French soldiers, and within a few months his son had formally allied with the English. This alliance was crucial, for it brought both men and money to the English side and provided an important base of operations. Between Normandy and Burgundy, Henry V at last had the resources he needed to win the war. In 1420 he was able to conclude the Treaty of Troyes, making him the heir to Charles VI and marrying Charles's daughter, Philippa of Hainault. The next year his new wife was crowned queen of England in London, and by the end of the year she had borne Henry a son, Henry VI. To all appearances, by the end of 1421 England had triumphed; yet within a decade, it all was slipping away.

One of the three objectives appeared won, for the king of England was also the king of France, although Henry VI would not be formally crowned until a few years later. There was, however, a rival. Charles VI was insane. His son, the Dauphin and future Charles VII (Charles the Well-Served), was not a strong leader, but the Armagnac party in particular used him as a rallying point. Also, although weak militarily, the French could still inflict damage, as in their victory at Bague in 1421. The battle itself was small and saw comparatively few casualties, but in it the Armagnacs destroyed the English force and killed the Duke of Clarence, who was Henry V's brother. This small engagement demonstrated that the English had not yet destroyed French resistance and that claiming the French Crown meant more than merely placing an English king on the throne of France—it also meant removing any other legitimate heir around whom resistance could form.

The third factor would ultimately prove to be the most important. English resources were stretched thin. Each English victory entailed ruling more of France. As long as a rival could claim to be the true king and resistance seemed possible, ruling France meant garrisoning or destroying castles and occupying towns. This proved to be an enormous drain on the English treasury, leading the English Parliament to soon decide that the occupied territories should pay for their own occupation. Crushing taxes, especially in Normandy, led to the steady impoverishment of that duchy. As long as the Burgundians were willing to help with the burden and as long as the French were being pushed back, this precarious financial balance could be maintained.

From 1422 on, however, that balance shifted. Henry V died at only age 35 while on campaign, and Charles VI died later that same year. This meant that an infant was now the king of England (and theoretically of France), while Charles VII could now claim to be the king. This shifted the political realities; in England there was fierce maneuvering for power among factions at court, and in France there was in contrast a unifying of forces around Charles VII. He was not a charismatic leader, but in 1429 Joan of Arc emerged and turned him into a symbol. She not only helped break the siege at Orléans, which would have given the English control of central France but helped him march to Rheims, there to be crowned the king of France. The final blow came in 1435, when Duke John of Burgundy switched sides.

This was the final act in the aftermath of Agincourt. England still insisted on finding a way to make the king of England also the king of France, and this aim was simply not negotiable from either side. By 1435, Normandy had been stripped bare. The English Parliament was split by factions and would fund expeditions only when one faction or another gained the upper hand. Most of those expeditions failed. Meanwhile, the French were growing stronger militarily. From this point on, the French goal was to drive the English completely out of France, while the English goal was simply to hold on to what they had.

In 1449 French forces recovered Rouen. The following year saw a significant French victory in the Battle of Formigny. The English suffered three times the number of casualties as the French. Compounding this was the loss of Bordeaux the following year. Gascony was the heartland of English holdings in France, and the loss of its key port was a severe blow. The English were forced to find a way to send an army to attempt recovery. That army was destroyed at Castillon in 1453. England was too exhausted to continue the struggle, and the long war came to an end.

Ellis L. (Skip) Knox

Perspective Essay 2. French Governmental and Military Reforms

England won the major battles of the Hundred Years' War; however, in the process the conflict awakened French nationalism and led to governmental and military reforms that prevented the English from winning the war itself. The Hundred Years' War between England and France began in 1337 and lasted on and off until 1453. Certainly one of the most protracted and bloody wars in history, it had major effects on both England and France. The war began as a feudal struggle but assumed a nationalist character and led to a worldwide rivalry between France and Britain that extended until the beginning of the 20th century.

The chief causes of the war were feudal and dynastic. The feudal issue arose from the complicated relationship between the kings of France and the kings of England. The kings of England were also the rulers of Aquitaine in southwestern France and thus owed liege homage to the kings of France. The dynastic issue arose from the kings of England claiming to be the kings of France. Along with these two major issues were the growing commercial influence of the English in Flanders, specifically the wool trade, and French influence in Scotland and the assistance rendered by them to the Scots in their wars with England.

In 1328, King Philip VI sent troops and established French administration of Flanders. English king Edward III responded with an embargo on wool in 1336, leading textile merchants in Flanders to conclude a treaty with England and prevail on Edward to declare himself king of France that same year. Philip then declared forfeit the English fiefs in France south of the Loire River and sent his troops into Guienne (Aquitaine). The war was on.

England, although far smaller than France, was much better governed, and its king had better access to its resources. Thanks largely to reforms begun by King William I the Conqueror (r. 1066–1087), power in England was highly centralized, and the king had great authority. William had reorganized England administratively, unifying the country under firm royal authority. He also introduced Norman law and justice. William broke the Scandinavian connection, but he also ushered in a long period of English confrontation with France.

In 1086 William had ordered a full inventory of property, known as the *Domesday Book*. Once this was ascertained, he insisted that taxes owed be paid directly to the king. This was of immense importance in strengthening the English Crown, especially in England's later dealings with France.

France was much larger in territory than England and more populous and enjoyed far greater wealth. It ought to have had every advantage in the war, but these great assets could not be utilized because power was diffuse, and the country was poorly administered and led. Because 14th-century France was so large and given the primitive communication systems of the time, local authority was strong. France also had a tradition of weak kings and a strong, fractious nobility, with some of them more powerful than the monarch. The Crown was thus unable to use the great resources of the realm effectively. In many ways, then, England was far better prepared for war than France.

Thanks in large part to far more effective leadership, the English won virtually all the major battles of the war, including the naval Battle of Sluys (June 24, 1340), which made possible the English invasion of France, and the land battles of Crécy (August 26, 1346), Poitiers (September 19, 1356), Agincourt (October 15, 1415), Cravant (July 31, 1423), and Verneuil (August 17, 1424). The war was also immensely lucrative for the English, with many participants making vast fortunes. With the English controlling the sea, the war occurred entirely on French soil. Considerable sums were also made from ransoming the many noble prisoners taken in battle, especially after the Battle of Poitiers and the capture of French king John II (r. 1350–1364) and so many of his nobles.

At the same time, chaos reigned in France with the collapse of the central government. This was perhaps the low point for France in the war. In the years immediately after the Battle of Poitiers, the English ranged over France almost at will. Those French who were able sought refuge in castles and fortified towns. Freebooters known as *routiers* also ravaged the countryside. These unemployed former soldiers lived off the land by looting, robbing, raping, and destroying. In 1358, a frustrated French peasantry rose up in a short-lived rebellion centered in the Oise River Valley north of Paris and known in French history as the Jacquerie. The nobles soon crushed it, however. Clearly something had to be done if France was to survive.

In 1364, Charles V came to the French throne. Ruling until 1380 and known as Charles the Wise, this physically weak yet able and realist monarch probably saved France, rescuing it from the military defeats and chaos that had occurred under his immediate predecessors Philip VI and John II. With the able assistance of the first great French military commander of the Hundred Years' War, constable of France Bertrand du Guesclin, Charles V reformed the French military. His reforms provided for new military units, established the French artillery, and created a permanent military staff. Charles also reorganized the navy and ordered the rebuilding of castles and city walls (most notably in Paris). He also dominated the new financial arrangements established by the noble-controlled Estates General.

Mercenaries, known as free companies, continued to prey on the civilian population, however, pillaging, raping, and looting. King Charles VII (r. 1422–1461), on the advice of his leading advisers, finally solved this problem by establishing a regular standing army. It was formed of the *compagnies d'ordonnance*, companies of 30–100 lances each commanded by a reliable captain and at first totaling 1,500 men but later expanded by Louis XI to 3,000 men. All were well paid and received rations, so there was no need for them to prey on the peasants. Also, their sole loyalty was to the Crown. The establishment of such professional armies signaled the end of feudalism and English military dominance.

The siege of Orléans (1428–1429), the great city on the Loire River, brought forward the person of Jeanne d'Arc (Joan of Arc). Jeanne's appearance was fortuitous. Answering what she believed to be a call from God to drive the English from France, she led the French relief expedition to Orléans, although she had only the empty title *chef de guerre*. Jeanne greatly inspired the French people. This was not diminished by her martyrdom following her capture by the Burgundians and execution by the English. Jeanne brought about an explosion of French nationalism. Even in death she has remained one of history's most powerful national symbols; certainly she was central in the French victory in the Hundred Years' War. The Maid of Orléans, as Jeanne was known, united her people and in the process helped produce the French nation.

Although the Hundred Years' War continued for another two decades, the relief of Orléans was the turning point in the long war. Peace between France and Burgundy in 1435, Charles VII's effective advisers (the king became known as "Charles the Well-Served"), and military reforms in France that provided for a standing army and an infantry militia finally brought the expulsion of the English. The Hundred Years' War ended with the fall of Bordeaux to the French in 1453. England also fell into its own disunion in the Wars of the Roses (1455–1485) between the houses of Lancaster and York.

Spencer C. Tucker

Perspective Essay 3. Superior French Resources Turn the Tide

How could the English continually win the major battles but ultimately lose the Hundred Years' War? Both the success in individual battles of the English and the final victory of the French in the war itself resulted, during the long course of the war, from the shifting of important strategic, tactical, and technological advantages from the English to the French.

Under Kings Edward III and Henry V, the English nullified the French strength in heavy cavalry through the use of superior technology (the longbow) and superior tactics (the innovative combination of longbow archers and dismounted men-at-arms in powerful defensive formations). These advantages won battles for the English. Under Kings Charles V and Charles VII, the French nullified these English strengths with their own superior technology (artillery and handguns) and adjustments in strategy and tactics (avoidance of large battles and greater expertise in siege warfare). In this way, the French eventually brought to bear their overwhelming superiority in resources and manpower and thus forced the English to end the war and withdraw from France.

During most of the 14th century the main English strategy was the *chevauchée*, a swift, destructive raid in force designed to cripple both French morale and France's ability to wage war. By moving rapidly through the French countryside destroying farms, villages, and crops, the English sought to advertise the French king's inability to defend his people and territory against the superior military might of his rival. The *chevauchée* was also easier and cheaper to organize and equip, less destructive of English manpower, and highly destructive of French economic resources. The *chevauchée* not only reduced the ability of towns and whole regions of France to pay the French king's war taxes but also forced local communities to divert resources to building expensive walls and fortifications needed to provide havens from English raiders.

In the wars that Edward I had fought in Wales and Scotland in the late 13th century, the English had learned the devastating effectiveness of the longbow, which in terms of distance, accuracy, and rate of fire far outstripped the crossbow, the preferred missile weapon of the French and continental armies. In these same British wars, the English also discovered the value of integrating bodies of archers armed with longbows into bodies of dismounted men-at-arms. This formation offered the English a formidable density of resistance; the men-at-arms gave cover to the archers, who in turn devastated enemy cavalry with a hail of arrows, thereby allowing the men-at-arms to wreak havoc among the disrupted enemy formations. Even more important to the English war effort was the development of the highly mobile mounted bowman, whose numbers steadily increased as the war progressed. Unknown to continental armies before Crécy, the longbow, the mounted bowman, and the ability of bowmen to act in unison with men-at-arms gave the English a technical/tactical battlefield advantage that the French in the 14th century could not match.

The vital importance of archers to English battlefield success prompted strategic adjustments by the French under Charles V to counter the advantage the longbow gave their enemies. If archers gave the English an advantage in pitched battle, Charles nullified that advantage by avoiding battle. The bitter experience of defeat at Crécy and Poitiers forcibly shifted the French military focus from huge armies of heavy cavalry comprising the personal contingents of the great nobility to smaller dismounted forces recruited, paid, and controlled by the Crown. These forces were used not to give battle but instead to defend fortified towns and castles and harass English troops.

The English use of the *chevauchée* also stimulated French advances in the design and construction of town walls and fortifications. By the time of Charles V's death in 1380, the French shift in strategy had rendered the English reliance on the *chevauchée* and on archer-dominated defensive battles ineffective. Unable to bring the French to battle or to capture walled towns, the English Rheims Campaign of 1359–1360 came to naught, while earlier English territorial gains in Gascony and the southwest were largely wiped out.

English military fortunes revived in the early 15th century thanks to the eruption of the French civil war and the accession to the English throne of the energetic and ambitious Henry V. Meanwhile, Charles V's son and successor, Charles VI, proved to be not only incompetent but also insane, and other members of the royal family, most notably the king's brother Louis, Duke of Orléans, and his cousin John, Duke of Burgundy, led factions that fought each other for control of the royal government. This turn of events completely undid the strategic and military reforms of Charles V and explains the French military disaster at Agincourt in 1415, when another large army of mounted French knights dashed itself to pieces against the classic English defensive formation of archers and dismounted men-at-arms. The English were allowed to regain their tactical/technological advantage by a French monarchy distracted by civil war.

Although when Henry V renewed the war in 1415 he largely abandoned the *chevauchée* and embraced a strategy of besieging and occupying strongpoints, the importance of archers to the English war effort continued to grow. However, the new English emphasis on siege warfare stimulated new French advances in military architecture and led to recognition by both sides of the growing importance of artillery. Henry V understood that if he was to conquer and control Normandy and other French provinces, he needed artillery to reduce strongpoints.

In the early 15th century the French also recognized the need for effective artillery to both defend and besiege town walls and fortifications. As the century progressed gunpowder became cheaper and easier to handle, as the invention of the powder mill in the late 1420s eliminated the need to laboriously mix powder in the field. The new powder increased projectile velocity tremendously. Shot also became more deadly as cast-iron cannon balls replaced stone projectiles, and new methods of casting cannon made them less prone to exploding in the faces of the operators and easier to site and fire. All of these advances heralded the beginning of a process that eventually allowed handguns and artillery to win the advantage over the bow.

French military architects also developed new types of fortifications designed to restore the balance between defender and besieger, which artillery had unbalanced in favor of the latter. Walls were made lower and thicker to better withstand artillery impacts, and towers were built only to the height of the wall to aid in the placement of defensive artillery and were rounded in order to better deflect cannon shot. Although archers were not without their uses in siege warfare, a growing expertise in artillery use and fortification design began by the 1430s to shift the technological advantage in the war to the French.

Beginning in the 1430s, a revived French monarchy began to press its growing tactical and technological advantages. Certainly luck played its part in placing the French Crown in this more advantageous position. The death of Henry V in 1422 deprived the English war effort of his excellent leadership, while the rise of Joan of Arc and the crowning and consecration of Charles VII in 1429 as well as the ending of the French civil war in the 1430s gave the French Crown a strength and prestige it had not enjoyed since the 1370s. Charles VII was thus able to revive the military and strategic reforms that had proven successful for his grandfather. In the 1440s royal edicts created a new army of 15 companies of 100 lances, with each lance consisting of one man-at-arms, two archers, and three armed attendants. The most revolutionary feature of this new force was that it was a standing force to be kept in existence even in time of peace rather than being disbanded when open hostilities ceased, as had been the custom on both sides throughout the war. Well trained, well paid, well supplied, and effectively led by men appointed by the king, this reformed French Army was quite impressive. Another edict in 1448 created the "franc-archers," standing companies of royal crossbowmen who were raised and maintained by local communities. Although paid only while on campaign, they were exempted from payment of royal taxes during peacetime.

Along with these military reforms, Charles VII acquired the finest collection of artillery on the continent thanks to the work of Jean Bureau, a civilian who made himself an expert in the collection and deployment of cannon. Although the English had artillery, they never had the quality or quantity of guns of the French, and they never had anyone with the expertise of Bureau. These French cannon proved their worth at the successful sieges of numerous English-held towns, such as Montereau in 1437, Meaux in 1439, and Pontoise in 1441. Bureau's handling of the artillery was also vital to the success of the Norman Campaign of 1449–1450. At Formigny in 1450, the French culverins (small cannon) so disrupted the archers in the traditional English defensive formation that the French were able to hold the field until reinforcements arrived and win the day. Thanks at least in part to the effective use of artillery, Formigny became the first major engagement not won by the English since Bannockburn in 1314.

In April 1451 with Normandy cleared of English troops, Jean d'Orléans, Comte de Dunois, invaded English-held Gascony accompanied by Bureau and an imposing artillery train. The French guns helped force the surrender of all English positions in Gascony by July 1452. Although John Talbot, Earl of Shrewsbury, retook Bordeaux several months later, Bureau returned in 1453 with companies of the reformed royal army and an artillery train of more than 300 guns. On July 17 Bureau's guns, carefully sited to provide enfilade or flanking fire as well as direct frontal fire, destroyed the attacking English at Castillon. With their formations broken, the English were easy prey for Bureau's troops. The French, standing on the defensive with superior artillery, had gained the tactical and technological advantage on the battlefield. Having lost the advantage that bowmen had long given them, the English could no longer win battles against a revived French monarchy. Although no treaty was ever signed, Castillon was the last battle of the war.

John A. Wagner

Further Reading

Allmand, Christopher. *The Hundred Years War: England and France at War, c. 1300–1450.* Cambridge: Cambridge University Press, 1988.

Allmand, Christopher, ed. *Society at War: The Experience of England and France during the Hundred Years' War.* Edinburgh, UK: Oliver and Boyd, 1973.

Allmand, Christopher, ed. *War, Government and Power in Late Medieval France.* Liverpool: Liverpool University Press, 2000.

Barker, Juliet R. *Agincourt: Henry V and the Battle That Made England.* New York: Little, Brown, 2006.

Barnies, John. *War in Medieval English Society: Social Values in the Hundred Years War, 1337–99.* Ithaca, NY: Cornell University Press, 1971.

Burne, Alfred Higgins. *The Agincourt War: A Military History of the Latter Part of the Hundred Years' War, from 1369 to 1453.* Westport, CT: Greenwood, 1976.

Burne, Alfred H. *The Crecy War: A Military History of the Hundred Years' War from 1337 to the Peace of Bretigny, 1360.* Ware, UK: Wordsworth Editions, 1999.

Curry, Anne. *Agincourt: A New History.* Stroud, Gloucestershire, UK: Tempus, 2005.

Curry, Anne. *The Hundred Years' War.* New York: Macmillan, 2003.

Curry, Anne, and Michael Hughes, eds. *Arms, Armies and Fortifications in the Hundred Years War.* Woodbridge, Suffolk, UK: Boydell, 1999.

DeVries, Kelly. *Joan of Arc: A Military Leader.* Gloucestershire, UK: Sutton, 1999.

Duby, Georges. *France in the Middle Ages 987–1460: From Hugh Capet to Joan of Arc.* Translated by Juliet Vale. Oxford, UK: Blackwell, 1991.

Favier, Jean. *La Guerre de Cent Ans.* Paris: Fayard, 1980.

Neillands, Robin. *The Hundred Years' War.* London: Routledge, 2001.

Nicolle, David, and Angus McBride. *French Armies of the Hundred Years' War, 1328–1429.* Oxford, UK: Osprey, 2000.

Perroy, Edouard. *The Hundred Years' War.* New York: Capricorn Books, 1965.

Potter, David, ed. *France in the Later Middle Ages, 1200–1500.* Oxford: Oxford University Press, 2003.

Prestwich, Michael. "English Armies in the Early Stages of the Hundred Years' War: A Scheme of 1341." *Bulletin of the Institute of Historical Research* 56 (1983): 102–113.

Reid, Peter. *Medieval Warfare: Triumph and Domination in the Wars of the Middle Ages.* New York: Carroll and Graf, 2007.

Rogers, Clifford J. "The Military Revolutions of the Hundred Years War." *Journal of Military History* 57 (1993): 241–278.

Rogers, Clifford J. *War Cruel and Sharp: English Strategy under Edward III, 1327–1360.* Woodbridge, UK: Boydell, 2000.

Seward, Desmond. *The Hundred Years; War: The English in France, 1337–1453*. New York: Atheneum, 1978.

Sumption, Jonathan. *The Hundred Years' War*, Vol. 1, *Trial by Battle*. Philadelphia: University of Pennsylvania Press, 1999.

Sumption, Jonathan. *The Hundred Years' War*, Vol. 2, *Trial by Fire*. Philadelphia: University of Pennsylvania Press, 2001.

Sumption, Jonathan. *The Hundred Years' War*, Vol. 3, *Divided Houses*. Philadelphia: University of Pennsylvania Press, 2009.

Vale, Malcolm. *The Angevin Legacy and the Hundred Years War, 1250–1340*. Oxford, UK: Basil Blackwell, 1990.

Villalon, L. J. Andrew, and Donald J. Kagay, eds. *The Hundred Years' War: A Wider Focus*. Leiden: Brill, 2004.

PART III

THE EMERGENCE OF MODERN EUROPE AND THE AMERICAS (1500–1825)

12. Was the English Civil War Primarily a Political Rebellion, a Constitutional Struggle, or a Religious Conflict?

The English Civil War was actually a series of three separate confrontations that took place during 1642–1646, 1648–1649, and 1649–1651. These conflicts pitted the supporters of Parliament (Parliamentarians) against supporters of the monarchy (Royalists), first under King Charles I and then, after his execution, under his son, King Charles II. Although such a Civil War proved to be a lengthy and costly affair with far-reaching effects on the English governmental system (including establishing the precedent that an English monarch could not rule without Parliament), its root causes remain a topic for scholarly debate. The conflict resulted in the trial and beheading of Charles I in 1649, the replacement of the English monarchy with the Commonwealth of England and then the Protectorate under Oliver Cromwell, and an end to the Church of England's monopoly on Christian worship in England. Whether the war was a political rebellion, a constitutional struggle, a religious conflict, or some combination thereof has been a long-standing matter of historical interpretation.

The three perspective essays that follow demonstrate the wide range of interpretations concerning the causes, course, and legacies of the English Civil War. In the first essay, Dr. James Daybell argues that the civil war was neither inevitable nor the culmination of a long history of religious or political tension; rather, he views it simply as the result of the constitutional pressures of immediately preceding events such as the Bishops' Wars. By contrast, in the second essay Dr. William B. Robison asserts that the English Civil War was primarily a religious conflict resulting from the monarchy's ecclesiastical policies. He traces the role of religion in a series of English crises dating back to the early 1500s, demonstrating how religion and its practice suffused other political, economic, and social issues. Dr. John A. Wagner takes a more personal approach to the question, examining the persona of Charles I and outlining how his personal defects and character flaws led to the civil war. Charles I was a staunch believer in the divine right of kings and was not in any way given to compromise or even explanation concerning his actions. Indeed, Charles believed that he was accountable only to God. In Wagner's view, the war was a rebellion against Charles, whose various negative qualities created unnecessary conflict.

Background Essay

The English Civil War emerged as a result of the conflict between Charles I and Parliament in regard to his attempts to circumscribe and curtail the authority of the representative institution of the English realm, in addition to his pursuit of forcing Anglicanism on his subjects. While imbued with the notion of divine right of kings to rule by the grace of God, which he inherited from his father James I and was an acceptable notion of kingship, Charles I was at odds with the fiscal limitations imposed on him by Parliament. Thus, he levied forced loans, and those who refused to contribute were imprisoned. Charles I did not realize that when Henry VIII gave Parliament the right to make him supreme head of the English Church he also gave Parliament a power over the Crown that it was willing to use to protect its rights as a group of property owners and taxpayers.

When Charles called a session of Parliament in 1628 to raise money, both the House of Lords and the House of Commons granted him funds in exchange for agreeing to the Petition of Right. This held that the king could not enact taxes or borrow without the consent of Parliament. This situation infuriated Charles, and he governed without a Parliament for 11 years and continued to circumvent Parliament's power over the purse by seeking loopholes to raise money. One such expedient was ship money. This was originally a levy imposed on maritime counties and was used for the purpose of maintaining the Royal Navy, but Charles utilized it for his expenses outside defense.

Charles also infuriated English Puritans (English Protestants who disapproved of Catholic rituals in Anglicanism) by placing Archbishop William Laud as head of the Anglican Church; Laud immediately set about persecuting Puritans. Moreover, Charles I and Laud aggravated the situation by imposing the Anglican Book of Common Prayer in Presbyterian Scotland, effectively triggering a rebellion (1638–1640).

The Scottish rebellion forced Charles I to convene Parliament in 1640 in an attempt to unify the realms amid a Scottish invasion after having dismissed a prior Parliament that refused to grant him funds. The Long Parliament, known as such due to its continuous session from 1640 to 1653, immediately outlawed Charles's extraparliamentary taxes and removed Laud. Some more radical members sitting in the House of Commons, mostly Puritans, were keen on extracting power from the Crown and granting it to Parliament, leading to divisions within that body and the emergence of the Royalist faction. This is illustrative of the fact that moderates resisted the more radical Puritan objectives and remained loyal to the Crown, despite their disagreements with Charles I. When Charles attempted to arrest parliamentary leaders in 1642, however, he triggered civil war.

The initial years of the civil war (1642–1646) pitted the Parliamentary Roundheads (who cut their hair short in the Puritan style), based in London and the wealthy southeast, against the Royalist Cavaliers, based in the northwest. While most early engagements were indecisive, in the Battle of Marston Moor (July 2, 1644) a Scottish-Parliamentary force decisively defeated a Royalist army under Prince Rupert. A devout Puritan officer, Oliver Cromwell, reorganized Parliamentary forces into the New Model Army, removing commanders with Royalist sympathies and replacing them with strict Puritan leadership. The New Model Army defeated Charles's Royalist forces in the Battle of Naseby (June 14, 1645), subsequently taking the monarch prisoner.

Painting of the Battle of Naseby, artist unknown. This battle of the English Civil War on June 14, 1645, ensured the defeat of the Royalists by the Parliamentary New Model Army. (Photos.com)

While the Royalists were defeated, the next two years were spent attempting to make a settlement with Charles. However, the Parliamentary coalition split up owing to religious and ideological differences regarding the future of England. Scottish Presbyterians, Puritan Independents, and radical factions (Levellers and Diggers) all sought different ends regarding religious matters. The Scottish Presbyterians sought to turn the Anglican Church into a national institution with elected leaders akin to theirs. Independents rejected any form of a state church and advocated religious toleration (except for Catholics). Levellers advocated for suffrage and popular sovereignty, and the Diggers pushed for the abolition of private property.

These divisions led to Scottish Presbyterians joining forces with resurgent Cavalier forces to fight for the king against Parliament, given that he had sent out feelers that he would accommodate their religious interests. However, Cromwell effectively crushed this attack and ended divisions within Parliament by staging a coup. In December 1648, Colonel Thomas Pride only allowed ministers of Parliament friendly to Cromwell to enter Parliament (Pride's Purge), effectively creating what was known as the Rump Parliament. This would also ensure the exclusion of more moderate members of Parliament who might oppose the execution of the monarch. Cromwell took the opportunity to deal with Charles I (now stripped of his title and referred to as Charles Stuart) and had him executed on January 30, 1649, thereby removing him as a source of contention for rebellion.

Cromwell thereby instituted an English Republic, effectively ruling through the New Model Army and the Rump Parliament, that was in essence a military dictatorship known to posterity as the Interregnum (1649–1660). Cromwell conquered Ireland (1649) and then Scotland (1650–1651), ensuring English control of all the British Isles and eliminating potential dissent. In 1653 he disbanded Parliament and instituted himself as lord protector of England due to continuing divisions within that body. While he was hesitant to have himself made king, Cromwell and his family enjoyed the royal trappings of the Crown. Moreover, taxation imposed on the realm to fund his wars were far greater than that of his royal predecessor. Cromwell ruled in this manner until his death in 1658, after which his son Richard became the next and final lord protector. Because Richard lacked military experience and Parliament continually ignored the army's requests for funding, the army demanded that he dissolve Parliament, a move that caused his resignation on May 25, 1659. In 1660, General George Monck forced the Rump Parliament to recall the Long Parliament to include those excluded during Pride's Purge. The Long Parliament dissolved itself, and a general election was held for the first time in 20 years. In 1660 the Convention Parliament invited Charles's son to return to the throne as Charles II, thereby restoring the Stuart monarchy.

Abraham O. Mendoza

Perspective Essay 1. A Crisis of Constitutional Reform

The English Civil War resulted from the development of Parliamentary and Royalist parties divided regarding issues of constitutional reform. The religious dimension of the conflict is intertwined with political and constitutional issues. Marxist interpretations of the English Civil War as a "bourgeois revolution" have now been debunked. Older interpretations see the outbreak of the war as inevitable, the result of long-term constitutional conflict between Parliament and the monarchy. At one time historians stressed the opposition of Parliament to arbitrary monarchy, an "opposition" they saw as unified and ideological, fueled by constitutional principle and self-confident Puritan zeal, that could be traced back to the late 16th century. More recently, revisionist historians have emphasized the consensual nature of politics during the 1630s and before, with politicians seeking agreement and compromise. Today's historians have also reassessed the nature of Parliament, downplaying its role and significance, and stressed the difficulties of pinning down political allegiances. Thus, two years before the war started no one could have foreseen the events as they unfolded.

We are left, then, looking at the years 1640 to 1642 for an explanation of the breakdown in relations between Parliament and the Crown. Viewed through the lens of constitutional issues, the real reasons relating to why King Charles I raised his standard in Nottingham on August 22, 1642, an act that declared civil war, center on a series of new and intriguing questions. What was it that drove men with seemingly moderate reforming aims at the beginning of 1640 along a more radical trajectory that ultimately ended with the execution of the monarch and the formation of an English republic? Moreover, for civil war to take place the king needed to have supporters, which was far from true at the start of the Long Parliament, which sat from November 3, 1640, until December 1648. Why, then, did Charles have a Royalist party by 1642, and in what ways were political allegiances drawn along constitutional lines? This focus on the years 1640 to 1642 means that the outbreak of civil war can only be understood against the pressure of events and was directly related to the Bishops' Wars in Scotland between 1639 and 1640 and the Irish Rebellion of 1641, both of which were poorly handled by the king.

Charles dismissed an ineffective Parliament in 1629, ushering in 11 years of personal rule. The years of personal rule were marked by arbitrary monarchy in that the king ruled without parliamentary consent. Although Charles employed the expedient of necessity and crisis to justify his actions for the good of the country, this was far from a new theory of sovereignty of the absolutist sort that developed in

Europe during the first half of the 17th century. Moreover, English government throughout the 1630s rested on cooperation with local elites. Charles relied on members of the county gentry who acted as local justices of the peace, sheriffs, and tax collectors. In other words, he governed through a network of local officials, many of whom were exactly the same men who sat in Parliament before 1629 and after 1640 and during the interim period collected taxes, mustered troops, and administered in local government. During the 1630s, Charles was able to raise revenues and govern without calling members of Parliament to Westminster. Far from being a tyrannical monarch, Charles ruled throughout the 1630s with a high level of political acquiescence. For much of that period he was in a strong position, running a balanced budget. The Bishops' Wars in Scotland changed all this, and by April 1639 the king was forced to call the Short Parliament (which sat for only three weeks) while facing in Scotland the failure of his religious policy and a challenge to his political authority.

Political acquiescence on the day-to-day running of the country, however, is not the same as lack of opposition to the Crown or its policies and advisers. There was a current of criticism throughout the 1630s in response to Charles's resurrection of ancient feudal rights. Furthermore, there were elements within the country wanting to protect parliamentary liberties. These critics were members of the establishment who believed in monarchy but within certain limits and were committed to social order. Rather than dismantling the monarchy, many of the key figures who went on to oppose the king, such as the Earl of Bedford, hankered after the rewards, power, and influence that flowed from high office and a position at the royal court. In 1640 government was still in working order, and it was not until the institutional collapse of Charles's government over war with Scotland in 1639 that political discontent found a means of expression in the Long Parliament.

When Parliament met in November 1640 there was a remarkable degree of unity among its members, who were galvanized around the desire to dismantle what they saw as the worst aspects of Charles's government. The first targets were the king's chief advisers. Parliament rounded on William Laud, the archbishop of Canterbury and the leading churchman in the country, and Thomas Wentworth, Earl of Strafford, a close royal adviser, who were blamed for the religious and fiscal innovations of the 1630s. Members of Parliament then sought to abolish the unpopular royal fiscal measures of the 1630s and the ancient royal prerogative courts.

Afterward, a series of parliamentary acts were passed in the first year to ensure that the monarch could not rule without Parliament. The Triennial Act of February 1641 obliged the monarch to call a new Parliament within three years of dissolving the last one, and an act of May 1641 specified that the present Parliament itself, rather than the king, should decide when it should be dissolved. These were short-term measures aimed at curbing royal authority and ensuring parliamentary powers, passed by those distrustful of the king. The May Act, for example, was a rather knee-jerk reaction to the Army Plots of May 1641, an alleged conspiracy of Royalist officers to raise an army in Scotland and lead it against Parliament.

Amid fear for its own safety, Parliament issued the Ten Propositions (June 1641). This imposed limitations on the king's choice of advisers and control of the army and sought to constrain the activities of his Catholic wife Henrietta Maria and her followers, whose religious interference aroused widespread suspicion. The more radical measures adopted by Parliament are part of the explanation of why Charles began to gain supporters from Parliament in 1641 and 1642.

Moreover, after the euphoria of the initial first few months of the Long Parliament, divisions and disagreements began to appear among its members. Discussions centering on the method of removing the unpopular Earl of Strafford revealed differences. The House of Commons's decision to move against Strafford by a parliamentary bill of attainder, decreeing that he was guilty of treason and therefore subject to the death penalty without any requirement to prove it by law, worried moderate members. At this point, some sided with the king. Deeper divisions emerged in relation to the issue of church reform. At first a majority in Parliament favored moderate religious reform and sought to remove Archbishop Laud and sweep away the unpopular changes he made to the church and also reduce the influence of the bishops.

From then on disagreements emerged, with those who actively sought a true "godly reformation" of the Church of England attacking bishops and tithes (taxes paid to the church) and petitioning for "root and branch reform." The Scots (who were Presbyterians) added pressure for further change, and there was an outbreak of iconoclasm (the destruction of church property, stained glass, and communion rails) that accelerated the polarization of opinions as people feared for their property and worried about social unrest. Religious and constitutional issues were fundamentally related. Many of those who were against the bishops also attacked landlords and tithes, which had clear implications for the vested interests of landowners.

Those who defended the existing Anglican Church saw it as a defense of the prevailing social order, a commitment to the traditional status quo and hierarchies within the state and wider society. There was therefore an Anglican party before there was a Royalist party, and many of those who supported the king did so for religious reasons. Those who sided with Parliament wished to see a radical overhaul of the church and the imposition of a strict moral and religious code. In addition, many reacted negatively to the parliamentary leadership's tactics of using thousands of Londoners picketing Parliament to intimidate members of both houses into approving controversial new measures.

There were similar fears about popular participation in politics among conservative elements in response to the publication of the Grand Remonstrance, which listed Parliament's grievances against the king's government and appealed to the people at large. Moderates were also concerned about its violent language and the proposals that it put forward to approve the king's ministers. It was approved only by the narrow margin of 159 to 148 in late November 1641.

The temperature of the political mood was rising on both sides. In January 1642 Charles attempted a coup against parliamentary leaders, impeaching John Pym, John Hampden, William Strode, Denzil Holles, and Lord Kimbolton but failing to arrest them in the Commons. This was interpreted as an attack on parliamentary liberties and strengthened the resolve of the parliamentary leadership to push forward a radical reform program. Parliament had for a while been distrustful of Charles's use of the army and sought to extend its own control of local militias. In December 1641, a militia bill had been drafted. It proposed that Parliament nominate commanders of the armed forces. Charles refused to consent to the legislation. The bill, however, was later issued as an ordinance in March 1642 (circumventing the need for royal assent), with Parliament effectively claiming that it was acting independently of the Crown in the interests of defending the nation.

Similarly, the Nineteen Propositions sent to the king in June 1642 by the House of Lords and the Commons was a radical and uncompromising set of proposals that sought to ensure parliamentary control of the army and oversight of foreign policy, to make the king's ministers answerable to Parliament, and to supervise the education and marriages of royal children. This unprecedented move worried growing numbers of constitutional Royalists such as Sir Edward Hyde, who saw unacceptable constitutional innovations that interfered with royal prerogative and encouraged popular participation in politics. Fears of the consequences arising from such measures were clearly articulated in the King's Answer (published in June 1642). It claimed that the parliamentary proposals would be "a total subversion of the fundamental laws," a dismantling of the ancient constitution.

In the end, then, it was a constitutional struggle—informed by religious beliefs—that led to the outbreak of civil war in England in August 1642. Events had reached such an impasse by that summer that there seemed no other solution. At the beginning of 1640 Parliament had a relatively moderate appetite for reform, and despite the fact that there were harsh critics of Charles and his advisers, such men were isolated firebrands and malcontents. Over the next two years against a backdrop of events in Scotland and Ireland, the parliamentary leadership was forced to adopt a more radical program of reforms, distrustful of the king's erratic and devious behavior and actions during these years. It was the nature of their demands, their encroachment on areas considered to be sacrosanct royal prerogative, and the populist expediency of their methods that drove people toward the king.

James Daybell

Perspective Essay 2. A Religious Conflict

The English Civil War was primarily a religious conflict resulting from the ecclesiastical policies of Charles I and Archbishop William Laud and the resulting hostility of English Puritans. Tensions building in England since the beginning of the Reformation were exacerbated by bloody sectarian wars on the European continent. These reached a breaking point when Arminianism—which bases salvation on free will rather than predestination—transformed the king and the archbishop into irreconcilable enemies of Calvinists. In the crisis that led to the English Civil War, religion suffused every political, social, and economic issue—it was the essential cause of and fundamental to the conflict.

Between the opening of Henry VIII's Reformation Parliament in 1529 and the beginning of Charles I's personal rule a century later, religion was the most consistent source of friction in Britain. Parliaments met only intermittently, court factions came and went, social tensions ebbed and flowed, the economy alternately flourished and declined, and individual aristocratic and gentry families rose and fell. But God, Satan, and their earthly adherents were ever present. At any point after the 1520s a significant portion of people in both England and Scotland opposed the official religion, and thus persecution and religious polemic became regular features of life. Both nationally and in the localities, religious hostilities produced or exacerbated factional strife. With disturbing frequency, sectarian stress gave rise to sinister plots or erupted into violence, and a cycle of reform, reaction, rebellion, and repression bred long-lasting bitterness and suspicion.

In England, every Tudor rebellion from the 1530s had a religious component. After Mary, Queen of Scots, was imprisoned there in 1568, she became the focus of a series of Catholic plots to overthrow Elizabeth I. In Scotland, Catholic-Protestant violence began in the late 1520s and continued even after James VI succeeded Mary. In Ireland the Reformation heightened existing anti-English sentiment, and Catholicism was a major factor in Irish rebellions under Elizabeth. Abroad, the Reformation spawned armed sectarian conflict in Germany and Switzerland, the French Wars of Religion, and the Dutch Revolt against Spain. Eventually England took the Protestant side in both France and the Netherlands and became involved in the Anglo-Spanish War (1585–1604), which included the famous Spanish Armada campaign in 1588. All of this left Protestants with lasting fears of an international Catholic conspiracy.

By the time the Scottish king became James I of England in 1603, Protestants there were fairly united in hostility to Catholicism and in allegiance to Calvinist theology. But while Anglicans were content with the status quo, Puritans wanted further reform to eliminate remnants of Catholicism. The Gunpowder Plot of 1605—in which a handful of Catholic fanatics nearly succeeded in blowing up Parliament—gave further credibility to conspiracy theories, inspired lingering anger and fear, and strengthened Protestants' providential view of history, wherein the Gunpowder Plot and defeat of the armada proved that God was on their side.

Despite James's brutal punishment of the plotters and support of harsher penal laws against Catholics, Puritans remained skeptical of his commitment to true religion. He made this worse in 1617 by issuing the Book of Sports, which encouraged Sunday recreation in apparent disregard for the Sabbath. Also, control of the church was a bone of contention in the Parliaments of 1621 and 1624. In Scotland, James antagonized Presbyterians by attempting to enforce Anglican practices in the Five Articles of Perth between 1616 and 1622. Further, some English clergy who attended the Synod of Dort (1618–1619) returned as converts to Arminianism, made alarmingly manifest by Richard Montagu's 1624 tract *New Gag for an Old Goose*. Also problematic was James's foreign policy, especially his pursuit of a Spanish marriage for his sons, Henry and Charles, and his failure to take the Protestant side in the Thirty Years' War (1618–1648).

Conflict sharpened when Charles I took the throne in 1625. His father's favorite, George Villiers, first Duke of Buckingham, remained the most influential man in the kingdom until his assassination in 1628. One of many reasons for his unpopularity was his Arminianism. The new king appointed dean of the chapel royal William Laud, who became Britain's most influential cleric and eventually replaced Buckingham as the preeminent royal adviser. Historians who contend that Laud was Arminian are more convincing than those who deny it, but in any case his opponents believed it, and his staunch anti-Puritanism and fondness for ritual did nothing to dissuade them. Montagu's *Appello Caesarum* (1625), which had support from Buckingham, Laud, and for the most part the king, provoked fierce attacks on Arminianism in the Parliaments of 1625, 1626, and 1628–1629.

Meanwhile, the religious overtones of the Anglo-Spanish War (1625–1630) and the Anglo-French War (1627–1629) heightened English anti-Catholicism, while failure in both conflicts raised questions about Charles and Buckingham's competence and commitment. The wars were expensive, and in 1627 Arminian clergy backed the king's "Forced Loan" when others refused. In 1628 Parliament laid out its political grievances in the Petition of Right, which stemmed in no small part from fear that the king was bent upon establishing divine right absolutism. The House of Commons also produced a remonstrance for enforcement of anti-Catholic penal laws. The 1629 session of Parliament witnessed more attacks on Arminianism due partly to Laud's elevation to the bishopric of London. At its close, the king's opponents in the Commons passed Sir John Eliot's Three Resolutions, one of which identified as "capital enemies" (criminals subject to the death penalty) anyone seeking to introduce "popery or Arminianism."

Charles then dissolved Parliament and began his "Personal Rule," but this in no way abated sectarian strife. Although many opposed the king's questionable measures for raising revenue, most subjects at least reluctantly complied. But even here there were religious overtones, for the authors of the king's policy were Laud and Thomas Wentworth, whose activities in Catholic Ireland were suspect. Where purely religious divisions were concerned the stakes were higher, for there could be no compromise with doctrines that Puritans saw as leading to eternal damnation. Worse, the proponents of such doctrines appeared to be winning. In 1626, Puritans had established the Feoffees for the Purchase of Impropriations to buy up church lands and ensure that the income they generated went to clergymen, but in 1632 Charles suppressed the group. In 1633 the king appointed Laud as archbishop of Canterbury, reissued the hated Book of Sports, and imprisoned Puritan lawyer and writer William Prynne. Meanwhile, after Buckingham's death the Catholic queen Henrietta Maria's improved relationship with the king added to widespread fears of a popish plot.

Although modern scholars discount a royal plot to establish Catholic rule, there were Catholics in England and abroad who tried to eliminate the penal laws or even convert the king. In 1637 Puritans Prynne, clergyman Henry Burton, and physician John Bastwick were charged with sedition, fined, and imprisoned in the Tower of London. Charles forced a Code of Canons on Scotland in 1636 and the next year attempted to impose the Anglican Book of Common Prayer. This provoked rioting among Presbyterians, inspired thousands to sign a national covenant early in 1638, and later that year led the General Assembly of Kirk to repudiate the Prayer Book and abolish episcopacy. Meanwhile, the conflict with Scotland led to rumors that Wentworth might bring in Catholic troops from Ireland.

The First Bishops' War in 1639 produced only a small skirmish before ending in the Treaty of Berwick, which broke down because Charles refused to compromise over religion. In 1640 seeking funds for war, he summoned Parliament for the first time in 11 years. But he dissolved it after three weeks because of opposition led by John Pym, William Fiennes, and others who sympathized with Scottish Presbyterians and had their own grievances concerning parliamentary privilege, royal fiscal expedients, and Arminianism. However, Charles and Laud browbeat the Convocation into approving the Canons of 1640, which required clergy to preach the divine right of kings and included the oath swearing support for episcopacy, "et cetera."

In the Second Bishops' War in 1640, some of Charles's own troops mutinied, destroyed Catholic altars, and were unsuccessful on the battlefield. The king's intransigence regarding Scottish Presbyterianism backfired. It forced him to accept a Covenanter army of occupation in northern England with the Treaty of Ripon that October and set the stage for trouble when in November he summoned the Long Parliament.

The first parliamentary session (November 1640–September 1641) failed to pass the Root and Branch Petition to abolish episcopacy but declared illegal the Canons of 1640, impeached Laud and Wentworth, reversed earlier doctrinal and liturgical changes, abolished the courts of the Star Chamber and High Commission (which enforced laws against heterodoxy), and passed the Triennial Act to ensure regular sessions of Parliament (a blow against divine right). It also agreed on the Ten Propositions, which among other things required Protestant education for the king's sons and included strictures against the queen, recusants, and papal agents.

The country was rife with rumors of conspiracy. Reformers, led by the Dukes of Bedford and Warwick in the House of Lords and Pym in the House of Commons, polarized opinion by issuing the Protestation, which required that subscribers pledge to defend true Protestant religion against popery and uphold the king, Parliament, and English liberties. Others gravitated to the king, who grew stronger after the Treaty of London in August led to the Scots' withdrawal. But in November the Protestants' worst fears were realized and the king's recovery was compromised by the Irish Rebellion, whose Catholic leaders claimed royal sanction.

In December, Parliament made funding the Irish war conditional on Charles's acceptance of the Grand Remonstrance, which enumerated over 200 grievances, called for removing bishops from the House of Lords, accused Jesuits of undermining law and encouraging the king's absolutist tendencies, and denounced his Scottish ecclesiastical policy. Charles retaliated in January 1642 with the failed attempt to arrest the five members (all Puritans), after which he fled London. Distrusting Charles to deal with Catholic rebels, Parliament refused him funds and passed the Militia Ordinance in March, allowing Parliament to raise its own troops.

In June Parliament sent Charles the Nineteen Propositions, a radical attack on royal prerogative (divine right again) replete with religious provisions, including the demand that he reform the church according to a national synod's dictates and enforce the laws against Jesuits and recusants. Charles refused and began raising troops on June 11. Parliament appointed a committee of safety on July 4, and the king raised his standard at Nottingham on August 22, beginning the war that led to revolution and his own execution in 1649.

It is impossible to imagine matters reaching this stage without the long-term divisive influence of religion. A diffuse group of revisionist historians have argued that the goal of Tudor and early Stuart politics was consensus and that the English Civil War resulted from a short-term crisis. More recently, postrevisionists have reemphasized long-term conflict, particularly in politics and religion. They rightly note that while political consensus may have been the ideal, conflict was common and repeatedly arose over similar issues, and it intensified over a period of many years preceding 1642. Arguably, though, the goal of opposing religious groups from 1529 on was never consensus but a victory of annihilation over enemies seen as minions of the Antichrist. Elizabeth I, moderate Anglicans, and perhaps even James I may have hoped for an inclusive church, but Catholics and Puritans made that impossible. Antipopery had a long history prior to the English Civil War, and if

Catholics never were sufficiently numerous to pose a real danger to the Calvinist majority under the Stuarts, the rise of Arminianism—which looked like popery to Puritans and whose adherents developed a countervailing anti-Puritan mind-set—posed a far more plausible threat. While it is risky to use events after 1642 to explain the civil war's causes, the explosion of religious discontent it unleashed had been brewing for a long time.

William B. Robison

Perspective Essay 3. A Rebellion against King Charles I

In the three and a half centuries since the English Civil War, the event has been characterized as a political rebellion, an ideological struggle, a religious war, and a social revolution. While there can be little doubt that the origins of the conflicts that convulsed the three kingdoms of Britain in the mid-17th century were complex and involved elements of each characterization, this essay proposes that the war was caused by Charles Stuart and his policies. The English Civil War and the related struggles in Scotland and Ireland in the 1640s constituted in essence a rebellion against the acts and omissions of the king.

Historians are virtually unanimous in pronouncing Charles a failed king. They are also in widespread agreement that the character flaws that caused Charles's personal failure also caused the national tragedy of the civil war. What were these personality defects? Here again there is broad consensus among historians. Shy, aloof, and afflicted with an embarrassing stutter, Charles was rigid, stubborn, and authoritarian. Convinced that he ruled by divine right, he lacked and saw no need for the attributes of a politician, such as negotiation, compromise, and a sense of the possible. Charles never understood the need for bargaining and concession; he simply declared what his conscience demanded and expected obedience. When forced by circumstances to give way, he usually did so with ill grace and sought always to take back what he had given when the opportunity arose. He could also be vindictive toward those who opposed him such as Sir John Eliot, who was left to die in the Tower of London in 1629 because he refused to submit publicly to royal authority. Affronts to Charles's conception of kingship were rarely forgotten or forgiven. Most historians trace the roots of Charles's inability to act effectively as king to a deep insecurity, a lack of confidence that ill-befitted a king in a personal monarchy. The virtues that are ascribed to Charles, including marital fidelity, family feeling, refined taste, and moral uprightness, made him a good husband and father but not necessarily a good king.

Although considerable work has gone into trying to determine how and why Charles's personality formed as it did, there is little consensus among historians on this question. The most notable work in this regard is Charles Carlton's 1995 biography of the king, which uses psychoanalysis to examine Charles's life, particularly his childhood. Born in 1600, Charles was the second son of James VI of Scotland, who became James I of England upon the death of his kinswoman, Elizabeth I, in 1603. Charles's childhood does not appear to have been particularly happy. He lived with foster families in Scotland and England until he was 12 years old and had no close relationships either with his parents or his older brother. His upbringing was probably not significantly different from that of other royal children of the time, however. In 1612 Charles became heir to the throne upon the death of his much-admired elder brother Henry, who, according to surviving anecdotes, teased and belittled his younger brother, perhaps thereby playing a role in the development of Charles's stutter.

As sole male heir, Charles was sheltered and protected but was little regarded by his father, who showered his affection on his charming but inept favorite, George Villiers, Duke of Buckingham. Although initially rivals, Charles and Buckingham became close friends after 1618 and remained so until the duke's assassination in 1628, three years after Charles succeeded his father on the English and Scottish thrones. Indeed, many of Charles's initial difficulties with Parliament involved attempts to protect Buckingham from the consequences of his own incompetence.

Charles's childhood may explain his insecurity, shyness, and lack of a common touch. Uncomfortable among people, he sought as king to restrict access to the court, which he made one of the most rigid and formal in Europe. Such remoteness was not popular; the English people preferred to see and hear their monarch as they had in the days of Queen Elizabeth.

Charles's upbringing does not, however, clearly explain his approach to governing, about which there is disagreement among historians. Charles Carlton argues that the king was lazy and uninterested in the daily routine of government. In 1630 the king personally attended only 9 of 99 recorded council meetings. In contrast, Kevin Sharpe views Charles as a hardworking king who stood "at the center of government," especially during the personal rule in the 1630s. But however diligently the king may have applied himself to business, his authoritarian manner made him a hard man to work for. His servants found that he would not take advice if it differed from his own beliefs. And historian Julian Davis cited the case of William Laud, the immensely unpopular archbishop of Canterbury, as proof that the king's minions often received the blame for policies and actions that were entirely those of the monarch.

Charles's views on his role as king, and especially on what was due him as ruler, are clear from his words and actions. First and foremost, he expected obedience, once reminding his advisers that in the end "the question was of obeying the king, not of counselling" him. Charles expected loyalty and willing service, which included financial support as a right, not as things that could or should be negotiated or compromised. Upon the dissolution of Parliament in 1629, Charles promised no new sessions until "our people shall see more clearly into our intents and actions and . . . shall come to a better understanding of us and themselves." As historian Norah Carlin observed, such a sentiment was typical of Charles, who never considered the reverse—that he might need to better understand his people.

By acting on such beliefs, Charles saddled himself with a reputation for duplicity and bad faith among his opponents. In 1628, for instance, the king promised the Commons that he would publish the Petition of Right along with his second, less equivocal, acceptance of it. However, once Parliament was dissolved, Charles ordered the printer to publish instead his ambiguous first answer, to which were added further qualifications and exceptions.

In 1641, Charles's involvement in various shadowy army plots to undo concessions he had made to the Long Parliament contributed to the growing belief in the Commons that the king could not be trusted with military forces and that he would eventually use any troops available to him to overawe Parliament and destroy his opponents. And, of course, after the end of the First English Civil War in 1646, Charles overthrew any faith the army leadership had in him by negotiating secretly with the Scots while negotiating openly with the army, thereby initiating the Second English Civil War. Oliver Cromwell and his colleagues were left to conclude that Charles could never be trusted to abide by his agreements. Charles's duplicity eventually eroded even the faith and loyalty of many of his supporters. Over the course of the 1640s, a significant portion of the political realm lost faith in the king, believing him unfit to govern the kingdom, command the army, or protect the Protestant religion.

Still, Charles was not without intelligence or a certain ability to inspire affection and loyalty, at least as leader of a faction or cause if not as leader of a government. His failures would have been much less catastrophic and war would likely have been averted if he had been merely incompetent. England knew how to deal with incompetent monarchs, as the histories of Edward II, Richard II, and Henry VI attest. Had Charles been devoid of any political skills or ability to inspire loyalty or affection, Parliament would have deposed him or he would have been unable to generate sufficient support to fight a war. War was only possible in 1642 because a significant part of the realm was ready to take up arms on the king's behalf.

Charles proved to be a competent military leader, being more adept at fighting enemies during wartime than accommodating opponents during peace. And had a king either more able or less able than Charles come to the throne in 1625, war would have been unlikely; it was the personality of Charles I, an unusual mix of ability and incompetence, that led to war.

In matters of religion, the area in which his penchant for secrecy and double-dealing generated the most fear and distrust, Charles had about him the rigidity of a fanatic. The entire crisis leading to war might well have been avoided if the king had not insisted, against advice, on imposing the Anglican Prayer Book on the Scottish Church. The policy was entirely the king's, and its implementation illustrated Charles's ignorance of and indifference toward the political and religious realities of a kingdom he knew little about. All Charles understood was that the Scots were his subjects, that as such they owed him obedience, and that his religious principles told him there should be uniformity of religion throughout his realms. When the Scots resisted, Charles eschewed negotiation with the Scots, seeing in the Covenant only a wicked attempt to diminish the powers of a divinely sanctioned monarch. On the subject of bishops, another religious point at issue between Charles and the Scots, the king affirmed his belief that "bishops are *jure divino*. . . . I find as much authority for them as for some articles of the creed." And in an unfortunate comparison that only supported rumors of his secret Catholicism, Charles declared Presbyterian government "absolutely unlawful . . . [and] more erroneous than the church of Rome." From such declarations it was but a short step to virtual acceptance of martyrdom, as the following lines, written by Charles in 1646, seem to suggest: "I have already cast up what I am like to suffer: which I shall meet (by the grace of God) with that constancy that befits me . . . as I may justly hope that my cause shall not end with my misfortunes." With such a mind-set and such a wide divergence in religious opinion from that of his subjects, Charles transformed religious dispute into open warfare.

In 1637, whatever its discontents, England seemed far from any possibility of civil war. How then did war come about five years later, and what role did Charles play in the transformation? The importance of the king's imposition of the Prayer Book on Scotland has already been mentioned. Charles could have refrained from doing this, could have reversed his decision once he met resistance, or could have consulted with the Scottish Privy Council, rather than just with his like-minded clerical appointees, before going forward. He did none of these things, and each omission accords fully with the king's unshakable convictions regarding the nature of his authority over church and state. Because of his expectation of unquestioning obedience, Charles was shocked by the violent reaction the Prayer Book aroused and was unwilling to accept that his miscalculation had provoked that reaction. He thus was not prepared with sufficient force and funds to quell dissent before it got out of hand and had to again summon Parliament, which again subjected Charles to a political process in which he did not believe. And when the king tried to stand strong he only made matters worse, as with the botched attempt to arrest the five members of Parliament in early 1642. By then, both the king and the House of Commons had come to see war as the only solution to a crisis that the king himself might, at any number of points, have prevented or defused.

John A. Wagner

Further Reading

Adamson, John. *The Noble Revolt: The Overthrow of Charles I.* London: Weidenfeld and Nicolson, 2009.

Braddick, Michael. *God's Fury, England's Fire: A New History of the English Civil Wars.* London: Allen Lane, 2008.

Carlin, Norah. *The Causes of the English Civil War.* Oxford: Blackwell, 1999.

Carlton, Charles. *Charles I: The Personal Monarch.* 2nd ed. London: Routledge, 1995.

Cogswell, Thomas, Richard Cust, and Peter Lake, eds. *Politics, Religion and Popularity in Early Stuart Britain: Essays in Honour of Conrad Russell.* Cambridge: Cambridge University Press, 2002.

Collinson, Patrick. *The Religion of Protestants 1559–1625.* Oxford: Oxford University Press, 1983.

Cust, Richard. *Charles I: A Political Life.* Harlow, UK: Pearson Longman, 2007.

Cust, Richard, and Ann Hughes, eds. *The English Civil War.* London: Arnold, 1997.

Fincham, Kenneth, and Peter Lake, eds. *Religious Politics in Post-Reformation Britain.* Rochester, NY: Boydell and Brewer, 2006.

Fletcher, Anthony. *The Outbreak of the English Civil War.* London: Edward Arnold, 1981.

Gentles, Ian. *The English Revolution and the Wars in the Three Kingdoms, 1638–1652.* Harlow, UK: Pearson Education, 2007.

Gregg, Pauline. *King Charles I.* New Haven, CT: Phoenix, 2001.

Hibbert, Christopher. *Charles I: A Life of Religion, War, and Treason.* 2nd ed. New York: Palgrave Macmillan, 2007.

Hughes, Ann. *The Causes of the English Civil War.* Basingstoke, UK: Palgrave, 2001.

Morrill, John. *Revolt in the Provinces: The People of England and the Tragedies of War, 1630–48.* London: Longman, 1998.

Purkiss, Diane. *The English Civil War: Papists, Gentlewomen, Soldiers, and Witchfinders in the Birth of Modern Britain.* New York: Basic Books, 2006.

Richardson, R. C. *The Debate on the English Revolution Revisited.* New York: Routledge, 1989.

Russell, Conrad. *The Causes of the English Civil War.* Oxford, UK: Clarendon, 1990.

Russell, Conrad. *The Origins of the English Civil War.* Oxford: Oxford University Press, 1984.

Sharpe, Kevin. *The Personal Rule of Charles I.* New Haven, CT: Yale University Press, 1996.

Sommerville, J. P. *Royalists and Patriots: Politics and Ideology in England, 1603–1640.* 2nd ed. London: Longman, 1999.

Stone, Lawrence. *The Causes of the English Revolution, 1529–1642.* London: Routledge and Kegan Paul, 1972.

Tyacke, Nicholas. *Anti-Calvinists: The Rise of English Arminianism c. 1590–1640.* Oxford: Oxford University Press, 1987.

Young, Michael B. *Charles I.* London: Macmillan, 1997.

13. Did the Inca Civil War Play an Important Role in the Spanish Conquest of the Inca Empire?

The Inca Civil War has also come to be known as the Inca Dynastic War, the Inca War of Succession, and the War of the Two Brothers. As the Spanish incursion into the Inca realms commenced, the Inca political structure was becoming increasingly unstable. This instability was caused chiefly by fighting between two brothers—Huáscar and Atahualpa, sons of Sapa Inca Huayna Capac—regarding succession to the Inca throne. Huáscar precipitated the war because he believed that he alone was the legitimate heir to his father's throne. But Atahualpa enjoyed a key advantage in the conflict, namely tactical superiority over his brothers' forces and supporters. At the same time, smallpox, introduced to the Incas by Spanish European colonizers, had already begun to decimate the Inca population. The Incas had no previous exposure or immunity to the contagious disease, so they were highly susceptible to it. The fighting that broke out as a result of this growing instability is believed by some historians to have contributed to Spanish success in extending its power over what is now Peru and ultimately toppling the Incas in South America. Certainly, internal power struggles contributed to the weakening of Inca power to a degree. However, it is also arguable that the Inca Civil War did not contribute directly to the downfall of the Inca Empire but instead sustained Inca power against Spanish encroachment for a period of time. While they ultimately fell to Spanish colonial authority, the Incas were able to maintain a modicum of their autonomy, at least for some time.

In the first perspective essay, Dr. Rebecca Seaman argues that although at first glance Spanish dominance seemed to be the deciding factor in the civil war, the internal political divisions that were already in evidence when the conflict began actually contributed to a fairly effective Inca resistance movement. That movement stymied the Spanish conquest for a time and, if anything, delayed Spain's final subjugation of the Inca people. She also points to smallpox as a contributing factor to the Incas' demise. In contrast, in his perspective essay David F. Marley asserts that conflict between the Incas and other neighboring groups, which had preceded the Spanish presence, contributed to the weakening of the Inca political and military position in relation to the Spanish. Given this situation, the Inca realms were ripe for Spanish conquest.

Background Essay

The Inca Civil War, also known as the Inca Dynastic War, the Inca War of Succession, and the War of the Two Brothers, occurred during 1519–1523. It was fought between two brothers, Huáscar and Atahualpa, sons of the Sapa Inca Huayna Capac, regarding succession to the Inca throne. The war followed Huayna Capac's death in 1527, although fighting did not begin until 1529 and lasted until 1532.

The Sapa Inca, a hereditary position, was supreme head of the government, the military, and spiritual matters within the Inca Empire. When the 10th Sapa Inca, Topa Inca Yupanqui, died in the latter part of the 15th century, his firstborn son, Sapa Inca Huayna Cápac, became ruler of the Tahuatinsuyu kingdom, an empire spanning the Andes for nearly 3,000 miles. Huayna Cápac's principal wife (first sister) lived in Cuzco with their sons, Ninan Cuyochi and Huáscar. Huayna Cápac had a third son, Manco Cápac, with another of his sisters. The Sapa Inca spent his last years in present-day Quito, Ecuador, with his Ecuadorian wife (daughter of the last *scyri* of Quito, whose kingdom Huayna Cápac had conquered) and their son Atahualpa. It was Atahualpa and his half brother Ninan Cuyochi, who accompanied Huayna Cápac on military campaigns and were his constant companions. Huayna Cápac died in 1527, possibly from smallpox, but Ninan Cuyochi had also succumbed to smallpox just before his father.

Huayna Cápac subverted the fundamental laws of the empire and decreed that Huáscar and Atahualpa would share power in the event of Ninan Cuyochi's death. Atahualpa would inherit the ancient kingdom of Quito, while Huáscar ruled the rest of the kingdom, centered on Cuzco. Along with the northern kingdom, Atahualpa inherited a large experienced and loyal army with two capable commanders: Quizquiz and Chullcuchima, Atahualpa's maternal uncle.

The two brothers effectively shared power for a time, but in 1529 civil war broke out. Huáscar's troops captured and imprisoned Atahualpa near Tumebamba within Quito territory. Managing to escape, Atahualpa marched his army to 60 miles south of Quito, defeating Huáscar's forces at Ambato. At Tumebamba, meanwhile, Atahualpa caused the slaughter of the Cañaris people, who were loyal to Huáscar, and razed the city. Atahualpa then created a base camp at Cajamarca, where he remained. As Atahualpa's troops neared Cuzco, Huáscar followed the poor advice of his priests and waited until Atahualpa's troops were near the city before joining battle on the plains of Quipaipan.

Atahualpa's men were more experienced. They were also well led and disciplined. Huáscar's army, however, had been hastily assembled and was not well organized. Fierce fighting followed. At the end of the day Atahualpa was victorious, and Huáscar was taken prisoner. He was subsequently held in a mountain stronghold at Xuaxa. Atahualpa then invited all Inca leaders to Cuzco to a meeting to partition the kingdom. Once they had gathered, Atahualpa's men slaughtered them to ensure

Atahualpa's claim to the throne. Atahualpa was then acclaimed Sapa Inca but only briefly, for these events occurred in the spring of 1532, only a few months before the arrival of the Spaniards.

Francisco Pizarro, who had arrived in Peru about a year earlier, learned that part of Atahualpa's army was encamped about 10–12 days' march distant, near Cajamarca. Pizarro had only 177 men and 67 horses by the time he arrived at Cajamarca on November 15, 1532. Entering the city, he used deception to take Atahualpa prisoner and then held the newly recognized ruler of the Inca Empire for ransom.

When Atahualpa learned that Pizarro was considering which brother to recognize as Sapa Inca, Atahualpa ordered Huáscar murdered. Pizarro, not satisfied with the sizable ransom Atahualpa has paid for his release, charged the Inca with the murder of Huáscar and sentenced him to be burned alive in the plaza at Cajamarca on August 29, 1533. When Atahualpa agreed to convert to Roman Catholicism, Pizarro had him garroted instead. The execution of the emperor, on the heels of the recent struggle for power, resulted in the kingdom falling into chaos.

Pizarro thought that the Spanish appointment of an heir to the Inca throne might restore social order and secure Spanish control. The plethora of immediate descendants presented the conquistador with a dilemma, however. Huáscar's younger

The "Battle" of Cajamarca of November 16, 1532, in which Spanish forces led by Francisco Pizarro surprised and took captive Atahualpa, emperor of the Incas. Engraving from *Historia Americae* (1602), by Flemish printmaker Theodore de Bry. (DeAgostini/Getty Images)

brother, Manco, still lived in Cuzco, but Atahualpa's younger brother, Toparca (Tupac Hualpa), was nearby in Cajamarca. Pizarro approved the appointment of Toparca, who briefly became Sapa Inca. When Toparca suddenly died, rumor spread that he was poisoned. Manco claimed the throne, and Pizarro supported the claim, using it as an opportunity to guarantee the placement of Spanish officials in important positions within the Inca imperial structure as well as to replace the Inca sun god worship with Roman Catholicism.

With Manco Inca on the throne in the traditional capital of Cuzco in 1535 and with Atahualpa's general, Challcuchina, executed, it appeared that the Spanish had firm control over the empire in and around the capital. Inca general Quizquiz tried to stop the Spanish takeover, but his own men killed him. Assured of Spanish hegemony, Pizarro left his younger brothers to rule Cuzco as advisers to the figurehead Inca ruler, Manco. This period also saw the rise of Catholic influence in the city, removing much of the indigenous religious practices and inserting Catholicism instead. In the midst of pious attempts by religious orders to gain control and the abusive treatment of Manco Inca by the Pizarro brothers, the military broke into factions. The rupture left an opening for the puppet Sapa Inca to flee from Cuzco and revive a government in exile.

The deaths of Huáscar and Atahualpa brought disarray to Tahuatinsuyu, and the confederation began to crumble. The resulting extension of the original civil war was the pivotal event that allowed the Spanish to achieve their goal of conquest, for without the revolution dividing the Tahuatinsuyus, the few Spaniards could never have prevailed over the military might of the largest civilization of the pre-Columbian Americas. The corruption of the Pizarro brothers in their ruling of the Incas almost resulted in the reunification of the empire. Yet, the division between the *panaqas* seeking control of the empire for the various branches of the ruling elite and the bitterness from almost 10 years of political and military struggles, combined with suspicions of Inca collaboration with the Spanish in poisoning legitimate heirs to the throne, proved too hard to overcome. Manco Inca did escape and began a decades-long struggle against the Spanish. However, the previous Inca Civil War prevented his authority from ever extending throughout the entire empire.

Debra J. Sheffer

Perspective Essay 1. The Inca-Spanish War Delayed Spanish Conquest

The Inca Civil War was a conflict during 1529–1532 between the ruling Inca half brothers Atahualpa and Huáscar for the position of Sapa Inca (Unique Inca) over the entire Inca Empire. The war was initiated by a set of circumstances that included Spanish transmission of a deadly disease (probably smallpox) via their exploratory contact along the coastal limits of the empire. Many Incas succumbed to the deadly epidemic, including the powerful Sapa Inca Huayna Cápac. Realizing that he would not survive, the emperor designated his son, Ninan Cuyochi as heir apparent. Huayna Cápac also provided for the possibility of Ninan's death, designating his son through his primary wife, Huáscar, as the subsequent Sapa Inca. Interestingly, Huayna Cápac also designated his son Atahualpa, through a non-Inca wife, as a coruler of the northern region of the more than 3,000-mile-long empire. It was this decision to split the empire's leadership following the deaths of Huayna Cápac and Ninan Cuyochi that led eventually to the Inca Civil War.

How the Inca Civil War began is not typically debated. Of more interest historically is the question about the role the war played in the eventual Spanish conquest of the empire. Did the civil war contribute directly to the demise of the Incas at the hands of the Spaniards? Or did the war simply contribute to the complexity of issues encountered by the conquering Spaniards and delay their eventual success? While on the surface the Inca Civil War appears integral to Spanish dominance, in reality the divisions that began the war contributed to the Inca resistance movement, delaying Spain's final subjugation of the Peruvian Empire.

Francisco Pizarro's expedition of war-hardened conquistadors arrived at a crucial time in the Inca Civil War. News of the conflict filtered through the countryside. To Pizarro, this presented a scenario similar to that encountered by Hernán Cortés in Mexico. Internal divisions in the Inca government and the impact of these divisions on the subjugated population seemed to reveal an opportunity for the Spaniards to leverage further. The Inca elites were divided in their allegiance to the two claimants to the title of Sapa Inca. However, that division was effectively resolved with Atahualpa's defeat and capture of Huáscar in 1532 shortly before Pizarro encountered the victorious emperor at Cajamarca.

Typical of the royal prerogative of the Sapa Inca, both Atahualpa and Huáscar sought to eradicate those leaders and elements of the population who sided against them. While Atahualpa had not yet completed this process, he had managed to compel obedience and allegiance in the empire before being forced to confront the Spaniards. Instead of being able to leverage a divided Inca population against their own emperor, Pizarro's minimal force discovered a united military under the leadership of their acknowledged god-king.

It is this imbalance of numbers and unquestioned loyalty of the Inca forces that surprisingly played into Pizarro's hands. Understanding the total authority of the Sapa Inca and viewing the few Spaniards as weak and incapable of defying the superior Inca forces, it is small wonder that the Spanish strategy of ambush and capturing Atahualpa as a hostage resulted in the native forces being caught off guard. The violence of the Spaniards, who initially indicated a willingness to negotiate, and the use of unfamiliar weaponry added to the success of the surprise attack. It did not, however, immediately revive the recently concluded Inca Civil War.

With Pizarro holding Atahualpa hostage, the Incas' response was to remain loyal to their ruler. Indeed, it is Atahualpa who suggested the offer of a ransom and gave orders to his people to gather the ransom in payment for his freedom. To all appearances Atahualpa, even as a hostage, retained authority in the eyes of the native population. This reality helps explain why the Inca forces failed to attack the Spaniards while the foreigners were unable to effectively resist. Instead of the delay being the result of internal division, the initial delay was the result of internal unity behind Atahualpa.

Nonetheless, division internally did exist. The societal structure of the elites, specifically of the imperial family, bred division. Descendants of the former Sapa Incas continued to care for their dead loved ones and professed loyalty to these honored dead. To the Spanish, who sought leverage through whatever societal fractures they could identify, these unusual practices represented alienated groups that could be manipulated. The Inca practice of assimilating non-Inca peoples, designating those especially loyal non-Incan societies as "Incas by privilege," offered additional clusters of potential Spanish allies against the dominating Inca government. The news of Huáscar's continued existence must have presented Pizarro with an opportunity to not only defeat the powerful forces under Atahualpa but also to win over the loyalty and allegiance of the imprisoned former Inca ruler.

Atahualpa, still more ruler than hostage, was well aware of Pizarro's intent. Orders by the emperor to have his half brother killed, while decried by the immediate family members of Huáscar, did not revive the Inca Civil War. Dismayed by this turn of events and enticed by greed that was further fed by the payment of the generous ransom for Atahualpa's release, Pizarro decided to condemn the Sapa Inca and have him executed. In this fashion, he hoped to win the loyalty of Huáscar's descendants and to place one as the new, now puppet Sapa Inca. Again this action shocked the people, but the apparent willingness of the Spaniards to acknowledge the position of the Sapa Inca and even to consult the priests and leaders on his appointment placated them.

What, then, revived hostilities among the Incas? Highly placed generals under Atahualpa, those responsible for the gathering and payment of the ransom, continued to oppose the Spanish following the death of their leader. The new puppet emperor had no opportunity to respond to this Inca resistance, as he soon died. While his death probably resulted from contracting an illness, the Incas readily accepted the rumor that Spanish collusion led to the poisoning of their new leader. This belief drove some Incas by privilege and those willing to peacefully cooperate with the Spanish into the resistance led by generals such as Quizquiz, who fought to punish the foreigners and place an heir of Atahualpa on the throne.

Pizarro again sought to win over large segments of the Inca Empire, selecting Manco Inca Yupanqui (next descendant from Huayna Cápac's sons) as the next Sapa

Inca. Manco and the priestly leadership of the Incas accepted his role as ruler. However, the Spanish soon alienated this legitimate and peaceful heir to the throne. Assuming that the Incas were well under control and that the seat of power in Cuzco was firmly under Spanish influence, Pizarro left his younger brothers to oversee the puppet government at the Inca capital. This decision proved fateful for the smooth transition of power to the Spaniards and extended conflict in the region for decades to come.

Left to the mercies of the greedy and lustful Pizarro brothers, Gonzalo and Hernando, Manco Inca at first protested and then fled the city of Cuzco. With his beloved wife still hostage of these abusive brothers, Manco Inca rallied loyal Incas and Incas by privilege to his rebellion. The attempt may well have succeeded had another half brother, Paulla, who obediently accompanied conquistador Diego de Almagro southward into Chile, not returned with these Spanish forces in time to thwart the native siege of the capital city. Almagro's forces dispersed Manco Inca's men. Meanwhile, Paulla was groomed for serving the Spaniards as the new puppet Sapa Inca. The result was a long-lasting conflict between the Spanish conquistadors vying for ultimate authority among themselves as well as the Spanish and their puppet Inca allies versus the rebel forces from an exiled Inca government.

This internal division, while referred to by some as a continuation of the Inca Civil War, was a resistance movement known as the Neo-Inca. Initially under the authority of Manco Inca Yupanqui, the rebellion turned the tide on the divided Spanish. The Neo-Inca captured and employed Spanish horses, weapons, and ammunition. Though never numerous enough to overcome the increased Spanish presence, especially with the use by Pizarro of Inca and other native allies, the rebellion managed to wreak havoc on Spanish control of the region. Unlike the relatively quick defeat of the Tainos in the Caribbean or the collapse of the Aztec Empire in Mexico, the Incas retained an effective opposition force to the Spaniards for almost three decades. Though the resistance was not a direct extension of the Inca Civil War between Atahualpa and Huáscar, the Neo-Inca movement emerged out of Pizarro's attempt to manipulate internal divisions among the Inca elites and within the Inca society in general.

Rebecca Seaman

Perspective Essay 2. The Inca Civil War Was Key to the Spanish Conquest

Inca fighting among themselves and against neighboring tribes had gone on for decades and was one of the principal reasons why the oversized Inca Empire fell so easily to the Spaniards. The latest round of Inca civil strife, known as the War of the

Two Brothers, ended with the victory of Atahualpa's northern armies over his younger half brother Huáscar, who was emperor in the capital city of Cuzco, just a few months before the Spaniards arrived in the autumn of 1532. This bloody triumph in no way brought an end to Inca quarreling, though. It was followed by the pursuit of remaining loyalist forces and a brutal purge of opponents within the ruling classes at Cuzco, which Atahualpa waited to have resolved before taking the throne himself.

The empire, forged in less than a century by campaigns directed by a small Inca elite, seems to have been in a constant state of conflict. The history of the Incas' sudden rise to power would only be recorded in bits and pieces by later Spanish and mestizo scribes, as the Incas themselves left no written language. Much of their oral folklore would also be lost forever, while descendants from among their former vassals remembered unfavorable versions (the exception, of course, being the Inca Garcilaso de la Vega, who not surprisingly portrayed his ancestors as kind and caring rulers in his 1609 *Comentarios reales*).

Yet enough information has survived to suggest that during the reign of the ninth Sapa Inca (emperor), Pachacútec (1438–1471), the Inca Empire had emerged as an Andean superpower. It is believed that he became emperor after defeating a Hanka Chanca invasion, then hunted down their armies and forcibly relocated any civilian survivors. Growing increasingly well disciplined and aggressive during his long rule, the Incas had subdued neighboring tribes—the Huancas and Taramas to their north, the Collas and Lupacas to the south—forcing them to submit and pay tribute and to participate in campaigns of further expansion.

Túpac Yupanqui, the warrior-prince who emerged as Pachacútec's successor from the dynastic intrigues at Cuzco, pushed Inca domination even farther south, to the Maule River, during his own 22-year reign. The Chachapoyas, Huambos, and Guayacondos were all overrun and long remembered the treachery and ferocity used in their defeats. During years of fierce campaigning, Túpac Yupanqui's armies and his allied auxiliaries probed as far north as Quito and even attempted to cross the Andes before a revolt by the Collas had to be crushed. The hatred felt against Túpac Yupanqui for his many victims would linger on so bitterly that even 40 years after his death, gleeful northern commanders would burn his mummy after capturing Cuzco.

Huayna Cápac emerged from yet another round of murderous court intrigues to become the 11th emperor, and his 30 years on the throne saw still more repression and a military penetration into Ecuador. His victory over the Caranquis was typical: he lured them out of their stronghold by pretending to retreat, then circled around behind their pursuit column and butchered them in a swamp, which is still known today as Yahuarcocha (Lake of Blood). After he died a brief truce ensued between the northern prince Atahualpa and Huáscar, the favorite crowned by the influential *panacas* at the imperial court in Cuzco, before open warfare exploded once more, with alliances redrawn on both sides.

Six months after Atahualpa's generals Chalcuchimac and Quizquiz had fought their way into Cuzco, putting all of the imprisoned Huáscar's family to death before his eyes and destroying many temples, the northern warlord still hesitated to travel south for his coronation because of continued resistance. When Spaniard Francisco Pizarro and his 168 men unexpectedly materialized from the coasts of Ecuador shortly thereafter, they found a sprawling empire that had been created during a few short decades of militaristic growth. Although it had forts, roads, cities and developed arts and agriculture, a closer examination also revealed a patchwork with many dozens of subject tribes, ruled over by a distant emperor they were forbidden to even look at and a communication system for quickly issuing instructions and orders that also discouraged local leaders from showing any initiative. There were also leaders (including the Inca royal family itself) who sired many children through harems of wives, producing multiple contenders for each succession; territories administered by four officials known as the curacas, who competed to govern their single province; and many people who could still remember when their tribes had been independent as well as the brutality in their conquest and administration.

Of the 12 million to 16 million people living within this empire, only a tiny minority were members of its ruling Inca caste—no more than 40,000 people, possibly as few as 15,000. Some Quechua-speaking nobles had been accepted as Hahuas or "Outer" Incas—"Incas by privilege or adoption"—yet descendants of the original Cuzcan nobility had jealously guarded their exclusive status as elite Capac Inca. Emperors could only be drawn from their ranks.

Therefore, when Pizarro suddenly seized Atahualpa and murdered his courtiers at the resort town of Cajamarca on November 16, 1532, the empire was thrown into fearful uncertainty. The northern generals occupying Cuzco knew that their leader would never be crowned as Sapa Inca, while all around them resistance stiffened, and their own native allies began to desert them. When they killed their captive Huáscar, the empire was left without any recognizable chieftain. As the Spaniards pushed inland the next summer, the once mighty empire remained utterly paralyzed, as traditional rivalries and suspicions between tribes reemerged, paving the way for these foreign invaders to advance.

David F. Marley

Further Reading

Angles Vargas, Víctor. *Historia del Cuzco incaico.* Lima: Industrial Gráfica, S.A., 1998.

D'Altroy, Terence N. *The Incas.* Oxford, UK: Blackwell, 2002.

Davies, Nigel. *The Incas.* Boulder: University Press of Colorado, 2007.

Espinoza Soriano, Waldemar. *Los Incas.* Lima: Amaru, 1997.

Gabai, Rafael Varón. *Francisco Pizarro and His Brothers: The Illusion of Power in Sixteenth-Century Peru.* Translated by Javier Flores Espinoza. Norman: University of Oklahoma Press, 1997.

Gamboa, Pedro Sarmiento de. *History of the Incas.* Translated and edited by Sir Clements Markham. Cambridge, UK: Hakluyt Society, 1907.

Hemming, John. *The Conquest of the Incas.* Tequesta, FL: Mariner, 2003.

Marrin, Albert. *Inca & Spaniard: Pizarro and the Conquest of Peru.* New York: Atheneum, 1989.

McEwan, Gordon F. *The Incas: New Perspectives.* Santa Barbara, CA: ABC-CLIO, 2006.

McQuarrie, Kim. *The Last Days of the Incas.* New York: Simon and Schuster, 2007.

Means, Philip A. *The Fall of the Inca Empire and the Spanish Rule in Peru, 1530–1780.* New York: Gordian, 1971.

Moseley, Michael E., and Alana Cordy-Collins, eds. *The Northern Dynasties: Kingship and Statecraft in Chimor.* Washington, DC: Dumbarton Oaks, 1991.

Rostworowski de Diez Canseco, María. *Historia del Tawantinsuyu.* Lima: FIMART, 2002.

Urton, Gary. *Inca Myths.* Austin: University of Texas Press, 1999.

Villanueva Sotomayor, Julio R. *El Perú en los tiempos antiguos.* Lima: Quebecor Perú, S.A., 2001.

14. WAS THE THIRTY YEARS' WAR A RELIGIOUS OR POLITICAL CONFLICT?

The Thirty Years' War (1618–1648) was a series of bloody conflicts waged in Central Europe. The war began as a clash between various Catholic and Protestant states in the increasingly fragmented Holy Roman Empire. The immediate catalyst for the war was the new Holy Roman emperor Ferdinand II's attempt to introduce religious homogenization into his realm by imposing Roman Catholicism on his subjects. The conflict, waged chiefly with mercenary forces, was one of the most destructive wars in European history, resulting in more than 5 million deaths. Although fought chiefly in what is now Germany, at one time or another the war involved almost every European power. The struggle also precipitated widespread famine and disease, particularly in the German and Italian states. Mercenary soldiers routinely resorted to looting and attempted to extort money from local officials in order to pay their salaries. The Thirty Years' War also bankrupted many combatants' treasuries. While its devastating effects are clear, historians continue to debate the true nature of this complex conflict.

In the first perspective essay, Dr. Skip Knox argues that the Thirty Years' War began as a religious conflict with political undercurrents but ended as a political conflict with religious undercurrents. He attributes this gradual shift to the entrance of foreign powers into the conflict and the generational changes that occurred when a number of older leaders died and were succeeded by their children. For Dr. Lee W. Eysturlid, the Thirty Years' War was not solely a political or religious conflict but instead was a combination of the two. As he traces the war through its four distinct phases, he points out that the religious aspect of the conflict was complex because it suffused all facets of early modern life, including politics, economics, and culture. By contrast, Dr. Peter H. Wilson posits that the Thirty Years' War was neither a religious nor an international conflict but rather a struggle over the imperial constitution. In his view, the root cause of the war was the fact that the imperial Estates disagreed on how to share power between themselves and the emperor.

Background Essay

The Thirty Years' War of 1618–1648 was one of the most destructive conflicts in European history. While it began as a war of religion between Catholics and Protestants, it soon devolved into a geopolitical struggle during which Catholics fought Catholics and Protestants fought Protestants. This was the Age of Faith, and rising religious tensions between Catholics and Protestants in Germany led to the formation of the Protestant Union in 1608 and the Catholic League in 1609.

The war began with a local revolt in Bohemia with the 1618 Defenestration of Prague. Protestant rulers in Bohemia favored Protestant Frederick V as successor to Holy Roman emperor Matthias, who was also the king of Bohemia, as opposed to his acknowledged heir, Ferdinand II, who was a staunch Catholic. With the death of Matthias and the succession of Ferdinand, Frederick, the leader of the Protestant Union, came to the aid of the Protestant Bohemians against the re-Catholicization policies implemented by Ferdinand. Soon the Protestant forces had a new ally in Transylvanian prince Bethlan Gabor, with financial and military backing from the Ottoman Empire, who would wreak havoc in Hungary. However, forces of the Catholic League, under Johann Tserclaes von Tilly, crushed the Bohemian resistance in the Battle of White Mountain (November 8, 1620), forcing Frederick to take flight.

From 1621 to 1625, Spain mobilized its forces to fight the Protestant Dutch, continuing what was known as the Eighty Years' War. Meanwhile in Germany, despite numerous subsequent tactical defeats, Protestant Union general Peter Ernst von

Mansfeld and Christian of Brunswick remained in the field (with Dutch, French, and British financial backing) against the Spanish until they were decisively defeated by Tilly in the Battle of Stadtlohn on August 6, 1623.

Meanwhile in France following the assassination of King Henry IV in 1610 and the accession of King Louis XIII, the French Protestants, known as Huguenots, began their own rebellion against the increasing religious intolerance of Louis's regent, Marie de Medici. Henry (a Huguenot turned Catholic) had protected the rights of Huguenots in the 1598 Edict of Nantes, but Marie, a staunch Catholic, moved to undo it. Although the English intervened to support the Huguenots, the latter were eventually defeated.

The next phase of the war was known as the Danish period. It lasted from 1625 until 1629. King Christian IV of Denmark, a Lutheran and also the duke of Holstein, intervened in hopes of not only defending Protestantism but also increasing his holdings within the Holy Roman Empire. While he had the financial backing of England and France, he went into the struggle virtually alone, unsupported militarily by England, France, Sweden, Brandenburg, and Saxony. After sustaining a series of defeats at the hands of the Catholic forces led by Albrecht von Wallenstein and Tilly, Christian signed the Treaty of Lubeck in which he agreed to abandon his support of the Protestant German cause.

Sweden now entered the war. The Swedish Phase (1630–1635) saw King Gustav II Adolf (Gustavus Adolphus) of Sweden take up the Protestant cause. Gustavus, a brilliant general and military reformer, invaded northern Germany with a well-trained force. Ferdinand had been forced by many of the German princes to relieve Wallenstein of command, and in an early victory Gustavus defeated Tilly in the Battle of Breitenfeld (September 17, 1631). After Tilly's mortal wounding in April 1632, Wallenstein commanded the imperial (Catholic) forces. He engaged Gustavus in the decisive Battle of Lützen (November 6, 1632). Although Wallenstein's army was defeated, Gustavus was killed. Sweden continued in the war thereafter but in a less prominent role, with France becoming the prominent member of the anti-Habsburg alliance for the remainder of the war. In 1634 Wallenstein, who was playing a duplicitous game, was assassinated.

The last and so-called French Phase of the war commenced in 1635. Although predominantly Roman Catholic, France, under its chief minister Cardinal Armand Jean du Plessis de Richelieu, was a geopolitical foe of the Habsburgs. Protestant military reversals now forced France not only to supply subsidies to those powers fighting the Habsburgs but also to enter the war openly with its own troops, contesting not only with Spain but also with the forces of the Austrian Habsburgs and their supporters. The first few years of this phase of the long war went badly for France, as Spanish troops invaded France and threatened Paris itself. To make matters worse, Richelieu died in 1642, followed by Louis XIII in 1643, leaving the five-year-old Louis XIV on the throne under his chief minister, Cardinal Jules

The first Battle of Breitenfeld, fought near Leipzig in Saxony on September 17, 1631, during the Thirty Years' War. An allied Protestant army of Swedes and Saxons commanded by Swedish king Gustav II Adolph defeated the Catholic forces under Johann Tserclaes, Count of Tilly. (Rischgitz/ Getty Images)

Raymond Mazarin, who had been schooled by Richelieu and followed his policies. However, anti-Imperialist fortunes began to change in 1643 when French forces under the Duc d'Enghien crushed the Spanish in the Battle of Rocroi, and in 1645 Swedish marshal Lennart Torstenson defeated the Imperialists in the Battle of Jenkau. Also that year Condé defeated the Bavarian Army in the Second Battle of Nordlingen.

With both sides exhausted, the 1648 Peace of Westphalia ended the Thirty Years' War in Europe and the Eighty Years' War between Spain and the Netherlands. Under the treaty terms, each German state was made virtually sovereign, resulting in the effective atomization of Germany. While other areas of Europe were coalescing into large unified nation-states, Germany was moving in the opposite direction. Its population reduced by a third to a half, physically devastated by 30 years of war, and now divided into many small states, Germany ceased to play a major role in world affairs. That place was now taken by the Atlantic powers of the Dutch Republic, England, and France. France and Sweden were made guarantors of the peace, and although Sweden became too weak to exercise that right effectively, the French used it as a legal excuse to intervene in Central Europe during the next century and a half. The Thirty Years' War was thus a major watershed in world history. With it also, the European wars of religion came to an end.

Spencer C. Tucker

Perspective Essay 1. The Transition from Religion to Politics

The Thirty Years' War began as a religious conflict with political undercurrents but ended as a political conflict with religious undercurrents. This shift happened gradually and unevenly, but the key turning points were the entry into the war of foreign powers and a change of generations.

When it began in 1618, the war was primarily a power struggle for control of Bohemia between Elector Frederick V of the Palatinate and Holy Roman emperor Ferdinand II. Religion colored the struggle in that Frederick was a Protestant, and some feared that if he became king of Bohemia it would give the Protestants controlling power in imperial elections. On the other side, the emperor saw it as his divine duty to prevent the further spread of Protestantism within the empire and indeed to reverse the Protestant tide.

During the first part of the 1600s, there was an increasing conviction among militant Protestants of an international Catholic conspiracy to eradicate Protestantism or at least to retake as much of Protestant Europe as possible. Events such as the assassination of King Henry IV in France (1610) and the Gunpowder Plot in England (1605) seemed to confirm these fears. In Germany, the tension can be seen in the formation of the Protestant Union in 1608 and the Catholic League in 1609, both associations of German princes formed on confessional lines. It can be seen also in the succession crisis in Jülich Cleves in 1609–1610. Lines were drawn on religious grounds.

As the war unfolded, the religious theme was strong. For example, when three Habsburg officials were thrown from a window (the Defenestration of Prague in 1618), Catholics explained their survival as a miracle by Catholics, while Protestants claimed that the men survived only because they had landed in a dung heap. A more practical example can be found in Prague when the rebels seized power, where they systematically replaced Catholic officials with Protestants while keeping the institutions themselves unchanged. This pattern was repeated frequently during the first half of the war, with each side replacing clergy and secular officials with new ones of their own. Indeed, one of the reasons why Protestants did not present a united front was that Lutherans feared suffering at the hands of Calvinists, and vice versa.

The high-water mark of the religious factor came in 1629, when Emperor Ferdinand issued the Edict of Restitution. A key provision of the edict stated that all property that had been taken over by Protestants since 1552 must be returned to the original owners (which nearly always meant returning it to Catholic control). Ferdinand went further, though, in that he authorized use of force to effect this property transfer. The war was now not only a matter of settling who should rule in Bohemia and restoring peace there but also of property rights throughout the empire. The Habsburgs were clearly identified as intending to reduce Protestantism to a few isolated and harmless enclaves. Ferdinand took this step not because it was politically advantageous or even sensible but because it was part of his program of re-Catholicization. This action galvanized Protestants, as it was a public confirmation of their worst fears.

The arrival of a Swedish army under King Gustavus Adolphus in 1630 was seen across Europe as almost a crusade against militant Catholicism. Indeed, it was portrayed this way by Swedish propagandists, who issued a letter that couched the invasion in religious terms. The king's practical aim, however, was to establish Swedish rule on the southern coast of the Baltic Sea. From the beginning, he indicated that he was willing to accept religious compromise as long as Sweden obtained Pomerania or some acceptable substitute. Moreover, he was dependent on money from Catholic France, so he could not really make the destruction of Catholicism a centerpiece of his policy.

The first factor that tipped the balance from religious to political motives and aims was the entry of the French into the war. France had been meddling in the conflict since the early years. French policy, under the direction of Armand Jean du Plessis, Cardinal Richelieu, aimed mainly at mitigating Spanish influence in the Low Countries, controlling key areas along the Rhine River, and keeping the Habsburgs from winning total victory in Germany. None of these goals were religious in nature. In fact, it was the threat felt by France with regard to the Habsburgs that led it to send huge subsidies to Sweden. Where convenient, however, France also allied with Catholics, such as Maximilian of Bavaria. In short, French aims from the beginning were more political than religious. Initially, support was purely financial and diplomatic. The death of Gustavus Adolphus followed by the great Habsburg victory at Nordlingen in 1634 made direct interference imperative. After 1635, the kingdom finally felt strong enough to risk men as well as treasure in pursuit of its goals.

By the mid-1630s another shift was becoming apparent, as embodied in the Peace of Prague (1635). By this treaty, the year of restitution was set at 1627. This was a major change from the original year of 1552 and removed a good many areas of dispute, although it left a few major places that would still be contested. The peace also abolished both the Catholic League and the Heilbronn (Protestant) League, which at least in theory meant an end to confession-based armies. Various territorial settlements were also made.

This should have brought an end to the war. Three issues, though, caused the peace to break down. These were the question of amnesty for those who had fought against the emperor, the matter of the year of restitution, and the demobilization of armies. The peace had addressed each, but the emperor proved incapable of enforcing the terms. It is important to note that religion was not addressed in the Peace of Prague, and this turned out to be a weakness as well.

The participants were ready to make peace, but two factors, one external and one internal, kept the war going. Within the empire there were still several armies in the field, and these refused to disband because of arrears in pay. The amounts were enormous, and the peace had not addressed how to settle this question, so there were still armies available to keep the fight going.

This is where the external factor came into play, for Richelieu began to send French troops into the war, fighting mainly in the Rhine River Valley to gain certain territories such as the towns of Metz, Toul, and Verdun. This was sufficient to keep at least some of the Protestant armies in the field and gave a reason for key Protestant leaders to continue the fight in hopes of winning better terms.

The conditions for the final decade of the war were now in place. Negotiations for a new peace treaty began only a few years after the Peace of Prague, but the war now involved so many participants that it took a long time to get them all together. When they finally did begin negotiations in 1643, religion was again on the table, as it had not been at the Peace of Prague.

By then, Gustavus Adolphus was dead (1632). Imperial general Albrecht von Wallenstein had been assassinated in 1634, and Ferdinand II had died in 1637. Cardinal Richelieu passed away in 1642, and Louis XIII died the following year. A new generation was directing the war, and all parties—Queen Christina of Sweden, Cardinal Mazarin (Richelieu's successor) in France, and Holy Roman emperor Ferdinand III—showed clear preference for a political rather than religious resolution. There was a new focus even in Spain.

In the war's final years, no one believed that there could be total victory. Battles continued not in order to defeat the enemy but rather in hopes of gaining some advantage in the field that could be of advantage at the negotiating table. The war had not become completely political, for one of the advantages sought was determining which confession would prevail in this district or that town, but religious advantage was increasingly a secondary consideration. Most of the participants in the talks were ready to agree to the neutral religious terms that were present in the final settlement.

The two peace treaties of Osnabrück and Münster in 1648 (collectively called the Treaty of Westphalia) were long and detailed. Most of the provisions have little or nothing to do with religion, though religious issues were directly addressed. The Peace of Augsburg was reconfirmed, with important revisions. For example, no prince was to force his religion on his people. If a prince converted, that was to be a private matter. This was a significant modification and shows how the experiences of the war had brought Europeans to realize the dangers of mixing religion with public policy. Another important aspect was that for the first time, Calvinism was recognized as a legitimate church within the empire.

That said, for the most part the Peace of Westphalia was about practical politics. There was almost no adjustment of boundaries along confessional lines and no change to the imperial constitution along confessional lines, something that the Protestant rebels had long fought for but at last had yielded on. The empire had exhausted itself in fighting over religion. Future wars would be about politics and economics.

Ellis L. (Skip) Knox

Perspective Essay 2. A Blend of Politics and Religion

The Thirty Years' War (1618–1648) was not solely a political or a religious conflict but instead was a combination of the two. It has been standard interpretation that it was at heart a "war of religion," the primary motivator coming from differing notions of Christianity between Roman Catholics and Protestants. Ever since the beginning of Martin Luther's religious revolution of the 1520s and the disintegration of the European continent into several significant faiths, there had been open conflict, at times resulting in warfare between the sides. In the religious split that occurred in Europe in the 16th century, there was anything but a clear differentiation of sides. First, the difference between Catholic and Lutheran as well as between Lutheran and Calvinist, or Huguenot, is best referred to as "confessional" and not "religious." All were Christian, but important factors of control of issues such as the sacraments, priestly duties, and institutional authority moved beyond reconciliation. In addition, there was a clear break between Lutheran and Calvinist states in the northern half of Europe and Scandinavia and Catholic states in France and the south. Germany itself divided north and south, Protestant and Catholic. There was never a single clear Protestant political or religious entity at any time during the conflict.

The Thirty Years' War was waged by states and leaders under a complex and messy collection of motivations. Personal and state motivations were not distinct from religious motivations. For monarchs such as Habsburg emperor Ferdinand II (Catholic), Elector Frederick V of the Palatinate (Calvinist), and Swedish king Gustavus Adolphus (Lutheran), motivations were held to be religious. For an early modern monarch there was no difference between the expansion of their states, personal glory, and defense of their faith. All were intertwined in the person and authority of the ruler. For example, Gustavus's ambitions to secure control of the Baltic region and the northern German states neatly linked with his campaign to preserve Protestantism in that area.

The bulk of the important decisions for war in the 30-year period after 1618 were religious *and* political. This being the case, it also becomes clear that one of the reasons the war lasted so long was the ability to combine these two powerful forces. For the common soldier, religion often did play a major role. However, a close examination of the limited records that remain makes evident that the primary motivator for the common soldier was money and plunder. Tens of thousands of soldiers, correctly referred to as mercenaries, moved from army to army seeking the best pay and employment. In many cases during the war, Catholic and Protestant armies marauded mercilessly through regions populated by people of the same confessional faith. Finally, the peasants of these lands did not offer up increasing taxes or sons to conscription in order to fund the wars with hopes of confessional victory or the victory of the true faith but largely through fear of the tax collector.

The catalyst for the war came with the rejection of the Habsburg Ferdinand as Holy Roman emperor in 1618. In a complex political situation that required the seven electors of the empire to choose the new emperor, the Bohemian nobility led a revolt against him, withholding Ferdinand's title as king of Bohemia. The Bohemians feared Ferdinand for both political and religious reasons. First, they feared that this German ruler, from whom they were separated by language and culture, would undermine their independence. Second, the Bohemian nobles knew that with Ferdinand came the powerful Catholic Jesuits, whom they despised as the shock troops of papal authority and Catholic evangelism. For good reason these independent-minded Calvinist nobles saw the combination of Habsburg political authority with papal authority as too much. The May 23, 1618, defenestration, or throwing from a window, of Ferdinand's representatives in the Hradschin castle in Prague opened the war. Announced as a move to preserve ancient Bohemian rights and to free Ferdinand from the evil Jesuits, it was in reality an act of political resistance, a rejection of Habsburg rule.

Instead of selecting Ferdinand as their king, the Bohemian leaders offered the crown to Frederick V of the Palatinate. At this moment as well with the death of the aged sitting emperor Matthias, the other Protestant electors and princes of the Holy Roman Empire (read: Germany) had a unique opportunity. This was their best chance to rebel and end Habsburg Catholic rule for nearly half a century. Despite this, both Protestant and Catholic electors chose, with the exception of Frederick V, to support the Catholic Ferdinand's election. The Protestant princes would now stand aside as Ferdinand sought to reassert himself politically in Bohemia. This first phase of the war ended in 1622, however, with the complete defeat of the Bohemians and Frederick V.

Following this first phase of the war (there were to be four phases), the Lutheran king of Denmark, Christian IV, moved into Germany in 1625 as the defender of the Protestant cause. While proceeding under the banner of religion, it became clear that the king feared Habsburg domination of the German states, a direct threat to his sovereignty. Christian IV also hoped to profit from the war in the acquisition of territories in northern Germany. However, John Georg, the elector of Saxony and a Lutheran, offered a defense of Ferdinand's efforts to reassert Habsburg control and a condemnation of Christian IV's invasion and anyone who might support it. He rejected the Danish invasion as foreign intervention and branded those who supported it, such as Bernhard, Duke of Saxe-Weimar, as traitors. The elector even evoked Martin Luther's call for Christians to obey the "powers that exist" as upholding the right of Ferdinand to rule, as he had not been the cause of the troubles. Ferdinand's reassertion of authority over the Protestant German parts of the empire was the fulfillment of the *cuius regio,* the rule that the religion of a state's ruler was the official religion of that state's people. In his statement, Georg evoked religion not to promote the war but instead, using Lutheran quietism, as a reason to restore peace and political unity.

In the third phase of the war, the Swedish Phase, the Edict of Restitution of 1629 (the edict was meant to restore Catholic lands to church control) and the involvement of Sweden again showed the mix of political authority and religious justification. In the edict, the military success to date of the Habsburg cause and the rise of Habsburg and Catholic mercenary captain Albrecht von Wallenstein's army put Ferdinand II in position to end the Augsburg Confession, the agreement that allowed for Protestant states in the empire. The emperor, having gained what he felt was the upper hand militarily, looked to reconvert and rule all of Germany. In subduing the Protestant princes, Ferdinand removed a source of political resistance that came from religion but could not be tolerated if he was to gain real control. It was clear that religion had become the catalyst for noble efforts to reject royal dominance (as in Bohemia and France) and imperialism (as the Habsburgs in the Spanish Netherlands and Spain). A Catholic Habsburg empire would therefore be a unified and politically dominated entity under the person of the emperor.

Swedish Lutheran involvement followed many of the same lines as Danish Lutheran involvement but also was seen as foreign and had trouble finding any German allies. Without support Gustavus's invasion might have floundered, but he was assisted by two political events. First was Ferdinand II's overreaching effort to force the German electors to recognize his son as the rightful imperial heir and to provide financial and military assistance to the Spanish Catholic Habsburg forces fighting in the Netherlands. They refused both as an overreach of his political authority. The second stroke of luck for Gustavus was the offer of substantial financial assistance by the French under chief minister Cardinal Armand Jean Richelieu. In a single move, the cardinal bolstered the Protestant cause in Germany while undermining the efforts of the Catholic Habsburgs in both Germany and the Netherlands. What is clear is that Richelieu did not care about confessional differences. He sought to undermine Habsburg power by an entangling war in Germany. This would secure the French effort in a war with Spain and assist their efforts to gain territory in the Rhineland. The Catholic cardinal, running the foreign policy of Catholic France, now became the chief financial supporter of the Lutheran Swedish army in Germany in its military effort against the Catholic Habsburg emperor.

The death of the Swedish king on the battlefield of Lützen in November 1632 did not end the war. Gustavus's capable chancellor Axel Oxensternia carried on, and Richelieu forwarded more money and men to sustain the war. Although Sweden's German allies of Brandenburg and Saxony had made peace, this counted for little. By 1635, the primary fight was no longer contained in the German lands regarding confessional or constitutional issues but was now a political or dynastic struggle for dominance between the Habsburgs and Bourbons (France). As both powers were Catholic, this meant that religion had ceased to be a serious issue.

The fourth and final phase, the French Phase, lasted from 1635 to 1648 and became the most purely political of the war in general. Owing to the relative balance of forces, no one side could gain dominance. General talks were entered into in 1644 to establish a peace. The treaty that was hammered out at Westphalia returned the religious question over confessional rights to the Augsburg Confession of 1555. Again, northern Germany was mostly Protestant and southern Germany mostly Catholic, with Calvinists in the Rhineland. This division was to remain permanent. All of the states involved gained something politically. France, Denmark, and Sweden gained new, if modest, territories. Holland gained its independence, and the son of Frederick V returned to resume his father's position as the elector of the Palatinate. Although the Habsburgs did not really gain any territories, the new emperor Ferdinand III exerted far greater political control over his German-Austrian and Bohemian lands than had his father in 1618.

Lee W. Eysturlid

Perspective Essay 3. The Crisis of the Imperial Constitution

The Thirty Years' War was neither a religious nor an international conflict but rather a struggle regarding the imperial constitution. The religious war argument sees this struggle as the culmination of an entire "age of religious wars" initiated by the Protestant Reformation and including the French civil wars of 1562–1598 and the Dutch Revolt against Spain (1568–1648). In its most common form, this argument claims that belligerents were divided primarily by religion, that they fought for religious goals and used theological arguments to legitimate their objectives, and that sectarian hatred accounts for the ferocity of the fighting. None of these assumptions stand up to closer inspection.

The Thirty Years' War began with the Defenestration of Prague on May 23, 1618, when Bohemian nobles threw three of the emperor's representatives from a castle window. Though beginning as a revolt in one part of the empire, the war spread as other areas joined in and foreign powers intervened. It is impossible to distinguish clear religious parties within these struggles. Spain and France were Europe's leading Catholic powers yet pursued opposing agendas that spilled over into a brief war fought in northern Italy during 1628–1631 and then a protracted struggle between 1635 and 1659. France already subsidized the Dutch rebels against Spain after 1624 before openly allying with them in 1635 and merging its own war with Spain and the Dutch Revolt until 1648, when Spain finally accepted Dutch independence. Yet, the Dutch leaders were mostly Calvinists, a form of Protestantism similar to that of the Huguenots in France who had a long tradition of opposing the Catholic French monarchy.

Both Spain and France were ruled by Catholic monarchs facing Protestant rebellions yet remained enemies throughout this period. Likewise, the two leading Baltic powers of Denmark and Sweden were Lutheran yet refused to cooperate to defend those German Lutherans and Calvinists who opposed the Catholic emperor during the Thirty Years' War. Denmark deliberately waited until 1625 before intervening in the empire, delaying until Sweden had become embroiled in a separate quarrel with Poland. Sweden then waited until Denmark had been defeated by the emperor before launching its own invasion of the empire in 1630. It then attacked Denmark in 1643 when it appeared that the Danes were assisting the emperor to secure a peace hostile to Sweden. Swedish intervention was partly financed by France, which had also brokered the truce with Poland in 1629 that freed the Swedes to land in Germany.

The conflict within the empire displayed a similar lack of religious solidarity. The emperor's principal opponents were disaffected nobles in his own hereditary possessions of Austria and Bohemia as well as some of the leading princes in the German part of the empire. These opponents were mainly Calvinists, but this did not stop some Calvinist princes from backing the emperor for considerable periods during the war. The majority of German Protestants were Lutherans. Some Austrian and Bohemian Lutheran nobles participated in the initial revolts during 1618–1620, but many remained neutral or sided with the Catholic minority among the nobility in supporting the emperor. The leading German Lutheran prince, the elector of Saxony, played a significant role in helping the emperor crush the rebellion by 1622. Thereafter the Lutherans remained split, with most preferring to remain neutral, as did some Calvinists, until the Swedish invasion left them no choice.

This leads us to the question of how religion fit into the constitutional dispute at the heart of the war. The imperial constitution was an accumulation of written charters, precedents, and accepted practices that had evolved since the ninth century. Many aspects were deliberately left vague, especially the relative position of the emperor and princes, since this allowed each to evolve new rights in response to circumstances. The empire's general character was that of a mixed monarchy, meaning the emperor had to share the exercise of key powers and responsibilities with other lesser authorities within the empire. These lesser authorities were collectively known as the Imperial Estates and consisted of the different territories comprising the empire. This did not make the empire a federation, since the Imperial Estates did not enjoy equal rights. They varied considerably in status, and there was no logical correlation between their constitutional rights and how large they were or how many inhabitants they had. There were around 65 larger and 135 smaller principalities as well as about 50 civic republics. These were not of independent status but instead were autonomous territories that managed their own affairs within the empire's legal and political framework. Just how much autonomy each enjoyed depended on formal rights, actual power, and circumstance.

The Reformation posed particular problems for the empire, not least because it was the part of Europe where Protestantism first emerged and developed. The fragmentation of Christian Europe into rival churches shattered the medieval unity of religion and law. The Protestants were seeking not to form new churches but instead to reform the existing one. Like the Catholics, they claimed that there was only one true religion. Rather than endorse a single faith, the empire tried to defuse tension by taking theology out of politics. The emperor and princes remained committed Christians, with each hoping that their version of Christianity would ultimately prevail. Beginning in the 1520s, disputes centered on the control of material assets needed to sustain churches and on political jurisdictions over communities of believers. This culminated in an agreement of the Imperial Estates meeting in the city of Augsburg in 1555. This has entered history as the "Religious Peace" but in fact was part of a wider series of measures revising the imperial constitution. The treaty tried to settle the disputes over assets and jurisdictions by allowing those Lutheran Imperial Estates to keep buildings, property, and rights they had taken from the Catholics within their territories. Princes were allowed to decide whether they and their subjects remained Catholic or embraced Lutheranism. Like other constitutional documents, the treaty was deliberately ambiguous to enable people of the two recognized faiths to remain within the same legal and political system.

The peace failed to remove all problems. Controversial issues included the position of subjects who rejected their ruler's faith as well as the status of Catholic property within Lutheran territories that had not yet been taken over. The most dangerous issue concerned the fate of the 35 large and 45 small ecclesiastical principalities, collectively constituting the imperial church, that were governed by senior clerics elected by cathedral or abbey chapters. These were denied the right to choose their subjects' religion. Some dozen north German prince-archbishoprics and bishoprics passed into Lutheran hands by 1600 because Protestants dominated their cathedral chapters and chose coreligionists who refused to step down. This process of course involved religion but was far from purely a matter of faith. The princes and aristocrats had dominated the imperial church since the Middle Ages because it offered suitable employment for younger sons and unmarried daughters and also allowed powerful families to extend their influence into neighboring territories. The northern German princely families were not prepared to relinquish these opportunities just because they had converted to Lutheranism.

Most accounts of the Thirty Years' War now jump ahead by arguing that these problems built inexorably toward war. Yet the period 1555–1618 was the longest period of tranquility in modern German history prior to the 21st century. Most princes wanted the 1555 peace to last. Self-interest was supplemented by the widespread ideal of a common fatherland. This was not nationalism in the 19th-century sense but rather the political conviction that all princes shared "German freedom," or the privilege of managing imperial affairs together to ensure that the emperor did not rule as an absolute monarch.

This leads directly to the war's real cause. The Imperial Estates disagreed on how to share power between themselves and the emperor. The emperor argued that he had to consult the Imperial Estates but was not bound to follow their advice. The senior princes (the electors) wanted to exclude the lesser princes and cities from deciding the more important issues. The latter felt that the existing system overburdened them with taxes without a corresponding voice in imperial institutions. Most Imperial Estates refused to join either the Protestant Union (1608) or the Catholic League (1609), recognizing these groups as vehicles for rival branches of the Wittelsbach family ruling the Palatinate and Bavaria, respectively. The league was dissolved in 1617, while the union was nearing collapse.

What made the Bohemian Revolt so serious was the general loss by 1618 of confidence in the Habsburg family, which held the imperial title. The Habsburgs had been unable to resolve the empire's various disputes because they had been distracted since 1576 by unrest within their own hereditary lands. These problems deepened when an expensive war against the Ottoman Turks ended in bankruptcy and defeat in 1606. The family turned in on itself in a relatively bloodless yet politically damaging dispute lasting six years. The Bohemian Revolt arose from these circumstances, as one group of local aristocrats sought to expand their influence at the expense of the Habsburgs.

The real tragedy of the war that followed was that it could have been ended much sooner. All the constitutional changes adopted in 1648 were already on the agenda before 1618. It was not religious hatred that prolonged the conflict but rather the refusal by the belligerents on each side to abandon their interpretation of the constitution.

Peter H. Wilson

Further Reading

Anderson, M. S. *War and Society in Europe of the Old Regime, 1618–1789.* Montreal: McGill-Queen's University Press, 1998.

Ashe, Ronald G. *The Thirty Years' War: The Holy Roman Empire and Europe, 1618–1648.* New York: Palgrave Macmillan, 1997.

Benecke, Gerhard. *Germany in the Thirty Years War.* London: St. Martin's, 1978.

Bergin, Joseph. *Cardinal Richelieu: Power and the Pursuit of Wealth.* New Haven, CT: Yale University Press, 1990.

Bireley, Robert. *The Jesuits and the Thirty Years' War: Kings, Courts, and Confessors.* Cambridge: Cambridge University Press, 2003.

Bireley, Robert. "The Thirty Years' War as Germany's Religious War." In *Krieg und Politik 1618–1648,* edited by Konrad Repgen, 85–106. Munich: Oldenbourg, 1988.

Bonney, Richard. *The Thirty Years' War, 1618–1648.* London: Osprey, 2002.

Cooper, J. P. *The New Cambridge Modern History,* Vol. 4, *The Decline of Spain and the Thirty Years War, 1609–48/59.* Cambridge: Cambridge University Press, 1970.

Cramer, Kevin. *The Thirty Years' War & German Memory in the Nineteenth Century.* Lincoln: University of Nebraska Press, 2007.

Croxton, Derek. *Peacemaking in Early Modern Europe: Cardinal Mazarin and the Congress of Westphalia, 1643–1648.* Selinsgrove, UK: Susquehanna University Press, 1999.

Dunn, Richard S. *The Age of Religious Wars, 1559–1715.* New York: Norton, 1979.

Guthrie, William P. *The Later Thirty Years' War.* Westport, CT: Greenwood, 2003.

Gutmann, Myron P. "The Origins of the Thirty Years' War." *Journal of Interdisciplinary History* 18(4) (1988): 749–770.

Helfferich, Tryntje, ed. *The Thirty Years War: A Documentary History.* Indianapolis: Hackett, 2009.

Kennedy, Paul. *The Rise and Fall of the Great Powers: Economic Change and Military Conflict from 1500 to 2000.* New York: HarperCollins, 1988.

Langer, Herbert. *The Thirty Years' War.* Poole, UK: Blandford, 1980.

Lockhart, Paul Douglas. *Denmark in the Thirty Years' War, 1618–1648: King Christian IV and the Decline of the Oldenburg State.* Selinsgrove, PA: Susquehanna University Press, 1996.

Mann, Golo. *Wallenstein: His Life Narrated.* New York: Holt, Rinehart and Winston, 1976.

Mitchell, John. *Life of Wallenstein, Duke of Friedland.* Westport, CT: Greenwood, 1968.

Mortimer, Geoffrey Wallenstein. *The Enigma of the Thirty Years' War.* Basingstoke, UK: Palgrave, 2010.

Oakley, Stewart. *War and Peace in the Baltic, 1560–1790.* London: Routledge, 1992.

Parker, Geoffrey. *Europe in Crisis, 1598–1648.* Oxford: Oxford University Press, 2001.

Parker, Geoffrey. *The Thirty Years' War.* London: Routledge and Kegan Paul, 1984.

Prinzing, Friedrich. *Epidemics Resulting from Wars.* Oxford, UK: Clarendon, 1916.

Pursell, Brennan C. *The Winter King: Frederick V of the Palatinate and the Coming of the Thirty Years' War.* Aldershot, UK: Ashgate, 2003.

Rabb, Theodore K. "The Effects of the Thirty Years' War on the German Economy." *Journal of Modern History* 34(1) (1962): 40–51.

Repgen, Konrad. "What Is a Religious War?" In *Politics and Society in Reformation Europe,* edited by E. I. Kouri and Tom Scott, 311–328. Basingstoke, UK: Macmillan, 1987.

Roberts, Michael. *Gustavus Adolphus.* New York: Addison Wesley, 1992.

Rogers, Clifford, ed. *The Military Revolution Debate.* Boulder, CO: Westview, 1995.

Steinberg, S. H. *The Thirty Years' War and the Conflict for European Hegemony, 1600–1660.* New York: Norton, 1967.

Sutherland, Nicola. "The Origins of the Thirty Years' War and the Structure of European Politics." *English Historical Review* 107 (1993): 587–625.

Wedgwood, C. V. *The Thirty Years' War.* New York: New York Review of Books, 2005.

Wilson, Peter H. "The Causes of the Thirty Years' War 1618–48." *English Historical Review* 123 (2008): 554–586.

Wilson, Peter H. "Dynasty, Constitution and Confession: The Role of Religion in the Thirty Years' War." *International History Review* 30 (2008): 473–514.

Wilson, Peter H. *Europe's Tragedy: A History of the Thirty Years War.* London: Allen Lane, 2009.

Wilson, Peter H. "The Thirty Years' War as the Empire's Constitutional Crisis." In *The Holy Roman Empire, 1495–1806,* edited by Robert Evans, Michael Schaich, and Peter. H. Wilson, 95–114. Oxford: Oxford University Press, 2011.

15. Was "Taxation without Representation" the Primary Cause of the American Revolution?

The American Revolutionary War was waged between 1775 and 1783. Initially, it involved an armed insurrection by Great Britain's 13 North American colonies against the power of the British king and Parliament. Although the fighting began in the northern colonies, by war's end the conflict had involved virtually all of the colonies as far south as Georgia and South Carolina. The first battles occurred in Massachusetts in April 1775; in July 1776, the Continental Congress formally declared its independence from British rule. An array of historians have quoted John Adams declaring that "The Revolution was effected before the War commenced. The Revolution was in the minds and hearts of the people." However, they often neglect to finish the quote: "a change in their religious sentiments of their duties and obligations. This radical change in the principles, opinions, sentiments, and affections of the people, was the real American Revolution." But on the question of what exactly caused the revolution, Adams becomes less quotable. That is reasonable—the question has a seemingly endless list of possible answers. Other than the words of Thomas Jefferson in the Declaration of Independence and Thomas Paine in Common Sense, *perhaps no phrase is more closely associated with the revolution or more frequently revived for a variety of purposes than "taxation without representation." Was that the cause of the American Revolution?*

Below, three scholars join the debate. Dr. John Ruddiman argues yes, but he also acknowledges that taxation without representation was inseparable from a host of other issues related to how the British Empire treated its colonists and how the colonists felt about the empire—indeed, it was the foundation on which the advocates of revolution built the edifice of a new nation. Dr. William Kashatus interprets the phrase "taxation without representation" as rhetoric that the colonists employed in pursuit of a larger goal: a free market economy that would liberate them from the mercantilist system that their colonial status dictated. Dr. James Volo also minimizes the importance of the phrase but for a different reason. According to Volo, colonists had grown accustomed to local control and resented the British government, and especially King George III, for trying to upend their way of life. The colonists themselves debated the relative importance of these issues; historians will continue to debate them for a long time to come.

Background Essay

Separated by both 3,000 miles of ocean and dissimilar circumstances, it was inevitable that differences would arise between the ruling class in Britain and the inhabitants of British North America. Statesmen in London did not understand this, and even when they did, they made little or no effort to reconcile the differences. Both groups had been growing apart for some time, but the British victory over France in the French and Indian War of 1754–1763, known in Europe as the Seven Years' War of 1756–1763, actually worked against British rule. The removal of the French threat gave free play to the forces working for separation. Although the war had been won largely by British regulars, Americans believed that their contributions to it diminished their obligations to Britain.

Almost immediately after the war, in 1763 Chief Pontiac of the Ottawa Indians led a rebellion along the western frontier. British regulars put it down, but London now decided to station 10,000 regulars along the frontier and have the Americans pay part of their upkeep. The plan seemed reasonable, especially as the mother country was hard-pressed for funds following the heavy expenditures of the French and Indian War and because the soldiers would be protecting the colonials both from Indian attack and any French resurgence. This decision, however, ignited a long controversy about Parliament's right to tax.

The question now became just what taxes the Americans would be willing to pay. Americans—that is, those who were not slaves or indentured servants—were probably the freest people in the world. Apart from import duties (much of which were evaded through widespread smuggling), they paid only those few taxes assessed by their own colonial legislatures.

Parliament's taxation effort began with the American Duties Act of April 1764, commonly referred to as the Sugar Act. Although lowering the duty on foreign molasses, it imposed a duty on all sugar or molasses regardless of its source. The act also included enforcement mechanisms and established a new vice admiralty court with jurisdiction over customs cases in the British colonies, located at Halifax, Nova Scotia, where British judges presumably would be safe from intimidation. The Sugar Act infuriated the colonists. James Otis of Massachusetts denounced it in his pamphlet *The Rights of the British Colonies Asserted and Proved*. This work enunciated the principle of no taxation without representation.

The Stamp Act of 1765 was a levy on all paper products, and such a tax was widespread in Europe. Opposition to the Stamp Act was strong, and Parliament repealed it the next year. Generally unnoticed in the excitement in the colonies over the repeal was the Declaratory Act of March 1766. It asserted Parliament's authority over its American colonies "in all cases whatsoever."

The next effort by Parliament to tax came in the Townshend Acts of 1767. These imposed customs duties on glass, lead, paint, paper, china earthenware, silk, and tea imported from Britain into the colonies. The resulting taxes would be applied to help pay the salaries of royal governors and judges as well as the cost of defending the colonies. But the acts were clearly an attempt to make British officials independent of colonial legislatures and to enable them to enforce parliamentary authority. The Townshend taxes too were repealed after colonial protests, in March 1770, except for the tax on tea.

Tensions between colonists and British soldiers also had been rising, in part for economic reasons (many British soldiers had, out of need, taken part-time jobs away from Bostonians). Another problem was the Quartering Act, by which Bostonians were forced to house and feed British troops. These factors led to a bloody confrontation on March 5, 1770: the Boston Massacre.

Matters were now coming to a head between the Crown and colonial agitators. The prolonged British effort to bring the colonies to heel and colonial resistance to it ended with the so-called Boston Tea Party. In May 1773, Parliament attempted to rescue the financially strapped British East India Company. The government authorized it to sell its considerable surplus of tea directly to its own agents in America. The tea would actually be cheaper—even with the tax in place—than smuggled Dutch tea, but the arrangement would cut out colonial middlemen, establishing a monopoly on what was the principal colonial drink and ending a major element of the smuggling trade. Public meetings in New York, Philadelphia, and Boston all condemned the act.

At the end of November 1773, three ships carrying East India Company tea arrived at Boston. Two large mass meetings at that port demanded that it be returned to England without payment of duty. With no action forthcoming, on the evening of December 16 some 8,000 people met in protest, and afterward a number of them, roughly disguised as Mohawk Indians, boarded the ships and dumped 342 chests of tea into Boston Harbor.

This event ended British government patience. Frustrated by its fruitless effort to tax the colonies and by colonial intransigence and lawlessness, London now adopted a hard-line approach. Determined to teach the rebellious American subjects a

The Boston Tea Party. In protest against the Tea Act of 1773, which imposed unpopular taxes on a heavily-consumed commodity, colonists disguised as Mohawk Indians boarded three British East Indiamen and cast some 300 chests of tea into Boston harbor. The British Parliament answered this action with the Intolerable Acts. (Library of Congress)

lesson, in March 1774 King George III and his ministers pushed through Parliament the first of what became known as the Coercive Acts, measures known in America as the Intolerable Acts. The first of these, the Boston Port Bill, closed the port of Boston, threatening the colony with economic ruin. Other legislation suspended the charter of Massachusetts, placed that colony under martial law, and gave the new government extensive new powers over town meetings. A Quartering Act required colonial authorities to provide housing and supplies for British troops. These actions created a firestorm of protest in America, lending credence to arguments by the New England radical leaders that the British were out to crush American liberties.

At the same time, although not part of the coercive program, the Quebec Act of May 1774 seemed to be a gratuitous British insult and one of the "intolerable" measures. Actually one of the most enlightened pieces of imperial legislation of its day, it sought to reconcile the large number of French Catholics to British rule by granting full civil rights and religious freedom to Canadians. This was, however, anathema to many Protestants in New England. It also defined the borders of the former New France as the French had drawn them, cutting the seaboard English colonies off from further westward expansion.

After the Intolerable Acts and the Quebec Act, colonists met in several colonies and sent delegates to a Continental Congress in Philadelphia in September 1774. It adopted the so-called Association that called for nonimportation of English goods after December 1. Individual colonies then organized Committees of Public Safety.

By the winter of 1774–1775, North America was a powder keg. British commander in North America Lieutenant General Thomas Gage reported to London that the situation was dangerous and that he lacked the manpower to keep the peace. Nevertheless, George III and his ministers were determined to pursue a hard line. In February 1775, Parliament declared Massachusetts to be in rebellion.

London disagreed with Gage's assessment of required troop strength and warnings that the Americans would fight. On April 19, 1775, Gage sent troops to destroy stocks of arms and powder at Concord, Massachusetts. On the way, at Lexington, there was an armed clash between colonial militiamen and the British regulars. The American Revolutionary War had begun.

Spencer C. Tucker

Perspective Essay 1. Power, Rights, and Revolution

The phrase "taxation without representation," which undoubtedly sparked the American Revolution, was shorthand for a struggle about power and rights in the

British Empire. The resulting arguments laid bare the irreconcilable political goals and conflicting constitutional premises of Great Britain and its colonists. Debate regarding taxation without representation lay at the heart of questions about the relationship between different parts of the empire, the liberties of colonial subjects in America, and the power of the British Parliament. The resulting conflict fueled three separate fires that blazed into the American Revolution: colonial resistance to British imperial control, the British government's attempts to compel subordination, and the subsequent political and social transformation of colonial American society into a new republican order.

The debate over taxation without representation unfolded in an environment of conflicting ideas about the relationships within the British Empire. While the American colonials viewed themselves as British, increasingly their imperial cousins did not. British officials acted accordingly in their attempts to reform the empire and deal with the crushing debt that Great Britain had accrued in its victory in the Seven Years' War. Rather than emphasize equality and cooperation within the empire, imperial officials subordinated the colonial provinces to English interests. The reforms began in 1763 by curbing absentee officeholding in the colonies and increasing the financial incentives for enforcing customs regulations. Confident that improved administration would collect more revenue, Parliament followed with the Sugar Act of 1764, lowering the duty on sugar from non-English plantations but ensuring its collection. Most intrusive, the Stamp Act of 1765 required colonists pay a tax on printed materials and legal documents and promised to impact every aspect of life.

Papers submitted in a lawsuit, land deeds and surveys, wills, licenses, diplomas, apprenticeship and indenture papers, newspapers, pamphlets, almanacs, and playing cards all required stamps. In addition, the Currency Act of 1764 aimed at preventing colonial assemblies from irresponsibly sinking their constituents' debts with depreciating paper currency. The Proclamation Line of 1763 similarly sought to impose external solutions to American disorder by temporarily barring colonial settlement beyond the Appalachian Mountains. Further "reforms" empowered vice admiralty courts to assume guilt and limit jury trials in customs cases. In all of these laws, American colonists saw that they were being treated as something less than wholly British—and that their traditional rights were being subordinated beneath the interests of those in England.

The new taxes gave American colonists direct means to voice their fears that Parliament viewed them as subordinate members of the empire. The Virginia Stamp Act Resolutions of 1765 laid out the central premise: "taxation of the people by themselves, or by people chosen by themselves to represent them, . . . is the only security against burdensome taxation." Equally important, however, was the connection between representation and taxation as "the distinguishing characteristic of British freedom." The Stamp Act Congress echoed that argument: the colonists "owe the same allegiance to the Crown of Great Britain" but also "are intitled to all the inherent rights and liberties" of those in England. This congress of politicians from across Britain's North American colonies insisted that "it is inseparably essential to the freedom of a people, and the undoubted right of Englishmen, that no taxes should be imposed on them, but with their own consent, given personally, or by their representatives." The Stamp Act Congress declared not only "that the people of these colonies are not. . . and . . . cannot be represented in the House of Commons in Great Britain" but also that "it is unreasonable and inconsistent with the principles and spirit of the British constitution, for the people of Great Britain to grant to his Majesty the property of the colonists." Taxation without representation both affronted their rights as Britons and denied their proper, equal place in the empire.

Across the imperial crisis of the 1760s and 1770s, American colonists linked taxation, representation, and liberty into a narrative that proclaimed the imminent threats of tyranny, poverty, and slavery. For John Dickenson in his 1768 *Letters from a Farmer in Pennsylvania,* the innovation of parliamentary taxes—either directly levied or imposed through trade duties—made it clear that Britain intended to treat the parts of its empire unequally. Worst of all, there would be nothing to stop Britain from impoverishing its colonials in pursuit of revenue. Dickenson and his fellow colonial protesters hammered on taxation as a stand-in for fears about a slippery slope of exploitation. In the logic of their politics, people who were dominated by the will and actions of others—those who did not have a voice in their own governance—were slaves. By imposing taxation without representation, Parliament would strip Britons in the American colonies of their rights as Englishmen and threaten them with worse degradation to come.

Parliament correctly saw colonial resistance as a rejection of its power to rule and control the future of the empire. By rejecting the supremacy of Parliament, the American colonials threatened to disrupt a delicate constitutional balance that had taken a century and a half of upheaval to achieve. As a result, Parliament also took a constitutional stand in the Declaratory Act of 1766, insisting that the American colonies "have been, are, and of right ought to be, subordinate unto, and dependent upon the imperial Crown and Parliament of Great Britain" and that Parliament possessed "full power and authority" to make laws "to bind the colonies and people of America, subjects of the Crown of Great Britain, in all cases whatsoever." Like the colonial insistence that taxation without representation would lead to tyranny and slavery, Parliament asserted complete power over the colonies for fear that any weakening of resolve would result in their departure from the empire. The destruction of the tea in Boston Harbor in December 1773 gave King George and his prime minister, Lord North, the opportunity to show their determination to rule over the colonials. Parliament closed the port of Boston to trade, dissolved Massachusetts's 1691 charter, and instituted a new government stripped of the traditional hallmarks of home rule and balanced government. On both sides of the Atlantic, the question of taxation without representation had exposed the absolutes of liberty versus slavery on one hand and subordination versus independence on the other.

The terms set by the argument over taxation without representation necessitated collective resistance in colonial America, which in turn strengthened relationships among the American provinces and expanded political participation in colonial society. Colonials responded to the Stamp Act by threatening and shaming the agents of empire who lived in their communities. The defense of their communities' traditional rights empowered the middling and lowly to humble the high and mighty. Merchants organized boycotts of English goods but, following Dickenson's observation, found that "opposition cannot be effectual unless it is the united effort of these provinces." Cooperation across colonial borders was necessary. Colonial unity reached unprecedented levels in 1774 in response to the British ministry's retaliation against Boston after the destruction of the tea. Fueled by the emotions of sympathy and rage, the Continental Association drew men and women of all levels of society to declare their political allegiance, organize for the relief of those suffering in Boston, and shun and punish their neighbors who violated the strictures against consumption of British goods. New committees focused the emotions and actions of common folk and became schools for broader revolution.

Arguments over taxation without representation, with their rhetoric of liberty and rights, fed the "stream of revolution," wrote historian J. Franklin Jameson, that, "once started, could not be contained within narrow banks, but spread abroad upon the land." The American Revolution was not simply colonial resistance to Parliament's imperial reforms; the revolution reordered colonial society and politics and the unified diverse provinces into a confederation of states and expanded the political order. The language of liberty and the experience of mobilization turned initially limited and conservative goals   defense of traditional English liberties, including no taxation without representation—into something radical and unpredicted: a movement that created a nation-state, set a new example of republican government, gradually broadened the body politic, and rooted sovereignty in we, the people.

John Ruddiman

Perspective Essay 2. Colonial Desire for Free Market Economy

The American Revolution was provoked by merchant-entrepreneurs who sought to eliminate British control over colonial trade and commerce in order to increase their own profits in a free market economy. Joining colonial legislators who shared the same economic interests, these large merchants manipulated their constitutional rights as Englishmen to affect a separation from Great Britain. "Taxation without representation" was one of the constitutional manipulations employed against parliamentary authority to further their cause. In the process, colonial merchants made "the pursuit of [economic] happiness" synonymous with "American independence."

From the beginnings of North American colonization in the 17th century, Anglo-Americans accepted and operated on the mercantilist theory that the British colonies existed solely for the economic benefit of the mother country. The colonies were to be used as a supplier of raw materials for British manufacturers as well as consumers of the finished products that flowed from London. The system was enforced by Parliament's authority to regulate colonial trade through regulatory (external) taxes via the Navigation Acts.

Farming and trade formed the foundations of the mercantilist relationship between Great Britain and its colonies. Philadelphia was the financial center of North America, second only to London in the economic influence it wielded throughout the British Empire. Through that port flowed the crops and timber of Pennsylvania's hinterland. Throughout the port cities of North America, merchant-entrepreneurs circulated in taverns and coffeehouses to propose maritime ventures or engage in land speculation. These commercial centers served as de facto stock exchanges and supplied the capital to finance the colonies' impressive economic infrastructure and ongoing development.

Originally, colonial merchants deferred to the authority of the vice admiralty courts, which were responsible for enforcing British mercantilist policy. But as the colonies grew more populated and the trade in colonial products increased, many merchants began circumventing the Navigation Acts to engage in the fairly lucrative practice of smuggling. The vice admiralty courts were inclined to ignore these violations because of the huge financial return the British government enjoyed from the colonies.

This policy of salutary neglect resulted in a huge expansion of the British economy as well as Britain's dependence on the American market. Between 1700 and 1765 the quantity of goods exported from the colonies to the mother country rose 165 percent, while imports from Britain to North America increased by more than 400 percent. Large American merchants complained very little about the system because they were profiting as never before. Soaring prices for agricultural exports, an increase in colonial manufacturing, and growing levels of consumption meant rising standards of living for farmers, small merchants, and artisans as well.

With the end of the Seven Years' War in 1763, however, the economic prosperity of the colonies was challenged. The British government, faced with a staggering £137 million debt from the war, had to raise revenue to pay for it. Parliament then decided to impose a series of revenue-raising (internal) taxes on its North American colonies to offset the burden.

Beginning in 1764, British prime minister George Greenville proposed new taxes to finance the 10,000 British troops who remained in British North America to police French-speaking Canada and the frontier. Among the several bills he presented to Parliament was the Sugar Act, which raised the duty on sugar, indigo, coffee, and wine imported into the colonies. Another measure, the Currency Act, prohibited colonial assemblies from issuing paper money, forcing them to deal strictly in English tender. A third piece of legislation, the Quartering Act of 1765, required the colonies to provide housing and accommodations for British troops in public buildings. The most troubling bill, however, was the Stamp Act of 1765, which placed a tax on documents used in court proceedings; papers used in clearing ships from harbors; college diplomas; appointments to public office; bonds, grants, and deeds for land mortgages; indentures, leases, contracts, and bills of sale; liquor licenses; playing cards and dice; and pamphlets, newspapers, and almanacs. The Stamp Act was widely criticized as a revenue-raising or direct tax on the American people. Most important, the measure angered printers and editors as well as lawyers, who now joined merchants in their opposition to Parliament.

This coalition of radical elites would lead the movement for American independence. They transformed an economic argument—how to protect their own financial interests against the new legislation—into a political one and turned to the English Constitution to make their case. All they wanted, they claimed, were the rights of Englishmen, and according to the constitution they could "not be taxed without Parliamentary representation." British officials rebutted their claim by asserting that while the colonists may not actually choose their own representatives, they were virtually represented in Parliament because each member was supposed to act on behalf of the entire empire, not just his constituents. In other words, Parliament was supreme, and it had full authority over the colonists.

The colonial elites aroused the attention of prosperous merchants and planters, artisans and craftsmen, and poor people who believed that their rights were being violated by British officials. In Boston, mob action made certain that the Stamp Act would not be enforced. Activists in other colonies shut down provincial courts so that no stamps could be used, and merchants agreed not to import any British goods until the act was repealed. Parliament, in March 1766, was forced to repeal the Stamp Act, though it was not unwilling to concede the constitutional point. To this end, it simultaneously issued the Declaratory Act of 1766, asserting its right "to make laws in all cases whatsoever."

When Parliament in 1767 imposed the Townshend Acts on glass, lead, paper, paint, and tea, the radicals once again rallied the masses around the cry "no taxation without representation." Most colonists limited their protests to petitions, but Bostonians mobbed British customs officials when they tried to enforce trade regulations. In response, Parliament sent two regiments of British soldiers "to bring the Bostonians to a proper state of subordination" and to make them examples to the rest of the colonies. Once again the radicals, using the rhetoric of the English Constitution, argued that the deployment of troops to restore order was in fact imposing a standing army on the colonies in peacetime, a direct violation of their rights as Englishmen. More effectively, the colonists organized an economic boycott that reduced all British exports by 60 percent. Unwilling to risk further revenue declines, Parliament on March 5, 1770, repealed all the Townshend duties except that on tea.

On the same day in Boston, a large mob gathered around a group of British soldiers and began throwing snowballs, rocks, and debris at them. In defense the soldiers fired into the crowd, killing five people. Although the soldiers were tried and acquitted, the widespread descriptions of the so-called Boston Massacre soon became propaganda to turn colonial sentiment against the British.

Between 1770 and 1773, there was a period of calm in the colonies. The radicals' efforts to organize a boycott against the remaining Townshend tax on tea failed. Colonists had become too fond of tea to give it up, enabling smugglers to carry on a thriving trade in untaxed Dutch tea. The point of no return came in late 1773 when Parliament, in an effort to assist the financially troubled British East India Company, passed another Tea Act that permitted the company to ship tea directly to America. By so doing, Parliament created a potentially significant loss of revenue for American importers and smugglers. Insisting that Parliament was imposing an import monopoly on colonial markets, the radicals made bolder claims of American rights against the "encroaching power" and "tyranny" of the British government. These merchant-entrepreneurs and their allies understood that they could profit handsomely if unencumbered by the restrictions of the mercantilist system. To that end, on the night of December 16, 1773, a group of activists loosely disguised as Mohawk Indians tossed 340 chests of tea owned by the East India Company into Boston Harbor.

Stunned by the Boston Tea Party, Parliament responded by passing the so-called Intolerable Acts, which closed the port of Boston until the colony paid for the destroyed tea, altered the charter of Massachusetts, and reestablished the demand to quarter British troops in the homes of private citizens without owners' permission. Shortly after Parliament passed the Quebec Act, restricting colonial settlement of the West. Viewed by many Americans as a blatant abuse of power by the British government, the Intolerable Acts prompted a call for a colonial congress to determine a response. That First Continental Congress, convened on September 5, 1774, organized a comprehensive embargo of trade against Britain and conveyed a petition of rights and grievances demanding the repeal of all parliamentary acts passed after 1763. The congress also asserted the rights of the colonies to regulate their own internal affairs. Before adjourning, the delegates agreed to convene another congress to be held the following spring.

By the time the Second Continental Congress convened in May 1775, the first battles of a war between the American colonists and Great Britain had been fought. It is no coincidence that the members of the new U.S. government had significant interests in trade and commerce. Of the 56 delegates who signed their name to the Declaration of Independence, 47 earned their livelihoods as merchants, shippers, or large planters, and more than half were trained in the law. Their incentive for independence had much less to do with political principles than with British regulation of colonial trade. Despite their bold claims of the inherent right of all Americans to "life, liberty and the pursuit of happiness," they were more concerned about financial profits than lofty democratic ideals.

William Kashatus

Perspective Essay 3. The Crown's Arrogance

On the night of December 16, 1773, several thousand people massed in the chilly streets of Boston to listen to a speech given by political radical and longtime colonial rabble-rouser Samuel "Sam" Adams, who targeted the shipment of tea belonging to the British East India Company in three ships tied up at Griffin's Wharf. The Boston Tea Party is one of the most iconic symbols of the American Revolution, but it may not have precisely mirrored the causes for which Americans went to war. It was instead the Crown's arrogance in tampering with the long-established systems of local governance and commerce that was a more significant cause of the revolution. In order to better understand the true nature of the prerevolutionary period, it may be necessary to decouple the historical anger over taxation and the grievances concerning colonial governance in British North America.

The people of Anglo-America showed their indignation toward the Crown not only when it came to taxation but, more important, with regard to the attempt by Parliament to fundamentally transform the political and economic relationships among the Crown, the colonies, and the people themselves. This essentially English question of political sovereignty and with whom sovereignty ultimately resides had been fought over many times in British history. Most Americans, like most Britons, had no right to vote, and they recognized the proper role of hierarchy in everyday life. Boston was a city governed by the typical New England town meeting, and the colonies all had active, if sometimes headstrong, representative assemblies—the delegates empowered to aid or restrict the royal prerogative as circumstances warranted. The common people relied on the latter group to defend their rights.

Increased taxation had angered the American people. Certainly British propaganda attempted to paint the Patriot Party in America as petty, cheap, and unwilling to pay its fair share of the cost of running the empire. Yet only a small part (some 3 percent) of the expense was tied to the American colonies. Public debt in

Massachusetts, on the other hand, had skyrocketed between 1739 and 1763, and local taxes had almost doubled to pay for three major military campaigns in as many decades.

Before the accession of George III in 1760, the Crown had seemingly chosen to govern its Atlantic colonies with what amounted to benign neglect. Thereafter Parliament, through the Board of Trade, seemed willing to sacrifice the rights, the property, and the liberties of the colonials for the profits enjoyed by its friends among the London investors in the British East India Company. The hypocrisy astounded political observers on both sides of the Atlantic.

In 1754, Benjamin Franklin had addressed the problem by visualizing a better-defined relationship between the Crown and the colonies in his Albany Plan of Union, and Joseph Galloway also suggested that the problem could be resolved by a federation of Anglo-American states—very much like the British Commonwealth accepted in the 19th century. Early in 1764, however, Patriot radical James Otis had publicly gone a giant step further than either man, launching for the first time the idea that Parliament had no authority to legislate for the colonies without their consent—a fundamental concept advanced by John Locke and other political theorists a century earlier. Otis suggested that the colonies be given their own representatives in Parliament in order to resolve the impasse. Yet the colonials had meaningful evidence that the Crown planned to dissolve their local governments—at least in Virginia and Massachusetts. Fully half of the complaints in the Declaration of Independence speak directly to the fundamental alteration of the role of royal government in America—a virtual disempowerment of the colonial legislatures and the desire by the Crown to extend an unwarrantable jurisdiction over its colonial assemblies or dissolve or limit their authority.

Parliament passed a number of pieces of legislation that proved to be very unpopular in America. Among these were the Proclamation of 1763; the Stamp Act, the Sugar Act, and the Navigation Acts of 1764; the Townshend Acts of 1767; the Tea Act of 1773; and the Coercive Acts of 1774. Each restricted colonial commerce and further attempted to dismantle the authority of the colonial assemblies. Stamp Act protests of 1764 are generally assigned as a point of departure between colonial acquiescence and active resistance to royal governance. The Proclamation of 1763 in particular closed off all the native lands west of the Appalachians to white settlement and required those settlers already there to remove themselves to the east without any form of compensation from the Crown for their losses in labor, crops, buildings, cleared fields, fences, and other improvements. During the following winter, a sensational series of anti-Indian and antigovernment riots broke out among a furious population of indignant backcountry settlers. In this regard, the profoundly commercial character of American resistance becomes evident.

For coastal New England, it was the vigorous and even arbitrary enforcement of the maritime regulations under the new administration that was the cause of much of the colonial alienation. A greatly enlarged customs bureaucracy annoyed the Bostonians and was met by protests and jeering crowds.

It would be an error to consider these attitudes concerning the customs and regulations a mere expression of colonial pique. Enforcement had been extended beyond the purview of local magistrates to sailing skiffs and rowboats passing a few hundred yards across a boundary river between colonies such as New York and New Jersey. After 1760, violations of many regulations had been raised for the first time to the status of major crimes, and the penalties had increased to confiscatory levels. Disgruntled merchants stood in long lines to have their paperwork processed by petty bureaucrats or risk an appearance before an admiralty court—somewhat akin to answering a modern-day parking ticket before a military tribunal.

The importance of all the aforementioned measures to the coming of the American Revolutionary War, however, was that they raised to prominence a group of extraordinary radical leaders from within the colonies. The voices of this new group rose above the normal background of discontent common to the colonial middle classes. Among these radicals was a largely disconnected assortment of political intellectuals, grassroots organizers, street thugs, and economic theorists. That the Americans instead became nationalists seeking an independent republic of their own was really a by-product of their initial success in forging a cohesive economic response among themselves and in uncovering the staggeringly arrogant attitude of the government to their complaints at almost every phase of the dispute. Herein a wider consensus had been forged for more than a mere tax protest. Thereafter, the cause of independence took on an emotional force and a life of its own that was shared by a large enough segment of the American population to come to fruition. The people wore liberty caps, gathered around liberty poles, designated liberty trees, and rang liberty bells. Yet the shift from discussing, speaking, and writing about liberty to shouting, shoving, and burning during a protest was a startling violation of decorum in an age when body language spoke volumes about royal authority and its vulnerability.

As ordinary Americans affirmed their trust in one another through unconventional acts, creative forms of protest, and the brilliant, if extralegal, formation of popular antimercantile collectives and the organization of paramilitary organizations and local militias, they discovered that the language of rights and liberties was more than mere rhetoric and faded scratchings on the ancient velum of the Magna Carta. The most radical among the protestors often suppressed their anger, their passion, and their natural recklessness in order to redeem their traditional rights as Englishmen. They initially undertook to regain the former structure of British polity, not to transform it. Yet in its consequences, the revolution that the Patriots undertook to avoid fundamental change imposed upon them from without was as radical as any that followed thereafter in that it also fundamentally transformed America from within.

James M. Volo

Further Reading

Anderson, Fred. *Crucible of War: The Seven Years' War and the Fate of the Empire in British North America, 1754–1766.* New York: Vintage, 2000.

Bailyn, Bernard. *The Ideological Origins of the American Revolution.* Cambridge, MA: Belknap Press of Harvard University Press, 1992.

Bailyn, Bernard, and Jane N. Garrett, eds. *Pamphlets of the American Revolution, 1750–1776.* Cambridge, MA: Belknap Press of Harvard University Press, 1965.

Breen, T. H. *American Insurgents, American Patriots: The Revolution of the People.* New York: Hill and Wang, 2010.

Breen, T. H. *The Marketplace of Revolution: How Consumer Politics Shaped American Independence.* New York: Oxford University Press, 2004.

Brewer, John. *The Sinews of Power: War, Money and the English State, 1688–1783.* Cambridge, MA: Harvard University Press, 1990.

Bushman, Richard. *King and People in Colonial Massachusetts.* Chapel Hill: University of North Carolina, 1987.

Carp, Benjamin L. *Rebels Rising: Cities and the American Revolution.* New York: Oxford University Press, 2007.

Countryman, Edward. *The American Revolution.* Revised ed. New York: Hill and Wang, 2003.

Dickerson, Oliver M. *The Navigation Acts and the American Revolution.* New York: A. S. Barnes, 1963.

Drake, Francis S. *Tea Leaves.* Boston: A. O. Crane, 1884.

Gardner, Brian. *The East India Company.* New York: Dorset, 1971.

Greene, Jack P. *American Revolution: Its Character and Limits.* New York: New York University Press, 1987.

Greene, Jack P. *Understanding the American Revolution: Issues and Actors.* Charlottesville: University Press of Virginia, 1995.

Holton, Woody. *Forced Founders: Indians, Debtors, Slaves, and the Making of the American Revolution in Virginia.* Chapel Hill: Published for the Omohundro Institute of Early American History and Culture by the University of North Carolina Press, 1999.

Jameson, James Franklin. *The American Revolution Considered as a Social Movement.* Princeton, NJ: Princeton University Press, 1926.

Jensen, Merrill. *The Founding of a Nation: A History of the American Revolution, 1763–1776.* Indianapolis: Hackett Publishing, 2004.

Koebner, Richard. *Empire.* New York: Grosset and Dunlap, 1965.

Labaree, Benjamin W. *The Boston Tea Party.* New York: Oxford University Press, 1964.

Leach, Douglas E. *Roots of Conflict: British Armed Forces and Colonial Americans, 1677–1775.* Chapel Hill: University of North Carolina Press, 1986.

MacFarlane, Alan, and Iris MacFarlane. *The Empire of Tea: The Remarkable History of the Plant That Took Over the World.* Woodstock, NY: Overlook, 2004.

Maier, Pauline. *From Resistance to Rebellion: Colonial Radicals and the Development of American Opposition to Britain, 1765–1776.* New York: Norton, 1972.

Maier, Pauline. *The Old Revolutionaries: Political Lives in the Age of Samuel Adams*. New York: Norton, 1990.

Morgan, Edmund S., and Helen M. Morgan. *The Stamp Act Crisis: Prologue to Revolution*. Chapel Hill: Published for the Omohundro Institute of Early American History and Culture by the University of North Carolina Press, 1953.

Morison, Samuel Eliot. *Sources and Documents Illustrating the American Revolution, 1764–1788, and the Formation of the Federal Constitution*. New York: Oxford University Press, 1965.

Morris, Richard B., and James Woodress, eds. *Voices from America's Past: The Times That Tried Men's Souls, 1770–1783*. New York: McGraw-Hill, 1961.

Moxham, Roy. *Tea, Addiction, Exploitation, and Empire*. New York: Carroll and Graf, 2003.

Nash, Gary. *The Urban Crucible: The Northern Seaports and the Origins of the American Revolution*. Cambridge, MA: Harvard University Press, 1979.

Schama, Simon. *A History of Britain: The Wars of the British, 1603–1776*. New York: Hyperion, 2001.

Stroll, Ira. *Samuel Adams: A Life*. New York: Free Press, 2008.

Wood, Gordon S. *The American Revolution: A History*. New York: Modern Library, 2002.

Wood, Gordon S. *The Radicalism of the American Revolution*. New York: Vintage Books, 1993.

Young, Alfred F., ed. *Beyond the American Revolution: Explorations in the History of American Radicalism*. DeKalb: Northern Illinois University Press, 1993.

16. Could the Patriot Side Have Prevailed in the American Revolutionary War without French Assistance?

France's decision to enter the American Revolutionary War on the Patriot side was a rather complicated affair. It came less from a burning desire to help the American insurrectionists and more from a thirst for revenge. Indeed, the French saw their intervention as a way to seek retribution against the British, who had humiliated them during the 1754–1763 French and Indian War. That conflict had effectively ended

France's North American empire. The French also hoped to blunt what they viewed as British ambitions to attain world dominance. After the American victory at Saratoga in the autumn of 1777, France, which had been observing the revolution in the British colonies from its beginning and covertly funneling equipment to the rebels, decided to go to war with Britain and openly support the revolutionaries. Some three years later on October 19, 1781, a combined Franco-American force secured the surrender of Lord Charles Cornwallis's large British army at Yorktown, Virginia, essentially bringing an end to the active military phase of the American Revolutionary War. During the course of the conflict France sent two expeditionary land forces to North America, numbering about 13,000 men in all. Nearly 240 years later, scholars continue to debate the importance of French assistance in the colonies' quest for independence.

In the first perspective essay, Dr. Jim Piecuch argues that without French assistance the revolution would have ended at a different time and place, but the outcome would have been the same. He traces the course of the war, revealing how in the early years the colonists managed to achieve successes despite a lack of foreign forces and how the addition of French troops from 1778 onward failed to produce battlefield victories except at Yorktown. In the second essay, Dr. Lee W. Eysturlid cautions against attributing American success to any one factor. Although he acknowledges the importance that French assistance played, he also discusses the equally important factors of American military leadership, the failure of British military strategy and logistics, the challenges of American climate and geography, and the myth of the superiority of the British Army.

Background Essay

France provided important assistance to the American colonies in their revolt against the British Crown. As early as September 1775, French agents were in America to assess the rebellion and its course. American privateers operating against British merchant shipping soon found welcome in French ports, and beginning in March 1776, the French government extended financial assistance to the American rebels. That same year, the French government ordered weapons and munitions sent to the West Indies for transshipment to North America. France thus became the chief source of arms supplies for the colonial cause.

This French support was largely the work of French foreign minister Charles Gravier, Comte de Vergennes, who sought to weaken Britain internationally and advance France's interests abroad but above all secure revenge for the humiliating defeat suffered by France in the Seven Years' War (1756–1763), which began first in America as the French and Indian War of 1754–1763.

French aid was handled by well-known playwright Pierre-Augustin Coron de Beaumarchais. He secured armaments, mostly from French government arsenals, and sent on to America either directly or through the West Indies more than 200 cannon and 25,000 small arms. The latter included the excellent .69-caliber Charleville musket, named for the principal French arsenal producing it. The Charleville was one of the finest muskets of the period and would remain the standard American infantry weapon well after the American Revolutionary War. The French also provided 100 tons of gunpowder, 20 to 30 brass mortars, and clothing and tents sufficient for 25,000 men. This was a tremendous amount of aid, especially considering that the maximum size of the Continental Army was just 20,000 men.

In the fall of 1777, the impact of this assistance was clear during the pivotal First and Second Battles of Saratoga (Freeman's Farm on September 19 and Bemis Heights on October 7). These decisive military encounters ended with the surrender of Lieutenant General John Burgoyne's army that had invaded upper New York state from Canada and represented about a third of the British army then in North America. While the battle was won solely by American forces, French weaponry and powder had made it possible.

Individual Frenchmen also volunteered for service in America. For the most part recruited by American representatives in Paris, they received commissions from the Continental Congress. Some came to occupy important positions in the Continental Army. The most important of these was certainly the Marquis de Lafayette. A member of one of the most prominent noble families of France, he became a major general and one of the Continental Army's major field commanders as well as virtually the adopted son of Continental Army commander General George Washington. Many other French officers served in the Continental Army in lesser but nonetheless important capacities, such as artillerist Louis Tousard, who later produced the first artillery manual for the U.S. Army.

The surprising Continental Army victory at Saratoga (October 1777) convinced French government leaders at Versailles that the Americans actually had a chance of winning the war, and they now decided to bring France into the war openly. In February 1778, France concluded with the United States both a treaty of Amity and commerce and a treaty of alliance. Both parties agreed to fight on until American independence was "formally or tacitly assured." In June 1778, hostilities actively commenced between France and Britain.

The entry of France into the war was a threat to every part of the British Empire, including India and especially the West Indies. The war now ceased to be wholly a land operation in North America and became largely a contest of sea power. From 1778 except in North America itself, Britain was on the defensive, compelled to surrender the initiative. This change was further accentuated in 1779 when Bourbon Spain followed France and declared war on Britain. Spain's interest was chiefly in securing Gibraltar. Although the British managed to hold on to that important possession and indeed maintain their empire outside America, this meant that few resources would be available for major offensive operations in North America. In December 1780, rising tensions over its claim to search Dutch shipping led the British government to declare war on the Kingdom of the Netherlands. While the Royal Navy was adequate to secure the Atlantic sailing lanes, it was not sufficiently dominant to meet all exigencies, the most worrisome being that France might actually invade the British Isles.

Although on paper the Royal Navy in 1778 was still more powerful than the French Navy, the latter was more efficient. In that year, the Royal Navy had 73 ships of the line (the capital ships of that day) at sea or in good repair. France had some 60 ships of the line, but many of these were finer warships than those of the British. When Spain entered the war it added another 49 ships of the line, and the Dutch added another 14. The British weathered the threat of a French invasion in 1779, but this was more from poor allied leadership and disease than any action by the Royal Navy.

In July 1781, a French Navy squadron under Commodore Louis Jacques, Comte de Barras, arrived at Newport, Rhode Island. It brought 4,000 French troops under the command of Lieutenant General Jean Baptiste Donatien de Vimeur, Comte de Rochambeau. In August, Washington learned that a powerful French fleet had arrived in the West Indies under Admiral François Joseph Paul, Comte de Grasse, and that de Grasse would be coming north during hurricane season. Washington preferred a campaign against New York, but de Grasse sent word that he would sail north to the Chesapeake Bay, bringing an additional 3,000 French land troops, and that he would be able to support allied land operations until mid-October. Rochambeau meanwhile moved his army south from Newport and placed it under the Americans' command. Washington's commander in Virginia, Lafayette, had earlier informed him that British lieutenant general Lord Charles Cornwallis had moved his sizable army to Yorktown.

Washington's combined American and French army marched south and arrived at Yorktown on September 28. The French constituted the largest regular army element in Washington's forces, and their military engineers directed the siege of Yorktown. On October 19 after French and American forces had each seized a key British redoubt, Cornwallis surrendered 8,077 men, one-third of the British army in America. Two-thirds of the 274 allied troops killed or wounded were French. Certainly one of the most important battles of the American Revolutionary War, Yorktown was made possible by the brief period of French naval supremacy and the turning back of British naval forces in the Second Battle of the Chesapeake the month before.

For all its efforts, France secured only the island of Tobago in the West Indies and Senegal in Africa in the Treaty of Paris of 1783. In all, some 44,200 Frenchmen took part in the American Revolutionary War: 31,500 in the navy and 12,700 in the

Continental Army commander General George Washington consults with Lieutenant General Rochambeau of the French army during the Siege of Yorktown in October 1781. Engraving by Jean Mathias Fontaine after a painting by Louis-Charles-Auguste Couder (1790–1873). (New York Public Library)

army. Of these, 5,040 died in the cause of American independence: 3,420 in the navy and 1,620 in the army.

Spencer C. Tucker

Perspective Essay 1. The Myth of French Assistance

When the British force commanded by Lieutenant General Lord Charles Cornwallis surrendered to a combined Franco-American army at Yorktown, Virginia, on October 19, 1781, it seemed clear that the Patriot side could not have achieved this decisive victory without French military support. A French fleet had turned back British naval forces, preventing Cornwallis from escaping or being reinforced by sea, and French troops under the Comte de Rochambeau made up about half of the allied force that surrounded Cornwallis. French assistance was certainly crucial to the outcome of the siege of Yorktown.

However, in the three and a half years between the American alliance with France and the triumph at Yorktown, the French Army and the French Navy had accomplished nothing of consequence against the British in North America. Even before Cornwallis surrendered, British forces in North America had clearly failed to subdue the rebellion, and both commander in chief General Sir Henry Clinton and Cornwallis had run out of strategic options for securing this. Without French intervention, the American Revolution would have ended at a different time and place, but the outcome would still have been an American victory.

From the beginning of the rebellion, British leaders waffled on how to conduct the war. Some believed that the rebels should be subdued using any and all means available, including widespread destruction of property, the employment of allied Native Americans, and even providing arms to slaves and encouraging insurrection. Others argued that reconciliation was the primary object and that the war should be fought with a musket in one hand and an olive branch in the other; only the minimum necessary military pressure should be applied to convince the colonists to return to their allegiance. This division existed in Parliament as well as in the army and forced King George III and his ministers, who preferred a policy of coercion, to accommodate the demands of those who favored conciliation. The resulting strategy, if it can be called such, was incoherent at best and counterproductive at worst.

By the time France entered the war in March 1778, British forces had occupied the northern theater's three major cities—Boston, New York, and Philadelphia—at one time or another, but possession of them had not brought the British victory. For the British to march from any of them into the American interior would only invite a debacle such as that suffered by General John Burgoyne in the Battle of Saratoga in October 1777. Before the first French forces arrived, the British had exhausted their available military options in the north, with little to show for the effort beyond the occupation of New York.

Meanwhile, General Sir Henry Clinton was appointed the new British commander in North America. French intervention did have an effect on British planning: officials in London gave Clinton permission to evacuate Philadelphia, which he did, and also ordered him to dispatch 8,000 troops to defend the West Indies and Florida from possible French or Spanish attack.

When French forces did reach America in July 1778, they did nothing to seriously disrupt the British. A French fleet and 4,000 troops under the Comte d'Estaing joined American major general John Sullivan's forces to attack Newport, Rhode Island, which the British had held since December 1776. The operation was a fiasco. The French ships were forced to sea to meet a British naval squadron, and after an indecisive battle a hurricane scattered d'Estaing's fleet. He decided to refit in Boston, effectively ending the attempt to take Newport. Many Americans, including Sullivan, denounced d'Estaing. Sullivan accused the French of "abandoning the United States."

If the French contributed nothing at Newport, they similarly failed to prevent the British from opening a new phase of operations in the southern states. Hoping to find the success that had eluded the British in the north, Clinton dispatched an expedition from New York in November 1778 that captured Savannah, Georgia, the following month.

The American desire to recapture Savannah led to the second effort at cooperation with the French and again strained relations between the allies while producing a military catastrophe. On September 1, 1779, d'Estaing's fleet and army arrived at Savannah. Major General Benjamin Lincoln, commanding the Continental Army in the South, promptly marched to join the French. Lincoln was surprised to learn on reaching Savannah that d'Estaing had demanded the garrison's surrender "to the arms of the King of France" with no mention of the United States. D'Estaing also continued his negotiations with the British commander, General Augustine Prevost, without consulting Lincoln. At a meeting on September 16, Lincoln protested both the original surrender terms and his exclusion from the negotiations. D'Estaing mollified him but continued to act independently. Nevertheless, the allies finally mounted an assault on Savannah on October 9. The British repulsed them, losing about 100 men while inflicting nearly 900 casualties on the attackers. Ignoring Lincoln's protests, d'Estaing embarked his troops and sailed away. The operations at Savannah had produced nothing except defeat and animosity between the French and Americans.

With Savannah secure, Clinton launched the next phase of his southern campaign with an attack on Charleston, South Carolina. Lincoln surrendered the city and its nearly 6,000 defenders on May 12, 1780, in the worst American defeat of the war. Clinton returned to New York, leaving Cornwallis to command in the South. Congress sent Major General Horatio Gates to take command of another army and retrieve the situation, but Cornwallis smashed the Americans in the Battle of Camden, South Carolina, on August 16. American fortunes were ebbing, and the French had done nothing to help arrest British progress in the South.

It was the Americans, unaided, who turned the tide. The British effort to hold Georgia and South Carolina demonstrated the difficulty of operating in the interior of a hostile territory. Partisans harassed British posts and supply lines, dispersed the Loyalist militia that was trying to organize, and destroyed a large militia force at Kings Mountain, South Carolina, on October 7, forcing Cornwallis to abandon his invasion of North Carolina. On January 17, 1781, a combined force of Continental troops and militia crushed a British detachment at the Cowpens, South Carolina. Cornwallis, vowing to release the prisoners taken at Cowpens, set off in pursuit of the Americans. He pursued Gates's successor, Major General Nathanael Greene, across North Carolina. Greene escaped to Virginia but soon returned to North Carolina, where Cornwallis attacked and defeated him at Guilford Courthouse on March 15. Cornwallis then marched into Virginia, united his depleted army with a 5,000-man British force there, and tried to force that state to submit.

Greene made the daring decision to ignore Cornwallis and return to South Carolina. Skillfully coordinating his army's actions with those of the partisans, Greene suffered a string of defeats at Hobkirk's Hill (April 25) and the siege of Ninety Six (May–June). However, while he kept the main British forces occupied, the partisans severed the supply lines from Charleston, forcing the British to abandon their posts in the southern interior. On September 8, Greene fought his last major battle at Eutaw Springs, South Carolina. Although the Americans gave up the field, the British suffered heavy losses and withdrew the next day. More than a month before the surrender at Yorktown, the British strategy in the South had failed, and their forces were confined to the environs of Charleston and Savannah. Greene had accomplished all of this without assistance from the French, whose army in America remained with Washington's forces in the North.

As for Cornwallis, his operations had not ended resistance in Virginia despite a campaign that devastated much of the state. By the time his army was trapped at Yorktown, he had no good options remaining. Georgia and the Carolinas were lost, and Virginia remained unconquered. Nor did Clinton have anything better to offer in the way of strategy. Believing that his army was not strong enough to risk a decisive battle with Washington, Clinton considered establishing havens for Loyalists near Norfolk, Virginia, and on the eastern shore of Maryland. He also hoped that if the British avoided defeat, the Americans would tire of the fight and give up.

None of these were viable strategies for victory. The British had occupied every major American city except Baltimore and Portsmouth, New Hampshire, at one time or another, and holding these cities had not brought victory. Operations far inland had produced disaster at Saratoga, Kings Mountain, and Cowpens. Had the French not been present to force Cornwallis's surrender at Yorktown, he could either have gone to New York and joined with Clinton in an effort to defeat Washington's army or returned to Charleston and attempted a second conquest of South Carolina. Neither option held any great promise.

Washington had deftly avoided battle for three years, recognizing that the existence of his army served as both a check on British activity and a symbol of American resistance. If Cornwallis returned to South Carolina and succeeded in defeating Greene, the British would simply face the same problem they had failed to solve earlier: suppressing a determined rural insurgency. Without a plan that offered hope of decisive victory, the British public and Parliament would have tired of the expensive, inconclusive struggle and eventually forced the king and his ministers to grant independence to the United States. The Americans had won the war before Cornwallis's surrender at Yorktown. Without that victory, the only one achieved with French military assistance, the war might have continued for a longer time, but the outcome would have been the same.

Jim Piecuch

Perspective Essay 2. Many Factors Lay behind the American Victory

The American Revolutionary War was a long, drawn-out affair. It is a popular contention among historians that the primary reason for the American victory over Great Britain was the financial, material, and especially military aid provided by France. Unfortunately, this overplays the impact of the French while disregarding a number of other critical factors. In the end, there is no single predominant factor to be found. American military leadership, the failure of British strategy and logistics, American geography, local colonial militias, and the myth of the British Army deserve equal consideration.

The French entered the war not as the supporters of a fledgling democracy on the other side of the Atlantic or simply for revenge for their defeat in the Seven Years' War (1756–1763). Rather, the French would commit resources as it suited their overall geopolitical need to combat growing British naval dominance and to reestablish French power in its colonial and military standing. For this reason, the French would often divert significant resources and military forces to elsewhere in their empire, with little consideration for American strategy or preferences.

The first factor of importance in the American victory was the overall quality of America's military and, to a lesser degree, political leaders. America produced some of the best military leaders of the 18th century. None of the American military leaders had any formal military education. However, they had practical experience handling both regular and militia troops and a real grasp of regional geography. This can be seen in three individual examples: George Washington, Nathanael Greene, and Francis Marion.

Washington's immediate appointment as army commander at the war's outset and his dogged tenacity, even in the face of his own failures, to see war through made him a powerful unifying symbol of the effort. Washington always realized the inherent limitations of the troop strength and supply base under which he operated. Only in his campaign to defend New York in the summer of 1776 against a sizable invasion can Washington be seen as making a serious mistake. By directly trying to match British strength, his ragtag army took a real beating. But he learned from this error and never repeated it. What became apparent was that as long as the Continental Army remained intact and operational, Washington could fight a long-term war of attrition against the British.

Washington also had several excellent subordinates who could operate to great effect without centralized control. Greene took command of forces in the American South in 1780. The situation on his arrival was critical, and he immediately displayed the common sense of rebuilding his force before engaging the British. Rather than directly fight, he embarked on a long, wearing campaign involving a great deal of maneuvering with the clear intention of grinding down the British forces. While his engagements, such as those at Cowpens and Guilford Courthouse, were often seen as defeats, Greene exhausted the British, who retreated north to Yorktown. It was only there that French troops actually came into action.

On a smaller but also important scale were the efforts of Marion, the notorious "Swamp Fox," in reducing British logistical capabilities in the southern theater. Marion commanded irregular forces and militia and possessed an intimate knowledge of the geography of South Carolina, where he constantly harassed English supply lines. He did not operate under a direct command or congressional order and received no assistance from the French. Rather, America's vast woods and primitive roads made guerrilla warfare, especially against a clearly uniformed enemy, effective. Marion and several other irregular force commanders like him could operate with near impunity, leaving the British unable to effectively counter.

The British military situation also suffered from a number of factors that contributed to its own defeat in the American Revolution. When the rebellion began in 1775, the British armed forces were not on a wartime footing and had been scaled back as a matter of economy after the Seven Years' War. Debts from this war, which were substantial enough to inhibit borrowing and spending during the revolution, undermined the British ability to raise and support troops and naval units.

Along with British debt was the need to develop a strategy that allowed them to suppress a revolt, ostensibly against taxation and government authority, while not alienating the population at large. This had to be accomplished, owing to economies of scale and distance, with an army that never numbered more then 35,000 men and without a local source of recruitment. The logistics of supplying an army 3,000 miles across the Atlantic was also problematic.

The British never evolved a single effective or coherent strategy. None of the heads of the British government—King George III, Prime Minister Lord North, or Secretary of State for the American Department Lord George Germain—did, or perhaps could, provide useful coordination of forces in America. For that reason, the British seemed to move without purpose between American regions, first the northern colonies, then the mid-Atlantic, and finally the South. Field commanders were left to their own devices or preferences, often with disastrous results, such as General John Burgoyne's defeat and surrender at Saratoga in 1777.

Another factor was the physical and human geography of the American colonies. In 1776, North America was a singularly poor place for the operations of an 18th-century army in a struggle against a popular uprising. The modern world now recognizes in trying to suppress an insurgency the need for a distinct superiority in troop numbers and vast resources, something the British could not manage. They looked to control tens of thousands of square miles with fewer than 50,000 men. Due to the lack of a distinct road network, significant population centers, and centers of political gravity, there were no decisive physical targets.

Part of the human geography was the success of Patriot militia forces, an indigenous and lasting source of strength. While lacking the discipline and firepower of regular troops, they were a regional potential advantage for American commanders and, more important, maintained themselves, making them a very inexpensive part of an overall operation. While American militia forces often performed in a spotty fashion, their numbers made possible fighting in battles such as those at Saratoga, King's Mountain, Cowpens, and Guilford Courthouse. Militia troops also meant that British efforts to gain and maintain control in a specific region were impossible unless sizable garrisons were left behind; the British did not have the numbers to accomplish this.

Historians often note the vast superiority of the British Army and the Royal Navy during the period of the war. This was not the case. The British Army, while a capable and very small professional force, was not the best in Europe. It is certainly open to debate whether there even was a "best" army in 1776, and if there was, that distinction would most likely fall to the Prussians or the French. The French Army was in the process of a series of reforms that marked a real improvement. In the 1781 siege of Yorktown, French troops bested their British counterparts in actual fighting. In addition, more than a quarter of British troops were German mercenaries, who combined mixed motivations with the ability to inspire hatred in the American colonists.

The Royal Navy, generously given the title "best in the world," was in the period of the American Revolution the product of funding cuts and outdated tactics. While it dwarfed anything the Americans could create, it was still limited. British naval strength had to defend British interests in Caribbean, Indian, and European waters while still protecting convoys to America and blockading ports. This overstretch meant that American privateers and foreign supply could be successful. It is also a sign of British limitations that they were driven off or suffered reverses at the hands of French naval forces on several occasions.

French military assistance was not the most important factor in the American victory in the Revolutionary War. Rather, it must be seen as one of several factors that assisted in the American victory. More important to the cause than French troops and ships were French military munitions and credit. French muskets and bayonets were more vital by far than manpower. The French Army in particular played only a small role in the fighting on land, and the French Navy was more an effective distraction than an actual combatant. Would the conflict still have ended at Yorktown had no French troops or ships been there? Probably not. Rather, the British would have likely retreated mostly intact, regrouping in New York. But what effect would that have had?

Failing repeatedly over a seven-year period, it seems unlikely that Great Britain would have continued operations into 1784 and 1785. While the Americans had clearly grown weary of fighting the war, so too had the British, who had nothing to show for their efforts since 1776 and no real options for victory. Had George III ordered the resumption of hostilities in 1784, assuming a lack of French military forces, British planners would have faced the same limits. They could have operated only in one theater and with a now demoralized army. Despite the British retreat, the Americans, emboldened by a victory at Yorktown, would still have had militia forces and geography on their side. In the end, it is hard to find evidence that might point to an American overall strategic defeat with or without French military forces.

Lee W. Eysturlid

Further Reading

Bemis, Samuel Flagg Bemis. *The Diplomacy of the American Revolution*. New York: D. Appleton-Century, 1935.

Brecher, Frank W. *Securing American Independence: John Jay and the French Alliance*. New York: Praeger, 2003.

Chartrand, René, and Francis Back. *The French Army in the American War of Independence*. London: Osprey, 1991.

Coakley, Robert M., and Stetson Conn. *The War of the American Revolution*. Washington, DC: Center for Military History, 1996.

Corwin, Edward S. *French Policy and the American Alliance of 1778*. New York: Archon Books, 1962.

Deconde, Alexander. "The French Alliance in Historical Speculation." In *Diplomacy and Revolution: The Franco-American Alliance of 1778*, edited by Ronald Hoffman and Peter J. Albert, 1–37. Charlottesville: University Press of Virginia, 1981.

Dull, Jonathan R. *A Diplomatic History of the American Revolution*. New Haven, CT: Yale University Press, 1985.

Dull, Jonathan R. *The French Navy and American Independence: A Study of Arms and Diplomacy, 1774–1787*. Princeton, NJ: Princeton University Press, 1975.

Ferling, John E. *Almost a Miracle: The American Victory in the War for Independence*. New York: Oxford University Press, 2009.

Higginbotham, Don. *The War of American Independence: Military Attitudes, Policies, and Practice, 1763–1789*. Boston: Northeastern University Press, 1983.

Hoffman, Ronald, and Peter J. Albert. *Arms and Independence: The Military Character of the American Revolution*. Charlottesville: University of Virginia Press, 1984.

Hoffman, Ronald, and Peter J. Albert, eds. *Diplomacy and Revolution: The Franco-American Alliance of 1778.* Charlottesville: University Press of Virginia, 1981.

Kennett, Lee. *The French Forces in America, 1780–1783.* Westport, CT: Greenwood, 1977.

Lengel, Edward G. *General George Washington: A Military Life.* New York: Random House, 2005.

Mackesy, Piers. *The War for America, 1775–1783.* Lincoln: University of Nebraska Press, 1993.

Middlekauff, Robert. *The Glorious Cause: The American Revolution, 1776–1789.* New York: Oxford University Press, 1982.

Perkins, James Breck. *France in the American Revolution.* Boston: Houghton Mifflin, 1911.

Piecuch, Jim. *Three Peoples, One King: Loyalists, Indians, and Slaves in the Revolutionary South, 1775–1782.* Columbia: University of South Carolina Press, 2008.

Rice, Howard C., and Anne S. K. Brown. *The American Campaigns of Rochambeau's Army.* 2 vols. Princeton, NJ: Princeton University Press, 1972.

Ross, Maurice. *Louis XVI, America's Forgotten Founding Father: With a Survey of the Franco-American Alliance of the Revolutionary Period.* New York: Vantage Press, 1976.

Stinchcombe, William C. *The American Revolution and the French Alliance.* Syracuse, NY: Syracuse University Press, 1969.

Wood, Gordon S. *The American Revolution: A History.* New York: Modern Library, 2003.

Wood, W. J. *Battles of the Revolutionary War, 1775–1781.* New York: Da Capo, 2003.

17. WAS THE FRENCH REVOLUTION A DIRECT RESULT OF THE ENLIGHTENMENT?

The French Revolution represented a crucial turning point in European history and transformed France from a monarchy to a republic. This social, political, and economic upheaval began modestly and was meant to limit royal absolutism. Yet as the revolution progressed, its proponents became more dedicated to the idea of creating a French democracy. What commenced as a call for constitutional monarchy eventually erupted into a decade of turmoil that resulted in six consecutive governments, the execution of the king, and finally a dictatorship that ushered in the Napoleonic era. Because the leaders of the revolution sought change based on many ideals stemming from the intellectual movement known as the Enlightenment that had spread across Europe during the 18th century, it is well worth examining the question of whether the French Revolution was a direct result of the Enlightenment.

In the first perspective essay, Dr. Tom Lansford discusses the confluence of events that contributed to the revolution. He argues that the Enlightenment had a more direct influence on the American Revolution but that the American Revolution in turn directly influenced the French Revolution in two primary ways. First, the success of the American Revolution inspired French political and social leaders to challenge the autocratic rule of King Louis XVI. Second, the enormous debt incurred by the French government in fighting on the side of the American colonists against Great Britain in the American Revolutionary War (1775–1783) directly contributed to the financial crisis that precipitated the outbreak of the revolution in France. Lansford concludes that the Enlightenment was thus a crucial element that helped bring about the French Revolution, which could not have occurred without the challenge presented by Enlightenment thought to the existing political, social, and scientific orders of Europe. Dr. Malcolm Crook asserts that while the upheaval of the French Revolution has traditionally been attributed to the Enlightenment, such an interpretation is problematic because both the Enlightenment and the origins of the French Revolution are extremely complex. In particular, recent scholarship has emphasized the fact that the Enlightenment was not solely a French movement and that the French Revolution itself was largely precipitated by the growing financial crisis that the French government was unable to resolve. He points out that the primary audience for Enlightenment thought was the educated elite, while the majority of the French population—the uneducated masses—had virtually no access to Enlightenment ideas. He concludes that the Enlightenment was not solely responsible for the revolutionary uprising in France. In the third essay, Dr. Spencer C. Tucker argues that France's prolonged financial crisis, precipitated largely by France's intervention in the American Revolutionary War, was the primary catalyst for the French Revolution. France thrust itself into that conflict primarily to counter Great Britain's geopolitical ascendancy and to exact revenge on the British as a result of the 1754–1763 French and Indian War, which had resulted in a humiliating French defeat and the loss of its North American colonies. Furthermore, he points out that bad weather during 1788–1789 had created food shortages and bread riots in France in the months leading up to the revolution. Compounding that was the Crown's decision to increase taxes on France's privileged classes, which set off its own chain reaction against the status quo.

Background Essay

The French Revolution was precipitated by a host of complex problems, but financial difficulties contributed most in bringing it about. Throughout the 18th century, France was troubled by the government's inability to balance its income and expenses. By this period, France had emerged from a medieval principality into the largest and most populous kingdom in Europe and seemed poised to dominate the entire continent. To maintain their position relative to other states, especially in an age-old rivalry against Great Britain, the Bourbon kings of France incurred increasingly high expenses that placed a heavy burden on the kingdom's economy. King Louis XIV's wars, notably his last, the War of the Spanish Succession, significantly weakened the French economy, which was further undermined by Louis XV's involvement in the Seven Years' War. After inheriting a financially and militarily weakened realm, Louis XVI stood by helplessly as France's traditional ally, the Kingdom of Poland, was partitioned by Austria, Russia, and Prussia in 1772. He was able to intervene in the rebellion of the British colonies in North America, where French expeditionary forces played an important role in securing their independence from Britain. However, this success cost France a great deal of investment and delivered no tangible rewards that could have rectified dire financial conditions. Furthermore, France's participation in the American Revolution had driven the French government to the brink of bankruptcy. This proved to be a major impediment to the pursuit of objectives abroad.

Financial difficulties were not linked to foreign policy and wars alone. French monarchs presided over an elaborate welfare system that maintained roads, undertook

Fearful that its cannon might be used against them, Parisians attacked and secured the surrender of the Bastille, an old armory-prison in a working-class area of Paris. This action was falsely interpreted at Versailles as an act of solidarity with the National Constituent Assembly meeting there. (Ridpath, John Clark. *Ridpath's History of the World,* 1901)

public works, and provided justice, education, and medical services, all of which required substantial investments. The royal court also drained huge sums of money as the king underwrote the expenses of courtiers and granted lavish awards and pensions. To make up for its inadequate sources of revenue, the French monarchy began to sell government posts, which reduced their efficiency, and created independent venal officeholders who could not be removed unless the government purchased back the seat. This policy consequently produced an independent-minded and cumbersome bureaucracy. The collection of taxes was leased out to individuals who paid the treasury a fee in exchange for the right to collect taxes in a specific region. While this system provided the monarchy with a steady flow of income, it also allowed officials in charge to squeeze as much as they could from an embittered population.

France could have easily managed these financial strains if not for the government's inability to implement the much-needed reforms. Although popularly described as an absolutist monarchy, the French kings, in reality, were far from exercising unlimited authority and were obligated to rule according to laws and customs developed over the ages. In this respect, the royal appeal courts—the 13 parlements—represented an important check on royal authority. Although nominally royal courts, the parlements were in essence independent bodies after their members purchased their seats from the monarchy. The parlements, especially the Parlement of Paris, emerged as a potent opposition to the Crown, claiming the right to review and approve all royal laws to ensure that they conformed to the traditional laws of the kingdom. In the absence of representative institutions, the parlements (although representing the nobility) claimed to defend the interests of the entire nation against arbitrary royal authority.

The late 18th century was a healthy period of French trade and created a prosperous elite of wealthy commoners (merchants, manufacturers, and professionals), often called the bourgeoisie, who resented their exclusion from political power and positions of privilege. In social terms, France was divided into three estates that corresponded to the medieval notion that some prayed, some fought, and the rest farmed or worked in some other capacity. The First Estate consisted of the clergy, who were subject to their own church court system and were entitled to collect tithes. During the course of hundreds of years the Catholic Church had become a wealthy institution, owning large tracts of land and real estate. While bishops and abbots led a lavish lifestyle, the parish clergy maintained a much more modest lifestyle, often in poverty. The Second Estate consisted of the nobility, who accrued numerous privileges over the centuries. Its status granted the nobility the right to collect taxes from the peasantry and to enjoy many privileges. Thus, top positions in the church, the army, and the royal administration were limited to nobles. The First and Second Estates were both privileged in that they had a privileged status with respect to taxes and opposed the government's reforms as a threat to their respective positions.

The Third Estate consisted of unprivileged commoners, that is, the remaining 95 percent of the French population. As such, it was a loose group, lacking common interests, since it included the wealthiest bourgeoisie, who mixed easily with the nobility, and the poorest peasants and townsfolk. The bourgeoisie saw a significant growth in the 18th century, and merchants in Bordeaux, Marseille, and Nantes exploited overseas trade with colonies in the Caribbean and the Indian Ocean to reap tremendous profits. These wealthy commoners were naturally dissatisfied with the social and political system in France, which placed a heavy tax burden on their shoulders yet failed to provide them with proper representation in government. The role of the bourgeoisie at the start of the French Revolution had been hotly debated and laid the basis for the so-called bourgeois revolution thesis, which argues that revolutionary upheaval was the inevitable result of the commoners' struggle for class equality. Recent historical research has downplayed such an explanation of the revolution, since the boundary between the nobility and the bourgeoisie was very fluid, and both classes often shared common interests.

Of the groups comprising the Third Estate, the peasantry was the largest. Unlike their brethren in Eastern and Central Europe, the majority of French peasants enjoyed legal freedoms, and some owned land; however, most rented land from local seigneurs or bourgeois landowners. Rural conditions differed depending on the region, and such differences later influenced peasants' reactions to revolutionary events. By the late 18th century, the heavily taxed peasants were acutely aware of their situation and were less willing to support the antiquated and inefficient feudal system. The peasantry enjoyed prosperous years between the 1720s and the late 1760s, which produced a growth in the population. However, climatic conditions changed in the 1770s, bringing repeated crop failures and economic hardships that were exacerbated by the increased population. Secular attitudes became prominent in the countryside, and tolerance for the existing social order began to wear thin.

The ideological origins of the French Revolution are directly linked to the activities of the philosophes, who championed radical ideas and called for social and political reform. The intellectual arguments of the Enlightenment had been read and discussed more widely in France than anywhere else. Applying a rational approach, the philosophes criticized the existing political and social system. In his *Spirit of the Laws* (1748), Baron de Montesquieu, a prominent political thinker, provided a detailed study of politics and called for a constitutional monarchy that would operate with a system of checks and balances between its branches. Voltaire directed his sharp wit and tongue at the social and religious ills afflicting French society, denouncing religious intolerance, fanaticism, and superstition and advocating the British system of constitutional government.

Starting in 1751, many philosophes participated in a monumental undertaking to produce the *Encyclopédie,* edited by Jean d'Alembert and Denis Diderot. Completed in 1765, the *Encyclopédie* applied a rational and critical approach to a wide range of subjects and became a best seller that, in part, shaped the newly emerging public opinion. The works of Jean-Jacques Rousseau proved to be especially important for the influence they exerted. In his famous *The Social Contract* (1762), Rousseau explained the rise of modern societies as a result of complex social contracts between individuals, who were equal and possessed a common interest—what he called "the general will." If the government failed to live up to its "contractual" obligations, Rousseau maintained, citizens had the right to rebel and replace it. Rousseau's ideas would eventually nourish the radical democratic section of the revolutionary movement.

One of the major outcomes of the Enlightenment was the growth of public opinion, which was formulated in an informal network of groups. In Paris, this network manifested itself in salons—informal regular meetings of artists, writers, nobles, and cultured individuals—that became the discussion forum for a variety of ideas. Essays and various literary works presented here eventually appeared in the growing number of newspapers and journals that further disseminated information. The spread of the Masonic movement, which was introduced from Britain in the early 18th century, further stimulated discussion, since it advocated an ideology of equality and moral improvement, irrespective of social rank. The process of secularization accelerated after 1750 and affected both the elites and the lower classes. Cafés in Paris and other cities established reading rooms where patrons could peruse and discuss a wide range of literature, notably the works of the philosophes. The late 18th century also saw the rapid growth of pamphleteering, which was largely directed against the government and provided ample criticism of the royal family, particularly the widely unpopular queen, Marie Antoinette. Some pamphleteers eventually emerged as leading revolutionary orators and journalists.

Alexander Mikaberidze

Perspective Essay 1. A Complex and Controversial Relationship

The relationship between the Enlightenment (1689–1789) and the French Revolution (1789–1799) remains complex and controversial. Many assert that the French Revolution began as a manifestation of the democratic and egalitarian ideals formulated during the Enlightenment, while others contend that the upheavals in France owed more to the country's political and social structures and forces as well as the influence of the American Revolution (1775–1783).

The Enlightenment prompted a period of dramatic intellectual, philosophical, and scientific growth. The roots of the Enlightenment lay in the work of figures such as John Locke (1632–1704) who argued in favor of natural rights, republicanism, limited government, and the social contract. Later Enlightenment thinkers (known widely as philosophes) further challenged conventional wisdom and accepted scientific, social, and religious norms. They were generally critical of absolutism and existing social hierarchies. Many of the philosophes were identified with the French Enlightenment (1715–1789), including figures such as Baron de Montesquieu (1689–1755), Voltaire (1694–1778), Jean-Jacques Rousseau (1712–1778), Denis Diderot (1713–1784), and the Marquis de Condorcet (1743–1794). One of the seminal achievements of the philosophes was the publication of the multivolume *Encyclopédie,* beginning in 1751, that included essays, articles, and illustrations on Enlightenment thought.

Most of the political theories of the Enlightenment were considered to be very radical at the time. Locke and Rousseau argued that individual rights were inherent and preceded government and that the political power should be constrained through a social contract between the governed and the government. Otherwise, governments would erode the freedom of individuals. Rousseau wrote in *The Social Contract* (1762) that "Man is born free, and everywhere he is in chains." However, Locke contended that government should exist mainly to protect property rights, while Rousseau believed that government's main role was to encourage equality and opportunity. Meanwhile, Montesquieu asserted that governments should have a separation of power in order to prevent the tyranny of any single branch. Such ideas challenged the notion that monarchs ruled by divine right.

Enlightenment thinkers were also critical of organized religion because of their preference for reason over faith and a belief that the world was governed by a set of rational laws that could be discovered through scientific observation and empiricism. Many philosophes rejected what they perceived to be the superstition of contemporary religion and instead became deists or atheists. Figures such as Voltaire were instrumental in the development of modern secularism.

Many of the ideals of the Enlightenment arose from the Glorious Revolution of 1688 in Great Britain, which limited the powers of the monarchy and laid the foundation for the British system of constitutional monarchy. The Enlightenment exerted a stronger influence on the American Revolution, and principles such as individual liberty, limited government, separation of powers, and the social contract were embodied in the founding documents of the United States, including the U.S. Declaration of Independence (1776) and the U.S. Constitution (1789).

The American Revolution subsequently contributed to the French Revolution in two ways. First, the success of the new nation inspired French political and social leaders to challenge the autocratic rule of Louis XVI (1754–1793). Many French soldiers who had fought alongside the Americans returned to their home country determined to reform the government and society. They joined those philosophes who called for reductions in royal power, since they perceived that the American

Revolution proved that the ideals of the Enlightenment could serve as the foundation for a new system of government. Second, France was an ally of the Americans during the war of independence. France provided both troops and funding. The war added more than 1 billion livres tournis to France's national debt and left the country essentially bankrupt. Efforts by the royal government to raise taxes in response to the costs of the conflict prompted popular unrest, which was exacerbated by food shortages among the lower classes.

In May 1789 the king summoned the Estates General, the French parliament, in an effort to address the nation's debt. However, infused with Enlightenment and revolutionary ideas, the deputies became increasingly bold in efforts to reform the government. In June the deputies voted to create a new national legislature, the National Assembly. The *Encyclopédie* was influential in spreading ideals and served as a common political reference for those who sought to overturn the existing order. Leaders of the French Revolution, such as Maximilien Robespierre (1758–1794), looked to Montesquieu and Rousseau for inspiration.

In July 1789 crowds stormed the Bastille, a political prison and a symbol of the old regime. Events progressed rapidly; feudalism was abolished, and on August 27 the Declaration of the Rights of Man and of the Citizen was promulgated. Broader in scope than the Declaration of Independence, the French declaration incorporated many of the main principles of Enlightenment political thought and was developed to serve as the main social contract between the French people and the government. "Liberty, equality, and fraternity" emerged as the slogan of the revolution.

Even as the revolution became more radicalized—the monarchy was abolished in 1792, and Louis XVI was executed a year later—leaders of the movement continued to embrace Enlightenment thought. For instance, beginning in 1790, the Civil Constitution of the Clergy created a separation of church and state, and the government began to confiscate church property across France. Secularism would remain a significant component of French political philosophy. Meanwhile, a succession of revolutionary regimes attacked the aristocracy in an effort to create a full democracy. The growing excesses of the succession of revolutionary governments and efforts by radicals to export the revolution throughout Europe led to armed conflict with other European powers. External threats reinforced the radicalization of some groups, and by 1799 the troubled republic had been replaced by the empire of Napoleon I.

The French Revolution could only have occurred because Enlightenment thought challenged the existing political, social, and scientific orders in Europe. The leaders of the revolution looked to the Enlightenment as well as contemporary events such as the formation of the United States as they recast French politics and society. The resultant themes of democracy, secularism, and individual rights trace their roots to the Enlightenment and the philosophes.

Tom Lansford

Perspective Essay 2. The Enlightenment and the Origins of the French Revolution

"It was the fault of Voltaire and Rousseau." Early efforts to explain the outbreak of the French Revolution were inclined to attribute the blame to subversive writers of the 18th-century Enlightenment, such as Voltaire and Jean-Jacques Rousseau. The fact that homage was paid to these philosophes during the 1790s, when the remains of Voltaire and Rousseau were transferred to a national shrine, while so many leaders of the revolution acknowledged their inspiration, seemed to offer conclusive proof that the movement of ideas preceding 1789 had indeed played a major role in bringing down the old regime in France. Yet this simple proposition is open to many objections, not least because both the nature of the Enlightenment and the origins of the revolution were extremely complex; their exact relationship thus remains a matter of considerable argument.

An emphasis on the diversity of the Enlightenment, no longer regarded as solely French or explicitly revolutionary, has made direct links to upheaval much harder to detect. There were radical elements, but their importance can easily be exaggerated by a selective reading of texts such as Rousseau's *Social Contract,* which was not his most widely read work. Even the philosophes' general hostility to established religion, especially the Catholic Church, criticized its organization as much as its dogma. Christians often responded positively to the onslaught, and the 18th century was an age of faith as well as doubt. In the political domain, the anarchic potential of the uneducated masses was feared, leading many writers to look to those in authority to implement their ideas. Rousseau, who hailed from a particularly humble background, should be seen as atypical, though when he was asked to legislate for Poland his prescriptions were cautious. Denis Diderot, whose more daring reflections were not published until the following century, counseled respect even for bad laws in order to encourage compliance with good ones. In the absence of a modern concept of revolution as a means of progress, the philosophes' watchword was "reform" or "improvement."

Moreover, the downfall of the old order in France resulted primarily from the financial collapse of the monarchy, a consequence of overexpenditure on a (largely unsuccessful) series of wars for both maritime and continental hegemony in Europe as well as an inadequate system of administration. Writers had sought to cure rather than exploit these growing difficulties, and some, like Anne-Robert-Jacques Turgot, had entered royal service. Harvest failures, high prices, and unemployment in the late 1780s, which coincided with impending state bankruptcy, were hardly a result of ideology but instead were a regular occurrence in a preindustrial society (though the philosophes were keen to foster economic growth). Finally, hostility between nobles and the bourgeois, which fatally divided the representative body (the Estates General) that was convened to help the king resolve the crisis, fractured the enlightened elite who had achieved consensus around ideas such as responsible government and greater individual freedom.

As numerous studies over the past few decades have underscored, the audience for Enlightenment was nothing if not well heeled and elitist. Only a minority could read and write, for education was the preserve of the wealthy in 18th-century Europe. Readers of expensive enlightened texts thus shared the same aristocratic, clerical, and middle-class characteristics as the philosophes themselves. Analysis of the book trade and membership in salons and academies in Paris and the French provinces has likewise demonstrated the limited diffusion of the Enlightenment in a largely illiterate society; peasants and artisans, who were the overwhelming majority of the population, had no direct access to what was a demanding and open-ended intellectual debate.

With historians having demolished the popular myths surrounding Edmund Burke's celebrated "conspiracy of educated men," it might appear that the Enlightenment had little impact on the origins of the French Revolution. However, in recent years the role of ideas has been convincingly integrated into the cultural origins of the revolution, which have claimed increasing attention. In this domain, which is concerned with attitudes and behavior, it is not so much the influence of specific texts—whose impact it is virtually impossible to measure—as of gauging shifts in the climate of opinion. Not only was skepticism encouraged about the literally God-given right of existing institutions and practices to prevail, but the status quo was challenged in unprecedented fashion. This is not to say that the revolution was imagined before it was put into effect after 1789, but a critical atmosphere was certainly created in which established ideas could no longer be taken for granted and change became feasible.

"The rise of the public sphere," a phrase borrowed from the German sociologist Jürgen Habermas, has gained significant currency among historians of the 18th century. It suggests that the ruled as well as rulers had a right to participate in debating affairs of state. Politics was accordingly no longer the preserve of the court, since with the rise of the press, information was being broadly disseminated and discussed not just in capital cities but also in provincial centers. The foundations of the old regime in terms of royalty, religion, and social hierarchy thus began to be sapped, while the business of government became more difficult in this increasingly open environment. As King Louis XVI discovered when attempting to rely on his traditional absolutist authority in 1788–1789, only an appeal to reason would convince the educated public, but proposals for reform merely whetted the appetite for more.

It was thus in a more subtle manner that the ideas of the Enlightenment played a role in the origins of the French Revolution as a crucial strand within the complicated web of developments that emerged in 18th-century France. That the universally acknowledged necessity for reform should topple into upheaval was not the work or the desire of the philosophes. Their writings would inform many of the policies that were subsequently applied, leading one participant to suggest that it was not the influence of the Enlightenment that brought about the revolution but rather the revolution that brought the ideas of the Enlightenment to bear after 1789. Revolution might previously have proved unthinkable, but change was placed firmly on the agenda, its terms clearly set by the philosophes' intellectual endeavors.

Malcolm Crook

Perspective Essay 3. The Financial Crisis Caused the French Revolution

Many writers assumed at the time and since that the French Revolution of 1789 was caused primarily by Enlightenment ideas and the "wind from America." As a number of prominent 20th-century historians have made clear, however, the prime catalyst was a financial crisis brought on by France's participation in the American Revolutionary War (1775–1783).

Intendant at Limoges (1761–1774), French controller general of finances (1774–776) and noted economist and philosophe Anne Robert Jacques Turgot had argued in 1775 that the only way that mounting French budget deficits could be handled was if there were no new wars and the government instituted a policy of fiscal restraint. France had begun to aid the American rebels secretly and was contemplating open intervention. Turgot had argued that the debt could be handled if there were no new loans or major new expenditures and that the costs of aiding the America rebels would postpone, perhaps forever, meaningful reform. He even went so far as to suggest that the fate of the monarchy might hinge on this one decision. In this he was correct, but he failed to convince King Louis XVI, and so the council and aid to the American revolutionaries proceeded.

French support for the American colonies in their revolt against Britain was largely the work of one man: Charles Gravier, Comte de Vergennes, French foreign minister during 1774–1787. Vergennes believed that the British were bent on world domination, and he sought to develop an alliance with Spain and the Dutch Republic to secure a balance of power and thwart British ambitions. Certainly he also wanted revenge for the humiliating defeat suffered by France in the Seven Years' War (1756–1763), known in America as the French and Indian War (1754–1763).

The vast sums necessary to fight the American Revolutionary War bankrupted France. The cost of the French military intervention was particularly high in the naval sphere. In 1781 alone France spent 227 million livres on the American war, with 147 million livres on the navy alone. This latter figure was five times the operating cost of the peacetime navy.

For the year 1774, the Crown had received 277 million livres in revenue, with expenses running at 325 million livres. The deficit, to be covered by loans, thus came to 48 million livres. In 1778 while income to the Crown had risen twofold to 504 million livres, the deficit had tripled to 630 million livres over what it had been 14 years previously. The cause of this was the American Revolutionary War, which may have cost France as much as 2 billion livres.

The man who found the money to fight the American Revolutionary War was Swiss banker Jacques Necker, who took Turgot's place as director general of finance in 1778. He simply paid too much for the money raised, much of it through annuities without following actuarial tables and sold to canny bankers. By 1788, some 51 percent of government revenues were going just to service the interest on the debt.

France was the richest country in Europe, but a number of factors contributed to the shortage of Crown revenue. Certainly one reason was the system of tax farming. Since 1726 a private group, the Company of the Farmers General, had charge of tax collection. The group included the king, who owned a full share and thus assisted in plundering his own kingdom. In the contract of 1786 the farm guaranteed to provide 116 million livres to the Crown. If the sum raised was between 116 and 125, the amount would be split between the Crown and the farm. Any revenues received in excess of 125 million livres would be kept entirely by the farm alone. In 1788 the farm paid the Crown 208 million livres but kept 200 million livres for itself.

Another reason for the lack of Crown revenue was a general economic decline in the last years of the Old Regime. Part of this was owing to a sharp increase in the French population, which had grown by 50 percent in the course of the 18th century. More people were now dependent on the same area of land at a time when agricultural production drove the economy. There was also an industrial recession, which threw many people, such as those in the textile industry, out of work.

Bad weather in the form of hailstorms in July 1788 aggravated an already serious situation by sharply reducing crop yields and driving up the price of grain. In many cities in the winter of 1788–1789 there were bread riots. France experienced sharp inflation, with the costs borne chiefly by the lower classes in skyrocketing prices for such essentials as grain and firewood. As noted historian George Lefebvre observed, "Had bread been cheaper, the violent intervention of the masses, which was essential for the overthrow of the Old Regime, would perhaps not have taken place, and the bourgeoisie would have triumphed less easily."

What were the paths open to the Crown to solve the financial crisis? One was to work to increase prosperity, but this was at best a long-term solution. The Crown might also curtail expenses, and some of this was done. Thus, France did not intervene in the Netherlands during civil strife there in 1787. The Crown also set up some economies in the court itself, but the effect of these was limited because in 1788 the court only accounted for some 6 percent of the budgetary expenses. The administrative system (including the court), public works, industrial development, and poor relief amounted to roughly 23 percent. The military and foreign affairs claimed 26 percent. These two broad areas could not be sharply reduced without danger to the nation. As noted, the largest portion of the budget was the 51 percent devoted to simply servicing the debt.

The Crown could, of course, repudiate the debt. While Spain had done this twice, the fact that much of the debt was held by important French individuals and institutions ran the great risk of revolution. Finally, there was the only logical course: tax the wealth that was previously exempt.

Although France was Europe's richest country, the church (the First Estate, with perhaps 1 percent of the population) and the nobility (the Second Estate, with some 2 percent of the population) were exempt from taxes, which were paid by everyone else (the Third Estate). As the First and Second Estates together possessed some half of the land of France (which was the chief source of wealth in the late 18th century), the government was chronically poor.

The financial crisis facing France now forced the Crown to move to tax the privileged classes. Necker was dismissed in 1781, and the new controller-general of finance, Charles Calonne, who held that office during 1783–1787, attempted to secure approval for a scheme to broaden the tax base by calling an Assembly of Notables in 1787. It failed. The nobles, who dominated the 13 parlements of France led by the Parlement of Paris (not parliaments in today's sense but quasi law courts that passed on the historic "laws" of the kingdom) insisted that for such a fundamental change the Estates General must be called. In the so-called Aristocratic Reaction (1787–1789), the nobles held firm, and the Crown at last gave way. It was thus the nobles who unwittingly began the French Revolution.

The Estates General had last met in 1614. It included representation of the three estates but with a vote by order. As they dominated the higher offices in the clergy, the nobles expected to control the Estates General in a vote of two to one, and while having to pay some taxes, the nobles expected to secure in return a degree of control over the Crown. The success of the nobles in forcing the meeting of the Estates General, however, led leaders of the Third Estate to rebel in turn. With the Third Estate having as much as 97 percent of the national population, its publicists demanded that it be allowed to elect more representatives, and the government foolishly agreed to the "doubling of the Third," giving the Third Estate the number of representatives equal to those of the clergy and nobility combined. This did not seem to be a major concession at the time, for voting was still to be by order.

When the Estates General met at Versailles in May 1789, however, representatives of the Third Estate refused to transact business until there was a vote by head (the Tennis Court Oath) and, supported by nonnoble members of the clergy and some liberal nobles, stood firm in this demand. Louis XVI, who had initially sided with the nobles, finally yielded, and the National Assembly came into being, with major changes enacted into law. Many thought that the revolution was now over. This was not the case, of course. It continued to evolve and become more radical, although throughout representatives of the middle class remained solidly in charge until Napoleon Bonaparte seized power in a coup d'état in 1799.

The radical changes came under the pressure of war and the possibility of a national defeat. Although there was little threat to France, the new leaders of France were convinced that their achievement would never be safe while France was surrounded by reactionary states. They hoped to spread the revolution abroad while at the same time securing the centuries-old goal of a natural frontier for France on the Rhine to the northeast. On April 20, 1792, revolutionary France therefore declared war on Austria and Prussia, beginning what would be 23 years of war in the French Revolution and Napoleonic periods and in 1793 ushering in the most radical period in the revolution.

Spencer C. Tucker

Further Reading

Berlin, Isaiah. *The Age of Enlightenment.* New York: Meridian, 1984.

Bouloiseau, Marc. *The Jacobin Republic, 1792–1794.* New York: Cambridge University Press, 1983.

Censer, Jack R., and Lynn Hunt. *Liberty, Equality, Fraternity: Exploring the French Revolution.* University Park: Pennsylvania State University Press, 2001.

Chaline, Olivier. *La France au XVIIIe siècle (1715–1787).* Paris: Éditions Belin, 1996.

Church, William F. *The Influence of the Enlightenment on the French Revolution: Creative, Disastrous or Non-Existent?* Boston: D. C. Heath, 1964.

Cobban, Alfred. *A History of Modern France,* Vol. 1, *Old Régime and Revolution, 1715–1790.* New York: Penguin, 1991.

Cobban, Alfred. *The Social Interpretation of the French Revolution.* Cambridge: Cambridge University Press, 1964.

Corzine, Phyllis. *The French Revolution.* San Diego: Lucent Books, 1995.

Doyle, William. *The Oxford History of the French Revolution.* Oxford: Oxford University Press, 2002.

Dupre, Louis. *The Enlightenment and the Intellectual Foundations of Modern Culture.* New Haven, CT: Yale University Press, 2004.

Egret, Jean. *Necker, Ministre de Louis XVI, 1776–1790.* Paris: Honoré Champion, 1975.

Ellis, Geoffrey. *The Napoleonic Empire.* London: Palgrave Macmillan, 2003.

Furet, François, and Denis Richlet. *The French Revolution.* Translated by Stephen Hardman. New York: Macmillan, 1970.

Gershoy, Leo. *The French Revolution and Napoleon.* Englewood Cliffs, NJ: Prentice Hall, 1964.

Gottschalk, Louis R. *The Era of the French Revolution (1715–1815).* New York: Houghton Mifflin, 1929.

Israel, Jonathan. *Revolutionary Ideas: An Intellectual History of the French Revolution from the Rights of Man to Robespierre.* Princeton, NJ: Princeton University Press, 2014.

Jacob, Margaret C. *The Enlightenment: A Brief History with Documents.* New York: Bedford/St. Martin's, 2001.

Jacob, Margaret C. *Living the Enlightenment: Freemasonry and Politics in Eighteenth-Century Europe.* Oxford: Oxford University Press, 1991.

Kaplow, Jeffry, ed. *France on the Eve of Revolution.* New York: Wiley, 1971.

Lefebvre, Georges. *The Coming of the French Revolution.* Princeton, NJ: Princeton University Press, 1947.

Manceron, Claude. *Twilight of the Old Order, 1774–1778.* Translated by Patricia Wolf. New York: Knopf, 1977.

Manuel, Frank E. *The Prophets of Paris: Turgot, Condorcet, Saint-Simon, Fourier, Comte.* New York: Harper and Row, 1962.

Martin, Xavier. *Human Nature and the French Revolution: From the Enlightenment to the Napoleonic Code.* New York: Berghahn Books, 2003.

Munck, Thomas. *The Enlightenment: A Comparative Social History, 1721–1794.* New York: Oxford University Press, 2000.

Murphy, Orville T. *Charles Gravier, Comte de Vergennes: French Diplomacy in the Age of Revolution, 1719–1787.* Albany: State University of New York Press, 1982.

Rudé, George. *The French Revolution: Its Causes, Its History, and Is Legacy after 200 Years.* New York: Weidenfeld and Nicolson, 1988.

Shennan, J. H. *The Parlement of Paris.* Ithaca, NY: Cornell University Press, 1968.

Soboul, Albert. *The French Revolution, 1787–1799.* Translated by A. Forrest and C. Jones. New York: Random House, 1974.

Solé, Jacques. *Questions of the French Revolution: A Historical Overview.* New York: Pantheon Books, 1989.

Sutherland, Donald. *France 1789–1815: Revolution and Counter-Revolution.* New York: Oxford University Press, 1986.

Thompson, J. M. *The French Revolution.* Oxford, UK: Basil Blackwell, 1962.

Vovelle, Michel. *The Fall of the French Monarchy, 1787–1792.* Cambridge: Cambridge University Press, 1983.

Williams, David, ed. *The Enlightenment.* New York: Cambridge University Press, 1999.

Yolton, John W. *Blackwell Companion to the Enlightenment.* Hoboken, NJ: Wiley-Blackwell, 1991.

Zysberg, André. *La Monarchie des Lumières (1775–1786).* Paris: Éditions du Seuil, 2002.

18. DOES NAPOLEON BONAPARTE DESERVE HIS REPUTATION AS A MAJOR MILITARY INNOVATOR AND BRILLIANT FIELD COMMANDER?

Napoleon Bonaparte is without doubt one of the most famous military leaders in human history. Except for two brief periods, he was involved in warfare almost continuously from 1792 until 1815. In addition to his many military exploits, Napoleon also shrewdly manipulated politics to his advantage, becoming France's first consul in 1800, emperor of France in 1804, and king of Italy in 1805. His Continental System, designed to strangle England economically, was for a time a great success. Napoleon enjoyed an unprecedented series of military victories, often defeating armies larger than his own. His greatest victory was the December 2, 1805, Battle of Austerlitz, where he defeated a much larger Austrian-Russian force. But his invasion of Russia in 1812 proved disastrous, as he waited too long to withdraw and fell victim to a brutal Russian winter.

The four perspective essays that follow examine Napoleon from a variety of perspectives and come to varying conclusions about his abilities as an innovator and a field commander. The first essay, by James R. Arnold, asserts that Napoleon does indeed deserve his sterling reputation as an innovator and commander. He was a superlative tactician and strategist and a great motivator for the men serving under him. He knew the importance of strong morale among his soldiers and thus favored individual merit above all else as the benchmark of good soldiering. Moreover, Napoleon took advantage of the power of offense in military campaigns. The second essay, by Dr. John T. Kuehn, also argues that Napoleon's reputation is well deserved. In addition to Napoleon's skills as a great military innovator and field commander, Kuehn claims that Napoleon's indefatigable work ethic, brilliant mind, and outsized ambition also served him well. Above all else, it was Napoleon's uncanny ability to improvise that made him such a great commander. In the third essay, by Dr. Lee Eysturlid, Napoleon is portrayed as a gifted commander but not as a great military innovator. Napoleon's innovations essentially ended in 1805, and his reputation for applying new ideas to military affairs is thus more myth than reality. Eysturlid also points out that Napoleon never faced off against a commander with skills equal to his own. In the last essay, Dr. Spencer C. Tucker argues that Napoleon was a great military and political leader but not a cutting-edge military innovator. He was a master planner, logistician, prop-agandist, and motivator, and he was an excellent political leader, having introduced the Napoleonic Codes and the concept of meritocracy to France. However, he devel-oped no new weapons or weapons systems, instead building on the ideas and concepts developed by others. He also tended to place self-ambition ahead of France's best interests.

Background Essay

French general and emperor Napoleon Bonaparte was born into the lesser nobility in Ajaccio, Corsica, on August 15, 1769. Genoa had ceded Corsica to France the year before, so Napoleon was born a citizen of France. He studied at the Brienne military school in France (1779–1784) and at the École militaire in Paris (1784–1785). Commissioned in the army, he was assigned to an artillery regiment.

The French Revolution of 1789 made possible Bonaparte's rapid advancement and brilliant military career. War began in the spring of 1792 and, with but two brief exceptions (1802–1803 and 1814–1815), 23 years of war followed, 17 of them dominated by him. Bonaparte welcomed the coming of the revolution, but for most of the next three years he was in Corsica. He hoped to advance the family position there, but running afoul of Corsican nationalist Pascal Paoli, his entire family fled the island in June 1793.

Bonaparte now had to provide for his mother and six brothers and sisters. Find-ing employment in the French Army siege of the British Royal Navy and French Royalists at Toulon (September 4–December 19), Bonaparte developed the artillery plan that drove the British from that port city on December 19. He was advanced from captain to brigadier general in December 1793 and given command of the artillery in the French Army of Italy in February 1794. In Paris as second-in-com-mand of the Army of the Interior, he put down the Royalist uprising of 13 Vendé-maire (October 5, 1795). His "whiff of grapeshot" killed several hundred people but prevented a coup d'état. His reward was command of the Army of Italy in March 1796. Before his departure, he married the widow Josephine de Beauharnais.

Taking the offensive on his arrival in Italy in April 1796, Bonaparte forced an ar-mistice on the Piedmontese and defeated the Austrians at Lodi (May 10) and entered Milan (May 15). He secured all of Lombardy and then won other notable battles over the Austrians, including at Arcole (November 15–17) and Rivoli (January 14–15, 1797). Advancing into Austria, he imposed the preliminary Peace of Leoben (May 12). Bonaparte then dictated the Treaty of Campo Formio with Austria (December 17) that secured the Austrian Netherlands (Belgium and Luxembourg) for France

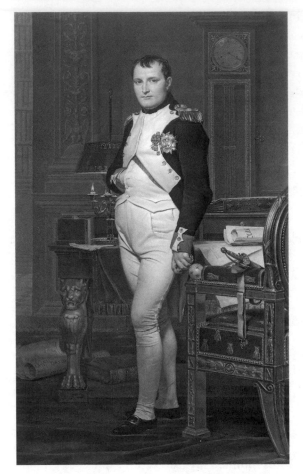

Portrait of French emperor Napoleon I, painted by Jacques-Louis David. Napoleon rose to prominence in France as a brilliant general in the French Revolutionary Wars. He came to power in 1799 and became emperor in 1804. At the height of his power, he controlled most of continental Europe. (National Gallery of Art)

and Austrian recognition of a northern Italian (Cisalpine) republic under French influence.

Bonaparte's reward was command of an expedition against Egypt. After stopping at Malta and seizing its treasury, the French landed at Alexandria on July 1. Bonaparte defeated the Mamelukes in the Battle of the Pyramids (First Battle of Aboukir, July 21), only to be cut off in Egypt by the destruction of most of his fleet by Admiral Horatio Nelson in the Battle of the Nile (Battle of Aboukir Bay, August 1). Bonaparte's forces subsequently overran all Egypt. In February 1799 he invaded Syria to forestall an Ottoman attack but failed to take the city of Acre by siege (March 15–May 17).

Returning to Egypt, Bonaparte defeated an Anglo-Turkish force in the Second Battle of Aboukir (July 25, 1799). Learning of unrest in France, he abandoned his army and sailed in a fast frigate. Returning to France on October 9, Bonaparte took the leading role in the coup d'état of 18 Brumaire (November 9, 1799).

Made first consul under the Constitution of the Year VIII in February 1800, Bonaparte solidified his position by invading Italy and defeating the Austrians in the Battle of Marengo (June 14, 1800). Following General Jean Moreau's brilliant victory over the Austrians in Germany at Hohenlinden (December 3), Austria sued for peace in the Treaty of Lunéville (February 3, 1801).

Bonaparte ended hostilities with England at Amiens in March 1802 and was rewarded by being made consul for life in May. His actions, however, prompted Britain to resume the war in May 1803. Bonaparte then ordered preparations for an invasion of Britain. He was crowned emperor of the French in Paris as Napoleon I on December 2, 1804, and king of Italy on May 26, 1805.

On the opening of hostilities with Austria in July, Napoleon broke up the camp at Boulogne and, marching quickly, surprised the Austrians and forced the surrender of an entire army at Ulm (October 20, 1805), then captured Vienna (November 13). Advancing against a larger Austrian and Russian force in Moravia, Napoleon won his most brilliant victory, at Austerlitz (December 2). He then forced peace terms on Austria at Pressburg (today Bratislava, Slovakia) on December 26.

Napoleon dissolved the Holy Roman Empire and reorganized much of Germany into the Confederation of the Rhine under French control in July 1806. His actions in the Germanies led Prussia to declare war on France in September 1806. Napoleon then advanced into Germany. On October 14 Marshal Louis Davout defeated the main Prussian army at Auerstädt, while Napoleon defeated another Prussian army at Jena. These two battles decided the campaign, although other engagements followed. Russian support for Prussia drew Napoleon into Poland where he suffered a check by the Russians at Eylau (February 8, 1807), then won at Friedland (June 14). Czar Alexander I then concluded peace at Tilsit (July 7).

Russia agreed to join Napoleon's Continental System, designed to ruin Britain financially by prohibiting its exports to Europe. Napoleon's efforts to impose this system on all of Europe led to unrest in Portugal and Napoleon's decision to take over that country and Spain. This in turn brought a popular uprising in Madrid against the French (May 2, 1808) and the Peninsular War, with Britain sending an expeditionary force.

Austria judged this the right time to go to war again, believing that all of Germany would join. This did not happen. Napoleon captured Vienna (May 12, 1809) but suffered defeat at Aspern-Essling (May 21–22), which he reversed with a decisive victory at Wagram (July 5–6). Napoleon dictated peace in the Treaty of Schönbrunn in October. Desperate for an heir, he set aside Josephine and married Archduchess Marie Louise on April 1, 1810. She gave birth to their son, Napoleon Francis Joseph Charles, the king of Rome, on March 20, 1811.

Russia meanwhile was unhappy with the French alliance and withdrew from the Continental System in December 1810. Napoleon resolved to invade Russia. Throughout 1811 he assembled the Grand Army, invading Russia with a half million men (June 24, 1812). He took Smolensk (August 7) but ignored wise counsel and pushed on for Moscow, which he believed would being the czar to terms. At Borodino (September 7) Napoleon won the bloodiest battle of the century, but the Russians were able to withdraw in good order. Although Napoleon captured Moscow (September 14), Alexander refused to treat with him. Napoleon waited too long before withdrawing, and Russia's winter and Russian Army attacks destroyed his army.

Napoleon had already returned to Paris to raise a new force. He could secure men but not the commissioned and noncommissioned officers as well as trained horses lost in Russia. Napoleon then fought what became known as the German

War of Liberation, winning costly battles at Lützen (May 2, 1813) and Bautzen (May 20–21), but a prolonged truce during June–August greatly benefited his enemies, especially with the addition of Austria. Although Napoleon was victorious in the Battle of Dresden (August 26–27), he was defeated in the largest battle of his wars, at Leipzig (October 16–19).

Rejecting peace terms that would have given France the Rhine frontier, in the winter of 1813–1814 Napoleon won a number of battles with dwindling resources but was unable to stop the allies from occupying Paris (March 30, 1814). His marshals then demanded his abdication on April 4. Exiled to Elba by the Treaty of Fontainebleau, Napoleon busied himself with his small kingdom. With unrest in France with the new government of King Louis XVIII and the allies quarreling at the Congress of Vienna regarding the peace settlement, Napoleon escaped from Elba and returned to France (March 1, 1815). Troops sent against Napoleon rallied to him, and he returned to power in Paris. Resolved to strike before his enemies could coalesce against him, he invaded Belgium on June 1 and defeated the Prussians at Ligny (June 16) and the British at Quatre Bras (June 16) but then was defeated by the allies at Waterloo (June 18), bringing the Napoleonic Wars to a close.

Napoleon abdicated for a second time and surrendered to the English, who sent him to the island of St. Helena in the South Atlantic, where he died from gastric cancer on May 5, 1821. In 1840 his remains were returned to France and entombed at Les Invalides in Paris.

Spencer C. Tucker

Perspective Essay 1. One of the Three Greatest Military Commanders

The world has witnessed many great generals whose dazzling displays of leadership changed the course of history. There have been only three great captains, men whose combination of inspiring leadership and consummate tactical and strategic skills elevates them above all others: Alexander the Great, Genghis Khan, and Napoleon. During his own time and for more than 100 years after, men related military theory and practice to Napoleon's concepts of warfare and measured ideas and performance against his standards.

In March 1796, Napoleon Bonaparte was 26 years old and largely unknown and unproven when he assumed command of the Army of Italy. His subordinates were extremely skeptical about the capacity of a jumped-up Corsican boy-general. His army was a near-starving rabble that included numerous mutinous units. Lacking a reputation, power, or largess, Napoleon relied on force of personality and intellect to convince his principal subordinates and his army to follow his directives. On his first day of command, he met with three divisional generals. He questioned them in detail about their forces, laid out his campaign plans, announced that on the morrow he would hold an inspection, and the following day would attack. At this first encounter he convinced his subordinates to obey.

On March 27, Napoleon issued a proclamation to his troops: "Soldiers! You are hungry and naked; the government owes you much but can give you nothing." He continued by praising their "patience and courage" and pledged to lead them to fertile plains where they would find "honor, glory and riches." Napoleon concluded by challenging the army to display the required "courage" and "endurance." His words inspired the army. Seventeen days and two victories later Napoleon had conquered Lombardy and taken the next step toward joining the ranks of history's great captains. Long afterward, he explained that a general's "most important talent is to know the mind of the soldier and gain his confidence."

Napoleon believed that in military encounters morale factors outweighed physical factors by three to one. He backed up this belief with a deep study of human motivation. Although he did utter his well-known aphorism "Men are led by baubles," he appreciated that bravery could not be bought. His goal was to convince his soldiers that their conduct, his rule, and France's future were all one. To solidify this union, he created a decoration that superseded all others. This was the Légion d'honneur, known as the Cross. Anyone who displayed exemplary service to France could earn the Cross. It was not a mere bauble but rather a symbol of equality, a measure of merit rather than a function of birth or wealth. On countless battlefields, men competed to earn the coveted Cross. Napoleon encouraged such rivalry because he thought that it produced an officer's best efforts. More than any contemporary general, he also understood the rank and file. He was a master of the theater of leadership. Whereas most of his avowedly class-conscious foes distanced themselves from the common soldier, Napoleon circulated among them, chatting with easy familiarity, proffering rewards, and remembering the faces of those he had met before. He extended his reach by keeping a mobile printing press at imperial headquarters. Its bulletins emphasized that the emperor shared his soldiers' burdens by eating the same food, sleeping amid them on the eve of battle, and feeling the same heat and cold, the same rain and snow. Thus the emperor, known to the rank and file affectionately as the "Little Corporal," reinforced the impression that he was one of them. The egalitarian familiarity between Napoleon and his men was unique and goes a long way toward explaining why his army achieved prodigies of valor.

Moreover, Napoleon intuitively appreciated what modern psychological research discovered regarding the power of the offensive: namely, that morale factors multiplied physical power when a soldier was on the advance and reduced power when a soldier was retreating. Napoleon perceived that the power of the offensive extended beyond a morale impact on individual soldiers; it affected entire national war machines. Therefore, he sought through his war strategy to impose his will by forcing his enemy to respond to his maneuvers. This was most apparent with his favorite strategic maneuver, *la manoeuvre sur les derrières* (the advance of envelopment). Napoleon's faith in the offensive was such that over his entire career he only truly fought on the defensive three times: Leipzig in 1813 and La Rothière and Arcis in 1814. He resorted to the defensive on these occasions only after the dismal failure of his initial attack.

Shining competence was a key to Napoleon's leadership. When he was a youth, his mathematical prowess led him to join the most scientific of the three military arms, the artillery. The French artillery of this time was undergoing major technical reform. Napoleon's intellect and energy well matched the dynamic drive to modernize. Having achieved a technical mastery of artillery, he came under the tutelage of Baron du Teil, who encouraged him to broaden his military knowledge. Napoleon responded, proving himself an avid reader and an apt pupil. He approached military history in analytical fashion. Step by step he collected strategic and grand tactical concepts and unified them into a whole. He was not an original military theorist. Rather, he took existing concepts and improved them. He labored tirelessly to build a solid foundation of knowledge for his chosen career. Intelligent men followed Napoleon because they recognized the power of his brain.

Among modern minds, Napoleon's towering intellect has overshadowed the fact that he also abundantly possessed the soldiery virtues of endurance and bravery. No leader in recorded history worked harder in a more focused way. Twenty-hour days were routine. Emmanuel Las Cases quotes him as asserting that "I was born and made for work. I have recognized the limits of my eye-sight and of my legs, but never the limits of my working power." Napoleon dictated orders while being shaved, conducted interviews while bathing, and plotted strategy while attending the opera. His *carnets,* the notebooks stuffed with statistical data about every imperial and enemy unit, were his favorite reading material.

Napoleon was an able, daring horseman who rode farther and harder than any contemporary ruler and most soldiers. January 1809 found him in Spain. He responded to news of Austrian war preparations by galloping back to Paris, reaching with one hand to whip his companion's horse so they could make better time. Napoleon completed the 700-mile journey in an astounding 6 days. In 1812 he covered nearly 1,300 miles of winter road in 13 days, arriving in Paris at midnight and putting in a full day's work beginning before daybreak. At moments of supreme crisis, Napoleon worked at a tremendous pitch. During the final planning of the Danube crossing in 1809 through the second day at Wagram, he spent 60 of 72 hours on horseback. During a 3-day period at Bautzen in 1813, he slept only a handful of hours, famously dozing beneath his thundering artillery. He rose upon hearing the combat beginning in a new sector and announced "Ney has made his maneuver, the battle is won." With his peerless sense of battlefield timing, he then committed his reserves.

Until the American Civil War had demonstrated the impact of accurate shoulder firearms, the catalog of martial leadership included willingness to expose oneself to enemy fire. Napoleon did not shy away from such exposure. During the course of his career, he had some 19 horses shot from beneath him. Throughout it all he exhibited exemplary sangfroid.

More extraordinary, Napoleon possessed what he called "2 a.m. courage," by which he meant the moral courage to make a decision and live with its consequences, even while knowing that he possessed imperfect information. He prepared himself for those critical choices by rigorous application to intelligence gathering and analysis. But he understood that the path to perfection had to be simple. So, he reduced the principles of military art to three: concentration of strength, activity, and a firm resolve to perish gloriously. He ignored all secondary issues to focus on the main chance. No contemporary possessed his battlefield coup d'oeil.

A final testament to Napoleon's supreme martial skills comes from the circumstances of his downfall. His penultimate defeat in 1814 followed almost a decade of costly attrition against a variety of hostile coalitions yet still required the unified action of all Europe's great powers to topple the colossus. Napoleon had served as commander in chief and political leader to carve a European empire not seen since Roman times. His legions paraded through Vienna, Berlin, Rome, Madrid, and Moscow. He established legal, social, educational, and administrative institutions that persist to this day. He was indeed a great captain.

James R. Arnold

Perspective Essay 2. A Well-Deserved and Enduring Reputation

Napoleon Bonaparte deserves his reputation as a major military innovator and brilliant field commander. Carl von Clausewitz, a man with firsthand knowledge of Napoleon, once wrote of him that "War, in his hands, was waged without respite until the enemy succumbed, and the counterblows were struck with almost equal energy." Similarly, prior to Napoleon's defeat of a combined Austrian-Russian-Prussian army group at Dresden in the summer of 1813, Baron Antoine de Jomini warned his new allies that Napoleon was "the ablest of men." What can one say when faced with this sort of evidence? Quite a bit, actually. However, to be clear, Napoleon's reputation as a military commander nonpareil is in no danger of losing its luster, earned in the hard school of war and defended with brilliance even in defeat. However, our understanding of it must perhaps be modified.

Napoleon, like many great commanders, learned the art of war in the hard school of combat at a very young age. However, unlike some other commanders of the era, he came at the problem of war with a ferocious ambition, a fierce work ethic, and a computerlike brain. His experience, oddly, seemed to skip the lower tactical levels of combat entirely—somewhat like the aforementioned Frederick who began his tutelage in war at the highest levels of strategy and grand strategy. The young Napoleon's first major battlefield accomplishment involved the expert siting of cannon in order to achieve an operational victory over a combined British-Neapolitan-Royalist force at Toulon in 1793. His next significant involvement with combat was the application of artillery firepower to put down a Royalist coup by an armed mob in Paris against the government of that period in 1795. Today this sort of operation is more in the realm of crowd control, counterinsurgency, or even police work, but its results reached the highest level, preventing the overthrow of the national government. Thus, Napoleon's early formative experiences of combat were in more nontraditional settings than one normally finds for a 20-something young officer.

A second point to be made was Napoleon's preference to solve problems with massive firepower, as befitted an artillerist. We must remember that in the old Royal Army only men of merit and talent could advance in the artillery, although their chances at high command were limited. Napoleon chose this route, as it appealed to his nature.

Victor Hugo famously observed in *Les Miserables* that Napoleon's entire style of warfare rested on this early training—he was the "gloomy pugilist of war." When one examines his engagements and campaigns, it is hard not to agree. Napoleon aimed divisions, corps, and armies like cannonballs at his enemies' centers of gravity in order to smash and annihilate them. This led Clausewitz to characterize Napoleon as the "God of War." Perhaps his greatest victory was his least bloody. Napoleon "threw" his entire 170,000-man army behind Baron Karl Mack's Austrian forces at Ulm (October 16–19, 1805), resulting in the surrender of most of the Austrian Army.

Finally, Napoleon's excellence as a commander was not primarily in tactical situations—he had plenty of other talented subordinates who excelled at this—but at what Jomini called "grand tactics" and strategy, what we today call the operational level of war. Napoleon practically invented, primarily in his conduct of his campaigns, what is now referred to as the operational art of war. This involves the construct of campaigns to achieve the political purpose of the war as well as the movements of major military forces prior to engagements and the echeloning of these units' routes of march and arrival locations on the field of battle.

Most of Napoleon's engagements, from his first as an army commander in northern Italy to his final engagements during the Waterloo Campaign (June 15–July 8, 1815) involved the arrival (or supposed arrival) over time of other operational forces at the right time and place on the battlefield. His most famous victories, at Austerlitz (December 2, 1805) and Marengo (June 14, 1800), for example, involved the arrival of forces over time as he calmly fed them into the fight, waiting for the right moment or combination to crack his enemy's composure. At Marengo this was done unintentionally, at Austerlitz intentionally. Historian Owen Connelly, one of Napoleon's most effective critics, attributes his greatness to his ability to "scramble" operationally to victory—to improvise with the situation he found in the theater of operation and the field of battle rather than the one he had planned for. Thus, Napoleon's true greatness as a commander was as an artist whose key ability was the capacity to improvise with the tools at hand and achieve an operational masterpiece.

The second part of Napoleon's reputation must rest on his skill as a military innovator. He was so highly effective at organizing and training that some things he did not invent or create—the combined arms division and many French tactics of the period—are credited to him. However, his innovations involved often putting together the many disparate elements he inherited from the French revolutionary armies into a coherent whole—the Grande Armée and its organizational structure built around the combined arms corps. In addition to these, we need name only a few others in the military sphere to emphasize his unique creativity and organizational skill. First, Napoleon institutionalized a system of advancement by merit, almost single-handedly creating the modern military decoration with his institution of the Legion of Honor, an award that any soldier or citizen of France, and then the empire, could earn by talent, hard work, and merit. As a motivational tool it was unexcelled. Another key innovation that Napoleon created, or rather re-created, involved leadership—his marshals. In creating a rank to correspond with command of his new *corps d'Armée,* he solved both a command-and-control problem as well as a means to propel the most talented generals created by the revolution into positions of operational command.

Napoleon deserves his reputation as a commander of unequaled insight, skill, and sheer willpower. However, the secrets of his success lay in his understanding of firepower, of the hearts of men, and of an emerging operational level of war for the modern era. As with his most famous interpreters, Clausewitz and Jomini, he was ahead of his time and remains a relevant study in commandership for our own time.

John T. Kuehn

Perspective Essay 3. A Gift for Military Command

During the course of his relatively long career as a military commander (1794–1815), Napoleon Bonaparte, first general and then emperor, established an undeniable and spectacular historical persona. If "genius" is accepted as meaning a person of rare and remarkable talent or intelligence, then Napoleon seems to qualify. His actual intellectual abilities were well attested to by both his admirers and his foes, and this reputation continues to be fodder for historians to the present day. However, genius or not, Napoleon was inconsistent in his ability to apply these intellectual gifts in the art of war. His meteoric rise, due in great part to his genius, was matched by his singular end and exile. Therefore, when looking at Napoleon's success operationally and tactically there is no doubting his talents, but when looking for originality or the application of new ideas or technologies, his record is somewhat more myth than reality.

Napoleon's great battlefield successes, such as Austerlitz (1805) and Jena (1806), and his great operational maneuvers, such as the envelopment of Karl Mack's Austrian army at Ulm (1805), owe much of their success to the reformers of the late French Royal Army and the innovations of the French Revolution. The formulation of units into smaller self-contained and permanent fighting forces, or "divisions," could be seen as early as Maurice de Saxe's all-arms "legions." The attack in massed columns to deliver an irresistible blow at a static enemy line was advocated by Joseph de Bourcet in imitation of the Greeks. Emphasis on tactical maneuverability as well as making troops live off the land rather than being fettered to supply depots was put forward by the Comte de Guibert. The increasingly effective use of artillery, a hallmark of the Napoleonic battle, was pioneered and later taught directly to Bonaparte by Jean-Pierre Duteil, his instructor when Bonaparte was a lieutenant in the La Fère artillery regiment at Auxonne.

These many critical changes in troop formations and tactics, a willingness to operate offensively and energetically, and improvements in artillery types and its deployment were but a few changes then being pioneered by young French officers in the 1770s and 1780s. Perhaps more important for Napoleon's success were the forces that the revolutionaries unleashed in the five years immediately after 1789. Innovative and strategic thinkers such as Lazare Carnot envisioned the entirety of France's physical forces, which were considerable, being brought to the use of the state. The vast potential mass of manpower that had been rejected by the Royal Army was tapped into by the radicals on the Committee of Public Safety. Rather than armies of tens of thousands, France would produce multiple armies with hundreds of thousands of men, and mandated production would outfit them with weapons and gear. Further, the destruction of noble control of the officer corps and an active willingness to promote men of talent and energy created a dynamic generation of French noncommissioned officers, field-grade officers, and generals. These were the men who would actually lead French armies during the era. It was that opening of command to meritocracy that allowed for Napoleon himself, a young man of decision, energy, and luck, to succeed in an army otherwise dominated by well-connected nobles. Lacking this change, his genius for command would have been stifled. The French Revolution's emphasis on the state and the service by men for the nation was the cornerstone for the personality cult that Napoleon would build after 1804. This personal and real attachment that he created with his troops, from the ranks into the officer corps, was also part of his greater success and his ability to bounce back after defeats, such as the invasion of Russia in 1812.

The first of two great innovations attributed to Napoleon—the use of the corps as a viable, independent combined force of infantry, artillery, and cavalry—was dependent on many of the ideas listed above. However, it did create a formation that was to be both a strategic and tactical asset. The second innovation, the so-called *battalion carré,* was based on the expanded size of the army, the flexibility of the corps system, and the ability of French commanders, now called marshals, to operate independently. Corps could move at some distance from each other, allowing for greater speed and logistical flexibility, but not so far that they could not concentrate the entire army quickly on contact with the enemy.

When the elements of Napoleon's gift for command are brought together with the innovations and energies released in France by the revolution, his abilities are clear. His success and his ability to take risks in the face of multiple enemies raise another concern. Were the enemies of Napoleon his equal? Were the troops and formations that he faced of real comparison to those that he commanded? Until at least 1809, and more likely until 1813, the answer is no. Arguably Napoleon never faced someone of equal mind or energies to himself. He almost always faced commanders that were, by comparison, of limited talent and energy and hamstrung by the systems they operated under. Napoleon's military genius was therefore facilitated by his opponents' inability to measure up. His encirclement of Mack's forces at Ulm was in part made possible by the lethargic, unresponsive, and outdated Austrian system of command and control. Austrian troops and logistical trains had to be pressed to cover 8 miles in a day, whereas the French Army of 1805 might force-march more than 16 miles in a day.

Since Napoleon, as opposed to the contemporary commanders with whom he is often compared, had absolute military and political power, viewing him as a military genius requires a broader view. His energy, his amazing ability to digest and mentally command maps and terrain, and his ruthlessness gave him dominance on the battlefield that was dynamic. In contrast, as a military innovator especially after 1805, there is little to show. Time and again Napoleon showed no mind for technology, dismissing spotting balloons, steam engines, musket improvements, and an expansion of the French semaphore system. In naval affairs it appears that Napoleon simply hoped that more ships might equal victory, suffering repeated defeat at the hands of the superior British Royal Navy. He never gained any effectiveness in the use of fleets, either tactically or strategically. Finally, his creation of a modern Praetorian guard in the units of the French Old Guard, while spectacular in uniform, denuded regular army units of men needed for its command.

In the end, perhaps a notion of military genius is really predicated on a subtle and visceral combination of charisma, energy, and ability to understand terrain rather than just intellect. In Napoleon's case the reforms of the Royal Army, the energies of the French Revolution, and the failures of his many enemies combined to set the stage for his success. It was his own efforts in exile and his admirers' panegyrics that glossed over his many failures and defeats to rank him as one of the great military geniuses in world history.

Lee W. Eysturlid

Perspective Essay 4. Great Captain but Not a Military Innovator

Napoleon Bonaparte was certainly one of the great captains in military history. He was a meticulous planner and logistician who sought to concentrate the maximum forces possible and bring them to bear quickly before an enemy commander could realize what was occurring. Until his later years in power, he was seemingly indifferent to fatigue. Certainly he excelled as a motivator and propagandist. He knew how to motivate men, and they responded by calling him affectionately "The Little Corporal."

Certainly, as first consul and then as emperor, Napoleon introduced many reforms in France and was a great lawgiver in the Napoleonic Codes, which he had a sizable role in drafting. He regularized the French administrative system, reformed taxation, created the Bank of France, instituted "careers open to talent" as opposed to circumstance of birth, concluded a concordat with the Catholic Church, and solidified many reforms of the French Revolution.

Contrary to myth, however, Napoleon was not a great strategist, theorist, or military innovator. Nor did he introduce new weaponry. The French artillery, which he would employ to such great effect, had already been reformed by Jean Baptiste de Gribeauval during 1765–1774, making it the best in Europe.

Napoleon's sole major operational innovation was the organization of the *corps d'armée* and the tactical deployment of the corps in what was known as the *bataillon carré* (battalion square). Each corps contained two to four divisions of infantry with their own organic artillery, a cavalry division, and corps artillery. Each corps was also self-sustaining. The *bataillon carré* was the employment of four corps with them so placed as together to form a diamond or square in shape, one leading, one on each flank, and the remaining corps a reserve in the rear. Each corps would be no more than one or two days' march from the other and able to fight on its own until other corps could join it. The route could thus be quickly changed depending on contact with an enemy, and yet the army could be massed rapidly. The front of the advancing *bataillon carré* might be as much as 120 miles. This system not only provided Napoleon flexibility in operations not seen before but also allowed him to deceive an enemy as to his real intention.

Apart from this, what Napoleon did was to take the ideas developed by others and make maximum use of them. He waged wars of rapid movement and concentration of resources in the expectation of prevailing in one decisive battle. Where he excelled was in his management of individual battles, in his ability to turn circumstances to his own advantage, making the utmost of the hand dealt him. As he put it in exile at St. Helena: "You engage and then you wait and see." As prominent Napoleonic historian Owen Connelly has put it, Napoleon's "forte was execution: fighting to perfection with the men and weapons available."

Napoleon was often lucky or saved by the actions of subordinates. Marshal Joachim Murat's epic cavalry charge against the Russians in the Battle of Eylau (February 7–8, 1807) plugged a gaping hole in the center of the French line and preserved Napoleon's army from destruction. He also could not abide a rival. General Jean Victor Marie Moreau won a brilliant victory over the Austrians in the Battle of Hohenlinden (December 3, 1800), accomplishing it at less cost than Napoleon's own victory over the Austrians at Marengo (June 14, 1800). Hohenlinden forced the Austrians to sue for peace, which they had rejected after Marengo.

Although Moreau had not shown any political aspirations of his own (he had in fact suggested to plotters seeking a "sword" in order to overthrow the Directory in 1799 that not he but Napoleon should be their man), Napoleon was undoubtedly jealous of Moreau's military successes and regarded him as a threat to his own reputation. Moreau found himself falsely implicated in a Royalist plot to unseat Napoleon in 1804. Arrested, Moreau protested his innocence but was sentenced to exile for life.

Napoleon was certainly a master propagandist; he took the credit for success and blamed others for his failures. The Battle of Marengo is perhaps the best example of both points.

Campaigning in Piedmont, Italy, in the summer of 1800 and believing that the Austrian forces opposing him (estimated by Bonaparte at only 22,000 men but actually 35,000) must have retreated, Bonaparte detached some 11,000 men to search for the enemy. Austrian field marshal Michael von Melas then pounced, catching by surprise Bonaparte with only 15,000 men. Napoleon immediately dispatched urgent appeals to his detached divisions to return as soon as possible. The commanders did not receive the messages in time, but General of Division Louis Desaix marched his division to the sound of the guns. His men arrived, only to see Bonaparte's forces in retreat. Desaix is said to have remarked that "The Battle has been lost; there is time to win another." He then led the attack against the unsuspecting Austrians and carried the day. Unfortunately for Desaix, however, he was shot and killed in the fighting.

Napoleon's victory bulletin made it appear that the battle had been brilliantly planned and executed: "The enemy was allowed to advance to within musket range of the village of San Giuilano, where Desaix's corps was drawn up in line of battle" as if by plan. Napoleon trumpeted a great victory, exaggerating enemy losses while listing his own at about half of the actual total. Some credit had to be paid to Desaix, the real hero of the battle, so the bulletin has his dying words as "Go tell the First Consul that I die regretting not having done enough to live in posterity." As Desaix had been shot through the heart, he cannot have said anything. Many such bulletins gave rise to the expression "To lie like a bulletin."

Napoleon certainly understood the appeal of nationalism and worked it to the maximum advantage in France. He also subordinated the interests of other European countries occupied by the French to those of France itself. Thus, he promoted industrial development in France while discouraging it elsewhere. Such policies made him a prime mover in the creation of European nationalism. The nationalism that swept first Spain and then the Germanies was largely prompted by opposition to heavy-handed French rule.

Napoleon also often ignored the wise counsel of his advisers, always putting his own ambition ahead of the legitimate interests of France. Glaring examples of this are found in his rejecting the sound advice of Charles Maurice de Talleyrand-Périgord, foreign minister of France during 1799–1807, that he moderate his conquests as being the only way to secure a lasting peace. Perhaps his most egregious failure in this regard, however, was ignoring the sound advice of General of Division Armand-Augustin-Louis de Caulaincourt, his former ambassador to Russia during 1807–1811, who argued in vain against the Russian Campaign of 1812 and whose wise advice during it Napoleon repeatedly ignored.

Napoleon did not know when to stop. Take the case of the Treaty of Amiens with the British in 1802. True, the British also violated the treaty, but Napoleon was not prepared to make the few concessions necessary for it to have had a chance of succeeding, and the peace lasted but 10 months. As late as November 1813, even after Napoleon's devastating defeat in the Battle of Leipzig (October 16–19, 1813), the Allies offered Napoleon peace, with France retaining the natural frontiers of the Rhine and the Alps for which so much blood had been shed in vain during previous centuries, but Napoleon rejected it. His refusal to yield anything meant in the end that he lost all.

A hundred years later, Marshal of France Ferdinand Foch, who led the Allied armies to victory in 1918, wrote of Napoleon that "He forgot that a man cannot be god; that above the individual is the nation, and above mankind the moral law; he forgot that war is not the highest aim, for peace is above war."

Spencer C. Tucker

Further Reading

Arnold, James R. *Marengo and Hohenlinden: Napoleon's Rise to Power.* Lexington, VA: Napoleon Books, 1999.

Arnold, James R. *Napoleon 1813: Decision at Bautzen.* Lexington, VA: Napoleon Books, 2015.

Arnold, James R., and Ralph R. Reinertsen. *Crisis in the Snows. Russia Confronts Napoleon, The Eylau Campaign, 1806–1807.* Lexington, VA: Napoleon Books, 2007.

Bonaparte, Napoléon. *Correspondance de Napoléon 1re.* 31 vols. Paris: Henri Plon, 1863.

Caulaincourt, Armand de. *Recollections of Caulaincourt, Duke of Vicenza.* 2 vols. London: Henry Colburn, 1838.

Chandler, David G. *The Campaigns of Napoleon.* New York: Macmillan, 1966.

Chaptal, Jean-Antoine. *Mes souvenirs de Napoléon.* Paris: E. Plon, Nourit et Cie, 1893.

Clausewitz, Carl von. *The Campaign of 1812 in Russia.* Reimpression of the London edition of 1843 with a historical introduction by Forrestt A. Miller. Hattiesburg, MS: Academic International, 1970.

Clausewitz, Carl von. *On War.* Edited and translated by Michael Howard and Peter Paret. Princeton, NJ: Princeton University Press, 1984.

Connelly, Owen. *Blundering to Glory: Napoleon's Military Campaigns.* New York: Rowman and Littlefield, 2006.

Elting, John R. *Swords around a Throne: Napoleon's Grande Armée.* New York: Free Press, 1988.

Englund, Steven. *Napoleon: A Political Life.* Cambridge, MA: Harvard University Press, 2004.

Epstein, Robert M. *Napoleon's Last Victory: 1809 and the Emergence of Modern War.* Lawrence: University Press of Kansas, 1994.

Esdaille, Charles. *Napoleon's Wars: An International History.* New York: Penguin, 2007.

Esposito, Vincent J., and John Robert Elting. *A Military History and Atlas of the Napoleonic Wars.* New York: Praeger, 1964.

Herold, J. Christopher. *The Mind of Napoleon.* New York: Columbia University Press, 1955.

Hugo, Victor. *Les Miserables.* Translated by Lascelles Wraxall. New York: Albert Cogswell, 1879.

Jomini, Baron Antoine de. *The Art of War.* Translated by G. H. Mendell and W. P. Craighill. 1862; reprint, Rockville, MD: Arc Manor, 2007.

Las Cases, Emmanuel. *Memoirs of the Life, Exile, and Conversations of the Emperor Napoleon.* 4 vols. New York: Redfield, 1855.

Lefebvre, Georges. *Napoleon.* 2 vols. Translated by Henry F. Stockhold and J. E. Anderson. New York: Columbia University Press, 1969.

Lynn, John A. "Toward an Army of Honor: The Moral Evolution of the French Army, 1789–1815." *French Historical Studies* 16(1) (Spring 1989): 152–173.

Markham, Felix. *Napoleon.* New York: New American Library, 1963.

Roberts, Andrew. *Napoleon: A Life.* New York: Viking, 2014.

Rothenberg, Gunther E. *The Art of Warfare in the Age of Napoleon.* Bloomington: University of Indiana Press, 1978.

Schneid, Frederick C. *Napoleon's Conquest of Europe: The War of the Third Coalition.* Westport, CT: Praeger, 2005.

Schom, Alan. *Napoleon Bonaparte.* New York: HarperCollins, 1997.

Thompson, J. M. *Napoleon Bonaparte*. New York: Oxford University Press, 1952.

Tulard, Jean, and Louis Garros. *Itinéraire de Napoléon au jour le jour, 1769–1821*. Paris: Librairie Jules Tallandier, 1992.

Wartenburg, Maximilian Yorck von. *Napoleon as a General*. London: Gilbert and Rivington, 1955.

19. WHICH SIDE WON THE WAR OF 1812?

The War of 1812, a sideshow to the ongoing Anglo-French confrontation across the world, pitted the United States against the British Empire. While Britain arguably won the conflict in terms of securing its modest war aims against its former colony in North America, the United States emerged from the conflict with a true national identity as well as a more secure hold over the North American continent, which would prove quite helpful later in the century. Indeed, a number of historians have argued that for the Americans the War of 1812 represented nothing less than a second war of independence. Distracted by events in Europe and the Napoleonic Wars, Britain was nevertheless able to conduct an effective military campaign in North America with the help of its Canadian militia and Native American allies. In spite of this, the United States held its own in various naval campaigns and even in many land battles. Ultimately, war fatigue on the part of Britain and a reluctance to engage in a long campaign of attrition contributed to the end of the war. Despite American attempts to seize it, Canada remained a British colony, and the United States preserved its "honor" and arguably emerged as an Atlantic power.

In the first perspective essay, Dr. James Daybell argues that from a purely military perspective, at least in terms of attaining its war aims, Britain won the War of 1812. In the conflict, Britain's main objective was to defend Canada from U.S. invasion, which it managed to do with the help of Canadian and Native American forces. Dr. Spencer C. Tucker asserts that while the War of 1812 was technically a draw for both the United States and Britain, it did have significant consequences for both belligerents. For the United States, the war resulted in the cementing of the power of the federal government and laid the foundation of American economic development for the remainder of the century. For Britain, the conflict contributed to the expansion of the Royal Navy and ensured a British-dominated Canada, albeit one with a strong sense of national identity after having survived the U.S. invasion.

Background Essay

Virtually forgotten in Great Britain and misunderstood in the United States, the War of 1812 ranks among the more obscure conflicts in the history of either country. The conflict featured a confusing array of political, economic, ideological, social, and maritime causes; very few set-piece battles; considerable bungling and mismanagement; and uncertain consequences. Yet the war laid the foundation of Canadian nationhood, while in the United States the conflict destroyed the Federalist Party, spurred industrialization, accelerated the professionalization of the armed forces, encouraged territorial expansion, fueled nationalism, and catapulted a new generation of political and military leaders into prominence. In short, the conflict produced consequences out of all proportion to the murkiness of its origins or the scale of the fighting.

To understand the conflict requires examining the early 1800s, when a confluence of American and European events placed the United States and Great Britain on a path toward war. In the United States, a critical shift occurred with the election of Thomas Jefferson as president in 1800. Jefferson was a Democratic-Republican who progressively abandoned the pro-British policies of his Federalist predecessors and eviscerated their programs for military preparedness, internal taxes, and financial stability. Overseas, the key development was the resumption of war between France and Britain in 1803. Each tried to prohibit neutral countries from trading with the other, and both seized hundreds of American vessels. Britain exacerbated the situation by searching U.S. ships for deserters and then impressing them into the Royal Navy, a practice that often included seizing American citizens as well. Public opinion in the United States turned against these insults to American honor but focused more strongly on Great Britain rather than France.

The British sought to avoid war and to reduce tensions with the Monroe-Pinkney Treaty of 1806, but Jefferson refused to submit it to Congress because he disliked treaties in general and distrusted the British in particular. As seizures of American ships continued, the U.S. economy suffered. In the United States Jefferson's policies fueled bitter partisan rancor between Federalists and Democratic-Republicans and contributed to the growing sectional split between New England (generally Federalist, pro-British, and highly dependent on seagoing trade) and the rest of the nation (generally agrarian, anti-British, and Democratic-Republican).

After Jefferson and a Democratic-Republican–dominated Congress imposed a U.S. trade embargo in 1807, the situation became desperate. They had hoped to deny Britain and France American-supplied products and thereby force concessions but succeeded only in devastating the American economy. James Madison (also a Democratic-Republican) assumed the presidency in 1809 and continued the embargo.

After 1810, Madison fell under the sway of the War Hawks in Congress who saw war with Great Britain as a means of resisting British economic aggression and an excuse to conquer neighboring Canada and neutralize the Native American danger along the western frontier. They saw war as a means of reasserting independence from Britain, protecting American shipping rights, strengthening their party, and unifying the country. Many southern and western settlers believed that the British were arming and inciting Indians on the frontier, and talk of war was generally met with considerable support everywhere but in New England.

Madison was persuaded, in large measure by the War Hawks, to ask Congress for a war declaration on June 1, 1812, despite personal misgivings regarding American preparedness and his hope that the mere threat of war would lead the British to suspend their interference with U.S. shipping. War nevertheless came as a surprise to many Americans, and astonished British leaders who were preoccupied with the war against France.

The ensuing conflict lasted just over two and a half years and featured a handful of two-ship victories by the U.S. Navy, an increasingly effective British blockade of the American Atlantic coast, and a series of failed efforts by the United States to conquer Canada by land. The British husbanded their limited resources and effectively integrated Canadian militia and Native Americans into their forces, while

Depiction of the victory of the new U.S. Navy sloop *Wasp* over the British sloop *Reindeer* on June 28, 1814, during the War of 1812. (National Archives)

the United States struggled with poor financing, ineffective leaders, inadequately trained and equipped troops, and a generally disorganized war effort.

After Napoleon's abdication in April 1814, the British dedicated more ships and men to the war effort. They subsequently burned Washington, D.C., and moved a large army to the coast of the Gulf of Mexico. Yet victory eluded them. Privateers on both sides ravaged enemy merchant shipping and drove up insurance rates, while naval victories scored by the Americans on the Great Lakes and in isolated incidents at sea in no way addressed the crushing supremacy of the Royal Navy.

In short order both sides recognized that they had little hope of securing a decisive victory or major territorial concessions, so each had strong incentives to end the fighting. Diplomats concluded the Treaty of Ghent, which ended the war, on December 24, 1814. In it, both nations agreed to essentially return to the status quo ante bellum, and no war aims on either side were addressed or fulfilled. Indeed, there was no mention of freedom of the seas, seizures of U.S. merchant ships, or impressments. The treaty released all prisoners of war and restored all territory seized by the other.

Yet the war mattered. In U.S. politics it led to the collapse of the Federalists and an era of one-party rule and brought a new generation of wartime heroes into power. The war also spurred industrialization and highlighted the need for banking systems, tax collection, and trade; in geographic terms, it demonstrated the importance of the Great Lakes and the St. Lawrence River as avenues of transportation; geopolitically, it foreshadowed America's territorial expansion largely at the expense of Native Americans and the increasing importance of Canada to the British Empire. On a social and cultural level, the war fueled American and Canadian nationalism. Militarily, the war demonstrated the general superiority of regular troops.

Robert Lance Janda

Perspective Essay 1. A British Military Victory

From a military perspective, the War of 1812 was "won" by Great Britain but only in the narrowest sense that the British achieved their one clear war aim: the retention of Canada. Aided by Canadians in British North America and First Nation alliances, British forces successfully and significantly repulsed the invading U.S. armies that crossed into their territory with the goal of annexing land and potentially subsuming Canada into the union.

At the start of the war in 1812 Great Britain was engaged in a prolonged and costly war with Napoleonic France, which diverted its attention from the American conflict and, more important, tied down manpower, ships, and resources in Europe. Consequently, the British were woefully underresourced for any sort of long-term military engagement in North America. An estimated 5,000 troops were in Upper Canada (modern-day Ontario). Their numbers were swelled by the local Canadian militia, and British naval presence was small, limited to a small number of ships.

These forces lined up against approximately 7,000 regular U.S. Army soldiers, but the army itself was hampered by problems. Despite the recent establishment of West Point, the military academy in New York, good officers were limited, and there was poor-quality strategic leadership. Furthermore, the large numbers of state militias (estimated at between 400,000 to 500,000 citizens who were prepared to take up arms and train to defend their homes) were necessarily localized, parochial in outlook and aims, not to mention poorly trained and equipped. They would be hard to galvanize into a nationally coordinated force fighting a common foe.

The United States grossly underestimated the difficulty of a victory in Canada: Thomas Jefferson thought that it would be "a mere matter of marching." This is perhaps understandable, since Florida had been acquired in this way in 1810. At the outset of the war U.S. forces attacked British Canada, as this was the only way to strike a blow at Great Britain because the U.S. Navy was weak in terms of numbers of ships, and British troops were there.

Early attempts at invasion were repulsed. This was owing to the effectiveness of the Canadian militia, the alliances forged with the First Nations, and the success of the British troops led by Major General Sir Isaac Brock, the British Army officer and administrator charged with defending Upper Canada. British successes included the capture of Detroit and the Battle of Queenston Heights.

The tide of military success, however, began to flow in the opposite direction when the United States won the strategically important Battle of Lake Erie in September 1813 and regained Detroit after the Battle of the Thames, which resulted in the death of the charismatic Native American leader Tecumseh, who led a large tribal confederacy that opposed the United States in the war. In the early part of the war British success was mixed, and victories were not achieved alone but instead in conjunction with Canadian and First Nation forces.

With the collapse of the Napoleonic Empire from 1812 and the French leader's abdication in 1814, the British were able to turn their entire attention to the situation across the Atlantic and redirect significant resources, so much so that by the summer of 1814 they had assembled something approaching 50,000 troops and upwards of 100 naval vessels to engage the Americans. Using their superior sea power, the British imposed an economic blockade of the Atlantic seaboard, which had a devastating impact on the U.S. economy. Alongside this stranglehold naval campaign, amphibious parties raided towns along the Chesapeake Bay, former slaves were treated as freemen and incorporated into British regiments, and advances were made in occupying key strongholds throughout Maine.

Perhaps the most devastating defeat inflicted by the British—an intentionally humiliating act of retribution for the U.S. sacking of York (now Toronto) in 1813—was the burning of public buildings in the U.S. capital city of Washington, D.C., in August 1814. Some 2,500 British troops were met by a 6,000-strong U.S. militia force, which, however, was soon put to flight. On withdrawal from Washington, the British concentrated their efforts on the nearby city of Baltimore, which was an important port from which American privateers operated with rather effective negative consequences for British merchant trade. The British were, however, unsuccessful in their amphibious landing, and Fort McHenry, which stood at the entrance of Baltimore Harbor, withstood a massive 25-hour bombardment from the British ships.

The war was not then a British "victory" in the more traditional sense of invading and occupying land in order to cudgel a foe into submission. Instead, the strategy was to protect British trade and interests in Canada as well as weaken U.S. military capabilities and humiliate the new nation. In these specific areas, the British achieved some degree of success.

It is, however, perhaps in the war at sea that the British would have wished their successes in the War of 1812 to be judged. Surprisingly for the post–Horatio Nelson generation, the Royal Navy experienced a series of setbacks in the early going. Superior U.S. frigates captured smaller British ships in a number of two-ship actions, and American privateers had a devastating effect on British merchant shipping, capturing well more than 1,000 vessels. By the summer of 1813 the British government had committed more ships, and the war at sea turned in its favor. An effective economic blockade was imposed, shutting down ports and harming trade; American privateers were captured, their activities curtailed; and a series of defeats were inflicted on the U.S. Navy as its warships were hunted down and forced to surrender.

Ultimately, though, the case for Great Britain "winning" the War of 1812 rests not merely on its retaining Canadian colonies and preventing American invasions of Canada but instead on the analysis of the peace conditions and the argument that the Treaty of Ghent gave no concessions to American claims for impressment and made no mention of noninterference with American neutrality and rights. The peace treaty came about in the first place as a direct result to the end of war against the French in Europe in 1814. Napoleon's empire had collapsed, and there was no need for impressment or for the British to interfere with U.S. commercial activities. It thus made sense for both sides—the Americans and the British—to come to the table for peace talks. The upshot of the treaty was the restoration of all occupied territories to the status quo ante bellum ("the state existing before the war"), an agreement to sort out formally the boundaries between the United States and Canada, and an additional agreement to move toward stopping the slave trade.

The Americans had declared war in 1812 with a clear set of expectations but came away without having achieved any of them. Canada remained British, and the seizure of ships in addition to blockades and impressment ceased with British victory against France in 1814. Moreover, the war had a profound impact on British North America, which experienced a new sense of national identity as a result of militias having successfully defended their country and land. There was an increased understanding between French- and English-speaking Canadians, forged by a mutual and embittered distrust of the United States.

From a U.S. perspective, the War of 1812 was a watershed. Americans believed that they had defeated the greatest military power in the world, which had a profound effect on nationalist pride; it was also viewed as the end of the American Revolution, ushering in a period of security as a sovereign nation without interference from the British, during which time the United States developed into a mighty industrialized world power. In a way, then, even if we argue that Britain won the war, the United States won the peace.

James Daybell

Perspective Essay 2. Fought to a Draw

The United States declared war on Britain on June 18, 1812. Peace was concluded two and a half years later on December 24, 1814. Neither side won the war, which was concluded essentially on the basis of status quo ante bellum. This did not mean, however, that the war did not have important effects and influences.

Without French emperor Napoleon Bonaparte there would have been no war, for the War of 1812 sprang from Britain's long struggle against Napoleonic France. In their effort to defeat Napoleon, British leaders pushed the Americans too far, bringing on the war. The chief stated causes of the war were maritime in nature. One was British impressment of American seamen. Ships of the Royal Navy routinely stopped U.S. merchant ships, supposedly to search for and take back deserters but also to impress many native-born Americans into involuntary service in the Royal Navy.

Another cause of the war was the British Orders in Council that allowed the Royal Navy to seize any ship sailing for a European port controlled by Napoleon. Britain and France had resumed fighting in 1803, and both sides attempted to destroy the commerce of the other: Britain by a blockade of France and the territories it controlled in Europe, and France by the Continental System, which sought to deny British manufacturers access to European markets, forcing Britain into ruinous inflation. By 1812, the British had captured some 400 American ships and were in effect destroying the American export trade.

Another principal cause of the war was the American desire to annex Canada, which was the chief U.S. war aim. Also, many Americans believed that the British authorities were arming Native Americans against settlers settling on Native lands in the Old Northwest.

On June 18, 1812, the U.S. Congress declared war. Ironically, this so-called War for Free Trade and Sailors' Rights was fought chiefly on land. Support came mainly from the west. The War Hawks, led by U.S. representative Henry Clay of Kentucky, championed armed conflict in the anticipation of an easy victory. The population of British North America (Canada) in 1812 was only about 300,000 people, while the United States had more than 8 million. The U.S. Navy was minuscule next to the Royal Navy, but given Britain's commitments in European waters and elsewhere, it would be some time before major British naval assets could be sent to North America. In any case, few expected the U.S. Navy to accomplish anything of note against the powerful Royal Navy. Indeed, Congress adjourned without making appropriations to expand the navy, a strange state of affairs given the supposed maritime causes. Americans expected the war to be decided early in their favor and on land.

In June 1812 the U.S. regular army numbered some 11,744 officers and men, while British Army strength in Canada was only about 8,125. Given British manpower commitments in Spain, there was little prospect of reinforcement. The majority of the population in Upper Canada, moreover, consisted of newly arrived Americans, attracted there by cheap land and low taxes, and they were expected to support any U.S. invasion.

The war did not go the way the James Madison administration had hoped. The United States lacked the economic means to fight a long conflict. The president had ignored Secretary of the Treasury Albert Gallatin's warnings about the financial vulnerability of the national government, which was forced to rely on import duties for revenue. Although the continental struggle continued after Napoleon met defeat in Russia, its naval assets were such that Britain could still apply sufficient resources to accomplish its strategic goals in North America.

The three-pronged American attack of 1812 to conquer Canada failed miserably. Although the British regulars were few in number, they were well-trained professionals and had an able commander in Major General Isaac Brock. In addition, many Native Americans, goaded by American land grabs, sided with the British. Shawnee chief Tecumseh and British Indian agents played a key role in the early British victories. A second American attempt against Canada in 1813 also failed.

Meanwhile, much to the surprise of all, especially the British, American frigates and smaller ships scored victories in two-ship actions against the Royal Navy at sea. Too late, in 1813 Congress voted funds for the navy. Inland American naval victories on Lake Erie on September 10, 1813, and Lake Champlain in September 11, 1814, proved critical for the Americans, however.

With the failure of their efforts in Canada, the British took the initiative. By 1813, they had imposed a crippling naval blockade of the American coasts. The blockade led to a tripling of the U.S. national debt and forced Washington to default on national interest payments and loans and made Madison amenable to a peace settlement.

The British took the offensive on land in 1814 with the release of regulars from Europe. The British mounted an offensive in Chesapeake Bay that led to their capture of Washington, D.C., and the destruction of its public buildings, but they met rebuff at Baltimore's Fort McHenry. The British also mounted an invasion of upper New York state from Canada and an effort to take New Orleans. By now, however, American land forces were much better trained and inept leaders had been weeded out. The Battle of Chippawa on July 5, 1814, was an American victory over hardened British regulars, and the American naval victory of Lake Champlain on September 11, 1814, ended the large British invasion of New York. The British expedition to Louisiana met disaster in the Battle of New Orleans on January 8, 1815, but that was after the conclusion of peace.

By the end of 1814, both sides were ready for peace. The British people were tired of 22 years of war, London wanted to be free to redraw the map of Europe at the Congress of Vienna, and British merchants were eager to resume trade with America. The Americans had also finally proven themselves a formidable opponent on land. With both sides hurting financially, there was considerable pressure to reach a settlement. Peace was concluded in the Treaty of Ghent on December 24, 1814.

The treaty saw a virtual return to the status quo ante bellum. Both sets of negotiators initially took a firm stance. The Americans demanded an end to impressment and blockades and the resolution of other matters. The British demanded the creation of a neutral Indian buffer state in the Old Northwest (in fulfillment of a pledge made to the Native Americans at the beginning of the conflict) and territorial concessions in the northeastern United States to the benefit of Canada. Eventually the British acceded to the U.S. position of status quo ante bellum with the prewar territorial situation. Thus, the United States failed to achieve its chief war aim—securing Canada. West Florida, taken by the United States from Spain during the war, remained in U.S. possession.

The treaty provided for the release of all prisoners but said nothing about the maritime differences that were the chief causes of the war. In addition, the treaty provided for a commission to settle the disputed northeast border between the United States and Canada, and both sides agreed to leave to future negotiations the military status of the Great Lakes and offshore fishing rights. There was no mention of an Indian state.

Britain "won" in that the War of 1812 was probably the most important factor preventing the absorption of Canada by the United States, for it fostered Canadian nationalism as well as heightening nationalism in the United States. In addition to its impact on Canadian and American nationalism, the war is important from a number of standpoints. The U.S. Navy firmly established its reputation from the very beginning of the war, and this led to a substantial increase in the navy afterward. The

U.S. Army, which had begun the war so poorly, found a new professionalism. The war also proved the importance of the young U.S. Military Academy at West Point, which had been established only a decade earlier. With the cutoff in British manufactured goods and military demands, the war also hastened the Industrial Revolution in the United States. The Native Americans, who had played such an important role in preserving Canada for the British in the war's early going, were the conflict's chief losers. Promised their own state in the Old Northwest by the British in 1812, they were abandoned by both sides at its end. Even many of those who sided with the United States soon lost their lands.

The War of 1812 also helped break down internal barriers in the United States and advanced the political fortunes of such individuals as Andrew Jackson and William Henry Harrison, although it contributed directly to the demise of the Federalist Party. The war also can be said to mark the inauguration of the so-called Era of Good Feelings, during which the United States was more united than ever before and dominated by a single political entity—the Democratic-Republican Party.

Spencer C. Tucker

Further Reading

Arthur, Brian. *How Britain Won the War of 1812: The Royal Navy's Blockade of the United States, 1812.* Woodbridge, Suffolk, UK: Boyswll and Brewer, 2011.

Black, Jeremy. *The War of 1812 in the Age of Napoleon.* Norman: University of Oklahoma Press, 2009.

Burt, A. L. *The United States, Great Britain, and British North America: From the Revolution to the Establishment of Peace after the War of 1812.* New Haven, CT: Yale University Press, 1940.

Coles, Harry L. *The War of 1812.* Chicago: University of Chicago Press, 1965.

Dangerfield, George. *The Awakening of American Nationalism, 1815–1828.* The New American Nation Series. New York: Harper and Row, 1965.

Dudley, Wade G. *Splintering the Wooden Wall: The British Blockade of the United States, 1812–1815.* Annapolis, MD: Naval Institute Press, 2003.

Elting, John R. *Amateurs, to Arms! A Military History of the War of 1812.* Chapel Hill, NC: Algonquin Books, 1991.

Fowler, William M., Jr. *Jack Tars and Commodores: The American Navy, 1783–1815.* Boston: Houghton Mifflin, 1984.

Gilje, Paul A. *Free Trade and Sailors' Rights in the War of 1812.* New York: Cambridge University Press, 2013.

Graham, Gerald S. *Sea Power and British North America, 1783–1820: A Study in British Colonial Policy.* Harvard Historical Studies, 46. Cambridge, MA: Harvard University Press, 1941.

Hickey, Donald R. *Don't Give Up the Ship! Myths of the War of 1812.* Champaign: University of Illinois Press, 2006.

Hickey, Donald R. *The War of 1812: A Forgotten Conflict.* Urbana: University of Illinois Press, 1989.

Hill, Peter P. *Napoleon's Troublesome Americans: Franco-American Relations, 1804–1815.* Dulles, VA: Potomac Books, 2005.

Hitsman, J. Mackay. *The Incredible War of 1812: A Military History.* Toronto: University of Toronto Press, 1965.

Horsman, Reginald. *The Causes of the War of 1812.* Philadelphia: University of Pennsylvania Press, 1962.

Horsman, Reginald. *The War of 1812.* New York: Knopf, 1969.

Ketcham, Ralph. *James Madison: A Biography.* New York: Macmillan, 1971.

Lambert, Andrew. *The Challenge: Britain against America in the Naval War of 1812.* London: Faber and Faber, 2012.

Latimer, Jon. *1812: War with America.* Cambridge, MA: Harvard University Press, 2007.

Mahan, Alfred T. *Sea Power in Its Relations to the War of 1812.* 2 vols. New York: Greenwood, 1905.

Mahon, John K. *The War of 1812.* Gainesville: University of Florida Press, 1972.

Nettels, Curtis P. *The Emergence of a National Economy, 1775–1815,* Vol. 2, *The Economic History of the United States.* New York: Holt, Rinehart and Winston, 1962.

Perkins, Bradford. *Castlereagh and Adams: England and the United States, 1812–1823.* Berkeley: University of California Press, 1964.

Perkins, Bradford. *Prologue to War: England and the United States, 1805–1812.* Berkeley: University of California Press, 1961.

Quimby, Robert S. *The U.S. Army in the War of 1812: An Operational and Command Study.* 2 vols. East Lansing: Michigan State University Press, 1997.

Roosevelt, Theodore. *The Naval War of 1812.* 1812; reprint, Annapolis, MD: Naval Institute Press, 1987.

Rutland, Robert Allan. *The Presidency of James Madison.* American Presidency Series. Lawrence: University Press of Kansas, 1990.

Smelser, Marshall. *The Democratic Republic, 1801–1815.* The New American Nation Series. New York: Harper and Row, 1968.

Stagg, J. C. A. *The War of 1812: Conflict for a Continent.* Cambridge: Cambridge University Press, 2012.

Stuart, Reginald C. *United States Expansionism and British North America, 1775–1871.* Chapel Hill: University of North Carolina Press, 1988.

Taylor, Alan. *The Civil War of 1812: American Citizens, British Subjects, Irish Rebels and Indian Allies.* New York: Vintage, 2010.

Updyke, Frank A. *The Diplomacy of the War of 1812.* Baltimore: Johns Hopkins University Press, 1915.

Webster, Charles K. *The Foreign Policy of Castlereagh, 1812–1815.* London: Bell, 1931.

White, Patrick C. T. *A Nation on Trial: America and the War of 1812.* New York: Wiley, 1965.

20. What Role Did the Enlightenment Play in Sparking the Latin American Revolutions?

The Enlightenment, a social and cultural movement principally associated with Europe in the 17th and 18th centuries, had a significant impact on European colonies in the Americas. Enlightenment political ideals, based on the reformation of society through the use of reason as well as the questioning of long-standing traditions and faith, were a distinct threat to the existing political power structures in Europe and its colonial possessions. Much like the Enlightenment contributed to the political environment that spurred the French Revolution and the American Revolution, it also shaped various 19th-century revolutions in Latin America. Nevertheless, it is important to point out that in some instances the revolutions in Latin America were as much a reaction to the Enlightenment as they were a consequence of it.

In the first perspective essay, Bruce Farcau argues that while the Enlightenment did influence Latin American revolutions, there were in fact examples such as Mexico, where reactionaries, while advocating separation from Spanish control, were reluctant to allow for greater political power for mestizos and indigenous peoples. Moreover, Spain, now advocating liberal policies, was to be resisted, lest it upset the power structure in Mexico with the Spanish American–born criollos (Creoles) at the apex of the social order. The second essay, written by Karl Yambert, illustrates—using Simón Bolívar as an example—how Bolívar's efforts against Spanish rule demonstrated that he was both a product and an instrument of the Enlightenment. While Bolívar did embrace the principles of the Enlightenment and sought to put them into practice in the new state named after him, he had reservations about how far these ideals should be extended. He still believed that the people of Latin America were not yet ready for the benefits of republican government. In the third essay, David F. Marley asserts that while Latin American revolutions were successful in removing Spanish dominion over the colonies, thus preserving power for the Creoles, the Enlightenment played only a negligible role in the way in which the revolutions unfolded.

Background Essay

During the late 19th and early 20th centuries, almost all of Latin America secured its independence from the European colonial powers of France, Spain, and Portugal.

Revolution occurred first in Haiti. It was unique among those in the Americas in that it was led by black slaves and mulattoes rather than whites. In August 1791, slaves in the French sugar colony of Saint-Domingue revolted, destroying plantations and killing numerous whites. The French government, having declared war on Britain, responded by abolishing slavery in Saint-Domingue and granting civil rights to blacks and mulattoes. Led by Toussaint L'Ouverture, most Haitians joined a few thousand French soldiers to defeat a joint invasion by Spain, which controlled the eastern portion of the island of Hispaniola, and Great Britain.

Although now supposedly back under French rule, L'Ouverture's Saint-Domingue was virtually autonomous. After defeating several challenges to his rule, he invaded the Spanish-held portion of Hispaniola in 1800 to free the slaves of Santo Domingo. In 1801, L'Ouverture declared himself governor for life; however, Consul Napoleon Bonaparte dispatched a large French expeditionary force to restore French control.

Although L'Ouverture was captured and sent to France, Napoleon's plan to reestablish slavery reignited the conflict. Preoccupied with European events, Napoleon refused to send reinforcements, and French forces were defeated in November 1803 in the Battle of Vertières. On January 1, 1804, Saint-Domingue became independent as Haiti, the first republic ruled by people of African descent.

The Spanish viceroyalty of the Rio de la Plata consisted of modern-day Argentina, Uruguay, Paraguay, and Bolivia. While the independence movements in most of Spanish South America were triggered by the Peninsular War in Europe (1807–1814), earlier events dictated this in the Rio de la Plata region.

In 1806 Britain, then at war with France and Spain, sent an expeditionary force to capture Buenos Aires. The viceroy and most of the Spanish elite fled, but local criollos ably defended the city. After turning back another British attempt a year later, the criollos refused to relinquish control of Buenos Aires to the Spaniards. In May 1810 a criollo junta declared independence from Spain.

For the next six years, most of the fighting in the Rio de la Plata region was between the junta and those who did not want to be controlled by Buenos Aires. Paraguay rejected rule by Buenos Aires, defeated a junta force under General Manuel Belgrano, and declared independence on May 17, 1811. Goucho Gervasio Artigas achieved independence from Argentina for Uruguay in 1815, but a year later Brazil, still under Portuguese rule, invaded. Artigas fought on until 1820, when he was defeated. Uruguay remained a province of Brazil until August 1828, when it secured independence at the end of the Argentine-Brazilian War.

The junta in Buenos Aires was convinced that independence throughout South America would be threatened if Peru remained royalist. In one of the greatest feats of the Latin American Wars of Independence, Argentine criollo José de San Martín led 5,000 men in a crossing of the Andes Mountains into Chile. Chilean criollos under Bernardo O'Higgins had been fighting the royalists since 1810. O'Higgins and San Martín joined forces and defeated the royalists in the Battle of Chacabuco (February 12, 1817). O'Higgins declared Chilean independence on February 12, 1818. Final victory was won in the Battle of Maipú (April 5, 1818).

With Chile now independent, San Martín sailed for Peru in August 1820. Peruvian independence was declared on December 29, 1820, yet fighting continued. Venezuelan revolutionary Simón Bolívar arrived in September 1823 and, along with Antonio José de Sucre, oversaw the last years of the fighting. The last major battle for Peruvian independence occurred at Ayacucho on December 8, 1824, although minor fighting continued until January 1826.

Sucre then conquered Upper Peru, controlled by Pedro Antonio de Olañeta, defeating him in the Battle of Tumusla (April 1, 1825). A new assembly declared Upper Peru independent. It was named Bolivia in honor of Bolívar.

Painting of General José de San Martín proclaiming the independence of Peru, July 28, 1821. (DeAgostini/Getty Images)

The independence movement in Venezuela began with a criollo revolt on April 19, 1810. Bolívar joined the fight and arranged for the return of the exiled Francisco de Miranda from Europe. A republic was declared on July 5, 1811, but the royalists mounted a counteroffensive in 1812. Miranda was captured, and Bolívar fled to New Granada (Colombia).

Fighting in Venezuela and Colombia continued for another decade. Bolívar emulated San Martín by crossing the Andes from Guayana to liberate Colombia, before moving against Venezuela. Aided by José Antonio Páez and Francisco de Paula Santander, Bolívar defeated Spanish royalists in the Battle of Boyacá (August 7, 1819) and soon thereafter captured Bogotá. With Colombia secure, Bolívar defeated the royalists at Carabobo in June 1821, captured Caracas, and declared the independence of the Republic of Gran Colombia (unifying Venezuela and Colombia).

Bolívar then sent Sucre south to Ecuador, where he defeated royalists in the Battle of Pichincha (May 24, 1822) and seized the capital of Quito. On July 13, 1822, Ecuador was incorporated into Gran Colombia. It split into Colombia (including present-day Panama), Venezuela, and Ecuador in 1831.

The path to independence in Brazil was relatively nonviolent. In 1807, the French invasion of Portugal prompted the Portuguese royal family to flee Lisbon for Brazil and reestablish the seat of government at Rio de Janeiro. In December 1816 the colony was elevated to a kingdom.

When King João VI returned to Europe in July 1821 to deal with the liberal revolution spreading through Portugal, his son, Dom Pedro, remained in Brazil as regent. The decision of the Portuguese Cortes in September 1821 to return Brazil to its original colonial status angered the criollos and fueled nationalist sentiments. Pedro, who had spent much of his life in Brazil, refused to obey the Cortes's demand that he return to Portugal. Instead, he declared Brazil independent on September 7, 1822. Pedro had the approval of his father, King João, who preferred an independent Brazil ruled by his family. The resulting war between the newly formed Brazilian Army and Portuguese troops stationed in the former colony saw few pitched battles but a number of sieges of royalist strongholds. João formally recognized Brazil's independence on November 15, 1825.

Dom Pedro, ruling as Emperor Pedro I, created a highly centralized and conservative government. This, along with his mismanagement of finances and continued interaction in the politics of Portugal, engendered significant dissent within Brazil. The empire was transformed into a republic in 1889.

In Mexico, the independence movement received its earliest impetus from mestizos led by Catholic priest Miguel Hidalgo y Costilla. Elites did not join the 1810 rebellion, and their fears grew as Indians and mestizos looted and seized crops, registering their discontent after two years of famine. Hidalgo was captured and executed in 1811, but warfare continued under another priest, José María Morelos. Morelos was also captured and executed in December 1815, although the independence struggle continued. When Spain's government came under the control of a liberal legislature in 1820, the Mexican military, clergy, and merchants became angered by the reforms attacking their privileges and plotted to establish an independent, conservative Mexico. Augustín de Iturbide, who had led the loyalist army in the fight against the patriot guerrillas, offered a peace plan to the rebels. The two united, routing the royalists and achieving Mexican independence on September 28, 1821.

Central America had been part of the enormous viceroyalty of New Spain since the 1500s. Numerous small rebellions occurred in 1811 and 1814 but were easily quelled by royalist troops. On September 15, 1821, a congress of criollos declared independence and met scant resistance. On January 5, 1822, newly independent Mexico annexed portions of Guatemala and El Salvador, but when Mexico became a republic in 1823, Central America was given the right of self-determination, and on July 1 the United Provinces of Central America was declared. It included present-day Guatemala, El Salvador, Honduras, Nicaragua, and Costa Rica. Tensions between liberals and conservatives soon led to civil war beginning in 1838, however. By 1840 Nicaragua, Honduras, Costa Rica, and Guatemala had all declared their independence.

Maxine Taylor

Perspective Essay 1. Conflicting Interpretations of the Enlightenment's Role

The philosophical movement known as the Enlightenment played a significant role in sparking the early 19th-century Latin American revolutions for a variety of conflicting reasons. The political concepts of the Enlightenment, as put forth by European philosophers and manifested in the American Revolution and the French Revolution, had certainly influenced the leaders of the various independence movements in Latin America. On the other hand, the reform efforts spawned during the turbulent years of the early 19th century in Spain, based on the theories of the Enlightenment, caused a significant backlash within the ruling class in Spain's colonial possessions, forcing them to break with the empire in order to preserve their own positions and status. Finally, in a very practical sense, if one can say that the French Revolution itself had its roots in the ideas of the Enlightenment, then the disruptions caused by the subsequent wars growing out of the revolution and Napoleon's subsequent conquests must be seen as physically shaking the foundations of the Spanish Empire.

Most of the principal leaders of the Latin American independence movements had studied and been influenced by the political philosophies of the Enlightenment and the events in North America and Europe that these prompted. The writings of Charles-Louis de Montesquieu, François-Marie Voltaire, Jean-Jacques Rousseau, and others destroyed forever the infallibility of the concept of absolute monarchy and the divine right of kings, which of course raised the possibility of a dramatic change of government by the will of the people. The dominant liberators, such as Simón Bolívar in the north and José Francisco de San Martín in the south, had ample opportunity to imbibe the teachings of the philosophers of the Enlightenment. This can be seen in their declarations throughout the struggle for independence and in the constitutions and edicts that they enacted thereafter.

One must also consider the practical example that the revolutions in America and France set for the liberators in the Spanish Empire. There is little doubt that both revolutions were inspired by the concepts rising from the Enlightenment. Therefore, one must assume that the subsequent revolutions in Latin America were, at least indirectly, also products of the Enlightenment. The American Revolution was arguably the first example in which a colony had successfully broken away from the mother country, at least since the age of ancient Greece, and this path was followed by the Latin Americans. Both the American Revolution and the French Revolution also attacked the institution of the monarchy, creating instead a political system on the democratic model.

In the American case, the revolutionaries did not attempt to overthrow the monarchy itself. They merely wanted to relieve themselves of the burden of monarchy, and the Americans were ultimately able to establish and sustain a democratic system, unlike France. The Latin Americans split the difference here, not addressing the survival of the monarchy in Spain, like the Americans, but ultimately failing to consolidate a nonauthoritarian political system at home, like the French. In any case, the underlying intellectual justification for their movements was based on the teachings of the Enlightenment.

If one can accept that the Enlightenment was the precursor of the French Revolution, one must also accept the connection between the Enlightenment and the subsequent political chaos in Spain that made the independence movements in Latin America feasible. The French Revolution opened the door to the rise of Napoleon, and the revolutionary ideas of the Enlightenment spread far beyond France's borders, facilitating Napoleon's subsequent conquests. Among those was Spain, where Napoleon overthrew the Bourbon monarchy. The Spanish people rebelled, however, and the resulting years of bloody insurgency diverted the attention of Spanish leaders from the maintenance of the overseas empire. Even after the defeat of Napoleon and the restoration of the Bourbon monarchy, Spain was unable to regain the level of power it had held prior to the French occupation. There can be no question that Spain would have been in an infinitely better position to resist the rebels had it not been for the massive military and financial losses caused by the Napoleonic Wars.

The Enlightenment also contributed to the drive for independence in Latin America in a negative sense. Both after the immediate collapse of the Spanish monarchy following Napoleon's initial invasion in 1806 and again after his fall in 1815, liberal regimes, referred to as juntas, emerged in Spain. Borrowing heavily from the teachings of the Enlightenment, the leaders of these nontraditional political structures fundamentally attacked the existing institutions and the power base of the landed aristocracy. As related to Latin America in particular, the juntas attempted to eliminate the system of *encomienda* and *mita* throughout the empire. The former essentially carved up the new territories and doled out vast estates to the conquistadores and their heirs, along with the people inhabiting them as virtual slaves. The latter was a system of forced labor that the native population was obliged to deliver to their new overlords, also resulting in something like slavery. The criollo aristocracy, the American-born but ethnically European rulers of Spanish America, were very comfortable with this system and took it as just compensation for being largely excluded from key administration positions within the empire. The actions of the juntas, notably the Constitution of Cádiz, seriously threatened the survival of this lucrative arrangement.

The original *grito,* the call for independence, in Mexico (with a similar situation arising in Guatemala) was essentially a grassroots movement by indigenous and mestizo peasants against the entire oppressive system. Led by Padre Miguel Hidalgo and Padre José Maria Morelos, this movement attacked the local criollo interests just as it attacked the concept of rule of Mexico by distant Spain. The movement was clearly both motivated by the spirit of the Enlightenment, with the concept of individual freedom, and facilitated by the evident collapse of Spanish power at home due to the Napoleonic Wars. However, the criollos quickly recognized that such a mass movement would not be to their benefit, and they swung their power behind the imperialist forces, decisively defeating the rebels in a conflict that Spanish imperialist forces alone would have been very unlikely to win.

However, after the fall of Napoleon, the short-lived government of the Constitution of Cádiz again raised the specter of the elimination of criollo domination of the economy in Mexico and Guatemala. These powerful men now decided that it was in their best interests to fend for themselves and led a new independence movement not to establish personal freedom and democracy but instead to ensure their continued position of privilege that the liberals in Cádiz were threatening. With the imperialist forces (now paradoxically fighting on the side of liberalism) greatly weakened by the Napoleonic Wars, the powerful criollo leaders had little trouble in seizing direct control in the name of independence, a conflict in which the lower classes now showed rather limited interest. This is one reason why in Mexico in particular independence day has always been a bit awkward to celebrate, focusing on the unsuccessful *grito* rather than the successful war of the local aristocracy to ensure their domination of society.

One significant argument against the influence of the Enlightenment on the independence movements in Latin America has been a notable lack of the development of truly democratic institutions in the region following independence, unlike in the United States. Of course, one could say the same about the French Revolution, although no one doubts the impact of the Enlightenment there, since the French did not establish a sustainable democracy for nearly a century. The early constitutions of the various Latin American states do pay lip service to the concepts of the Enlightenment, but they are bounded by caveats protecting special interests based on race, class, or institution (notably the military). Furthermore, there is the question of the iron law of oligarchy under which oppressive regimes have a tendency to re-create themselves with new personnel even after being overthrown. The United States started with a far less repressive regime than that which existed in the rest of the hemisphere and thus had a much better chance of developing democracy after the American Revolution.

The theories of the Enlightenment did have a significant effect on the movements toward independence in Latin America. In a positive sense they provided an intellectual justification for what was at the time revolutionary concepts of disavowing monarchical authority and for a colony breaking away from imperial power. The leaders of the various movements were certainly aware of these concepts, and some had even participated in their practice earlier. There was the practical example provided by the American Revolution and the French Revolution, both of which clearly owed a great deal to the Enlightenment. And the subsequent Napoleonic Wars created a physical environment in which the independence movements could succeed. Finally, in some cases, notably Mexico and Guatemala, the actual achievement of independence was a product of a negative reaction to the ideas of the Enlightenment.

Bruce Farcau

Perspective Essay 2. Simón Bolívar: Product and Instrument of the Enlightenment

The Enlightenment played a key role in Latin America's revolutions, as exemplified by Simón Bolívar's espousal of Enlightenment principles—sovereignty of the people, legal equality of citizens, constitutional government of divided powers, abolition of slavery—and his attempts to realize those principles in the constitutions of republics newly liberated by him.

The Enlightenment was a mostly North American and West European intellectual movement that occurred over the course of the 17th and 18th centuries and generally promoted the use of reason, rather than faith or tradition, to make sense of the world and to reform society. On that account it is also called the Age of Reason.

Several thinkers stand out as exemplars of Enlightenment political theory. In England, Thomas Hobbes contended that monarchies exercise legitimate authority not by divine right but instead by the consent of the people they govern. Fellow Englishman John Locke contended that while people submit to a common authority that enacts and enforces laws, authority in turn is limited by the terms of the social contract and therefore must not threaten certain innate human rights, including those of life, liberty, and property. Jean-Jacques Rousseau, born in Switzerland, considered the social contract to be the submission of the individual to the general will, ideally taking the form of the rule of law as formulated through the direct vote of the people. French theorist Charles-Louis de Montesquieu advanced several tenets of political thought that have become givens in republics of the modern world. He proposed that political liberty depends on a separation of powers—executive, legislative, and judicial—thus creating a system of checks and balances to ensure that no one aspect of government overpowers the others. Most of these Enlightenment thinkers commonly urged an end to slavery, as it was incompatible with their precepts of liberty and equality.

Enlightenment political theories commonly converged in their articulation of the natural or inherent rights of people, government according to the consent of the governed, and the government's protection of liberty and equality for all. Freedom of religion was supported, though the practices of particular religious institutions, such as the Catholic Church, were sometimes criticized for propping up traditional structures of authority and impeding the progress of reason and science. But Enlightenment political theory did not necessarily favor republics over monarchies. In fact, certain monarchies embraced Enlightenment principles and sought to apply them to the politics, economics, sciences, arts, and education of their realms. Nor, despite the prominent examples of the French Revolution and the American Revolution, did Enlightenment principles explicitly endorse revolution or colonial independence except in Thomas Paine's *Common Sense* (1776).

Simón Bolívar, the eventual liberator of what would become six Latin American countries—Venezuela, Colombia (which at the time of its independence included Panama), Ecuador, Peru, and Bolivia—was born into an aristocratic family of Caracas, Venezuela, in 1783. Bolívar traveled twice to Europe as a young man, meeting several social and intellectual leaders of the day. In his time abroad he also read ancient classics and modern philosophers, including John Locke, Voltaire, Montesquieu, and Jean-Jacques Rousseau.

Bolívar's embrace of Enlightenment thinking is evident in his subsequent writings and speeches. On his return to Venezuela, he joined the insurrectionists who seized Caracas in 1810 and declared independence from Spain. However, royalist forces soon regained the upper hand, and Bolívar moved to New Granada (Colombia) to continue the struggle. There in Cartagena in 1812 he delivered his first major political address, explaining the political situation in Venezuela. Two points stand out in particular, both of them bearing on open or implicit comparisons to the American Revolution. First, what had most weakened the first attempt at a new Venezuela republic, Bolívar maintained, was adherence to a decentralized federal system of government. The provinces, and even the cities within provinces, governed themselves essentially independently, leaving the central government virtually powerless. With a glance at North America, Bolívar proclaimed the federal system the most perfect and the most capable of providing for human happiness. But that was in times of peace and prosperity; in turbulent times of war and internal dissension, the government needed to be stern and firm and needed to override, if need be, laws and constitutions until happiness and peace could be restored.

Besides the demands of wartime, a second reason for what became Bolívar's lifetime advocacy of a strong central authority was rooted in what he believed to be a lack of "virtue" in the South American populace. Bolívar complained that under the absolute control of the Spanish government for centuries, the people in Spanish South America had never been able to exercise their rights in full measure. He expanded on this point in his so-called Jamaica Letter (1815), arguing that the colonists had been denied participation in even local administrations and thus were in a state of permanent infancy with respect to managing public affairs.

To buttress his analysis, Bolívar drew upon Montesquieu's suggestion that climate and geography interacted with local culture to produce a particular "spirit" of a given people. Bolívar often cited Montesquieu's maxim but imparted to it his own sociological rather than geographical spin. With large populations of Spanish, Creoles (American-born people of Spanish descent), Indians, free blacks, and mixed bloods (white-Indian mestizos and white-black-Indian *pardos*), the peoples of South America were far more heterogeneous than were the white citizens of the United States. The many social groupings had distinct and competing interests that they might pursue rather than support the common cause of a new republic. Furthermore, the Spanish American colonists lacked the "virtue" of their North American counterparts that comes with the experience of participation in self-government. Bolívar argued that until Spanish American patriots could acquire those talents and virtues, more strongly centralized governments were necessary to ensure the eventual implementation of the principles of justice, liberty, and equality.

The murderous example set by Haiti's black slave revolution troubled many of Bolívar's fellow Creoles. Bolívar himself exhibited ambivalence toward *pardos* out of concern that they might unite to achieve their own particular ends instead of joining with the Creole-led revolution. Nonetheless, for Bolívar, liberty and equality in any new republic should extend not just to those who were already free, regardless of color, but also to slaves. He advocated the prohibition of slavery as a general principle, and in 1816 he issued a decree for the emancipation of slaves along the Venezuelan coast, though in that instance the would-be ex-slaves needed to join the army to earn their emancipation. Addressing a form of Andean peonage and explicitly invoking the principle of equality among all citizens, Bolívar in 1825 decreed an end to the centuries-long practice of exacting personal services without recompense from Peruvian Indians.

As a liberator of much of Spanish America, Bolívar was in a historic position to influence the realization of Enlightenment ideals in practical terms, notably within constitutional proposals for Venezuela and Bolivia. His address to the Congress of Angostura (1819) set forth his recommendations for drafting a new Venezuelan constitution. In his speech, he endorsed Venezuela's efforts to establish a democratic republic that supported the rights of man and the freedoms of action, thought, expression, and writing. However, he felt that Venezuelans were not ready to receive or manage the benefits of a completely representative government. Accordingly, Bolívar urged the congress to create a presidency with strong executive power, to be complemented by a hereditary senate. He proposed that courts be presided over by permanent and independent judges and that a "fourth power"—in addition to the executive, judicial, and legislative—be instituted to foster national spirit and civic virtue.

Having defeated the Spanish in Peru in 1824, Bolívar in 1826 wrote the constitution for Upper Peru, which had named itself the Republic of Bolivia in his honor. His presentation of his draft constitution expressed his vision of the social contract: that true freedom lies in civil liberty and that the inviolability of the individual is the true purpose of society and the source of all other safeguards of liberty. Bolívar declared that slavery is the negation of all law and a perversion of social rights and obligations. In terms of institutions for the new republic, the judiciary would enjoy an unprecedented degree of freedom, according to Bolívar. A Chamber of Tribunes would initiate laws of finance, peace, and war and oversee several administrative departments. Senators would write codes of law and appoint a number of public officials. Censors would constitute a division of government responsible for defending popular rights and the constitution, safeguarding morality, and bestowing public honors, all in a manifest effort to promote a common sense of patriotism and instill republican virtue in Bolivia's citizens.

Not all of Bolívar's suggestions were accepted by either the Venezuelan or the Bolivian congress, particularly his wish for a potent president, with a lifetime tenure, or for a hereditary senate, which Bolívar had modeled after the English House of Lords. The Venezuelan constitution never went into effect because it was quickly superseded by an even newer constitution for Gran Colombia, which briefly (1819–1831) combined Venezuela with Colombia/Panama, Ecuador, northern Peru, and northwestern Brazil.

Bolívar was a leading example of the Enlightenment's political principles put into action within a context of revolution and colonial independence. His influence, along with the influence of Enlightenment ideals from a multitude of other sources, was evident in the attempts of the new republics of South America to be, in fact, representative democracies that derived at least nominal sovereignty from their peoples and exercised the popular will through constitutional governments of divided powers, with the goals of ending slavery and protecting the liberty, equality, and other civil rights of their citizens.

Karl Yambert

Perspective Essay 3. Spanish America's Unenlightened Revolutions

The intellectual movement known as the Enlightenment, which spread through learned circles in Europe and crossed the Atlantic during the 18th century, played only a negligible role in sparking the uprisings that brought about independence for colonial Latin America. Of the four causes commonly cited by modern scholars as having paved the way toward the continent's insurrections—openings created by Bourbon dynasty reforms, sociopolitical aspirations inspired by the Enlightenment, resentments harbored by Creoles against Peninsular domination, and the rupture in imperial rule after French emperor Napoleon I ended the Bourbon dynasty in Spain in 1808—only the latter two factors proved to be truly significant.

In the Enlightenment, thinkers sought to apply rational theories derived from their studies of nature into scientific or technological advances. Some had then gradually expanded these to entail economic and sociopolitical experimentation. However, political ideals espoused by such men as England's John Locke and France's Jean-Jacques Rousseau were by no means universally embraced within their own countries, much less beyond their borders.

The more conservative ruling classes of Spain had accepted certain facets of Enlightenment thought in scientific and technological matters yet not in any broader political or societal context. King Charles III had set the Spanish standard by enacting his own brand of enlightened despotism, selectively introducing reforms throughout his empire as early as the 1760s. However, most were merely aimed at overhauling outdated administrative practices, increasing commercial and industrial output, and broadening the overall quality of education. A few more liberalizing concepts were entertained by the regime of his successor Charles IV, yet the Spanish Enlightenment remained pragmatic, primarily focused on benefits for the status quo.

Spanish society viewed democratic reforms such as those unleashed by the American Revolution and the French Revolution with detachment and misgivings, particularly given the violence that accompanied the radical doctrines of the First French Republic. These were greeted throughout Spain and its empire by purges of Francophile or republican sympathizers. Newspapers in Spain and its empire reported on events in Paris, contrasting them unfavorably with Spain's seemingly stable monarchy and comfortable Catholicism.

Well-to-do citizens in the Spanish colonies preferred the more restrained and officially sanctioned Enlightenment emanating from the Sociedades Económicas de Amigos del País (Economic Societies of Friends of the Nation), of which there were numerous local chapters modeled after the original in Madrid. With membership drawn almost exclusively from among the merchant and landowning elites and high-ranking colonial bureaucrats, these organizations remained limited to the study and dissemination of technological innovations and scientific improvements, not discussions regarding a reordering of society. Works by the French philosophes and other theorists were not unknown in the Spanish colonies; it was just that their dogmas did not seem to apply to local circumstances.

The French revolutionaries' military successes pulled a weakened Spain into an uneasy alliance by August 1796, which brought about a crippling transatlantic blockade by the British Royal Navy. A few disaffected young Creole officers serving in Europe, such as the Venezuelan Francisco de Miranda in London and the Chilean Bernardo O'Higgins in Cádiz, founded secret Masonic lodges with the aim of achieving independence for Spanish America. Yet they were only a tiny minority. Most colonials were not inspired by Madrid's French allies. Indeed, they abhorred the revolutionary attacks in France on the Catholic Church and aristocratic privileges during the Reign of Terror. And despite isolated clashes against British forces, most Spanish viceroyalties in the Americas were not threatened during the ensuing six years of hostilities, so their internal commerce continued unaffected, with even some overseas trade becoming possible aboard American or other neutral carriers.

European peace and direct rule from Madrid were briefly restored but then abruptly severed again in the autumn of 1804, as Spain was drawn back into the global conflict as an unequal partner of France. The American colonies were again isolated by the Royal Navy. Then in 1808 Napoleon deposed Charles IV and his youthful heir Ferdinand VII, only to install his own brother Joseph Bonaparte as king of Spain. Most Spaniards rose against this action, convening local juntas (assemblies) to govern themselves. These disparate organizations soon coalesced into the single chaotic Junta Suprema Central.

The first French emissaries who slipped through the Royal Navy blockade to the Americas to announce King Joseph's ascension were met with derision. Concerned

Spaniards in the colonies moved to ensure loyalty to the metropole. In Mexico City, for example, 300 armed Peninsulars pushed into its viceregal palace on the night of September 16, 1808, and removed the sitting viceroy, José de Iturrigaray, in favor of the octogenarian Field Marshal Pedro de Garibay, whom they believed to be more firmly loyal to Spain. Five days later, a similar ultraloyalist junta appeared in Monte-video because of suspicions against the acting viceroy in Buenos Aires, French-born Santiago de Liniers. Two months later, a group of wealthy Caracans were arrested for simply proposing the establishment of a Venezuelan junta to their governor.

Yet after the passage of several months, some American Creoles began moving into this political vacuum to assert their own interests, all the while paying lip service to the captive Ferdinand VII. In the summer of 1809 a handful of Peninsular governors were removed from office in Upper Peru (modern-day Bolivia) and Ecuador, although they were soon restored by a royalist counterexpedition from Lima. The following spring, coups established more permanent Creole juntas in Venezuela and Buenos Aires, which in turn began extending their authority into neighboring Colombia and Paraguay. The royalist occupiers of Quito responded to these upheavals on August 2, 1810, by purging that city of suspected sympathizers and massacring 200 civilians, prompting the radical junta at Buenos Aires to retaliate a week later by executing numerous royalists at Córdoba and sending their own small army up into the Andes.

Finally, the viceroyalty of New Spain was to be rocked by its own massive Creole insurrection, sparked by 57-year-old village priest Miguel Hidalgo y Costilla. He was no poor country cleric but instead was a wealthy and urbane gentleman, fluent in several languages, who owned numerous properties. Hidalgo had been one of many Creole leaders who believed that Mexico could govern itself without supervision from Madrid until the French were expelled from Spain and Ferdinand VII was restored to the throne. Hidalgo eventually came to entertain the notion of outright Mexican independence.

After some initial successes, Hidalgo's revolt in 1810 failed. Fighting nonetheless flared with varying degrees of intensity throughout most of Spanish America during the next dozen years, until the imperial grip was at last broken. But scarcely a hint of the Enlightenment can be detected in the motivations of these early rebels. There was no groundswell in favor of democratic rights, only broad-based and ingrained resentment against the inequities and restrictions of colonial rule, such as the self-interested and privileged status of Peninsular Spaniards, annual exactions in royal taxes sent overseas, monopolies on trade, and wrongheaded decrees and judicial decisions emanating from faceless ministers in Madrid.

Most insurgent leaders showed little desire to uproot their traditional colonial societies. Once independence was attained, it was notable how many young republics continued to honor ancient land titles, left the Catholic Church in its preeminent position, retained special privileges for high-ranking military officers, severely restricted suffrage, and reserved education largely for sons of the wealthy, while the masses of rural and urban poor were expected to resume their lives of servile labor. Not even slavery was abolished. The most basic tenets that any modern reader would identify with the Enlightenment would not begin to emerge until the triumph of liberal forces during the 1850s.

David F. Marley

Further Reading

Acemoglu, Daron, and James Robinson. *Why Nations Fail.* New York: Crown, 2012.

Briggs, Ronald. *Tropes of Enlightenment in the Age of Bolívar: Simón Rodríguez and the American Essay at Revolution.* Nashville: Vanderbilt University Press, 2010.

Brown, Matthew, ed. *Simón Bolívar: The Bolívarian Revolution; Introduction by Hugo Chávez.* London: Verso, 2009.

Bushnell, David, ed. *El Libertador: Writings of Simón Bolívar.* Translated by Frederick H. Fornoff. Oxford: Oxford University Press, 2003.

Chasteen, John Charles. *Americanos: Latin America's Struggle for Independence.* New York: Oxford University Press, 2008.

Chust, Manuel, and José Antonio Serrano, eds. *Debates sobre las independencias iberoamericanas.* Madrid: Iberoamericana, 2007.

Collier, Simon. "Simón Bolívar as Political Thinker." In *Simón Bolívar: Essays on the Life and Legacy of the Liberator,* edited by David Bushnell and Lester D. Langley, 13–34. Lanham MD: Rowman and Littlefield, 2008.

Durant, Will, and Ariel Durant. *Rousseau and Revolution.* New York: Simon and Schuster, 1967.

Dym, Jordana. *From Sovereign Villages to National States: City, State, and Federation in Central America, 1759–1839.* Albuquerque: University of New Mexico Press, 2006.

Griffin, Charles C. "The Enlightenment and Latin American Independence." In *Latin America and the Enlightenment,* 2nd ed., edited by Arthur P. Whitaker, 119–141. Ithaca, NY: Cornell University Press, 1961.

Harvey, Robert. *The Liberators: Latin America's Struggle for Independence.* New York: Overlook, 2000.

Humphreys, R. A., and John Lynch, eds. *The Origins of the Latin American Revolutions, 1808–1826.* New York: Knopf, 1965.

Jacob, Margaret C. C. *The Enlightenment: A Brief History with Documents.* New York: St. Martin's, 2000.

Kinsbrunner, Jay. *Independence in Spanish America: Civil Wars, Revolutions, and Underdevelopment.* Albuquerque: University of New Mexico Press, 2000.

Langley, Lester D. *Simón Bolívar: Venezuelan Rebel, American Revolutionary.* Lanham, MD: Rowman and Littlefield, 2009.

Lasso, Marixa. *Myths of Harmony: Race and Republicanism during the Age of Revolution, Colombia, 1795–1831.* Pittsburgh: University of Pittsburgh Press, 2007.

Lynch, John. *Latin America between Colony and Nation: Selected Essays.* Basingstoke, UK: Palgrave, 2001.

Lynch, John. *Simón Bolívar: A Life*. New Haven, CT: Yale University Press, 2006.

Madariaga, Salvador de. *Bolívar*. Madrid: Espasa-Calipe, S.A., 1984.

McFarlane, Anthony. "Identity, Enlightenment and Political Dissent in Late Colonial Spanish America." *Transactions of the Royal Historical Society*, series 6, 8 (1998): 309–335.

Paquette, Gabriel B. *Enlightenment, Governance, and Reform in Spain and Its Empire, 1759–1808*. Basingstoke, UK: Palgrave Macmillan, 2008.

Rippy, J. Fredo. *Latin America: A Modern History*. Detroit: University of Michigan Press, 1959.

Robinson, David J. "Liberty, Fragile Fraternity, and Inequality in Early-Republican Spanish America: Assessing the Impact of French Revolutionary Ideals." *Journal of Historical Geography* 16(1) (January 1990): 51–75.

Schmidt-Nowara, Christopher. "Politics and Ideas in Latin American Independence." *Latin American Research Review* 45 (2010): 228–235.

Skidmore, Thomas. *Modern Latin America*. New York: Oxford University Press, 2009.

Stein, Stanley, and Barbara Stein. *Apogee of Empire: Spain and New Spain in the Age of Charles III, 1759–1789*. Baltimore: Johns Hopkins University Press, 2003.

Tarragó, Rafael E. "Science and Religion in the Spanish American Enlightenment." *Catholic Social Science Review* 10 (2005): 181–196.

Van Young, Eric. *The Other Rebellion: Popular Violence, Ideology, and the Mexican Struggle for Independence, 1810–1821*. Stanford, CA: Stanford University Press, 2001.

Weber, David. *Bárbaros: Spaniards and Their Savages in the Age of Enlightenment*. New Haven, CT: Yale University Press, 2005.

Whitaker, Arthur P. *Latin America and the Enlightenment*. 2nd ed. Ithaca, NY: Cornell University Press, 1961.

21. WAS THE CONGRESS OF VIENNA A DIPLOMATIC SUCCESS?

The 1814–1815 Congress of Vienna stands as a definitive moment in the attainment of the Concert of Europe in the 19th century. It was the first of a series of agreements among European ambassadors that strove to maintain a balance of power on the European continent in the post-Napoleonic era. The congress occurred in the immediate aftermath of Napoleon Bonaparte's surrender in May 1814. Prior to that, most of Europe had been enveloped by 25 years of nearly constant warfare. The congress can also be seen as an attempt to reverse Europe's nascent liberal and nationalist movements and as a boost to European monarchies. On the other hand, it can be viewed as a genuine attempt to bring peace and long-term stability to a continent that had been badly damaged by a quarter century of conflict. Indeed, the congress served as the blueprint for European power politics until the outbreak of World War I in 1914. However, historians have long debated its true effectiveness at establishing a workable balance of power as well as an effective and long-lasting peace.

In the first perspective essay, Dr. Pavel Murdzhev views the Congress of Vienna as a useful diplomatic foundation that maintained a long-term balance of power in Europe but nevertheless failed to recognize the burgeoning spirit of nationalism that would ultimately upset the peace of Europe by the dawn of the 20th century. In the second essay, Dr. Ralph Ashby asserts that the Congress of Vienna often appears successful in comparison to later diplomatic agreements such as the 1919 Treaty of Versailles, which attempted to restore order after World War I. Indeed, he argues that the Congress did prevent a full-scale war in Europe for 40 years. However, he points out that on closer inspection, the Congress of Vienna failed in its attempt to crush nationalism or the liberal revolutionary spirit of the Napoleonic era, making it only a partial success.

Background Essay

With Napoleon having rejected peace terms that would have left him on the French throne and given France what it had sought for so long in the natural frontiers of the Rhine, in January 1814 the allied armies invaded northeastern France. Napoleon fought a brilliant campaign; however, faced with dwindling resources and with his marshals turning against him, he was forced to abdicate in April. On May 30, the allies imposed on France the remarkably lenient Treaty of Paris of 1814. They had claimed all along that Napoleon, not France, was the enemy, and the treaty was designed both to preserve a strong France and to get new Bourbon king Louis XVIII off to a good start. France was reduced to its frontiers of 1792, which included Avignon, Venaissin, parts of Savoy, and some border strongholds in the northeast, none of which had belonged to France in 1789. France agreed to recognize the independence of the Netherlands, the German and Italian states, and Switzerland. There was no indemnity.

Given the complexity of territorial settlements elsewhere, the allied leaders agreed to a general peace conference in Vienna. Britain simply announced that it would return the Netherlands Indies but retain Malta, Helgoland, Trinidad, the Cape of Good Hope, and Ceylon (Sri Lanka); Britain also secured a protectorate over the Ionian Islands. Britain agreed to return to France its overseas colonies except for Tobago, Ste. Lucia, and Mauritius.

In September 1814 representatives of virtually all European states—and those of a number no longer existing—began gathering at Vienna in what was one of the most important diplomatic assemblies of modern times. Emperors Alexander I of Russia and Francis I of Austria were present, along with the kings of Prussia, Bavaria, Württemberg, and Denmark, but the real work was carried on by their first ministers. The key players were Prince Klemens von Metternich of Austria; Robert Stewart, Viscount Castlereagh, of Britain; Prussian chief minister Prince Karl August von Hardenburg; and Charles Maurice de Talleyrand-Périgord of France.

A serious split developed at Vienna between Austria and Britain on the one hand and Prussia and Russia on the other. Russia wanted all of Poland in a reconstituted Kingdom of Poland with Alexander as its ruler, while Prussia sought all of Saxony. Austria and Britain feared an increase in Russian and Prussian influence. The discord almost brought war and enabled Talleyrand to play a key role, supporting Austria and Britain. Metternich proposed a defensive alliance of Austria, Britain, and France, and this secret treaty was signed on January 3, 1815.

Napoleon was well informed of events in Vienna, and these encouraged him to try one final roll of the dice, whereupon the Allies quickly settled their differences. Indeed, already on news of the secret treaty, Russia and Prussia backed down. Russia received most of Poland, and Prussia received part of Saxony.

Napoleon now departed Elba, which he had been given to rule under the terms of his abdication, and returned to France. Although he reestablished himself

Delegates assemble during the Congress of Vienna, held during September 1814–June 1815, to redraw the map of Europe following the defeat of Napoleon. (Library of Congress)

in power, his rule was short. The Hundred Days ended in defeat at Waterloo on June 18.

Napoleon's venture was costly for France. In the Treaty of Paris of November 20, 1815, France lost additional territory (being restricted to the borders of 1790 rather than 1792) and had to pay an indemnity of 700 million francs, support an allied army of occupation until it was paid, and return all captured artworks to their countries of origin.

In the Final Act of the Congress of Vienna of June 8, 1815, Austria received Lombardy and Venetia, the Illyrian Provinces (the former French kingdoms of Illyria and Dalmatia), and Salzburg and the Tirol, both from Bavaria. Austria, however, gave up the Netherlands.

Prussia gained two-fifths of Saxony, Posen and Danzig (Gdansk), Swedish Pomerania, and Rügen (for which Denmark received Lauenburg). Prussia also secured territory in Westphalia as well Neuchâtel. In return Prussia yielded Ansbach and Baireuth to Bavaria, East Friesland to Hanover, and part of its Polish territory before 1807 to Russia.

To offset any future French threat to the northeast, the Dutch Republic secured the former Austrian Netherlands (Belgium), the new enlarged state being known as the Kingdom of the Netherlands. Metternich hoped that this step would enhance the possibility of future cooperation between France and Austria. The Netherlands, however, was sharply divided along religious and linguistic lines.

One of the most difficult problems to resolve was that of the German states. Napoleon had consolidated some 350 into a 10th that number. German nationalism, so evident in the German War of Liberation of 1813, was now deliberately set aside in favor of a loose-knit German Confederation of 39 states, including 5 free cities, with Austria as its permanent president. The Act of Confederation was signed on September 8, 1815.

The new Polish state (Congress Poland) encompassed much the same territory as Napoleon's former Grand Duchy of Warsaw. Its king, Czar Alexander, granted Poland a liberal constitution (which Russia did not have), with Polish as the official language, and its own army. Kraków (Cracow) became a free state under the protection of Russia, Austria, and Prussia.

Sweden was confirmed in possession of Norway (acquired in the Treaty of Kiel of January 14, 1814), with Norway receiving a guarantee of its rights and a separate constitution. In the Act of Union of 1815, Norway was confirmed as an independent kingdom, merely united with Sweden under the same ruler. Denmark was compensated by receiving Lauenburg.

Switzerland became an independent confederation of 22 cantons. Spain, Sardinia (which secured Genoa), Tuscany, Modena, and the Papal States were all reconstituted. The duchies of Parma, Modena, Lucca, and Tuscany were given to members of the Habsburg family. The Bourbons were not reestablished in the Kingdom of

Naples until 1815 (then the Kingdom of the Two Sicilies). In Italy as in Germany, nationalism was deliberately stymied, with Habsburg predominance reestablished.

Concurrent with the Treaty of Paris of 1814, the major powers had agreed to the Quadruple Alliance. Britain, Austria, Prussia, and Russia pledged to maintain for 20 years the arrangements they made at Vienna and Paris. They also agreed to meet periodically in order to discuss problems of common interest and to maintain the peace of Europe, establishing what became known as the Concert of Europe. The British government, however, served notice that it did not regard this as a license to meddle in the internal affairs of other states and that it would intervene only to maintain the territorial boundaries agreed to.

Spencer C. Tucker

Perspective Essay 1. The Beginning of Collective Security

The Congress of Vienna occurred from September 1814 to June 1815. Major powers sending representatives included Russia, Great Britain, Austria, and Prussia, the allied states that had defeated Napoleon and put an end to two decades of warfare. France was also represented.

The ultimate goal of the four victorious powers was to establish a lasting peace in Europe by a fair settlement, which would free the continent from French domination and restore the territorial status quo before the Napoleonic Wars. At Vienna, the Concert of Europe established a new principle of international settlement, according to which disputes between the states would be settled by diplomacy and negotiation involving all the great powers to reconcile contending claims and to attain a reasonable compromise and a "real and permanent balance of power."

The Congress of Vienna marks a turning point in the political organization of Europe, and its short- as well as long-term impact on political development has been the subject of study of a wide range of specialists. Undoubtedly, the failure of the peacemakers in 1814–1815 to understand and thus to draw the implications and consequences of the surge of nationalism ultimately eroded their capacity to maintain peace. Beyond doubt, however, the balance of power established by the Vienna Settlement led to the first, the longest-lasting, and the most successful attempt at collective security in Europe, compared perhaps only to that of the post–Cold War era.

Except for Britain, where rapid industrialization had taken hold, at the opening of the 19th century agriculture still held first place on the European continent. Political power continued to be based primarily on land and population. More land clearly benefited the state in terms of more taxes, greater security, and more power. Bargaining regarding territories and economic interests during 1814–1815 was thus extremely important for neutralizing internal weaknesses and enforcing the strategic strengths of each of the great powers. Regrettably, in an effort to provide each party some satisfaction, the representatives of the great powers did not hesitate to redistribute territories and status as if they were pieces of a gigantic puzzle, often ignoring the will of the people involved and historical backgrounds. The Poles failed to win independence, while northern Italy was given over to Austrian rule, Norway was transferred from the Danish to the Swedish Crown, and the Belgians were subjected to the Dutch in a new Kingdom of the Netherlands. In their effort to preserve lasting peace, the negotiators at Vienna built their consensus on the quicksand of suspended national sentiments.

The redrawing of the European map followed two main principles: containment of France and reciprocal territorial compensation for "the grand allies." Rather than restoring the pre-Napoleonic frontiers, the great powers had to align the new territorial arrangements with the concept of balance of powers. Balance of power remained the main concern of the peacemakers, superior not only to national sentiments and aspirations but also to the restoration of dynastic rights. Indeed, there were far more rulers who were not restored by the Vienna Settlement, most obviously in Germany where Napoleon had reduced some 350 states to 39. The thus created power vacuum in Germany served the balance of powers well: it cleared the arena of the two main rivals for German leadership, Prussia and Austria, and at the same time guaranteed that Germany would remain too fragmented and weak to counter French and Russian ambitions.

The Vienna conferees gave more consideration to liberalism in the form of constitutions, but even for Britain, the most eager advocate of liberal causes, political liberalism was of secondary concern to economic interests. Public opinion in Britain was captivated by domestic antislave rhetoric, and British secretary for foreign affairs Viscount Castlereagh felt obliged to press for the abolition of the slave trade at Vienna but made very little progress, apart from extracting vague promises from the other great powers. No doubt, Castlereagh would have been happy to see the European countries adopting the British governmental system but only where appropriate for British interests, which, as the French Revolution had proved, could be easily jeopardized by radical political change.

On the other end of the political spectrum, among the major players in 1814–1815 was Austrian foreign minister Klemens von Metternich, who was determined to minimize the spread of liberalism and nationalist ideas because these would be destructive for the multinational Habsburg Empire. The aim of Austrian foreign policy therefore was "a just equilibrium," and most of Metternich's brilliant diplomatic skills were directed at preventing other powers from achieving their aims rather than creating opportunities for Austria. The balance of powers was understood by Austria as a neutralization of the double threats from Russia to the east and France to the west and the forestalling of Prussian expansion within Germany at Austrian expense.

There was not much to lose for France in Vienna, for it had already been stripped of most of its conquests under the Treaty of Paris of May 1814. France's chief representative at the congress, Charles Maurice de Talleyrand-Périgord, was, however, successful in exploiting the differences between "the grand allies" in order to limit the punishment of France and restore its status and influence as part of the Concert of Europe.

The political views of Czar Alexander I of Russia were a strange mixture of traditional authoritarianism on the one hand and liberal generosity from his Christian mysticism on the other. Alexander's strategic aims, however, were no different than those of the previous Russian rulers. His priority was the annexation of the whole of Poland, a goal that he had already settled with Prussia in the Treaty of Kalisz of February 28, 1813. Alexander agreed in return to support Prussia in securing all of Saxony, France's most loyal German ally. Both Castlereagh and Metternich viewed this arrangement of Russia getting all of Poland and Prussia getting all of Saxony as threatening the European balance of power. In addition, Alexander, as was the case with his predecessors, sought to secure an outlet on the Mediterranean, preferably through Istanbul (Constantinople) that would see the Ottoman Empire excluded from Europe.

The Congress of Vienna offered the best insights to the mechanism of the balance-of-power system. Britain and Austria firmly opposed the demands of Russia and Prussia for Poland and Saxony. The dispute escalated in the late fall of 1814. By December Karl August von Hardenberg, chief Russian representative, announced that any attempt to alter the Treaty of Kalisz might be taken as a cause for war. Talleyrand seized this opportunity to align France with Castlereagh and Metternich in opposing Russian and Prussian demands. The conclusion of this alliance ended France's diplomatic isolation.

At the beginning of January 1815, France was admitted as the fifth great power in the Directing Committee of the congress. A compromise was then reached whereby Russia acquired most of Poland, while Prussia secured half of Saxony. This agreement paved the way for progress in other areas under consideration, and on June 9, 1815, the Final Act of the Congress of Vienna was approved, with each of the victorious powers securing some of its key demands.

In the following years the Vienna Settlement was regarded as the cornerstone of European equilibrium, with an increasingly shifting alignment. In 1826 Russia and Britain, in pursuit of their own interests, violated the aims of both the Holy Alliance and the State Paper, respectively, and demonstrated a readiness to resolve the Greek question. In 1829, together with France they extracted semi-independence for the Greeks from the Ottoman Empire and isolated Metternich's efforts for mediation.

When the former Austrian Netherlands (Belgium) declared its independence from the Kingdom of the Netherlands in 1830, the Concert of Europe again demonstrated that legitimacy was of secondary importance to the balance of power and that lesser states could benefit from the pursuit of self-interest. The balance-of-power system prevailed during and after the great wave of European revolutions in 1848, when Russian forces helped the Austrians crush the Hungarian Revolution of 1848–1849. Russian support of Austria also helped discourage Prussian king Frederick William IV from accepting the crown of a unified Germany offered to him by the revolutionary Frankfurt Assembly.

The Concert of Europe was undermined by the Crimean War (1853–1856), in which Russia, isolated and deserted by "neutral" Austria, faced a coalition of France, Britain, the Ottoman Empire, and the Kingdom of Sardinia. The Treaty of Paris of 1856 that ended the war left Russia embittered and keen on revenge. The coup de grâce for the Vienna Settlement and its related balance-of-power system came from Camillo Benso de Cavour, chief minister of the small Kingdom of Sardinia (Piedmont-Sardinia) who, aided by France, went to war in 1859 against Austria in order to unify Italy. Within a few years the unification of Italy had been accomplished, and the Vienna Settlement was effectively at an end.

Piedmont-Sardinia's victory confirmed the suspicions that appeared during the Crimean War that the ancient axiom of power resting on land and population was no longer valid. It seems that by the 1860s, as also confirmed by Prussia, sheer physical size was no longer as important as the combination of industrialized economy, efficient infrastructure, and modern military establishment. There was, of course, a new balance reached in Europe after the wars between Austria and Prussia in 1866 and between France and Prussia during 1870–1871. But the arrangement among the European great powers was unstable, temporary, and susceptible to the attacks from nationalist movements and the ambitions of the lesser states in Europe. At the turn of the century, the era of consensus, limited warfare, and collective security achieved by the European diplomats at Vienna in 1815 was gone, replaced by chauvinism, contest for resources, and an arms race that culminated in a world war.

Pavel Murdzhev

Perspective Essay 2. A Success for Some

The Congress of Vienna was a success, but this was partial, uneven, and certainly impermanent. When considering to what extent the Congress of Vienna was a success, we must quantify and qualify success against the goals of the negotiators and also consider short-, medium-, and long-term results. Its success can be judged in relation to other such conferences. Thus, if we compare the results of the Congress of Vienna to the results of the Paris Peace Conference of 1919, we can judge the Congress of Vienna to have been a smashing success. The Paris Peace Conference failed to establish a long-lasting peace, and indeed regional conflict followed immediately, and World War II occurred two decades later. The Congress of Vienna, in contrast, was followed by a much longer period of peace, at least among the major powers.

The national delegations came to the Congress of Vienna with quite different goals. Broadly, besides seeking their own territorial aggrandizement, they had two principal goals: establishing a durable peace and suppressing revolutionary tendencies in Europe. Most of the participants saw these two goals as not only compatible but also inextricably linked. The trick, then, was how to accomplish these goals while harmonizing them with the individual national interests.

After nearly a quarter of a century of bloody warfare in Europe, the negotiators at Vienna were strongly motivated to achieve a durable peace. In this respect, the diplomatic efforts of the 1814–1815 Congress of Vienna were largely successful, at least in preventing a large-scale war in Europe for nearly four decades. As far as the goal of suppressing revolutions was concerned, the notion that these could be overcome was essentially delusional. The premise that the suppression of revolutionary ideals was necessary for the establishment of peace was flawed to begin with.

Peace in Europe rested on establishing a balance of power. How to create a balance of power with Europe or even define it was a matter of disagreement among the negotiators. The basic concept of balance of power meant that there would have to be at least several strong powers whose military, economic, and geopolitical potential was sufficient to prevent any one power from dominating. Ideally, the powers would have systems of alliances and spheres of influence so as to discourage aggression or the instigation of warfare.

Historians have generally lauded the main participants in the Congress of Vienna for their skill, judgment, and intelligence. Prince Klemens von Metternich of Austria, Charles Maurice de Talleyrand-Périgord of France, and Robert Stewart, Viscount Castlereagh for Great Britain, all played key roles. Czar Alexander I of Russia was his own chief negotiator and also played an important role. The long period of peace in Europe between the Napoleonic Wars ending in 1815 and the start of the Crimean War in 1853 can be traced to their work. Indeed, war involving all the major powers did not again occur until World War I in 1914, nearly a full century after the end of the Congress of Vienna. This says much for the balance of power created by the congress. At the same time, the revolutions and "small" wars that characterized much of the 19th century were significant and were also the legacy of the Congress of Vienna.

The tasks immediately before the diplomats at the Congress of Vienna beginning in September 1814 involved redrawing the map of Europe to ensure a balance of power while at the same time rewarding and strengthening the powers that had defeated Napoleon I, especially Russia, Prussia, and Austria. The "restoration" of Europe was hardly a matter of selfless altruism on the part of these powers. Their leaders were not about to leave the bargaining table without territorial gains for their countries. Indeed, Napoleon had cynically assessed the territorial ambitions of the Allied powers more than a year before the Congress of Vienna. In a meeting with Metternich in 1813 in which the French emperor sought to dissuade Austria from again declaring war on France, Napoleon informed the Austrian foreign minister that "In fact, you want Italy, Russia wants Poland, Sweden wants Norway, Prussia wants Saxony, and England insists on the possession of Holland and Belgium." This Napoleonic analysis essentially outlines almost precisely the territorial gains confirmed by the Congress of Vienna. While Britain did not secure control of Holland and Belgium, Castlereagh was able to achieve the unification of those two in the Kingdom of the Netherlands, friendly to the British.

Creating a balance of power in Europe meant that France could not be left in a position of potential dominance. As a corollary, the same should apply to all the other major powers of Europe. While it was easy for the Allied powers to impose limits on French territory, it was another matter altogether as to how to distribute territory that would reward the victors yet achieve a relative balance. Indeed, this set the stage for much diplomatic wrangling. Most territorial adjustments were accomplished by early 1815, but before the negotiations could play out fully, Napoleon shocked Europe with his escape from exile in Elba and return to France in what became known as the Hundred Days.

After the Allies had definitively defeated Napoleon in the June 1815 Battle of Waterloo, the diplomats at Vienna confirmed the original decision to limit the power and territory of France. The Treaty of Paris of November 20, 1815, cost France some additional territory beyond that of the Treaty of Paris of 1814. France reverted to the frontiers of 1790. In addition, France was forced to pay reparations, and there would be temporary occupation by Allied troops until this was forthcoming. In addition, France had to surrender all the artworks looted from the rest of Europe.

Napoleon had made great use of nationalism in France, and it had also swept the Germanies in 1813, but its impact had yet to be felt in much of Europe. Nationalism held that people of a common language, culture, and historical experience should form an independent state, free of foreign control. Nationalism was linked to liberalism, itself a broad and vaguely defined movement. The development of nationalism in the 19th century was at least partly the result of Enlightenment influence. It held that nations were not the possessions of kings or rulers but instead were the embodiment of the people and therefore the will of the people. Both nationalism and liberalism were growing in influence throughout Europe. The fact that they were identified in large part with the French Revolution and Napoleon and nearly a quarter century of warfare meant that most of the diplomats at Vienna were bound to oppose them. Suppression of nationalism and liberalism was considered essential to a long-term peace.

By this point the powers had resolved most of their major differences. For all practical purposes Poland became an adjunct of the Russian Empire, although small slices of Polish territory were given to Austria and Prussia. Austrian territorial gains were mostly in Italy. In addition to direct annexations of large sections of ethnically Italian territory to the Austrian Empire, other Italian states were clients of Austria. Not gaining ethnically German territory but rather lands containing Italians, Poles, Croatians, etc., the Habsburg Austrian Empire only added to its polyglot nature. At least 15 different languages were spoken within the empire, an ominous portent at the dawn of the Age of Nationalism.

Prussian territorial gains were chiefly in ethnically German territory. Having lost much of its earlier Polish holdings to Russia, the Prussians sought to be compensated with all of Saxony. Issues of legitimacy concerned the Congress of Vienna diplomats in regard to the king of Saxony. They did not wish to see him stripped entirely of his realm, so he was left with a fragment, and Prussia received about half of Saxony. Prussia also received territory on the Rhine. The end result was a Prussia that was less Polish and more purely German, an advantage in the new Age of Nationalism. Prussia was in a position to dominate not only northern Germany but also potentially all of Germany.

While many of the arrangements made at Vienna during 1814–1815 were of long duration, other Congress of Vienna constructions fell apart relatively quickly. The Revolutions of 1830 constituted a direct challenge to the conservative mindsets of 1815 and afterward. The Poles rose in revolt against the Russians. This bloody revolution during 1830–1831 ended, inevitably, in Polish defeat and Poland's direct incorporation into the Russian Empire. In 1831 the Belgians rose in revolt, ending the artificial union of the Kingdom of the Netherlands, which was sharply divided along linguistic lines.

The Revolutions of 1848, which occurred among other places in Austrian-controlled northern Italy and also in Vienna itself, ended Metternich's political career, and a revolution in Hungary threatened the existence of the Austrian Empire. Only the aid of large Russian forces enabled the Austrians to defeat the Hungarians in 1849. The implications of a strong and interventionist Russia eventually brought an end to the period of peace between the major powers of Europe. The Crimean War of 1853–1856 would see Britain and France in the unaccustomed role of allies against Russia, which now appeared to be the greatest threat to the precarious balance of power.

The successes of the Congress of Vienna were greatest where the diplomats were able to focus on the map of Europe and create a workable balance of power, all the while smoothing over differences with quid pro quo arrangements. Yet the inherent conservatism of their regimes doomed aspects of the Vienna Settlement to eventual failure. The main failures of the Congress of Vienna were largely the fault of individual governments, which too often looked at the map of Europe as though it were a chess board occupied by playing pieces rather than lands inhabited by real people with rising aspirations.

Ralph Ashby

Further Reading

Anderson, Matthew Smith. *The Rise of Modern Diplomacy, 1450–1919*. London: Longman, 1993.

Black, Jeremy. *British Diplomats and Diplomacy, 1688–1800*. Exeter, UK: University of Exeter Press, 2001.

Chapman, Tim. *The Congress of Vienna: Origins, Processes, and Results*. London: Routledge, 1998.

Charmley, John. "Castlereagh and France." *Diplomacy & Statecraft* 17(4) (December 2006): 665–673.

Derry, John W. *Castlereagh*. New York: St. Martin's, 1976.

Downs, George W. *Collective Security beyond the Cold War*. Ann Arbor: University of Michigan Press, 1994.

Dwyer, Philip G. *Talleyrand*. London: Longman, 2002.

Gulick, Edward Vose. *Europe's Classical Balance of Power: A Case History of the Theory and Practice of One of the Great Concepts of European Statecraft*. Westport, CT: Greenwood, 1982.

Jarrett, Mark. *The Congress of Vienna and Its Legacy: War and Great Power Diplomacy after Napoleon*. London: I. B. Tauris, 2013.

King, David. *Vienna, 1814: How the Conquerors of Napoleon Made Love, War, and Peace at the Congress of Vienna*. New York: Harmony Books, 2008.

Kissinger, Henry. "The Congress of Vienna, Reappraisal." *World Politics* 8(2) (January 1956): 264–280.

Kissinger, Henry. *A World Restored: Metternich, Castlereagh and the Problems of Peace, 1812–22*. Boston: Houghton Mifflin, 1957.

Krasner, Stephen. *Sovereignty: Organized Hypocrisy*. Princeton, NJ: Princeton University Press, 1999.

Nicolson, Harold. *The Congress of Vienna: A Study in Allied Unity, 1812–1822*. New York: Harcourt Brace Jovanovich, 1946.

Palmer, Alan. *Metternich: Councillor of Europe*. London: Orion, 1997.

Rendall, Matthew. "A Qualified Success for Collective Security: The Concert of Europe and the Belgian Crisis, 1831." *Diplomacy & Statecraft* 18(2) (June 2007): 271–295.

Robinson, James Harvey, and Charles Beard, eds. *Readings in Modern European History*. 2 vols. Boston: Ginn, 1908–1909.

Schroeder, Paul. W. *The Transformation of European Politics, 1763–1848*. New York: Oxford University Press, 1994.

288 | Enduring Controversies in Military History

Sked, Alan. *Metternich and Austria: An Evaluation.* Basingstoke, UK: Palgrave Macmillan, 2008.

Sofka, James R. "Metternich's Theory of European Order: A Political Agenda for 'Perpetual Peace.'" *Review of Politics* 60(1) (Winter 1998): 115–150.

Webster, Charles. *The Congress of Vienna.* New York: Barnes and Noble, 1966.

Zamoyski, Adam. *Rites of Peace: The Fall of Napoleon and the Congress of Vienna.* New York: HarperCollins, 2007.

Zartman, William, and Viktor Kremeniuk. *Peace versus Justice: Negotiating Forward- and Backward-Looking Outcomes.* Lanham, MD: Rowman and Littlefield, 2005.

PART IV

THE RISE OF IMPERIALISM AND NATIONALISM (1825–1914)

22. Was the United States Justified in Annexing Texas and Taking California from Mexico in Its Pursuit of Manifest Destiny?

The notion of U.S. manifest destiny was an ideological set of assumptions employed to rationalize westward territorial expansion to the Pacific Ocean during the 1840s and 1850s. This mind-set held that the United States had a divinely ordained right and duty to occupy the entire continent south of Canada. Indeed, those who subscribed to manifest destiny saw westward expansion as inevitable and a reflection of American exceptionalism. By implementing manifest destiny, its adherents also believed that they were bringing U.S.-style democracy to areas where freedom was in short supply. There were, however, other motives involved in manifest destiny, and some of them were less than altruistic. Many slaveholders in the southern United States, now largely supported by the Democratic Party, sought additional U.S. territory so that more lands could be opened for agricultural cultivation fueled by slave labor. This was particularly the case with Texas, where cash crops such as cotton could be grown with relative ease. A by-product of slavery's expansion would be the strengthening of the slaveholding South against the increasingly prosperous and industrialized northern states. Although California was less suited for cotton cultivation, it nevertheless offered abundant natural resources, fertile soil, and fine harbors and would serve as an ideal entrepôt for expanding Pacific trade. For Native Americans, however, manifest destiny was nothing short of catastrophic. At the same time, manifest destiny demonstrated a blatant disregard of Mexico's territorial rights as a sovereign nation.

In the first perspective essay, Dr. Gregory S. Hospodor asserts that the United States did not have a legitimate claim to Texas or California because the Americans had already recognized Mexico's existing borders, chiefly in the 1819 Adams-Onís Treaty in which the United States specifically relinquished any claims to Texas. America's unlawful annexation of Texas in 1845 and the ensuing dispute over its border with Mexico provided the pretext for the Mexican-American War (1846–1848). By war's end, the United States had claimed California and other former Mexican territory in the American West. Jeffery O. Mahan argues that the Mexican-American War resulted from the clash between manifest destiny and Mexico's hypernationalism. Furthermore, because of the stark differences in the two nations' economies, foreign policy viewpoints, and governmental setups, conflict seemed almost inevitable. In addition, Mahan points out that U.S. racism and attitudes toward slavery also played a role in the conflict with Mexico. In the third essay, Dr. Lee W. Eysturlid states that manifest destiny was the primary justification used by American politicians to seize Mexican lands. Strategic and ideological considerations strongly influenced the U.S. drive into the West. Moreover, the desire to open more territory for slavery and the relative weakness of its southern neighbor were also key factors in the U.S. government's decision to instigate the Mexican-American War.

Background Essay

By the 1830s, the Mexican provinces bordering the territory of the United Stares were attached to the mother country by the thinnest of ties. At the same time, many Americans strongly supported territorial expansion, fueled by a steady influx of immigrants, most of them from Europe, and strong westward settlement.

Many if not most Americans saw it as their nation's right to possess all the land between the Atlantic and the Pacific. Known as manifest destiny, this doctrine included the Mexican territory that today constitutes present-day Texas, California, Arizona, Nevada, and New Mexico. For many Americans, taking and securing this land constituted no less than a divinely sanctioned mission during which the new territory would be infused with American values and government. A number of southern planters and politicians meanwhile saw in westward expansion the opportunity to open up new lands to agricultural cultivation (most notably the South's cash crop of cotton). This would also mean the expansion of slavery, upon which cotton cultivation so depended.

Americans had begun settling in Texas in the 1820s. The Mexican government had encouraged this, as few Mexicans wished to do so because of the threat from Comanche Indians. Although President James Monroe had recognized the Sabine and Red Rivers as the southwestern boundary of the United States, later American presidents had endeavored to purchase Texas, creating considerable resentment in Mexico as a result. By the 1830s, there were four times as many Americans in Texas as Mexicans. A number of issues estranged Texans from Mexico, including administrative practices,

Mexican political chaos, religion (all settlers in Texas were supposed to be Roman Catholics, but few actually were), and slavery. During 1835–1836 Texans fought and won their independence and established their own republic. Although Mexico's population outnumbered that of Texas by more than 10 to 1, Mexico made no effort to reconquer Texas.

Most Texans wanted annexation by the United States, but slavery, which Texans supported, was a growing issue for many Americans. Finally, in February 1845 the United States annexed Texas by a joint resolution of Congress. This procedure did not require a two-thirds majority vote.

In 1845, James K. Polk became president. A champion of manifest destiny, Polk sought to secure California, where there were then only some 6,000 whites. He sent an agent to Mexico City with an offer to purchase the future Golden State, but Mexico's leaders refused to sell. Polk then baited Mexico into war, in which California was the prize.

Mexico had broken off relations with the United States over the annexation of Texas but made no hostile moves. In July 1845 Polk ordered much of the U.S. Army under Brigadier General Zachary Taylor to take up position along on the Nueces River, the southwestern border of Texas, but there was then no reason to assume that Mexico was preparing to attack.

Later in 1845 Polk attempted to stir up revolt against Mexican rule in California and even sent a small military "exploring" mission there. At the same time, he made another effort to secure the Rio Grande as the southern border of Texas in return for the U.S. government assuming the claims owned by Americans and also to purchase for cash New Mexico and California. The Mexican government rejected the offer, which indeed caused so much resentment that it led to another Mexican revolution.

Polk reacted quickly. On January 13, 1846, the day after he received word of Mexico's refusal to receive his agent, he ordered Taylor to cross the Nueces River and occupy the left bank of the Rio Grande. This was in effect an act of war. The Nueces had been the recognized southern boundary of Texas, even by the Lone Star Republic.

Taylor's men occupied the north (left) bank of the Rio Grande on March 23 and rejected demands by the Mexican authorities to return to the Nueces. On May 9, dispatches from Taylor gave Polk what he wanted. On April 25 a Mexican force had crossed the Rio Grande and engaged in a cavalry skirmish with a troop of U.S. dragoons, inflicting several casualties. Polk promptly produced a war message, sent to Congress on May 11. In it Polk declared that "The cup of forbearance has been exhausted. After reiterated menaces, Mexico has passed the boundary of the United States, has invaded our territory and shed American blood upon the American soil." Congress responded with a declaration of war.

The ensuing Mexican-American War saw U.S. forces triumphant, with Mexico forced to conclude the Treaty of Guadalupe Hidalgo of February 2, 1848. In it Mexico

Lithograph depicting the U.S. victory in the Battle of Palo Alto, fought in northern Mexico on May 8, 1846. The battle was the first major clash of the Mexican-American War. (Library of Congress)

ceded Texas with the Rio Grande boundary, New Mexico (including Arizona, Colorado, Utah, and Nevada), and Upper California (including San Diego). The victor assumed the unpaid claims and paid $15 million in addition. The United States had rounded out its continental area, excepting Alaska. The question remained whether this new territory would be slave or free. This significantly intensified the national debate over the question of slavery, which brought on the American Civil War in 1861.

Spencer C. Tucker

Perspective Essay 1. No Legitimate Claim for the United States

With the ratification of the Treaty of Guadalupe Hidalgo by the Mexican and U.S. Senates in 1848, the Mexican-American War ended and more than 500,000 square miles of territory officially passed into American hands. Although Mexico retained a legitimate historical claim to Texas and California, the treaty reflected the military situation on the ground, in which American forces occupied most of the land claimed and indeed much of Mexico that was not. Mexico was forced to relinquish any claim to Texas, whose independence and later annexation by the United States the Mexican government had until now refused to officially recognize. Mexico also surrendered title to land west all the way to the Pacific Ocean, including the future state of California.

Mexico's legitimate historical claims to the ceded land stem from two key factors. First, the United States officially recognized the territorial boundaries of Mexico before that issue was clouded by the Texas Revolution of 1835–1836. Second, the primary cause of the Mexican-American War was American hunger for Mexican land.

During their early history, Mexico and the United States traveled a similar path. Both based their claims to territorial sovereignty on the imperial past. Both broke away from their mother countries after successful revolutions and established republics (Mexico achieved independence in 1821 and established a republic in 1824 after overthrowing Emperor Agustín de Iturbide). Early on, both understood each other as fellow travelers along a common republican path. Mexico's 1824 constitution, for example, intentionally bore many similarities to that of the United States.

Mexico and the United States also shared a well-defined border. In 1819, the Adams-Onís Treaty between the United States and Spain established the border along the Sabine River. Furthermore, the United States relinquished any claim to Texas in Article III of the same treaty. Mexico inherited both the boundary and the claim to Texas when the United States became one of the first countries to recognize Mexican independence in 1822.

Expansionism, a perpetual theme in antebellum American history, eventually overwhelmed the incipient republican amity between the two countries as well as the border. Spanish colonial authorities had long eyed their northeastern neighbor's expansionist tendencies with suspicion. Thus, Joel Poinsett, the first U.S. ambassador to a newly independent Mexico, surprised no one when he advised the Mexican government of the American desire to acquire Texas, California, and New Mexico. Encouraged by the Mexican government, which hoped thereby to pacify the Comanches, thousands of Americans moved across the Sabine River into Texas during the 1820s and early 1830s. Most accepted Mexican citizenship. Later, these same immigrants would fight for their independence. The Texas Revolution proved popular in the United States, which made it clear to many Mexicans that acquisitiveness for land had trumped republican sympathy and respect for the border in American hearts and minds. Mexico quickly rejected the Treaties of Velasco, "negotiated" by Antonio López de Santa Anna after his capture in the war, that had recognized Texan independence and set the Lone Star Republic's border on the Rio Grande. The United States, on the other hand, recognized Texan independence on March 3, 1836. Predictably, U.S.-Mexican relations gradually soured until the year 1845 saw them come to a head with the annexation of Texas and the inauguration of James K. Polk as president of the United States.

President Polk's small physical stature was no reflection of the size of his expansionist plans. Indeed, Polk, who styled himself an agent of manifest destiny, sought to enlarge the country by a half in adding Oregon, Texas, and California to its domain. John Tyler, the previous president, took care of Texas by joint resolution of Congress in 1845, and an agreement had been worked out with Great Britain regarding the Oregon Territory by early 1846. This left California and other Mexican territory to the east. American expansionists had long sought California, especially for its port of San Francisco. Polk considered several methods of satisfying his and his countrymen's desire for California, the most notable of which was John Slidell's 1845–1846 diplomatic mission to Mexico. Slidell's instructions were simple—offer money for land. When Mexico failed to deal, Polk sought to play the military option.

The annexation of Texas and the consequent dispute over its border with Mexico provided the pretext for armed confrontation. Mexico continued to regard Texas as its sovereign territory and broke off diplomatic relations with the United States. As half of the U.S. Army marched to Corpus Christi to "protect" the new state, a Mexican army gathered at Matamoros 150 miles to the south. Between the two armies rested what historians now and many people then referred to as "disputed territory." Texans claimed the Rio Grande as their state's border, although it had never served as a provincial boundary, nor was it ever "controlled" by the Lone Star Republic. In Mexico, even those willing to accept the loss of Texas would only concede the Nueces River as its border. Polk then made a fateful decision; on January 13, 1846, he ordered U.S. forces to march south. This aggressive move made war a probability. Diplomacy, the president understood, offered little hope of achieving his aims regarding California. War, Polk told his cabinet in April 1846, was the answer to the Mexico question. And so it proved.

Gregory S. Hospodor

Perspective Essay 2. Mexico Was Goaded into War

The Mexican-American War resulted from the collision of manifest destiny—in which Americans claimed not only Texas but also the future states of California, Arizona, and New Mexico—with Mexican pride and nationalism. European leaders were preoccupied with revolutionary developments that drew their attention away from the Western Hemisphere. The James K. Polk administration took advantage of these dynamics, which were only enhanced by the 1803 Louisiana Purchase and ascendant American views of superiority and exceptionalism, particularly after the War of 1812. American public opinion had favored territorial expansion since the American Revolutionary War, first into Louisiana and then into Florida and Texas because of the steady migration of American farmers into these areas. And the many Americans who championed or benefited from slavery saw western expansion as a way to spread slavery beyond the general confines of the Southeast.

Economic systems, foreign policy goals, and the governments of Mexico and the United States were also starkly different. Like the United States, Mexico had been a European colony. However, Mexico was a debtor nation largely dependent on its North American neighbor and European powers. The postindependence period (since 1821) was beset by economic crises and political unrest. The Mexican government was very unstable, with as many as 23 different governments between 1836 and 1848. Added to that were several independence movements in the northern states.

The U.S. government, on the other hand, enjoyed stability during the same period. For much of the 19th century, the American economy and U.S. foreign policy were geared toward the ideal of manifest destiny. This was the belief that it was a divine right or preordination for the United States to occupy the North American continent from the Atlantic to the Pacific. Also inherent in this belief was that no obstacles—be they Native Americans or Mexico—would stand in the way of this goal. Additionally, manifest destiny suggested that Anglos were ideologically and racially superior to Mexicans (and Native Americans). Historian Norman A. Graebner suggests that economic considerations in the West also drove manifest destiny. Northeastern merchants had long-standing relationships with trading partners in the Pacific. These merchants sought ports on the West Coast for trade with Asia; therefore, they lobbied U.S. presidents from Andrew Jackson to James K. Polk to pursue western expansion. Proslavery forces, of course, hoped to extend slavery into newly won lands in the West.

American goals under this rubric were to keep imperial European powers out of the Americas and to compete economically all around the world. Certainly, the 1823 Monroe Doctrine was a clear enunciation of this thinking. But some American leaders were also concerned that European powers might invade Mexico or other Latin American nations, thereby threatening American sovereignty in the Western Hemisphere. According to many policy makers of the era, the only logical way to avoid this scenario was to invade Mexico.

Race was also a factor in the differences between Mexicans and Americans. Mexico was a hybrid society that had emerged from the interplay of Spanish and Native American cultures. Conversely, the United States in the early 19th century was an essentially racist society that relegated all but white Anglo-Saxon Protestants to the sidelines, enslaved African Americans, legally barred miscegenation, and believed fervently in Anglo superiority.

There were differing racial ideologies and views on slavery in Mexico. First, slavery's importance had been diminished in Mexico under Spanish rule. The Mexican government did not want slavery in Texas; however, it lacked the resources to enforce this policy. Second, most Mexicans realized that if the United States annexed Mexico, they would most likely be treated in the same manner as African Americans, Native Americans, and other ethnic and religious minorities.

By the 1830s and 1840s, meanwhile, slavery had become a divisive issue in the United States. Southern slave owners sought to expand slaveholding areas in the United States, and toward this end they strongly pushed for the annexation of Texas in 1845. Many Whigs and northern Democrats decried the potential expansion of slavery, but their sentiments were in the minority, at least in Congress.

However, most of the American Southwest is arid and not well suited for slave-based agriculture. Some scholars have argued that because of manifest destiny, the American government coveted not only the Southwest but also all of Mexico as a way to dull the growing divisions surrounding slavery. The acquisition of all of Mexico would have given proslavery forces all of Mexico below the Compromise of 1821 line and would not have upset the balance between free and slave territories.

Another cause of the war was the tension between the American and Mexican governments over Texas. Mexico had allowed settlement in Texas by American citizens after 1821, provided that they obeyed Mexican laws and respected Mexican culture. However, many white settlers in Texas refused to comply with these policies, producing an ideological conflict and causing resentment among Anglos over their harsh treatment at the hands of the Antonio Lopéz de Santa Anna government.

By 1836, however, demographics in Texas had changed, with American settlers now greatly outnumbering Mexican citizens. Mexican leaders now feared that they would lose the entire Southwest to American expansion. The May 1836 Treaties of Velasco, negotiated by Texans and Santa Anna, brought finis to the Texas Revolution, granted Texans their independence, and established the Rio Grande as the southern border of Texas. However, these agreements caused great resentment in Mexico. The Mexican government refused to ratify the treaties or recognize the border at the Rio Grande. Instead, Mexico claimed that the Texas border was the Nueces River, near Corpus Christi.

After Texan independence, raids by bands of Mexican nationals across the border caused nearly $2 million in property damage to Texas residents. The failure of the Mexican government to deal with these raids caused outrage among Texans. The Mexican government actually borrowed money from the United States to pay for the damages but defaulted on these loans because it was nearly bankrupt. In 1845, President James K. Polk demanded repayment and suggested that Mexico cede territory to the United States to cover the cost of the loans. Mexican president José Joaquín Herrera, seeking to avoid a war, actually considered such a move but was removed from power in a military coup. Herrera was replaced by Mariano Paredes y Arrillaga, who seemed to relish a conflict with the United States and flatly refused Polk's demands.

The U.S. annexation of Texas in February 1845 did not bring war. That came when Polk sought to provoke Mexico into an armed conflict by sending U.S. forces south of the Nueces River, the traditional southern boundary for Texas, to the Rio Grande in support of Texas claims of that stream as its border with Mexico. Pursuant to orders, Brigadier General Zachary Taylor and 3,500 U.S. Army troops had occupied Corpus Christi, allegedly to protect Texas from Mexican attack. On January 13, 1846, Polk ordered these forces to move south and proclaimed a naval blockade of the Rio Grande. The Mexican government viewed this as an act of war.

Upon reaching Port Isabel on March 8, 1846, Taylor's men discovered that flee-ing residents had burned the settlement. By March 28, Taylor's men had secured the mouth of the Rio Grande. Mexican general Pedro de Ampudia warned Taylor that if he remained in the area, armed conflict would result. Sure enough, on April 25, 1846, a Mexican cavalry unit crossed the Rio Grande and skirmished with American troops at Carricitos Ranch, killing several and taking 47 as prisoners in what came to be known as the Thornton Affair.

Polk had already drafted a declaration of war based on Mexico's failure to repay loans and the refusal of its government to receive U.S. presidential envoy John Slidell. Slidell had been sent to Mexico City to negotiate the boundary dispute and other issues, including the purchase of territory. Upon hearing the news of the April 25 skirmish, Polk claimed that the Mexican Army had "invaded" the United States and "had shed American blood upon American soil." Congress declared war on May 9, 1846. Under the guise of manifest destiny, the United States waged a war of aggression against Mexico.

Jeffery O. Mahan

Perspective Essay 3. U.S. Acquisition of Mexican Territory Justified

When the war between the United States and Mexico came to an official end on February 2, 1848, the political nature of the North American continent had changed forever. With the signing of the Treaty of Guadalupe Hidalgo, the United States increased in size by some 500,000 square miles and gained the mineral and agricul-tural riches of the Southwest and California. Within a half century, Americans had largely settled and developed the region. Fulfillment of U.S. manifest destiny can be viewed as justification for the U.S. seizure of all that land from Mexico.

The rights and wrongs of the U.S. acquisition of Texas, California, and other lands in the Southwest from Mexico are a matter of debate. The historian can show relatively clearly that there were legal documents in which the United States agreed to the de facto boundaries and that the area belonged to Mexico. The 1819 Adams-Onís Treaty made this clear, especially as it concerned Texas. But the ideological U.S. vision of the time and strategic realities came to outweigh the niceties of treaty restrictions.

Manifest destiny was a clear motivator and, in a way, a legitimate reason for the American acquisition of Texas and California. The mind-set of the 1840s made it clear that Americans linked access to new lands with its growing and evolving notion of a democracy. To unnaturally limit that access was to limit freedom. The man who coined the term "manifest destiny," John L. O'Sullivan, feared that foreign intervention would act at "limiting our greatness and checking the fulfillment of our manifest destiny to spread over the continent allotted by Providence for the free development of our yearly multiplying millions." For the majority of Americans at the time, the need to expand was clear. Other presidents had acted on this, including Thomas Jefferson with his unconstitutional Louisiana Purchase of 1803, certainly a brilliant move.

Although it is outside U.S. society's present norms, taken in the context of the time the fact that Texas, and to some degree California, were already filling with American settlers seemed to have superseded supposed legalities. The U.S. population at the time was growing rapidly, and the lands in dispute would never have been effectively populated or governed by Mexico. Since the Mexican government had encouraged the settlement of Americans in Texas with the goal of subduing the Comanche Indians and developing the land for Mexico, the U.S. government had certain responsibilities toward its citizens. As early as the 1830s, when Mexico realized that it could not retain control due to the burgeoning settlement of Americans in Texas, it again sought to advance its own purposes by closing off that settlement. Finally, where the Mexicans looked to retain a historical claim to the land, in reality the land belonged to the Spanish Crown, which the then government of Mexico had won from it. Actually real ownership, if that can be said to exist, belonged to the Native Americans from whom the Spanish had taken the land. Legalities are always waved as a source of evidence by the last power to take something.

In 1848 the United States still faced a geopolitical situation in which it was at best a second-rate power. The notion of the Monroe Doctrine and American dominance over this hemisphere was based on the power of the British fleet. Clearly, there were European powers that had an interest in Mexican territory, especially the California-Oregon area. At that time the Europeans—British, French, Germans, and Russians—were all interested in these areas for imperial expansion. If any or all had gained toeholds on the continent, creating new legal and historical claims (as the British had in the Oregon Territory), it is hard to imagine that they might later have abandoned these. Rather, the move by the United States to secure its frontiers to the south and west made geopolitical sense.

The argument that it was for Mexico to protect these borders fails, as Mexico had as a state. Whereas the United States had experienced long-term stability since its founding, in the short time since its independence in 1821 Mexico had experienced rebellions, coups, and the catastrophic leadership of the dictator Antonio López de Santa Anna. There was no good reason for the United States to look at the unstable failed state of Mexico as a neighbor that could secure the continent's borders. It was a strategic necessity for the U.S. government to acquire both Texas and the West Coast, especially the port of San Francisco. In doing so, this fulfilled a clear defensive need. President James K. Polk did initially offer to purchase these territories but was rebuffed. That he allowed the country to move to war to resolve the issue was a logical, if unfortunate, progression.

That Texas and California and the vast lands in between should become part of the United States served multiple purposes. It fulfilled the political will of Americans at the time and took care of America's greatest geopolitical liability as well. Historians have often put a modern face on the American acquisition, labeling it an illegal land grab that led to the American Civil War. While this might be true from a 21st-century perspective, it fails to see the United States and the world as they were in the 1840s.

Lee W. Eysturlid

Further Reading

Alcaraz, Ramon. *The Other Side: Notes for the History of the War between Mexico and the United States.* Translated and edited by Albert C. Ramsey. New York: Wiley, 1850.

Bauer, K. Jack. *The Mexican War, 1846–1848.* New York: Macmillan, 1974.

Bergeron, Paul H. *The Presidency of James K. Polk.* American Presidency Series. Lawrence: University Press of Kansas, 1987.

Bill, Alfred Hoyt. *Rehearsal for Conflict: The War with Mexico, 1846–1848.* New York: Knopf, 1947.

Brack, Gene M. *Mexico Views Manifest Destiny, 1821–1846: An Essay on the Origins of the Mexican War.* Albuquerque: University of New Mexico Press, 1975.

Brooks, N. C. *A Complete History of the Mexican War, 1846–1848.* Baltimore: Hutchinson and Seebold, 1849.

Camp, Roderic A. *Mexican Political Biographies, 1884–1935.* Austin: University of Texas Press, 1991.

Carleton, James Henry. *The Battle of Buena Vista.* New York: Harper and Brothers, 1848.

Clary, David A. *Eagles and Empire: The United States, Mexico, and the Struggle for a Continent.* New York: Bantam Books, 2009.

Conway, Christopher, ed. *The U.S.-Mexican War: A Binational Reader.* Translated by Gustavo Pelón. Indianapolis: Hackett Publishing, 2010.

Eisenhower, John S. D. *So Far from God: The U.S. War with Mexico, 1846–1848.* New York: Anchor Books, 1990.

Francaviglia, Richard V., and Douglas W. Richmond, eds. *Dueling Eagles: Reinterpreting the U. S.-Mexican War, 1846–1848*. Fort Worth: Texas Christian University Press, 2000.

Fuller, John D. P. *The Movement for the Acquisition of All Mexico, 1846–1848*. New York: Da Capo, 1969.

Graebner, Norman A. *Empire on the Pacific: A Study in American Continental Expansion*. New York: Ronald, 1955.

Henderson, Timothy J. A *Glorious Defeat: Mexico and Its War with the United States*. New York: Hill and Wang, 2007.

Hietala, Thomas. *Manifest Destiny: Anxious Aggrandizement in Late Jacksonian America*. Ithaca, NY: Cornell University Press, 1985.

Johannsen, Robert W. *To the Halls of the Montezumas: The Mexican War in the American Imagination*. New York: Oxford University Press, 1985.

Johannsen, Robert W., John M. Belohlavek, Thomas R. Hietala, Sam W. Haynes, and Robert E. May. *Manifest Destiny and Empire: American Antebellum Expansion*. Edited by Sam W. Haynes and Christopher Morris. The Walter Prescott Webb Memorial Lectures 31. College Station: Texas A&M University Press, 1997.

Peterson, Norma Lois. *The Presidencies of William Henry Harrison and John Tyler*. Lawrence: University Press of Kansas, 1989.

Pletcher, David M. *The Diplomacy of Annexation: Texas, Oregon, and the Mexican War*. Columbia: University of Missouri Press, 1973.

Polk, James K. *The Diary of James K. Polk during His Presidency, 1845 to 1849*, Vol. 1. Edited by Milo Milton Quaife. Chicago: A. C. McClure, 1910.

Price, Glenn W. *Origins of the War with Mexico: The Polk-Stockton Intrigue*. Austin: University of Texas Press, 1967.

Raat, W. Dirk. *Mexico and the United States: Ambivalent Vistas*. Athens: University of Georgia Press, 1992.

Raat, W. Dirk, ed. *Mexico: From Independence to Revolution, 1810–1910*. Lincoln: University of Nebraska Press, 1982.

Ruiz, Ramon Eduardo, ed. *The Mexican War: Was It Manifest Destiny?* New York: Holt, Rinehart and Winston, 1963.

Schroeder, John H. *Mr. Polk's War: American Opposition and Dissent, 1846–1848*. Madison: University of Wisconsin Press, 1973.

Weber, David J. *The Mexican Frontier, 1821–1846: The American Southwest under Mexico*. Albuquerque: University of New Mexico Press, 1982.

Weems, John Edward. *To Conquer a Peace: The War between the United States and Mexico*. Garden City, NY: Doubleday, 1974.

Weinberg, Albert K. *Manifest Destiny: A Study of Nationalist Expansion in American History*. Chicago: Quadrangle, 1963.

23. WERE THE OPIUM WARS DECISIVE IN THE HISTORY OF MODERN CHINA?

The Opium Wars (1839–1842 and 1856–1860) pitted China's Qing dynasty against Britain and its European allies. At the time the Chinese were highly resentful of foreign intrusion, while the Europeans were all too eager to capitalize on China's economic potential. The conclusion of the First Opium War compelled China to cede Hong Kong to the British and forced open five Chinese port cities to Western trade. Shortly thereafter, the British forced China to grant them most-favored-nation status in trade; they also demanded and received judicial immunity for all British citizens in China. France received the same privileges the following year. When the Second Opium War ended, China was compelled to exempt foreign goods from internal transit duties and to open more ports to trade, which eventually opened China to trade with all foreign nations. These developments were certainly important milestones in the evolution of geopolitics during the mid-19th century. Scholars disagree, however, as to whether these two conflicts played a significant role in shaping the history of modern-day China.

In her perspective essay, Dr. Kathryn Meyer asserts that the Opium Wars were indeed the most significant event in the history of modern China because they broke the traditional dynastic cycle that had existed for more than two millennia. She points out that the conflicts between China and Britain were fundamentally conflicts between two opposing worldviews. Through its defeats in the Opium Wars and the unequal treaties that followed, China was forced onto a path that led to the emergence of the country we know today. Although Dr. Andrew Robinson agrees that the Opium Wars were pivotal in the creation of modern-day China, his essay is focused through a different lens. Dr. Robinson argues that in conceptualizing their histories, postcolonial nations cite the trauma of colonialism as the founding event that eventually brought about the formation of the modern state. Although China was never fully colonized, the Opium Wars served as this "founding trauma," inaugurating the Century of Humiliation that figures prominently in modern-day Chinese discourse. For China, later conflicts with foreign powers were viewed simply as a reiteration of the pattern established by the Opium Wars. By contrast, Dr. John T. Kuehn posits that the Opium Wars were not the most significant event in the history of modern China. Rather, he considers a combination of internal and external pressures to be the root cause of China's gradual transformation into a modern state. He cautions against the futility of ascribing sweeping historical changes to single events and also questions whether the Opium Wars were even the most integral external pressure exerted on the crumbling Qing dynasty.

Background Essay

The First Opium War was fought during 1839–1842 between China and Britain, while the Second Opium War of 1856–1860 pitted China against Britain and France. The conflicts were waged over the trade and trafficking of opium. China, which did not want foreign goods, had insisted on payment from Britain in silver bullion for its exports of tea, porcelain, and other products highly prized in the West. British traders then introduced opium, smuggled into China from India, as a means of regaining the silver. The Chinese court resorted to force to halt the illegal trade, and this brought on war. Chinese military reversals then forced the court to sue for peace.

The First Opium War was ended by the Treaty of Nanjing on August 29, 1842. The first such agreement signed by China with the Western powers, the treaty stipulated that China open five major seaports for trade, cede Hong Kong to the British, and pay an indemnity of 21 million silver dollars. In 1843, the Qing dynasty signed two addendums to the Treaty of Nanjing. These documents stipulated that Chinese tariffs on imported British goods be limited to 5 percent and that the British be given the right to rent land and build homes in the five trading ports. The latter provision paved the way for the so-called concessions in the trading port cities. Additionally, the British acquired the right of consular jurisdiction and most-favored-nation status.

In 1844, the United States and France signed the Sino-American Treaty of Wangxia and the Sino-French Treaty of Huangpu, respectively. Through these two agreements, the Americans and French acquired all the privileges provided in the Treaty of Nanjing and its supplementary documents except the war indemnities clause. In addition, the Americans also secured the special privilege of sending warships to Chinese ports for protecting American commerce and building churches and hospitals in the five port cities. Meanwhile, the French had succeeded in convincing the Chinese government to lift the ban against missionary activities on the part of Roman Catholics who, from then on, could propagate their faith in China as they wished. Protestant missionaries soon gained the same privilege.

After Qing officials refused to revise the treaties 12 years later, tensions heightened between China and the Western powers. From 1856 to 1860, the allied forces of Britain and France defeated the Qing Army and captured Guangzhou and Tianjin, threatening Beijing. In June 1858, the Qing government signed the Treaties of Tianjin with Britain, France, the United States, and Russia. These stipulated that the Western powers be granted permanent representation in Beijing; that 10 more port

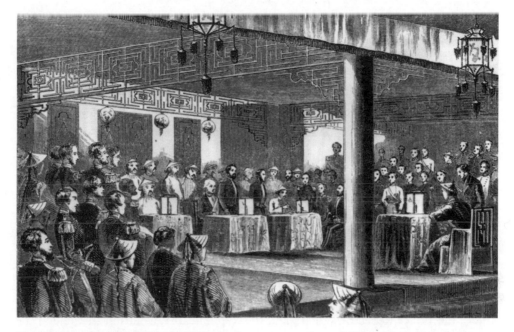

The signing of the 1858 Treaty of Tianjin by representatives of China, Great Britain, France, Russia, and the United States, ending the Arrow War, the second of the Opium Wars of 1839–1842 and 1856–1860. (Library of Congress)

cities be added as trading ports; that foreigners be allowed to tour, trade, and preach their religious faith in China's hinterland; that foreign merchant and naval vessels be allowed to ply between the trading ports; and that the Chinese government pay an indemnity of 2 million taels of sliver each to Britain and France. Later, the Chinese government was also forced to legitimize the opium trade and to employ the British to administer Chinese maritime customs.

The Opium Wars had long-term effects on China and changed the nature of its foreign relations for the worse. The wars were humiliating defeats for the Chinese Empire. The Qing dynasty fought the European powers with outdated weapons and with no cohesive strategy. Chinese military weakness was exposed to the world, and as a consequence of the wars, China was opened to Western influence and imperialist exploitation. The various treaties meant that China had essentially lost its rights as a sovereign nation. The inflow of foreign goods into China without restriction precipitated the slow but sure disintegration of China's native economy. It also began to erode Chinese culture. Thereafter, step by step, China was transformed from an isolated, traditional society into a semicolonial state.

The great Qing Empire gradually lost the central position and powerful status established by the Han dynasty. The wars ended China's regional tributary system, which had depended on recognition of Chinese superiority and dominance in exchange for Chinese goods for nearly half a millennium. The British and French effectively destroyed this distinctly Chinese advantage, eventually forcing the Chinese to take a completely different approach to international relations.

As a result, the Chinese court began to pay closer attention to modern military technology and military reform. The military disasters in the Opium Wars forced the government to improve its military structure and modernize its armies along Western lines. The Self-Strengthening Movement and establishment of the Qing's New Army were part of these efforts, although the progress of Chinese military modernization was too little and too slow to prevent more foreign incursions during the last quarter of the 19th century and the early 20th century.

The Opium Wars marked the beginning of the end for the Qing dynasty. After the Opium Wars, the Manchu rulers retreated further into tradition and continued to reject Western ideas. China's once dominant power was fractured between Qing elites and the Han population, the latter of which became stronger in the late 19th century. The weakening of Manchu rule led to a series of conflicts. Domestic troubles went hand in hand with foreign wars, including the Taiping Rebellion (1850–1864), the Boxer Rebellion (1900), and the Republican Revolution that ended the Qing dynasty in 1911. That revolution did not substantively end until the communists came to power in 1949.

Xiaobing Li

Perspective Essay 1. The Most Important Event in Modern Chinese History

The Opium Wars (1839–1842, 1856–1860) were the most important event in modern China's history. They forced the traditional Confucian political and economic system to develop in a radically different direction.

By 1840, when Chinese troops first fought the British Royal Navy, the Qing dynasty (1644–1911) was already in decline. In the drama leading up to the First Opium War, the war itself, and the diplomacy that followed, Chinese political and military leaders faced a new kind of organization. The modern warships of the Royal Navy defeated the antiquated Chinese forces. More to the point, the unequal treaty system that began with the Treaty of Nanjing in 1842 forced China to come to terms with a new way of organizing production and commerce.

The trade in opium was part of this modern commercial order. British merchants did not invent the practice of smoking opium. They did, however, create an efficient delivery organization for the drug, similar to the growing global commerce in sugar, tobacco, rum, and tea. The century following the First Opium War, popularly known as One Hundred Years of Humiliation, was the story of China's struggle to come to terms with the modern world.

Qing rule began when the imperial house came to power with the fall of the Ming dynasty (1368–1644). Three strong emperors reinvigorated the bureaucracy, were patrons of the arts, and reinstated Confucian rituals. By the end of the reign of the Qianlong emperor in 1796, a court bodyguard gained the favor of the aging monarch. Corruption spread through the kingdom, causing hardship and unrest in the countryside. Signs of trouble came in a series of peasant revolts. The White Lotus Rebellion (1796–1804) revealed both the crisis in the heartland and the weakness in the Qing military. Like earlier peasant revolts, the movement was religious in its rhetoric and violent in its tactics and was repressed with considerable ferocity.

At that time foreign trade was not important to the state; rather, it risked attracting dangerous barbarians to Chinese shores. The Qing government ensured the safety of overseas trade in 1760 when it limited foreign commerce to Canton, far from the capital. Licensed merchants held monopoly rights to trade with their foreign counterparts during the winter months. Merchants from Europe came to Canton to buy tea and silk. No exchange commodity was required by self-sufficient China. The Chinese demanded payment in silver, which the British were reluctant to provide. The trade in opium filled the void.

In the beginning this system worked for European merchants. They were controlled by monopolies in the form of the East India companies established when mercantilism was the philosophy of commerce. But as the 1700s ended, British advocates of free trade strained against such restraints at home and abroad. By the end of the Napoleonic Wars, British merchants called for the right to open more areas to commerce. Their government sought to place consuls in ports to facilitate trade and diplomats in the Chinese capital to negotiate problems between nations as equals.

If Chinese policy makers needed proof that foreign merchants caused trouble, they found it in the growing sale of illicit smoking opium. Chinese officials grew concerned as the number of addicts increased and its use spread inland. By 1821, authorities discovered opium smokers in the capital. Even more worrying was the sudden drain of silver from China. Chinese smugglers paid for contraband with silver, more than was brought back later to legally purchase tea. Foreign trade was not important to the government; silver was. The currency worked on a copper to silver ratio. Loss of silver caused hardship in the countryside by inflating the copper currency used by the peasants.

Meanwhile, British merchants had no room to develop legitimate markets in the Chinese system and no channel to present grievances to the government. Representatives of other lands submitted to Chinese court ritual, bowing to the ground before the imperial throne in the formal *kotou* (the word became known in English as "kowtow") to gain an audience with the emperor. The kowtow became controversial, as British merchants and diplomats, eager to rationalize the commercial relationship between the two nations, sought to send a diplomatic mission to the capital to discuss a change in the commercial situation on the Chinese coast. However, British diplomats refused to kowtow.

Behind the seemingly absurd argument over bowing lay a conflict of worldview. Great Britain represented an evolving system of nation-states that viewed history as a chronicle of progress, diplomacy as an art of statecraft, war as a development of science, and commerce as a legitimate source of wealth. China, however, was self-sufficient within its borders and could find no reason to treat foreign drug smugglers as equals.

Both sides of the debate made legitimate points. The Chinese side saw pirates and drug traffickers demanding that changes be made to a system that worked well for two millennia. British officials wished to change a limited Chinese foreign trade system in ways that would conform to laissez-faire commerce developing in the West. The impasse led to war after Commissioner Lin Zexu publicly destroyed 3 million pounds of raw opium in June 1939 in Canton.

British ships blockaded Canton (today Guangzhou), then continued along the Chinese coast until they threatened forts protecting Beijing. With danger near his capital, the Chinese emperor dismissed Commissioner Lin and sued for peace. On August 29, 1842, China signed the first of the unequal treaties, the Treaty of Nanjing. It laid the foundation for a system of treaties that would grow in complexity and scope, eroding Chinese sovereignty. Immediately it gave the British, and soon after the Americans and the French, the right to trade in five ports, the right to be judged by their own consuls for crimes committed in China, and one-sided most-favored-nation status. There was no mention of opium.

Less than 15 years later in 1860 a Second Opium War ended, with the Chinese emperor fleeing his capital as foreign troops looted his summer palace. The Convention of Beijing (1860) opened more Chinese ports to foreign trade, legalized opium, and arranged for foreign government representatives to reside in Beijing.

More trouble was brewing even as the Opium Wars ran their course. Chinese religious prophet Hong Xiuquan organized a new religion that combined elements of Christianity and challenged Confucian society and Qing rule. This led to the Taiping Rebellion of 1850–1864. Soon the Taipings controlled the Yangtze River Valley, and in 1853 they captured Nanjing and made it their capital. Ultimately the Taipings were crushed, but by 1860 the Qing court had begun to accommodate Western trade and diplomacy.

Both the Opium Wars and the Taiping Rebellion exposed influential Chinese officials to a new worldview. Modernizing occurred in the Chinese military, transportation, and industry, while Chinese envoys traveled abroad. Such efforts, intended to strengthen the old order, in fact put in motion a process that would ultimately destroy it. Chinese intellectuals began to embrace reform in the traditional political system. When the Qing dynasty finally collapsed in 1911, it was replaced with a fragile republic. Soon China had become an amalgam of territorial fiefdoms controlled by warlords, who fought each other for control. China would not be reunited until the communists took power in 1949.

Kathryn Meyer

Perspective Essay 2. A Central Event for Modern China

The Opium Wars (1839–1842 and 1856–1860) were the central event for modern China because of their impact on later events. The importance of the Opium Wars stems from their centrality to Chinese nationalism. Modern Chinese nationalism is noted for its calculated celebration of national insecurity and humiliation. This is evident in the Century of Humiliation, a period running from the First Opium War to the founding of the People's Republic of China in 1949. There are textbooks, atlases, songs, theme parks, and monuments in China devoted to this theme.

The Century of Humiliation consisted of a wide range of events. In the 1842 Treaty of Nanjing, which ended the First Opium War, Britain secured the cession of Hong Kong and trading concessions. Other countries secured similar agreements. For instance, the Treaty of Whampoa (1844) extended the Nanking concessions to France, and the Treaty of Shimonoseki (1895) conceded territory and payments to Japan. These treaties were a continual series of humiliations. But the Opium Wars are iconic as the founding moment of the century and the frame through which later humiliations are viewed.

Chinese national identity is constructed in anti-imperialist and postcolonial terms. The theme of humiliation is widely invoked in international politics. It is most prevalent, however, in postcolonial narratives around the foundation of the modern nation-state. Most postcolonial nations were not modern nations prior to colonization. They formed nationalist ideologies during their modernization and as a reaction to colonialism. In these narratives the national history is reinvented, often presented as a glorious past followed by a period of loss and shame.

In this sense, China is fundamentally a postcolonial nation. Its leaders talk, act, and relate in postcolonial ways. Chinese nationalism is primarily a reaction against subordination to foreigners, even though that subordination was not territorial. It is the Opium Wars that locate China thus.

The Opium Wars were when national insecurity became fully apparent. Prior to the wars, China was a significant world power. In the Century of Humiliation narrative, the First Opium War was when the Chinese Empire as center of the world is replaced by the "sick man of Asia." The Opium Wars brought foreign-controlled trade ports and immunity of foreigners from prosecution, which the Chinese people usually identify with imperialism.

While there had been previous encounters with Europeans and earlier wars with "barbarians," the First Opium War was the first real challenge to the earlier Chinese worldview premised on the eternal nature and superiority of the empire.

The Opium Wars were crucial because of their relationship to nationalism and modernity. Prior to the wars, China can largely be viewed as a premodern empire. Thus, historian Joseph Levenson argues that before the Opium Wars, China was a cultural rather than a national phenomenon. Belonging was established by identification with universalizing moral goals and values, not national identity. For example, the Chinese emperor took on different titles and claims to power in each region. This period is retrospectively constructed in nationalist narratives as "5,000 Years of Civilization," ending with the Opium Wars.

In China, the Opium Wars are the founding event of the modern nationalist narrative. The Century of Humiliation is placed between the glory of the "5,000 Years of Civilization" and the rebirth of the modern nation. The term "Century of Humiliation" was only invented in 1915, many decades after the Opium Wars. Coinciding with China's passage from empire to republic (in 1911), it was based on a selective reading of Chinese history. During the Opium Wars, Manchu soldiers killed Han civilians based on ethnic rivalry. There was no clear sense of a unified nation. Yet the constructed common experience of imperialism, however artificial, was to become the driving force in Chinese politics.

It is thanks to the Century of Humiliation and hence the Opium Wars that the Maoist and post-Maoist regimes could claim to be the saviors who restored the Chinese nation to greatness. The discourse is not only used against foreign enemies but is also used to criticize individual Chinese leaders for corruption or failure. Such failings are seen as allowing events such as the Opium Wars to happen. Classic studies of Chinese communism suggest that the Communist Revolution was as much about nationalism as socialism. When Chinese Communist Party leader Mao Zedong took power in 1949, he told the world that China "will no longer be a nation subject to insult and humiliation." The discourse of this period treated the Opium Wars as the triumph of capitalism in China. Capitalism was viewed as pure imperialism and plunder. The anti-imperialist narrative saw China going through a period of victimization and redemption. The Maoist-era film *Lin Zexu,* set during the Opium Wars, showed a heroic struggle by ordinary peasants against foreign invaders and corrupt officials. This use of the Opium Wars is not exclusive to the Mao era. It has also been notable in the post–Tiananmen Square period (1989–present).

The Opium Wars and the Century of Humiliation also impact Chinese foreign policy, one of the goals of which is to cleanse the memory of national humiliation.

The regime takes any opportunity to create an appearance of foreign pressure or interference, referring back to the shame of the Century of Humiliation. Chinese leaders and people often read international events through this lens, seeing a repeat of the Opium Wars in each slight. For instance, the 2001 spy plane incident in which a U.S. reconnaissance aircraft was forced to land on Hainan Island is seen as yet another in a series of humiliations by foreigners. The failure to obtain the 2000 Olympics was seen as a result of foreign bullying. The 1989 prodemocracy movement was presented as a foreign-led effort to overthrow Chinese independence. Even the exposure of drug use among Chinese athletes was reported as a conspiracy to humiliate China. A "never again" mentality toward the Century of Humiliation makes Chinese oversensitive to slights. China still feels a need to "cleanse national humiliation" by regaining Taiwan and holding on to Tibet, Xinjiang, and Hong Kong.

It could be argued that the Century of Humiliation is not as important as has been suggested here. Scholars such as Prasenjit Duara argue that Chinese national identity was in some part already formed prior to the Opium Wars. Han ethnonationalism was implicit in various movements from the late 18th century to the Boxer Rebellion of 1900. Yet even if the modern break with the past is not as sharp as most scholars suggest, the Century of Humiliation had tremendous impact.

It may also be asserted that influences other than nationalism are central to modern Chinese outlook. Maoist China was as much class-based as nationalist, and contemporary China is as much consumerist as nationalist. Nonetheless, the nationalist narrative remains paramount. China has pursued economic growth primarily in order to strengthen itself as a world power.

It might be held that the Opium Wars were less important in cementing Chinese nationalist ideology than the Twenty-One Demands of 1915 or the Japanese invasion of China in 1937. Yet the Opium Wars remain the most important event in modern Chinese history, the traumatic moment when the Chinese Empire lost its claim to universality and that set in motion the events that led to the emergence of a modern nation.

Andrew Robinson

Perspective Essay 3. Collapse of the Qing Dynasty Was the Most Important Event

Many Sinologists and historians in the West identify events associated with the imperialist West's impact and collision with China in the 19th century, especially the Opium Wars, as central to the modernization of China. Others have rejected this viewpoint and instead ascribe China's modern trajectory to internal developments and factors that reflect China's long and turbulent cycle of dynastic rise and fall. This essay takes a middle course and argues that the turbulence and violence of the collapse of the Qing dynasty is the most important event in modern Chinese history.

Within the "Western impact" position, the key points of contact are the First Opium War (1839–1842) and the Arrow War or Second Opium War (1856). The Opium Wars were significant but not the most significant event in modern China. More recent and objective scholarship identifies the Western factor as subordinate to the internal factors that led to imperial stagnation of the Qing dynastic state throughout the 19th century, culminating in its collapse in the early 20th century. Others have focused more intently on the role of the Japanese as a sort of proxy Western imperialist agent contributing to the establishment of a communist state in China. However, none of these interpretations give as much weight to the Opium Wars as did the Chinese Communists themselves.

The Opium Wars and China's concurrent internal troubles must be examined against the backdrop of more than three millennia of Chinese dynastic history. Each dynasty rose and fell due to unique factors contingent on time, place, and context. What is important is how each dynasty's collapse contributed to the shape of what followed. Beginning with the Shang dynasty in 1523 BCE and continuing to today, China has followed a pattern of the rise and fall of principally authoritarian dynastic regimes; only the current authoritarian People's Republic of China (PRC) can be considered nondynastic. It is against this backdrop that the most expansive and ambitious dynasty in imperial history wielded power in the late 18th century.

After the collapse of the Ming dynasty during the mid-17th century, China as we know it today came under the control of the Manchu (or Jürchen) ethnic group, whose homeland is often referred to as Manchuria. These non-Han (the primary Chinese ethnic grouping) warrior-aristocrats established a "barbarian" dynasty that came to be China's most powerful. Its founders quickly adopted Chinese culture to their purposes, retaining the Mandarin bureaucratic elites along with their own foreign "Banner" armies to spread their control of China from Formosa (Taiwan) all the way to Tibet and the distant Muslim lands of Xinjiang to the west. Naming itself the Qing (meaning "pure" or "clear") dynasty, it established a vast empire. However, just as this empire reached its peak of military conquests and influence, it came into contact with the maritime powers of Europe eager to trade, develop new markets, and exploit the riches of the East.

During this roughly 150-year period, China had been ruled primarily by three prominent Qing emperors: Kangxi (the founder), Youngzheng, and, longest of all, Qianlong. It was in the 80th year of Qianlong's reign (1793) that the British

Macartney Mission—named after Earl George Macartney—arrived ostensibly to salute Qianlong. In actuality, King George III had sent Macartney to relax trade restrictions with the Chinese and to open a diplomatic residence in Beijing. Macartney judged the situation far more accurately than many later historians in commenting that "The Empire of China is an old crazy, first rate man-of-war, which a fortunate succession of able and vigilant officers has contrived to keep afloat for these one hundred and fifty years past, and to overawe their neighbors merely by her bulk and appearance." He predicted that once sound leadership was absent, China would be "dashed to pieces on the shore." This was written almost a half century before the First Opium War.

Macartney had identified China's fundamental problem as a looming lack of competent leadership. Qing China's huge size generated immense problems in the face of profound changes under way as a consequence of outside pressures. China's dynastic decay abetted these problems. As the Europeans began to slice off pieces of China's coast and humiliate the Qings with imposed trade treaties, inside the empire massive rebellions challenged the authority of the "barbarian" regime in Beijing. These challenges were religious and ethnic based and also included the often peasant-led indigenous rebellions that congealed around popular "bandit" leaders. This type of rebellion had unseated the Ming dynasty, but the religious revolts proved to be just as dangerous. The real problem with these mid-19th-century revolts is that they occurred at the same time the Western powers were penetrating China from the outside.

The most important of these uprisings was the Taiping Rebellion of 1850–1864. Hong Xiuquan tapped into the great uncertainty of the times. Incorporating certain elements of Christianity, he sought to "reestablish" the "heavenly kingdom" of Taiping (Great Peace) on Earth. The movement tapped into various strains of monotheism in Chinese culture and even Nicheren Buddhist ideas of an apocalyptic battle between good and evil. It also built on demands for reform. The Taipings captured Nanjing (the southern capital) in 1853. The rebellion claimed 20 million lives before it was crushed. The end result, however, was a fundamental breakdown in institutions and families and a fatal undermining of the Manchu "Mandate of Heaven."

Concurrently, the peasant-bandit–based Nian Rebellion occurred during 1851–1858 in northern China. It too was crushed with great loss of life. The final set of rebellions was also somewhat based on religion, having to do with Muslim minorities and a breakaway Muslim state in central and western China.

Qing arms defeated all of these challenges, but the warfare took its toll. It also led to a fatal sharing of power by the emperor with his generals. In some sense this established the precursor for the warlord institution that would dominate China until the communist victory in the Chinese Civil War 80 years later. The 18th-century warfare also delayed much-needed military and economic reforms. Only a Westernizing program, such as that of the Japanese, could have saved China. However, 40 years of revolt delayed reform too long. When external enemies, especially the Japanese, began to encroach on Chinese sovereignty, China was ill-prepared, poorly led, and already more a collection of loosely aligned provinces than a functioning state.

The Qing dynasty's failures to defend new encroachments to its sovereignty by the Russians, Germans, and Japanese were the final nails in the imperial coffin. From this standpoint the Boxer Rebellion (1900), the Sino-Japanese War (1894–1895), and even the Russo-Japanese War (1904–1905) have better claims in initiating collapse than do the Opium Wars.

The life of the last Qing emperor, Pu Yi, encompassed the period of the Chinese Revolution that finally led to the establishment in 1949 of the new communist regime led by Mao Zedong. This regime, like its dynastic predecessors, was authoritarian and tended to focus on the personality and even infallibility of the supreme leader; however, without this revolution and without Mao, it is hard to imagine the accession of the profound reformer and organizer Deng Xiaoping. If any event or succession of events has a claim to the most significant for modern China, then the process by which Deng and his disciples gained power and reorganized the PRC must also be acknowledged and compared to the Opium Wars.

The Opium Wars were only one of many Western events that influenced the slowly building change that swept over China in the 19th and 20th centuries. It is even arguable if they were the most important of Western events, since a case can be made that European Marxism (ironically), late 19th-century imperialism, and even Christianity (by way of the Taipings) were more profound in their impact. However, in the dynamic of change and slow stagnation internal to Qing China and the startling violence of the mid-19th-century rebellions, we find a powerful argument for these factors being the primary agents of change. Clearly revolution, revolt, and internal collapse trump foreign imperialism in significance and in scale.

John T. Kuehn

Further Reading

Beeching, Jack. *The Chinese Opium Wars.* San Diego: Harcourt Brace Jovanovich, 1975.

Chang, Hsin-pao. *Commissioner Lin and the Opium War.* Cambridge, MA: Harvard University Press, 1971.

Chang, Maria Hsia. *Return of the Dragon: China's Wounded Nationalism.* Boulder, CO: Westview, 2001.

Collis, Maurice. *Foreign Mud: The Opium Imbroglio at Canton in the 1830s and the Anglo-Chinese War.* New York: Norton, 1946.

Courtwright, David T. *Forces of Habit: Drugs and the Making of the Modern World.* Cambridge, MA: Harvard University Press, 2001.

Duara, Prasenjit. "De-Constructing the Chinese Nation." *Australian Journal of Chinese Affairs* 30 (1993): 1–26.

Elleman, Bruce A. *Modern Chinese Warfare, 1795–1989.* London: Routledge, 2001.

Elvin, Mark. *The Pattern of the Chinese Past.* Stanford, CA: Stanford University Press, 1973.

Epstein, Israel. *From Opium War to Liberation.* Hong Kong: Joint Publishing, 1980.

Fairbank, John K. *The Great Chinese Revolution, 1800–1985.* New York: Harper and Row, 1986.

Fay, Peter Ward. *The Opium War, 1840–1842.* New York: Norton, 1997.

Graff, David, and Robin Higham. *A Military History of China.* Boulder, CO: Westview, 2003.

Gries, Peter. "Nationalism, Indignation and China's Japan Policy." *SAIS Review* 25 (2005): 105–113.

Janin, Hunt. *The India-China Opium Trade in the Nineteenth Century.* Jefferson, NC: McFarland, 1999.

Kuhn, Philip A. *Rebellion and Its Enemies in Late Imperial China: Militarization and the Social Structure, 1796–1864.* Cambridge, MA: Harvard University Press, 1980.

Polachek, James M. *The Inner Opium War.* Cambridge, MA: Harvard University Press, 1992.

Spence, Jonathan D. *God's Chinese Son: The Taiping Heavenly Kingdom of Hong Xiuquan.* New York: Norton, 1996.

Spence, Jonathan D. *The Search for Modern China.* New York: Norton. 1990.

Unger, Jonathan. *Chinese Nationalism.* Armonk, NY: Sharpe, 1996.

Wakeman, Frederic, Jr. *The Fall of Imperial China.* New York: Free Press, 1975.

Wong, J. Y. *Deadly Dreams: Opium, Imperialism, and the Opium War (1856–1860) in China.* Honolulu: University of Hawaii Press, 1999.

Zhong, Yongnian. *Discovering Chinese Nationalism in China: Modernization, Identity, and International Relations.* Cambridge: Cambridge University Press, 1999.

24. How Was a Relatively Small British Army Able to Conquer the Subcontinent of India?

British interest in establishing commercial ties with India began in earnest in 1600, when Queen Elizabeth I granted a royal charter to the privately held English East India Company (later the British East India Company). Thereafter, the company systematically penetrated India in search of raw materials, trade, and profits. In the process, the company imposed de facto British dominance over the subcontinent that would last for several centuries, which was accomplished with minimal military power. In 1857 a major rebellion in India broke out, but by 1859 the uprising had been quelled, and India achieved the status of a British crown colony. The British government ruled India directly until 1947, at which time it was granted independence. By then, a potent Indian nationalist movement and precarious finances made the British presence in India untenable.

In the first perspective essay, Dr. James B. McNabb argues that superior leadership— both civilian and military—as well as better military organization and technology permitted the British to move into and then dominate India for several centuries without resorting to large standing armies. He also asserts that the British East India Company took the time to understand the local culture and subdued the subcontinent through chiefly financial and diplomatic means. The second essay, written by Dr. Alexander Mikaberidze, suggests that India was subdued by the clever use of British diplomacy and the establishment of alliances that benefited both British interests and those of the local Indian rulers who became parties to them. The British East India Company first established commercial dominance before asserting political and military control in India. In addition, the British were able to exploit the lack of indigenous centralized power in the region and played local rulers against each other. In the third essay, Dr. Lee W. Eysturlid asserts that British military organization and logistical superiority proved invaluable to their dominance of India. Furthermore, the British East India Company shrewdly employed bribes to curry favor with local rulers and to keep them divided at the same time. Profits, rather than conquest, drove the British in India, who routinely trained and used indigenous soldiers to help impose order.

Background Essay

Europeans had long been interested in India. The first to attempt to establish control over the subcontinent was undertaken by Macedonian ruler Alexander the Great in the fourth century BCE. Later, the Romans established direct trading links to India. Securing highly sought after spices by opening up a westward water trading route to India was the chief motivation behind the European voyages of discovery that incidentally led to the discovery of America in 1492 by Christopher Columbus.

The Portuguese were the first Europeans since the ancient Romans to establish a direct trading link with India. In 1498 Vasco de Gama, having sailed around the Cape of Good Hope, arrived in Calicut (now Kozhikode). In 1600 English merchants established the English (later British) East India Company, and by 1612 the English and Portuguese were fighting over trading rights in the subcontinent. The

Indian rulers actively encouraged competition between the English, Portuguese, Dutch (who had arrived during 1601–1603; the Dutch East India Company was established in 1602), and Danes (1616). The French were latecomers in India, arriving there only in 1666.

Beginning in the early 17th century, the English and Dutch began to challenge the Portuguese for influence in India. In 1621 Mughal emperor Jahangir granted additional trading rights to the English in return for East India Company ships serving as an auxiliary naval force for the Mughal Empire, which was in decline.

In 1639 the English secured a small strip of land on the Coromandel Coast of southeastern India and established a trading post there. The next year they built Fort St. George, nucleus for the colonial city of Madras (present-day Chennai), later one of the largest cities in India. This was followed by a post in West Benghal at Hooghly in 1651. In 1668 the English established a post at Bombay (today Mumbai) in west-central India to facilitate trade with the interior, and in 1668 the East India Company transferred its headquarters there.

Trading rivalries led to four major 17th-century wars (1652–1654, 1665–1667, 1672–1674, and 1780–1784) between the English and Dutch for worldwide trading mastery. These resulted in Dutch naval dominance and trading power in Asia. With the Glorious Revolution in 1688, however, William of Orange became the king of England. England and the Netherlands then concluded a trading arrangement whereby the Dutch controlled the more valuable spice trade of the Indonesian archipelago and the English controlled the textile trade of India. Textiles, however, soon overtook spices in terms of profitability.

In 1757 the British agreed to support Mir Jafar, commander of the army of the nawab of Bengal and others who were conspiring to overthrow the nawab. Although East India Company forces were numerically far inferior to those of Bengal, they were instrumental in the great victory of the Battle of Plassey (June 23, 1757). Mir Jafar was duly installed in power but largely under British control. The British went on to parlay the victory into an effort to conquer outright or control smaller Indian states indirectly through behind-the-scenes control of their rulers.

In the 18th century, Britain and France engaged in a series of worldwide wars (1740–1748, 1756–1763, and 1778–1783). In India, the two sides waged war through both proxy rulers and direct action. Partly because the French never expended sufficient effort, by the mid-19th century the British controlled virtually all of India either directly or indirectly. Their efforts to strengthen this control brought the great Rebellion of 1857 (the Sepoy Rebellion or Indian Mutiny of 1857–1858). Although quelled after six months with heavy loss of life on both sides, the revolt led to the British decision to take rule from the East India Company, which was dissolved in 1858. In 1887 Queen Victoria took the title of empress of India, then regarded as the "jewel" in the imperial crown.

Spencer C. Tucker

Robert Clive, commander of British forces, greets Mir Jafar following the British victory in the Battle of Plassey, June 23, 1757. This British victory decided the fate of Bengal. (Hulton Archive/Getty Images)

Perspective Essay 1. A Matter of Superior British Capabilities

The British were successful in their conquest of India through a combination of superior leadership and organization that reinforced effective diplomatic, military, and other elements of their national power that Indian forces proved incapable of overcoming. Moreover, the British were fortunate that at the time of their initial activities in South Asia, the overland trading route known as the Silk Road from East Asia to Europe had been effectively blocked by the Ottoman Turks. This created incentives for merchants and rulers to discover new ways in which to conduct commerce between East and West. As a result sea power became increasingly important, and Great Britain's efforts in India were supported by its superior seafaring capabilities.

In addition, British soldiers and their allies in India had the benefit of arms, technology, discipline, and leadership that were far superior to those of their native opponents on the subcontinent. Indian forces facing British arms favored cavalry tactics adopted from those of Turkestan in Central Asia and employed artillery purchased from the Ottoman Turks. Their infantry weapons tended to be obsolete, and the British outclassed their opponents' weapons in terms of both rate of fire and range. British forces in India employed superior weaponry and tactics to overcome the traditional advantage of the cavalry charge, used so successfully for centuries and perfected in the Central Asian steppes. Armed with the new longer-range and more accurate European musket, a soldier could fire three shots before the cavalry was able to close on his position. The traditional cavalry charge against disciplined and well-organized infantry formations, backed by longer-range, more accurate artillery, became increasingly suicidal.

A key to the early British success in India was a singular focus on opening trade relations, which made the English seem like a profitable partner rather than a military conqueror. In pursuit of these commercial objectives, Queen Elizabeth I supported the establishment of the English East India Company in December 1600. In 1707, it became the British East India Company (BEIC). A privately held company, the East India Company was created to be the sole agent for the Crown in developing trade with India and was granted a monopoly on all British commercial activity on the Indian subcontinent.

In the beginning, company representatives were unsuccessful in generating any tangible trade accords. After English captain Thomas Best's small armed flotilla defeated Portuguese warships in the Battle of Swally (November 29–30, 1612), Mughal emperor Jahangir began distancing India from Portuguese influence. Following these developments, English ambassador to the Mughal court Sir Thomas Roe negotiated an accord through which the company secured trading rights and the right to build factories in India in exchange for providing naval protection to the Mughals. British sea power and the resourcefulness and courage of East India Company sailors were essential in London securing the first agreements in India. Added to this was the skill of the English diplomats, which was instrumental in developing the necessary bilateral relationships that, from the initial entreaties in 1612 through the ongoing trade wars with European competitors in the 18th century, outmaneuvered British competitors.

Britain's eventual ascendancy to political and military control in India followed a dual-track strategy encompassing a range of national capabilities including trade, diplomacy, administration, and military power. The two tracks complemented and supported one another and can be loosely described as inside-out and fortified-seaport-in. The inside-out aspect involved gaining a foothold within India itself by offering lucrative trade agreements to key Indian elite leaders.

Upon obtaining its initial trade agreements, the East India Company was able to place representatives inside India who worked diligently to understand and appreciate the nuances of the values, beliefs, and preferences contained within India's various established ethnic and cultural groups. These early representatives were skillful in keeping a relatively low profile and interfacing with the major power figures within the country as they developed relationships and knowledge that provided understanding of the intricate workings of Indian society.

From these early beginnings, the East India Company expanded its trade activities from inside the country and made political and military contacts. In doing so, the company positioned itself for an increasingly influential role in political and governance issues. Rather than a foreign country trying to penetrate a society from the outside in, Britain achieved its desired results by conducting an inside-out approach. These efforts generated not only valuable contacts and relationships but also served in providing London with a treasure trove of economic, political, and military intelligence.

From inside, the East India Company representatives became aware of princes who did not trust each other or were too busy fighting one another to join in a common cause unless a clear foreign threat presented itself. Accordingly, a key objective for East India Company leaders was to establish trust with key decision makers while maintaining a low profile. From this point and armed with expert knowledge of the country, the company's representatives subsequently engaged in a complex manipulation of coalitions and alliances and leveraged the various infighting and distrust among the quarreling factions within India to create a bloc of power sufficient for prevailing against any internal opponents or group of opponents.

Serving to support and complement the inside-out track was the East India Company's efforts in a fortified seaport-in approach. Here the objective was to leverage Britain's advantages in sea power by taking control of a seaport initially achieved through trade and political influence and then establishing a fort to secure that port facility. Near the seaport, fortified factories were built and towns were established as satellites of the seaport-fort complex. From this base, the British moved inland by identifying a distant but key strategic town or location and, when necessary, building a railway that aided in connecting the seaport and the strategic inland objective. The East India Company relied on its own private military force beginning in 1652, when an officer and 30 men were hired to guard the factory in Calcutta. By the mid-19th century, its private army had expanded to include 30,000 Europeans and 250,000 native soldiers, or Sepoys.

During the first two centuries of BEIC involvement in India, the British first secured their position on the west coast of India by outcompeting and outmaneuvering the Portuguese. This was then followed by the consolidation of its power in what would become the important west coast port city of Bombay (modern-day Mumbai) from which it projected power inland. This process was repeated when the BEIC successfully outmaneuvered the French on the east coast as the company consolidated its hold around the key seaport of Madras (Chennai). After establishing footholds on the west and east coasts of southern India, the BEIC solidified its position in the north when it established a fort at the seaport of Calcutta (today Kolkata), strategically located at the mouth of the Ganges River. From Calcutta, rail links were established that extended inland across northern India to Delhi.

In pursuing the inside-out and fortified-seaport-in approach, the British transitioned from a focus primarily on trade to one that gave the BEIC a higher-profile role in both governance and taxation. With the extension of British power from Calcutta in the north and moving inland through the Bengal province to Delhi, the low-profile nature of British visibility began to expand and gave way to a greater concern within India of unwelcome foreign interference. Earlier in the mid-18th century, various elites located in the north had refused to accept increased British influence, and the BEIC was forced to fight its way across northern India with its private army and associated allies to the objective at Delhi. In the Battle of Plassey (1757) and the Battle of Buxar (1764), the BEIC defeated the forces of the native leaders who opposed an increased British role in northern Bengal Province.

Following those engagements, the BEIC cemented its control over trade and governance in Bengal Province and began involving itself in tax collection. The strongest challenge to British rule in the 19th century occurred during 1857–1858 in what has been variously described as the Indian Rebellion, the Indian Mutiny, and the First War for Indian Independence. In 1857, Indian soldiers assigned to the Bengal Army revolted against measures that they perceived were designed to impose British culture on Hindus and Muslims. At the time, there were only 35,000 British soldiers scattered across the Indian subcontinent. They were charged with the control of three separate armies located at Bombay, Madras, and Bengal. The rebellion broke out in the north within the Bengal Army, while the two remaining armies were relatively unaffected during the upheaval. If the mutiny had spread to all three armies, given the light European military footprint, British control in India might not have survived.

During 1857–1858, British-led forces suppressed the mutiny and retained control. However, these events led to the withdrawal of the BEIC's charter by London and the direct governance of India by the British Crown. London followed this announcement by sending 80,000 British troops for garrison duty within India. The Indian Army was subsequently restructured so that there was at least one British officer for every three Indian soldiers. Further, the rifles that were then issued to non-British troops were of inferior quality compared to those issued to European soldiers. Artillery batteries were also kept strictly under British control. The Crown's control of India was supported by its ability to project both military power and political influence.

In the 20th century, millions of soldiers from India served in both world wars and in campaigns throughout the world. However, the costs of those wars reduced both the resources and the will in Britain to continue its dominant role in India. Continuing in such a position would have demanded from a war-weary British public support for coercive measures and extensive costs. The British Labour Party government decided against such a course, and the British treasury simply could not afford continued rule in India. British rule in India ended with its recognition of independence for India and Pakistan in 1947.

James Brian McNabb

Perspective Essay 2. Diplomacy and Alliances Pave the Way

In its securing control of India, diplomacy and alliances were more important to Britain than military victories. Remarkably, Great Britain's Indian empire was created through the actions of a private commercial organization that held a monopoly on British trade in Asia. The British presence in India began in earnest during the reign of Elizabeth I (1558–1603), when the first English merchants received trading concessions from the powerful Mughal emperor of India. In 1608, the English East India Company, later the British East India Company (BEIC), an English joint-stock trading company formed just eight years earlier to conduct commerce in Asia, set up its first trading posts in India. Together with a monopoly of trade with India, the BEIC also secured from the English Crown the right to acquire territory and raise a military force. During the next century and a half, the BEIC gradually moved beyond commercial activities to pursue a political agenda.

By the early 18th century, India was already a great land with a sophisticated civilization and a population estimated at between 110 million and 150 million, or nearly a fifth of the world's population. But it was not, in the Western sense, a single nation. The Mughal dynasty, which came to power in the 16th century, governed a vast array of states with a vast assortment of ethnic groups and religions. The Mughal Empire reached its height in the 17th century but after the death of the last great emperor Aurangzeb in 1797 suffered from political turmoil, social unrest, and sectarian violence.

The authority of the Mughal emperors was sharply limited by rebellious warlords and rival kingdoms that sprang up throughout the Indian subcontinent. As Mughal central authority began to decline, Europeans, most notably the BEIC, began to intervene in Indian politics. Its leaders skillfully manipulated and exploited rivalries between Indian states, slowly building up alliances to secure political and commercial advantages.

The BEIC proved to be equally successful in its struggle against European rivals, especially the French, who with their Mughal allies were defeated at Plassey in 1757 and Pondicherry in 1761. Under the leadership of Governor-General Robert Clive, the BEIC laid the foundation for British rule by its military conquest of Bengal in northeastern India. From its base in Bengal, the BEIC steadily expanded its authority to the rest of India, eventually becoming the main instrument of British imperial dominance in India. The Regulating Act of 1773 and the India Act of 1784 secured British government control over the BEIC.

Flush with profits and already maintaining its own armed forces, the BEIC fought a series of wars—most notably the Anglo-Mysore Wars (1767–1799), the

Anglo-Maratha Wars (1775–1819), and the Anglo-Sikh Wars (1845–1849)—that extended its influence and administrative system to almost the entire Indian subcontinent. Success in these conflicts allowed the BEIC to bring new administrative order to a region that had never had strong central control. Finally, in 1859 the British government took over the administrative system developed by the BEIC during the previous 100 years and laid the foundation for the British Raj (empire) in India for the next nine decades.

But how did a few thousand people from a small island in Northwestern Europe succeed in conquering and ruling this distant and vast subcontinent? Many advocates of British colonialism in India credited it to the "finer character" of the British, arguing that white Europeans, especially North Europeans, had a culture that was superior to others. British poet Rudyard Kipling's famous poem "White Man's Burden" reflected the perception that Britain had the responsibility to "civilize" the colonized peoples described as "half-devil and half-child." On the other hand, historians often credited British success in India to the superiority of the British military. The reality, however, is more complex, and BEIC success can be explained by a variety of long- and short-term factors.

Compared to other parts of the world, European states were generally more prepared for modern warfare and more ruthless in prosecuting it. Europe's close confines compelled all competing political units to innovate constantly in order to deal with different terrains and climates as well as ensure technological parity with their rivals. More efficient military finance and taxation systems emerged in Europe to deal with the endemic wars. In Asia, meanwhile, the great empires, such as the Mughal Empire of India, felt less military pressure to adapt and could afford remaining lax as far as military modernization was concerned. Thus, Indian armies incorporated a huge variety of tribal troops, who supplied their own weapons and horses. This lax approach to military innovation can be partly explained by the fact that India was spared the vicious wars of religion and trade that afflicted Europe until the 18th century.

It is often argued that inadequate armies—that is, the lack of trained infantry and the weakness of indigenous artillery—placed the Indian states at a great disadvantage compared to the British. However, this argument seems to ignore important military developments in India in the 18th and early 19th centuries. Recent studies have shown that the technological gap between Indian and British forces narrowed by the end of the 18th century. This was largely the result of borrowing European technology as well as the recruitment of European officers and mercenaries to train Indian troops. Indeed, popular perceptions of the British expansion in India oftentimes overlook that the British were not always successful on the battlefield. Thus, in 1779 a BEIC force suffered a setback at the hands of the Marathas at Wadgaon. A year later, Haidar Ali of Mysore invaded the Carnatic and destroyed a BEIC force under Lieutenant Colonel William Baillie at Pollilore.

The late 18th century also saw continued improvements in the efficiency of Indian infantry and artillery. British officers noted improvements in the Indian artillery in the battles at Buxar and Patna in 1764. The performance of the Maratha forces in 1803 in the Second Anglo-Maratha War revealed a high level of infantry and especially artillery capability.

The BEIC military force did not operate alone, and its continued presence in the Indian subcontinent was dependent on British control of the sea. Certainly, the BEIC was attentive to any threat to its naval dominance. Throughout the 1770s and 1780s British squadrons patrolled the seas around India, destroying native fleets, maintaining the imperial lifeline to Britain, and facilitating sustained British expansion in India.

India in the 18th century did experience an increasing struggle for political power, but instead of leading to the consolidation of central power, the ensuing wars actually undermined it and sped up the breakup of the Mughal Empire. Indian armies reflected contemporary India, which lacked not only central political leadership but also a sense of single identity and common cause. Indian troops were devoted not to their nation but instead to their leaders, the political ambitions, rivalries, and jealousies of whom often sustained continued civil strife in the subcontinent. This meant that the BEIC never faced a united front of Indian forces and could exercise coercive action and diplomacy to prevent the local rulers from putting up a united struggle.

It was this disunity of Indian states that played the decisive role in British expansion in the subcontinent. The BEIC skillfully exploited local rivalries within and between the Indian states and successfully advanced its economic and political interests in the region. For this purpose, the BEIC frequently resorted to raising armies of Indian sepoys trained in the European manner. Such armed forces were sufficiently effective on the battlefield and cost less in pay than regular European troops.

The BEIC's use of subsidiary alliances—a type of alliance between a dominant nation and a nation that it dominates—underscores this point. In the mid-18th century, BEIC governor-general Clive sought to secure power in India while minimizing responsibilities the BEIC had to bear. He thus preferred an indirect approach that secured actual power for the BEIC while leaving titular authority power to native rulers. He began this policy by placing his ally, Mir Jafar, as the nawab of Bengal. In return, Mir Jafar pledged to provide financial support to the BEIC. As the BEIC's influence grew, more Indian states entered into subsidiary alliances with it. Such alliances entailed loss of the Indian state's autonomy, as the ruler pledged not to enter into alliance with any other power without the BEIC's permission. The ruler also agreed to deploy British forces within his territory and pay for their maintenance. In return for the ruler accepting its conditions, the BEIC pledged to protect the state from any external dangers and internal disorders. Frequently, in lieu of payments the ruler forfeited part of his territory to the BEIC, which further increased the company's hold over the region.

Naturally, one may wonder why the Muslim and Hindu rulers failed to foresee the risks they were running in allying with the BEIC. Partly this was because of the BEIC's ability to conceal its ambition. Publicly it made no claims to titular authority, and it preserved the ruling class intact; its governor-generals might have had more power than some Indian kings, but they made no display of royal behavior or symbols. Thus, until 1857 the BEIC continued to recognize the sovereignty of the Mughal emperor and claimed to have acted in his interests. On the other hand, many Indian rulers faced a choice between two evils—accepting the BEIC's seemingly "benign" services or facing more immediate and threatening dangers from their rival neighbors. Amid intermittent warfare between regional rulers, subsidiary alliance with the BEIC could deliver a crucial advantage over a rival. In practice, this meant that the BEIC could use Indian resources and manpower to overcome Indian resistance.

In many respects, the BEIC was best suited to expansion. Although there was considerable squabbling among the BEIC's offices in Bombay, Madras, and Bengal, the company nevertheless was a much more centralized and consolidated institution than any of the Indian states it faced, and at key moments its offices tended to cast their rivalries aside and mobilize necessary resources. The Indian states, on the other hand, faced considerable challenges in effectively competing with the BEIC. Understanding the need for stronger armed forces, Indian rulers sought to increase revenues that had to be squeezed from all social groups, but this generated many potential conflicts, which the BEIC then exploited to its own advantage.

The BEIC's use of diplomacy and subsidiary alliances played a decisive role in its struggle for control of the subcontinent. It exploited existing dynastic and territorial struggles of Indian states, siding with some rulers against the others. The armies that expanded the BEIC's authority were not manned exclusively by British soldiers but in fact were largely recruited from native populations. Finally, the British conquest was made possible through the BEIC's willingness to negotiate with the ruling elites and offer protection against outside threats. The BEIC made no claims to titular authority and did not interfere with native law, religion, and tradition, making its authority more palatable to indigenous rulers.

Alexander Mikaberidze

Perspective Essay 3. British Military and Logistical Superiority

British military and logistical superiority compensated for Britain's small military numbers, allowing Britain to take control of the Indian subcontinent with minimal military action. The British achieved this rather remarkable feat with a limited commitment of men and resources against remarkable numerical odds. For example, the census of 1861 showed just more than 83,000 European officers and men serving in the British Raj. Whereas Great Britain's population was some 23 million people, India's population was at least 100 million.

How could the British build an empire at such a great distance from Britain itself without a very considerable effort? The answer is in the organizational genius of Britain, for its logistical services proved decisive. These facts, combined with often ruthless efficiency and a succession of effective leaders, resulted in victory for the British again and again.

India, when the English first arrived early in the 17th century, was in no way a unified state. First, the fractured state of affairs in India fueled the initial success of the British and for that matter other Europeans, including the Portuguese, Dutch, Danish, and French. The Mughal Empire, which had ruled the bulk of the subcontinent in the centuries previous to the arrival of the English, had significantly declined as a power. The armed forces of the Mughals and their ability to raise and pay for troops had been undermined by wars with the Marathas and Persia.

The armies of India were not primitive. The Mughal armies possessed effective matchlock and flintlock firearms and were effective at using and supplying them. More important perhaps, they also possessed a considerable quantity of artillery that was often of superior design and casting to that available to the British in India. The changes in military technology—in this case firearms and cannon—occurred in European and Mughal armies simultaneously. Mughal armies also possessed significant infantry forces. They had long before realized the importance of infantry and heavy cannon in the reduction of fortifications and towns and in the occupation of places. When the British arrived, they faced a technologically equal military.

The British did possess a clear advantage in logistics. How they achieved and maintained this superiority is not, however, obvious. Logistics has to do with the ability to maintain troops in the field. The British were also able to raise and sustain funds for the long-term purchase of supply and for bribes as needed, which were so effective with the multitude of minor Indian rulers, playing them against each other. For this reason the argument of British superiority requires the inclusion of the use of money as a logistical weapon along with that of armed force. Consistently, British governors and generals were able to undermine their Indian enemies' strength by bribing certain princes not to fight.

To say that the British possessed a human superiority on the battlefield is often deemed as racist. It is not. The British did not take over the subcontinent with a great wave of troops and superior weaponry. Rather, they brought to bear, in the civilian form of the British East India Company (BEIC), a bureaucratic machine that was far more relentless, efficient, and single-minded than anything then present in the courts of the indigenous princes. This can be seen in the leadership of men such as Robert Clive and the Wellesley brothers. Importantly, the BEIC engaged in war in India for power and profit, not for honor or dynastic reasons, as the Indian princes often did. It was also an institution and was thus not subject to the vagaries of changes in leadership like in the Indian ruling families of the many numerous states that it would come to subjugate. The rise of the BEIC freed the British in India to use money removed from the direct control of the home government and Parliament. Further, British leadership on the ground, because of the great distance from home, could and often did make bold, sometimes reckless decisions that most often resulted in great successes.

In the realm of leadership and logistics for field forces the British also triumphed, as seen in the campaigns of Clive and Arthur Wellesley (later the Duke of Wellington). Both men's exploits featured brilliant logistical work topped off by great success on the battlefield. In the first case Clive, who operated against a far superior foe, recognized the limits of his logistics and acted accordingly. Moving in 1765 to engage and replace Siraj-ad-daula, the nawab of Bengal, Clive took a force of 2,000 Sepoys and 600 British troops. Also attached were 200 well-trained British artillerists and 12 pieces of artillery. This was a tiny force when compared to Siraj's nearly 40,000 men, 50 cannon, and war elephants. Clive knew that even his small force, operating as a unified body, would quickly strip the limited agricultural reserves of the area. This would bring starvation for the locals, resulting in potential unrest and an increase in food prices for the Sepoys, who paid for their own food. Through strict discipline he was able to maintain his forces, which advanced in three separate columns and then reunited in the face of the enemy.

The two armies met at a bend in the Hughli River just north of the town of Plassey. Clive's forces were drawn up in three tight divisions, fronted by his guns. The battle opened with a brief cannonade, but after half an hour this ended with the crash of thunder and a torrential downpour. Here the British gained a critical advantage. Thinking fast, the British covered their guns with tarpaulins, but the Indians did not. When the rain ended, the Indians, assuming that the British guns had been soaked and therefore rendered useless, advanced. The Indians were met with devastating cannon and musket fire and quickly retired. Siraj, fearing defeat, fled, and the rest of his army went with him. The British effectively gained control of all of Bengal.

The second example, some 50 years later, involved both Richard and Arthur Wellesley. As the British governor-general in India, Richard Wellesley realized that the growth and increasing professionalization of the local armies, especially the Marathas, required preemptive action. An early battle fought against them at Laswari on November 1, 1803, was considered a narrowly won victory and a sign of future problems. It became clear that the Marathas were imitating the keys to British success and doing so rapidly. Arthur Wellesley was given command of an army and moved to defeat and reduce the power of a Maratha ruler, Daulut Rao Scindia, in order to deprive him of the ability to continue his resistance.

Wellesley made great use of British resources and abilities to meticulously plan the logistics of his campaign, allowing him to pursue the Marathas and force them to engage in a set-piece battle. Having reduced the enemy forts that offered resistance, Wellesley faced an enemy numbering 20,000 regular and irregular infantry with another 10,000 or more irregular cavalry and 100 cannon. Even though he possessed only 9,500 troops and 17 guns, many of his men were seasoned British regulars.

Wellesley immediately moved his guns across the Katina River near the village of Assaye in the face of his opponent, with the intention of flanking them. To his surprise, the Maratha regular infantry and guns wheeled, much like a European force, and faced him. In the face of heavy fire, Wellesley ordered a brief artillery bombardment followed by a frontal assault. The intensity and discipline of the British and British-trained Sepoys smashed the Marathas, who eventually broke and fled. Both sides suffered heavy losses, but the Marathas had almost all their cannon taken, and their leaders lost the will to fight on.

Another of the great successes of the British in the manipulation of forces was the creation of effective Sepoys, or native forces. Here perhaps more than in any other area, the British achieved real success. When the British first arrived, it was already apparent that the Mughals were no longer capable of generating the military power to fully control their territories or retake those that had rebelled. The reality of the Indian military manpower pool was that it was fluid. For those men involved there was a far greater sense of service as a profession but one more akin to business than the Western concept of the loyal soldier serving the state.

The Indian of military experience and ability was paid to serve and often saw his concept of soldierly honor as being tied to serving as long as it made sense. Further, the intense notion of military discipline that became the norm for Europeans after 1650 did not exist in India. The European model had moved from the idea that soldiers were sustained by loot during a war and then left to support themselves by civilian occupations, trying to create for themselves a peacetime role in society. The Indian model did not change, as its society had not changed. This manpower pool was, for lack of a better term, taken over by the British and turned into an effective and essential source of local soldiers in India and later throughout Asia and the Middle East.

Rather than allowing the native contingents to exist as they had, within a construct of the large army of brave, relatively skillful, but individual fighters, the British imposed European order and discipline. Also, the British hired and retained these men on a near-permanent basis, removing them from the local society that might distract them and thus keeping them from the manpower pool that might have made them available to their Indian opponents. It was a brilliant success, as it gave the British what they needed: effective, well-trained, and renewable manpower while removing it from the indigenous market. Soldiers received regular pay, were subject to strict discipline, and enjoyed the promise of a pension and land upon being mustered out. Finally, under the control of the BEIC, the British did effectively and systematically disarm the local and numerous militias that were not subject to specific state control. All of these were either co-opted or eliminated.

In conclusion, British superiority in arms and logistics is based on the development of an effective system. The British military, which made use of strict and effective discipline combined with regular pay, made for an effective military force that gave them dominance. For the rise of an effective service-oriented bureaucracy, the British also made use of a cultural model that their Indian opponents simply could not match. Therefore, British success in India was based on its military and logistical superiority, made possible by cultural preferences and developments established over time.

Lee W. Eysturlid

Further Reading

Armitage, David. *The Ideological Origins of the British Empire.* Cambridge: Cambridge University Press, 1967.

Bayly, C. A. *Empire and Information: Intelligence Gathering and Social Communication in India, 1780–1870.* Cambridge: Cambridge University Press, 1999.

Bayly, C. A. *Indian Society and the Making of the British Empire.* Cambridge: Cambridge University Press, 1988.

Bayly, C. A. *The Raj: India and the British, 1600–1947.* London: National Portrait Gallery Publications, 1990.

Bowen, H. V. *The Business of Empire: The East India Company and Imperial Britain, 1756–1833.* Cambridge: Cambridge University Press, 2006.

Cain, P., and A. Hopkins. *British Imperialism: Innovation and Expansion, 1688–1914.* White Plains, NY: Pearson Longman, 1993.

Chaudhuri, K. N. *The Trading World of Asia and the East India Company, 1660–1760.* Cambridge: Cambridge University Press, 1978.

Cooper, Randolph G. S. *The Anglo-Maratha Campaigns and the Contest for India: The Struggle for Control of the South Asian Military Economy.* New York: Cambridge University Press, 2003.

Dirks, N. *The Scandal of Empire: India and the Creation of Imperial Britain.* Cambridge, MA: Belknap Press of Harvard University Press, 2006.

Edney, Matthew H. *Mapping an Empire: The Geographical Construction of British India, 1765–1843.* Chicago: University of Chicago Press, 1997.

James, Lawrence. *The Making and Unmaking of British India.* London: Little, Brown, 1997.

Johnson, R. A. *British Imperialism.* New York: Palgrave, 2003.

Johnson, R. A. *The Great Game: The Imperial Secret Service and the Defence of India.* London: I. B. Tauris, 2006.

Johnson, R. A. "Russians at the Gates of India? Planning the Defence of India, 1885–1900." *Journal of Military History* 67(3) (July 2003): 697–743.

Judd, Denis. *The Lion and the Tiger: The Rise and Fall of the British Raj, 1600–1947*. Oxford: Oxford University Press, 2004.

Lawson, Philip. *The East India Company: A History*. White Plains, NY: Pearson Longman, 1993.

Marshall, P. J. *East Indian Fortunes: The British in Bengal in the Eighteenth Century*. Oxford: Oxford University Press, 1976.

Marshall, P. J. "Western Arms in Maritime Asia in the Early Phases of Expansion." *Modern Asian Studies* 14(1) (1980): 1–28.

Marston, Daniel P., and Chandar S. Sundaran, eds. *A Military History of India and South Asia: From the East India Company to the Nuclear Age*. Westport, CT: Praeger, 2006.

Misra, B. B. *The Central Administration of the East India Company*. Manchester, UK: Manchester University Press, 1959.

Parsons, Timothy. *The British Imperial Century, 1815–1914: A World History Perspective*. New York: Rowman and Littlefield, 1999.

Popplewell, Richard J. *Intelligence and Imperial Defence: British Intelligence and the Defence of the Indian Empire, 1904–1924*. London: Routledge, 1995.

Watson, Ian B. *Foundation for Empire: English Private Trade in India, 1659–1760*. New Delhi: Vikas, 1980.

Wickremsekera, Channa. *"Best Black Troops in the World": British Perceptions and the Making of the Sepoy, 1746–1806*. Delhi: Manohar, 2002.

25. WHAT WAS THE SINGLE MOST IMPORTANT FACTOR IN BRINGING ABOUT THE CRIMEAN WAR?

The Crimean War (1853–1856) was an important turning point in 19th-century European history. The struggle pitted Great Britain, France, the Ottoman Empire, and the Kingdom of Sardinia against Russia. Ostensibly, the conflict was sparked by a dispute between Russian Orthodox monks and Roman Catholics over jurisdictional rights to the Christian holy sites in Muslim Ottoman-controlled Jerusalem. However, most historians agree that this issue is not central to understanding how the war came about. Further complicating the scene was Russian czar Nicholas I's desire to take possession of Ottoman possessions in Europe and to secure the Turkish Straits connecting the Black Sea with the Mediterranean Sea, the latter of which had long been an objective of Russian foreign policy. The war began in the Balkans after Russian forces took possession of the Danubian Principalities and soon involved Sevastopol and the Crimean Peninsula. Eventually the conflict devolved into a costly siege and spread to the Baltic Sea, the Caucasus, and even the Russian Far East. The underlying cause of the Crimean War, however, remains a topic for scholarly debate.

In the essays that follow, three historians offer their own views on the subject. Dr. Spencer C. Tucker asserts that the true cause of the war was the British and French desire to prevent Russia from securing direct access to the Mediterranean Sea through the control of territories surrounding the Black Sea. He argues that Russia constituted the greatest threat to West European imperial power at the time. He also points out that the British and French encouraged the Ottomans not to consider any compromises with Russia. Had a compromise been reached, war might well have been averted. In the second essay, Dr. John Wagner argues that it was the indecision and division within the British government that precipitated the war. He suggests that either the Russians or the Ottomans might have backed down if Britain had taken a clear stance in favor of one of the two countries. Dr. Alexander Mikaberidze rejects the idea that there was one single factor that caused the war. Instead, he cites a combination of geopolitical, religious, and domestic factors. He does, however, illustrate the central importance of the so-called Eastern question in shaping these complex circumstances. Indeed, the perceived decline of the Ottoman Empire and the desire of the great powers to safeguard their interests in the Middle East lay at the heart of the conflict.

Background Essay

The Crimean War began in October 1853 and ended in February 1856. The war saw a coalition of the Ottoman Empire, France, the United Kingdom, and Sardinia defeat the forces of the Russian Empire in a bloody conflict marked by considerable military incompetence on both sides. The Crimean War is chiefly remembered today for a mistaken cavalry charge and the courage of one woman, Florence Nightingale, but it was an important event in European history.

The war's chief cause was the desire of Russian czar Nicholas I to secure the Ottoman possessions in Europe and, specifically, to gain control over the straits connecting the Black Sea to the Mediterranean, a long-term Russian goal.

Toward this end, the Russian government approached Britain and other powers about dividing up the Ottoman Empire, the "sick man of Europe." Britain, however, regarded Russian control of the straits as a threat to its naval dominance in the Mediterranean. French emperor Napoleon III also assumed an aggressive stance against Russia.

The catalyst for war was a dispute regarding protection of Christians and control of the shrines in the Holy Land. Sultan Abdülmecid I (r. 1839–1861) had assigned this to the Roman Catholic Church. The deeply religious Nicholas, however, demanded that control of the religious sites be vested in the Greek (Eastern) Orthodox Church, the faith of the vast majority of the Ottoman Empire's Christians. Frantic diplomatic activity followed but failed to avert war.

The Russian government sent the Porte an ultimatum demanding the right to act as protector of the Ottoman Empire's 12 million Christian subjects. If granted, this would allow Russia to intervene almost at will in Ottoman affairs. Confident in British and French support, Sultan Abdülmecid I rejected a possible compromise. In July 1853 Nicholas sent troops into Ottoman-controlled Moldavia and Wallachia (the so-called Danubian Principalities, today joined as Romania), and on October 4, 1853, the sultan declared war on Russia. Able Ottoman general Omar Pasha (Croatian-born Michael Lattas) was able to halt the Russian land advance.

The Ottomans did not fare as well at sea, however. A Russian squadron obliterated an Ottoman squadron at the northern Anatolia seaport of Sinop (Sinope) on November 30, 1853. This Ottoman disaster was, however, a key factor in bringing Britain and France into the war.

With British and French public opinion demanding decisive action, the allies decided to attack the great Russian naval base of Sevastopol on the Crimean Peninsula. Following considerable preparation, an allied expeditionary force landed on the Crimean Peninsula in September 1854. After a series of costly battles, the allies reached Sevastopol and opened a siege there (October 17, 1854–September 9, 1855). Meanwhile, there was also fighting in the Baltic (principally naval actions), in the Caucasus, on the White Sea, and in the North Pacific.

Sevastopol fell on September 9, 1855, and while the Russians won the last major action of the war when they took the surrender on Kars in far northeastern Anatolia following its siege (June–November 1855), Russia was now effectively isolated diplomatically and facing the prospect of invasion from the west. Russia sued for peace in March 1856. France and Britain welcomed this, as public opinion in the two countries had turned against the war. Under the terms of the peace agreement hammered out in the Congress of Paris (February 25–March 30, 1856), Russia was forced to give up its ambitions regarding the Ottoman Empire. The Ottoman Empire was admitted to the Concert of Europe, and the signatories pledged themselves to respect its independence and territorial integrity. Russia also lost control of the mouth of the Danube River, and an international commission was appointed to ensure safe navigation on the Danube. Russia was also forced to cede the southern part of Bessarabia to the Ottoman Empire and to return Kars to the Ottomans. The Danubian Principalities were to be placed under a joint guaranty of the powers, with their exact status to be determined later. Britain also secured its chief goal, for Russia was forced to agree to demilitarize the Black Sea.

Commencement of the Siege of Sevastopol, a painting of the principal battle of the Crimean War by Thomas Packer. (Photos.com)

The war witnessed considerable advances in military technology. It had begun with the old-style warfare of smoothbore muskets, brightly colored uniforms, cavalry charges, and wooden ships; it ended with trench warfare, the rifle, explosive shells, the telegraph, long-range rifled artillery, the ironclad warship, and mine warfare at sea. The atrocious handling of the wounded, which was exposed in the dispatches of war correspondents and actual photographs, led to improvements in military medicine and the care of patients.

Spencer C. Tucker

Perspective Essay 1. Russia's Determination to Secure Mediterranean Access

The war between the Ottoman and Russia Empires that began in October 1853 was caused by the desire of Russian czar Nicholas I to seize Ottoman territory in Europe and gain control over the straits connecting the Black Sea to the Mediterranean. This had been a long-standing Russian goal since at least the reign of Catherine the

Great (r. 1762–1796). That being said, British and French support caused Ottoman leaders to reject possible compromise with Russia that might have avoided war, and this led to the wider Crimean War that saw Great Britain, France, the Kingdom of Sardinia, and Ottoman forces fighting Russia.

France and especially Britain were determined to prevent Russia from achieving its aims of controlling the straits. Britain had long been locked in an imperial struggle with Russia over its desire to gain access to a warm-water port on the Mediterranean. The two powers were also at loggerheads regarding the North-West Frontier (India) and in the Middle East.

The Russian government had on several occasions approached Britain and the other European powers about dividing up the Ottoman Empire, often referred to as the "sick man of Europe." Britain, however, saw Russian control of the straits as a threat to its own naval dominance in the Mediterranean and rejected the Russian overtures. Emperor Napoleon III of France also took an aggressive stance. The French emperor had been snubbed by Czar Nicholas I as an upstart and now saw a chance to assert himself as a key player in European affairs as well as bolster his stance as a defender of Catholicism. Napoleon III ordered a French naval squadron to Istanbul (Constantinople), and the British followed suit.

The immediate catalyst for the war was a seemingly trivial dispute over control of the Christian shrines in the Holy Land. Thanks to France's aggressive stance against Russia, Ottoman sultan Abdülmecid I had placed these under France and the Roman Catholic Church. Nicholas demanded that the Greek Orthodox Church control these sites and dispatched an ultimatum demanding the right to act as protector of the Ottoman Empire's 12 million Christian subjects as well as Orthodox Christians who made pilgrimages to the holy sites. Nicholas justified his demands by the fact that the vast majority of Christians within the Ottoman Empire were Orthodox as opposed to Roman Catholic Christians. If Nicholas's demand had been granted, however, it is obvious that this would have allowed Russia to intervene almost at will in Ottoman affairs.

To press the Russian demands, Czar Nicholas I dispatched to Istanbul as special envoy Prince Alexander S. Menshikov, who proved to be a disaster as a diplomat, however. Menshikov blustered, took delight in ignoring Ottoman protocol, and threatened war on every possible occasion unless Russian demands were met. Confident that the naval show of support by Britain and France would dissuade the Russians, the Ottomans rejected Menshikov's demands.

The sultan was thus shocked when on July 3, 1853, Russian troops entered Ottoman-controlled Moldavia and Wallachia (the Danubian Principalities, today joined as Romania), pressing toward the Danube River. Russia's leaders reasoned that Britain and France would not fight and that Austria would not object to Russian acquisition of several Ottoman border provinces, given Russia's vital assistance in crushing the Hungarian Revolution of 1848–1849. Thus far there had been no fighting. Frantic diplomatic activity now occurred in Vienna by representatives of Britain, France, Austria, and Prussia but not those of the Ottoman Empire or Russia. The conference produced a compromise agreement accepted by all the representatives.

Confident in the support of Britain and France, Sultan Abdülmecid I rejected the Vienna compromise, and the Ottoman Empire declared war on Russia on October 4, 1853. Russia responded with its own declaration of war on November 1. The sultan dispatched an army of 90,000 men under able commander Omar Pasha (Croatian-born Michael Lattas) across the Danube against the Russians. The Ottomans then defeated the Russians (seemingly always poorly organized at the beginning of a war) at Oltenița on November 4.

The war took a different turn on the water. Following the near annihilation by Russian ships equipped with shell guns of an Ottoman squadron at Sinope (Sinop) on November 30, 1853, there was a wellspring of support in Britain and France for the Turks. The British press labeled the Battle of Sinope, which had been a legitimate act of war, "a foul outrage" and a "massacre." Sinope and the ensuing public reaction to it led London and Paris to commit their naval assets to the defense of the Ottomans. On January 3, 1854, French and British warships entered the Black Sea. And on March 12, both nations pledged themselves to protect the Ottoman Empire's coasts and shipping against Russian attack.

Czar Nicholas I had hoped that the war would be restricted to Russia and the Ottoman Empire, but this was not to be. On March 28, Britain and France declared war on Russia; then on April 10, the two Western powers concluded a treaty of mutual alliance with the Ottoman Empire. Although the French people displayed little enthusiasm for the war (France would end up supplying the greatest number of troops and suffering the most casualties), there was great enthusiasm in Britain for the anticipated "glories" the war would bring.

A British-French expeditionary force then landed at the Bulgarian port of Varna on the Black Sea. It became the headquarters for their forces in the war. Although Austria did not declare war, it refused to guarantee its neutrality and, with Ottoman permission, sent an army of 50,000 men into Moldavia and Wallachia. The Russians now decided to withdraw from Ottoman territory. They raised the siege of Silistra on June 9 and retired across the Danube. Habsburg forces would remain in the Danube provinces until 1857.

The war could have ended at this point but became the Crimean War largely because of the British position that the Russian fleet remained a threat to its Mediterranean maritime interests. British public opinion, moreover, demanded a decisive victory. Napoleon III was also anxious for glory and prestige for French arms. Having beaten the war drums, it was difficult for the leaders of these two countries to tamp down public sentiment especially in Britain, where public opinion was more important than in France.

The allies put forward a four-part peace proposal: Russia was to give up its protectorate over the Danubian Principalities, abandon any claim to interfere in Ottoman affairs on the behalf of Orthodox Christians, agree to a revision of the Straits Convention of 1841, and agree to free access for all nations on the Danube. When the Russians rejected the allied demands, the war continued. Although fought elsewhere, including in the Baltic, the war centered on a land campaign on the Crimean Peninsula, which gave name to the war.

Following numerous examples of poor generalship, military bungling, and considerable bloodshed on both sides, coupled with widespread poor medical care, in September 1856 the allies secured their chief object—the capture of the great Russian base of Sevastopol. They then lost interest in continuation of the war.

Spencer C. Tucker

Perspective Essay 2. Weakness and Vacillation by the British Government

Although the Crimean War was the result of a complex series of events and decisions, the most important factor in its outbreak was the political weakness and internal division that afflicted the Aberdeen Coalition, the British government of the day. Because of its naval power, economic strength, and diplomatic influence, Great Britain, of all the powers involved, had the greatest opportunity and ability to arrest the movement toward war in 1853. Unfortunately, Britain was in the midst of a period of political confusion caused by the breakdown of its two-party system following repeal of the Corn Laws in 1846. The bitter political battle required to settle that issue destabilized the British party system and led to the formation of a weak and divided coalition government at the very moment when events abroad demanded a strong ministry able to formulate and implement a clear and decisive foreign policy.

In 1852, a coalition government formed under the leadership of George Hamilton Gordon, Earl of Aberdeen, a Peelite. Containing six Whigs, six Peelites, and one Radical, the Aberdeen Coalition commanded an unstable parliamentary majority that made the formation and implementation of any strong policy difficult. This was particularly true in terms of foreign policy, because two of the coalition's leading members were former foreign secretaries with very different views on conducting foreign affairs. Aberdeen preferred a more pacific policy that emphasized peace, diplomacy, and cooperation with other powers. Henry Temple, Lord Palmerston, the Whig home secretary, exemplified a more bellicose approach that emphasized independent action and the threat or use of British naval and economic power.

When the Russo Turkish dispute of 1853 again aggravated the so called Eastern question, these contradictory approaches to foreign policy prevented the Aberdeen Coalition from taking any strong stand that might have prevented war.

The Eastern question concerned the issues arising from the gradual political and military decline of the Ottoman Empire, a Muslim state that consisted of territories stretching from Southeastern Europe through the Middle East and North Africa. The question of whether the Ottoman state should be preserved or allowed to dissolve had exercised European diplomats for decades. Russia, as an Orthodox, expansionist state, was most willing to support dissolution both to win access to the Mediterranean through the Ottoman-controlled straits of the Bosporus and Dardanelles and to expand its influence with the sultan's Orthodox subjects, who were almost one third of the empire's population. Although Britain had no direct interests in the Balkans and was on friendly terms with Russia, it favored preservation as a means of checking the czar's ambitions elsewhere especially in Central Asia, where Russian expansion was seen as a threat to British control of India.

The dispute between the Ottoman Empire and Russia, which involved control of the main Christian sites in the Ottoman-controlled Holy Land, was of great importance to France. In 1852, French emperor Napoleon III won concessions for the Catholics from the Turkish government. Napoleon had overthrown the French Republic in 1851 and, after winning a national plebiscite, had himself crowned emperor in 1852. He intervened in the Holy Land dispute both to curry favor with French Catholics and thereby win support for his political coup and to split Catholic Austria from Orthodox Russia and thereby weaken the Holy Alliance, a cooperative grouping of three conservative autocracies—Austria, Russia, and Prussia—that had worked to limit French power since 1815.

Napoleon's success angered Czar Nicholas I of Russia, who demanded that Constantinople recognize Russia's right to act as protector of the sultan's Orthodox subjects. Fearing that such recognition threatened the sovereignty and integrity of the Ottoman state, the sultan refused. Thus, what began as a petty clerical quarrel was escalated by the self-interested intervention of both France and Russia into an international crisis. Britain, which in 1853 still viewed France, not Russia, as its chief European rival, was faced with a serious foreign policy question: Should it stand with a French government it distrusted in behalf of a Muslim state it disliked against a Russian government to which it was allied, or should it back Russia or refuse to intervene and risk the expansion of Russian power and influence in the Balkans and Asia? A firm stand either way would likely have averted war, but this was beyond the power of the Aberdeen government.

The British government's entire approach to the crisis that led to the Crimean War was characterized, even at the time, as a "drift" into war. This policy of drift was the result of an attempt to prevent the fall of the government by steering a course between two contradictory approaches to the crisis, either one of which, if followed firmly and consistently, would probably have averted war. Aberdeen, a devout Christian, and to a somewhat lesser extent most of the Peelite ministers evinced less fear of Russian expansion and more concern over the possible expenditure of British blood and treasure on behalf of Muslims. Meanwhile Palmerston, supported by Russell, Clarendon, and the other Whig ministers, wanted first and foremost to check Russian territorial ambitions and thus urged a firm statement to the czar of Britain's willingness to fight if Russian belligerence against the Ottoman Empire passed a certain point.

As the crisis unfolded British intentions remained unclear, and neither policy was followed to the exclusion of the other. The czar thus proceeded in the belief that Britain would not go to war for the Ottoman Empire, while the sultan acted in the belief that Britain would support the Ottoman Empire, even to the point of war with Russia. In March 1853 Palmerston wanted the government to tell Russia that any aggression toward the Ottomans would mean war, but the cabinet, following Aberdeen's lead, refused. In an effort to force Britain's hand, Napoleon, who had no intention of involving France in a war with Russia without Britain, ordered the French Mediterranean Fleet to Salamis, near Athens. But the Aberdeen government refused to order the British Mediterranean fleet from its base at Malta. In May, however, the government, as part of an internal compromise, authorized Stratford Canning, the British ambassador in Constantinople, who had extraordinary influence with the Turkish government, to summon the fleet if he believed that the situation warranted it. To make Stratford's new authority effective, it was necessary to move the fleet closer to Constantinople, an action ordered by the cabinet in early June.

Although annoyed by the movement of the British fleet, the czar still did not believe that Britain would go to war and so ordered Russian troops to occupy the Danubian Principalities in early July. Russia had undertaken similar actions during 1829–1834 and 1848–1851 and had encountered no resistance from Britain on either occasion, so the czar had no reason to expect that war with Britain might result. However, the Ottomans had likewise received no definite statement of limits to Britain's support, and with Stratford's tacit encouragement and the British fleet in the Aegean, the Ottoman government believed that it had a golden opportunity to fight Russia with Anglo-French backing. In this belief, on August 18 the Ottomans rejected the Vienna Note, a compromise devised by the British, French, and Prussian ambassadors meeting with the Austrian foreign minister in Vienna.

This rejection shocked the British ministers. The Aberdeen government, like the other governments involved, had assumed that the Christian powers could simply impose a settlement on the Turks. It now dawned on the British ministers that they faced an awkward dilemma. They had backed the Ottomans thus far and could not now honorably abandon them.

The Ottoman forces attacked the Russians in the principalities in late October, and the czar responded with a declaration of war against the Ottoman Empire on

November 1. The subsequent Russian destruction of an Ottoman fleet in the Black Sea on November 30 unleashed a storm of outrage in Britain, where the press characterized the battle as a "massacre" and public opinion demanded a strong response. Palmerston and Russell demanded action against the Russians. Aberdeen suspected that his Whig colleagues would bring down the government if it did not bend to public opinion. Thus, on December 22 the cabinet authorized offensive naval operations in the Black Sea in concert with the French. The war no one wanted was about to erupt.

Although the crisis of 1853 was complex and involved many unstable elements, the indecision and division of the British government was clearly a prime factor in the eventual outbreak of war. Either the Russians or the Turks might well have backed down if a politically stable British ministry had been able to firmly follow a clear policy from the start of the crisis.

John A. Wagner

Perspective Essay 3. The Eastern Question

The Crimean War resulted from a combination of geopolitical, religious, and domestic factors that had profound geopolitical impact on contemporary Europe. The simple explanation often given to the roots of this conflict is that the war was the result of Franco-Russian tensions surrounding the Christian holy sites in Palestine. However, the reality is much more complex. The Crimean War reflected deep-seated tensions and diplomatic problems in the European political order. But the so-called Eastern question—the perceived decline of the Ottoman Empire and the desire of the great powers to safeguard their interests in the Middle East—was at the heart of the conflict. Since the 15th century, when the Byzantine Empire collapsed under the onslaught of the Ottoman Turks, the rising Russian state claimed the leadership of Orthodox Christianity.

Russia had long sought to reclaim the Byzantine lands conquered by the Ottoman Turks. Russia's political ambitions went hand in hand with its religious claims of leading and protecting the Christians of the Ottoman Empire. Russia and the Ottoman Empire shared a long border and were rivals since the 17th century. They directly competed for territory and influence in the Balkans, the Crimea, and the Caucasus but were also often brought into conflict with each other because of their alliances with other great powers in Europe.

The Russo-Ottoman War of 1768–1774 was particularly important in the context of the Crimean War. The war ended badly for the Ottomans, and the peace treaty signed at the village of Kuchuk Kainardji (Bulgaria) on July 21, 1774, had long-term effects on the history of the Middle East. Among its 30 articles, the most consequential was Article 7, which granted Russia the right to represent (and protect) a Russian Orthodox Church and its parishioners in the Galata district of Constantinople (Istanbul). This provision proved to be highly controversial, as disagreements over its interpretation quickly emerged. Russia interpreted the article as granting it the status of the protector of Ottoman Orthodox Christians, which allowed it to actively interfere in Ottoman domestic affairs. Russia was keen on exploiting its newly acquired status to secure its positions on the shores of the Black Sea and the Mediterranean Sea. Yet from 1774 to 1815, Russian efforts had been stymied by resolute Ottoman resistance that was buttressed by Great Britain and France, which sought to prevent any Russian territorial expansion that could threaten their interests in the region.

The Eastern question became an acute international problem only after the Napoleonic Wars ended in 1815. Three main factors played a role. First, the Ottoman Empire decayed internally as corruption and administrative and economic mismanagement sapped valuable resources and delayed much-needed reforms. Second, the Ottomans struggled to contain the nationalist sentiments of the Balkan peoples. The first decade of the 19th century witnessed a major uprising of the Serbs (supported by Russia), who came close to achieving independence. The Serbian Uprising was barely over when the Greeks rose against the Turks in 1820, launching a decade-long brutal conflict. The Ottoman quandary was further amplified by the struggle of the people in North Africa to free themselves from Turkish dominion. By the 1830s, the rise of the powerful Egyptian state under the leadership of Mehmed Ali clearly manifested the weakness of the once-mighty Ottoman Empire. Egypt triumphed over the Ottomans in two wars that came close to redrawing the balance of power in the Middle East.

The third factor was the intervention of the European great powers. The Egyptian success against the Ottomans prompted the great powers to intervene to prevent Mehmed Ali from enjoying his success. In 1833, Russia set aside its long-standing rivalry with the Ottoman Empire to come to its defense when the Egyptians invaded the Ottoman heartlands. The Russian support, however, came with strings attached, and the Treaty of Hunkar Iskelesi required the Turks to close the straits of the Dardanelles and the Bosporus to all ships in case of war, thereby safeguarding Russia's southern provinces. Upon learning about the treaty Britain and France became suspicious of its secret provisions, fearing that they had given Russia freedom of action in the Ottoman Empire. During the eight years it was in force, the treaty was a point of major concern between the great powers that ultimately insisted on replacing it with the London Straits Convention of 1841. The convention, masterminded by Britain, was a major setback to Russia's ambitions in the Middle East.

France, on the other hand, had long cultivated its interest in the Levant (eastern Mediterranean). Back in the 16th century, French king Francis I, "the most Christian king," shocked his contemporaries when he allied himself with the Ottoman sultan against the Catholic Habsburgs. The Franco-Ottoman alliance of 1535 was renewed in 1740, forming the basis for closer relations. Thus, in the 1770s and 1780s French military advisers helped the Ottomans in reforming their military. The French Revolutionary Era (1789–1799) saw a brief rupture in this relationship as France, in an effort to defeat Britain, launched a military expedition to Egypt in 1798.

Following the French departure in 1801, Mehmed Ali, an Ottoman soldier blessed with charisma, military skills, and political savvy, exploited the political vacuum to seize power and significantly altered the Middle Eastern status quo. With French help, Egypt rapidly developed economically and militarily so that by the 1830s it could challenge the Ottoman Empire. But France also sought to revive its ties to the Ottoman Empire. France's efforts redoubled after Emperor Napoleon III came to power in 1851.

Britain sought to uphold the territorial integrity of the Ottoman Empire. By the mid-19th century, India had become the most important colony of the rapidly industrializing British Empire. London was apprehensive of any overland threats to India and considered Russian expansion into the Ottoman Empire as one such possibility. Both the British public and government routinely condemned the Ottoman government for being despotic and believed that its collapse would only benefit the people residing in the empire. Yet, geopolitical considerations compelled Britain to side with a regime that it despised. The Ottoman Empire was both an important market for British industrial products, especially textiles, and a major source for raw materials and provisions. Russian expansion into the Middle East or French expansion into Egypt could pose a direct threat to British interests in the Mediterranean Sea and, more important, in the Indian Ocean. Such concerns were only further heightened when Russian emperor Nicholas I approached the British with an offer to dismember the Ottoman lands. On the eve of the Crimean War, Nicholas famously described the Ottoman Empire as the "sick man of Europe," urging his British counterparts to act in concert with Russia.

Religion played an important role in amplifying these international rivalries. The 19th century saw a bitter rivalry in Palestine between the Catholics (backed by France) and the Greeks (supported by Russia) over who should have control of the Church of the Holy Sepulcher in Jerusalem and the Church of the Nativity in Bethlehem. A deeply devout man, Emperor Nicholas developed a special interest in the holy places and was keen on securing the Russian Orthodox Church's position at the Church of the Holy Sepulcher. The 1830s saw thousands of Orthodox believers, many of them Russians, visiting Jerusalem and Bethlehem on religious pilgrimages. As the number of Orthodox visitors increased, a rivalry between Christian churches in Palestine intensified, forcing the Ottoman governor of Jerusalem to position Ottoman soldiers inside and outside the church to preserve order.

The religious strife between the Orthodox Church and the Roman Catholic Church gradually caused their respective countries to exert political power to protect their interests and shore up support back home. In France, Emperor Napoleon exploited the issue of the holy sites to bolster support of the Catholic Church, which had watched the increased influence of the Orthodox Church in Palestine with mounting distrust. Between 1842 and 1847, Jerusalem saw Christian communities rapidly expanding: the Anglicans founded a bishopric, and the French built Catholic schools and churches and helped Pope Pius IX establish a resident Latin patriarch, the first since the Crusades of the 12th century. On the other hand, Russia established a hostel, a hospital chapel, and a school and supported the Greek patriarch of Constantinople in asserting his power in the holy city. Britain was suspicious of Russia's religious activities and considered them harbingers of future political claims in this strategically important region. France was equally alarmed by the growing Russian presence.

Thus, the control of the holy sites in Palestine soon transcended religious boundaries and became deeply enmeshed in populist rhetoric of national honor and history. Both the British and French governments exploited such discussions to whip up rabidly Russophobe sentiments in their societies and shape public opinion into supporting their policies designed to achieve geopolitical goals. Napoleon III seized power in France just two years before the Crimean War began. An ambitious man, he was eager to consolidate his power and restore France to its former glory enjoyed under his great-uncle Napoleon I.

Meanwhile, more divisive politics reigned across the English Channel in Britain. In 1852 the government of George Hamilton-Gordon, Earl of Aberdeen, included Henry John Temple, Lord Palmerston, as home secretary, and John Russell as foreign minister, even though neither man could see eye to eye on many issues. As a result, the government suffered from instability and indecision. Aberdeen feared France and was willing to ignore Russia's growing influence in Southeastern Europe, a position that gave Emperor Nicholas I the impression that Britain would not risk going to war over the Ottoman Empire. Palmerston, on the other hand, was firmer in his opposition to Russia, and many historians agree that had he been the prime minister, the Crimean War might have been averted.

Alexander Mikaberidze

Further Reading

Anderson, Matthew S. *The Eastern Question, 1774–1923: A Study in International Relations.* New York: St. Martin's, 1966.

Badem, Candan. *The Ottoman Crimean War, 1853–1856.* Boston: Brill, 2010.

Barker, A. J. *The War against Russia.* New York: Holt, Rinehart and Winston, 1971.

Baumgart, Winfried. *The Crimean War, 1853–1856*. New York: Bloomsbury, 1999.

Bridge, F. R., and Roger Bullen. *The Great Powers and the European States System, 1814–1914*. London: Pearson Education, 2005.

Conacher, J. B. *The Aberdeen Coalition 1852–1855: A Study in Mid-Nineteenth-Century Party Politics*. Cambridge, MA: Cambridge University Press, 1968.

Curtiss, John S. *Russia's Crimean War*. Durham, NC: Duke University Press, 1979.

Edgerton, Robert B. *Death or Glory: The Legacy of the Crimean War*. Boulder, CO: Westview, 1999.

Figes, Orlando. *Crimea: The Last Crusade*. London: Allen Lane, 2010.

Goldfrank, David M. *The Origins of the Crimean War*. London: Longman Publishing Group, 1994.

Gooch, Brison D. "A Century of Historiography on the Origins of the Crimean War." *American Historical Review* 62(1) (October 1956): 33–58.

Hoppen, K. Theodore. *The Mid-Victorian Generation, 1846–1886*. Oxford, UK: Clarendon, 1998.

Markovits, Stefanie. *The Crimean War in the British Imagination*. Cambridge: Cambridge University Press, 2009.

Ponting, Clive. *The Crimean War: The Truth behind the Myth*. London: Chatto and Windus, 2004.

Pottinger Saab, Anne. *The Origins of the Crimean Alliance*. Charlottesville: University of Virginia Press, 1977.

Puryear, Vernon J. "New Light on the Origins of the Crimean War." *Journal of Modern History* 3(2) (June 1931): 219–234.

Rich, Norman. *Why the Crimean War? A Cautionary Tale*. New York: McGraw-Hill, 1991.

Royce, Simon. *The Crimean War and Its Place in European Economic History*. London: University of London Press, 2001.

Royle, Trevor. *Crimea: The Great Crimean War, 1854–1856*. New York: Palgrave Macmillan, 2004.

Schmitt, Bernadotte E. "The Diplomatic Preliminaries of the Crimean War." *American Historical Review* 25(1) (October 1919): 36–67.

Schroeder, Paul W. *Austria, Great Britain, and the Crimean War: The Destruction of the European Concert*. Ithaca, NY: Cornell University Press, 1972.

Sweetman, John. *The Crimean War, 1854–1856*. New York: Osprey, 2001.

Taylor, A. J. P. *The Struggle for Mastery in Europe, 1848–1918*. Oxford, UK: Clarendon, 1954.

Troubetzkoy, Alexis S. *A Brief History of the Crimean War: History's Most Unnecessary Struggle*. New York: Carroll and Graf, 2006.

Wetzel, David. *The Crimean War: A Diplomatic History*. New York: Columbia University Press, 1985.

26. WAS SLAVERY THE PRINCIPAL CAUSE OF THE AMERICAN CIVIL WAR?

Sometimes it seems as though the amount of ink spilled in writing about the American Civil War exceeds the amount of blood that flowed during the conflict—and with more than 600,000 dead, the war was a bloody one indeed. When the Civil War broke out in April 1861, the United States was deeply divided—economically, culturally, and socially. A good deal of this division revolved around the institution of slavery. In the South slave labor was employed extensively, particularly in warmer areas along the coast and in the piedmont from the Carolinas to Texas. There were approximately 4 million enslaved African Americans in the South on the eve of the Civil War, meaning that slave labor powered much of the Southern economy. In the North, by 1861 slavery had either petered out or had been specifically prohibited in some states. For years, historians have argued especially strongly about the role that slavery played in causing the war. At one time, historians asserted that it was and had to be the only cause: the South wanted to protect and even expand slavery, while the North wanted to limit and eventually abolish it. However, that argument has become subtler and more refined, and it has evolved as some historians have even gone so far as to contend that slavery played no role at all, a limited role, or a less important role than originally believed, especially in comparison with problems such as economic disputes, a lack of cultural affinity, extremists dominating the political debate, and differing views of the role of government.

The following three essays address the question about the role of slavery in decidedly different ways. Dr. Brooks Simpson agrees on the importance of other potential causes but points out that all of them ultimately grew out of the dispute over the existence and spread of slavery. Indeed, he posits that the changing nature of the institution of slavery, including how it was perceived nationally and internationally, and the inability of U.S. leaders to reach a lasting compromise ultimately led to civil war. Dr. Scott Stabler takes the discussion in a different direction by explaining the role that the long history of American westward expansion played in defining the debate over slavery—and how slavery did a great deal to define westward expansion. Furthermore, the centrality of cotton cultivation to many Southerners as well as Northerners was a major impetus for westward expansion. Dr. Steven Woodworth has no doubt that slavery was the primary cause of the Civil War. He argues that the war was the culmination of a 40-year sectional clash between North and South over the issue of slavery, a struggle that commenced in earnest with the Missouri Compromise of 1820.

Background Essay

The United States underwent great territorial expansion during the first half of the 19th century as a consequence of the Louisiana Purchase (1803), the acquisition of Florida (1819), and the Mexican-American War (1846–1848). The country also experienced rapid population growth from both a high birth rate and immigration. By June 1860, with a population of some 31.4 million people (3.9 million of them slaves), the United States was more populous than Great Britain and almost as large as France.

By 1860, however, the United States was coming apart. North and South were entirely estranged. The South had an agricultural economy based on the production of cotton, tobacco, rice, sugarcane, and naval stores. It was the world's largest producer of raw cotton, but seven-eighths of this was exported, chiefly to the United Kingdom. Southerners therefore sought a low tariff in order to be able to purchase cheaper manufactured goods from Britain, then leading the Industrial Revolution. The North, on the other hand, had a balanced economy. It was rapidly industrializing, and Northern business interests sought a high tariff to protect their finished goods against cheaper British manufactures. Capital also tended to multiply in the North, and banking, insurance companies, and railroads all concentrated there. Increasingly the railroads were tying the West to the North. There was also a large and growing population imbalance between North and South; new immigrants could not compete with free slave labor in the South and settled primarily in the North. Most whites in the South were also hurt economically by the slavery system.

The Mexican-American War set up the Civil War, for the chief issue regarding the newly acquired territories was whether they would be slave or free. The Missouri Compromise of 1820 provided that new states would be admitted to the Union on the basis of one slave and one free in order to maintain rough parity in the U.S. Senate and in presidential elections. But California was admitted singly as a free state in 1850. In the ensuing Compromise of 1850 the North agreed to enforce laws on runaway slaves. This, however, ran counter to increasing abolitionist sentiment in the North that fueled violence in the territories, especially Kansas.

As abolitionism gained strength in the North, white Southerners increasingly saw their way of life threatened. Political parties and even churches split along regional lines. Increasingly there was talk of secession; most Southerners believed that a state had the right to secede from the Union, whereas Northerners rejected this notion.

In October 1858 militant abolitionist John Brown led a raid on the federal arsenal at Harpers Ferry, Virginia (now West Virginia), with the intention of setting up a base in the Appalachian Mountains for fugitive slaves and using arms from the arsenal to raid the South. The raid was easily put down, and Brown was tried and

Engraving by Patrick Reason entitled "Am I not a man and a brother?" This 1835 woodcut image of a supplicant African male slave in chains appeared in the 1837 broadside publication of John Greenleaf Whittier's antislavery poem, "Our Countrymen in Chains." (Library of Congress)

hanged, but the event greatly alarmed Southerners, who saw in it true Northern sentiment, and led to increasing numbers of state militia units in the South.

In November 1860, Republican Party candidate Abraham Lincoln was elected president of the United States with a plurality of the vote and largely because the Democratic Party split on the issue of slavery. The Republican platform called for no more slavery in the territories but promised no interference with slavery in the states. Nonetheless, many Southern leaders refused to accept a "black Republican president," and on December 24, 1860, South Carolina voted to secede from the Union. State conventions in Alabama, Georgia, Florida, Mississippi, Louisiana, and Texas followed South Carolina's lead. On February 8, 1861, representatives from the seven seceded states met in Montgomery, Alabama, and formed the Confederate States of America. The next day its congress elected Jefferson Davis president.

U.S. president James Buchanan's Democratic administration had almost a month to go, but Buchanan was afraid of using force and alienating the border states, chiefly Virginia, and took no action. But after taking office, Lincoln also did nothing for six weeks. In his March 4, 1861, inauguration, he renewed his promise to respect slavery where it existed and to enforce the fugitive slave laws, but he also said that he would not countenance secession.

The Confederates had now taken control of all federal forts and navy yards in the seceded states except the key installations of Fort Pickens in Pensacola, Florida, and Fort Sumter in Charleston Harbor, South Carolina. Lincoln reluctantly concluded, against the advice of a majority of his cabinet, that he had to send relief expeditions to these two installations even though this would probably cause Virginia to secede as well. Lincoln informed Davis that this would be only for provisioning, but Davis ordered Major General P. G. T. Beauregard at Charleston to demand the surrender of Fort Sumter. If refused, he was to reduce it. Following an unsatisfactory reply from its commander, Major Robert Anderson, Beauregard ordered fire opened on Fort Sumter before the Union relief expedition could arrive.

Shelling commenced at 4:30 a.m. on April 12, 1861. After 34 hours of bombardment and short of ammunition and provisions, Anderson surrendered. The bloodiest war in American history began with the only casualty being a horse.

Spencer C. Tucker

Perspective Essay 1. Other Factors Were Also at Play

Without the institution of slavery, it is hard to imagine the growing sectional rift between the slaveholding South and the rest of the United States evolving into civil war. Nevertheless, it is also true that slavery alone did not spark secession and civil war. The American republic had been founded even as slavery was losing its character as a national institution and was becoming more and more identified with the South, yet for decades politicians successfully crafted compromise after compromise that appeared to stave off more serious conflict. Thus, even as disagreement over slavery proved to be a necessary prerequisite for disunion and conflict, slavery by itself did not cause that result. Rather, it was the changing nature of the issue coupled with the inability of political institutions to achieve lasting compromise that led Americans to civil war in 1860–1861.

Of course, there are those people who argue that something else was at the heart of the sectional divide. Some favor an explanation resting on the concept of states' rights, others argue that economic or cultural differences were at the root of the conflict, and there are those who remain attached to the notion that the South sought to escape Northern domination of politics, especially when it came to such issues as the tariff, and that white Southerners, in the words of Confederate president Jefferson Davis, simply sought to be left alone. There is something to be said for each of these explanations. In each case, however, slavery lay at the root of the differences.

Take states' rights. White Southerners cited states' rights as a way to defend slavery when they felt it was under attack by Northerners acting through the federal government, but they had no problem in using national power when it came to the protection and expansion of slavery. In defending the Fugitive Slave Law of 1850, in fact, white Southerners rejected Northern efforts to use states' rights to provide civil rights safeguards for blacks accused of being escaped slaves.

The matter of economic and cultural differences can be wildly exaggerated. Both the North and the South embraced commercial capitalism, and one can view plantation agriculture as a form of agribusiness that did not differ all that much from manufacturing. Moreover, although the North did have more industry than the South, more Northerners were farmers than factory workers in 1860, and one should not overlook the importance of farming in shaping the economy of the United States outside the South. That some differences existed is true, although there was also a common national heritage and history born in the struggle for American independence. But these differences in themselves did not cause the crisis. As for a distinct Southern way of life, much of its distinctiveness tended to rest on the existence of plantation slavery and the society that emerged around it.

Even less persuasive is the argument that the political domination of the South by the North resulted in a Southern quest for independence. The South had exercised disproportionate political power in the affairs of the republic ever since its founding. The three-fifths rule adopted at the Constitutional Convention in 1787 augmented Southern political power in the House of Representatives and in the electoral college by counting every five slaves as equal to three white people for purposes of determining the allocation of representation by population. The Southern wing of the Democratic Party had proven especially successful in getting its way through 1860, and it was the secessionist fire-eaters who shattered that party when they walked out of the 1860 presidential convention at Charleston. The U.S. Supreme Court remained a bastion of Southern political power, as its ruling in the 1857 case *Dred Scott v. Sandford* clearly demonstrated: that decision opened up all federal territories to slavery, overturning decades of congressional compromises. It is more to the point to say that white Southerners would not accept any electoral verdict that would relegate them to minority status.

To the degree that states' rights, economic and cultural differences, and the struggle over political power caused the American Civil War, they did so because each was inextricably entangled with slavery. The existence of slavery made those clashes far more explosive than they otherwise would have been and complicated efforts to reach compromise. Remove slavery from the equation and it would be difficult to discover any issue that could not be resolved through the normal operation of the political process. That said, the mere existence of slavery did not by itself cause the American Civil War. Rather, it was the changing nature of the issue and the collapse of the political institutions that had managed to negotiate compromises that led to division and disunion.

At the time of the Constitutional Convention, slavery was undergoing a transformation from a national to a sectional institution. Between 1780 and the early 19th century, state after state north of the Mason-Dixon line did away with slavery or set it on the road to ultimate extinction. However, the invention of the cotton gin in 1793 and the expansion of the United States westward across the Mississippi offered hopeful prospects for slavery. New lands provided promising locations for cotton plantations, and the Louisiana Purchase in 1803 secured the port of New

Orleans for shipping cotton abroad and brought even more land within U.S. boundaries. Before long more and more people in the South spoke of slavery as a positive good for both whites and blacks, providing economic opportunity for the former and offering a more humane existence for the latter under white paternalism. The efforts of some white Americans to eradicate slavery made little headway, and the Missouri Compromise of 1819–1821 opened up more western lands for slavery.

The abolitionist movement that emerged in the 1830s characterized slavery as a sin and called for its abolition as soon as possible. That movement worried white Southerners who were already concerned about the very real possibility of slave insurrections. Afraid of what might happen should slaves be inspired to rebel by the abolitionist message and determined to shut down discussion among whites who harbored doubts about slavery, many white Southerners blocked abolitionist efforts to use the mails and political petitions to Congress to spread their message and spark debate. The resulting struggle over the so-called Gag Rule angered some Northerners, who began to complain that white Southerners seemed determined to get their way regardless of the consequences.

Unpopular as these efforts at constricting civil rights might have been among some Northerners, slavery's opponents still faced a difficult road to climb. During the 1840s the question of slavery's expansion westward was a legitimate subject for political debate, given the assumption that Congress determined where and if slavery could expand. This debate heated up during the Mexican-American War as Northern Democrats, dissatisfied with the behavior of their party's Southern wing under President James K. Polk, backed the Wilmot Proviso, which would have barred slavery from any territory gained as a result of the war. The proviso never passed, but voting patterns revealed a clear North/South split in both houses of Congress.

Efforts to organize California as a free state in the wake of the discovery of gold and Southern unhappiness over Northern efforts to block the execution of the Fugitive Slave Law of 1793 opened the way to yet another grand compromise in 1850. This time, however, senators and representatives gave little ground, and the components of Kentuckian Henry Clay's initial bill only passed due to the superior legislative tactics of Democratic senator Stephen A. Douglas of Illinois, who pushed forward each bill separately. Included in that compromise was an option for several territories to decide whether to admit slavery through local voting, a process called popular sovereignty. That process would remove from Washington the responsibility of determining where slavery would be allowed in the trans-Mississippi West. Many Northerners disliked the new Fugitive Slave Law of 1850: they looked askance at the possibility of being impressed into service to help capture fugitive slaves and deplored the omission of a jury trial to determine the fate of the alleged fugitive. Still others found themselves moved by Harriet Beecher Stowe's novel about the evils of slavery, *Uncle Tom's Cabin*.

By 1854, a few things were clear. There was only limited interest in slavery as a moral issue, and one could not mobilize many voters to support a call for its abolition. Even as white Southerners increasingly dwelled on the benefits of slavery, white Northerners were slow to respond so long as slavery's gains did not come at their expense. However, Northern whites were not nearly so pleased at evidence of Southern political dominance: a growing number were becoming convinced that slavery was getting its own way at the expense of their rights, opportunities, and interests. Talk of a "slave power" in which white Southerners were prepared to rule or ruin circulated throughout the North, and it would not take much to invigorate that notion. So long as there were bisectional political parties that sought compromise on the issue as essential to institutional survival, however, the issue remained muted.

All of that changed between 1854 and 1860. Douglas's introduction of the Kansas-Nebraska Act ripped apart the Missouri Compromise and opened to slavery land once reserved for free soil in the West. The actions of Missouri's so-called border ruffians in carrying territorial elections by fraud and violence made a mockery of popular sovereignty. Politics became warfare on the plains of Bleeding Kansas. The crumbling of the Whig Party left the Democratic Party as the only remaining national political organization, and even there Southern demands were stretching it to the breaking point. A Southern-dominated Supreme Court tore away what remained of the Missouri Compromise and popular sovereignty in the *Dred Scott* decision, and some white Northerners, including Illinois Republican Abraham Lincoln, speculated that before too long the Supreme Court might apply its reasoning to nullify the prohibition of slavery in the free states. In short, it was the insistence of a growing number of white Southerners that they get their way on slavery, whatever the cost, that provided the fertile soil upon which the Republican Party quickly took root.

As politics became polarized along sectional lines, white Southerners found it difficult to endure the mounting attacks against slavery and worrisome when some white Northerners did what they could to thwart such federal laws as the Fugitive Slave Law of 1850. John Brown's violent actions in Kansas and Harpers Ferry suggested that at least some white Northerners were also willing to embrace violence instead of politics. Douglas's efforts at salvaging popular sovereignty among Northern voters raised questions about whether Northern Democrats would continue to support Southern interests and risk electoral defeat to a party that was explicitly antislavery and anti–slave power. Fire-eaters, convinced that the South must make its own way to independence, aided in disrupting the Democratic Party in 1860, slicing apart the last remaining national political institution. Lincoln's victory that November signaled the coming to power of an avowedly antislavery president sworn to block the designs of the slave power. Secessionists argued that it was better to act now and launch a preemptive first strike by leaving the Union before Lincoln and his minions took over.

In short, it was not the mere existence of slavery that by itself caused disunion and civil war. It was the changing nature of slavery in the 19th century as a political and economic institution that made it a polarizing political issue, taking away the possibility for the construction of any lasting compromise that would have allowed white Northerners and Southerners to pursue their own interests and exercise their own rights unfettered by sectional concerns. Having ruled for so long, white Southerners saw the loss of political power as inevitably leading to their ruin and responded accordingly to protect the institution that was at the core of their political and economic order as well as their way of life.

Brooks D. Simpson

Perspective Essay 2. Slavery Had Deep Roots in American History

Slavery served as the root cause of the American Civil War, but related economic factors played a key role as well. There is little doubt that slavery helped produce the number one export of the United States in the antebellum era: cotton. The importance of this crop to the livelihood of a majority of white Southerners and thousands of Northerners cannot be dismissed. To protect this valuable economic interest, the white South used federal power to preserve slavery. The wielding of federal power often revolved around territorial expansion. Therefore, to protect their economic interests based on slavery, rich white slave owners used the federal government to keep their wealth and power.

Geography formed a major component of why slavery became essential in the minds of white Southerners. When the country formed, slavery existed in every state, but the South, with its climate and landscape, served as an excellent place for large plantations to form and make money. The money made by the rich white plantation owners, which many called the slave power, existed in the South primarily due to its geography.

The slave power was a minority of rich white plantation owners who were often politicians and gained great wealth via cotton picked by slaves. This wealth was unprecedented, and these rich men understandably wanted to keep wealth and power. To stay wealthy, the slave power manipulated the federal government. From the beginning of the United States to 1860, 23 of 36 Speakers of the House, 24 of 26 president pro tempores of the Senate, and 20 of 35 justices on the U.S. Supreme Court were from the South. In addition, in 49 out of 72 years the president had been from the South; during 12 other years the presidents were Northerners who favored the South. Although it represented a fraction of the population, the slave power held a lot of clout in the federal government.

From the beginning, with the Three-Fifths Compromise as part of the 1787 U.S. Constitution, the white South realized that it had to protect its minority power in Washington. However, this compromise did not serve as the only way the slave power kept hold. The manner in which the slave power survived for so long involved the issue of westward expansion. From the 1787 Northwest Ordinance to the *Dred Scott* case 70 years later, settler expansion westward created questions and conflicts over the role of slavery in new territories and states. This originated many debates about the admission of states as either free or slave.

The issue of slavery's expansion came prior to the U.S. Constitution in the form of the Northwest Ordinance. Nonslaveholders desired free land that they could farm without having to face competition from other farmers who used slave labor. Slave labor's low costs, many believed, would make small farmers noncompetitive and drive them out of business. The banning of slavery in the Old Northwest led to some Southern politicians in the 18th century adopting a rigid policy of giving no ground on the issue of slavery's expansion. However, that tide of slavery protection grew alongside the country's expansion west and the increase in the value of cotton.

The Missouri Compromise in 1820 created clear state divisions regarding slavery, in turn generating sectionalism. By 1820, the cotton gin had made cotton and slavery staples of the South. Through this compromise, Congress granted Maine statehood under the conditions that it remain a free state, with Missouri named a slave state. This would continue to maintain the balance of equal representation within the Senate for slave and nonslave states. This compromise came due to the Senate's rejection of Missouri's initial application for statehood. The so-called Tallmadge Amendment would have allowed Missouri to become a state but also allowed for the gradual abolition of slavery. The House, which by now had a majority of free state representatives due to immigrants most often choosing to seek a new life in nonslaveholding states, approved the Tallmadge Amendment. But the Senate rejected it. The Senate proved to be the power seat for the slave power in the federal government and forced the Missouri Compromise.

The Senate was not the only place the slave power manipulated the federal government, particularly in the 1830s. In 1832, the Nullification Crisis arose in which South Carolina threatened to secede over a federal law involving tariffs. The state wanted to nullify a federal law. Though the effort at nullification did not succeed, the mere threat of secession eventually led to a compromise in which the federal government agreed to South Carolina's demands by lowering tariffs over time.

In 1835, President Andrew Jackson utilized the federal postal system to end the sending of abolitionist pamphlets to the South. The postal ban came at the behest of the slave power, which did not worry about illiterate slaves reading the literature but instead worried about literate white Southerners who were not slaveholders contemplating abolition.

The next year, the slave power had the House of Representatives establish the gag rule as part of a compromise with free states to stop citizens from submitting antislavery petitions. Specifically, the slave power introduced the gag rule to postpone petitions by the American Anti-Slavery Society. Some nonslaveholding Northerners went along due to sympathy with the South, dislike for abolitionists, and/or political reasons. John Quincy Adams led the opposition to the gag rule, which he believed was unconstitutional, but repeal did not occur until the House voted 105 to 80 in 1844.

The 1830s also involved the question of the annexation of the newly independent country of Texas. In 1837, Texas appealed to the administration of President Martin Van Buren for annexation but was rejected. The rejection partly came due to fears of war with Mexico, which did not recognize Texas's independence, but also because the possibility of adding a new slave state set off protests over annexation in many of the free states. Van Buren avoided the issue of annexation during his presidency, fearful of creating even more tension within an already straining union.

The 1840s again involved the slave power and westward expansion. The eventual annexation of Texas created violent debate, leading the Senate to reject the annexation treaty. In a legislative maneuver, President John Tyler used a joint resolution to annex the state by rallying sympathetic Whigs with Democrats in the House to obtain the simple majority needed for annexation. The support came due to the implicit connotation that Oregon would soon join the Union as a free state.

Texas's annexation helped provoke the Mexican-American War, which many in the North saw as an explicit attempt to expand slavery. Many in Congress, including new representative Abraham Lincoln, opposed the war. This debate over extending slavery into any acquired Mexican territory sparked Pennsylvania Democrat David Wilmot's proviso. The proposed bill would demonstrate that the war was not about the extension of slavery by proposing to ban slavery in any newly acquired territories. Against President James K. Polk's advice, those wanting the new territories to be slave-free tried passing the proviso more than once in Congress. The bill passed the House but faced defeat in the Senate, where the slave power still held sway. The slave power entertained the idea that if the government would not let them bring slaves into new states, their Senate power would vaporize. These two divergent opinions caused the House and Senate to have the most intense debates over slavery since the 1820 Missouri Compromise.

The 1850s served as the harbinger of the Civil War. Many incidents in this decade further demonstrated how the slave power and westward expansion interacted with the issue of slavery. The Compromise of 1850 led the way to civil war. This complex piece of legislation basically gave the free states a majority in the Senate and gave the slave power a more rigid Fugitive Slave Law. The cause of the compromise involved the slave power and westward expansion. Californians desired to enter the Union as a free state. Slavery, as many Northerners feared, would provide slave owners with an unfair labor advantage, thus forcing free labor competitors out of business. The admission of California as a free state led to an imbalance in the Senate.

The Compromise of 1850 contained many stipulations that gave the South some territorial concessions but, most important, proffered a bolstered Fugitive Slave Law. The slave power's new Fugitive Slave Law brought the full force of the federal government to the North by forcing fugitives and some free slaves to return to bondage. Not only did the federal government set up special courts and hire more U.S. marshals, but the law also allowed the marshals to require free Northerners to join posses in order to track down fugitive slaves. This act brought slavery to the doorstep of those who had never had the issue affect them and caused Northerners previously unconcerned with politics to appreciate the impact of the slave power on a personal level.

In 1854 Senator Stephen Douglas, Democrat of Illinois, proposed the Kansas-Nebraska Act to gain federal funding for a railroad that would run from his home city of Chicago to California. To do this he needed the support of the slave power, and in return the slave power sought and received popular sovereignty for the territories of Kansas and Nebraska. Popular sovereignty allowed citizens in the two territories to vote on the issue of free versus slave. The act infuriated Northerners, who by now fully understood how a fraction of the U.S. population, wealthy white slaveholders, manipulated the federal government to their own benefit. The backlash came in the death of the Whig Party, the growth of a Northern party firmly against the spread of slavery (the Republican Party), and a virtual miniature civil war in Kansas. Nevertheless, by the time Kansas applied for statehood in 1857, President James Buchanan fully supported its admission as a slave state. The submission of the fraudulent proslave Lecompton Constitution for Congress's approval went down in defeat, and Kansas would not become a state until 1861. The defeat of Lecompton served as the first significant setback to the slave power.

The 1856 election between John C. Fremont of the new Republican Party and the Democrat Buchanan showed the first national electoral split in the country. Though Buchanan won, Fremont, despite not winning a single Southern state, did surprisingly well in the free states, where the Republican denouncement of slavery's extension proved popular. As Buchanan agreed to serve only one term, the Republicans realized that they could win the presidency in 1860 without a single Southern electoral vote.

The next year demonstrated the other federal hold the slave power had: the Supreme Court. The 1857 *Dred Scott* decision outlawing slavery's restriction in the western territories caused an outcry in the North, as free states feared that the ruling would eventually allow slavery in their states. Again the slave power injected itself through the federal government on the issue of slavery's expansion westward.

The Lincoln-Douglas debates of 1858 demonstrated the impact that slavery had on politics. The seven three-hour "debates" (that were really discussions) took place as part of the two men's quest for the U.S. Senate. The prime topic of these debates revolved not around Illinois but instead around the issue of slavery that so threatened the nation. Shortly before the debates, the then nationally unknown Lincoln had made his famous "House Divided" speech in the Illinois state capitol. The issue of slavery and its expansion and the slave power proved prominent throughout the country. The slave power wanted to ensure that another doughface (a politician from the North who supported slave power) would hold the oval office after Buchanan's presidency, and Douglas was the Democrats' prime candidate. They would be sorely disappointed after Douglas issued his Freeport Doctrine in which he implied that the *Dred Scott* decision could be ignored in territories. The fact that the potential chief federal law enforcement officer would not enforce a court ruling favoring slavery did not sit well with the slave power. This produced the Democratic Party split in the 1860 election, leading to Lincoln's election as president.

Lincoln's election marked the defeat of the slave power and the secession of the Deep South. White Southerners thought that by making a preemptive strike of secession they could protect the South's peculiar institution. They were wrong.

Scott L. Stabler

Perspective Essay 3. The War of the Slaveholders' Rebellion

During and shortly after the American Civil War, many Northerners referred to the conflict as "The War of the Slaveholders' Rebellion"—and they were right. Slavery was the only significant cause of the Civil War. Other issues, such as states' rights, were dragged along in the conflict, and later writers would tack on such themes as the industrial North versus the agrarian South, but the war was no more about these topics than it was about the relative merits of blue woolen uniforms versus gray cotton ones. The issue that brought the United States to the point of internecine conflict in 1861 was slavery and slavery alone.

The disputes that led up to the war all centered on slavery. The Civil War came as the culmination of a four-decade-long succession of sectional clashes over the issue of human bondage. Dispute over slavery first occurred when in 1819 Missouri sought admission to the Union as a slave state and Northern congressmen proposed an amendment to the statehood bill stipulating that slavery should be phased out in the new state over the next several generations. Southern politicians reacted with outrage, and a lengthy political wrangle ensued, ended by the famous 1820 Missouri Compromise, which admitted Missouri as a slave state but drew a line through the remainder of the Louisiana Purchase, limiting slavery to the area south of 36 degrees, 30 minutes latitude.

In the 1830s the country did experience political strife over the issue of tariffs, though even then the disagreement was most bitter and dangerous when mixed with slavery. It was not Illinois or Indiana that challenged the federal government over the tariff, though high tariffs affected those states as negatively as they did any slave state. Rather, it was South Carolina, the state with the highest proportion of slaves, that attempted the nullification of the tariff in 1832 and 1833. The clear implication is that even when Americans squabbled over the tariff, the issue of slavery was not far in the background, providing the real impetus behind every clash.

Also in the 1830s, pressure from Southern congressmen brought about the decision to prohibit the U.S. Postal Service from delivering abolitionist literature in the Southern states and the congressional policy of not even accepting petitions from American citizens requesting restrictions on slavery in the territories or the District of Columbia. Outside the halls of government during those years, slavery advocates twice destroyed the printing press of antislavery newspaper editor Elijah P. Lovejoy and the third time killed the abolitionist editor as well.

When the Mexican-American War began in 1846, Congressman David Wilmot offered his famous Wilmot Proviso as a proposed amendment to a spending authorization bill for the war. The proviso stipulated that slavery should not spread into any territories the United States might gain as a result of the war. Wilmot's goal was to make clear to all Americans, especially his constituents back in Pennsylvania, that the war then commencing was being fought to spread American ideals of freedom and not America's shameful institution of slavery. The reaction from Southern congressmen was outrage. The House adopted the proviso, but the Senate rejected it. When antislavery congressmen renewed their attempts to gain its adoption, tempers steadily rose. Southerners began to talk openly of secession if their demands for added slave territory were not met.

When California petitioned for admission as a free state in 1849, Southerners complaining loudly that the admission of the new state without slavery amounted to a backdoor adoption of the Wilmot Proviso. In debates that eventually led to the sectional cease-fire known as the Compromise of 1850, John C. Calhoun and other Southern orators repeatedly stated that the issue at stake was the right of slaveholders to bring their human chattel into any and all of the republic's new territories and to secure those territories as slave states. Demands grew louder for secession of the Southern states in order to form a republic in which slavery would never be questioned, and most of the slave states sent delegates to a summer 1850 convention in Nashville whose all-but-announced purpose was to facilitate secession. Passage of the Compromise of 1850 temporarily assuaged the prosecession furor.

One of the most salient features of the Compromise of 1850 was a new and stronger Fugitive Slave Act, designed to defeat the personal liberty laws passed in some Northern states. These personal liberty laws had in turn been designed in part to ensure that legally free black citizens of the Northern states were not wrongly caught up by the operation of the old Fugitive Slave Act (1793) and carried away into slavery. The 1850 Fugitive Slave Act swept aside the legal protections of the personal liberty laws by providing a short and summary legal process for any black accused of being an escaped slave. The law was used to kidnap freeborn blacks and make slaves of them. It also demanded the cooperation of free-state law enforcement authorities and even the citizenry in the business of slave catching.

The significance of the Fugitive Slave Act of 1850 in a discussion of the cause of the Civil War is that it gives the lie to the oft-repeated claim that the Confederacy was somehow fighting for states' rights. Far from being the defenders of states' rights, Southern politicians were ready and eager to see the rights of Northern states trampled when it would serve the cause of slavery. Prior to the 20th century, no policy of the federal government infringed on states' rights as blatantly as did the fugitive slave laws, by which slave-state law, wielding the power of the national government, regularly reached into free states and imposed its will in defiance of the wishes of the citizens of those free states.

The rampant assertion of national authority in the operation of the Fugitive Slave Act of 1850 found its clearest expression in the 1859 U.S. Supreme Court case *Ableman v. Booth*. When newspaper editor Sherman Booth was arrested for helping to rescue an accused escaped slave from federal marshal Stephen Ableman, the Wisconsin state courts ruled in Booth's favor, declaring the Fugitive Slave Act of 1850 unconstitutional. Ableman appealed to the Supreme Court, and in an opinion written by ardent proslavery chief justice Roger B. Taney, the Court slapped down the Wisconsin judiciary, upholding the Fugitive Slave Act and decreeing that state courts could not interfere with federal laws.

Meanwhile, the course of the growing sectional crisis of the 1850s showed again and again that slavery was the only issue fueling the disagreement. When in 1854 Senator Stephen A. Douglas wanted to organize the remaining lands of the Louisiana Purchase so as to build a transcontinental railroad, the price of Southern congressmen's support was outright repeal of the Missouri Compromise's limitation on the northward spread of slavery and a reorganization of the new territories in such a way as to present the lands immediately west of Missouri, the new Kansas Territory, as an easy target for Southern acquisition and transformation into a slave state. In the subsequent guerrilla war that broke out in Kansas, the contending parties were not pro- and antitariff. Nor was Lecompton the capital of the territory's agrarian faction and Lawrence the headquarters of a rival corporate-capitalist regime. Rather, those two prairie settlements were the seats of pro- and antislavery factions, each bidding to govern the territory.

Throughout the conflict over Kansas and subsequently during the debates over the Supreme Court's *Dred Scott* decision and the election campaigns of 1858 and 1860, the issue of contention was virtually always slavery. If there were other issues of dispute between North and South in the years leading up to the Civil War, it is strange that neither side thought it necessary to debate any portion of their differences besides those pertaining to slavery. If the South was being unfairly characterized as the defender of slavery, its politicians certainly had plenty of opportunities during the debates of the 1850s to stake out some other position, but instead they repeated again and again the charge that Northern abolitionists were trying to interfere with the rights of slaveholders.

When Abraham Lincoln won election to the presidency in 1860, the State of South Carolina responded by declaring itself no longer a part of the United States. In its "Declaration of the Immediate Causes Which Induce and Justify the Secession of South Carolina from the Federal Union," the state's secession convention complained of the Personal Liberty Laws in 14 Northern states, which, so the South Carolinians claimed, interfered with their right to retrieve their slaves. Continuing, they accused the Northern states of having "denounced as sinful the institution of slavery," of having permitted the organization of abolition societies, of having assisted the escape and encouraged the insurrection of slaves, and of electing, without the aid of Southern votes, a president "whose opinions and purposes are hostile to slavery" and who had "declared that . . . the public mind must rest in the belief that slavery is in the course of ultimate extinction." As a further indignity, the South Carolinians complained, some Northern states had accorded citizenship to free blacks and allowed them to vote. Finally, the new regime in Washington did not propose to allow slavery to spread into the territories. For all of these reasons, the secessionists maintained, South Carolina was justified in leaving the Union.

As six other Deep South states followed South Carolina in secession, all attempts at compromise during the winter of 1860–1861 foundered on the issue of slavery expansion. The Republicans, stiffened by Lincoln's firm resolve, would readily agree to respect slavery's claims in the states where it existed but would not accept the institution's further expansion in the territories. Southerners refused to make any compromise that did not allow for slavery's expansion.

With the Confederacy up and running, its new vice president, Alexander Stephens of Georgia, in a March 21, 1861, speech in Savannah, enumerated the differences between the United States and the Confederate States. He congratulated himself and his listeners that their new form of government had "put at rest, forever, all the agitating questions relating to our peculiar institution[,] African slavery as it exists amongst us," which he claimed had been "the immediate cause of the late rupture"— meaning secession. Thomas Jefferson and the other men of the founding generation had been "fundamentally wrong," Stephens claimed, in asserting that slavery was a moral evil. Their mistake lay in their "assumption of the equality of races."

"Our new government," the Confederate vice president continued, "is founded upon exactly the opposite idea; its foundations are laid, its cornerstone rests, upon the great truth that the negro is not equal to the white man; that slavery, subordination to the superior race[,] is his natural and normal condition. This, our new government, is the first, in the history of the world, based upon this great physical, philosophical, and moral truth." No Confederate leader saw fit to contradict him, nor did any outcry among Southern newspaper editors or the Southern populace indicate any different view of the reasons for the conflict. Only in the years after the war did Stephens and others like him "discover" that in fact their cause had nothing at all to do with slavery but had instead concerned states' rights, constitutionalism, limited government, or resistance to Northern economic oppression.

In conclusion, the Civil War was the culmination of decades of dispute within American politics, and that dispute was about slavery. The seceding states announced slavery as the reason for their secession, and slavery was the breaking point for all attempts at compromise. Then vice president of the Confederacy proclaimed slavery as the cornerstone of the new nation and the reason for secession. For all of these reasons there can be no doubt that slavery was the only cause and the sole significant issue in the Civil War and that the conflict can justly and accurately be called the War of the Slaveholders' Rebellion.

Steven E. Woodworth

Further Reading

Abrahamson, James L. *The Men of Secession and Civil War, 1859–1861.* Wilmington, DE: Scholarly Resources, 2000.

"The Address of the People of South Carolina, Assembled in Convention, to the People of the Slaveholding States of the United States." Furman University, Nineteenth Century Documents Project, http://history.furman.edu/~benson/docs/SCaddress.htm.

Barney, William L. *The Secessionist Impulse: Alabama and Mississippi in 1860.* Princeton, NJ: Princeton University Press, 1974.

Channing, Steven A. *Crisis of Fear: Secession in South Carolina.* New York: Norton, 1974.

"Declaration of the Immediate Causes Which Induce and Justify the Secession of South Carolina from the Federal Union." Furman University, Nineteenth Century Documents Project, http://history.furman.edu/~benson/docs/decl-sc.htm.

Dew, Charles B. *Apostles of Disunion: Southern Secession Commissioners and the Causes of the Civil War.* Charlottesville: University Press of Virginia, 2001.

Fehrenbacher, Don E. *The Dred Scott Case: Its Significance in American Law and Politics.* New York: Oxford University Press, 1978.

Freehling, William W. *Prelude to Civil War: The Nullification Controversy in South Carolina, 1816–1836.* New York: Oxford University Press, 1992.

Holt, Michael F. *The Political Crisis of the 1850s.* New York: Wiley, 1978.

Levine, Bruce. *Half Slave and Half Free.* 2nd ed. New York: Hill and Wang, 2005.

McCardell, John. *The Idea of a Southern Nation: Southern Nationalists and Southern Nationalism, 1830–1860.* New York: Norton, 1979.

McPherson, James M. *Battle Cry of Freedom: The Civil War Era.* New York: Oxford University Press, 1988.

Miller, William Lee. *Arguing about Slavery: The Great Battle in the United States Congress.* New York: Knopf, 1996.

Morrison, Michael. *Slavery and the American West: The Eclipse of Manifest Destiny.* Chapel Hill: University of North Carolina Press, 1997.

Potter, David M., with Don E. Fehrenbacher. *The Impending Crisis, 1848–1861.* New York: Harper and Row, 1976.

Stampp, Kenneth. *The Causes of the Civil War.* 3rd ed. New York: Touchstone, 1992.

Walther, Eric H. *The Shattering of the Union: America in the 1850s.* Wilmington, DE: Scholarly Resources, 2004.

Waugh, John C. *On the Brink of Civil War: The Compromise of 1850 and How It Changed the Course of American History.* Wilmington, DE: Scholarly Resources, 2003.

27. In What Ways Did African Americans Affect the Outcome of the American Civil War?

Although it is true that endemic racist attitudes and beliefs kept many African Americans from enlisting to fight in the early years of the American Civil War (1861–1865), both the Union Army and the Confederacy used slaves and former slaves for manual labor and in other capacities. Following the Emancipation Proclamation of 1863, the Union Army established the United States Colored Troops (USCT), and while members of the USCT were initially placed in labor rather than in combat positions, ultimately they proved themselves to be worthy soldiers in battle. African Americans also played a large role in the Union Navy, constituting some 16 percent of all the sailors who served. Although it was not until the waning days of the war that the Confederacy considered the possibility of using African Americans in combat positions, it is estimated that about 9 percent of the 2 million soldiers and sailors who fought for the Union were African Americans. Thus, African Americans' contributions to the war effort, particularly in the North, cannot be overlooked or taken lightly.

Below, Dr. Julie Holcomb discusses how the actions of slaves and former slaves, both on and off the battlefield, hastened emancipation. She explains how Union occupation disrupted slave life on plantations, giving slave families a chance to escape and thereby weakening the institution of slavery. Whether by enlisting to fight as soldiers or by serving in a variety of supporting roles, African Americans went from supporting the liberators to becoming liberators themselves. Dr. William Pencak demonstrates that by 1863, African American soldiers had decisively proven their mettle in Union armies, perhaps nowhere more so than during the July 1863 assault against Fort Wagner near Charleston, South Carolina. He also points out that the desertion rate among Union soldiers was some 15 percent, while the desertion rate among African American troops was only 5 percent. Nevertheless, African American veterans were treated poorly after the war, particularly in comparison to white veterans, and were disproportionately impoverished. Dr. Paul Cimbala discusses the realization among many African Americans that in order to defeat slavery, they needed to take an active role against the Confederacy. They also had to prove that they could be as good as, if not better than, white soldiers. In addition, Cimbala notes that the Confederacy never committed itself to the idea of employing African Americans as combatants until it was close to defeat.

Background Essay

African Americans made a major contribution to the Union war effort during the American Civil War. By the end of the war, the United States Colored Troops (USCT) constituted approximately 10 percent of the Union Army. Yet during the first two years of the war, President Abraham Lincoln was reluctant to allow African Americans to join the army. Indeed, he was concerned that African American recruitment might further alienate the South, anger Northern whites, and jeopardize the loyalty of the border states. Consequently, many free African Americans who tried to enlist for service early on were turned away.

African Americans made up less than 1 percent of the population of the North, but the need for manpower led Frederick Douglass and the abolitionists to press Lincoln to let African Americans serve. Douglass and others expected that military service would produce full citizenship rights. The first official black enlistment system, although the total was set low, began after the summer of 1862 under U.S. congressional authorization.

By late 1862, Lincoln had determined that enlistment of African American troops would not only strengthen Union forces but, more important, also weaken the Confederate cause. Consequently, Lincoln threw his full-hearted support behind African American enlistment with the issuance of the Emancipation Proclamation, which took effect on January 1, 1863, as a war measure. The proclamation stated that slaves in rebelling states as of that date were freed from slavery and that the Union

Soldiers of the 4th U.S. Colored Infantry at Fort Lincoln, part of the defenses of Washington, D.C., during the Civil War. (Library of Congress)

would do everything in its power to ensure that they would remain free. Furthermore, the proclamation extended the first well-publicized invitation for African Americans to join Union military forces on land and at sea and served to entice many Northern and Southern African Americans to join the Union Army.

African American soldiers encountered much discrimination. They served in strictly segregated units led by white officers, many of whom were reluctant to promote African Americans because they feared that white soldiers of lower rank would not take orders from black superiors. As a consequence, by the end of the war only 100 or so African Americans were commissioned officers, and none rose higher than the rank of major. African Americans were also initially paid less than their white counterparts; they received $10 per month compared to $16 per month for white soldiers. Some USTC units refused to accept their pay in protest of the unequal treatment. Yielding to public pressure, Congress finally approved equal pay for the USTC in June 1864.

Duty assignments were also unequal. The USTC was often placed in labor rather than combat positions. Major General William T. Sherman, for example, refused to deploy African American troops to the front lines because he doubted their willingness and ability to fight. Instead, Sherman utilized African Americans in manual labor and support capacities. Furthermore, USTC troops often went into battle with inferior clothing, equipment, and weapons. African Americans also had to contend with the constant fear that Confederate forces might execute them on the spot or sell them into slavery if they were captured.

On July 18, 1863, the 54th Massachusetts (Colored) Infantry Regiment led an assault on Confederate Fort Wagner guarding Charleston, South Carolina. The unit suffered heavy casualties that day—281 of 600 men—in desperate hand-to-hand fighting. This battle and its meaning is the subject of the film *Glory* (1989). The courage displayed by the 54th Regiment that day was a strong signal to Washington and the North that freed men and liberated slaves could indeed prove highly effective soldiers.

Some 200,000 African Americans served, mostly in labor units. In fact, more than 15 percent of the 1860 free African American population of the North served, while more than 80 percent of the USTC hailed from the South. Total African American enlistment ultimately comprised as much as one-eighth of the Union Army in 166 regiments (145 infantry, 13 artillery, 7 cavalry, 1 engineer). African Americans also made up about 16 percent of Union naval strength. Although most African American soldiers were led by white officers, there were more than 100 African American lieutenants, captains, and surgeons, and this figure does not include some African Americans who passed as whites. It is estimated that more than 180,000 African Americans took part in more than 40 major battles and about 450 smaller engagements throughout the conflict. Some 68,000 African Americans lost their lives on the battlefield, and 23 black soldiers and 4 black sailors were awarded the Medal of Honor.

The USCT were disbanded at the end of the war, although Congress authorized four African American regiments thereafter. The 9th and 10 Cavalry and the 24th and 25th Infantry Regiments served with distinction in the American West and were the first regiments for black volunteers in the peacetime U.S. Army. Not until 1877 did the first African American graduate from West Point, however.

Military service remained a source of pride for African American families. For many years after the war, these families honored their relatives who had served in the war for the cause of freedom. Military service was also a source of respect in African American communities, and more than 130 African American veterans became political leaders during the Reconstruction era. However, with the end of Reconstruction in 1877, persistent racism and the emergence of Jim Crow laws blotted out the importance of African American military service during the Civil War. In fact, it was not until the 1950s that historians revived scholarly interest in the subject.

Rolando Avila

Perspective Essay 1. From Enslaved to Liberators

In 1860 as the United States hovered on the brink of civil war, 4 million African Americans living in the South were legally defined as articles of property. As such, African

American families could be separated at will by white masters, who wielded absolute power over them. Laws excluded slaves from education, property ownership, and even the freedom to leave their master's property. When the war came, many African Americans saw the need to participate directly in the fight to free the slaves. Whether on the home front or the battlefield, African American actions shaped the black experience of the American Civil War and hastened the arrival of black emancipation.

At the outbreak of war in 1861, African American men and women offered their assistance to the war effort. However, in the first several years of the war, Northern and Southern whites generally rejected all such offers from African Americans. Because secession, not slavery, was the pretext for the war, President Abraham Lincoln rejected any consideration of abolition or black military assistance through government means.

Still, the disruption of the Civil War, which forced men and women, black and white, free and enslaved, to labor in new settings and in new ways, ensured that black emancipation would be central to the war effort regardless of Lincoln's assurances to the contrary. By the time the war officially began with the surrender of Union forces to the Confederates at Fort Sumter, South Carolina, in April 1861, the ideas of war and secession had already severely disrupted plantation life throughout the South.

Moreover, as the war progressed, Union occupation affected slave families both positively and negatively. The presence of Union troops and the exigencies of the Civil War provided an unprecedented opportunity for slaves to escape. Although the bulk of escaped slaves in the antebellum years were men, during wartime large numbers of women, children, and older slaves sought safety behind Northern lines. Their escapes further disrupted life throughout the South.

For Northern whites, black freedom, however vague, carried a host of social problems that the federal government had yet to solve. In August 1861, Congress voted on the First Confiscation Act in an attempt to deal with the contraband question. The act allowed only for the confiscation of property, including slaves, used directly in the Confederate war effort; it did not grant freedom or deal with the question of freedom for slaves confiscated under the act's authority.

By mid-1862, the tide against emancipation had started to turn. In the summer of 1862 Congress passed the Second Confiscation Act, which prohibited under penalty of court-martial the return of fugitive slaves even to masters who claimed loyalty to the Union. Congress also abolished slavery in Washington, D.C.

Lincoln realized the inconsistency of fighting a government based on slavery without striking a blow at the institution. Slavery was indeed the core of Southern economic and social life; even though slaves were not engaged in combat, their service in support roles continued to aid the Southern cause.

As the summer of 1862 wound down, Lincoln drafted his Emancipation Proclamation. Union success in the Battle of Antietam on September 17, 1862, gave Lincoln the victory he needed, and on September 22 he issued his Preliminary Emancipation Proclamation. The final proclamation took effect on January 1, 1863.

African Americans recognized the implications of the Emancipation Proclamation and celebrated those who had brought about its existence. For slaves, the Union Army had always been seen as an army of liberation. After Lincoln issued his Preliminary Emancipation Proclamation, the army of liberation included a following of runaway slaves and free blacks.

Still, many Northern whites feared the consequences of arming black soldiers to fight for black freedom. In the summer of 1863 draft riots broke out throughout the North, revealing class and racial tensions. In New York City, antiblack and antidraft rioters burned a draft office and destroyed a black orphanage as well as the homes of well-known abolitionists and Republicans. Rioters linked black emancipation to amalgamation, a charge that antiabolitionists had leveled against abolitionists since at least the 1830s. The New York City riots, fueled in part by fears of miscegenation and loss of jobs to free African Americans, targeted New York City blacks.

The support rendered by Northern blacks to the Union war effort was critical. Just as white women took action to support Union troops in 1861 and 1862 through volunteer efforts and aid societies, African American women similarly focused their voluntary efforts on helping other African Americans. Initially, they sent aid to former slaves in the South. After the Emancipation Proclamation was issued, black women took a more active role in soldier relief. Just as white women had done at the outset of the war, African American women formed soldiers' aid societies.

On May 22, 1863, the Union War Department established the Bureau of Colored Troops to oversee black recruitment and create examining boards to screen applicants for officers' commissions. The United States Colored Troops (USCT) mustered 7,122 officers and 178,895 enlisted men. By war's end, African Americans made up 12 percent of the Union Army, had participated in 41 major battles and 449 smaller actions, and had earned 16 Medals of Honor.

In sharp contrast, African American sailors were an active part of the Union Navy from the beginning of the Civil War. Indeed, the navy provided African Americans with the best opportunity to actively support the Union war effort. African American naval service dated back to the American Revolution, and many African Americans possessed maritime skills gained through service in the merchant marine in the first half of the 19th century. Black sailors received equal pay and an equal share of all prize money from captured Confederate merchant ships and blockade-runners. An equal standard of equipment, decent medical care, similar opportunities to earn distinction in combat, and an equitable naval criminal justice system also ensured that black sailors had a better wartime experience than did black soldiers. Furthermore, the navy retained control of its recruiting responsibilities, thus eliminating much of the racism that pervaded state recruitments for the army. Black sailors were primarily urban Northern free blacks or foreign blacks, while black soldiers were largely rural slaves.

Although black men were consistently barred from military service for the Union Army early in the war, they were included in the Confederate Army from the beginning. However, black Confederate military service was built on the conventions of Southern society, which put blacks to work performing the menial tasks of heavy labor. Slaves and conscripted blacks also built fortifications, expanded river defenses, repaired rail lines, and assisted in the manufacture of armaments. In the early years of the war, there was no talk in the Confederacy of arming slaves for combat. Generally, black soldiers who served the Confederacy did so because they were conscripted, coerced by their masters or other whites, or sought economic gain or protection for their families and communities. There is no evidence that blacks fought to support the South or its so-called peculiar institution.

The adoption of the Thirteenth Amendment in January 1865 forever settled the status of slavery in the United States and "placed reunification at the forefront of ex-slave families' quest for freedom." Although the Emancipation Proclamation did not free a single slave, the amendment prepared the way for the expansion of civil rights that were later guaranteed for African Americans in the Fourteenth and Fifteenth Amendments.

Popular support for abolition grew as war casualties mounted. The elections in the fall of 1864 provided the final impetus for passage of the amendment. Lincoln claimed his overwhelming victory in his reelection bid as a mandate on the abolition amendment.

With ratification of the Thirteenth Amendment and Union victory in 1865, African Americans witnessed and participated in their transcendence from slavery to freedom. In February 1865 after the Confederate evacuation of Charleston, South Carolina, the Twenty-First USCT and detachments of the Fifty-Fourth and Fifty-Fifth Massachusetts Regiments were the first Union troops to enter the city. As Colonel Charles B. Fox of the 55th Massachusetts put it,

> Words would fail to describe the scene which those who witnessed it will never forget—the welcome given to a regiment of colored troops by their people redeemed from slavery. . . . Cheers, blessings, prayers, and songs were heard on every side. Men and women crowded to shake hands with men and officers.

The enslaved had become the liberators.

Julie Holcomb

Perspective Essay 2. The African American Experience in the Civil War

Some 178,000 African American soldiers served in the Union Army during the American Civil War. Before 1862, those who sought to serve openly were turned away. However, some African Americans definitely served as members of their local units. Only as white volunteers became scarce were African Americans welcomed to enlist. Benjamin Butler, military commander of Louisiana, organized the Louisiana Native Guard when the Union conquered New Orleans and much of that state in 1862. He employed African American officers who had served with distinction in earlier battles, but when Butler was replaced, so were the African American officers. The 54th and 55th Massachusetts Regiments were the first African American regiments mustered in the North and accepted recruits from other Northern states as well as escaped slaves.

Perhaps a quarter of all African Americans who enlisted were from the North; the rest were mostly former slaves from the South. As with all other African American units during the war, they were segregated and commanded by white officers. Some 19,000 African Americans served in the U.S. Navy, which had always had black sailors. All in all, at the end of the war 9 percent of about 2 million soldiers and sailors who were mustered out of the service were African Americans.

At first African American soldiers were given noncombatant duties building camps and roads, repairing rail lines, and driving wagons, as white officers feared that they would not do well in combat. One African American soldier wrote to Secretary of War Edwin M. Stanton that "we expected to be treated as men but we have been treated more like dogs." African Americans were originally paid $10 per month regardless of rank. They mainly served as corporals and sergeants, although 111 were commissioned officers by the end of the war. They had $3 per month deducted from their pay, whereas white privates, in contrast, earned $10 a month in addition to a $3 clothing allowance, and higher ranks earned more money. The Massachusetts regiments refused to accept any pay at all rather than accept an inferior wage, even when the Commonwealth of Massachusetts offered to make up the difference. A few soldiers mutinied and were executed.

By the end of the war African American soldiers had proven themselves, most spectacularly in the heroic but disastrous assault on Fort Wagner near Charleston, South Carolina, on July 18, 1863, when two-thirds of the officers and half the rank and file of the 54th Massachusetts Regiment lost their lives. Union general in chief Lieutenant General Ulysses S. Grant employed large numbers of African Americans in the Overland and Petersburg Campaign against Richmond, as did Major General George Thomas in the final battles at Franklin and Nashville against Confederate general John Bell Hood's Army of Tennessee.

More than a fifth of the African American troops—36,000—died, 80 percent from disease, as opposed to 60 percent for the disease-related deaths of white soldiers because of inferior camps and also because more African Americans were in poorer health than their white comrades when they had enlisted. However, despite poor treatment, only about 5 percent of black soldiers, as opposed to 15 percent of whites, deserted.

The war provided African Americans with some of the skills needed for civilian occupations. Sixteen percent became noncommissioned officers and thus became leaders. Although there was no general policy, Northern abolitionists and white officers established schools to teach the mostly illiterate African American soldiers to read and write. The corporals and sergeants were taught, and they in turn taught the privates. Their protests for equal pay and combat duty, in addition to being able to march and fight alongside large numbers of other African Americans, instilled pride and a willingness to use their rights as citizens.

Most African Americans had enlisted in 1863 or later, and their three-year enlistments had not expired when the war ended. Thus, the Union regarded them as ideal occupation troops for the defeated South. Most African Americans resented this; they wanted to return to their families, correctly fearing that Southern whites not policed by Union troops would retaliate against African Americans. Those sent to Texas for garrison duty along the Mexican border mutinied as the United States was pressuring the French to leave that republic. African American troops in Jacksonville, Florida, mutinied, and several were executed. The African American troops who remained on garrison duty in the South proved to be targets for the governments reconstituted by ex-Confederates that President Andrew Johnson allowed to take power.

After the war, African American veterans suffered more from poverty and unemployment than white veterans. Over four times as many black as white veterans were jobless in the immediate postwar era. The Freedmen's Bureau had to feed and clothe thousands of homeless African American veterans discharged in Washington, D.C. Largely because African American Southerners did not obtain land at the end of the Civil War, most remained poor. Nevertheless, the 1890 census shows that there was a significant degree of geographic and economic mobility for African American veterans. Although most remained in their region of birth, there was a pronounced movement from the South to the North and from the country to cities—in short, to places where opportunity and freedom would be greatest.

A smaller percentage of African American veterans received government pensions. This was even more true of widows, because many African Americans did not legitimate their unions with official marriage ceremonies. Until 1890 veterans had to prove disability, and this required assembling witnesses and paperwork, notarizing documents, and traveling to pension offices. With average yearly incomes of about $250, many African Americans could not assemble the funds even to hire pension agents to take their cases. Others who did receive pensions often were obliged to take out loans at high rates, anticipating future checks.

Some African Americans used their war service to achieve distinguished careers. Most notable was Lewis Latimer, who served aboard the steamer *Massasoit* in the Union Navy and returned to his home city of Boston, where he learned mechanical drawing and later worked for Thomas A. Edison. Other well-regarded African

Americans received patronage posts in the Republican Party. Sergeant William H. Carney of the 54th Massachusetts was among 16 African Americans to win the Medal of Honor during the war.

African American veterans became involved in politics primarily during Reconstruction, when governments consisting of African Americans and Southern Unionists were protected by Union troops. Robert Smalls, who served as congressional representative from South Carolina for 10 years in the 1870s and 1880s, was perhaps the most famous of all the African American veteran politicians, having become known for leading the slaves who seized and captured the Confederate steamer *Planter.* One acting governor and three lieutenant governors of Louisiana were veterans of the Native Guard. Two of the men were the principal sponsors of Homer C. Plessy's lawsuit in 1896 that unsuccessfully challenged the segregation of railroad cars and led to the U.S. Supreme Court's famous "separate but equal" decision.

Some African American veterans used their education to instruct their countrymen. John H. Murphy founded the *Baltimore Afro-American,* which at the time of his death in 1922 had the highest circulation of any African American newspaper on the East Coast. Alexander Augusta and Charles B. Purvis were African American medical professors at Howard University and founded the National Medical Society of the District of Columbia when white doctors would not admit them into the American Medical Association.

Other veterans saw migration as their solution to prejudice. Entitled to 160-acre homesteads, African American veterans were among the leaders of the Exoduster movement of Southern blacks to Kansas in 1879. Alfred Fairfax of Louisiana was the first African American member of the Kansas legislature. Henry McNeal Turner, chaplain of the First United States Colored Infantry, served in the Georgia state legislature and as postmaster of Macon before deciding that African Americans could not live peaceably with dignity in the United States. A bishop of the African Methodist Episcopal Church, Turner never obtained many followers for his back-to-Africa movement because of lack of funds and reports of high death rates among those who emigrated.

For many years, the most notable monument to African American Civil War veterans was the frieze outside the the State House in Boston. Executed by Augustus Saint-Gaudens and completed in 1897, it depicts African American soldiers led into battle by Colonel Robert Gould Shaw. In 1998, the African American Civil War Memorial was dedicated in Washington, D.C. Here several 11-foot-tall statues of African Americans titled *The Spirit of Freedom* stand alone and do not share their glory with white officers. The names of more than 208,000 African American soldiers and sailors who served in the war are also etched into the memorial.

William Pencak

Perspective Essay 3. African Americans in the Union Army

After President Abraham Lincoln's call to arms, free African Americans in the North shared their white neighbors' eagerness to put down the rebellion. They offered their voluntary companies to the cause, and some men set out to form new fighting organizations for that purpose. These men understood that the war, at its heart, was a war against slavery. In 1861 unfortunately for these black patriots, the war remained a white man's fight, excluding blacks from state and federal service, a reality that had its legal foundation in federal law.

The bloody circumstances of a war that dragged on beyond anticipation led many Northerners to reconsider their stand on black soldiers. Even racists came to accept that African Americans, who in their minds were the root cause of the war, should share in the burden of death. During 1862 as the nation moved toward emancipation, Congress passed the Second Confiscation Act and the Militia Act, both of which pointed to the enlistment of black troops. Thus, African Americans would become a critical component of the Northern war machine.

During 1862 freemen and ex-slaves in Kansas, Louisiana, and South Carolina joined newly formed black regiments, not entirely with the support or the satisfaction of the federal government. After the beginning of 1863, however, Northern state governments, pressed to fill quotas, courted the African American population with heretofore unseen vigor within their state boundaries and beyond. The first Northern black regiment, the 54th Massachusetts, came into existence early that year, and soon Northern governors were competing for black volunteers. From its inception the 54th Massachusetts drew blacks into its ranks from across the North. Massachusetts was not alone in relying on far-flung recruiting. African American Martin Delany, for example, recruited in Illinois for Connecticut and Rhode Island regiments. Indiana, Illinois, and other states attempted to ward off this poaching to preserve the black male population for their own 1863 quotas. Because of the large numbers of escaped slaves who had entered their borders early in the war, those midwestern states had much larger populations of black men on which to draw than indicated by their 1860 census data.

Recruiting African Americans in many respects was no different from recruiting white men. Illinoisan James T. Ayers, who in 1863 was recruiting in Alabama, employed all the tactics that recruiters used to lure white men into the ranks. Some of Ayers's counterparts, especially among substitute brokers, were not necessarily as honest as he was in their dealings, sometimes promising extravagant bounties or tricking black men into enlisting by other means. For example, a New York newspaper reported substitute brokers kidnapping blacks after plying them with alcohol.

There were substitute brokers who threatened black men with arrest if they did not enlist, and some soldiers carried out similar threats.

There were some problems, however, that were unique to enlisting blacks both for the recruiters and the recruits. Recruiting for black regiments, as an officer of the 54th Massachusetts later reported, "was attended with much annoyance." Massachusetts agents recruiting in Philadelphia had to collect their volunteers in secret, keep them in small groups, and get them aboard trains to Massachusetts "one at a time . . . or under the cover of darkness," all "to avoid molestation or excitement." Also, recruiters had to deal with whites who ridiculed them and harassed their families for their associations with black regiments. As for the black men who joined, they too suffered ridicule and violence at the hands of "white rowdies, or pretended citizens." In June 1863 in Washington, D.C., blacks in uniform were attacked on the streets and could not count on the local police for assistance.

Eager to meet their quotas, states competed with one another for black enlistees in the occupied parts of the Confederacy as well as among the refugees in the North. Estimates of the numbers of blacks serving in the U.S. Army during the war vary, with numbers ranging from upwards of 179,000 to over 186,000. Of the lower figure, over 102,000 came from the Confederacy, with almost another 43,000 coming from the slave border states. Most of these enlistees from the slave states had probably recently been slaves, which suggests that the bondsman could legitimately claim to have participated in his own emancipation.

Northern free blacks and Southern contrabands enlisted for all the reasons their white counterparts did, including for the state and local bounties that were available to them. African Americans also understood from the start that they had to prove they were just as good as, if not better than, white men at war to earn a place as citizens when peace came. Blacks knew that the war's outcome would greatly shape their future as well as the future of their families, their communities, and their race. Black Massachusetts soldier James H. Gooding made it clear when he proposed that there were only two outcomes to the war: "one is slavery and poverty and the other is liberty and prosperity." Black men therefore had to take an active role in securing the positive outcome or forever face ridicule for not helping to bring about the end of slavery. As Gooding explained, "the least false step, at a moment like the present, may tell a dismal tale at some future date." But the risks they assumed were greater than those of their white counterparts. If captured, they could end up being enslaved or executed for participating in a slave rebellion.

Even slaves, who may have relished the thought of avenging the wrongs of slavery by fighting their former masters, understood the larger noble consequences of their enlistments. Their actions and sacrifices indicated their commitment to the cause of freedom. Some border state slaves risked their lives traveling through hostile country to join the Union Army.

The Confederate government never committed itself to tapping into the manpower reserves of its black population for soldiers until it was much too late to matter. The Confederacy relied on thousands of blacks to perform support duties that ranged from playing music to building defenses. But using free blacks and slaves as laborers and servants was one thing; sanctioning the arming of black men was another matter. The ideological contradiction of armed black men was simply too difficult to circumvent until March 1865, when the Confederacy agreed to enlist slaves.

There were nevertheless free blacks in the Southern states who sought places in the Confederate service. The Louisiana Native Guards of New Orleans, over 900 elite free men of color, volunteered for the state militia; after the fall of the city, only 108 of them joined the Union Army's First Regiment of Native Guards. In March 1863 in South Carolina, free black John Wilson Buckner was able to join an artillery regiment despite state law forbidding the arming of blacks because of his family's good reputation. There were probably some free people of color who passed for white and enlisted to complete their racial transition.

There were no black regiments regularly mustered into the Confederate Army. Groups of black men, slaves and free, however, helped to defend their communities on an ad hoc basis, while individual black slaves probably came to the aid of masters on the battlefield, even though the Confederate government did not sanction such actions. Some Union soldiers, for example, claimed to have witnessed blacks fighting against them.

Some of these black Confederates possibly fought willingly, but local commanders, in spite of government policy, forced blacks to take up arms against Union troops. For example, African American John V. Givens noted that in Virginia in July 1861, he encountered free blacks fighting in Confederate uniforms "that were pressed into the rebel service." Forty black deserters had been "forced to leave their families" by the Confederates. They wished to join the Union ranks, "but how disappointed they were when they found that they could not fight in our ranks against their oppressors." Some willing black men may very well have been found in the Confederate ranks. They became fine symbols for the postwar Lost Cause, but their contribution to the secession was negligible compared with what their brothers accomplished for the Union.

Paul A. Cimbala

Further Reading

Bennett, Michael J. *Union Jacks: Yankee Sailors in the Civil War.* Chapel Hill: University of North Carolina Press, 2004.

Berlin, Ira, Joseph P. Reidy, and Leslie S. Rowland, eds. *Freedom's Soldiers: The Black Military Experience in the Civil War.* Cambridge: Cambridge University Press, 1998.

Blight, David W. *Frederick Douglass' Civil War: Keeping Faith in Jubilee.* Baton Rouge: Louisiana State University Press, 1991.

Buckley, Gail. *American Patriots: The Story of Blacks in the Military from the Revolution to Desert Storm.* New York: Crown, 2003.

Clinton, Catherine. *The Black Soldier, 1492 to the Present.* Boston: Houghton Mifflin, 2001.

Cornish, Dudley Taylor. *The Sable Arm: Black Troops in the Union Army, 1861–1865.* Lawrence: University Press of Kansas, 1987.

Forbes, Ella. *African American Women during the Civil War.* New York: Garland, 1998.

Glatthaar, Joseph T. *Forged in Battle: The Civil War Alliance of Black Soldiers and White Officers.* New York: Free Press, 1990.

Haskins, Jim. *Black, Blue & Gray: African Americans in the Civil War.* New York: Simon and Schuster, 1998.

Mays, Joe H. *Black Americans and Their Contributions toward Union Victory in the American Civil War, 1861–1865.* Lanham, MD: University Press of America, 1984.

McPherson, James M. *The Negro's Civil War: How American Negroes Felt and Acted during the War for the Union.* Urbana: University of Illinois Press, 1982.

Ramold, Steven J. *Slaves, Sailors, Citizens: African Americans in the Union Navy.* DeKalb: Northern Illinois University Press, 2002.

Smith, John David, ed. *Black Soldiers in Blue: African-American Troops in the Civil War Era.* Chapel Hill: University of North Carolina Press, 2002.

Taylor, Amy Murrell. *The Divided Family in Civil War America.* Chapel Hill: University of North Carolina Press, 2005.

Tucker, Spencer C. *Blue and Gray Navies: The Civil War Afloat.* Annapolis, MD: Naval Institute Press, 2006.

Vorenberg, Michael. *Final Freedom: The Civil War, the Abolition of Slavery, and the Thirteenth Amendment.* New York: Cambridge University Press, 2004.

28. WHAT WAS THE PRIMARY REASON FOR THE CONFEDERATE DEFEAT IN THE AMERICAN CIVIL WAR?

From the moment the American Civil War ended, participants and then historians, as one wit once observed, have spilled more ink in writing about the events than the men who participated in them spilled blood—and more than 600,000 Americans were casualties during what historian James McPherson once called the central event in the

American historical consciousness. One of the key questions that contemporaries and scholars have addressed has been framed in two ways: why did the North win or, conversely, why did the South lose? Although historians have even argued over which is the better question, most of them can agree that the North was stronger industrially, politically, and diplomatically. Yet the South entered the war with a seeming advantage in military personnel and experience, and the Confederacy's battlefield successes in the war's first two years certainly attest to the possibility that the North could have lost. But it did not, and thus there is debate as to the primary reason for the South's military defeat in the Civil War.

Appropriately enough, three historians find different reasons. Dr. Jennifer M. Murray argues that the South's inability to develop and execute a viable military strategy proved to be the Confederacy's undoing. While the South had key moments to capitalize militarily, such as in the summer of 1863, poor decision making ultimately rendered them vulnerable to Union attack. Dr. Lee Eysturlid provides an economic interpretation of the South's defeat: an underdeveloped industrial base that could not keep pace with the demands of a long, drawn-out war. Eysturlid asserts that the Confederacy simply lacked what it needed, whether it was men or arms, money or food, to defeat the Union. Dr. Ethan Rafuse cites the "strategy of exhaustion"—the Southern hope that Northerners finally would tire of fighting—and its ultimate failure on several levels besides the battlefield. Nearly a century and a half after the Civil War ended, many of the battles at the heart of it continue to be fought, and historians continue to fight on their own ground as well.

Background Essay

During the American Civil War, the Union and the Confederacy were dissimilar in a number of ways—they had different political goals, military strategies, economic resources, and cultures. During the course of the war, many of those differences placed the Confederacy in a disadvantageous position that would bring its defeat in 1896.

Demographics might seem an obvious explanation for the Confederate defeat. Although a larger percentage of the population in the South joined the war (13.1 percent as compared to only 10.7 percent for the North), the Confederate states had a much smaller population. During the war the Union mobilized 2,800,300 men, while the Confederacy could muster only 1,064,200. The South's manpower shortage was complicated by the fact that slaves constituted a third of its total population. Although white Southerners were understandably reluctant to arm them, slaves and free blacks did contribute substantially to the Southern war effort as noncombatant laborers, wagon drivers, cooks, and messengers. In February 1865 with the South's prospects of victory slim, the Confederate Congress did authorize the use of black troops, to be granted their freedom in exchange for military service. Although several thousand enlisted, this change in policy came too late in the war to have any real effect.

Other aspects of its military hampered the Confederate cause. Although the South had military academies—the Virginia Military Institute, the South Carolina Military Academy, and the Georgia Military Institute—it lacked a national military academy. These schools were all relatively new (the oldest founded in 1837 and the newest founded in 1851), while the U.S. Military Academy at West Point had been in existence since 1802 and had a highly developed and standardized curriculum. Although several notable Southern generals (including Robert E. Lee, Thomas J. "Stonewall" Jackson, and Albert S. Johnston) were graduates of West Point, most Confederate officers were either graduates of one of these newer Southern academies or had no formal military education.

Military strategy was also an issue for the Confederacy. Although the Confederate Army won a number of battles, many historians have questioned the effectiveness of the offensive-defensive strategy used by the Confederacy. These scholars have suggested that the South should have remained more on the defensive in order

Major General Ulysses S. Grant's Union troops assault Confederate defenses in the Siege of Vicksburg. The surrender of this Confederate bastion on the Mississippi River in July 1863 was one of the most important Union victories of the American Civil War. (Library of Congress)

to achieve its goal of driving out Union forces. They have also pointed out that often the Confederate Army did not push the advantage when it possessed it. The South's forces were also spread too thin over a large expanse of territory, which also made communication and coordination difficult.

Economic differences also favored the North. It enjoyed a relatively balanced industrialized economy and far more developed infrastructure, which made the prosecution of a war much easier. By contrast, the South was almost entirely dependent on agriculture, with its chief export crop being cotton grown with slave labor. The manufacture of weapons and other essential military supplies was more difficult than in the North. Railroads were an excellent illustration of this economic disparity between the Union and the Confederacy. At the beginning of the war the North had 21,276 miles of track, while the South had only 9,000. This gap only grew larger during the war, when the Union laid down an additional 4,000 miles, compared to fewer than 400 miles in the Confederacy. Additionally, the North's railroads, which were accustomed to moving large volumes of goods and passengers from one place to another, were better maintained and used more innovative technologies. The South's railroads were antiquated and could not handle the enormous amount of traffic the war required. For the Union, the United States Military Rail Roads handled the transport and supply of troops, but no such centralized organization existed to regulate and coordinate Confederate railroads, which in any case sharply deteriorated during the war.

The nature of the Southern economy also negatively impacted the Confederacy's international relations. Southern diplomatic policies were based on King Cotton, which held that countries such as Great Britain and France would be inclined to recognize and assist the Confederacy because of their need for raw cotton for their textile industries. But this proved to be faulty thinking: large crops in previous years had created surpluses in European storehouses, and the Union blockade of the South drove the price of Confederate cotton so high that Britain and France turned to other suppliers. In the end, the large amounts of grain from farms in the North to Western Europe proved much more persuasive than the South's cotton.

In a more intangible sense, it can also be argued that it was harder for the South to win the war simply as a result of what winning would have required. In order to achieve its objective of becoming an independent nation, the Confederacy had to accomplish the daunting tasks of driving Union forces out of the South and maintaining—permanently—territorial sovereignty. It also needed to establish the new political, military, and economic institutions necessary for the functioning of the new nation. Not only was military morale important, but nationalist sentiment within the general Southern population was also critical to success. The fact that the majority of battles were fought on Confederate soil meant that the South witnessed much more devastation than the North, which both lowered morale and made the feeding and supply of armies more problematic. The Union, on the other hand, saw relatively little fighting on its own soil and needed only to subdue a rebellion through military might and return things to more or less the prewar status quo. It could also depend on well-established and smoothly operating institutions to accomplish this goal.

It is clear, then, that there were a number of factors that contributed to Confederate defeat and Union victory. The question of which, if any, was the most significant is a topic for historical debate.

Maxine Taylor

Perspective Essay 1. Ineffective Southern Military Strategy

The South lost the American Civil War primarily because of poor military strategy. When Confederate general Robert E. Lee surrendered his Army of Northern Virginia to Union lieutenant general Ulysses S. Grant at Appomattox Court House, Virginia, on April 9, 1865, Lee offered an explanation for the South's defeat: "The Army of Northern Virginia has been compelled to yield to overwhelming numbers and resources." Lee's statement does not, however, fully explain the Confederacy's defeat. Superior resources and overwhelming manpower do not guarantee victory, as is shown by the British defeat during the American Revolutionary War and by the United States in Vietnam. The South placed hundreds of thousands of courageous soldiers on the field led by competent generals, including Lee and Thomas J. "Stonewall" Jackson, but within four years Confederate armies and the Confederate nation were forced to surrender. A key factor in explaining the South's defeat was its inability to formulate and execute a viable strategy.

President Jefferson Davis and Confederate officials maintained that they were on the defensive. Yet the Confederacy's grand strategy was offensive-defensive. This strategy, designed to protect the vast territory of the South from a Union invasion, raised large armies and placed them in defensive postures in the South. This defensive strategy, however, became secondary at times. Whenever circumstances were thought to favor success, Confederate armies launched offensives, as seen in Lee's two invasions of the North in the fall of 1862 and the summer of 1863.

This was not the most effective strategy, and in the midst of the war Confederate generals debated the merits of the offensive-defensive policy. Thus, General Pierre G. T. Beauregard was foremost in criticizing this strategy. After the South's victory in the First Battle of Bull Run (Manassas) on July 21, 1861, Beauregard, eager to maintain the strategic initiative, urged Davis to amass Confederate manpower and drive on Washington, D.C. Davis rejected Beauregard's plan, and any momentum gained from victory in the war's first major battle was lost. If Davis had not remained steadfast to the offensive-defensive strategy and allowed Beauregard to exploit the advantaged gained from victory at Bull Run, the war might have turned out differently.

To some degree, however, the nature of the rebellion and the expectations of the Southern people dictated military strategy. In *The Confederate War,* historian Gary Gallagher argues that the key to success lay in maintaining high morale and nationalistic sentiment, which could only be achieved through decisive battlefield victories. Gallagher believes that the adoption of the offensive-defensive strategy fits into this mind-set. When Confederate armies scored victories, morale increased; when Southern armies suffered defeats, morale plummeted. Confederate officials, however, failed to appreciate the role of morale and failed to understand that battles, military strategies, and popular support were intrinsically linked.

Perhaps Confederate victories came at too high a cost. In *Attack and Die,* Grady McWhiney and Perry Jamieson contend that in the early stages of the war the "Confederates bled themselves nearly to death" by adhering to archaic tactics, particularly frontal assaults. They argue that the South would have benefited by adapting a more defensive strategy that would have helped negate their numerical disadvantage in manpower. McWhiney and Jamieson calculate that "the South lost more than 175,000 soldiers in the first twenty-seven months of the war." Clearly, the South failed to appreciate its most precious resource, the Southern soldier, and should have pursued a strategy such as that employed in the Battle of Fredericksburg rather than that of the Battle of Gettysburg.

Another contributing factor to the South's defeat was the failure of government and military officials to understand the larger picture of the war, specifically the importance of the western theater. Lee seems to have been guilty of this misunderstanding. In the summer of 1863 instead of pushing Davis to send reinforcements to Confederate armies in the West, Lee pushed for his own offensive into Pennsylvania. Little effort was given to reinforce Lieutenant General John C. Pemberton's forces at Vicksburg, and as a result on July 4, 1863, the fortress fell, and the Mississippi River was opened to Union forces. Only after the Army of Northern Virginia's defeat at Gettysburg and the surrender of Vicksburg did Lee approve the transfer of troops from his army to the West.

By the time the South came to recognize problems with its military strategy, it was too late. Only when the Confederacy's final hours approached did its leaders consider altering their strategic policies and war aims to reconsider the idea of arming and emancipating slaves. In *Confederate Emancipation,* Bruce Levine argues that the proposal might have been more "viable" if enacted earlier in the war, perhaps as early as 1861 after the Confederate victory at Bull Run, when slavery and black freedom were secondary to the North's war aims.

Arguably, the South should have adopted a different military strategy. For the North to win the war, it had to conquer and subjugate the South and its people, an objective finally accomplished by the spring of 1865. On the other hand, the Confederacy's best course of action would have been to mirror the strategies of the colonists during the American Revolutionary War, adopting a defensive strategy with minimal but well-timed and well-placed offensives. The colonists focused on keeping a viable army on the field and wearing down Britain's support for the war. The South, however, failed to recognize the advantages of assuming a defensive military strategy. Adopting a more efficient strategy, recognizing the importance of the western theater, refraining from bloody and costly offensives, and making use of all available manpower, including slaves, may have changed the outcome of the Civil War.

Jennifer M. Murray

Perspective Essay 2. Economics Was the Primary Cause

"We are resisting revolution. . . . We are not engaged in a Quixotic fight for the rights of man. . . . We are conservative." The revolution that *De Bow's Review,* perhaps the most influential of Southern journals, is here referring to was the Industrial Revolution. The outcome of this revolution could clearly be seen in the American North, while the rejection of the revolution could be seen with equal clarity in the South. The South's resulting lack of an industrial base (a necessity in modern warfare) would prove to be the primary reason, although by no means the only reason, for its defeat in the American Civil War.

In many ways, the Civil War was the first modern conflict in that it was the first war conducted by an industrialized power (the North) whose goal was the conquest of the entirety of its enemy (the South). Wars in Europe that occurred after the end of the Napoleonic Wars and since the coming of industrialization had given a notion of the potential economic needs of modern armies. But none of these wars (for example, the Crimean War and the Prusso-Danish War) had been on a somewhat similar scale to the American Civil War. They also lacked the motivating differences in ideology that the American war brought.

When the war began on April 12, 1861, neither the North nor the South were prepared for the economic demands of the conflict. Neither side could foresee the necessity of fighting a war to the bitter end, which is what would come to pass. As would happen in all modern wars since, both sides assumed that the war would be a short if brutal affair, with the other side quickly giving way. This was shown to be a false hope.

In every critical measure of what would be economically important, the North had a distinct advantage. As the war started, for example, the entire industrial output of the Confederacy was only half that of the state of New York. There was only one major ironwork facility in the South capable of producing heavy cannon, the Tredegar Iron Works in Virginia. The railroad, which was the greatest of 19th-century logistical innovations in war, was another area of Northern dominance. Large-scale troop movements, plus the continual movement of thousands of tons of supplies daily, became more difficult as the far fewer Confederate rail lines and rolling stock wore out or were destroyed.

The Confederacy therefore lacked any major industrial centers. It had less than half the rail lines of the North (some 9,000 miles versus more than 21,000). Also, more than 90 percent of steam locomotives and rolling stock were manufactured in the North. Further, railroads in the South were considered light service, geared to move cotton to ports. There was only one rail link between the western and eastern theaters of operation in the South, a grave strategic liability during the war.

Because of its lack of industry, the South could not produce critical items such as boots and uniforms. The South was also incapable at the war's start of feeding itself. Since its production was of nonedible agricultural goods such as cotton and tobacco that were destined for industry, it was actually the American Midwest that was the heart of corn and grain output. Northern agricultural output, thanks to machines such as the McCormick reaper, actually grew during the war, not only feeding Northerners but also making up for European crop failures through exports that tied those countries to the North.

Since Southern leaders realized that catching up would be impossible as well as socially unappealing, they pinned much of their hope on buying what they needed from Europe. When the Northern blockade made this increasingly more difficult, Southern national leadership, which ironically was based on the concept of minimal government, had to turn to direct control of production. The South never did develop an effective industrial policy nor, it can be argued, could it have. It failed to organize production, and the lack of any effective banking system meant that cash to fund industrial growth floundered in the hyperinflation created by the printing of ever more paper money.

Such a lack of war materials necessarily dictated Confederate strategy, at least to a greater degree than is generally the case, and also limited Confederate effectiveness tactically. There was always a lack of supplies, be they guns, ammunition, uniforms, shoes, or food. Hopeful of foreign recognition and potential intervention, which meant access to British and French industry, the South launched two costly and failed invasions of the North. The need for boots drove Robert E. Lee's advance elements during his Pennsylvania invasion to detour into the town of Gettysburg for supplies, a move that precipitated the fatal battle there. Although there are too many variables in a war for any one reason to be *the* reason for its outcome, clearly economics was the primary cause of the Confederate defeat in the American Civil War.

Lee W. Eysturlid

Perspective Essay 3. A Triumph of Northern Will and Power

In the Amrican Civil War, Southern military leaders faced the challenge of convincing the North to accept Confederate independence, while the North's challenge was to persuade the Southern people to give up establishing an independent nation. As President Abraham Lincoln correctly pointed out in July 1861, the Civil War was essentially "a people's contest" in which the hearts and minds of the people in both the North and the South would be the ultimate determinant of victory and defeat.

The failure of the Confederacy to achieve military victory in the Civil War was attributable to many factors. In the aftermath of the surrender of his army at Appomattox in April 1865, Robert E. Lee told his army that it had been "compelled to yield to overwhelming numbers and resources." Others have blamed weak military and political leadership, the outcome of specific military engagements, a faulty strategy for applying the South's military resources, the contradiction between the South's claim to be fighting for liberty and freedom and its commitment to slavery, the fact that the South's particular geography provided too many viable routes of invasion for Union armies, the South's failure to secure recognition and more vigorous assistance from France and Great Britain, and the inadequacy of a political ideology that prized states' rights and limited government when military, economic, and diplomatic success demanded the vigorous exercise of centralized power.

All of these factors played important roles in shaping the outcome of the Civil War, and few serious historians accept singular explanations for Confederate defeat. Thus, debate largely revolves around how much one emphasizes one factor relative to the others in explaining why the South's will and ability to wage war was inferior to that of the North. It is clear, though, that there was a principal reason behind this: Confederate military and political leaders, owing to military realities and the society they served, had to ultimately stake the success of their cause on their ability to defeat the North in a conventional war of exhaustion, which the superiority of Northern material and human resources and the North's unshakable resolve to preserve the Union made an exercise in futility.

Lee certainly had a point in citing the North's great material and manpower superiority in his explanation for defeat. Given the scale of the challenge it faced in bringing the South back into the Union, it is hard to see how the North could have prevailed had it not possessed considerable advantages over the South in terms of resources. Yet the North's quantitative advantage in resources would have been meaningless if its society had not possessed the qualitative human capital necessary to mobilize and manage resources effectively. That the North had this was a consequence of the decades prior to the war, when its society had developed in a different and, as events proved, decidedly superior way to that of the South. While the South remained a largely agricultural and reactionary Jeffersonian society politically, socially, and economically, the North developed in a progressive, modern, Hamiltonian direction. Thus, the wartime North was a far more industrial, commercial, mechanical, educated, and open society that had the political, economic, and cultural tools—above all the acceptance of an activist central state—necessary to possess and benefit from its advantages in resources.

The Confederacy's political and military leadership organized and maintained armies that were capable of effectively conducting conventional operations. They did not, however, fully take advantage of the resources at their disposal to develop a truly effective guerrilla force whose efforts, if properly directed, encouraged, and coordinated, could have complemented the efforts of the Confederacy's conventional forces and further complicated Union efforts to conduct operations or reassert federal authority in the South. Nor did the Confederate leadership secure the sort of assistance from foreign governments that the Patriot side had secured during the American Revolutionary War.

While the ability to secure foreign assistance was largely beyond the control of the Southern political and military leadership, their failure to develop an effective guerrilla force and incorporate it into their strategy and take advantage of potential areas of sanctuary were the consequence of fundamental strategic choices. These decisions were largely dictated by the nature of the society they were defending and the purposes for which the South had left the Union and the government of the Confederate States of America had been organized. According to the men who created it and directed its defense, the rationale for an independent Confederacy that made it worth fighting for was a belief that the South's distinctively traditional way of life was mortally threatened—and the cornerstone of this was the institution of black chattel slavery. Southern leaders convinced their followers that only by breaking away from the old Union and forming their own independent government could the people of the South truly secure their society.

Moreover, the white people of the South arrogantly believed that the society they created a separate government to defend fostered qualities in its people that made them superior to the people of the North. Aware of this sentiment, Confederate military leaders understood that they risked losing popular support if they appeared unwilling to confront any Northern effort to violate the South's territorial integrity. This made it necessary that they attempt to defend as much territory as possible. Also compelling in convincing the South's military and political leadership that they had to contest every possible inch of Confederate soil through conventional military means was the fact that the South's most valuable regions in terms of manpower, agricultural resources, and industrial production were close to the frontier. Thus, a strategy of abandoning parts of the Confederacy to take advantage of sanctuary or lure the Union troops into the South so they would be vulnerable to guerrilla operations was neither suitable nor acceptable.

To be sure, pro-Confederate Southerners did not hesitate to engage in guerrilla warfare, which was often very effective. Yet the idea of making unconventional operations a central feature of Confederate strategy received a decidedly cool reception from Southern military leaders—and for compelling reasons. First, the chaotic and informal nature of guerrilla warfare could not be easily reconciled, if at all, with the conservative, hierarchical social, economic, and political ethos that the South seceded from the Union to preserve. In addition, to most effectively employ guerrilla warfare, Northern armies would have to actually be in occupation of significant sections of the South. This was something that moral, economic, and political factors—not least of which was the large segment of the Southern population that remained loyal to the Union—made it impossible for the Confederacy's leadership to accept.

The enthusiasm for guerrilla warfare was surely dimmed by the Confederacy's battlefield victories in 1861 at Big Bethel, Wilson's Creek, and, above all, First Manassas. The results of these engagements seemed to offer compelling evidence that the South could prevail in a conventional war with the North. Any doubts that might have subsequently arisen regarding a mainly conventional strategy by a tidal wave of Union military victories in early 1862 were undoubtedly allayed by a series of Confederate victories that followed Robert E. Lee's ascendance to command in June 1862. These probably delivered the final blow to those who championed making unconventional warfare a focus of Confederate strategy. Thus, the people of the Confederacy staked their fate on their armies' ability to win a conventional war against a foe possessing overwhelming advantages.

The problem for the Confederacy, however, was that the North's major armies proved too powerful and resilient for the South to achieve the truly decisive battlefield successes necessary for a strategy of annihilation to succeed. Likewise, a strategy of attrition that would gradually destroy Union armed forces over time, rather than in a single engagement or campaign, was unfeasible for the materially inferior Confederacy.

This left Confederate strategists to pursue a strategy of exhaustion in which they endeavored to erode the North's will to wage war. Here, however, was the most significant obstacle to Confederate victory. The terms that the Confederacy demanded for ending the war were simply never acceptable to the North. For all the great battlefield successes achieved by Southern armies, at no point did the South come close to pushing the North to the point that it was willing to consent to recognition of an independent Confederacy. Northern politicians understood that to the vast majority of their constituents, Confederate independence was unacceptable. Republican electoral victories reflected not so much the determination of the Northern populace that to let the Confederacy survive was unacceptable but more so confidence that the Lincoln administration and its policies were the most effective means for achieving that end.

Of course, Republican politicians recognized that the overwhelming sentiment of the Northern public was for making whatever effort was necessary to preserve the Union. Otherwise, they would not have made so great an effort to foster in the minds of the electorate a perception (which many Republicans no doubt sincerely held to be true) that opposition to their party and its policies was synonymous with disunionism. Thus, the outcome of the Civil War was determined by this combination of the Southern people's decision to pit the fate of their nation on winning a conventional war of exhaustion and the superiority of Northern resources and its people's unbreakable resolve to preserve the Union.

Ethan S. Rafuse

Further Reading

Anderson, Bern. *By Sea and by River: The Naval History of the Civil War.* New York: Da Capo, 1989.

Beringer, Richard E., Herman Hattaway, Archer Jones, and William N. Still Jr. *Why the South Lost the Civil War.* Athens: University of Georgia Press, 1986.

Bradford, Ned, ed. *Battles and Leaders of the Civil War.* New York: Appleton-Century-Crofts, 1956.

Buell, Thomas B. *The Warrior Generals: Combat Leadership in the Civil War.* New York: Crown, 1997.

Clark, John Elwood. *American Railroads in the Civil War.* Baton Rouge: University of Louisiana Press, 2004.

Davis, William C. *Look Away! A History of the Confederate States of America.* New York: Free Press, 2003.

Davis, William C. *Stand in the Day of Battle: The Imperiled Union, 1861–1865.* Garden City, NY: Doubleday, 1983.

Donald, David, Jean H. Baker, and Michael F. Holt. *The Civil War and Reconstruction.* New York: Norton, 2001.

Donald, David Herbert, ed. *Why the North Won the Civil War.* Baton Rouge: Louisiana State University Press, 1960.

Eicher, David J. *The Longest Night: A Military History of the Civil War.* New York: Simon and Schuster, 2001.

Ekelund, Robert B., Jr., and Mark Thornton. *Tariffs, Blockades, and Inflation: The Economics of the Civil War.* Wilmington, DE: SR Books, 2004.

Escott, Paul D. *Military Necessity: Civil-Military Relations in the Confederacy.* Westport, CT: Praeger Security International, 2006.

Foote, Shelby. *The Civil War: A Narrative.* New York: Random House, 1958–1974.

Gallagher, Gary W. *The Confederate War: How Popular Will, Nationalism and Military Strategy Could Not Stave off Defeat.* Cambridge, MA: Harvard University Press, 1997.

Grimsley, Mark, and Brooks D. Simpson, eds. *The Collapse of the Confederacy.* Lincoln: University of Nebraska Press, 2001.

Hattaway, Herman, and Archer Jones. *How the North Won: A Military History of the Civil War.* Urbana: University of Illinois Press, 1981.

Levine, Bruce. *Confederate Emancipation: Southern Plans to Free and Arm Slaves during the Civil War.* New York: Oxford University Press, 2006.

Linderman, Gerald. *Embattled Courage: The Experience of Combat in the American Civil War.* New York: Free Press, 1987.

McPherson, James M. *Battle Cry of Freedom: The Civil War Era.* New York: Oxford University Press, 1988.

McPherson, James M. *Drawn with the Sword: Reflections on the American Civil War.* Oxford: Oxford University Press, 1996.

McWhiney, Grady, and Perry D. Jamieson. *Attack and Die: Civil War Military Tactics and the Southern Heritage.* University: University of Alabama Press, 1982.

Rafuse, Ethan S. *Robert E. Lee and the Fall of the Confederacy, 1863–1865.* Lanham, MD: Rowman and Littlefield, 2008.

Sutherland, Daniel E. *A Savage Contest: The Decisive Role of Guerrillas in the American Civil War.* Chapel Hill: University of North Carolina Press, 2009.

Tucker, Spencer C. *Blue & Gray Navies: The Civil War Afloat.* Annapolis, MD: Naval Institute Press, 2006.

Weigley, Russell F. *A Great Civil War.* Bloomington: Indiana University Press, 2004.

Wise, Stephen R. *Lifeline of the Confederacy: Blockade Running during the Civil War.* Columbia: University of South Carolina Press, 1988.

29. WAS OTTO VON BISMARCK LARGELY RESPONSIBLE FOR THE UNIFICATION OF GERMANY IN 1871?

On January 18, 1871, at the Palace of Versailles and with the princes of the various German states in attendance, King Wilhelm I of Prussia announced the formation of the German Empire, with himself as emperor. Otto von Bismarck, who had been minister-president and foreign minister of Prussia since 1862, was named chancellor of Germany a few months later. A conservative Prussian statesman with an uncanny knack for politics and adroit diplomacy, Bismarck helped create the first modern welfare state and remained doggedly loyal to his king even when the two men disagreed, which was not an infrequent occurrence. At the same time, Bismarck was headstrong, outspoken, and authoritarian. But his revolutionary conservatism served Germany well, as did his vision for great power politics, which aided in the establishment of a long period of peace on the previously war-torn European continent. At the helm of Prussian and German politics for more nearly 40 years, Bismarck certainly spurred on the formation of Germany as a modern, unified nation-state, although historians continue to debate whether unification would have happened without his influence.

In the first perspective essay, Dr. Timothy C. Dowling asserts that Bismarck was indeed the key force behind German unification. He ultimately achieved unification through his calculated creation and then management of a series of crises, most notably the Prussian war against the Habsburgs and the Franco-Prussian War. Dowling does, however, explore several alternate (albeit unlikely) paths that might have led to unification without Bismarck's guiding hand. In the second essay, Dr. Spencer C. Tucker acknowledges the critical role played by Bismarck in uniting the German states. Tucker carefully traces the events in Bismarck's life and career, including the postunification era. In doing so, he views Bismarck's archconservative worldview and his devotion to realpolitik (reality politics) as the pivotal keys to his success, for Bismarck accomplished what the liberals who had preceded him could not. Nevertheless, Tucker suggests that Bismarck's actions helped lay the foundations of World War I, which in turn precipitated World War II. By contrast, Dr. Lee W. Eysturlid contends that unification could have happened without Bismarck's influence. Eysturlid examines the rise of German nationalism and highlights two previous moments in history—the German Revolution of 1848–1849 and the constitutional crisis of 1859–1861—in which unification might also have occurred.

Background Essay

Born at the family estate of Schönhausen in Brandenburg (now Saxony-Andhalt) just east of the Elbe on April 1, 1815, Otto Edward Leopold von Bismarck came from a prominent noble family. After briefly studying law at the University of Göttingen, he finished his education at Friedrich Wilhelm University, Berlin. Entering the Prussian civil service as a court reporter, he had to resign for neglect of his duties. Bismarck then took over management of the family estates.

Marriage and election to the Prussian United Landtag in 1847 changed the sometimes wild Bismarck. In Berlin he was known as a conservative, even a reactionary. After the reversal of the Revolution of 1848 in Prussia, he served as Prussian representative to the Diet of the German Confederation at Frankfurt during 1851–1859, then Prussian ambassador to Russia during 1859–1862 and to France in 1862.

Recalled to Berlin in September 1862 by his friend, Minister of War Albrecht von Roon, Bismarck accepted from King Wilhelm I the post of minister-president (premier) of Prussia. The king was then in a deadlock with the Landtag (lower house of parliament) regarding expansion of the army and the means to pay for it, and Bismarck believed that the Crown should openly defy the wishes of the nation's elected representatives. Bismarck became, as he put it, "the best hated man in the country," knowing that if successful his running roughshod over the Landtag would be forgotten. Bismarck believed that it was not "speeches and the will of the majority" but "iron and blood" that would bring the unification of Germany under Prussian leadership.

Using taxes collected in defiance of the Landtag, Roon and chief of the Prussian General Staff General Helmuth von Moltke expanded, reformed, and readied the Prussian Army. Bismarck then engineered war with Denmark over the duchies of Schleswig and Holstein, persuading Austria to fight on Prussia's side in 1864. Under Bismarck's orchestration, relations with Austria steadily deteriorated. Securing the neutrality of France and Russia, he goaded Austria into a conflict that saw Prussia and Italy at war with Austria and virtually all the other German states.

The Austro-Prussian War (Seven Weeks' War) of June–August 1866 went as Bismarck planned, establishing Prussia as the dominant German power. Bismarck treated Austria leniently, taking some territory in northern Germany and forming the states north of the Main River into the North German Confederation. The war also brought Bismarck's triumph over the Landtag, which passed a bill of indemnity that legalized his actions since 1862.

Bismarck isolated France diplomatically, then secretly secured nomination of a Prussian Catholic prince as king of Spain. Bismarck then manipulated the ensuing diplomatic crisis, in which the French government declared war on July 19, 1870. The Franco-Prussian War (1870–1871) pitted France against Prussia and the remainder of the

Otto von Bismarck, minister-president of Prussia (1862–1890) and chancellor of Germany (1871–1890). Late in life he boasted that he had caused three wars. He is usually credited with having masterminded the unification of Germany. (Chaiba Media)

German states and ended in a decisive German victory. While the war was still in progress, at Versailles Bismarck proclaimed establishment of the German Empire on January 18, 1871. In the ensuing Treaty of Frankfurt (May 1871), he took from France most of Alsace and Lorraine and imposed an indemnity of 5 billion francs, two and a half times the cost of the war to Prussia.

Now raised to prince and made chancellor of the new German Empire, Bismarck devoted his energies to establishing the new imperial institutions. In foreign affairs his chief goal was to isolate France. He first tried for a tripartite arrangement with Austria-Hungary and Russia, but when this fell apart he opted for the Dual Alliance with Austria in 1879. He then secured a secret bilateral arrangement with Russia known as the Reinsurance Treaty in 1887.

While Bismarck enjoyed great success in foreign affairs, his record in domestic developments was far less satisfactory. The 1870s were marked by a struggle with the Catholic Church, and in the 1880s there was a struggle with the socialists. Both were failures for Bismarck. When Wilhelm II became kaiser in 1888, he and Bismarck clashed on a number of issues—chiefly who would rule Germany—and Wilhelm forced him to quit his post on March 18, 1890. From retirement, Bismarck criticized Wilhelm II's policies of dropping the Reinsurance Treaty in 1890 and opposed the kaiser's plan to build a powerful navy, which he predicted would drive Britain into the arms of France. Bismarck died at his estate of Friedrichsruh on July 30, 1898.

Bismarck changed the face of Germany and of Europe, but his exaltation of the policy of blood and iron encouraged his countrymen to worship power at the expense of justice and helped bring on World Wars I and II. In domestic affairs he placed excessive power in the hands of the kaiser and failed to train the German people in the art of self-government. As Georg von Bunsen summed up, Bismarck "made Germany great and Germans small."

Spencer C. Tucker

Perspective Essay 1. The Father of German Unification

Otto von Bismarck was the key figure in the unification of Germany during the 19th century because he created and managed a series of crises between 1859 and 1870 that resulted in the creation of a German nation-state.

While serving as the Prussian representative to the German Confederation since 1851, Bismarck garnered a reputation as a staunch conservative, a devout Prussian monarchist, a devoted opponent of Austria, and a casual, pragmatic supporter of

German nationalism. These qualities earned him a term in virtual exile as Prussian ambassador to St. Petersburg shortly after the appointment of the moderate regent Prince William in 1858. Upon becoming king, however, William also became more conservative and soon found himself in conflict with the Prussian House of Deputies (Abgeordnetenhaus) over the military budget. Convinced that Bismarck was the only politician capable of resolving the crisis, William appointed him minister-president and foreign minister of Prussia in September 1862. In his famous "Blood and Iron" speech, made only a week after his appointment, Bismarck tried to convince the House of Deputies that providing the military with money would lead to German unification. The gambit failed, as the parliamentarians refused to grant increased taxes in return for promises. Bismarck nonetheless proceeded to collect the monies, exploiting a legally dubious loophole in the Prussian constitution. To validate this maneuver, over the next eight years Bismarck managed and created a series of crises that essentially reversed the process: he worked to unify Germany under Prussian authority.

The first opportunity presented itself with the death of Frederick VII of Denmark in November 1863, which reopened the Schleswig-Holstein question. The matter boiled down to whether Holstein would remain in the German Confederation; Bismarck chose to make his stand on this issue. He convinced the Habsburg representative to the confederation to join in an ultimatum to the Danish ruler of Holstein, which led to a joint war against the Danes. Bismarck convinced the Habsburg leaders first that an invasion of Denmark proper was necessary and then, in 1864, that the annexation of the two provinces was desirable. He next contrived a spat with the Habsburgs over administrative issues, convinced by his friends Helmut von Moltke, the Prussian chief of staff, and Albrecht von Roon, the Prussian minister of war, that even though the Habsburg troops had garnered most of the laurels in the Danish War, the Prussian Army could defeat the Austrians in a short war.

This proved correct in 1866, as the Prussians decisively defeated the Habsburg forces at Königgratz (Sadowa). Although most Prussian leaders wanted to press on to conquer Vienna, Bismarck convinced the Prussian king to not only call a halt but also negotiate a relatively lenient peace. The Habsburgs lost no land and paid a relatively small indemnity; the only price Bismarck asked was that the Austrians remove themselves from German affairs. The Prussian deputies, swept up in the glory of the moment, approved his monetary policy retroactively. The northern German states were organized into a confederation under Prussian leadership, and the southern states (which had mostly sided with Austria) were obliged to sign treaties of defensive alliance. Bismarck believed that he had moved as far toward German unification as possible and turned his attention to internal affairs.

In 1870, however, another opportunity presented itself in the question of succession to the throne of Spain. Bismarck supported the rather weak claim of a minor German prince against the candidate backed by France. This upset Emperor

Napoleon III, who believed that Prussia owed France for its neutrality during the 1866 war. Bismarck readily withdrew, but the French demanded further guarantees. Bismarck subtly altered the Prussian king's rejection of these demands in the infamous Ems Telegram. The French took offense, as Bismarck had hoped, and declared war—an event for which the Prussians were completely prepared and the French not at all. Prussia's army once again carried the day, aided by the other German states, which had joined in not simply out of obligation but also in a spasm of nationalism. The treaty ending the Franco-Prussian War in 1871 thus also created a unified German state, led by Prussia.

No other political figure in Germany likely could have accomplished this. Few other politicians had the connections that Bismarck enjoyed with the leaders of the Prussian Army, and these—along with the force of his personality—allowed him to convince the Prussian leaders to settle the war with Austria quickly and with little apparent gain. Finally, it is hard to imagine another politician who would have dared alter an official message from the king to spur a war. German unification was largely the work of Bismarck.

The Habsburgs and their chancellor, Prince Klemens von Metternich of Austria, had actually worked to stifle all manifestations of German nationalism after the Napoleonic Wars ended in 1815. In the war scare of 1840–1841, Metternich led the smaller German princes to oppose any action that might lead to German unification on the grounds that this would deprive them of their independence. Time after time, the German princes followed this principle: freedom before unity.

The German Confederation was thus ironically one of the main obstacles to unification. Created in 1815 by the Congress of Vienna, it is sometimes viewed as a step toward unification because it reduced the number of German states from well over 2,500 to a mere 41. The aim of the union, however, was to keep Germany divided. Prussia was strengthened against France, while Austria was weakened in Germany by the loss of its territories on the Rhine, but the Habsburgs, as presidents of the confederation, were still the leaders within Germany. The new larger states remaining were intended to hold the balance between Prussia and Austria. The British, Danish, and Dutch monarchs, moreover, were still represented in the confederation by virtue of their holdings within Germany. In 1854 when the most important middle German states favored intervention in the Crimea, Prussia blocked any action for fear that Austria would benefit. Five years later, the confederation was similarly paralyzed during the Austro-Italian War. The confederation could not act independently in international affairs, and it was almost always divided internally.

The depth of the political and ideological divisions within the German Confederation made both reform and revolution unlikely—as the events of 1848–1849 revealed. Rebellions sparked by economic disruptions took on political dimensions early in 1848 and forced rulers in nearly every state of the confederation to promulgate a constitution or institute liberal, democratic reforms. Advocates of German unity, however, could not agree on a political program. The National Assembly that met at Frankfurt in May 1848 debated endlessly whether Germany should be a republic or a constitutional monarchy and what states should be included. When the Habsburg restoration of late 1848 finally forced the issue and the National Assembly offered Frederick William IV the title of German emperor on favorable (nonrepublican) terms, the Prussian king refused. There was no political force within the confederation strong enough to create a unified state.

Recognizing this, both Austria and Prussia attempted to use economic means to foster unity. Prince Felix von Schwarzenberg, the new Habsburg chancellor, proposed the creation of a broad free-trade zone, the "Empire of 70 Millions," which would include the states of the German Confederation and all of the Habsburg lands. Prussia naturally declined. The Prussian foreign minister, Josef Maria von Radewitz, suggested instead that the remaining states of the German Confederation join the Prussian customs union (Zollverein) that had dominated northern Germany since 1835. Scholars have often noted its potential for creating a unified German state, but the Zollverein purposely lacked a political program. The smaller states guarded their independence jealously, and in 1849 Hanover, Bavaria, Württemberg, and the Habsburg territories refused to join Radewitz's "Prussian Union" for fear that they would be subject to Prussian law. In the end, Austria and Prussia negotiated the Punctuation of Olmutz (1850), which essentially restored the German Confederation of 1815. All subsequent attempts to foster the creation of a German nation-state on either economic or political foundations collapsed as well.

It is impossible to know what would have happened if Bismarck had not appeared on the scene. Austria's projects for the reform of the German Confederation based on free trade might eventually have won an overwhelming majority and forced Prussia to the table. It is equally likely that the Progressive Party, successor to the Nationalverein, might have won enough support for its vision of a reformed federal German state led by Prussia. The two German powers might also have resorted to war in any case. Had Bismarck not cut the Gordian knot and allowed the Prussian military reforms to continue, however, Austria might have triumphed. The two states might also have fought to a draw, exhausting themselves in the process and leaving the door open for Bavaria, Saxony, or some other state to seize leadership of the confederation. Even if Prussia did win, without Bismarck's restraining influence King William and his military advisers would likely have carried out their plans to humiliate the Habsburgs, thus alienating the other German states and preventing unification. Bismarck played an indispensable role in the unification of Germany. It is possible, but extremely difficult, to imagine how a German state might have come into being otherwise. It certainly was not inevitable.

Timothy C. Dowling

Perspective Essay 2. German Unification Largely Bismarck's Work

The realization of the long-sought German goal of national unification was achieved in 1871 largely due to the work of one man, minister-president (premier) of Prussia Otto von Bismarck. The great powers of Europe had long played on the division of Germany, seeking to keep the various German states in rivalry with one another. The French Revolutionary and Napoleonic Wars had revealed German weakness but also worked to create strong German nationalist sentiment rooted in a common language and culture. The customs union known as the Zollverein, established in 1819 and expanded thereafter, was also working to unite the German states economically. Yet liberal efforts to achieve the unified German state by peaceful means had met resounding failure in the Frankfurt Assembly during the revolutionary year of 1848–1849. It was the archconservative Bismarck who accomplished what the liberals could not.

In 1847, Bismarck won election to the United Diet in Berlin. There he established himself as a staunch conservative. In 1848, he was one of only two deputies to vote against King William I giving Prussia a constitution. After the reversal of the Prussian Revolution of 1848, the Crown rewarded Bismarck for his loyalty by appointing him the Prussian representative to the Diet of the German Confederation at Frankfurt. Bismarck served there during 1851–1859 and went out of his way to offend the Austrians whenever possible. Prussia had long played second fiddle to Austria in the Germanies, and in November 1850 in the Punctuation of Olmutz, Austrian pressure forced King Frederick William IV to abandon his plan for a federation of the German states without Austria in favor of a restoration of the German Confederation of 1815 under the presidency of Austria. In his dispatches from Frankfurt, Bismarck reiterated his conviction that the chief principle of any union of the German states had to be the exclusion of Austria.

Fearful that his confrontations with the Austrians at Frankfurt might actually bring war, in 1959 the Crown assigned Bismarck as ambassador to Russia. During the next three years in St. Petersburg, he established a close relationship with Russian minister of foreign affairs Prince Aleksandr Gorchakov. This would subsequently pay handsome dividends for Prussia.

Appointed ambassador to France in the spring of 1862, Bismarck was recalled to Berlin that September by his friend, Minister of War Albrecht von Roon, and accepted from William I the post of minister-president of Prussia. Prussia was then in political crisis because the king had deadlocked with the Landtag (lower house of parliament) over expansion of the army and the means to pay for it. Bismarck held that the Crown should simply collect taxes and spend the money as it wished in defiance of the wishes of the nation's elected representatives.

The master practitioner of realpolitik (politics of reality) and a staunch Prussian nationalist, Bismarck was determined to make Prussia the preeminent power in the Germanies and believed that any steps were justified in achieving that end. Using state revenues spent in defiance of the Landtag, Roon and the chief of the Prussian General Staff, General Helmuth von Molte, worked to expand, reform, and ready the Prussian Army for war. Bismarck meanwhile won the gratitude of the Russian government by closing Prussia's borders with Poland during the Polish revolution against Russia during 1863–1864.

Bismarck set the stage for future confrontation with Austria in the first of his wars, that against Denmark in 1864. The cause of the war was bound up in the fate of the two duchies of Schleswig and Holstein, which had large German populations. Bismarck cleverly manipulated a crisis caused by the Danish parliament's determination to make the two duchies part of Denmark (they were then under the personal rule of Danish king Christian IX). Danish incorporation of the duchies led to war with the German Confederation, a conflict that was popular throughout Germany and in which Austria was obliged to fight on Prussia's side. Prussia took the lead in the fighting, and the Danes went down to defeat; the war proved the value of the Roon-Moltke reforms. Bismarck then arranged a settlement in August 1865 whereby Prussia administered former Danish Schleswig while Austria controlled Holstein, an enclave between Schleswig and Prussian territory to the south.

Under Bismarck's careful manipulation, relations between Russia and Austria steadily deteriorated. Before war could occur, Bismarck needed to secure the neutrality of Russia and France. Russian neutrality was ensured because Russia was Austria's rival in the Balkans, and its leaders were grateful to Bismarck for his actions regarding Poland.

Bismarck traveled to France in October 1865 and secured a pledge from French emperor Napoleon III that in the event of war between Prussia and Austria, France would remain neutral. In return, Bismarck promised compensation to France in the form of territory along the Rhine. Foolishly, for it helped Prussia win the subsequent war, Napoleon encouraged Prussia to take the Kingdom of Italy as an ally against Austria. Napoleon believed that Austria would win a war with Prussia, but he calculated that in any case the struggle would be prolonged and that with both Austria and Prussia weakened, France would then be able to intervene and impose a settlement of its own on the exhausted adversaries.

Having now secured his flanks, Bismarck goaded Austria into war. In April 1866, he instructed the Prussian representative to the Frankfurt Diet to propose abolition of both the German Confederation and the Diet, establishing in its place a new German assembly that would be elected by universal suffrage but exclude Austria and all its lands. Proof that Prussia was the culprit in this is seen in that virtually all the other German states sided with Austria against Prussia and Italy.

The conflict lasted just seven weeks, far too short for France to intervene and impose a settlement as Napoleon had planned. Italy tied down Austrian forces in the south, while the Prussian Army easily defeated the other German states in the north and then ended the war in the great set-piece Battle of Koniggratz (Sadowa) in Bohemia on July 3, 1866. The war decided 120 years of dynastic rivalry between Prussia and Austria over which power would dominate the Germanies. Bismarck brushed off King William I's demands for a harsh settlement and treated Austria with great leniency, taking some territory in northern Germany, dissolving the German Confederation, and forming the states north of the Main River into the North German Confederation. There was no indemnity. The war also brought Bismarck's triumph over the Landtag. He secured from that body passage of a bill of indemnity legalizing all of his illegal actions since 1862.

Bismarck knew that he could not complete his work of German unification without first defeating France, and he now worked to isolate that country. In a masterful deceit, Bismarck manipulated a crisis over his efforts to install a Prussian prince on the throne of Spain. The French foolishly stepped into his trap and declared war on July 19, 1870.

The Franco-Prussian War of 1870–1871 found France isolated in Europe. Austria was angered over revelations of French intrigue in the 1866 war, and Russia was still friendly to Prussia. The war pitted France against not only Prussia but also the southern German states. (After the Austro-Prussian War, Bismarck had asked Napoleon to put in writing his aspirations regarding the Rhineland. Bismarck then shared this draft treaty with the rulers of the southern German states of Baden, Württemberg, and Bavaria and secured from them military alliances that bound all to fight together in the event of a French attack.)

The Franco-Prussian War ended in a decisive French defeat. Already before the end of the war, with Paris under siege, Bismarck had proclaimed at the German military headquarters of Versailles the establishment of the German Empire. In the Treaty of Frankfurt on May 10, 1871, that ended the war, Bismarck handed France a harsh settlement. Germany took from France most of the French eastern provinces of Alsace and Lorraine and imposed an indemnity of 5 billion francs—2.5 times the cost of the war to Prussia—to be paid within three years. German troops were permitted a triumphal parade through Paris and then were to remain in occupation of northeastern France until the indemnity was paid. This punitive settlement ensured a burning French desire for revanche (revenge) that would find fruition in World War I.

Raised to the status of prince and made chancellor of the new empire, Bismarck reigned as the dominant European statesman of the second half of the 19th century. He now devoted his energies to establishing the institutions of and then preserving and strengthening his new creation. A new constitution granted universal suffrage and placed final authority in the hands of the emperor and Prussian king William I, whom Bismarck largely controlled.

Bismarck changed the face of Germany and of Europe, but his exaltation of the policy of blood and iron encouraged his countrymen to worship power at the expense of justice. In domestic affairs he had placed excessive power in the hands of the kaiser and had failed to train the German people in the art of self-government. Bismarck boasted in retirement that he had personally caused three wars, yet there is every reason to assign him responsibility for laying the stage for World War I, which in turn spawned World War II.

Spencer C. Tucker

Perspective Essay 3. German Unification Would Have Occurred Even without Bismarck

To read most histories, there is only Otto von Bismarck, the politician; Albrecht von Roon, the minister of war and military reformer; and Helmuth von Moltke, the chief of the Prussian General Staff—the trio who unified Germany from scratch against all odds. This is at best simplistic, although all three men by the 1860s played pivotal roles. The fact that a unified German political state did not emerge for 60 years after the Napoleonic Wars was more the result of a series of failures than the result of a deliberate process.

Could the German states have united before 1871 without Bismarck to force unification? While this did not happen, there were two significant periods when it was possible. This was during the Revolutions of 1848–1849 and the constitutional crisis of 1859–1861. In both of these, the pillars of Prussian absolutism and the complex force of German liberalism came together but also in both cases failed.

The forces of nationalism that motivated Germans to contemplate a unified political state emerged in full force during the period of the French Revolutionary and Napoleonic Wars. Outside of France, the Germans were probably the people most affected by the new ideas unleashed by the revolution. Linked to nationalism—the concept that peoples of the same language and cultural background should live together in one nation-state—was the other great mover of the early 19th century: the Industrial Revolution. It added powerful economic forces to the changes already begun by the rise of nationalism.

Prussia was the key state in the creation of Germany, mostly because of its overall size and the military prominence it had gained as the dominant Central European state outside that of Austria since the Thirty Years' War (1618–1648). Prussia's success was owing to a combination of three factors. The first was a series of astute and aggrandizing rulers, most famously Frederick II (the Great), who ruled during 1740–1786. Second was the fact that the landed nobility, the Junkers, had been converted into supporters of the monarchy as military officers and civil servants. Third and of critical importance was the rise of a highly centralized, effective, and dedicated bureaucracy, one of the foundations of the modern German state.

German idealism and liberalism were the intellectual underpinnings that would give Prussian and then German imperial absolutism their moral legitimacy. Liberalism, as a philosophy, first came to the fore in the great period of intellectual and cultural creativity that the German lands experienced between 1770 and 1830. This period produced intellectual giants such as Immanuel Kant, Johann Gottfried von Herder, and Georg W. Hegel, all pillars in German thought. They departed from the rationalism of the rest of the Enlightenment period and moved toward a more intense humanism. Herder's concept of the organic individuality of each national culture combined with the unique character of the *Volksgeist* (people's spirit) laid the foundations for German nationalism.

The economic and demographic revolution was also important. In the first half of the 19th century, the population in the area that would become Germany rose from just over 25 million to more than 34 million. The same area also saw serious economic problems in its primary sector, agriculture. Prices remained depressed during the period, and many peasant families, due to debts, were forced off their lands, becoming laborers. Many of the nobility did poorly as well, with large numbers selling ancestral lands to the rising bourgeoisie. The old prenational ties of nobility and peasant were disintegrating. Also critical was the creation by Prussia of the Zollverein, or "German" customs union, which enhanced trade and railroad construction. German business began to seek the advantages of further union: a single currency, centralized banking, uniform weights, and commonly recognized law for all the territories within the treaty area.

The first of the great potential moments for German unification came with the Revolutions of 1848. The grievances felt in the German states concerning poor harvests, declining trade, and notions of social injustice brought revolutionary action across the German states. Prussian king Frederick William IV often spoke of German unity, although his notions were more romantic than realistic. When unrest broke out in Berlin in March 1848, the king initially offered concessions, including a willingness to draw up a constitution and the imminent calling of the Prussian United Diet (the Landtag). An event that saw cavalry dispersing a crowd in front of the palace, the removal of troops from Berlin, and the humiliation of the king ended Frederick's willingness to cooperate. Had the incident at the palace not occurred, he might have gone along with the nationalistic events that were occurring. The king had offered to "merge" Prussia with a new German empire and to assume leadership of the German princes. While this floated as a possibility, Frederick William also called an assembly into being that drafted and offered a constitution.

In 1848, liberal nationalists from the German states and German parts of the Habsburg monarchy met in Frankfurt to form a parliament. Their intention was to establish a unified state under a relatively liberal constitution. One of the great hurdles to be overcome at Frankfurt was agreement on a form of government, although all wanted a single German state. Had the parliament met when Frederick William was in a conciliatory frame of mind, it might have drawn up a modestly representative constitution for a unified state. Because Frederick William was not interested in democracy, the state structure would have been at best a federation, loosely linked by a general assembly and the princes. In 1849 when another pressing issue, that of what constituted Germany territorially, was resolved and the Frankfurt Assembly offered the imperial crown to Frederick William, it was too late, and he rejected it as "a crown from the gutter."

The real questions of an 1848 unification came with the potential reaction of a powerful Habsburg monarchy, which likely would not have accepted a unified Germany under Prussian (as opposed to Austrian) control. Russia also could not be expected to favor a unified German state on its borders. The possibility that German unification would be opposed by force materialized when Frederick William advanced his own plan for a federated state but then backed down under direct Austrian pressure with the support of Russia in the Punctuation of Olmutz in 1850, what German nationalists referred to as the "Humiliation of Olmutz."

The second potential pre-1871 unifying period came after the 1858 mental breakdown of Frederick William, who was then succeeded by his brother William (who officially became king as William I on Frederick William's death in 1861). During the constitutional conflict that ensued, the result of William's effort to reconcile existing constitutional limitations with his notion of kingly power, he seriously toyed with abdicating. Had he taken this course, his son, Crown Prince Frederick William, would have taken the throne. Far more liberal-minded and backed by his strong-willed English wife, William looked to establish a Prussian parliament along British lines. Such a liberalized representative government would have cleared the way for a progressive move to a federated, economically linked German state. William, however, chose to rule, and the chance for the installation of a real democratic government in Prussia was lost.

Finally, had William chosen not to pick Bismarck as minister-president in 1861, it is still difficult to see Prussia and the rest of the non-Austrian German states remaining politically adrift into the 20th century. Even without Bismarck, the Prussians certainly would have rejected Denmark's efforts to gain control of Schleswig-Holstein. Without Austrian assistance, something concocted by Bismarck, it seems likely that Prussia could have handled the war and come out as Germany's protector. Minister of War Roon, however, might not have been able to get the funding he needed to reform and build the Prussian Army, thereby delaying Prussia's ability to fight Austria alone. Rather, a later war between Austria and Prussia and its northern German allies could have cemented a northern German-Prussian political-economic state. Bavaria, and perhaps Saxony, would have waited to join until later, then likely motivated by the wish to be a part of growing German economic power. It is possible to envision by 1900 a limited federated German state, with Prussia as its core but perhaps not dominated by it. This is a much preferable picture, as it is hard to see a less threatening Germany as one of the primary causes of World War I.

All of these cases remain counterfactual history. What is clear is the reality of the growth of a real sense of German nationalism in the 19th century. Divisions would remain, especially between southern Catholics and northern Protestants, but those divisions exist today. What is hard to imagine, Bismarck or no Bismarck, is that nationalism—the great emerging driver of so many modern states—would not have succeeded in the German states due to the lack of a single man.

Lee W. Eysturlid

Further Reading

Breuilly, John. *Austria, Prussia and Germany, 1806–1871.* London: Longman, 2002.

Breunig, Charles. *The Age of Revolution and Reaction, 1789–1850.* New York: Norton, 1970.

Cecil, Lamar. *Wilhelm II: Prince and Emperor, 1859–1900.* Chapel Hill: University of North Carolina Press, 1989.

Crankshaw, Edward. *Bismarck.* New York: Viking, 1981.

Darmstaedter, Friedrich. *Bismarck and the Creation of the Second Reich.* New York: Russell and Russell, 1965.

Eyck, Erich. *Bismarck and the German Empire.* New York: Norton, 1964.

Feuchtwanger, Edgar. *Bismarck.* New York: Routledge, 2002.

Geiss, Immanuel. *The Question of German Unification, 1806–1996.* London: Routledge, 1997.

Hamerow, Theodore S. *The Social Foundations of German Unification, 1858–1871: Ideas and Institutions.* Princeton, NJ: Princeton University Press, 1969.

Hargreaves, David. *Bismarck and German Unification.* London: Palgrave, 1991.

Headlam, James Wycliffe. *Bismarck and the Foundation of the German Empire.* New York: Putnam, 1899.

Heuston, Kimberley Burton. *Otto von Bismarck: Iron Chancellor of Germany.* New York: Franklin Watts, 2010.

Hollyday, Frederic B. M. *Bismarck.* Englewood Cliffs, NJ: Prentice Hall, 1970.

Hope, Nicholas Martin. *The Alternative to German Unification: The Anti-Prussian Party, Frankfurt, Nassau, and the Two Hessen, 1859–1867.* Wiesbaden, Germany: Franz Steiner, 1973.

Kent, George O. *Bismarck and His Times.* Carbondale: Southern Illinois University Press, 1978.

Lerman, Katharine Anne. *Bismarck.* New York: Pearson Longman, 2004.

Palmer, Alan. *Bismarck.* New York: Scribner, 1976.

Pflanze, Otto. *Bismarck and the Development of Germany*, Vol. 1, *The Period of Unification, 1815–1871*. Princeton, NJ: Princeton University Press, 1990.

Price, Arnold H. *The Evolution of the Zollverein: A Study of the Ideas and Institutions Leading to German Economic Unification between 1815 and 1833*. New York: Octagon Books, 1973.

Rich, Norman. *The Age of Nationalism and Reform, 1850–1890*. New York: Norton, 1977.

Siemann, Wolfram. *The German Revolution of 1848–49*. New York: St. Martin's, 1985.

Steinberg, Jonathan. *Bismarck: A Life*. New York: Oxford University Press, 2011.

Taylor, A. J. P. *Bismarck: The Man and the Statesman*. New York: Knopf, 1969.

Wiener, George S. *Bavaria and the German Confederation, 1820–1848*. Cranbury, NJ: Associated University Presses, 1977.

30. DID THE UNIFICATION OF GERMANY MAKE A GENERAL EUROPEAN WAR INEVITABLE?

Prussian king Wilhelm I declared the unification of Germany on January 18, 1871. This occasion came at the end of the Franco-Prussian War, the third and last of Otto von Bismarck's wars to unify Germany. During the course of the first two conflicts, the Danish-Prussian War of 1864 and the Austro-Prussian War of 1866, Bismarck had managed to unite the northern German states in a confederation under Prussian control, leaving only the southern German states outside of the Prussian sphere. By 1870 France and its leader Napoleon III were the last significant obstacles to complete German unification, so Bismarck endeavored to provoke a war with France. He succeeded when France declared war on Prussia in July 1870, and the resulting Prussian victory brought the remaining southern German states under Prussian control, enabling the establishment of the Second German Empire. The replacement of numerous independent German states with a single nation-state did much to upset the balance of power in Europe in the latter part of the 19th century. This became particularly evident as the European political culture became increasingly antagonistic toward the end of the century, fueled in large part by competition among the European powers for overseas colonies. The major European powers soon began positioning themselves within the entangling web of military alliances that set the stage for World War I. While there is little doubt that the unification of Germany upset the balance of power in Europe, the question of whether or not German unification made a general Euro-pean war inevitable is not so easily answered.

In providing their own assessments of this historical dilemma, three historians each make clear that there were a multitude of factors that contributed to the outbreak of World War I. In the first perspective essay, Dr. Thomas Adam begins with a discussion of what he characterizes as "several misconceptions about the creation of the German Empire in 1871." In his subsequent discussion of German unification, Adam asserts that Bismarck was fully aware of the fact that the unification of the German states upset the balance of power and assesses the diplomatic steps he subsequently took to preserve European peace. Avoiding any conflict that could threaten the new German state quickly became Bismarck's overriding goal. In the second essay, Dr. Eleanor L. Turk points out that the European response to the wars of German unification re-vealed no great sense of threat. She also argues that Bismarck's diplomatic actions following those wars indicate that the new German Empire was not immediately in-terested in further continental conquests. Dr. Frank W. Thackeray agrees with that assessment, asserting that the new Germany only became interested in expansion fol-lowing the rise to power of Kaiser Wilhelm II in 1888. Nevertheless, Thackeray ac-knowledges the significant challenges to European peace resulting from the unification of Germany.

Background Essay

It is often said that wars settle nothing. This is rarely if ever the case, and certainly it was not the case with the Wars of German Unification, for there were significant immediate, intermediate, and long-term consequences not only for the countries involved but also for all of Europe.

The German-Danish War of 1864 immediately changed the status of Schleswig and Holstein, with Schleswig being administered by Prussia, while Holstein was administered by Austria. Holstein is German to this day, while Schleswig remained German until a 1920 plebiscite sent parts north of what had been the Dannevirke Line to Denmark and parts south to Germany, where things remained after the defeat of Nazi Germany (which had overrun Denmark in 1940) in 1945.

After defeating Austria in 1866, Prussia annexed Schleswig, Holstein, Hanover, Hesse-Kassel, Nassau, and Frankfurt am Main. This powerful "army attached to a state," as it was said earlier of Prussia, formed the core of the North German Con-federation from 1866 and the German Empire from 1871 to 1918.

The Austro-Prussian War of 1866 also permanently removed Austria from Ger-man affairs, which it had variously controlled or manipulated since the Middle

Ages. Austria was forced to concede an autonomous position to the Magyars of Hungary, whom they had defeated centuries earlier, bringing into being the cumbersome Austro-Hungarian Empire (Dual Monarchy), which lasted until 1918.

After the Franco-Prussian War of 1870–1971 Germany took the provinces of Alsace and Lorraine from France, which would not regain them until the Treaty of Versailles in 1919 following World War I.

The second and third wars of German unification realized a large, unified German state, what liberal nationalists could only dream about for the previous 50 years. The first step was the North German Confederation after the defeat of Austria, the second and more significant step was the creation of the German Empire, proclaimed in January 1871 during the Franco-Prussian War.

Having resolved two important parts of the German question—whether there would be a German state and whether Austria would be included in it—German chancellor Otto von Bismarck moved quickly to resolve the rest of the question: whether the German state would possess representative institutions with a meaningful, orderly, and lawful role in governmental decision making.

Minister-President of Prussia Otto von Bismarck reads Prussian king Wilhelm I's proclamation establishing the German Empire, in Versailles, France, on January 18, 1871, during the Franco-Prussian War. (Three Lions/Getty Images)

Bismarck's answer was most definitely a compromise. Both the North German Confederation and its successor, the German Empire, had a diet in Berlin, the Reichstag, elected on the basis of universal manhood suffrage and equipped with the power of the purse: taxes would never be collected illegally again. This crucial concession, written into the so-called Indemnity Bill of 1866, was very explicit about the rule of law, which immediately resolved the problem of raising loans to fund the expensive military establishment of the new state.

However, the political power of the Reichstag did not extend as far as, for example, the British House of Commons, for the kaiser (emperor) retained significant unlimited decision-making powers, such as the signing of treaties with foreign powers and the declaration of war. That Germany was not a democratic nation where elected representatives ruled the country was evident.

This authoritarian side of Bismarck's constitution began to create crises in German politics 20 years later with the rise of the labor movement and its political arm, the Social Democratic Party of Germany, which demanded a genuine democracy. These long-term sources of instability tore the country apart domestically during World War I and explain the eventual creation of that genuine—albeit unsuccessful—democracy in 1918/1919.

That Austria and Prussia could defeat Denmark came as little surprise to the other European powers, nor did its defeat upset relations between the great powers. Prussia's lightning victory over Austria and much of the German Confederation, on the other hand, caused considerable diplomatic jockeying. When France entered the fray against Germany alone in 1870, Paris, London, and St. Petersburg anticipated a French victory and, when the opposite occurred, reacted with alarm.

European history in the 19th and 20th centuries would be haunted by the new German question, namely what to do about the mighty military juggernaut in the center of the continent. In past centuries when one of the great powers grew too strong, the others had formed coalitions to bring the threatening country down, most recently in the Napoleonic Wars when Great Britain, Prussia, Austria, and Russia defeated France and then formed their Concert of Europe. Bismarck's immediate concern was that widespread alarm about German power could undo his many accomplishments.

As long as the empire's first chancellor remained in office, relative calm prevailed as he sought to allay the fears of other countries and convince them that it was not in their best interests to ally against Germany; instead, it made more sense to join a German alliance system. Russia, the Austro-Hungarian Empire, and Italy agreed, while Britain was successfully cultivated as a friendly power. But when the young, headstrong, impetuous Kaiser Wilhelm II dismissed Bismarck in 1890, relations quickly deteriorated, as France was able to break free of the isolation arranged by Bismarck's skillful diplomacy and seek alliances with Russia and Britain. Eventually this three-way counterbalance to Germany resulted in the defeat of the empire in World War I.

The German question had not been resolved, however, for the juggernaught rose again, even more powerful than before in the 1930s under Adolf Hitler and the Nazis, overrunning almost all of Europe before the Allies—Britain, the Soviet Union, and the United States—ended the German question once and for all in 1945, not least for the German people themselves, who had no desire to repeat the tragedies of the two world wars.

Eric Dorn Brose

Perspective Essay 1. Preservation versus Expansion: Otto von Bismarck and Wilhelm II

There are several misconceptions about the creation of the German Empire in 1871. Often referred to as German unification, the new nation-state included millions of Polish, Danish, and French speakers and at the same time excluded millions of German speakers in the Austrian lands. The architect of German unification, Otto von Bismarck, was a Prussian by heart and considered the integration of the principalities of Saxony, Bavaria, Württemberg, Baden, etc., into the new state as the enlargement of Prussian dominance and power. The Catholic south (Bavaria, Württemberg, and Baden) was to him an alien society, with its integration warranted for reasons of international relations and domestic pressure by nationalists rather than by Bismarck's conviction that these territories were essential for the new state. Bismarck's respect for the monarchical principle also forced him to accept a German state that was in fact a federation of German principalities and princes—a federation of kingdoms and duchies with an almighty Prussia that dominated the federal government, the legislature, and the emperorship. The German Empire created in January 1871 at Versailles was certainly not unified, nor was it centralized.

The creation of a new nation of 41 million people in the center of Europe was certainly Bismarck's greatest accomplishment. Bismarck was fully aware that the newly created Germany upset the power balance in Europe. He claimed that he did not favor the annexation of the provinces of Alsace and Lorraine as a result of the war against France during 1870–1871 but was unable to resist their integration into the new German Empire. This major mistake prevented a German-French rapprochement and forced Bismarck to develop a complex and comprehensive foreign policy that had the sole goal of keeping France isolated from other European powers and from collaborating with Russia in particular.

In an effort to isolate France, Bismarck negotiated the Dual Alliance with Austria in 1879 and secretly the Reinsurance Treaty with Russia in 1887. The problem was that both treaties were mutually exclusive, since Germany promised Austria military support in case of a foreign attack and at the same time also promised Russia neutrality in case of a military conflict. The disintegration of the Ottoman Empire that exposed a power vacuum in the Balkans, which both Russia and Austria-Hungary considered to be their zone of influence, made conflict between both powers over the Balkans extremely likely. However, Bismarck concluded the Dual Alliance and the Reinsurance Treaty not to encourage both sides to go ahead and seek a military solution to the disputes over land and people in the Balkans but instead as a power broker who sought to keep both sides apart.

Bismarck's overarching goal was to keep the young German state together and avoid any conflict that might result in its dissolution and return to the existence of several German kingdoms, as had been the case before 1871. He tried to convince the other European powers that Germany was not seeking any further territorial gains within Europe. He even opposed domestic demands for Germany to acquire colonies outside of Europe, suggesting that "for Germany to acquire colonies would be like a poor Polish nobleman buying silks and sables when he needed shirts." Economic considerations, domestic pressures, and simple pragmatism, however, forced Bismarck to abandon this position in the mid-1880s and become involved in the European scramble for Africa.

With the coronation of Wilhelm II as emperor in 1888, Bismarck faced a new ruler who had a very different vision for Germany's future. While Bismarck was intent on preserving German unification, Wilhelm II looked to the expansion of Germany's power in the world, including Africa and Asia and on the seas. Wilhelm's decision to let the Reinsurance Treaty lapse in 1890 cut Russia adrift and opened the door to French-Russian cooperation, freeing France from its political isolation. Wilhelm II's desire to build up a navy capable of challenging that of Britain and his interference in colonial disputes contributed to a British-French rapprochement and subsequently turned Bismarck's nightmare of a two-front war with France in the west and Russia in the east into a conceivable possibility. Moreover, alienating Britain turned the two former archenemies and colonial competitors, Britain and France, into allies.

By 1907, two hostile camps faced each other: the Triple Entente with Russia, France, and Britain and the Triple Alliance with Germany, Austria-Hungary, and Italy. Such a situation was inherently dangerous, since a single localized conflict between two countries could easily turn into a European-wide military conflict. The unstable situation in the Balkans and the unwillingness and inability of Austria-Hungary and Russia to find peaceful ways to solve their disputes over territorial claims in that region made the Balkans the most likely spot for a military confrontation to begin.

While the creation of the German Empire in 1871 upset the balance of power in Europe significantly, Bismarck's restrained foreign policy prevented, at least for the duration of his tenure as chancellor, military conflict in Europe. After his dismissal in 1890, his carefully created treaties and alliances fell apart because of Wilhelm II's desire to increase Germany's power and status. However, by 1914 the attitudes of people and politicians across Europe had been deeply penetrated by extreme nationalism, social Darwinism, and general irrationalism. Conflict—and colonial warfare in particular—was glorified, and war was viewed as a purifying and ennobling experience that could not be banished from history. The outbreak of war in the summer of 1914 was greeted and celebrated by millions of people across the European continent. Everyone expected a short war that was supposed to be over by Christmas.

Thomas Adam

Perspective Essay 2. General European War Not Inevitable

"The Allied and Associated Governments affirm and Germany accepts the responsibility of Germany and her allies for causing all the loss and damage to which the Allied and Associated Governments and their nationals have been subjected as a consequence of the war imposed upon them by the aggression of Germany and her allies" (Article 231, Treaty of Versailles, 1919).

This "War Guilt" clause of the treaty that ended World War I with Germany has been seen as controversial ever since. While Germany declared war, was it alone responsible for the war? Historians continue to debate the war's causes. Many have rejected the simplistic dictum of the Treaty of Versailles. But a notable exception was Hamburg University historian Fritz Fischer. In *Griff nach der Weltmacht: Die Kriegzielpolitik des kaiserlichen Deutschland, 1914–1918* (1961), published in English as *Germany's Aims in the First World War* (1967), Fischer argued that the conservative power elite who had achieved German unification in 1871 planned for world domination. He further argued that their successors sabotaged the postwar Weimar Republic and assisted the rise of Adolf Hitler, an ominous continuity that caused World War II as well. Was World War I inevitable? Did the founding of the German Empire make it so?

German unification was essentially a matter for the German Confederation, established by the Congress of Vienna in 1815. Austria chaired this organization of 39 sovereign German states in Central Europe. But member state Prussia wanted to oust Austria from Central Europe and replace the German Confederation with one headed by its own Hohenzollern monarchy. Otto von Bismarck, Prussian minister-president, was the architect of two wars (the Danish-Prussian War of 1864 and the Austro-Prussian War of 1866) that achieved those goals. The North German Confederation formed in 1867, incorporating the German states north of the Main River but excluding Austria, Bavaria, Baden, and Württemberg. Prussia's kaiser Wilhelm I was its president, and Bismarck was his chancellor.

The European response to these two unification wars revealed no great sense of threat. France's emperor Napoleon III had actually negotiated with both Prussia and Austria for territorial "compensations" in return for neutrality. Although the king of Hanover was related to the king of England, the British chose not to intervene to save him. Nor did any state outside those of the confederation come to Austria's aid. Afterward when Napoleon III pressed Prussia for territory on his eastern frontier as had been pledged by the chancellor earlier, Bismarck rejected this summarily and used the French pressure to secure defensive alliances with Bavaria, Baden, and Württemberg in case France should invade. Then with deliberately provocative diplomacy, he goaded Napoleon into declaring war in April 1870. The three south German states joined with Prussia to defeat him. Napoleon III surrendered on September 1, although fighting continued. On January 18, 1871, the heads of the German states met at the Palace of Versailles and, by treaty, created the Second German Empire. Wilhelm I of Prussia was proclaimed emperor. No other European country took up arms to reverse that development.

While Bismarck's wars had forged the new German Empire, his skillful diplomacy consolidated its place in Europe. The Treaty of Frankfurt (May 1871) required France to cede Alsace and Lorraine to the empire and pay it an indemnity of 5 billion francs. That humiliating defeat placed a permanent enemy on Germany's western frontier, and Bismarck's first task was to keep France diplomatically isolated. Moreover, since Austria had now been turned toward the east, Bismarck wanted to prevent conflict there, especially between Austria and Russia over the Balkans. His strategy was evident in the defensive Dual Alliance with Austria (1879): Germany would aid Austria if it was attacked by Russia, and Austria would aid Germany if it was attacked by France. Only those specific causes could join them together in a war; otherwise, each would maintain neutrality in the event of a conflict. Bismarck encouraged the Three Emperors' League Treaty (1881) to maintain neutrality in case of war with a fourth party and added the Reinsurance Treaty with Russia (1887), ensuring German neutrality if either country went to war with countries other than France or Austria-Hungary.

Bismarck's diplomacy demonstrates that the German Empire was not bound on world conquest. When problems in the Balkans threatened to escalate tensions between Russia and Austria, he acted as an honest broker by calling the Congress of Berlin (1878) to settle the Eastern question peacefully. Similarly, when the "Scramble for Africa" erupted, he convened the Berlin Conference (1884–1885) to help establish ground rules for the continent's peaceful partitioning. He actually argued, unsuccessfully, against Germany securing colonies there. Thus, during the Bismarck years (1871–1890) there was little evidence that the world felt sufficiently threatened to prepare for war with the German Empire. The major powers accepted Germany as a partner in European and world affairs.

German unification therefore did not make a world war inevitable; other significant factors triggered that conflict. As their empires expanded in Africa and Asia, the United Kingdom, France, and Russia confronted each other abroad. France and England barely avoided war in the Sudan (the Fashoda Crisis) in 1898. England and Russia faced each other across the Indian frontier. They all and the United States competed for spheres of influence in China. This competition and tension led to arms buildup and to a web of treaties. Significantly, France escaped isolation by concluding an alliance with Russia in 1894. It mirrored the Dual Alliance: France would aid Russia if it was attacked by Austria or Germany, and Russia would aid France if it was attacked by Germany.

The accession of Wilhelm II as German emperor in 1888 only stirred up the mix. His restless mind and brash manner, unchecked by common sense, antagonized Europe as he started a naval race with Britain (1898) and interfered in Morocco (1905–1906 and 1911), where Germany had no major national interests. The British and French drew closer (the Entente Cordiale). But Germany's gambits were defeated by diplomatic pressure, not war.

World War I was triggered in the Balkans, where as the Ottoman Empire collapsed Russia, Austria, and Serbia vied to claim its European parts. Independent since the Congress of Berlin in 1878, Serbia had accepted Austrian protection and built the region's largest army in the hope of driving out the Turks and controlling the region. The First Balkan War (1912) and the Second Balkan War (1913) ended Ottoman control and redrew the map. But Serbia wanted an outlet to the sea and, in the spirit of Pan-Slavism, to liberate the Slavs in Austria. Increasingly Serbia depended on Russia, Europe's leading Slavic nation, for support.

A European war became probable after the assassination on June 28, 1914, of Archduke Franz Ferdinand, heir to the Austrian and Hungarian thrones, by Gavrilo Princip. Princip was a Bosnian trained by the Black Hand, a secret Serbian military organization. This direct blow to the Habsburg monarchy could not go unanswered, and all of Europe knew it. France warned both parties to stay calm; Russia warned only Austria. But going to war required the decision of men. Austrian emperor Franz Joseph I looked to Germany for support. On July 5 Wilhelm II, ignoring the defensive principles of the Dual Alliance, assured the Austrian ambassador of Germany's support (the famous Blank Check) and began a summer cruise. On July 23 Austria delivered a harsh ultimatum to Serbia, which appealed to Russia for protection; the following day Czar Nicholas II initiated mobilization of the Russian Army. On July 28 Austria declared war on Serbia (without invading), and a diplomatic frenzy erupted across the continent as the powers, including Germany, tried to prevent a larger conflict. Military timetables and strategic plans now came into play. Unwilling to let Russia fully mobilize its considerable resources and have to fight a two-front war with it and France, on August 1 Germany declared war on Russia and then on August 3 declared war on France, intending to defeat the latter before turning to face the larger Russian Army. Inexorably as the web of treaty mechanisms clicked in, the war that began in the Balkans became global.

Eleanor L. Turk

Perspective Essay 3. Bismarck Sought Peace

The concept of inevitability in history is a chimera, an absurd creation of the imagination. History is not a science; identical factors do not always yield consistent results. Rather, history is an art: an infinite number of causal factors, each bearing a weight or importance that changes continually, constantly interacting with each other over an infinite period of time to produce an infinite number of results, virtually none of which are the same. Even so, if one chooses to speak of inevitability in history, one would be well advised to look to Adolf Hitler's Germany rather than the German Empire created by Otto von Bismarck in 1871.

Certainly it is true that the new German Empire dominated Europe; however, it was a satiated Germany that envisioned no further expansion. Bismarck had used force to achieve his goal (three wars in 1864, 1866, and 1870–1871). Now he worked to maintain the peace that so favored Germany. To that end, he allied Germany with the important nations of Russia and Austria-Hungary. Later, he added Italy to his alliance system. All of this took great ingenuity, since the interests of Russia and Austria-Hungary and those of Italy and Austria-Hungary frequently clashed.

Moreover, Germany enjoyed cordial relations with Great Britain, in no small measure because their interests coincided or at the least did not clash. Britain, focused on its overseas empire, as always wanted peace and quiet on the European continent. So did Germany, since its hegemonic position in Europe provided great benefits. Moreover, Germany had no substantive interest in building a colonial empire to rival Great Britain, and these two countries were each other's largest trading partners.

France was the only European nation likely to upset the apple cart. Smarting from its defeat in the Franco-Prussian War of 1870–1871 and the harsh terms imposed on it, France entertained thoughts of revanche (revenge). However, Bismarck's diplomacy effectively isolated France, and France was not strong enough to start a

European conflict without at least one major ally. Furthermore, Bismarck flattered France and encouraged it to expand its overseas empire, an initiative that met with only partial success but, together with the passage of time, served to lessen somewhat the French desire for revenge.

Nevertheless, significant challenges to the European peace lurked beneath this relatively placid surface. The nature and structure of the German state presented the greatest problem, and like the creation of Germany itself, Bismarck was largely responsible. Proudly tracing his heritage back to Prussia's landed gentry, Bismarck never really thought of himself as a German, and he viewed the German Empire that he created as an expanded Prussia more than anything else. Bismarck was clever enough to harness the raging hormonal sentiment of nationalism to further his aims. Calling his new state "Germany" rather than "Greater Prussia" was a small price to pay for achieving his goals. Moreover, in a bow to progressive sentiments then popular in Europe, Bismarck gave Germany a decidedly liberal facade with a constitution, a parliament (the Reichstag), and universal male suffrage. This was, however, all a sham, as real power resided elsewhere.

In addition to being a Prussian and an aristocrat, Bismarck was also a staunch conservative. He impressed on Germany the old Prussian governing structure that featured an authoritarian clique ruling efficiently and paternalistically over an obedient, deferential, and docile population that knew its place. The monarch, the aristocracy, and the army's officer corps—drawn from the sons of the aristocracy—comprised the ruling group. Moreover, it was understood that the monarch would share power with his supporters rather than rule absolutely.

Furthermore, the brusque, supremely self-confident Bismarck was power hungry. This brilliant but self-centered prima donna claimed the position of chancellor (prime minister) for himself and guided Germany's destiny for almost two decades. Thanks to his imaginative structuring of the state, few sources of countervailing power existed to challenge his role as power broker. Those that did exist, such as the army and the nobility, resolutely supported the chancellor, the Germany that he had created, and the policies that he devised. As to the emperor, Wilhelm I was old, weak willed, and more than happy to defer to his chancellor on most occasions. Wherever the emperor did voice doubts, Bismarck would threaten to resign, and Wilhelm capitulated. However, Wilhelm died in 1888, and following the brief reign and death of Frederick III that same year, the throne went to Wilhelm II. Young, energetic, and intellectually gifted, he was also arrogant, blustering, bullying, and unstable, an insufferable egomaniac who intended to rule rather than govern. Not surprisingly, Bismarck and Wilhelm II clashed, resulting in Bismarck's forced resignation in March 1890.

Thanks to Bismarck, the Germany that Wilhelm II inherited possessed no effective institutions to restrain its headstrong new ruler. Under Wilhelm, Germany jettisoned Bismarck's Eurocentric commitment in favor of *Weltpolitik,* an indecipherable policy that appeared to signal Germany's intent to project its power beyond continental Europe. Not satisfied with having the world's premier army, Germany began construction of a massive fleet despite its lack of an overseas empire to defend. Not unexpectedly, Great Britain took exception. Even earlier Wilhelm's Germany refused to renew its alliance with Russia, thereby setting the czarist state adrift. Russia's isolation did not last long. France was able to ally with Russia, ending its own isolation. More than ever, Germany had to rely on a decaying Austria-Hungary. Finally, Germany's posture roiled the waters. Arrogance, belligerence, irrationality, and aggressiveness came to characterize Germany's behavior.

Did the creation of the German Empire in 1871 make World War I inevitable? Not hardly. However, the nature of the Germany that Bismarck created allowed for irresponsible figures such as Wilhelm II and his advisers to play a disproportionate role in shaping Germany's destiny, and the policies they pursued in an unchecked manner made war considerably more likely.

Frank W. Thackeray

Further Reading

Afflerback, Holger, and David Stevenson, eds. *An Improbable War? The Outbreak of World War I and European Political Culture before 1914.* New York: Berghahn Books, 2007.

Berghahn, Volker R. *Imperial Germany 1871–1914: Economy, Society, Culture, and Politics.* New York: Berghahn Books, 2003.

Blackbourn, David. *History of Germany, 1780–1918: The Long Nineteenth Century.* New York: Blackwell, 2002.

Bloch, Camille. *The Causes of the World War: An Historical Summary.* Translated by Jane Soames. New York: H. Fertig, 1968.

Breuilly, John. *19th Century Germany: Politics, Culture and Society, 1780–1918.* New York: Oxford University Press, 2001.

Carr, William. *A History of Germany, 1815–1985.* London: E. Arnold, 1987.

Cecil, Lamar. *Wilhelm II.* 2 vols. Chapel Hill: University of North Carolina Press, 1989, 1896.

Clark, Christopher. *Kaiser Wilhelm II.* London: Longman, 2000.

Cowles, Virginia. *The Kaiser.* New York: Harper and Row, 1963.

Crankshaw, Edward. *Bismarck.* New York: Viking, 1981.

Feuchtwanger, Edgar. *Bismarck.* New York: Routledge, 2002.

Hamilton, Richard F., and Holger H. Herwig, eds. *The Origins of World War I.* New York: Cambridge University Press, 2003.

Jefferies, Matthew, *Contesting the German Empire, 1871–1918.* Malden, MA: Blackwell, 2008.

Joll, James. *The Origins of the First World War.* 2nd ed. London: Longman, 1992.

Kennan, George F. *The Decline of Bismarck's European Order: Franco-Russian Relations, 1875–1890.* Princeton, NJ: Princeton University Press, 1979.

Lerman, Katharine Anne. *Bismarck*. London: Longman, 2004.

Meyer, Henry Cord, ed. *The Long Generation: Germany from Empire to Ruin, 1913–1945*. New York: Walker, 1973.

Orlow, Dietrich. *A History of Modern Germany, 1871 to Present*. Englewood Cliffs, NJ: Prentice Hall, 1987.

Palmer, Alan. *Bismarck*. New York: Scribner, 1976.

Rosenberg, Arthur. *The Birth of the German Republic, 1871–1918*. Translated by Ian F. D. Morrow. New York: Russell and Russell, 1962.

Ross, Stewart. *The Causes of World War I*. Austin, TX: Raintree Steck-Vaughn, 2003.

Tucker, Spencer C. *The Great War, 1914–18*. London: UCL Press, 1998.

Whittle, Tyler. *The Last Kaiser: A Biography of Wilhelm II, German Emperor and King of Prussia*. New York: Times Books, 1977.

Williamson, D. G. *Bismarck and Germany, 1862–1890*. London: Longman 1998.

31. DID THE AMERICAN INDIAN WARS CONSTITUTE GENOCIDE?

While no exact figures exist, it is estimated that the area of North America that would eventually become the United States was home to 8 million to 12 million Native Americans at the time of first contact with North European explorers and settlers. That first contact began in the early 17th century. Before long, European settlers, in an attempt to secure more land, found themselves in conflict with Native Americans, to whom European concepts of landownership seemed wholly foreign. Clashes over land and water rights often erupted into war. European powers also frequently took sides in wars among Native American tribes, making those conflicts longer and bloodier than they had to be. Rivalries and wars among European colonial powers, most notably the French and Indian War and the American Revolutionary War, drew in many different Indian tribes, often with catastrophic results for Native American interests. After the establishment of the United States, white hunger for land and American concepts of manifest destiny resulted in a dizzying array of Indian wars and conflicts, which decimated Native Americans and their land holdings. Not surprisingly, the centuries-long American Indian Wars witnessed a precipitous decline in the Native American population, perhaps by as much as 90 percent by the time the conflicts ended with the Wounded Knee Massacre in 1890. By the close of the 19th century, the number of Native Americans had plummeted to a mere 250,000. Today, scholars continue to debate whether the lengthy Indian Wars constitute genocide as the term is under-stood today.

In the first perspective essay, Dr. Justin Murphy uses Raphael Lemkin's broader definition of the term "genocide" to argue that the Indian Wars indeed represented cultural genocide. Murphy examines the ways in which Indians were deprived of land and economic resources and forced to adopt white cultural practices. By contrast, Dr. Jerry Morelock argues that the Indian Wars were not genocide but instead were a clash of two entrenched, incompatible cultures. He believes that to call the wars genocide is a gross oversimplification and demonstrates a seriously flawed under-standing of what was a complex interaction of multiple cultures. In his perspective essay, Dr. Jim Piecuch asserts that the Indian Wars did indeed constitute genocide. Beginning in colonial times, he examines a number of important conflicts, including the Pequot War, King Philip's War, the Trail of Tears, the Sand Creek Massacre, and the Battle of Wounded Knee, all of which underscore his conclusion that, taken as a whole, the American Indian Wars proved to be genocidal for Native Americans.

Background Essay

Warfare between Native Americans and European settlers represents the most pro-tracted conflict in American history. While most Americans now associate the term "Indian Wars" with the fighting on the Great Plains in the period after the American Civil War, the first major recorded battle between Native Americans and colonists in the New World occurred on the island of Hispaniola in March 1495. Conflict in North America between Native Americans and white settlers began with European colonization in the early 17th century. This struggle may be said to have ended definitively sometime in the first decade or two of the 20th century.

Fighting not only occurred between the English-speaking colonists and the Na-tive Americans but also involved immigrants of the other colonial powers, includ-ing the Spanish, French, Dutch, and Swedes. There was even fighting between the Russians and Native Americans in the Pacific Northwest and Alaska.

Early on, Native Americans helped save European settlements by sharing with the colonists their knowledge of the land and local conditions, but hopes of peace-ful coexistence were soon dashed by the European desire to own the land and to fence it off. The native peoples did not adhere to the concept of private ownership of land. The ensuing warfare is chiefly explained by the presence of an expanding colonial population that sought to secure land westward from the Atlantic sea-board. Reprisals for perceived and very real attacks by the other side also played a key role, as did the belief held by many Europeans into the 19th century that Native

Americans were racially inferior. In 1803 the United States acquired the Louisiana Territory from France, and manifest destiny, which held that the United States was destined to expand from coast to coast, then came into play as settlers streamed westward. In the 1830s the U.S. government enacted Indian removal policies, designed to move and resettle in the west Native Americans who had lived east of the Mississippi in order that their ancestral lands might be open to European settlers. Thousands of Indians perished in the Trail of Tears of this forced migration. At the same time, settlers and the U.S. Army were also able to take advantage of rivalries between tribes and within some tribes themselves.

The fighting introduced the Europeans to a new type of warfare. Europeans were used to standup battles by close formations of men facing one another in the open and trading gunshots at dueling pistol ranges or slashing at one another with pikes or charging one another with horse cavalry. Conditions along the largely forested Atlantic seaboard in North America in the early 17th century did not lend themselves to this type of fighting. The Native Americans thus introduced skulking war, which emphasized stealth, the bow and arrow as well as tomahawks and knives at close quarters, along with hit-and-run raids. Although such tactics worked astonishingly well at first, they could not bring the native peoples victory against superior European firepower and, as it turned out, numbers.

The Indian Wars ended as they only could, in victory for the U.S. Army. A proliferation of tribes and clans with a long record of antagonism between them and

Troopers of the U.S. 7th Cavalry, led by Lieutenant Colonel George Armstrong Custer, shown attacking Cheyenne chief Black Kettle's peaceful village on the Washita River on November 27, 1868, killing all its inhabitants. (Library of Congress)

competing goals and leaders prevented the native peoples from effectively mobilizing their resources to oppose the growing numbers of white immigrants. Even when they were able to mobilize larger numbers, as in the Great Sioux War of 1876–1877, the Native Americans' lack of logistical services kept them from maintaining a sustained presence in the field. Diseases brought by Europeans such as smallpox for which the native peoples had no immunity killed off large numbers of Native Americans from the first settlement. Some estimates place the death toll at 80–90 percent of the population. At the same time, the European population was steadily increasing. Population imbalances, the superior military technology of the Europeans (including artillery), the coming of the railroads, and the demise of the buffalo all contributed to the inevitable Native American defeat and the movement of many Native Americans onto government-prescribed reservations.

Still, the cost of European settlement and warfare has been heavy. The native population of pre-Columbian America has been estimated by scholars at anywhere from 2 million to 18 million people. Although the Indian Wars may have claimed only some 19,000 people of European descent and 30,000 Indians, today Native Americans constitute only 5.4 million of the total U.S. population, or just 2 percent.

Spencer C. Tucker

Perspective Essay 1. Cultural Genocide of Native American Peoples

Although the word "genocide" usually provokes images of the Holocaust—the effort by the Nazis in World War II to exterminate the Jews—it is important to note that Raphael Lemkin, who coined the term "genocide" from the Greek word *genos,* which means "tribe or race," and the Latin word *cide,* which means "killing," did not restrict the definition to the mass extermination of a race but also included the destruction of a group's political, social, and cultural identity as a people. By applying Lemkin's broader definition and considering the broader policies toward Native Americans (using Prussian general Carl von Clausewitz's famous dictum that "war is a mere continuation of policy by other means"), it becomes clear that the Indian Wars constituted cultural genocide.

Although the Indian Wars are normally restricted to the series of 19th-century conflicts produced by westward expansion, it is important to remember that the policies the United States pursued toward Native Americans followed a pattern set by the first English colonists. For example, when the Puritans arrived in Massachusetts in 1629, the Narragansetts and other smaller tribes sought an alliance against the Pequots. When the Pequot War broke out in 1636, the Puritans, who viewed

New England as their "promised land," descended upon the Pequots with an Old Testament fury. After surrounding the chief Pequot village on the Mystic River on May 26, 1637, the Puritans and their native allies set fire to the village, killing some 400–700 men, women, and children. The remaining Pequots were hunted down and slaughtered near New Haven on July 28, ending the Pequot War. Almost all adult males were dead, and the few remaining women and children were either sold as slaves to the West Indies or taken in by the Mohegans. Forty years later in King Philip's War (1676–1677), the Puritans effectively destroyed the Narragansetts. To the extent that the policies of the Puritans toward the Pequots and Narragansetts resulted in their virtual annihilation, they meet the standards of genocide.

The chief cause of the fighting was the seizure of native lands by the colonists as their own population expanded westward from the Atlantic seaboard. After the Powhatan Confederacy launched its last uprising against Virginia in 1644–1646, Virginia authorities forced it to sign a treaty confining it to a small portion of territory beyond the Piedmont, in effect establishing the first reservation in North America.

Unlike the French and Spanish, the English made little effort to incorporate Native Americans into colonial society. Although Puritan missionary John Eliot was an exception in attempting to convert Native Americans to Christianity, native converts were segregated into so-called praying towns and forced to adopt English cultural customs. Depriving Native Americans of their ancestral hunting lands, upon which their existence and culture depended, and forcing them to convert and adopt white culture constituted cultural genocide.

The British victory in the French and Indian War (1754–1763) forced the French to cede Canada and all their lands east of the Mississippi to Britain and the Louisiana Territory to Spain. This placed tribes east of the Mississippi in a far weaker position. To prevent Indian unrest, the British issued the Proclamation of 1763 forbidding white expansion beyond the Appalachian Mountains. But as demonstrated in Pontiac's Rebellion in the Ohio Valley and Great Lakes region during 1763–1765, enforcement was problematic.

American independence placed Native Americans in a precarious position because the Treaty of Paris of 1783 granted the new United States sovereignty over the land south of the Great Lakes and east of the Mississippi River (excluding Florida, which went to Spain). The tribes soon discovered that the structure of the U.S. Constitution meant that they had to contend not only with the federal government but also with state governments, which often pursued their own policies against Native Americans especially in regard to Indian lands. In addition, the federal government proved ineffective in forcing white settlers to abide by treaties negotiated with tribes.

The Louisiana Purchase in 1803 nearly doubled the size of the United States with the acquisition of the Louisiana Territory west of the Mississippi River. This opened the prospect of removing eastern tribes west of the Mississippi as a new aspect of federal policy by encouraging trade that would lead to indebtedness and in turn force tribes to cede land. Thomas Jefferson also promoted assimilation as a policy, with Congress appropriating funds to induce Native Americans to abandon hunting and adopt agriculture.

In 1819 Congress established the Civilization Fund for Indian education, dispensing funds through missionary organizations, which established missions and schools among Native Americans. While many of the tribes of the Old Northwest resisted under the leadership of Tecumseh and fought with the British during the War of 1812 to preserve their culture and land, the five leading southern tribes—the Cherokees, Choctaws, Chickasaws, Creeks, and Seminoles—became referred to as the "Five Civilized Tribes" because intermarriage with white traders resulted in a mixed-blood leadership that actively adopted aspects of white culture, including plantation agriculture, black slavery, schools, churches, newspapers, and written laws and constitutions. Nonetheless, the southern tribes were divided, for traditionalist factions, generally led by full-bloods, sought to retain hunting lifestyles. This factionalism produced fighting within the tribes themselves but also contributed to the Creek War in 1813–1814 and a series of Seminole Wars (1817–1818, 1836–1838, and 1855–1858).

President Andrew Jackson's election in 1828 made removal official policy with the Indian Removal Act in 1830. This is one of the most controversial actions of federal Indian policy, especially as applied to the southern tribes that had assimilated so closely to white culture. Indeed, the Cherokees resisted the Indian Removal Act and Georgia's extension of state jurisdiction regarding Cherokee lands by filing suit in the U.S. Supreme Court. In *The Cherokee Nation v. Georgia* (1831), however, Chief Justice John Marshall ruled that Native American tribes were "domestic dependent nations" subject to the jurisdiction of the United States, with tribal members in the position of federal wards. Although Jackson has been vilified for the resulting Trail of Tears in which approximately 25 percent of Cherokees, Choctaws, Chickasaws, Creeks, and Seminoles died of exposure and starvation during their forced removal to Indian Territory, this resulted from the policy's flawed implementation rather than a stated objective of the policy per se. Historian F. P. Prucha forcefully argues that Jackson's policy was not based on hatred of Indians but instead was more a practical matter of denying them dual sovereignty. Those willing to enter white society could remain behind and become citizens, while those wishing to retain their tribal identity could do so by removing to Indian territory, where they would gain the time to evolve further on the path to civilization, which in Jackson's view would prevent their extinction.

The annexation of Texas in 1845, the acquisition of the Oregon Territory in 1846, and the Mexican Cession following the Mexican-American War marked the beginning of the Indian Wars that ended with the Battle of Wounded Knee in 1890 and

Included numerous individual actions that in themselves were genocidal. In the infamous Sand Creek Massacre on November 29, 1864, Colonel John M. Chivington led Colorado militiamen in an attack on Cheyenne chief Black Kettle's peaceful village of 500 Indians near Fort Lyon and ruthlessly slaughtered at least 300, mostly women and children. Then on November 27, 1868, Lieutenant Colonel George Armstrong Custer led the 7th Cavalry on a dawn attack of Black Kettle's peaceful village on the Washita River, killing Black Kettle and more than 100 Cheyennes, mainly women and children. A few months later Lieutenant General Philip H. Sheridan is reputed to have said that "The only good Indians I ever saw were dead." Although this infamous phrase may be anecdotal, many individuals and soldiers on the frontier embraced it, even though it was not official government policy.

Although the Indian Wars against the Plains Indians and the Apaches and Navajos in the desert Southwest do not meet the standard of genocide in that there was no systematic attempt of mass extermination, many aspects of federal Indian policy systematically sought to destroy Native American culture and constitute cultural genocide. Nevertheless, it must be noted that Native Americans resisted efforts to eradicate their culture. As a result of their incredible perseverance, Native Americans have managed to survive and retain their cultural heritage, even though the extreme poverty and appalling health conditions on reservations clearly demonstrate that Native Americans continue to suffer the long-term effects of the cultural genocide inflicted on them.

Justin D. Murphy

Perspective Essay 2: A Clash of Incompatible Cultures

The Indian Wars did not constitute genocide as we understand that monstrous term and the horror that it implies today. As acclaimed Holocaust scholar Daniel Goldhagen has convincingly argued, genocide is a conscious, deliberately chosen policy of extermination of a targeted population through organized, state-sanctioned mass murder. Instead, what we refer to as the Indian Wars, particularly the western Indian Wars circa 1860–1890 upon which this essay concentrates, were a tragic clash of two entrenched, incompatible cultures in which neither side was willing to accept compromise on the other's terms.

Although Indians eagerly adopted some items and elements of European American culture (for example, horses, steel implements, and firearms) that made their daily lives easier, they were determined to preserve and pursue their eons-old way of life that, by the mid-19th century, was impossible to maintain indefinitely and was ultimately doomed to be overwhelmed by the Industrial Age. European Americans, as was typical of that era, were racists and cultural imperialists. They saw Indians as impediments to what they were convinced was "progress" and considered them inconvenient roadblocks resisting the increasing pressure of westward expansion. To European Americans, Indians were simply in the way. Indian assimilation or removal, not genocidal extermination, was U.S. government Indian policy.

Clearly, many individuals on both sides would have enthusiastically welcomed the extermination of the other; the most infamous and oft-quoted examples of such an attitude on the European American side are the appalling May 28, 1868, remarks by Representative James M. Cavanaugh in the U.S. House of Representatives (usually incorrectly attributed to General Philip H. Sheridan): "I have never in my life seen a good Indian . . . except when I have seen a dead Indian" (typically shortened to the egregiously callous "The only good Indian is a dead Indian"). Yet, the U.S. government throughout the western Indian Wars was committed to controlling Indians through assimilation or removal, not exterminating them. In retrospect, the calamitous result of this collision of Stone Age culture and Industrial Age culture seems as predictable as it was, by the middle of the 19th century, inevitable; the way of life of the former was doomed to be confronted, overwhelmed, and eventually destroyed by the immense power and irresistible pressure of the latter. It was an American tragedy, the final act of which played out across the vast expanse of the West.

Neither side, Indian or European American, showed much willingness (or, arguably, even the ability) to understand the other's culture or to pursue interaction within their opposite number's very different cultural framework and worldview. One telling indication of this cultural bias and stubbornly pursued blindness is the European Americans' naive and unrealistic insistence on dealing with the many individual Indian tribes as "nations," as if each tribe was just a rustic version of a Westphalian-style state in which tribal chiefs not only spoke for the entire tribe (typically made up of various smaller bands that might have only infrequent contact with each other) but were also expected to force tribal members to abide by treaty provisions. As historian Gregory Michno has shown, Native Americans violated the treaties more often than did European Americans; yet, this is completely understandable and predictable given the individualistic nature of Indian culture and the artificial, alien process to Indians of the typically one-sided (usually to the Indians' detriment) treaties.

European Americans either did not understand the nature of Indian culture or, more likely, were arrogantly unwilling to even try to understand it and work within the Indians' frame of reference, since this made dealing with the numerous tribes incredibly complicated. Both sides' cultural blindness was also evident in the way Indians and European Americans retaliated for wrongs against them committed by the other: Indians attacked European Americans who had nothing to do with the act being retaliated for, and European Americans murdered Indians who may not have even been members of the same tribe responsible for the incident that had set the European Americans on a quest for bloody revenge. Both sides could—and did—kill the other's women and children, mutilate their opponents' corpses, and perpetrate massacres in brutal no-quarter combat.

Applying the term "genocide" to what transpired in the West during the 19th century is not only an inappropriate use of the term (given what it has come to mean today) but also reveals at best a gross oversimplification and at worst a seriously flawed understanding of what was a complex interaction of multiple cultures. As Patricia Nelson Limerick has shown, historians cannot present an accurate account of the history of the 19th-century West without including the complicated, frequently conflicted relationships between several competing cultures. Among these are European American, Hispanic, Chinese, African American, mixed-race, and Indian cultures.

Even the term "Indian" is misleading and imprecise (beyond the fact that it was a monumental misnomer when it was first applied to mean the indigenous peoples of the Americas by European explorers in the 15th century), since it implies a monolithic entity with shared values and a single common culture. In fact, the term "Indian" encompassed numerous different tribes and cultural groupings with often quite different customs, attitudes, and behavior. Many tribes had traditionally warred against other tribes for ages before European Americans arrived on the scene, and the latter hardly introduced warfare to the western tribes. Indeed, some Indian tribes could be as imperialistic as European Americans. For example, the Lakota people erupted from their original Minnesota homeland in the late 18th and early 19th centuries to conquer huge tracts of territory in present-day Montana, Wyoming, and the Dakotas, including the sacred Black Hills, forcibly displacing the Crows and other less powerful tribes that had traditionally occupied that region (and providing a major and quite understandable explanation of why the Crows later became U.S. Army allies in the 1866–1867 and 1876–1877 Sioux Wars).

The various western Indian tribes reacted to the aggressive European American encroachment in different ways. Some, such as the Lakotas, Cheyennes, Comanches, and Apaches, fiercely resisted. Others, as with the Crows, Tonkawas, and Pawnees, allied themselves with European Americans in wars against other tribes for such reasons as revenge, loot, payment, and gaining leverage for better treatment of their own tribe from European Americans. The western Indian Wars did not constitute a single genocide-motivated war of extermination waged by European Americans against all Indians; the wars played out as a series of widely scattered separate campaigns waged against individual tribes in which Indians were allies as well as opponents.

Genocide—as we have observed its horrific and most infamous occurrences in the 20th century with Armenians in 1915; European Jews, Poles, and Russians during 1933–1945; and Rwandan Tutsis in 1994—implies essentially defenseless victims powerless to prevent their mass murder by the irresistible force of those bent on their extermination. This is another reason why the term "genocide" fails to accurately describe the western Indian Wars. Those who hold such a view rob Indians of what social scientists and anthropologists refer to as "agency"—the power and ability to influence the events that have an impact on one's life—by treating them merely as helpless victims of European American aggression and as if nothing any Indians (as individuals or as tribal groupings) did had any influence on what transpired or on their ultimate fate. This seems to be an unnecessarily condescending attitude and is simply wrong.

To find only one notable example among many illustrating how Indians were actors in this American tragedy and not merely helpless victims, one need only examine the Comanche people of the southern Plains region. Numbering perhaps as few as 30,000 individuals with only about one-sixth of this number warriors, the various bands that made up the people known as Comanches dominated a huge area (Comancheria) stretching from Colorado to Mexico and from central Texas to eastern New Mexico. These "Lords of the southern Plains" reigned as the region's true power brokers for more than a century—overwhelming and displacing less powerful tribes, such as the Apaches and Tonkawas; stopping the Spanish colonization of the Plains in its tracks; preventing the French from advancing into the Southwest; and effectively blocking European American settlement of western Texas for a half century, circa 1820 to 1875.

The Comanches' power was only finally ended when their European American enemy, desperate to devise a military strategy that would work, ruthlessly targeted and eliminated the key elements that made their very way of life possible: the horse and the buffalo. European Americans' wholesale slaughter of the immense buffalo herds that provided Comanches and other Plains tribes with sustenance (a process largely carried out by civilian commercial hunters but encouraged by U.S. military leaders) and the mass killings of Comanche pony herds captured during winter campaigns that robbed the tribe of its mobility, which was absolutely vital to maintaining its way of life, seem today to represent brutal and unnecessarily harsh acts. Yet, the draconian strategy's aim was Indian removal—forcing the tribes onto government-run reservations—not genocidal extermination.

Indeed, the culminating action of the 1874 Red River War, the final campaign that forced the Comanches onto a reservation at Fort Sill, was the September 28, 1874, surprise attack by Colonel Ranald Mackenzie and the U.S. 4th Cavalry Regiment on the tribe's Palo Duro Canyon sanctuary. During the attack, only one soldier and three Indians were killed. Mackenzie had achieved complete surprise, yet instead of committing a wholesale slaughter of sleeping Indians, he targeted and destroyed the Indians' pony herd and winter supplies. This gave the Comanches no choice but to seek shelter and food at the Fort Sill reservation. The fact that European Americans had to resort to such an extreme strategy, borne out of frustration and desperation, of eliminating Comanche mobility and sustenance starkly emphasizes the real power the Comanches wielded for over a century. Indians were actors in the American tragedy that was the western Indian Wars, not helpless victims.

Although today often portrayed as the willing perpetrators of Indian genocide, the U.S. Frontier Army was often caught in the middle in this clash of incompatible cultures. Never numbering more than about 25,000 cavalrymen and infantrymen, the U.S. regular army, as historian Russell Weigley has pointed out, was essentially a "constabulary force" carrying out what today would be classified as "police" functions. This force was scattered in small detachments across an area of about 2 million square miles. Led by a small, largely West Point–trained officer corps, the U.S. Frontier Army was manned mostly by soldiers recruited from the bottom tier of American society. Many were foreign-born immigrants seeking a fresh start, and drunkenness, desertion, and psychologically numbing isolation were constant plagues that vexed commanders even more than their infrequent (albeit sometimes bloody and frustrating) armed clashes with Indians. One Frontier Army officer, former American Civil War hero Colonel John Gibbon, undoubtedly spoke for most of his fellow officers when he described service in the West as "being shot at from behind a rock by an Indian and having your name spelled wrong in the newspapers." Frontier army service was typically an onerous duty that the army was compelled to perform, carrying out frequently misguided policies originating in Washington formed by politicians and government officials who usually had no idea of the actual situation on the ground in the West. In this regard, it was not unlike what took place a century later in Vietnam.

One of the most notorious Indian Wars incidents used to justify claims that the U.S. Army pursued genocide is the infamous 1864 Sand Creek Massacre; yet, the wholesale killing of 70–160 Cheyenne men, women, and children at Sand Creek was neither perpetrated nor condoned by the U.S. Army. Poorly trained, ill-disciplined Colorado territorial militia (many reportedly drunk at the time) under the command of a racist bigot, Colonel John M. Chivington, committed this crime, which was later repudiated by the U.S. Congress Joint Committee on the Conduct of the War, which termed it a "dastardly massacre" and censured Chivington and his civilians in uniform for their unwarranted attack that "surprised and murdered, in cold blood, the unsuspecting [Cheyenne] men, women and children on Sand Creek who had every reason to believe they were under protection of the United States authorities." Indeed, some U.S. Frontier Army regular officers later became public champions of Indian rights. Probably the most notable of these is Brigadier General George Crook, who was one of the army's most successful Indian fighters but who spent the last decades of his life fighting for Indian rights and justice for the tribes.

Claims that this clash of incompatible cultures constituted genocide typically focus on only a select few of the more than 1,500 armed clashes—from minor skirmishes to pitched battles to undeniable massacres committed by both sides in the

West from 1850 to 1890. Gregory Michno in *The Encyclopedia of Indian Wars* calculates that there were about 21,000 total casualties in these armed clashes, with European Americans (soldiers and civilians) accounting for about 6,600 (31 percent) and Indians suffering about 15,000 (69 percent). Although these casualty figures do not include Indian deaths from disease, sickness, or displacement-induced starvation, they are hardly lopsided enough to support claims of genocide. In addition to Sand Creek (committed, as noted, by civilian volunteers), the other most often cited example used to support genocide claims does involve the U.S. regular army: the 1890 tragedy at Wounded Knee.

The tragedy that took place on December 29, 1890, at Wounded Knee Creek, South Dakota, is the final armed encounter usually taken to mark the end of the western Indian Wars. It is a compelling illustration of how the clash of Indian and European American cultures could produce a horrific and bloody outcome that neither side intentionally sought. What we today call the Wounded Knee Massacre was set in motion by desperation and fear, not by some desire for revenge by the 7th Cavalry Regiment for its losses at the 1876 Battle of the Little Bighorn (a motivation attributed to the troopers after the fact, created by sensationalist eastern newspaper accounts).

The Lakotas, by 1890 confined to a bleak existence on South Dakota reservations and desperate over the loss of their way of life, turned for solace to the Ghost Dance religion. Misunderstanding this new Indian religious movement, reservation agents and the area's European American settlers feared that it was a precursor to a Lakota uprising and sent panicked pleas to Washington to send troops. In turn, the arrival of U.S. Army soldiers (including the 7th Cavalry Regiment and African American buffalo soldiers of the 9th Cavalry Regiment) spread equal fear among the Lakotas, and some bands, including one of about 350 men, women, and children led by Big Foot (Spotted Elk), fled the reservation.

Intercepted by 7th Cavalry troopers, Big Foot's band was being escorted back to the reservation when, at a campsite on Wounded Knee Creek, the soldiers' attempt to disarm the Lakotas went horribly wrong. Surrounded by armed troopers but refusing to reveal and surrender the numerous repeating rifles they had been seen carrying when they surrendered the day before, about 100 Lakota warriors were being harangued by a medicine man, Yellow Bird, to resist: "Do not be afraid. Their bullets will not penetrate you!" As the soldiers grabbed the rifle of an unstable Indian named Black Coyote (some accounts attribute his actions to his being deaf), the weapon discharged; simultaneously, Yellow Bird threw a handful of dust into the air.

At this signal, several Lakota warriors threw back their blankets, raised their Winchester rifles, and fired a volley into the troopers' ranks, killing or wounding several soldiers and possibly hitting women and children in the Lakota camp beyond. The troopers fired back and, supported by four rapid-firing Hotchkiss guns, delivered an overpowering fusillade that struck down Lakota warriors, women, and children.

Once the shooting started it was difficult to stop, but given the 7th Cavalry's over-whelming firepower advantage, the end result was tragically inevitable. A total of 84 Lakota warriors, 44 women, and 18 children were killed. Yet, soldier casualties were also heavy, totaling 64 (25 killed and 39 wounded), representing 7th Cavalry losses during the Indian Wars second only to the regiment's disastrous losses in the Battle of the Little Bighorn.

Some accounts claim that the high soldier casualties were mainly due to friendly fire. This claim may have some degree of merit, since the soldiers' initial box forma-tion surrounding the Lakota warriors, while efficient for disarming them, unneces-sarily put soldiers in the line of fire when both sides began shooting. Yet, the evidence to support heavy soldier friendly fire casualty claims is sketchy and inconclusive, mainly based on the opinion that since the army set out from the start to massacre the Lakotas, any casualties they suffered must have been from friendly fire. In fact, the army's box formation—totally inappropriate for engaging in combat—seems to be clear evidence that the 7th Cavalry did *not* set out that day to intentionally kill all of the Lakotas. And in the wake of the shooting, 7th Cavalry troopers loaded surviving Lakotas (51 were found in the area) into wagons and transported them to shelter from the bitter cold and to receive medical treatment at the reservation hospital. This was hardly the action of soldiers who were intent on killing all of the Indians that tragic day.

Claims that the western Indian Wars constituted genocide—a term no one in the 19th century had even heard of, let alone had the prescience to foresee the horrific state-sponsored mass exterminations in the deadly 20th century that have come to define the term—grossly misread and incorrectly label a complex clash of incom-patible cultures in which the Stone Age one, unwilling or unable to adapt, could at any rate never have survived long-term as a way of life in the Industrial Age. Calling the American tragedy that was the Indian Wars "genocide" not only condescend-ingly idealizes and oversimplifies Indian culture while unfairly demonizing Euro-pean American culture but also demeans the experience of the victims of actual genocide in the 20th century.

Jerry D. Morelock

Perspective Essay 3. Three Centuries of Genocide

Between 1607 and 1890, one of the greatest acts of genocide in human history occurred as European colonists and their descendants in the United States nearly exterminated the region's native population. In 1492, nearly 4 million Native

Americans inhabited the area that is now the United States. By 1890, the native population of the United States had been reduced to about 250,000. The attitudes and policies that resulted in the annihilation of millions of the original North American inhabitants and millions more born during the four centuries since Europeans began colonizing the Americas were established in the early years of the colonial period and continued until the last native resistance was crushed in 1890.

When English colonists settled at Jamestown, Virginia, in 1607, the natives had already suffered serious population losses. Spanish explorers had introduced diseases such as smallpox to which the natives had no natural immunity, sparking waves of epidemics across the continent. Violent assaults on the natives and slave raids to supply workers for Spain's colonies took a further toll. Although the English colonists cannot be directly blamed for the epidemics, they took advantage of the chaos that such high mortality rates produced in native society.

As English leaders began the colonization of North America they recommended a policy of kindness toward the natives, but this advice conflicted with the colonists' other goals: to gain control of the land and find ways to make a profit. Indeed, English colonists showed little respect for the landownership rights of the Powhatan Confederacy of native nations that inhabited the Chesapeake Bay region.

Violence against the Native Americans and seizure of their lands were justified in English eyes by the claimed inferiority of the native peoples. John Smith of Virginia described the Powhatans as "savage" and "malicious," which made them dangerous to the English. A similar attitude toward the natives prevailed in New England, where Puritan colonists believed that they had to preserve their godly society from the threatening "savages."

The English colonists' sense of superiority led to a callous disregard for native lives. Virginians' violent raids to obtain food and their seizure of native land caused the Powhatans to retaliate, resulting in three wars that ended in 1646 with the complete defeat of the natives. The brutalities committed by the colonists included what became customary English practice: devastating the natives' dwellings and food supplies. Less than 40 years after the English landed at Jamestown, the Powhatans, who had numbered 14,000 in 1607, had been "so rowted, slayne and dispersed, that they are no longer a nation," declared an English observer.

In New England, war broke out in 1636 between Puritan settlers in Connecticut and their 3,000 Pequot neighbors. The next year a New England expedition set fire to a Pequot village and slaughtered the inhabitants, most of them women and children. By the time the war ended in 1638, some 2,000 Pequots had been killed. The remaining New England tribes were nearly annihilated in King Philip's War. Wampanoag leader Metacom, called King Philip by the English, attacked the colonists in 1675 to protect what remained of his people's land and autonomy. Despite some native victories, the English struck back in a campaign that saw the widespread massacres of noncombatants. In Rhode Island, the English slaughtered about 2,000 Narragansetts. Fighting subsided when Metacom was killed in 1676. As many as 6,000 natives were killed or sold into slavery.

The destruction of the natives of Virginia and New England in the 17th century established a pattern that was repeated over the next two centuries. Native nations that resisted English expansion, such as the Tuscaroras in North Carolina in 1711 and the Yamasees in South Carolina four years later, were ruthlessly crushed. Thousands of other natives, most of them allies of the French, died during the colonial wars between France and England that began in 1689, in Pontiac's Rebellion against the British in 1763, and during the American Revolution (1775–1783) and the War of 1812 (1812–1815), when many natives supported the British side.

The independent United States continued to expand westward, and in 1794 American forces defeated a Native American coalition in the Northwest. A decade later, Tecumseh of the Shawnees made a new effort to unite the region's natives against the Americans. He led his followers alongside the British in the War of 1812 but was killed in 1813, and native resistance in the North ended. In 1814, Andrew Jackson's defeat of the Creeks destroyed the last native opposition in the South. When Jackson became president in 1829 he put his Indian removal policy into effect, relocating tens of thousands of southeastern natives to present-day Oklahoma. About 4,000 Cherokees died in the Trail of Tears.

Americans moving west of the Mississippi River faced resistance from local natives. Between 1849 and 1890, the U.S. Army fought over 1,000 battles to defeat the natives and force land cessions. Little effort was made to spare the members of peaceful native nations or the lives of noncombatants. Major General Philip Sheridan was said to have remarked in 1867 that "the only good Indians I ever saw were dead," a phrase that was transformed into a popular slogan of the era: "The only good Indian is a dead Indian."

Soldiers and civilians killed large numbers of natives in incidents such as the Sand Creek Massacre of 1864, the Camp Grant Massacre of 1871, and the Wounded Knee Massacre of 1890. Native leaders, including Mangas Coloradas of the Apaches and Crazy Horse and Sitting Bull of the Lakotas, were murdered in captivity or on the reservations.

When the Indian Wars ended in 1890, only 250,000 natives remained in the United States. Weakened by epidemic diseases, the natives had been slaughtered in one conflict after another as the English colonies and then the United States pursued a policy of eliminating people whom they considered inferior and taking their land. The destruction of millions of natives, carried out over nearly three centuries, constitutes nothing less than genocide. The fact that some natives survived, as did many intended Jewish victims of Nazi genocide in the 1940s, does not mitigate the crime.

Jim Piecuch

Further Reading

Axtell, James. *Natives and Newcomers: The Cultural Origins of North America*. New York: Oxford University Press USA, 2001.

Bolt, Christine. *American Indian Policy and American Reform*. London: Unwin Hyman, 1987.

Brandon, William. *The Rise and Fall of the North American Indians: From Prehistory through Geronimo*. Lanham, MD: Roberts Rinehart, 2003.

Brown, Dee. *Bury My Heart at Wounded Knee: An Indian History of the American West*. New York: Holt, Rinehart and Winston, 1970.

Cave, Alfred A. *The Pequot War*. Amherst: University of Massachusetts Press, 1996.

Foreman, Grant. *Indian Removal: The Emigration of the Five Civilized Tribes of Indians*. Norman: University of Oklahoma Press, 1955.

Goldhagen, Daniel J. *Worse Than War: Genocide, Eliminationism, and the Ongoing Assault on Humanity*. New York: PublicAffairs, 2009.

Hine, Robert V., and John Mack Faragher. *The American West: A New Interpretive History*. New Haven, CT: Yale University Press, 2000.

Hoxie, Frederick, ed. *Indians in American History: An Introduction*. Arlington Heights, IL: Harlan Davidson, 1988.

Karr, Ronald Dale. "'Why Should You Be So Furious?' The Violence of the Pequot War." *Journal of American History* 85(3) (December 1998): 876–909.

Keller, Christian B. "Philanthropy Betrayed: Thomas Jefferson, the Louisiana Purchase, and the Origins of Federal Indian Removal Policy." *Proceedings of the American Philosophical Society* 144(1) (March 2000): 39–66.

Lepore, Jill. *The Name of War: King Philip's War and the Origins of American Identity*. New York: Vintage Books, 1998.

Michno, Gregory F. *The Settlers' War: The Struggle for the Texas Frontier in the 1860s*. Caldwell, ID: Caxton, 2011.

Michno, Gregory F., and Susan Michno. *A Fate Worse Than Death: Indian Captives in the West, 1830–1885*. Caldwell, ID: Caxton, 2009.

Mieder, Wolfgang. "'The Only Good Indian Is a Dead Indian': History and Meaning of a Proverbial Stereotype." *Journal of American Folklore* 106(419) (January 1993): 38–60.

Ordahl Kupperman, Karen. *Indians & English: Facing Off in Early America*. Ithaca, NY: Cornell University Press, 2000.

Prucha, F. P. "Andrew Jackson's Indian Policy: A Reassessment." *Journal of American History* 56(3) (December 1969): 527–539.

Rickey, Don, Jr. *Forty Miles a Day on Beans and Hay: The Enlisted Soldier Fighting the Indian Wars*. Norman: University of Oklahoma Press, 1973.

Smith, John. *Captain John Smith's History of Virginia: A Selection*. Edited by David Freeman Hawke. Indianapolis: Bobbs-Merrill, 1970.

Thornton, Russell. *American Indian Holocaust and Survival: A Population History since 1492*. Norman: University of Oklahoma Press, 1987.

Tyler, S. Lyman. *A History of Indian Policy*. Washington, DC: Washington, DC: United States Department of the Interior, 1973.

Utley, Robert M. *A Clash of Cultures: Fort Bowie and the Chiricahua Apaches.* Honolulu: University Press of the Pacific, 2005.

Utley, Robert M. *Frontier Regulars: The United States Army and the Indian, 1866–1890.* New York: Macmillan, 1973.

Utley, Robert M. *Frontiersmen in Blue: The United States Army and the Indian, 1848–1865.* Lincoln: University of Nebraska Press, 1981.

Utley, Robert M. *The Indian Frontier of the American West, 1846–1890.* Albuquerque: University of New Mexico Press, 1984.

Wallace, Anthony F. C. *The Long, Bitter Trail: Andrew Jackson and the Indians.* New York: Hill and Wang, 1993.

Woodworth, Steven E. *Manifest Destinies: America's Westward Expansion and the Road to the Civil War.* New York: Knopf, 2010.

Worster, Donald. *Under Western Skies: Nature and History in the American West.* New York: Oxford University Press, 1994.

32. WHAT WAS THE PRIMARY CAUSE OF THE SPANISH-AMERICAN WAR?

The sinking of USS Maine, *a 6,682-ton battleship, in the Cuban harbor of Havana on February 15, 1898, precipitated a major military conflict between the United States and Spain, the Spanish-American War. Although there was a public outcry that it had been caused by a Spanish mine, Spanish authorities asserted that the explosion originated internally, and several immediate U.S. investigations came to differing conclusions as to the cause. A few months before the incident the United States had taken an interest in the Cuban struggle for independence, requesting that Spain settle the dispute peacefully. To back up its position, the United States sent the* Maine *to Havana to protect U.S. interests. When an explosion sank the* Maine *less than a month after the ship arrived, the yellow press, led by journalists William R. Hearst and Joseph Pulitzer, used the incident to inflame public opinion against the Spanish and encourage a declaration of war.*

The Spanish-American War marked the entrance of the United States entrance into the arena of international imperialism; prior to 1898, U.S. expansionist efforts had been confined to North America. For that reason, many scholars cite the U.S. desire to branch out internationally as a primary cause of the war. However, other scholars point to the highly effective campaign waged by yellow journalists to intervene in Cuba as well as the excessive nationalism—or jingoism—sweeping across the United

States at the time as key factors in the U.S. government's decision to declare war against Spain in April 1898. The war was over quickly, with a victory for the United States. The Treaty of Paris on December 10, 1898, gave the country control of the former Spanish colonies of Puerto Rico, the Philippines, and Guam as well as the right to occupy Cuba. With several contributing factors to consider, including U.S. expansionist designs, yellow journalism, and the sinking of the Maine, *the debate continues over what was the primary reason for America's decision to go to war with Spain in 1898.*

In the perspective essays, each author presents different arguments as to what caused the United States to enter the conflict. Dr. Robert B. Kane argues that the tactics of yellow journalists, primarily newspaper owners William Randolph Hearst and Joseph Pulitzer, were key to initiating the Spanish-American War. The newspaper print wars that these two engaged in led each to publish stories about Cuba's fight for independence that were increasingly sensationalistic, inflammatory, and sometimes false. Faced with the powerful pressure their coverage created, U.S. president William McKinley approved a declaration of war against Spain. James Pruitt takes the opposite viewpoint, contending that the influence of yellow journalism may have contributed to the U.S. decision to go to war, but it would be oversimplifying the issue to claim that it was the sole cause. Instead, Pruitt argues, the United States elected to go to war ultimately to protect its foreign interests and to expand imperial leanings. He points out that the Cuban Revolution, which began in 1895, threatened U.S. economic interests in Cuba, giving the U.S. government a strong incentive to intervene there. Dr. Spencer C. Tucker asserts that the primary reason the United States decided to go to war with Spain in 1898 was the Cuban insurrection. He points out that Cuba and the United States had already developed close relations because of their geographic proximity, and the American people were very concerned about the rough treatment of the Cubans by Spanish forces, which was sensationalized in the press.

Background Essay

The Spanish-American War stemmed from international dislocations that began during the 1890s and eventually led to the long era of global warfare and cold war from 1914 to 1991. At this time the international balance of power, which had been largely stable though dynamic after the Napoleonic Wars, began to destabilize, a consequence of imposing changes during the 19th century. Among these unsettling developments were the urban Industrial Revolution, the rise of strong nation-states in the Western world that enjoyed the loyalty of their citizenry, and the expansion of European empires in Africa and Asia.

The Spanish Empire, once the greatest in the world, largely disappeared during the Napoleonic era, leaving only a few colonies in Africa (Morocco), the West

Indies (Puerto Rico and Cuba), and the Pacific Ocean (the Philippines and smaller island groups, among them the Carolines and Marianas). During the latter years of the 19th century anticolonial movements emerged in the most important of Spain's possessions, the Philippines and Cuba. Spain's Restoration Monarchy, which had been established in 1875, decided to put down these insurgencies rather than grant either autonomy or independence. The Spanish Army crushed the first outbreaks, the Ten Years' War in Cuba (1868–1878) and the First Philippine Insurgency (1896–1897). A second insurgency in Cuba that began in 1895 evolved into extended guerrilla warfare, which proved most troublesome to the Spanish Army, although by the end of 1897 General Valeriano Weyler, known as the "Butcher" because of his stern methods, succeeded in largely containing it.

This success, however, came too late. Spain's Conservative Party, led by Antonio Cánovas de Castillo, had authorized drastic measures in Cuba to counter the insurgents' recourse to partisan tactics. This initiative aroused growing opposition in the United States, especially after Weyler ordered a cruel reconcentration of rural civilians in urban areas to deprive the insurgents of support in the countryside. The United States did not have large investments and commercial interests in Cuba, but anti-Spanish sentiment grew as newspapers published reports of terrible civilian suffering and aroused latent dislike of Spain.

President William McKinley, who took office in April 1897, exerted increasing pressure on Spain to adopt reforms that would at least grant Cuba a significant degree of autonomy. When an anarchist assassinated Cánovas in 1897, the Liberal Party, headed by Práxedes Mateo Sagasta, soon took power, recalled Weyler, and finally granted home rule to both Cuba and Puerto Rico. This gesture, however, came too late. The Cuban leaders rejected autonomy, sensing that this concession signaled Spanish weakness and that perseverance might soon lead to independence.

The Cuban question, although of growing importance, was but one of several great issues that concerned Americans at this time, but the situation was suddenly transformed. On February 15, 1898, the battleship *Maine,* which had been sent to Havana Harbor to establish a U.S. naval presence, exploded and sank, causing the deaths of 266 crew members and many injuries among the survivors. Thereafter, the Cuban question dominated public attention. The nation jumped to the conclusion that the Spanish had placed a mine in the harbor to destroy the *Maine.* A naval inquiry confirmed this view, although years later it became clear that the probable cause was internal combustion in the ship's coal bunkers adjacent to stockpiles of ammunition.

The cautious McKinley opposed armed intervention, seeking instead to emphasize economic reforms, but public pressure eventually forced him to call for Cuban independence. His supporters in the business community, the most important constituency in the Republican Party, were concerned chiefly with the monetary system and the tariff. They feared the unsettling effects that might stem from war, which often leads to unexpected and undesirable outcomes for business.

An artistic rendering of the destruction of the U.S. battleship *Maine* in Havana Harbor on February 15, 1898. (Library of Congress)

When Spain did not bow to the American demand for Cuban independence, Congress authorized armed intervention but also adopted the Teller Amendment, which proclaimed that the purpose of armed intervention was to help Cuba achieve independence, a resounding repudiation of imperialist intentions. For various reasons many Democrats supported war, which influenced McKinley. He reluctantly went along with Congress, in all probability fearing that his failure to do so would compromise the Republican Party in the fall elections and eventually return the Democratic Party, the champion of free silver and free trade, to power in Washington, D.C.

Spain attempted to gain support from the great powers of Europe but failed to do so. The nation had no international ties of importance, having followed a policy of isolation from other nations during many years of internal political challenges, notably the agitation of Carlists, Basques, Catalonians, and other groups. Widespread domestic unrest raised fears of revolution and the fall of the Restoration Monarchy. Given these domestic challenges, Spain did not involve itself in external affairs. The European powers, preoccupied with great issues of their own, including difficulties with their own empires, refused to help Spain, having no obligations and no desire to earn the enmity of the United States. Bereft of European support, Spain had to fight alone against a formidable enemy.

Popular emotions influenced the Madrid government to some extent; many Spaniards believed that the empire had been God's gift as a reward for the expulsion of the Moors from Europe and also believed that no Spanish government could surrender the remaining colonies without dishonoring the nation. War seemed a lesser evil than looming domestic tumult. In addition, many believed that Spain could give a good account of itself because the Americans seemed unprepared for war. Spain possessed a large army, already in place in the likely combat zones, and also possessed a respectable navy, which it deemed superior to that of the United States. Even if Spain experienced defeat, an honorable military effort rather than craven acceptance of the American demands might preserve the established order.

Spain declared war on April 23, 1898, and the United States followed suit on April 25, predating its action to April 21 because it had already begun naval operations.

David F. Trask

Perspective Essay 1. The First Press War

The Spanish-American War is understandably viewed by some historians as the first press war. President William McKinley felt pressured to declare war on Spain in April 1898 because of growing outrage from many Americans and U.S. Congress members over Spanish actions in Cuba. That outrage had developed primarily from the newspaper war between William Randolph Hearst and Joseph Pulitzer. In an attempt to increase the number of readers for their respective newspapers, they outdid each other in telling lurid and sensationalized stories of Spanish atrocities against the Cuban people. The mass media, as represented by Hearst's and Pulitzer's newspapers, had developed from the urbanization, industrialization, and modernization of American society after 1865, which had produced in turn significantly larger numbers of literate adults with a desire to read and the technological means to publish large numbers of newspapers at very low costs.

As the 19th century drew to a close, newspapers increasingly became the major source of news in America. Free public education had resulted in a growing literacy rate in the United States and with it a rapidly growing demand for cheap newspapers. At the same time, the Industrial Revolution had produced machines that could easily print thousands of papers in a single night. Rather than producing objective journalism, a newspaper would routinely give the editor's interpretation of events, and no one had any effective means of testing the veracity of the reports. This served to give top newspapers significant political power. Thus, to increase the number of readers, top papers would exploit this power by printing news that was flamboyant or even false.

Newspaper owners, epitomized by Pulitzer, owner of the *New York World,* and Hearst, owner of the *San Francisco Examiner* and later the *New York Morning Journal,* competed with one another to increase circulation and obtain more revenue from advertising. To do so, in the mid-1890s Pulitzer and Hearst transformed their bland newspapers of seemingly endless columns of political debate and staid stories, read only by the social and political elite, to mass newspapers with sensational and scandalous news stories, drawings, and features such as comic strips to gain the readership of the growing literate masses. Older publishers, envious of Pulitzer's success, criticized the *New York World,* harping that its sensationalism came at the expense of more serious reporting.

In early 1896, Pulitzer began publishing color comic sections that included a strip called "Hogan's Alley," featuring a yellow-dressed character named "the yellow kid," drawn by Richard F. Outcault. After nine months Outcault went to work for Hearst's papers and brought his strip with him, where it competed with a Pulitzer-sponsored version. Journalists soon filled the increasingly cheap papers with gaudy, sensationalist, and lurid stories for reading by the common people. Soon this type of news received the label "yellow journalism."

In February 1896, conflict erupted in Cuba between rebels who wanted to free Cuba from a corrupt and inefficient Spanish colonial government and a Spanish government that wished to keep the last vestiges of its once great Latin American empire. Recognizing "a story when they saw it," Hearst and Pulitzer sent well-known reporters to Cuba to report on the fighting as a means to advance the battle over circulation. The *New York Morning Journal* fervently declared its support for the Cuban rebels against Spain, and Hearst even refused to carry news from Spanish sources, stating that only rebel informants were trustworthy.

These reporters sent back stories designed to tug at the hearts of Americans. Many of the stories that filled the Hearst and Pulitzer newspapers contained horrific tales about the ill treatment of female prisoners, executions of civilians, valiant Cuban rebels fighting for independence, and starving women and children in concentration camps. The yellow press vilified the new Spanish commander General Valeriano Weyler y Nicolau, who had a reputation as a ruthless fighter and was known as "Butcher Weyler." When Spanish prime minister Antonio Cánovas del Castillo was assassinated in June, Weyler lost his principal supporter in Spain. He resigned his post in late 1897 and returned to Europe.

As the fighting between the rebels and the colonial government escalated through early 1898, McKinley ordered the battleship *Maine* to Havana Harbor as an American show of force and as a means to protect American economic interests in Cuba. On the night of February 15, 1898, a mysterious explosion caused the *Maine* to sink, killing 254 crew members and injuring another 59. This event gave Hearst his big story for war with Spain. Without any evidence to support his accusation and the inability of a U.S. Navy board of investigation to determine the "perpetrators," the Hearst newspapers unequivocally blamed the Spanish, and the *New York World* supposedly sold 5 million copies the week after that disaster.

Quickly, American public opinion and many U.S. Congress members demanded intervention. Given the views of the increasingly prowar press, McKinley feared that the Republicans would suffer if he decided not to go to war with Spain. As a result, on April 20, 1898, McKinley reluctantly asked Congress for and received a declaration of war against Spain. Hearst, as he so proudly boasted, got his war against Spain.

Today, many historians see the Spanish-American War as the first press-driven war. Although claiming that Hearst and the other yellow journalists had started the war is probably an exaggeration, it is fair to say that the press fueled the public's passion for war and led the charge toward the involvement of the United States in Cuban affairs. Illustrations such as those of Frederic Remington and stories written by well-known authors helped to fuel the war, while graphic stories of brutality and often untrue events created a frenzy among the public. Without sensational headlines and stories coming out of Cuba, many Americans might have been less inclined to opt for war with Spain over Cuba. By early 1899 the United States had emerged as a world power from this "splendid little war" with Spain, and the American press had demonstrated its influence to frame public opinion.

Robert B. Kane

Perspective Essay 2. Destined for Empire

The Spanish-American War launched the United States onto the world stage and foreshadowed the larger role it would play in international relations during the 20th century. Initially, many historians writing on the causes of the war oversimplified the factors involved and attributed the conflict to the influence of yellow journalism on the American public. As the traditional explanation went, the circulation wars between rival newspapers led to increasingly sensational stories of Spanish atrocities committed against noble Cuban patriots. These stories, often accompanied by graphic illustrations, whipped up interventionist sentiment among the American public and forced the William McKinley administration to intervene. Although yellow journalism did play a part, the traditional interpretation ignored other significant factors and failed to place the conflict into the historic pattern of expansion by the United States.

A closer look at American foreign policy leading up to the Spanish-American War reveals a country seeking to develop a foreign policy compatible with its growing national power and reflective of its values and interests. A clear understanding of the factors involved provides insight into the complex nature of American foreign policy and highlights the competing interests that often propel that policy forward. For most of the 19th century, the United States limited its engagement in foreign affairs to continental expansion, matters of trade, and protecting the Western Hemisphere from encroachment through the Monroe Doctrine.

Geographically distant from the European powers and without any powerful regional rival, internal American development proceeded unabated by external threats for most of the 19th century. Such a long period of uninterrupted isolation allowed the United States to develop its internal resources (geography, population, and natural resources) and hone its social institutions to project a level of national power that soon surpassed European capabilities. The rising level of national power allowed the United States to turn its attention abroad. In some cases the very elements of national power demanded that the country turn its focus abroad and to economic and/or territorial expansion.

A remarkable level of economic growth and a desire to tap the potential of foreign markets focused the attention of many Americans abroad in the 1890s. Over the course of the previous century, the United States had undergone a profound economic transformation from a rural agricultural society to a large, highly industrialized urban society. Increasingly, industrialization, immigration, and advancements in technology combined to create an economic infrastructure that harnessed the scattered resources of the country to create an industrial and agricultural powerhouse regularly producing more than Americans could consume. Rather than face the stagnation and recession brought on by overproduction, Americans began to look abroad for new markets and economic opportunities. Spanish Cuba offered an attractive investment opportunity for American capital, a potential market for American products, and a potential source for important agricultural products, such as sugar. In 1894, one year prior to the 1895 Cuban Revolution, "the United States took 87 percent of Cuba's exports and provided 38 percent of its total imports, slightly more than Spain itself." By 1898, the destruction caused by the revolution threatened these economic interests and led to calls for American intervention.

If economic self-sufficiency provided the means for that expansion and the need to find markets to dispose of the surplus production supplied on at least one end, the growing power of the federal government provided the ways. While the United States underwent its economic transformation, other internal forces centralized political and military power in the federal government and eliminated major regional and sectional conflicts to create a high level of national unity. The Populist and Progressive crusades in the 1890s marked the willingness of the people to entrust the emerging federal government with more power and control over their daily lives. Their attempt to correct the social problems of the day did much to modernize federal and local governments and contributed to the flow of power to the national level. Furthermore, the Progressive drive for efficiency and profession-alism also honed the power of both the U.S. Army and the U.S. Navy, thus provid-ing the federal government with effective instruments for expansion.

The Progressive movement's commitment to social progress combined with an older belief in American exceptionalism to further orient American attention abroad. Even before the founding of the country in 1776, Americans viewed them-selves as destined by Providence to lead the world into a golden age of liberal de-mocracy and enlightened self-government. Best embodied in John Winthrop's "City upon a Hill" sermon and Abraham Lincoln's characterization of the United States as "the last best hope," American exceptionalism constitutes a definitive theme in American foreign policy. The theme proved especially powerful at the turn of the 20th century, when many expansionists combined it with social Dar-winism and a growing nationalism to call the nation to its "rightful place" in the world and to carry the benefits of its superior civilization and morality beyond its borders. None did so more consistently or with more conviction and power than Theodore Roosevelt, a popular reformer, politician, historian, public speaker, and unofficial leader of a political coalition of progressives and expansionists that in-cluded Alfred Thayer Mahan, Henry Cabot Lodge, William Howard Taft, Elihu Root, and Leonard Wood.

As the son and namesake of a well-to-do philanthropist, Roosevelt inherited a deep concern for the less fortunate and believed it the duty of those with power to assist them. In the realm of foreign policy, this led him to conclude that the United States had an obligation, even a divine charge, to spread the benefits of civilization to as many as possible. Roosevelt rejected the social Darwinist belief in the "survival of the fittest" and adopted a reformed Darwinist approach that sought to equip as many as possible for survival. Roosevelt believed that the uncivilized races were not inherently inferior and could be taught by the more advanced in the ways of civili-zation. According to Roosevelt, "It is our duty to the people living in barbarism to see that they are freed from their chains and we can free them only by destroying barbarism itself."

As the 19th century marched toward the 20th century, economic concerns, the growing power of the federal level, and a belief in America's divine role in the world increasingly turned the country's attention to foreign pursuits. Although the Cu-bans had revolted against Spain numerous times before, the revolt in 1895 found the United States more receptive to intervention. When the forces for intervention combined with the humanitarian concerns raised by the yellow journalists, the United States embarked on a conflict that not only liberated Cuba but also created an American empire that stretched from the Caribbean to the Philippines. The growing American presence on the world stage embroiled the United States in in-tense colonial rivalries with European and Asian countries. The U.S. government dictated a greater adherence to international relations and called for a massive reevaluation of American military power. In short, the war gave birth to modern America and set the course for American foreign policy into the 20th century.

James Pruitt

Perspective Essay 3. The Cuban Fight against Spanish Rule

Fighting in Cuba lay behind the U.S. decision to go to war against Spain in 1898. Located only 110 miles off the southern coast of Florida, the island of Cuba had necessarily been forced into a close relationship with the United States. There had been several revolts in Cuba against inept but not overly oppressive Spanish rule, including the Ten Years' War (1868–1878) and the Small War (1879–1880). The failure of the Spanish government to implement promised reforms following these conflicts and a high tariff on sugar into the United States imposed by the Dingley Tariff of 1897 led to a new widespread Cuban insurrection. Spanish captain General Valeriano Weyler attempted to put down the rebellion in compartmentalization of the island through *trochas* (fortified lines) and the establishment of concentration camps to isolate the insurgents from support by the civilian population.

The so-called yellow press in the United States reported widely on events in Cuba. Eager to sell more newspapers, media moguls such as Joseph Pulitzer and William Randolph Hearst took up the cause of the Cubans. Their sensationalist and sometimes untrue news stories were remarkably popular with an increasingly literate American population. They capitalized on the deteriorating situation in Cuba and reported on events there on a nearly daily basis. Pulitzer and Hearst sent artists and illustrators to Cuba to provide pictures for their newspapers. When artist Frederic Remington requested to return to the United States for lack of anything to report, Hearst allegedly replied "Please remain. You furnish the pictures, I'll furnish the war."

American sympathy was particularly stirred by the plight of those in the concentration camps, and Cuban exiles in the United States adroitly fanned the flames of anti-Spanish sentiment.

The struggle in Cuba threatened to go on indefinitely, as 150,000 Spanish troops were unable to subdue an estimated 40,000 rebels. U.S. presidents Grover Cleveland and William McKinley had both refused to get involved. Then in October 1897 a new Spanish premier, Práxedes Mariano Mateo Sagasta y Escolar, proposed abandonment of the concentration policy, recalled General Weyler, and promised Cuba a measure of home rule. The crisis apparently had passed.

The continuing Cuban insurgency, the Dupuy de Lôme Letter, and the sinking of USS *Maine* all brought rapid deterioration in U.S.-Spanish relations. Spanish ambassador to the United States Enrique Dupuy de Lôme wrote to an acquaintance in Cuba covering events there for a Spanish newspaper. In the letter Dupuy de Lôme was sharply critical of President McKinley, characterizing him as "weak" and a "low" politician who pandered to the "rabble." Cuban revolutionaries intercepted the letter and turned it over to the Hearst publishing empire. The letter appeared in the *New York Journal* on February 9, 1898, and played a significant role in increasing popular support in the United States for war against Spain. Dupuy de Lôme meanwhile promptly resigned his post and returned to Spain.

In a provocative act, the U.S. government had dispatched the second-class battleship *Maine* to Havana, ostensibly to protect U.S. interests in Cuba but actually to intimidate Spain into granting concessions to the Cuban insurgents. On the night of February 15, 1898, the *Maine* was riding at anchor in Havana Harbor when its forward magazines, with nearly 5 tons of powder charges, exploded, sinking the ship and resulting in the deaths of 266 members of its crew. A naval court of inquiry blamed the blast on an external mine. More recent scientific research has concluded that the explosion resulted from excessive heat caused by spontaneous combustion in a coal locker that touched off the magazines.

Encouraged by the yellow press, most Americans held the Spaniards responsible, although it is impossible to see how sinking a U.S. warship would have been in their interest. If it was a mine, it could well have been the work of the Cuban insurgents. In any case, Americans took up the cry "Remember the *Maine*—to hell with Spain!"

McKinley, a veteran of the American Civil War, did not want war with Spain. But Congress, the press, and the so-called congressional Young Republicans did. Imperialism was in the air, and American expansionists were eager to join the race for overseas territory. Influential figures such as U.S. Navy captain Alfred Thayer Mahan saw this as an opportunity for the United States to secure overseas bases and assert itself as a world power.

On March 8 the U.S. Congress passed a $50 million national defense appropriation bill, to be spent at the discretion of the president, and on March 17 moderate Republican senator Redfield Proctor, just returned from an inspection trip to Cuba, delivered a major speech before the U.S. Senate denouncing the methods employed by the Spanish authorities in Cuba. This speech helped convince many that the United States had a humanitarian duty to intervene in Cuba.

McKinley finally gave way to the argument that failure to act regarding Cuba would split the Republican Party. On March 22, the day after the report of the board of inquiry concerning the loss of the ship, the president sent Madrid an ultimatum demanding an immediate armistice, the release of prisoners, and American mediation between Spain and Cuba. Spain's formal reply to this unwelcome demand was unsatisfactory, but the Sagasta government did not want war with the United States and took steps to avert it. On April 9 the governor-general of Cuba offered an armistice to the insurgents, and on April 10 U.S. ambassador to Madrid Stewart L.

Woodford cabled Washington that if nothing was done to humiliate Spain, the Cuban situation could be settled on the basis of autonomy, independence, or even cession of the island to the United States.

On April 11, McKinley sent the Congress a long review of the situation with only a passing, deceptive reference to Woodford's dispatch, concluding that he had "exhausted every effort to relieve the intolerable condition of affairs which is at our doors" and asking for authority to intervene. On April 19 Congress passed a joint resolution (311 to 6 in the House of Representatives and 42 to 35 in the Senate) that recognized the independence of Cuba, demanded the withdrawal of Spanish armed forces from the island, called on the president to use the U.S. armed forces to carry out these demands, and disclaimed any U.S. intention to exercise sovereignty over the island (the Teller Amendment). President McKinley signed the resolution on April 20 and that same day sent it to Spain. The Spanish government held the ultimatum to be a declaration of war and declared war itself on April 23. The United States responded in kind on April 25. However, because of McKinley's order of a naval blockade of Cuba on April 22, the U.S. declaration was made retroactive to that date.

Spencer C. Tucker

Further Reading

Allen, Thomas B. "What Really Sank the *Maine*?" *Naval History* 12(2) (February 1998): 92–111.

Balfour, Sebastian. *The End of the Spanish Empire, 1898–1923.* New York: Oxford University Press, 1997.

Barrett, James Wyman. *Joseph Pulitzer and His World.* New York: Vanguard, 1941.

Beale, Howard. *Theodore Roosevelt and the Rise of America to World Power.* Baltimore: Johns Hopkins University Press, 1956.

Blow, Michael. *A Ship to Remember: The* Maine *and the Spanish-American War.* New York: William Morrow, 1992.

Bradford, James C., ed. *Crucible of Empire: The Spanish-American War & Its Aftermath.* Annapolis, MD: Naval Institute Press, 1993.

Cohen, Stan. *Images of the Spanish-American War.* Missoula, MT: Pictorial Histories Publishing, 1998.

Damiani, Brian P. *Advocates of Empire: William McKinley, the Senate, and American Expansion, 1898–1899.* New York: Garland, 1987.

Healy, David. *Drive to Hegemony: The United States in the Caribbean, 1898–1917.* Madison: University of Wisconsin Press, 1988.

Hendrickson, Kenneth E., Jr. *The Spanish-American War.* Westport, CT: Greenwood, 2003.

Milton, Joyce. *The Yellow Kids: Foreign Correspondents in the Heyday of Yellow Journalism.* New York: Harper and Row, 1989.

Nofi, Albert A. *The Spanish-American War, 1898.* Conshohocken, PA: Combined Books, 1996.

Offner, John L. *An Unwanted War: The Diplomacy of the United States and Spain over Cuba.* Chapel Hill: University of North Carolina Press, 1992.

O'Toole, G. J. A. *The Spanish War: An American Epic, 1898.* New York: Norton, 1984.

Silbey, David J. *A War of Frontier and Empire: The Philippine-American War, 1899–1902.* New York: Hill and Wang, 2006.

Swanberg, W. A. *Citizen Hearst: A Biography of William Randolph Hearst.* New York: Scribner, 1961.

Trask, David F. *The War with Spain in 1898.* Lincoln: University of Nebraska Press, 1996.

Tucker, Spencer C. *The Encyclopedia of the Spanish-American and Philippine-American Wars: A Political, Social, and Military History.* Santa Barbara, CA: ABC-CLIO, 2009.

PART V

THE WORLD AT WAR (1914–1945)

33. What Was the Primary Cause of World War I?

On June 28, 1914, Archduke Franz Ferdinand of Austria-Hungary was assassinated by Serbian nationalist Gavrilo Princip in Sarajevo. A mere month later, Europe was plunged into a gruesome conflict that would last for more than four years and claim the lives of 9 million combatants. The conflict was the first truly modern total war, meaning that the conflict affected all aspects of the combatants' societies and brought wide-scale suffering to civilian populations. As such, World War I wrought major societal, cultural, and economic changes from Russia all the way to the United States and many places in between. In some nations such as Russia, these changes morphed into full-scale revolution, which ended centuries of czarist rule and inaugurated the world's first major communist power. The war's legacy was even more momentous. Indeed, it upended the world's economy and ushered in fascist rule in Italy and Nazism in Germany. A number of historians have even argued that World War I and its aftermath paved the way for World War II less than a generation later. The sudden outbreak of World War I and its underlying causes, however, remain the subject of intense scholarly debate to this day.

In his perspective essay, Dr. Richard L. DiNardo argues that in 1914 there was an expectation among the major European powers that a general war was inevitable. This expectation was based on a number of factors, including a century-long history of frequent conflicts, rising nationalist sentiments, long-standing territorial disputes (particularly over Alsace-Lorraine and Bosnia and Herzegovina), and an internecine system of military and diplomatic alliances. Additionally, there was an expectation—which proved erroneous—that when war did occur it would be brief and decisive. For Dr. Mark D. Karau, the root cause of World War I can be ascribed to fear. He asserts that Austro-Hungarian leaders feared the dissolution of their empire, while their German counterparts fretted that if they could not prevent the collapse of the Dual Monarchy, they would lose their only European ally and would fall prey to Russian encroachments. Dr. Michael S. Neiberg expands on this theory, pointing out how these fears caused a number of strategic miscalculations among military and political leaders that pushed Europe into war in August 1914. He emphasizes the fact that war was

not inevitable and that most Europeans did not believe the assassination of the Aus-
tro-Hungarian archduke would lead to a larger conflict; World War I was instead the
result of a small crisis that was disastrously mismanaged.

Background Essay

Impetus for a general war had been building for decades, and all the major European powers bore some measure of responsibility for its outbreak in 1914. Historians usually identify five underlying causes: nationalism (the triumph of statism over internationalism but also the desire of subject minorities to have their own nation-states), two hostile alliance systems, imperialist and trade rivalries, an arms race, and economic and social tensions.

Nationalism was a major impetus, and nowhere was this more obvious than in Austria-Hungary, a mélange of at least a dozen minorities. Germans (23 percent) and Magyars (19 percent) dominated, but by the beginning of the 20th century Slavic nationalism, championed by neighboring Serbia, threatened the Dual Monarchy. Enjoying the support of Slavic Russia, Serbia had long sought to be the nucleus of a large state embracing all the South Slavs. In 1908 in an effort to diminish Serbian influence and cut Serbia off from access to the sea, the Dual Monarchy annexed Bosnia-Herzegovina, almost bringing war with Russia. Austria-Hungary also insisted on the creation of an independent Albania.

Germany—Europe's preeminent military power—was Austria-Hungary's closest ally and supported its action in Bosnia-Herzegovina. The German Empire had come into being as a consequence of the Franco-Prussian War of 1870–1871. Having imposed a draconian peace settlement on France, German chancellor Otto von Bismarck sought to isolate that country, which was bent on revenge. An arrangement with both Austria-Hungary and Russia (the Dreikaiserbund, or Three Emperors' League) shattered over their competition in the Balkans. Forced to choose, Bismarck selected Austria-Hungary as Germany's principal ally. This Dual Alliance of 1879 was the bedrock of German foreign policy into World War I. Not prepared to cast Russia adrift, however, in 1887 Bismarck concluded the so-called Reinsurance Treaty with Russia, which he kept secret from Austria.

As long as Bismarck was chancellor France remained isolated, but in 1888 Wilhelm II became emperor. Young, rash, and headstrong, he soon clashed with Bismarck and in 1890 dropped him as chancellor and dramatically changed Germany's foreign policy. Relations with Russia were already frayed, but the situation was made worse when Wilhelm ordered that the Reinsurance Treaty not be renewed in 1890. Russia was rapidly industrializing and seeking foreign capital, and France stepped into the breach. By 1894 the two had forged a military alliance against Germany.

Thus, by 1914 there were two mutually antagonistic alliance systems in Europe. The first consisted of Germany and Austria-Hungary. Separate from it was the Triple Alliance of 1882 of Germany-Austria-Hungary and Italy, made possible because of Italian anger over France's seizure of Tunis, but Italy was an increasingly reluctant ally. France and Russia formed the second alliance, to which Britain was informally linked.

Wilhelm II was not content with Germany being the preeminent European power; he wanted it to be the preeminent world power. He reversed Bismarck's wise policy of keeping the navy small so as not to antagonize Britain, and the result was a naval-building contest between the two powers beginning in the mid-1890s. Wilhelm II and Grand Admiral Alfred von Tirpitz saw Germany challenging Britain, even Britain and the United States, on the seas for world mastery. Wilhelm's policies alienated would-be allies and created a climate of uncertainty. Many Germans, however, saw themselves encircled and denied their rightful place in the sun. At the same time, Germany was undergoing social change, worker unrest, and political upheaval. Some German leaders saw a general European war as a means to unite the country.

France also looked forward to war. In addition to an indemnity of more than twice the cost of the war to Prussia, the Treaty of Frankfurt of 1871 had stripped France of Alsace and Lorraine. French foreign policy after 1871 is said to have been dominated by one word: revenge. In 1904 France and Britain ended decades of overseas rivalry in an agreement on colonial issues. Britain and Russia concluded a similar arrangement in 1907.

Russia was beginning to enter the modern age, although Czar Nicholas II would make no concessions to political change. Russia sought ascendancy in the Balkans and control of the straits to ensure free access from the Black Sea into the Mediterranean. Humiliated in the Russo-Japanese War (1904–1905), Russia had expended considerable resources in rebuilding its military. Russian industrial and military growth, which included the construction of new strategic railroads, raised alarm bells in Berlin. Chief of the German General Staff Colonel General Helmuth von Moltke said in May 1914 that in several years Russia would be rearmed and that the Entente powers would then be so powerful that it would be difficult for Germany to triumph. Germany therefore had no alternative but to seek a preventive war while there was a chance of victory.

Britain followed its traditional pattern of involving itself in continental affairs only to preserve vital national interests or the European balance of power, but Germany's decision to build a powerful navy drove it to the side of France. The British also saw growing German industrial might and world trade as a threat. Although aligned with France and Russia, Britain's sole military responsibility in 1914 was a 1912 pledge to protect France's coasts from German naval attack.

Several crises almost brought general European war in the decade before 1914. Two, in 1905–1906 and in 1911, involved Morocco when Germany, with no vital interests at stake, threatened war to block a French takeover. In 1908 war almost erupted over Austria's annexation of Bosnia-Herzegovina, but Russia backed down. In 1911 Italy went to war with the Ottoman Empire to secure present-day Libya and the Dodecanese Islands. Then in 1912 and 1913 two regional wars raged in the Balkans, both of which had threatened to draw in the big powers and bring world war.

As Bismarck had predicted, the situation in the Balkans triggered the war. In 1914 a Serb nationalist organization linked to the Serbian military undertook the assassination of Archduke Franz Ferdinand, heir to the Austrian throne and believed to favor greater rights for Slavs within the Dual Monarchy, a threat to Serbian aspirations. On June 28, 1914, in Sarajevo, Bosnia, young Bosnian Serb nationalist Gavrilo Princip shot to death Franz Ferdinand and his wife as they rode in an open car.

Austrian leaders sought to use the assassination to advantage, envisioning a localized Balkan conflict in which the Serbian question would be settled "once and for all." But Austria required German support, as this might bring on a general

Gavrilo Princip, who assassinated the Archduke Franz Ferdinand and his wife Sophie in Sarajevo on June 28, 1914, shown being taken into custody. (The Illustrated London News Picture Library)

European war. Russia had backed down in 1908, but this made a second retreat less likely. German leaders were well aware that Austria-Hungary intended to attack Serbia, but because the Dual Monarchy was its only reliable ally, on July 6 Berlin again pledged its support in the famous Blank Check.

To cloak the intention to crush Serbia and overcome Hungarian government hesitation, the Austro-Hungarian council of ministers approved an ultimatum couched so that Serbia must reject it. On July 22 Germany approved the terms, and a day later it was sent to Belgrade with the demand for a reply within 48 hours. To great surprise, Serbia responded within the time limit, accepting all the Austrian demands except those directly impinging on its sovereignty but offering to accept arbitration regarding these. Vienna declared the response unsatisfactory, severed diplomatic relations, and ordered partial military mobilization; Serbia had already mobilized.

In St. Petersburg the Russian government hoped to bluff Vienna into backing down by ordering "preparatory measures" for a partial military mobilization. This step on July 26 had the support of the Russian General Staff, which believed that war was inevitable.

On July 28 the Third Balkan War began when Austria-Hungary formally declared war on Serbia. On July 29 the Russian government ordered actual mobilization in four Russian military districts, and on July 30 Russia ordered a general mobilization. This ensured that the war would become a general European conflict, for military timetables now came into play.

In planning for the likelihood of a two front war against France and Russia, General Alfred von Schlieffen, chief of the German General Staff during 1891–1906, envisioned sending most German military strength against France with a holding action against a slowly mobilizing Russia. Following the rapid defeat of France, Germany could then deal with Russia. Thus, Germany could not allow the Russians to mobilize and still win the war. The German government therefore demanded that Russia halt its mobilization. When Russia refused, on August 1 Germany ordered general mobilization.

The French cabinet had refused to mobilize the army but did order troops to take up position on the frontier, although far enough from it so as to convince British public opinion that France was not initiating hostilities. The Schlieffen Plan mandated that there be no delay in opening an attack against France. Thus, on August 1 the Germans demanded to know how France would respond to war between Germany and Russia. Berlin insisted that even if France pledged neutrality, it would have to surrender certain eastern fortresses as proof of sincerity. No French government could agree to these terms, and Premier René Viviani replied that France would act in accordance with its interests. That same day France ordered military mobilization. On August 3, Germany declared war on France.

Spencer C. Tucker

Perspective Essay 1. The Expectation of War

The primary cause of World War I was a sense of expectation among the major powers of Europe in regard to both the possibility of a general war and its duration. The first expectation was that a major war between at least two of the great powers of Europe was considered to be almost an inevitability. Europe saw its share of armed conflicts between 1815 and 1914. The sense of expectation that a major war was in the offing was further heightened by the rise of nationalism in large parts of Europe over that same time period. Nationalism aroused aspirations for independence among peoples in Europe then under the rule of either the Russian, Austrian, or Ottoman Empires.

The expectation of a general European war was increased by the presence of long-standing issues between countries, usually involving territorial disputes. At the top of this list was the issue of Alsace-Lorraine and its impact on Franco-German relations. Prussia had taken the French provinces of Alsace and Lorraine early in the course of the Franco-Prussian War in 1870. The loss of Alsace and Lorraine stuck in the collective French craw, as these provinces had been French for almost two centuries. Thus, over the ensuing decades, the one constant objective of French foreign policy was the recovery of Alsace and Lorraine.

A similar situation involved Austria-Hungary and Serbia. The Dual Monarchy, seeking to maintain a polyglot empire under the auspices of the Habsburg dynasty, had gained de facto control of Bosnia-Herzegovina in 1879 after the Congress of Berlin. In 1908 Austria-Hungary formally annexed Bosnia-Herzegovina, triggering a crisis that brought Europe to the brink of war. Serbia, having gained its independence from the Ottoman Empire in 1829, by the late 19th century had become an equally expansionist power. For the Serbian governments at the end of the 19th century, Bosnia-Herzegovina represented unredeemed Serbia, a territory that could be gained only by force.

The expectation of countries that war would occur sooner or later was also increased by the changes in the alliance system that developed in Europe between 1879 and 1908. In 1879 after the Congress of Berlin had caused a strain in Russo-German relations, German chancellor Otto von Bismarck thought it a most propitious time to sign a 20-year secret alliance with Austria-Hungary. The terms of this Dual Alliance—that each power would come to the aid of the other if attacked by another power—were regarded by Bismarck as a good way of keeping Austrian adventures in the Balkans in check while also binding Germany with its closest natural ally. Italy was added to this arrangement in 1882 through a separate treaty, thus forming the Triple Alliance. Aside from the Austrian alliance, Bismarck also sought to obtain Russian neutrality. This would serve to keep Germany in some sort of friendly relationship with at least three of the five major powers in Europe. The alliance would also serve to keep France isolated diplomatically.

Bismarck's first attempt in this endeavor was the League of the Three Emperors, formed by Germany, Russia, and Austria-Hungary in the aftermath of the assassination of Russian czar Alexander II in 1881. This rather loose entente collapsed, however, owing to conflicts between Russia and Austria-Hungary over the Balkans and the outcome of the Serbo-Bulgarian War in 1885. With an alliance involving both Austria-Hungary and Russia now effectively dead, Bismarck resorted to the alternative course of pursuing a bilateral agreement with Russia. In 1887, he concluded the Reinsurance Treaty with that country. According to the terms of this agreement, both countries promised to remain neutral if the other became involved in a war.

After Bismarck's dismissal in 1890 by Kaiser Wilhelm II, many of Bismarck's policies became anathema. The German government let the Reinsurance Treaty lapse in 1890. Thereafter, Russian diplomacy began to gravitate toward France, culminated in the signing of a Franco-Russian alliance in 1894. From then on France, still desirous of regaining Alsace and Lorraine, could expect that if it did become involved in a war with Germany, it would do so with Russia fighting by its side. The kaiser's naval policy also served to exacerbate Germany's difficulties. The extensive German effort to build a powerful battle fleet alienated the potential German ally of Great Britain. The naval race, won by the British with the introduction of the modern Dreadnought-class battleship, left Germany in the worst of all possible worlds; Britain had maintained naval superiority and had also moved toward the French.

The worsening of Germany's diplomatic position changed the character of the Austro-German alliance. After 1905, German leaders could expect that the only country on whose help they could rely was Austria-Hungary. Although Italy was a member of the Triple Alliance, after the 1908 Bosnian Crisis it began to slowly back out of the alliance. By 1912 German military leaders had concluded that an Italian appearance on the Rhine was not to be expected, which meant Austria-Hungary had to be supported no matter what.

The issue of expectation and war also operated in another way: namely the length and conduct of a war. By 1914, all of the major powers had industrial economies capable of keeping large armies supplied. These economies were all supported by railroad networks of varying density and efficiency. All of these networks played major roles in the process of military mobilization, so much so that by the onset of the 20th century, the mere act of mobilization was the equivalent of an act of war. Since the military establishments of that day relied on a regular army that would be rapidly expanded by the immediate incorporation of millions of trained reservists, mobilization would have a double impact on the economy. First, millions of men would be removed from factories and farms. Second, the railroad system of a country would have to be devoted to supporting military mobilization and deployment, thus disrupting the normal system of transporting goods. Before 1914, it was widely held that these two things would serve to bring a modern economy to a complete halt. The perception that European economies were too fragile to withstand the strain of a prolonged and bloody war led to the expectation that when war did come, its duration would be brief.

Such expectation was buoyed by some selective cherry picking from recent history. In 1866, the Prussian Army needed just seven weeks to defeat Austria. Four years later the outcome of the Franco-Prussian War was decided in the first two months, with the trapping of the main French armies in Metz and Sedan. Although the forces raised by the French Provisional Government were able to drag the war on into 1871, the ultimate result was hardly in doubt.

The expectation that a new war would necessarily be of short duration was manifested in the war plans of the major continental powers. The most notable of these was the so-called Schlieffen Plan, named for General Alfred von Schlieffen, who formulated it during his tenure as chief of the German General Staff from 1896 to 1906. Confronted with the prospect of a two-front war against France and Russia, Schlieffen believed that Germany could only win if it could defeat France quickly. With France disposed of, the slower-to-mobilize Russians could then be dealt with. Schlieffen came up with a plan that called for the German Army to deploy the vast majority of its strength in the west. Most of this force would then invade Belgium and Holland, thus skirting the fortresses erected by France along the Franco-German border after 1875. The invading force, with its right wing moving parallel to the English Channel, would move into France and then wheel to the left, toward Paris. The bulk of the French Army, which presumably would be advancing into Alsace and Lorraine, would be caught in a vast battle of encirclement between Paris and the Franco-German border.

For its part, France, inspired with an offensive mentality based on the writings of military thinkers such as Ferdinand Foch, also produced a plan that called for a quick victory. This Plan XVII called for the French Army to drive to the northeast, straight into Alsace. This, combined with Russian pressure on East Prussia, was expected to bring about Germany's defeat. For their parts, both Russia and Austria-Hungary also developed plans that called for quick victories.

To conclude, the primary cause of World War I was indeed a sense of expectation, first that there would be a war and second that it would be short. In the first case, the expectation that a war would occur—fueled by the hypernationalism, militarism, and alliance systems—indeed became a prophecy. When war did come, however, the result of the opening campaigns was certainly not what was expected.

Richard L. DiNardo

Perspective Essay 2. Fear and the Outbreak of War

Germany and Austria-Hungary chose to risk war in 1914 out of fear. The initial decisions for war were made first in Vienna, where the Austro-Hungarian government chose to go to war with Serbia, and then in Berlin, where the German government chose to support Austria-Hungary even if it meant war with Russia, France, and Great Britain. What drove them was fear: fear on the part of the Austro-Hungarian government that if it failed to take a strong stand against Serbia, it would appear weak and the forces of separatism within the empire would be strengthened. This was echoed by fears on the part of German leaders that if they allowed Austria-Hungary to collapse, Germany would be entirely bereft of allies in a hostile Europe.

In addition, the leaders of Germany feared the growth of Russian military power. Both Germany and Austria-Hungary feared that a failure to take strong action in the 1914 crisis would lead to their inevitable decline. It was better to risk a continental war than to accept such a fate.

Although Austrian leaders had no concrete evidence, there was little doubt in Vienna that the Serbian government had been involved in the assassination of Archduke Franz Ferdinand on June 28, 1914. The two nations had been at odds for the previous decade. In fact, the Austro-Hungarian government saw the assassination as an opportunity to rectify two of the greatest problems facing the Dual Monarchy—what was called the "South Slav" problem and what was seen as a looming encirclement of the monarchy orchestrated by Russia.

The two problems worked hand in hand. The South Slav problem was that of nationalism. Austro-Hungarian leaders feared that their South Slav population, particularly in areas such as Bosnia-Herzegovina, was not loyal to the monarchy. In order to avoid the loss of those South Slav lands, Serbia had to be either contained or destroyed. The assassination provided an opportunity to destroy Serbia. The leaders of Austria-Hungary believed that failure to do so would demonstrate weakness on the part of the government and would encourage other minorities, such as the Czechs in Bohemia, to make demands for greater autonomy. The second problem, that of encirclement by Russia, stemmed from Russian support of the Serbians and from Russian entreaties to Romania, a secret ally of Austria-Hungary. The Austro-Hungarians feared that Russia intended to use the small Balkan nations to first contain and then destroy the monarchy.

The leaders of the Dual Monarchy chose war with Serbia out of fear of their continuing decline. The question remains, however, as to why the German government, which as recently as 1913 had restrained Austria-Hungary from war in the Balkans, decided to support an Austro-Hungarian war with Serbia. The answer here too was fear. Germany was Europe's economic and military powerhouse. Germany produced more coal, iron, and steel than any of its continental rivals. In addition, Germany possessed what most observers considered the finest army in the world and had an impressive and growing navy. Yet Germany's leaders also feared the future in the summer of 1914. As with the Austro-Hungarians, they saw themselves being encircled by their enemies, who would strike when the time was right. That fear stemmed from the signing of the Franco-British Entente Cordiale in 1904 and the strengthening of the Entente that took place as a result of the First Moroccan Crisis of 1905–1906. It was driven by a conviction that Great Britain in particular sought to prevent Germany from attaining its place in the sun as a major imperial power.

That fear was accentuated by the arms race that all the European powers were engaged in during the first decade of the century. In 1914, the Germans were particularly concerned by the fact that the French government had recently extended the term of military service for its enlisted men from two years to three and that the French were loaning large sums of money to Russia so that the latter could modernize its railroad network, particularly in Russian-controlled Poland. In addition, the Russians themselves were in the middle of a massive modernization and expansion of their military that by 1917 would leave them with not only the largest army in Europe but also one of the most modern. The German nightmare was that once that program was complete, the Franco-Russian allies would strike at Germany. The German government assumed that this war was inevitable, and therefore it would be better for Germany to fight the war sooner rather than later.

Tied into this fear of encirclement was concern over the fate of Austria-Hungary. The Germans doubted the reliability of their other ally, Italy, and therefore were all the more determined to maintain the viability of their Austro-Hungarian ally. For the Germans as well, then, the nationalist forces within the Austro-Hungarian Empire were a threat. Since Serbia was a potential source of loyalty for many South Slavs, the Germans concurred with the Austro-Hungarian assessment that the assassination should be used as a pretext for a reckoning with Serbia.

German leaders also had very real concerns over internal developments, in particular the German socialists. The German state and system, as set up by Chancellor Otto von Bismarck, entrenched the power of the monarchy and the old nobility. The kaiser, while technically a constitutional monarch, retained nearly all power. The one check on his authority, the Bundesrat, was staffed by officials appointed by the other German states, which were also monarchies and could usually be counted on to support imperial power. The Riechstag—the elected body of the people—was, however, falling increasingly under the sway of the Social Democratic Party (SPD), the largest party in Germany and still growing. The SPD took control of the Reichstag after the 1912 elections and was seen by many in the German establishment as a threat to the future of the monarchy. They hoped that a successful war would strengthen the position of the monarchy at home as well as abroad. The key decision makers in Germany saw war as the best way to deal with all of these problems.

The decision for war was not the result of years of military and political planning by national leaders aimed at the conquest of most of Europe. Nor was it the result of a series of accidents. The alliance system conditioned the thinking of the leaders of Austria-Hungary and Germany as did the arms races, but neither caused the war. Nationalism played a role, in particular within the Austro-Hungarian Empire, but it was not decisive. Neither was imperialism, although social Darwinism and the belief in the struggle between the races certainly played a role. Both domestic politics and foreign policy factored into the decisions made in July 1914, but neither was dominant. In the end, none of the traditional explanations for the outbreak of the war is sufficient. The war was not inevitable; it was the result of choices taken by the leaders of Austria-Hungary and Germany, and those leaders acted for one of the most human reasons of all: they feared the future.

Mark D. Karau

Perspective Essay 3. Strategic Miscalculation

The primary cause of World War I was the strategic miscalculation of the military and political leaders of Europe. A war was neither necessary nor inevitable, but the leaders of the continent mismanaged a relatively minor crisis and turned it into a world war.

The greatest tragedy of the war, once called "the war to end all war," is that it didn't need to be fought. Europe was not a place of intensive nationalist hatreds awaiting a spark. Only in the Balkans were such passions hot enough to start wars, and the Balkans seemed to most citizens of the West European great powers to be a long way away. By 1914, most of the issues that had Europe on edge over the past 15–20 years had been resolved or had lost their ability to drive political discourse on the continent. These issues included imperialism in Africa, grudging French acceptance of the German possession of Alsace-Lorraine, and the peaceful resolution of two recent crises in Morocco. In the weeks before the assassination of Archduke Franz Ferdinand in Sarajevo on June 28, 1914, most contemporaries observed that Europe was as peaceful as it had been for decades.

Nor did the assassination of Franz Ferdinand lead people to think that a war was imminent. His death put the much more moderate Archduke Karl in line for the Austro-Hungarian throne, which most close observers saw as a positive sign for the future peace of Europe. Almost no one in Europe thought that the assassination would lead to what they called a "general war." Having survived much more serious crises in the past decade, Europeans were sure that this one would quickly fade.

The crisis arising from the assassination became a world war because the leaders of Europe not only misread the crisis but also lacked a fundamental understanding of the ways their own military and political systems worked. This knowledge gap was greatest in the autocratic states of Austria-Hungary, Russia, and Germany. As a result of this widespread bungling, what should have been at worst the Third Balkan War became instead a world war.

The first and most serious miscalculation came in Vienna. The senior leaders of the Austro-Hungarian Empire, especially its army's chief of staff General Franz Conrad von Hötzendorff, assumed that the assassination of the archduke was an existential crisis for the empire. Conrad believed that the assassination had to be avenged in order to reverse the slow decay that he feared the Austro-Hungarian Empire was experiencing. More important, Conrad believed that the diplomatic situation in the Balkans would never be so favorable to his country again. Austria-Hungary, most often seen as an aggressor and a bully in the Balkans, could now depict itself as a victim. That Serbian officials might have been directly involved in the assassination gave Conrad all the justification he needed to argue for the most extreme measures.

Conrad had argued for a preemptive war against Serbia for years, but the political leadership of the Austro-Hungarian Empire had always refused his pleas. This time, however, they went to their allies in Berlin and asked for German support if they moved against Serbia. They needed that support in case Russia decided to support Serbia. Austria-Hungary had enough military power to defeat the Serbs but not enough to fight Serbia and Russia at the same time. A German guarantee of support would give the Austrians sufficient confidence to turn their armies south, against Serbia, without worrying about being invaded from the north by the Russians.

The Germans gave Austria-Hungary their unqualified support and in so doing set in motion the second tragic set of miscalculations. The German political and military establishments also assumed that the time for war would never be better. Anxious about Russia's growing rearmament in the wake of its disastrous defeat in the Russo-Japanese War, the German military leadership assumed that by 1917 the Russians might be too strong to defeat. Russia was also building a massive rail network (with French financing) that would enable the Russian Army to move men and supplies rapidly across its vast empire. Thus, the German General Staff assumed that Germany's chances of winning a war were better in 1914 than they would be in the future. They therefore decided to support Austria-Hungary and issue a diplomatic challenge to the Russians. If the Russians backed down, then Austria-Hungary would have a free hand in the Balkans, and German influence would grow there as Russian influence waned. If Russia chose to fight, then Germany would get a war in 1914 that its leaders thought they could win.

These political miscalculations made the crisis over the assassination seem far more important than it was. Austria-Hungary could easily have satisfied its honor over the matter without resorting to war. Instead, on July 23 the Austro-Hungarians issued an ultimatum to Serbia that contained conditions they knew the Serbs could never accept. Europeans were stunned by the severity of the ultimatum.

Military miscalculations followed political miscalculations. Shockingly, the German and Austro-Hungarian armies had done almost no joint planning. In part, this lack of coordination came from the very low opinion German generals had of their Austro-Hungarian counterparts. Their assessment seemed to be confirmed by the discovery in 1913 that the head of Austria-Hungary's counterespionage bureau was in fact a Russian spy. The Germans therefore feared that any sensitive information they shared with their most important ally would find its way into the hands of the Russians, who might well pass it on to their own ally, France. Thus, the Germans and Austro-Hungarians made their military plans in isolation from one another.

The outbreak of war also showed how poorly the political and military systems worked together. Neither German kaiser Wilhelm II, Austro-Hungarian emperor Franz Josef, nor Russian czar Nicholas II understood how their own militaries functioned. None of them knew the details of their own country's war plans. The kaiser thus asked his generals to mobilize on the Russian frontier only, and the czar asked his generals to mobilize against the Austro-Hungarians only. Both were told that partial mobilizations were impossible; assuming that any war in Europe would involve entire alliance systems, the generals had made no plans for war against just one enemy.

War planning thus proved to be another costly miscalculation. The German war plan assumed that any war, no matter what the cause, would force them to fight both France and Russia. Those two nations were allied, and French money had helped the Russians to rearm. The Germans also had an intense fear of having to fight on two fronts. German generals thus developed a war plan that focused on fighting France and defeating that country in just six weeks. The Germans would then transport their forces by rail to the east to fight off the presumably slower-to-mobilize Russians. While it is likely that France would have declared war on Germany to support Russia, the fact that the Russians were the first great power to mobilize might have given France the opportunity to remain neutral. Germany's war plans removed that option and dragged France into a war that was not in its interests to fight.

The risky and dangerous German war plan had dire consequences. It guaranteed French involvement in the war, and because it called for an invasion of neutral Belgium as well, it brought the entire British Empire into the war. Germany was therefore at war with three massive empires—the Russian, British, and French—that had ample resources to fight for many years. The German deployment of seven-eighths of its units to the west also meant that there was no sizable force to help the

Austrians in the east. Although the German Eighth Army did win two large victories against the Russians, even these successes could not help the Austro-Hungarians, who suffered terrible casualties at the hands of the Russians in the war's early months.

By the end of 1914, Europeans found themselves trapped in a general war. Too much blood had been spilled for the two sides to end this unnecessary war through negotiation. Determined to repel the aggressors, Britain and France were willing to commit to a total war effort, as were the Russians until 1917. Convinced that they had earned their gains by the blood of their own men, the Germans were just as determined not to surrender at the negotiating table what they had won on the battlefield. The war thus continued despite a tactical and operational stalemate that produced casualties far in excess of any battlefield gains. As a result of these tragic miscalculations, millions of men would die and kill for the next four years to complete a war that need never have happened.

Michael S. Neiberg

Further Reading

Albertini, Luigi. *The Origins of the War of 1914.* 3 vols. New York: Enigma Books, 2005.

Brittain, Vera. *Testament of Youth: An Autobiographical Study of the Years 1900–1925.* New York: Penguin, 1994.

Echevarria, Antulio J. *After Clausewitz: German Military Thinkers before the Great War.* Lawrence: University Press of Kansas, 2000.

Fischer, Fritz. *Germany's War Aims in the First World War.* New York: Norton, 1967.

Hamilton, Richard, and Holger H. Herwig. *Decisions for War, 1914–1917.* Cambridge: Cambridge University Press, 2004.

Herwig, Holger H. *The First World War: Germany and Austria-Hungary 1914–1918.* London: Arnold, 1997.

Herwig, Holger H. *Luxury Fleet: The Imperial German Navy 1888–1918.* London: Ashfield, 1980.

Herwig, Holger H., and Richard F. Hamilton. *The Origins of World War I.* New York: Cambridge University Press, 2003.

Hochschild, Adam. *To End All War: A Story of Loyalty and Rebellion, 1914–1918.* Boston: Houghton Mifflin Harcourt, 2011.

Horne, John, and Alan Kramer. *German Atrocities, 1914: A History of Denial.* New Haven, CT: Yale University Press, 2002.

Kennan, George F. *The Decline of Bismarck's European Order: Franco-Russian Relations, 1875–1890.* Princeton, NJ: Princeton University Press, 1978.

Kennan, George F. *The Fateful Alliance: France, Russia and the Coming of the First World War.* New York: Pantheon Books, 1984.

Mombauer, Annika. *Helmuth von Moltke and the Origins of the First World War.* New York: Cambridge University Press, 2001.

Neiberg, Michael S. *Dance of the Furies: Europe and the Outbreak of War, 1914.* Cambridge, MA: Harvard University Press, 2011.

Neiberg, Michael S. *Fighting the Great War: A Global History.* Cambridge, MA: Harvard University Press, 2005.

Stevenson, David. *Cataclysm: The First World War as Political Tragedy.* New York: Basic Books, 2004.

Strachan, Hew. *The First World War,* Vol. 1, *To Arms.* New York: Oxford University Press, 2001.

Tuchman, Barbara. *The Guns of August.* New York: Macmillan, 1962.

Tucker, Spencer C. *The Great War, 1914–18.* Bloomington: Indiana University Press, 1998.

Tunstall, Graydon A., Jr. *Planning for War against Russia and Serbia: Austro-Hungarian and German Military Strategies, 1871–1914.* Boulder, CO: East European Monographs, 1993.

White, George W. *Nationalism and Territory: Constructing Group Identity in Southeastern Europe.* New York: Rowman and Littlefield, 2000.

Williamson, Samuel R., and Russel van Wyk. *July 1914: Soldiers, Statesmen, and the Coming of the Great War; A Brief Documentary History.* New York: St. Martin's, 2003.

34. WAS GERMANY'S WORLD WAR I SUBMARINE WARFARE CAMPAIGN AGAINST NONMILITARY SHIPPING JUSTIFIED?

Most historians argue that World War I was history's first truly total war, meaning that it forced total mobilization on both the war front and the home front. Because the fighting was not limited to battlefields and soldiers but also included industry and civilian populations, innovative methods were devised to wage this new type of conflict. One of them was submarine warfare against enemy merchant shipping, known as guerre de course. *Submarines at the time were a relatively new tool of war. When World War I broke out in 1914 the British instituted a total naval blockade of Germany, which threatened to strangulate the German economy and deprive its citizens of basic items, including food. This compelled the Germans, whose navy was inferior to that of the British, to resort to submarine warfare. By 1916 Germany was beset by food shortages and riots, threatening its entire war effort. It was in fact Germany's decision to extend submarine warfare to include neutral shipping that caused the most problems.*

Dr. Paul J. Springer, in the first perspective essay, argues that Germany had no choice but to resort to submarine warfare. Germany was fighting a two-front war, was endangered by Britain's preemptive blockade, and possessed a relatively weak navy, and as such German leaders were entirely justified in declaring submarine warfare. Furthermore, the Allies' practice of arming merchant ships and using passenger ships to transport war matériel gave Germany no choice but to attack ships without warning. In the second essay, Robert P. Broadwater also argues that submarine warfare was justified. Germany had to overcome Britain's blockade and make use of its limited resources. By 1915 German food prices had gone up by 100 percent, while food shortages and rioting became endemic. German submarine warfare was a success, he asserts, at least until the Allies instituted the convoy system in 1917. Walter F. Bell, in the third essay, asserts that German leaders resorted to submarine warfare out of frustration and inflexibility and because they had badly mismanaged their economy. Indeed, he states that Germany's decision to reimpose unrestricted submarine warfare in February 1917 was its "worst decision" of the war. Ultimately that decision brought the United States into the conflict in April 1917, which virtually ensured a German defeat.

Background Essay

With the start of World War I, Great Britain announced a distant naval blockade of Germany. With its own surface navy inferior to that of Britain and unsuccessful in its effort to whittle away substantially at British naval strength, the Germans responded with a *guerre de course* (war against commerce) utilizing the submarine, the success of which had been demonstrated on September 22, 1914, when one German U-boat ("U" for *Untersee*, or "underwater") sank three old British armed cruisers within a single hour.

The Royal Navy meanwhile tightened its blockade of Germany, and in February 1915 Germany announced a policy of unrestricted submarine warfare, declaring the waters around Great Britain and Ireland a war zone, with every ship, including those of neutral states, subject to attack. The German Navy began this first unrestricted submarine campaign against merchant shipping with only some two dozen operational U-boats, with about a third of these on station at any given time. Nonetheless, between March and the end of September U-boats sank 480 ships totaling 787,116 gross tons. In this same period the British sank 15 U-boats, but the Germans commissioned 25 new ones.

The British Cunard passenger liner *Lusitania* was torpedoed and sunk by a German U-boat on May 7, 1915, off the south coast of Ireland. Twelve hundred people lost their lives, including 128 Americans. (Library of Congress)

Of course, this policy ran the risk of alienating neutral states trading on the high seas, especially the United States. On May 7, 1915, a German submarine torpedoed the British passenger liner *Lusitania* off southwestern Ireland. At least 124 of the 1,201 dead were Americans. The U.S. government lodged a vigorous protest, but President Woodrow Wilson set himself firmly against war.

By the end of September 1915 the British merchant marine had lost nearly 1.3 million tons of shipping from all causes, outstripping new construction by some 100,000 tons. From October 1915 to February 1916, U-boats sank 209 ships totaling 506,026 gross tons. Beginning on February 29, the Germans authorized attacks without warning against armed merchant vessels, and during the next two months U-boats sank 143 ships totaling 347,843 tons.

On March 24, 1916, however, there was another incident precipitating a diplomatic crisis with the United States when a German U-boat torpedoed the French cross-channel steamer *Sussex* without warning off Dieppe, with the loss of some 50 passengers and crew, including 25 Americans. President Wilson reacted by warning Germany that any further incident would cause the United States to sever diplomatic relations. On April 24, the Germans therefore reinstated the order requiring submarines to operate within the Prize Regulations, meaning that merchant ships would not be sunk without warning and provision for the safety of those aboard.

British merchant ship losses fell immediately. Nevertheless, British shipping losses for the first half of 1916 approached 500,000 tons, well over twice the rate of new construction and considerable grist for the arguments of those Germans demanding unrestricted submarine warfare.

The Battle of Jutland, fought in the North Sea on May 31–June 1, 1916, and the largest naval engagement of the war, ended in a strategic British victory in that the Germans now halted major surface operations, while the British naval blockade remained firmly in place. Germany's economy was now reeling, and much of the civilian population was undergoing privation (the winter of 1916–1917 was known as the Turnip Winter for the lack of food). In these circumstances, Berlin took what was probably the most fateful decision of the entire war in a resumption of unrestricted submarine warfare. This decision, announced on January 31, 1917, to take effect the next day, changed the entire course of the war.

Great Britain imported more than half its food and raw materials, and the German high command believed that an all-out submarine offensive would force it from the war. If this occurred, France would surely have to give up. Germany's leaders accepted the fact that unrestricted submarine warfare would bring the United States into the war, but they reasoned that the fighting would be over before this could have a major impact.

With German torpedoes claiming increasing numbers of American lives, on April 6 the United States declared war. German submarines were soon sinking ships at a prodigious rate: 520,412 tons in February, 564,497 tons in March, and 860,334 tons in April, for only nine U-boats lost. This was the peak, however. Allied technology in antisubmarine detection, depth charges, and mines played roles, but the main factor in the defeat of the U-boats was the institution of the convoy system. The submarines still registered kills, but the proportion of ships sunk to those sailing was far less than that of merchant ships traveling singly. Shipping losses generally dropped: 616,316 tons in May, 696,725 tons in June, 555,514 tons in July, 472,372 tons in August, 353,602 tons in September, 466,542 tons in October, 302,599 tons in November, and 411,766 tons in December. Forty-three U-boats were also sunk during July–December.

The entrance of the United States into World War I decided the war against Germany. In addition to being a tremendous morale boost for the Entente, the United States provided immediate financial assistance in the form of loans as well as huge quantities of food and industrial goods (U.S. annual steel production was three times that of Germany and Austria-Hungary combined). Without the U.S. declaration of war, Russia would still have collapsed, and without U.S. forces in the field, Germany probably would have been successful in its offensives on the Western Front in the spring of 1918, giving it victory in the war.

Spencer C. Tucker

Perspective Essay 1. A Necessary Step to Avoid Defeat

During World War I, Germany faced a two-front war that Germans perceived as a war for national survival. While the land campaigns produced military stalemate on the Western and Eastern Fronts, the German economy suffered, in large part owing to the British distant blockade of German ports. Out of a growing sense of desperation, in 1915 lest the twin forces of attrition and exhaustion wear down national capabilities, morale, and will to continue the war, Germany's leaders authorized several actions to obtain a significant advantage. These included zeppelin bombing raids on London, the use of chemical weapons, and the commencement of submarine attacks against civilian merchant vessels trading with the Allied powers fighting Germany.

In a submarine campaign against commercial shipping, the Germans hoped to cripple the British economy, which depended heavily on imported raw materials. This would weaken the British forces in the field and drive Britain from the war. Left alone, the French would surely have to sue for peace, leaving Germany free to pursue its annexationist aims in the East against Russia.

The submarine campaign utilized a relatively new technology but followed the centuries-old practice of *guerre de course* (war against commerce), a naval strategy of attacking enemy international trade. Traditionally, this approach was adopted by a weaker naval power against an enemy with a large commercial fleet. Prior to World War I the most frequent target of the strategy was Britain, the nation with the largest navy and heavy dependence on imports, and so it was only natural that Britain would protest any attempt to overturn its major naval advantage. In most wars the British used their naval supremacy to secure access to global resources while throttling the seaborne trade of the enemy, and World War I was no exception. Germany was under no obligation to cede control of the seas to its enemy or to fight in the manner of the enemy's choosing. Rather, Germany utilized submarines to take the naval war to the enemy, sinking significant tonnages of merchant shipping and triggering a protest from London.

When Germany began its first major submarine campaign in 1915, the British argued that the laws of war at sea allowed the capture of merchant vessels but not their destruction without providing for the safety of their crews. However, submarines moved far slower than most surface vessels and were extremely vulnerable to attack when surfaced. Initially German submarine captains tried surfacing to offer warnings before attacking, allowing merchant crews time to evacuate before their ships were sunk. Radio made this dangerous, as a merchant ship crew could transmit its coordinates to an antisubmarine patrol. The British also began arming merchant vessels, dubbed Q-ships, hiding ordnance that was revealed only when an enemy submarine surfaced. This duplicity all but forced the Germans to launch their attacks submerged and without warning.

The British regarded the German attacks as a barbaric escalation of warfare, while the Germans saw them as merely a new form of blockade adapted to the modern era. The British claimed that attacks against unarmed cargo vessels carrying nonwar materials were illegal under the laws of war and should be halted, while the Germans accused the British of transporting war materials in civilian vessels in order to circumvent the submarine campaign.

The sinking of neutral ships ran the risk of bringing other nations into the war against Germany, and the leading trading neutral was the United States. On May 7, 1915, a German submarine sank the British passenger liner *Lusitania* off Ireland, killing 1,191 passengers, including 128 Americans. As a result of U.S. threats, on May 4, 1916, Germany promised to halt all attacks on passenger liners, to attack merchant vessels only if weapons were present, and to provide for the safe evacuation of merchant crews before sinking their ships. This pledge held for only eight months before the unrestricted submarine attacks resumed, in large part due to reverses on the European continent.

In January 1917 with the situation on both fronts in danger of complete collapse, the German high command decided to resume unrestricted submarine warfare. This decision was taken in the full knowledge that it would likely bring U.S. intervention in the war, but the Germans gambled that the campaign could drive Britain from the war within six months, long before American intervention could upset the military balance. The alternative, in the German view, was their defeat in the war.

Given the options, there was truly no choice at all. The Germans had to utilize any tools at their disposal if they wished to have any hope of victory. Therefore, the decision to use unrestricted submarine warfare against all enemy merchant shipping was justified, particularly when it was resumed in 1917, as the alternative was embracing defeat in the war.

Paul J. Springer

Perspective Essay 2. A Justified Response to the British Naval Blockade

It has long been debated whether the German policy of attacking nonmilitary shipping was a sound response of military necessity or simply the barbaric act by the leaders of a frustrated nation. The former is correct. Germany was bound to do all in its power to win the war, and the unrestricted use of U-boats against merchant shipping offered a viable plan.

In October 1914 the Royal Navy imposed a distant naval blockade of Germany, aimed at crippling the country's economy and war effort. Germany relied on imports to feed its population, and Great Britain correctly assessed that restricting the flow of goods into that country would seriously hamper its ability to wage war. Within a year of the imposition food prices had risen some 100 percent, and shortages had become so severe as to cause food riots.

Britain also relied on agricultural imports to feed its people. The German high command estimated that a total blockade would starve the island nation into submission in three months. But Germany lacked the resources to impose a retaliatory blockade of its own. The British held overwhelming superiority in surface warships, which meant that a traditional blockade of British ports was impractical. Vice Admiral Hugo von Pohl, chief of the Admiralty Staff, advocated the use of submarines to wage unrestricted warfare against merchant shipping. Such a policy was seen by many as a violation of the Hague Convention, which required that such vessels be stopped and searched, with provision made for the safety of their crews, before any destruction took place. German chancellor Theobald von Bethmann Hollweg opposed such a step. He believed that if adopted, unrestricted submarine warfare would have a negative effect on neutral countries, especially the United States, and would far outweigh any advantages it might bring militarily. But the military leaders who now controlled German affairs claimed that unrestricted submarine warfare was no less discriminate or more reprehensible than the sinking of ships by British minefields in the North Sea. In the end Bethmann lost out, and in February 1915, just two days after Pohl was promoted to command the German High Seas Fleet, unrestricted submarine warfare went into effect.

The German high command declared that the waters surrounding the British Isles were considered a war zone. It was declared that any enemy merchant vessel could be sunk within these waters and that current conditions might make it impossible for crews and passengers to be protected from harm. Neutral ships were also warned that they would be risking a similar fate because of alleged British authorization for the use of neutral flags on their ships to prevent them from attack. Those supporting this policy believed that this statement of intent to enforce a blockade would be sufficient for neutral vessels to avoid British ports altogether, as was the case with the British naval blockade of Germany. Such did not prove to be the case.

The submarine blockade averaged nearly 100,000 gross register tonnage sunk per month during 1915, or about 1.9 ships per day. While these are staggering statistics, the blockade was not effective in producing the desired response. Though there were severe shortages in Britain, these occasioned only moderate belt-tightening and were not sufficient to bring the nation to its knees. In the meantime, neutral nations voiced outrage regarding the indiscriminate sinking of their merchant ships. The U.S. government, following the sinking of the British passenger liner *Lusitania* in May 1915 with the loss of 128 American lives, informed the German government that it would view any further such acts as "deliberately unfriendly." While the implied threat of American intervention prompted the Germans to shift emphasis of their submarine warfare to the Mediterranean Sea, unrestricted attacks continued into 1916, with a total loss to the Allies of 1,307,996 gross tons of shipping.

Rising pressure from the neutral nations, especially the United States, caused Germany to suspend its unrestricted submarine campaign in early 1916. Attempting to even the odds in surface ships, the leaders of the German High Seas Fleet planned to isolate and destroy part of the British Grand Fleet, but the British were aware that the entire German High Seas Fleet was at sea, and the resulting Battle of Jutland (May 31–June 1, 1916) saw the entire Grand Fleet at sea. Despite Britain's heavier losses in ships and personnel, Jutland was a strategic British victory, for the High Seas Fleet now largely remained in port for the rest of the war.

German naval leaders now proposed a resumption of unrestricted submarine warfare, claiming that this would force Britain from the war within six months if 600,000 tons of shipping per month were sunk. Although it would likely bring the United States into the war, Britain would be forced to sue for peace before U.S. forces could have a major impact. With Britain out, France also would be forced to sue for peace. Germany could then realize its war aims in the east against Russia.

With the German civilian population now experiencing extreme hardship, even starvation, chief of the German General Staff Field Marshal Paul von Hindenburg strongly supported the plan. On February 1, 1917, Germany resumed unrestricted submarine warfare. In its early going, it seemed to be working. In the first three months of the campaign, German U-boats sank some 1,945,243 gross tons of shipping for the loss of only nine U-boats. By April, Britain had been reduced to only a six-week supply of wheat.

In May, however, the Allies adopted a convoy system, sharply reducing the shipping losses as a result, while more submarines were sunk by the escorting warships. The Allies gained the advantage in 1918, although German U-boats had sunk more than 2.5 million tons of shipping before the end of the war that November. During the course of the war, more than 5,000 ships counting nearly 13 million tons fell victim to U-boats. Germany had inflicted grievous losses in both British and neutral shipping and thus supplies coming into the island nation. Although the unrestricted submarine warfare campaign brought the United States into the war, Germany's unrestricted submarine warfare campaign gained optimum results from limited resources and must therefore be seen as a military success and a justified response to the strangling British blockade that was bringing starvation to the German people.

Robert P. Broadwater

Perspective Essay 3. Submarine Campaign Cost Germany Victory

The unrestricted submarine warfare offensive launched by the German Navy in February 1917, three years into World War I, reflected equal parts desperation on the part of Germany's political and military leaders, exaggerated confidence in the capabilities of their U-boat arm, arrogant disregard of the rights and lives of Allied and neutral citizens on the high seas, and a serious underestimation of the consequences of war with the United States. For the Germans it proved to be the worst decision of the war.

Submarines were a relatively new weapon of modern war. Prior to 1914, naval strategists paid little attention to their potential as a weapon against other warships or as commerce raiders. War against belligerent merchantmen was governed by the rules of blockade and of cruiser warfare as set out by the Hague Conventions of 1899 and 1907. Because of the stop-and-search requirements of these agreements, submarines were believed to be too vulnerable and therefore not viable weapons against enemy commerce.

Nevertheless, shortly after the war's outbreak in August 1914, Germany's naval leaders took a closer look at the potential of submarines after a U-boat sank three British cruisers in one day in the North Sea. With a British naval blockade closing off Germany's overseas imports, German leaders searched for ways to retaliate. The apparent acquiescence of the United States and other neutrals regarding the Allied blockade and the growing American trade in munitions and other war materials with Britain and France fed German resentment and frustration.

Fueled by this growing anger and seeking a greater role in the war for the navy, a small but strident group of senior naval officers in the German Admiralty and the Imperial Naval Office pressed for unrestricted submarine warfare against Allied and neutral shipping. Their main spokesman and leader was Admiral Alfred von Tirpitz, Germany's secretary of state for the Imperial Naval Office. Early in 1915 without consulting either Kaiser Wilhelm II or Germany's civilian leaders, Tirpitz issued a public statement claiming that Germany's salvation lay in an unrestricted submarine blockade of British waters.

Neither Tirpitz nor any of his supporters mentioned that the navy lacked sufficient numbers of long-range submarines to make such a campaign effective or that this shortage resulted from the emphasis placed prewar by Tirpitz and the kaiser on building a large surface fleet. The measure appealed to important elements of the German public determined to prosecute the war to complete victory.

A struggle ensued between the naval leadership, led by Chancellor Theobald von Bethmann-Hollweg, Foreign Minister Gottlieb von Jagow, and moderates who feared war with the United States. In this contest, the German Army high command held the balance while Wilhelm II vacillated. The shifting balance manifested itself in an initial unrestricted blockade in British waters in early 1915. The torpedoing in May 1915 of the British passenger liner *Lusitania* with the loss of more than 1,100 lives (including 128 Americans) proved to be a political disaster for Germany. Vigorous protests from U.S. president Woodrow Wilson and the lack of long-range submarines to prosecute an effective campaign gave Germany's civilian leaders the upper hand and in early 1916, with additional losses of American lives, Germany ended unrestricted submarine warfare.

Nonetheless, the German Foreign Office warned Wilson and his advisers that continued restraint depended on the United States forcing Britain to relax the "starvation blockade" of Germany. Most Americans, however, sympathized with the Entente powers because of German atrocities in Belgium as well as civilian deaths caused by U-boat sinkings. Although German anger at the United States for following a double standard on neutral rights toward the Allied blockade while shipping them the sinews of war was understandable, it could not justify killing civilians on the high seas. Moreover, German protests about the "starvation blockade" did not address their own government's mismanagement of manpower and agricultural resources.

Amid mounting casualties, food and fuel shortages, and popular discontent, pressure for unrestricted submarine warfare mounted. Germany and its allies were experiencing a material and morale crisis at the turn of 1916–1917. Heavy fighting in 1916 left the armies of Germany and Austria-Hungary exhausted. Their populations greatly suffered in a severe winter, with the failure of the German potato harvest worsening an already strained food supply.

Furthermore, a negotiated compromise peace seemed unlikely. After his reelection in November 1916, Wilson appealed for peace negotiations and asked both camps to state their basic aims. In maneuvers designed more to shore up their domestic support, both Bethmann-Hollweg and British prime minister David Lloyd George made proposals, but each rejected the other's terms.

German inflexibility reflected the illusion nursed by the German Army high command and the navy that a complete victory was still possible. By this time the direction of German affairs was firmly in the hands not of the kaiser or civilian leaders but instead of Field Marshal Paul von Hindenburg and Lieutenant General Eric Ludendorff.

Hindenburg and Ludendorff were determined to continue the fight, despite worsening conditions both at home and on the fighting fronts. Germany's leaders played their last card in again unleashing the U-boats. Starving Britain into submission now seemed an acceptable option. Only fear of war with the United States had deterred German leaders before. In January 1917 with the high command ascendant, these concerns carried as much weight as the false assessment that German submarines could force Britain from the war before American power could make itself felt.

What led the German military to this conclusion? In December 1916, the German Admiralty staff produced a memo pointing out that Britain's wheat supply, which came mostly from India and the Western Hemisphere, was vulnerable. The authors claimed that an unrestricted submarine campaign could sink 600,000 tons of shipping a month and force from the seas another 1.2 million tons of neutral shipping. Under this pressure Britain's economy would collapse, and the government would be forced to capitulate no later than August 1917. This goal could only be achieved through the introduction of U-boat tactics unhampered by international law or the customs of cruiser warfare. The arguments put forth in this memorandum, along with the support of Hindenburg and Ludendorff, led Wilhelm II to approve unrestricted submarine warfare on January 9, 1917. The campaign commenced on February 1.

Unfortunately for Germany, the Admiralty's claims and statistics masked a number of faulty assumptions. The Admiralty underestimated the strength and flexibility of modern industrial economies. The planners' belief that Britain could not counter food shortages generated by submarine war turned out to be wrong. The British were able to bring more land into production. Most of all, the German's did not foresee the effectiveness of a convoy system, introduced by the British and Americans in May 1917.

Most disastrous for Germany was its military leaders' failure to grasp the consequences of the United States entering the war. In the months following the American declaration of war on April 6, 1917, the Wilson administration mobilized and trained an army of 3.7 million men and shipped 2 million of them to France. Once they entered the fighting on the Western Front in 1918, U.S. troops tipped the military balance overwhelmingly in favor of the Allied and associated powers. Furthermore, American participation in the war made the already tight blockade of the Central Powers even more devastating for the populations of Germany and Austria-Hungary and sped the political, military, and economic collapse resulting in their ultimate defeat.

Ironically, had Germany continued to exercise restraint at sea, it could have gained a much better settlement if not outright victory. Britain and France were themselves near exhaustion and desperately short of manpower and money. Without unrestricted submarine warfare, U.S. entry into the war would have been unlikely. The Wilson administration was deeply divided over the issue of war with Germany, and the president himself would have preferred to come to any peace conference as an honest neutral broker. In opting for unrestricted submarine warfare, Germany's leaders lost the war.

Walter F. Bell

Further Reading

Asprey, Robert B. *The German High Command at War: Hindenburg and Ludendorff Conduct World War I.* New York: Quill, 1991.

Bailey, Thomas A., and Paul B. Ryan. *The Lusitania Disaster: An Episode in Modern Warfare and Diplomacy*. New York: Free Press, 1975.

Ballard, Robert D., with Spencer Dunmore. *Exploring the Lusitania: Probing the Mysteries of the Sinking That Changed History*. New York: Warner, 1995.

Birnbaum, Karl E. *Peace Moves and U-Boat Warfare: A Study of Imperial Germany's Policy Towards the United States, April 18, 1916–January 9, 1917*. Stockholm: Almqvist and Wiksell, 1958.

Butler, Daniel Allen. *The Lusitania: The Life, Loss, and Legacy of an Ocean Legend*. Mechanicsburg, PA: Stackpole, 2000.

Compton-Hall, Richard. *Submarines and the War at Sea, 1914–1918*. London: Macmillan, 1991.

Coogan, John W. *The End of Neutrality: The United States, Britain, and Maritime Rights, 1899–1915*. Ithaca, NY: Cornell University Press, 1981.

Doenecke, Justus D. *Nothing Less Than War: A New History of American Entry into World War I*. Lexington: University Press of Kentucky, 2011.

Gibson, Richard H., and Maurice Prendergast. *The German Submarine War, 1914–1918*. Annapolis, MD: Naval Institute Press, 2003.

Grant, Robert M. *U-Boat Intelligence, 1914–1918*. Hamden, CT: Archon, 1969.

Grant, Robert M. *U-Boats Destroyed: The Effect of Anti-Submarine Warfare, 1914–1918*. London: Putnam, 1964.

Gray, Edwin. *The U-Boat War, 1914–1918*. Conshohocken, PA: Combined Books, 1994.

Halpern, Paul G. *A Naval History of World War I*. Annapolis, MD: Naval Institute Press, 1994.

Herwig, Holger H. *"Luxury" Fleet: The Imperial German Navy, 1888–1918*. London: George Allen and Unwin, 1980.

Lake, Deborah. *Smoke and Mirrors: Q-Ships against the U-Boats in the First World War*. Stroud, Gloucestershire, UK: Sutton, 2006.

Messimer, Dwight R. *Find and Destroy: Antisubmarine Warfare in World War I*. Annapolis, MD: Naval Institute Press, 2001.

Preston, Diana. *A Higher Form of Killing: Six Weeks in World War I That Forever Changed the Nature of Warfare*. New York: Bloomsbury, 2015.

Rose, Lisle A. *Power at Sea*, Vol. 1, *The Age of Navalism, 1890–1918*. Columbia: University of Missouri Press, 2007.

Terraine, John. *The U-Boat Wars, 1916–1945*. New York: Putnam, 1989.

Watson, Alexander. *Ring of Steel: Germany and Austria-Hungary in World War I*. New York: Basic Books, 2011.

Wegener, Wolfgang. *The Naval Strategy of the World War*. Translated by Holger Herwig. Annapolis, MD: Naval Institute Press, 1989.

Welch, David. *Germany, Propaganda, and Total War, 1914–1918: The Sins of Omission*. New Brunswick, NJ: Rutgers University Press, 2000.

Williamson, Gordon, and Ian Palmer. *U-boats of the Kaiser's Navy*. Oxford, UK: Osprey, 2002.

Winton, John. *Convoy: The Defence of Sea Trade, 1890–1990.* London: M. Joseph, 1983.

Zeman, Z. A. B. *A Diplomatic History of the First World War.* London: Weidenfeld and Nicolson, 1971.

35. Is the Balfour Declaration of 1917 to Blame for the Long-Running Arab-Israeli Conflict?

On November 2, 1917, in the midst of World War I, British foreign secretary Arthur James Balfour issued what has come to be known as the Balfour Declaration. The statement declared Great Britain's support for the creation of a national homeland for Jewish people in Palestine. The declaration also pledged that such a homeland would not be permitted to impinge on the rights of non-Jewish people already residing in Palestine. Thus, from the start Balfour's message seemed entirely contradictory. The Balfour Declaration was designed chiefly to rally the support of Jews around the world for the Allied cause. In the end, it gave a considerable lift to the Zionist movement and encouraged Jewish immigration to Palestine, particularly in the 1920s and 1930s. That in turn contributed to rising tensions and eventual violence between Arabs and Jews living in Palestine, which had become a British mandate at the conclusion of World War I. The declaration not only created confusion with its two contradictory promises but also contradicted a prior British commitment to support an independent Arab nation in Palestine after World War I.

In the first perspective essay, Lawrence Davidson argues that the Balfour Declaration is indeed responsible for the Arab-Israeli conflict. That contradictory policy statement, rooted as it was in the historical and religious beliefs of its creators and time, set the stage for nearly constant conflict in the region of Palestine both before and after the establishment of the State of Israel. The British sowed the seeds of this conflict by making promises they could not keep, encouraging Zionism, and facilitating massive Jewish immigration into Palestine, which radically altered the area's demography, social structure, and culture. Jennifer Jefferis maintains in the second essay that the declaration was not responsible for the Arab-Israeli conflict. She asserts that historical, philosophical, intellectual, and political events all gave rise to Arab-Israeli animosity, the three most important ones being Zionism, competitive political interests in the region, and state sponsorship of Zionism. In the third essay, Spencer C. Tucker argues that while the Balfour Declaration was an important development, it was not by itself the main catalyst for the Arab-Israeli conflict. Instead, he argues that a long series of miscues, conflicting policies, and international politics all conspired to spark animosity between Arabs and Jews, which continues to the present day.

Background Essay

Throughout history, Jews had been subjected to widespread discrimination, segregation, and even savage persecution. As a result many embraced Zionism, the movement that called for the creation of a Jewish state or homeland in Palestine. Only when this was achieved, they believed, would Jews be safe from persecution. The key figure in the growth of political Zionism was Theodor Herzl. A journalist, Herzl covered the trial in Paris of Captain Alfred Dreyfus, a Jewish French Army officer wrongfully accused of treason, which brought considerable anti-Semitism to the fore. Herzl was then moved to write a book, *The Jewish State* (1896), in which he urged the establishment of a Jewish state in Palestine. In August 1897 Herzl convened the First Zionist Congress in Basel, Switzerland. The congress attracted more than 200 delegates from 24 states and territories who voted in favor of a "publicly recognized, legally secured homeland" for the Jews in Palestine.

Palestine at that time was part of the Ottoman Empire, and in 1901 and again in 1902 Herzl met with Ottoman sultan Abdul Hamid, but his efforts to establish a Jewish state failed. Herzl then turned to the British government, seeking a grant of territory near the Holy Land that could be used as a refuge for Jews primarily from the Russian Empire. In 1903 Arthur James Balfour, then British prime minister, offered the Zionist movement on behalf of his government some 5,000 square miles on the Uasin Gishu (Gwas Ngishu) plateau in then what was part of British East Africa (present-day Kenya). Zionists were split on the issue, but a majority opposed any territorial solution other than the Holy Land itself.

The World Zionist Organization committed itself irrevocably to Palestine and reopened negotiations with the Ottoman government. These talks ran afoul of the Young Turk Revolution of 1908 and its virulent Turkish nationalism. This did not, however, reverse increasing Jewish immigration to Palestine. In 1907 the so-called practical Zionists centered in Russia established the Jewish National Fund to be used to support Jewish settlement in the Holy Land. Wealthy West European Jews, including French baron Edmond de Rothschild, assisted the generally financially strapped Jews wishing to relocate to Palestine.

World War I brought great changes to the Middle East, as the leaders of the Ottoman Empire decided to join the war on the side of the Central Powers. In July 1915 British high commissioner in Egypt Henry McMahon opened negotiations with Hussein, the sharif of Mecca, calling on the Arab ruler to lead a revolt against the Ottomans in conjunction with British forces and promising—upon the defeat of the Ottomans—the establishment of an independent Arab state. It was understood that this state would include Palestine. British efforts led to the 1917 Arab Revolt. But the British played a double game, as they and the French had their own designs on the Middle East. In May 1916 British Middle Eastern expert Sir Mark Sykes and French diplomat François Georges Picot concluded a secret partition agreement, which received the subsequent concurrence of Russia. With an Allied victory, Palestine was to fall in the British sphere. This, of course, flew in the face of the British government's overture to the Arabs and itself would be at odds with a pledge to the Jews in November 1917.

Arthur James Balfour, British prime minister during 1902–1905 and foreign secretary during World War I. He is known for the Balfour Declaration of November 1917, a proclamation designed to win Jewish support for the war effort and that proposed creation of a "Jewish homeland" in Palestine. (Library of Congress)

Zionists saw an opportunity with World War I, and they actively sought the support of the warring governments for a Jewish state in Palestine. The British government proved to be the most receptive. Although few in number, British Jews included influential figures such as prominent Liberal Party leader Sir Herbert Samuel and the Rothschild banking family. But the acknowledged Zionist leader in Britain was biochemist Dr. Chaim Weizmann at Manchester University, who would one day become the first president of the State of Israel. Weizmann had developed the acetone-butanol-ethanol fermentation process for the production of acetone through bacterial fermentation. This was of immense importance to the production of munitions and thus the British war effort. His prominence gave Weizmann entrée to the highest levels of government.

Weizmann played on the belief of many Christian Britons that there was now an opportunity to right a great historic wrong by facilitating the return of Jews to their historic homeland. Weizmann also argued that Jews were among prominent leaders of the March 1917 Russian Revolution and were more likely to keep Russia in the war on the Entente side if there was support for a Jewish settlement in Palestine. The entry of the United States, with its large influential Jewish population, into the war in April 1917 was another key. Having their enthusiastic support for the war effort would be another plus for the Entente. Finally, there was a negative card. German Jews might be persuaded to work against the German war effort if they believed that it was the Entente side that most favored the Zionist cause.

In December 1916, Balfour had become British foreign secretary. On a trip to the United States he conferred with prominent Zionist and U.S. Supreme Court justice Louis Brandeis, who was also a close adviser to U.S. president Woodrow Wilson. Brandeis assured Balfour of Wilson's support for a Jewish homeland. Wilson was at the time reluctant to give this support openly, as the United States had declared war only against Germany and thus was not formally at war with the Ottoman Empire.

Members of the Zionist movement in Britain helped draft the declaration that was then approved by the British cabinet. Balfour officially announced it on November 2, 1917. The declaration read as follows:

> His Majesty's government view with favour the establishment in Palestine of a national home for the Jewish people, and will use their best endeavours to facilitate the achievement of this object, it being clearly understood that nothing shall be done which may prejudice the civil and religious rights of existing non-Jewish communities in Palestine, or the rights and political status enjoyed by Jews in any other country.

The declaration employed the words "national home" instead of "state" because of some opposition within the British cabinet to the idea of a Jewish state. Indeed, British officials continued to deny that the creation of a Jewish state was the intention of the declaration, although privately many admitted that such was expected once a Jewish majority had been achieved. Arabs in Palestine certainly believed that this was the intent. The French government pledged its support for the Balfour Declaration on February 11, 1918, and President Wilson finally gave his open approval in a letter to Rabbi Stephen Wise on October 29, 1918.

Spencer C. Tucker

Perspective Essay 1. The Founding Document for the State of Israel

The Balfour Declaration, which was announced by Great Britain's war cabinet in November 1917, was indeed responsible for the subsequent Arab-Israeli conflict.

The declaration reflected the power of both colonial and religious sentiments of its time. For instance, in 1917 European and other imperial powers controlled most of the globe and believed that circumstance gave them the right to do as they willed. The British government believed that it held "sovereignty" over Palestine by virtue of having conquered the territory during World War I.

It should also be noted that many Western leaders, in particular British prime minister David Lloyd George and U.S. president Woodrow Wilson, were what we would today refer to as fundamentalist Christians. That is, they believed in the literal truth of the Bible and thus that European Jews, as supposed descendants of a biblical people, had a God-given right to settle in Palestine. This same sentiment was also expressed by British secretary of state for foreign affairs Arthur James Balfour.

It is this thinking that allowed the authors of the declaration to ignore its contradictory nature—that is, the statement also set the stage for intercommunal violence in Palestine. The first part of the Balfour Declaration, which promised to facilitate a "Jewish national home," could not in the long run be accomplished while remaining faithful to the second part, which stated "that nothing shall be done which may prejudice the civil and religious rights of existing non-Jewish communities in Palestine." The Zionists' ambitions for an exclusively Jewish state and the obvious priority they gave to their specific religion and culture had to eventually clash with the "civil and religious rights" of the Arabs already living in Palestine. In addition, omitting political rights for what was at the time 90 percent of the population and failing to foresee the trouble this would cause can only be explained by the blinding disdain with which both the British and the Zionists viewed native Palestinians.

For their part, the Zionists would also come to have an inflated notion of what the Balfour Declaration stood for. In the modern era, the declaration is recognized by many Zionists as a founding document for the State of Israel. In the announcement declaring the establishment of a Jewish state on May 14, 1948, the Balfour Declaration was described as giving "international sanction" to the Jews' historical connection to Palestine and their right to build their national home there.

The Balfour Declaration established an alliance between Great Britain and the World Zionist Organization. In exchange for promising to facilitate a Jewish national homeland in Palestine, the British expected Zionists to use their influence to solidify the support of Jews in the United States for the war effort and also expected influential Jews in the Russian government to throw their support behind continuing the war against Germany. If accomplished, these would greatly help the British war effort. This expectation on the part of the British was based on an exaggerated belief in Jewish influence in these two countries, which in turn was part of an age-old myth of clandestine Jewish world power. There is no convincing evidence that Zionist influence accomplished what the British wanted.

The Balfour Declaration is often coupled with the San Remo Conference of 1920. It was at San Remo that the victors of World War I divided up the conquered Ottoman

Empire and assigned portions of it to Britain and France. They then arranged for the League of Nations, a new creation that came into being by virtue of the treaty that ended World War I, to ratify the San Remo distribution in the form of mandates. In the process the British had the Balfour Declaration incorporated into the League of Nations mandate that granted Britain control of Palestine.

The Zionists have always seen this as a legally binding process—binding not only on the international community but also on the native population of Palestine. This is a highly questionable assumption. While this argument may have made sense to Europeans in an age of colonial conquest, it cannot be considered acceptable in an age of democratic self-determination. And, of course, in 1917 the inhabitants of Palestine were not given a voice in any of these decisions. In all cases the decisions were forced on them. Subsequent resistance was both morally and historically justified.

Once the British had control of Palestine, they began to facilitate the immigration of European Jews into the region, using the Balfour Declaration as a justification for this policy. Thus, as a direct consequence of the Balfour Declaration, thousands of European Jews immediately immigrated to Palestine. By 1945, over 400,000 Jewish immigrants had arrived. This caused a radical demographic change over a very short time period. From the Arab point of view, this migration constituted an invasion of European settlers and led to ongoing violence.

The violence began to play itself out soon after the British mandate went into effect. By 1920 organized demonstrations against Zionist immigration were being held in Jerusalem, which precipitated outbreaks of sporadic intercommunal violence elsewhere in the region. That same year to protect themselves against Arab attacks, Zionists in Palestine founded Haganah, an underground Jewish militia that later became the basis of the Israel Defense Forces. Soon irregular Zionist paramilitary organizations such as the Irgun and the Stern Gang appeared as well. The next year, 1921, saw riots erupt in Jaffa, resulting in hundreds of dead or wounded Jews and Arabs. Intercommunal violence continued sporadically thereafter.

The year 1929 saw renewed violence on a greater scale throughout the territory. In recognition of the role that Zionist immigration played in inciting the violence, the British investigatory report into the situation, the so-called Passfield White Paper, recommended limiting new immigration into the region. The government in London, acting under the influence of the Zionists, failed to implement that recommendation, however. Thus, the same pattern of the waning and waxing of violence repeated itself. Violence remained relatively sporadic until 1936, when renewed rioting led to the declaration of a general strike called by the Arab Higher Committee. This in turn led to the outbreak of a widespread Arab rebellion.

The British government harshly suppressed the Arab Revolt but soon thereafter, with a new world war looming, issued the White Paper of 1939. This policy statement promised that a unified and independent Palestine with a government based on majority rule would be granted following World War II; it also imposed substantial limits on Zionist immigration. The British did this to minimize the possibility of Arab collaboration with Nazi Germany during the impending war. The White Paper of 1939 resulted in a decrease in Arab violence but an increase in Zionist violence against British forces in Palestine because the Jews felt betrayed by the British. Driven forward by this sense of betrayal and subsequent Nazi persecution of Jews in Europe, the Zionists organized large-scale clandestine immigration into Palestine.

After World War II ended, the British did not fulfill their promise of 1939. Instead, they found themselves under mounting pressure to allow open immigration of Holocaust survivors into Palestine. That same pressure produced United Nations General Assembly resolutions that recommended the formal partitioning of Palestine. At that point law and order broke down in the territory, resulting in the British decision to abandon Palestine in May 1948. Palestinian Jews declared the State of Israel that same month.

Since the moment of its conception, the State of Israel has seen nearly constant turmoil. The reason for this is not complicated. The ill will established by the Balfour Declaration and the ensuing takeover of a non-European land via the mass migration of European people continues to persist. Indeed, the only way Israel could and can justify itself both in the broader region of the Middle East and among its own Arab population is through the use of force. The many wars and other conflicts in which Israel has engaged since its founding testify to this fact.

Lawrence Davidson

Perspective Essay 2. Historic and Intellectual Factors Overshadow Declaration

The Balfour Declaration was not responsible for the long-running Arab-Israeli conflict. Written in 1917 by Foreign Secretary Arthur Balfour of Great Britain, the short missive conveys the British government's sympathy for the Jewish quest for a homeland. The statement was used as a point of leverage by Zionist Jews to secure territory in Palestine, where decades later they would declare the establishment of a Jewish state. That declaration preceded decades of violent conflict between Arabs and Israelis, which continues today. However, to lay responsibility for this prolonged rancor at the feet of Balfour is to misunderstand the underpinnings of the conflict and to ignore an expansive swath of historic and intellectual factors that have played a far more sustained role in prolonging it.

To reasonably conclude that the Balfour Declaration is responsible for the Arab-Israeli conflict, one must be able to prove two things: first, that the declaration reflected the intent and capability of the British government to provide a homeland for the Jews in Palestine, and second, that temporal British support for such an endeavor was sufficient to spur enmity for generations to come. In fact, neither of these assumptions is accurate.

The Balfour Declaration was made at a time when the Zionists had been struggling to gain international support for the idea of a Jewish homeland. A persistent and politically astute effort by members of the Zionist Congress finally resulted in a rather restrained declaration of British sympathy. Balfour simply noted that "His majesty's Government view with favor the establishment in Palestine of a national home for the Jewish people, and will use their best endeavors to facilitate the achievement of this object." The declaration is awarded significance because it was the first time a world power had acknowledged the legitimacy of the Zionist cause. However, the British had offered similar expressions of sympathy to Arab groups seeking autonomy over the same territory at the same time. Thus, it is inaccurate to conclude that the British government intended the declaration to result in the creation of the State of Israel.

Moreover, in order to assign British support for the creation of such a state, one would have to ignore Britain's ambivalence toward Zionist immigration in the period between the Balfour Declaration and Israel's establishment of a state in 1948 and Britain's demonstrable lack of support for any political developments in the territory in question post-1948, when it withdrew from its Palestine mandate. Britain's withdrawal was met with a confluence of other states anxious to wade into the emerging conflict between the Arabs and Israelis. Over the course of the next seven decades, the interests of both neighboring and far-flung states have expanded the Arab-Israeli conflict from a dispute over territory to disagreements encompassing ideological identity, political influence, and military prowess.

Three main factors have characterized the Arab-Israeli conflict for its duration: the role of Zionism, the competitive political interests among players in the region, and the impact of great power sponsorship. When looking at these factors, it will be clear that while the Balfour Declaration is reflective of each of them, it did not cause any of them.

The Balfour Declaration was not a spontaneous outburst of British fondness for the Zionist cause. In fact, it was the result of a decades-long, hard-fought campaign on the part of political Zionists to secure sponsorship of a major power for the idea of a Jewish state. The campaign began with an Austrian Jew, Theodor Herzl, who believed that the only safe place for the Jewish people was the creation of a state run by the Jews themselves. Herzl articulated this perspective in his manifesto, *Der Judenstaat,* published in 1896. The historical land of Palestine held a nostalgic pull, and Herzl pursued these places by tirelessly lobbying the sultan of Turkey, who as ruler of the Ottomans had control over the territory at that time. But Herzl also petitioned Great Britain for permission to establish a Jewish state in East Africa, and in *Der Judenstaat* he also raised the possibility of settling in other locations. Herzl's geographic flexibility ensured that the process of statehood was separated from the place of statehood. Thus, the effort to secure both could occur simultaneously. To that end, in 1897 Herzl spearheaded the creation of the international Zionist Congress, an entity committed to the functional development of a Jewish state.

The Zionist Congress's herculean diplomatic efforts played a huge role in laying the groundwork for what would become the State of Israel. The ability of Herzl and others to leverage the competing political interests of international powers was extraordinary. Herzl prodded British prime minister Joseph Chamberlain and eventually secured assurances of territory in Kenya, but others in the Zionist movement urged waiting to secure the historic territory of Palestine. To advance this objective, Herzl continued to lobby the Ottoman sultan. This did not work out, but the lead-up to World War I offered an expansive playground for the politically astute, and Zionists used it to great effect. Herzl presciently anticipated the coming war and understood that even the initial rejections were temporary.

In the interim, the Zionists continued to play the great and regional powers against each other. When the sultan of Turkey rejected their petition, they began meeting with Arab leaders and pitched the Jewish state as a means for the Arabs to counterbalance the Turks. When this failed, they redoubled their efforts in Europe, this time promising that the state they sought could be a bastion of economic development and political stability in a swiftly deteriorating region.

When World War I began in 1914, the Allied powers at least began to more realistically consider the idea of the Jewish state, motivated at least in part by the desperate need to mobilize both resources and support, including that of the Zionists. Moreover, as the push for a Jewish state gained popularity among American Zionists, Britain recognized that support for such an endeavor could open an avenue toward solidifying American support for the war effort from its large and influential Jewish community as well as for the planned British reorganization of the Middle East at the war's end.

The Russian Revolution of March 1917 also became a vehicle of persuasion to the Zionist cause. Zionists emphasized the role of Russian Jews in the revolution and argued that the unifying nature of Zionism could serve as a bulwark against uprisings elsewhere in the world.

The Zionists were not, of course, the only ones leveraging the interests of the world's great powers to advance their own political aims. In 1914, Sharif Hussein of Mecca began a campaign to obtain Britain's support for Arab independence from the Ottoman Empire. The British government assured Hussein that if he were to aid Britain in the war against the Ottoman Empire, he could count on British support for Arab independence following an Allied victory. In 1915 Sir Henry McMahon,

British high commissioner in Cairo, responded to Hussein by saying that "Great Britain is prepared to recognize and support the independence of the Arabs in all the regions within the limits demanded by the Sherif of Mecca."

Adding a further degree of intrigue to the continuing conflict was the 1916 Sykes-Picot Agreement. This secret accord between Britain and France—and at least tacitly agreed to by Russia—divided the territory of the Middle East into sectors of British and French control upon the conclusion of World War I. The agreement sharply contradicted what Britain had negotiated with both the Zionists and the Arabs.

In the end, the land that became the State of Israel was a territory reflective of the interests of Britain, France, and the United States, informed by their economic, political, and ideological visions for the region. The various agreements and declarations that each of these states made over the course of two world wars must be recognized as political machinations designed to cultivate alliances in pursuit of victory in conflict, not a commitment to the cause promoted by one side or the other.

To fully understand the long-running Arab-Israeli conflict, we must also examine the role that external-power sponsorship has played in exacerbating it, not just leading up to the creation of Israel but in the many decades since World War I. The reaction of external states was immediate after the State of Israel was declared in 1948. The United States formally recognized the new state only 11 minutes after it was declared into existence. The Soviet Union followed three days later, and over the course of the next five months 19 other countries did the same.

The rapid support of the United States was only the start of a long relationship between the two states that endures to the present day. The United States has made Israel a pillar of its foreign policy in the Middle East and has repeatedly jeopardized its relationships with Arab states in the region to preserve that friendship. The United States has been the catalyst for many peace talks between Israel and its neighbors, including the successful 1978 Camp David Accords, when Egypt formally recognized Israel.

However, not all states have reacted so favorably to Israel's existence. Only one day after Israel was created, the new country's five neighboring states launched a war against it. Lebanon, Egypt, Syria, Jordan, and Iraq attacked Israel from all sides in a war that resulted in hundreds of thousands of Arab refugees fleeing to the states ostensibly fighting on their behalf. By the time the war ended in 1949, Israel had so effectively repelled the efforts of these five states that Israeli territory was expanded by 60 percent. Moreover, for the next two and a half decades, the Arabs struggled to decide who would speak for the Palestinians.

The Palestinians finally decided to take on the leadership role themselves with the creation of the Palestine Liberation Organization (PLO) and the declaration of Yasser Arafat as the only legitimate voice for the Palestinian cause. But this path toward statehood was not much straighter. Any decisions Arafat made about peace agreements with Israel were subject to the surrounding countries' views, particularly about the right of return of the refugees living within their borders. Arafat also sparked the ire of most states in the region when he supported Saddam Hussein's invasion of Kuwait in 1990, and in consequence some Arab states shifted their support to the PLO's main rival, Hamas. As a result of all these competing interests, the ability to secure peace between the Palestinians and the Israelis is greatly limited by external actors.

In conclusion, the Balfour Declaration was a product of the swirling dynamics of an important time in human history. The growing strength of the Zionist movement as new state boundaries were being created gave a prospect of feasibility to its cause. The competitive interests of Britain, France, Russia, and eventually the United States meant that the states that were eventually created would go to the groups that would prove most useful to the war effort. And the impact that the creation of the State of Israel had on the indigenous Palestinian population ensured that proximate and ideological neighbors would define the Arab-Israeli conflict long into the future. The Balfour Declaration was certainly significant but less for what it can be credited as having caused and more as a harbinger of conflict to come.

Jennifer Jefferis

Perspective Essay 3. British Missteps Led to the Arab-Israeli Conflict

The Balfour Declaration of November 1917 was not in itself decisive but instead was just one in a long progression of missteps by British leaders regarding Palestine that helped bring about the Arab-Israeli wars. Antagonism between Arabs and Jews in Palestine had been steadily building, largely as a consequence of increased Jewish immigration and land purchases, well before British foreign secretary Arthur James Balfour declared British support for the establishment of a Jewish homeland there.

The Balfour Declaration did indeed achieve its aim of winning enhanced Jewish support for the Allied war effort, but it had far-reaching and unintended effects as well. Interestingly, there was no dramatic Jewish migration to Palestine immediately after the war. By 1931, however, the number of Jews had sharply increased to 174,606, while the Arab population was 858,788. Tensions were heightened not only by this population influx but also by Jewish land purchases. Often the latter were fueled by wealthy absentee Arab landowners, and the transactions brought the eviction of Arab tenants.

The real rise in Jewish immigration to Palestine came, however, with the virulent and rampant anti-Semitism of the 1930s, the Holocaust of World War II, and the influx of surviving Jewish refugees immediately thereafter. The official census of

1945 shows the dramatic increase in the Jewish population, with 553,660 Jews and 1,211,100 Arabs (1,061,270 Muslims and 149,830 Christians). Jews now made up some 31 percent of the population, up from 11 percent in 1922. The Jewish population percentage thus increased dramatically not as an immediate consequence of the Balfour Declaration and World War I but instead as a result of Zionism and the events of the 1930s and World War II.

As a consequence of the Allied victory in World War I and a wartime agreement with the French, the British had been granted control of the new state of Palestine as a mandate by the League of Nations in 1920, but London soon had cause to regret this. British rule in Palestine during 1920–1948 failed to keep the peace between Arabs and Jews. The escalating violence between the two groups was the result of the impossible British policy of permitting Jewish immigration while at the same time attempting to safeguard Arab rights. Continued immigration brought more Jewish land purchases, and these led in turn to Arab violence and riots. The British would thus suspend Jewish settlements and land purchases for a time but then, under pressure from world Jewry, reverse this policy.

In 1920 Arabs began sporadically attacking Jewish settlements, and in response Jews formed the Haganah, a clandestine defense organization. Heightened violence by 1929 led the British to halt all Jewish settlement in Palestine, but Jewish outcries caused the British to reverse this policy. In 1936, a full-fledged Arab revolt began. Lasting until 1939, it forced the British to dispatch to Palestine 20,000 additional troops and resulted in the deaths of some 5,000 Arabs and many more injured. It also brought a temporary alliance between the British and the Jews.

In 1937, the British government considered partitioning Palestine into separate Arab and Jewish states but a year later rejected this as not feasible. In 1939 London announced that Palestine would become an independent state within 10 years. The British also sharply curtailed Jewish immigration and restricted the sale of Arab land to Jews. This policy of attempting to favor the Arabs continued during World War II, when the British even diverted warships to intercept and turn back ships carrying Jews attempting to escape the Holocaust. Jewish extremists now took up arms against the British in Palestine, and a three-way war ensued among Arabs, Jews, and the British.

News of the Holocaust that had brought the deaths of more than 6 million Jews dramatically changed attitudes throughout most of the world in favor of Jewish settlement in Palestine and even the creation of a Jewish state there. Probably most Jews now believed that the only way to prevent a new Holocaust was the creation of a nation-state that would safeguard their interests. Jewish terrorist organizations were increasingly at war with the British administration in Palestine, which was refusing to allow the resettlement in Israel from Europe of more than 250,000 Jewish survivors of the Holocaust. For their part, the Arabs failed to understand why they should be made victims for something not of their doing in the Holocaust.

On February 14, 1947, exasperated by its inability to solve the Palestinian problem, the British government turned matters over to the new United Nations (UN). That August the United Nations Special Commission on Palestine (UNSCOP) recommended that the British mandate be terminated and that Palestine be granted its independence on the basis of separate Arab and Jewish states. Although the Arab population was 1.2 million and the Jewish population just 600,000, the Jews would have had some 56 percent of the land. Jews supported the plan; understandably, the Arabs opposed it. Now desperate to quit Palestine, the British government announced acceptance of the UNSCOP recommendation and declared in September 1947 that the mandate of Palestine would terminate on May 14, 1948.

On November 29, 1947, the UN General Assembly officially approved the partition of Palestine. This assured the establishment of a Jewish state in Palestine, and in January 1948 the Arab Liberation Army invaded Palestine. Although the Arab forces enjoyed initial success, Jewish forces took the offensive in the spring of 1948 and, by design and/or circumstance, caused many Arabs to flee their homes and land. Then, on May 14, 1948, the Jews of Palestine declared the establishment of the State of Israel. The next day the Arab armies of Egypt, Lebanon, Jordan, Syria, and Iraq invaded Palestine, thus beginning the Israeli War of Independence.

This outcome was the result not solely of the Balfour Declaration but also of a long-standing convoluted and opportunistic British Middle Eastern policy often at odds with itself. The British government proved unable to bridge the animosity between Arab and Jew and then simply gave up. The result of the overly hasty British exit would be a number of costly Arab-Israeli wars and animosity that extends to the present.

Spencer C. Tucker

Further Reading

Ahlstrom, Gosta W. *The History of Ancient Palestine.* Minneapolis: Augsburg, 1993.

Avi-Yonah, Michael. *The Jews of Palestine: A Political History of Palestine from the Bar Kokhba War to the Arab Conquest.* New York: Schocken Books, 1984.

Biale, David. *Cultures of the Jews: A New History.* New York: Schocken Books, 2002.

Bickerton, Ian J. *A Concise History of the Arab-Israeli Conflict.* Upper Saddle River, NJ: Prentice Hall, 2005.

Bright, John. *A History of Israel.* 4th ed. Louisville, KY: Westminster John Knox, 2000.

Cleveland, William L. *A History of the Modern Middle East.* 3rd ed. Jackson, TN: Westview, 2004.

Coogan, Michael D. *The Oxford History of the Biblical World.* New York: Oxford University Press, 2001.

Davidson, Lawrence. *America's Palestine: Popular and Official Perceptions from Balfour to Israeli Statehood.* Gainesville: University Press of Florida, 2001.

Dimont, Max. *Jews, God and History.* New York: Simon and Schuster, 1962.

Dowty, Alan. *Israel/Palestine.* Malden, MA: Polity, 2005.

Farsoum, Samih K., and Naseer H. Aruri. *Palestine and the Palestinians: A Social and Political History.* 2nd ed. Jackson, TN: Westview, 2006.

Gelvin, James L. *The Israel-Palestine Conflict: One Hundred Years of War.* Cambridge: Cambridge University Press, 2007.

Grief, Howard. *The Legal Foundation and Borders of Israel under International Law: A Treatise on Jewish Sovereignty over the Land of Israel.* Jerusalem: Mazo Publishing, 2013.

Kamrava, Mehran. *The Modern Middle East.* Berkeley: University of California Press, 2005.

Khalidi, Rashid. *The Iron Cage: The History of the Palestinian Struggle for Statehood.* Boston: Beacon, 2006.

Lenczowski, George. *The Middle East in World Affairs.* Ithaca, NY: Cornell University Press, 1952.

Masalha, Nur. *Expulsion of the Palestinians: The Concept of "Transfer" in Zionist Political Thought, 1882–1948.* Washington, DC: Institute for Palestine Studies, 1992.

McCarthy, Justin A. *The Population of Palestine: Population History and Statistics of the Late Ottoman Period and the Mandate.* Institute for Palestine Studies Series. New York: Columbia University Press, 1990.

Pappe, Ilan. *The Ethnic Cleansing of Palestine.* Oxford, UK: Oneworld Publications, 2007.

Pappe, Ilan. *A History of Modern Palestine: One Land, Two Peoples.* Cambridge: Cambridge University Press, 2004.

Parkes, James. *A History of Palestine from 135 AD to Modern Times.* Elibron Classics Replica Edition. Brighton, MA: Adamant Media, 2005.

Provan, Iain W., et al. *A Biblical History of Israel.* Louisville, KY: Westminster John Knox, 2003.

Russell, Michael. *Palestine: Or the Holy Land from the Earliest Period to the Present Time.* Kila, MT: Kessinger, 2004.

Sachar, Howard M. *A History of Israel: From the Rise of Zionism to Our Time.* New York: Knopf, 1976.

Sanders, Ronald. *The High Walls of Jerusalem: A History of the Balfour Declaration and the Birth of the British Mandate for Palestine.* New York: Holt, Rinehart and Winston, 1983.

Schneer, Jonathan. *The Balfour Declaration: The Origins of the Arab-Israeli Conflict.* New York: Random House, 2010.

Shafir, Gershon. *Land, Labor, and the Origins of the Israeli-Palestinian Conflict, 1882–1914.* Cambridge: Cambridge University Press, 1989.

Shepherd, Naomi. *Ploughing Sand: British Rule in Palestine, 1917–1948.* New Brunswick, NJ: Rutgers University Press, 1999.

Smith, Charles. *Palestine and the Arab-Israeli Conflict.* Boston: Bedford/St. Martin's, 2007.

Stein, Leonard. *The Balfour Declaration.* New York: Simon and Schuster, 1961.

Tessler, Mark A. *A History of the Israeli-Palestinian Conflict.* 2nd ed. Bloomington: Indiana University Press, 2009.

Thompson, Thomas L. *Early History of the Israelite People: From the Written & Archaeological Sources.* Leiden: Brill Academic, 2000.